Dynamic Management in Marketing

DYNAMIC MANAGEMENT IN MARKETING

By

RALPH S. ALEXANDER, Ph.D., LL.D.

Philip Young Professor Emeritus
Columbia University

and

THOMAS L. BERG, Ph.D.

Associate Professor of Marketing
Graduate School of Business Administration
New York University

1965
RICHARD D. IRWIN, INC.
HOMEWOOD, ILLINOIS

First Printing, January, 1965

The Library of Congress Catalog Card No. 64-25728

PRINTED IN THE UNITED STATES OF AMERICA

This book is respectfully dedicated to the memory of

ROSS CUNNINGHAM

who participated in planning it and in writing the initial draft but whose death came before its final revision and publication.

Preface

When we set ourselves the task of writing a marketing text that would truly present the management approach to the subject, we quickly encountered several roadblocks which threatened to stop the project before it got well started. In order to understand what the management of marketing involves, the student must know about marketing, its functions and institutions. In the process of acquainting him with these matters, we ran the risk of making our treatment so descriptive that it would obscure the management aspects of the subject.

Professor Howard Westing of the University of Wisconsin in casual conversation suggested a way out of this dilemma. This was to organize the entire treatment of the subject around the problems and activities involved in managing the marketing work of a manufacturing firm. We have tried to adhere to this approach consistently throughout the book.

In doing so we have almost completely ignored the traditional system of marketing functions and have sought to focus our attention on the kinds or families of problems the marketing manager must worry about. As a result, we do not treat separately such time-honored functions as assembling, standardization and grading, transportation, risk management, and storage, but discuss the activities that comprise them in connection with the marketing manager's problems, such as product-mix management, providing customer service in stock carrying and delivery, selecting and managing marketing channels.

Our approach also tends to de-emphasize the treatment of the marketing agencies or institutions. They are described and their problems are discussed in the course of our study of the marketing manager's selection and administration of marketing channels.

There is no doubt that our approach unsuits the book as a text in schools whose marketing courses must be slanted in the direction of the problems of agriculture or the other extractive industries. On the other hand, we hope and feel that it will prove useful to those teachers of marketing who have for long wished to use the management approach and have suffered from the lack of a textbook that rigorously adhered to that approach.

In spots, our writing was facilitated by the generosity of Ginn and Company in assigning to us the copyright of *Marketing* by Alexander, Surface, and Alderson, which is now out of print. The present book is in no sense a revision of that earlier one. But since the earlier one was the first attempt at the managerial approach, fragments of it proved usable.

In the body of the material, we have used source footnotes sparingly, trying to confine them to passages in which we have drawn heavily from ideas or facts presented in specific sources. To compensate, we have included chapter bibliographies which we have sought to make fairly complete.

To facilitate the use of the book by teachers who like the case method, we have included in an Appendix references to cases in the published marketing case books. These are arranged by the chapters to which they are applicable.

We have not included in the text any section dealing specifically with the new tools of marketing management, such as operations research, motivation research, mathematical techniques, and the social sciences. Nor have we put in any formulas expressed in symbolic terms. We freely confess that this is due in part to our own deficiencies in math, but a sounder reason lies in our strong feeling that the manager needs to know when and where to use mathematical models and what to do with their results—but not necessarily how to construct them or operate them. So where mathematical technique or any other new tool is applicable, we have said so and suggested that the technical part of the job be turned over to an expert.

In spite of judicial opinion to the contrary, managers do worry about matters of ethics. Much that has been written on the subject seems to us to be on Cloud 9. So we have included a final chapter in which we have tried to get down to brass tacks and point out some of the areas in marketing management where the conscientious executive must face up to questions of right and wrong and make ethical judgments. We have not tried to answer many of the moral questions we raise because we are not disposed to fancy ourselves as keepers of the marketing conscience.

We are well aware that there are no pat answers to problems of marketing management. As a result our book probably raises more questions than it answers. We have tried to let the student know what the problems of marketing are, to give him some insight into their nature and implications, and to offer some suggestions as to how to go about solving them in the specific forms in which they present themselves in the actual practice of business management.

Professor Ross Cunningham of Massachusetts Institute of Technology worked with us as coauthor during the planning stage of this book and wrote a share of the initial draft. His untimely death prevented his participation in the work of revision and publication. We acknowledge his substantial contribution to whatever virtues it may possess. For such weaknesses as survived revision we assume final and complete responsibility.

R. S. ALEXANDER
THOMAS BERG

January, 1965

Table of Contents

CHAPTER 1

The Marketing Manager's Job

What is marketing management? This is not an easy question to answer by general description or by the exposition of abstract concepts. Nor would such an answer be easy to understand.

We have a feeling that the student can most quickly and easily get a working notion of the activities we will be discussing in this book and of the problems we will be attacking if he starts by reading about the case of a specific marketing manager. In describing his experiences we will not confine ourselves to activities and problems that are purely marketing in nature but will follow him in his contacts with and participation in several much broader areas of decision and action that have an impact on marketing. We do this not out of any mischievous intent to confuse the student but to impress on him from the beginning the fact that the marketing activities of a firm are not carried on in any hermetically sealed compartment of the business, that a business is all one body, and that there is a constant stream of influence and effect flowing both ways between the marketing department and every other functional unit of the firm.

From time to time we will refer to certain problems or activities as belonging to marketing, and to others as outside it but influencing it or being influenced by it. In making this distinction we will use the definition of marketing suggested by the Definitions committee of the American Marketing Association: "the performance of business activities that direct the flow of goods and services from producer to consumer or user." It is possible to quarrel with several features of this definition, but it is one that is widely used and sponsored by an arm of an organization whose membership consists mainly of marketing research men, collegiate teachers of marketing, government officials dealing with marketing activities, and persons engaged in managing the marketing work of business concerns.

1

The hero of our piece, Mr. William Highman, is not in a strict sense a real person. Although he is a figment of our imagination, in another sense he and his adventures are very real because many marketing managers undergo the experiences we will describe and must meet and solve the problems which Bill encounters in our story.

On August 1, Mr. Highman assumed the duties of vice president for marketing of a firm that shall remain nameless. He came from a much smaller company, which operated in a part of the industry in which his new firm was a leader. There he was executive vice president, having worked his way up through the sales and advertising groups to be director of marketing, and then into general management. Since his former firm was family-owned and Bill did not belong to the family, he knew he could go no higher there, and so he joined his new company in search of other worlds to conquer.

The firm which Mr. Highman joined made (*a*) a group of materials which it sold to concerns in several industries for further processing into end products, which they in turn marketed, some to ultimate consumers and some to other firms for use in their businesses, and (*b*) a line of consumer products which it sold to wholesalers who, in turn, sold them to retailers for resale to the ultimate consumers. Bill was in charge of the work of marketing both these groups of products. Sales of the two groups were about equal in dollar volume.

The customer firms, which used the materials, generally employed groups of specialized buyers under the management of a purchasing agent or director of purchases. Most of them wished to buy in fairly large lots, often committing themselves in a single contract for all or a large percentage of their requirements for a year or half a year. These professional buyers chose their suppliers mainly on the basis of the precision with which the quality of the materials they offered fitted the needs of the firms they served, the consistency of this quality, the speed and certainty of delivery, the reliability of the supplier as indicated by his reputation for doing what he promised to do, and the prices at which the materials were offered. Many of these buyers were technical men and shrewd and skillful bargainers. The buying firms often needed and expected technical service in the form of advice and help in using the materials to make the end products they wished.

The wholesalers and retailers who bought the company's consumer products purchased them for resale. Since they handled many products, made by many manufacturers, they did not want to and, in fact, could not do much of the selling work themselves—but depended on the manufacturers to do it. In order to market these products, therefore,

Mr. Highman's new company sought to put them in attractive packages, to brand them, and to advertise them widely and intensively to ultimate consumers. Each product had its own brand and the company name was printed in small type at the bottom of the package.

The company carried on an intensive and costly program of research to discover new products in both the materials and consumers' goods areas. It constantly added new products to its line and deleted old ones as their usefulness or popularity waned.

When Mr. Highman moved into the office of vice president for marketing he decided that, for a period of two weeks, he would stay out of the day-to-day management of his new department as much as he could and devote his time and effort to studying his organization: the way it operated, its relations with the other parts of the business, the people he would have to deal with, and the general orientation of the management he would have to work under and the executives he would have to supervise. Inevitably, though, his deliberations were disturbed by a number of matters upon which the responsibilities of his office demanded that he take a position and either approve or reject.

For example, the manager of materials sales and the marketing research manager presented for his approval a proposal to conduct marketing research with respect to a material on which the company was meeting severe price competition both from foreign imports and from one or two competitors whose costs were suspected to be lower than those of Bill's new firm. As a result of this some customers had diverted their patronage to these sources. Others had stuck with the company, indicating that perhaps Bill's firm had something else to sell beside the material itself and its price. What this "something else" was, and how important it was, the marketing executives did not know, but if they could find out the information might be of great help in planning countermeasures.

A marketing research study, costing $25,000, was proposed to try to find out what factors influenced users of the material in placing their orders with one source or another. Such a study had its dangers, for it might cause some faithful customers to examine their buying motives more carefully and, perhaps, switch their patronage. If Bill approved the proposal, he would have to carry it into the president's office and defend it—for the $25,000 exceeded the budget of the marketing research department and would have to be obtained by transfer from some other budgetary item.

Bill studied the organization chart and job descriptions of the marketing division. It looked something like what is shown in Figure 1-1.

He found that the managers of materials sales and consumers' goods sales were responsible for most of the work of planning the marketing of their respective groups of products, for recommending changes in prices, for originating helps for salesmen, for providing technical service to users, for recommending product modifications and deletions, and for keeping informed about trends in their fields and about the comparative performance and plans of the company and its competition.

FIGURE 1–1

MARKETING DIVISION ORGANIZATION AND JOB DESCRIPTION CHART

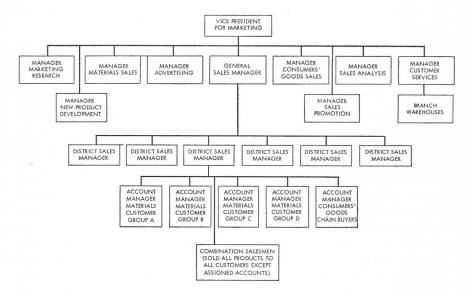

The manager of advertising administered a budget about ten times that of the sales promotion manager. Both, however, had to manage the preparation of promotional matter for materials which, in one instance, required exact, carefully drawn, somewhat technical copy dealing with provable claims; and in the other instance with consumers' goods which needed much more flamboyant copy, carrying claims that sometimes partook more of the fanciful than the factual.

The manager of new product development had a rather nebulous assignment. He and his very small staff were expected to originate or gather ideas for new products, assemble information on which development decisions could be made, follow new product projects through research, and prepare comprehensive plans for the introduction and market development of the chosen products. Bill found that a small, very high-powered new product unit operated out of the president's office, and that the manager of new product development was more than a little uncertain about where the responsibilities and powers of this high-level unit ended and where his began (although he was under the impression that the "presidential group" dealt with possible new categories of products and with products or firms available for purchase or merger).

The next morning Bill, talking with the leader of the new product group, learned that this gentleman had proposed to the president that he take over the functions of the manager of new product development and add a small staff of technical and production people, with whom he could run pilot plant operations, and a small force of salesmen. The new product manager explained that this way he could manage all phases of the introduction of a new product up to the point where it could be turned over as a full-fledged member of the line and be made and sold by the regular production and marketing divisions. Mr. Highman made a note to the effect that this was a matter about which he must make up his mind and prepare for a showdown. He felt that while new product development was not purely a marketing matter, it certainly had marketing implications, and there were definite advantages to having his men live with a product during the early stages of its introduction on the market.

The manager of customer services had charge of the branch warehouses (from which deliveries to customers were made), of processing orders, of requisitioning stocks for the branches and determining inventories of finished goods, and of handling customer complaints about delivery. A talk with him disclosed that all orders were processed in the same manner in spite of the fact that materials had to be stored differently from consumers' goods, that orders for them usually called for much larger quantities than those for consumers' goods, and that delivery requirements for the two types of products differed materially.

From him Bill also picked up the fact that some months previously an executive task force had been designated to study the whole question of the management of all kinds of inventories, raw materials, goods in process, and finished goods. Talking with the leader of this group he found out that there was strong likelihood that the task force would recommend the appointment of a manager of inventories, who would have charge of determining the amount and location of finished-goods inventories, along with all other stocks.

Bill made note of this as another matter on which he would sooner or later have to take a position. He fully approved the idea that the amount of company funds tied up in inventories should be reduced to the lowest point consistent with proper operations, but he was also keenly aware of the facts that the purpose of finished-goods inventories was to service customers' wants, and that customers' wants were the peculiar business of the marketing division.

The account managers, operating under the district managers, performed a dual function. Each had a number of large customers who belonged to a specific customer group: agricultural, food, textile, and the like, and each handled the company contacts with these customers. Even the president or the vice president for marketing did not visit such a customer without taking the account manager along with him. These men also traveled with the "combination salesmen" in the district from time to time and tried to train them and help them to sell to less important accounts in their several customer groups.

The combination salesman, reporting to the district sales manager, sold all the products of the company to all customers in his territory who were not assigned to an account manager. By the very nature of his work he could have no very complete knowledge either of the products he sold or of the operations of the customers he sold them to.

In the course of his organizational explorations the new vice president learned that a small group of the marketing executives had been working on a plan for reorganizing the structure of the marketing department. They were motivated by a feeling that the several customer groups were not getting the kind of specialized sales service they needed since the combination salesman had to be all things to all customers, and really could be of no very valuable service to any of them. They also deplored the fact that no executive with authority was responsible for obtaining the business of any one of the customer groups.

One of the marketing executives then described and charted several plans they had considered. The one that looked best to them is shown in Figure 1–2. This plan, Bill thought, made a lot of sense. One reservation he had regarding it lay in the fact that it was the brainchild of the general sales manager, who had "had a lightning rod up" when the vice president job was vacant and was much disappointed when an outsider was chosen. Bill wanted badly to win his support and confidence and was afraid that this desire might have influenced his appraisal of the plan.

This proposed plan contemplated setting up the operating units of the marketing organization on the basis of groups of customers who were differentiated either by their purpose or manner of using the

FIGURE 1–2

MARKETING DEPARTMENT REORGANIZATION CHART

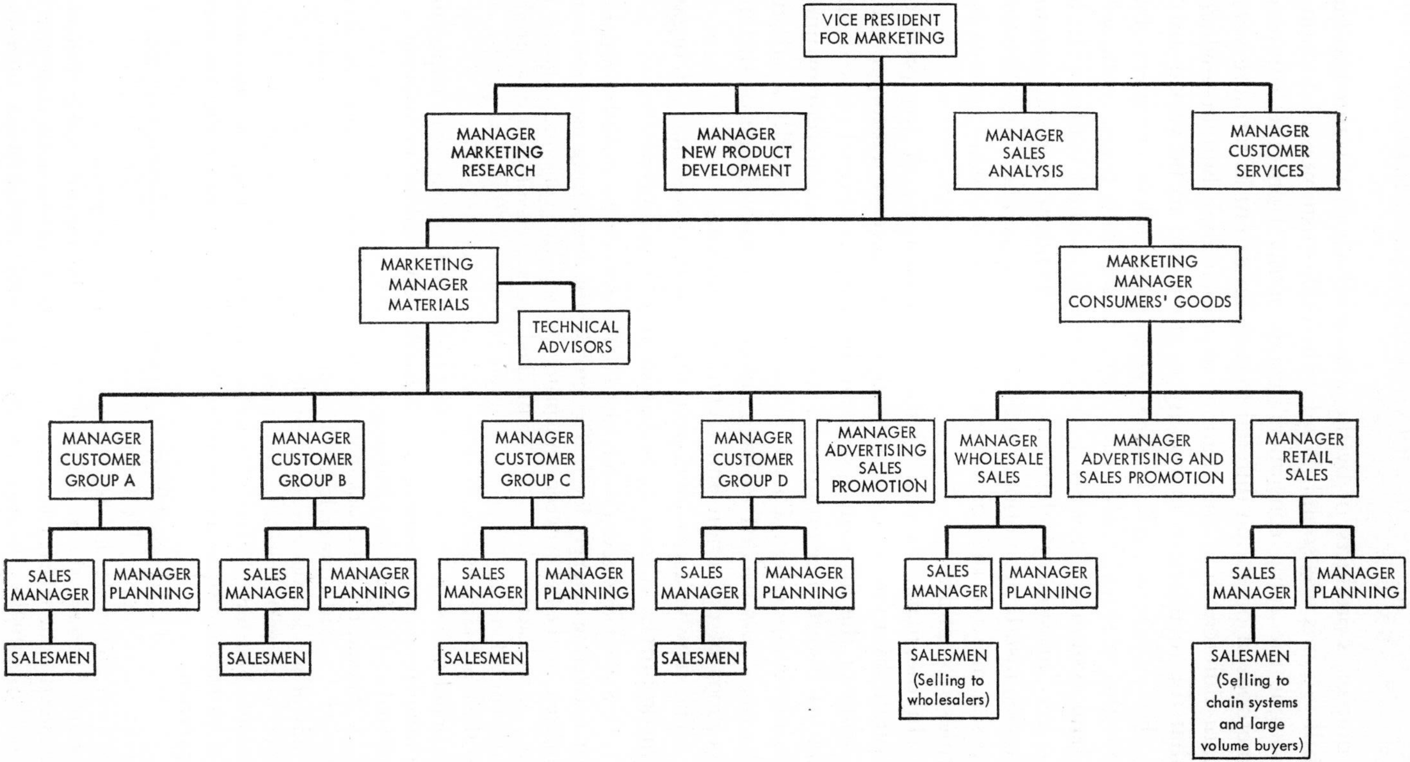

company's products, or by the way in which they wanted to buy them. Bill felt this was sound. While wholesale customers and chain systems bought the same consumers' goods items from the company, their methods of operation differed to such an extent as to cause very significant differences in the manner in which they bought—which meant that the methods of marketing to them had to be varied also.

For example, wholesalers and independent retailers habitually bought to stock, each order being a separate transaction, whereas a chain system often wished to buy on an annual contract. It was easy to get "missionary salesmen" into independent stores to arrange shelf stocks, install promotional material, and urge and train the storekeeper to sell more of the company's products. Many chain systems had strict rules against this.

In the materials part of the business many of the products were bought by more than one customer group, each customer group consisting of the firms in a separate industry or several related industries, but each customer group used the product in a different manner or for a different purpose. To sell to an industry successfully a salesman and his managers needed to have an intimate knowledge of the industry's methods of operation and technical problems.

The new vice president felt that before this system of organization was approved certain questions should be answered:

1. Should the new product development work be shoved down to at least the marketing manager level? The problem of discovering user needs and wants differed markedly between the materials and the consumers' goods business, and all the factors that made or blocked the success of each new product were different. Materials buyers were interested in such things as precise suitability to their purposes, cost reductions, and consistency of quality, while such things as brand names, packaging, and advertising were much more important in the consumers' goods business. The activities involved in introducing a product differed vastly in the two markets.

2. Should the functions of the customer services department be divided and shoved down to a lower level? The differences in storing and handling the two kinds of goods have already been noted. In addition a warehouse, properly located to serve the needs of consumers' goods customers, was not always where it could best serve buyers of materials. But to set up separate systems of warehouses for the two would undoubtedly increase the cost of the customer service operation .

3. Would it be possible to set up each of the marketing managers as a cost-profit center, responsible for preparing his own budget (subject to top management approval) and for showing a satisfactory profit on the operations of his area? Perhaps this principle might even be applied to the customer group managers under these executives. This would have the advantage that it would probably stimulate in each of the responsible executives a high degree of

personal involvement in the performance of his area and would focus that involvement on profits rather than on mere volume of sales. There was a wide variation in the net profit margin of different products, and often those that were easiest to sell returned the least profit. On the other hand, the application of this principle would demand almost complete delegation of authority, something not previously known in the company.

4. Are there enough able executives to man the new managerial positions? The general sales manager was mainly interested in consumers' goods, which would have the largest sales force. Bill thought the present manager of materials sales had executive as well as planning ability, but was uncertain of the availability of men to fit in the lower managerial posts. Most of the men who would go into these positions were not used to making their own decisions, so the mortality among them would probably be high, and the company's marketing efforts would be disrupted while they were being tried out and were learning their jobs. This learning process might be expected to be a fairly long one.

5. Will the new organization structure require more, or less, salesmen than the present one? Bill decided to ask the general sales manager if he could pry his assistant (who was an expert on salesmen's territories) loose from his regular work and have him plan the probable territorial set-up under the new organization.

6. Will we need managers of marketing planning as far down in the organization as we have them on the proposed chart? Would a planning unit under each of the marketing managers do just as well? Bill realized that if a customer group manager were to be a cost-profit center, he might need a planning unit.

7. Is it wise to divide the advertising and sales promotion work for materials from that for consumers' goods?

As for the last point, Mr. Highman very much approved the inclusion of advertising and sales promotion in one managerial package. The need for coordination of the two seemed urgent enough to require it. But the division shown on the chart might lead to two different advertising policies for the company and, perhaps, to the use of two agencies. Not much advertising was needed for materials, and so the advertising budget of the materials area might not be big enough to interest a first-rate agency—or even to justify the salary of a good man to administer it. Placing the materials advertising in the hands of a small agency might not be so bad, however, for some of the smaller agencies specialized in servicing industrial goods accounts and the company's materials advertising therefore might enjoy more expert handling than it now received as a minor, sideline fragment of a major account with a large agency. This would take some thinking.

At this point Bill's deliberations were interrupted by the managers of materials sales and new products development, who sought counsel and decision on the pricing of a new material that was about ready to be put on the market. The former thought that it should be priced very high at the beginning, to yield a gross margin of about 70 percent on sales. He felt that even at that inflated price there would be enough demand to absorb all the company could produce in the early stages and enable it to get back fast its research and development "seed corn" expenditures. The new products man did not deny this but felt that competition was bound to develop in about a year, and that customer loyalty should instead be cemented by a price somewhere near what it might be expected to be under competitive conditions.

In talking with these gentlemen the new vice president learned that the company had no recognized policy applying to a situation like this; in fact it had no general pricing policy at all. He further learned that the work of analyzing pricing problems was done in the marketing department and that the department was expected to come up with recommendations for all pricing actions. All but the most trivial of these recommendations had to be approved by top management. The others assured him, however, that very rarely was a well-reasoned and carefully considered proposal for pricing action rejected. Bill added another note to a file that was now growing rather thick, to the effect that it might be a good idea to develop a statement of pricing policy to guide the members of the department in gathering and analyzing pricing information and in thinking about pricing actions.

At lunch in the company cafeteria one day, Bill sat at a table with executives in the production division, including the vice president for production. There was considerable jesting about the inaccuracy of the sales forecasts made by the marketing division, and Bill countered by casually mentioning several recent quality failures. But he detected in the joking enough serious dissatisfaction with the sales estimates to justify his digging into the matter.

He found that estimates or forecasts of sales were assembled by the sales analysis unit of the marketing division. Since two of the chief uses of such forecasts were (*a*) in planning production schedules and (*b*) in making annual commitment contracts for materials, they had to be made for individual products and in terms of physical units. Since dollar income was important in planning the marketing work and the financial needs of the company, the physical unit forecasts were turned into dollar sales estimates by means of a system of price forecasts assembled also by the manager of sales analysis.

Sales forecasts were for one year but they were reviewed, and, if need be, revised every quarter. They were timed so that they could be used as the basis of the budget for the coming year, which had to be approved before December 15 of the preceding year. So the work of estimating occurred mainly during September, October, and November. The procedure of estimating was about as follows.

a) The sales analysis unit supplied each account manager a list of his assigned accounts with actual sales by product groups made to each account during the past three years and estimated sales and actual sales to date for the current year.

b) In conference with his district manager the account manager estimated how much he expected to sell each account during the coming year.

c) A similar list of the accounts serviced by the combination men in his district was furnished each district manager who then estimated next year's sales to these accounts.

d) These estimates were then reviewed by the general sales manager, and the manager of material sales and consumers' goods sales.

e) The manager of sales analysis checked the estimates against his statistical projections, and also reviewed them for internal consistency.

Mr. Highman studied past forecasting performance and found that, on the whole, estimates of sales of consumers' goods were much more accurate than those of materials—although chain store estimates were farther from the mark than were those for wholesalers. Estimates of sales of materials sometimes varied widely from actual sales, usually because of changes made by big customers in their sources of supply. He did not see how this could be remedied, although he felt that it was worthwhile to try to make these forecasts more accurate.

Bill had a serious talk about the matter with the production vice president and the treasurer, both of whom expressed gratification for his good intentions but no great confidence in the possibility of much improvement. He found that both sometimes made their own estimates in planning production schedules and working capital needs. Both expressed some concern about the lack of long-run forecasts, covering five to ten years, which they could use in planning future needs for equipment and capital. He promised to try to do something about the matter, but was undecided whether this should be the province of the sales analysis unit or of marketing research. Perhaps these units should be combined into a marketing information and statistics department, under one man. This would also help solve another problem which was beginning to trouble him: his span of control; he had too many people reporting to him, and this would reduce the list by one.

The manager of materials sales was unhappy and let Bill know it. Most of the consumers' goods products of the company were made of materials manufactured by it. Many of the company's competitors in the consumers' goods field did not make their own materials and so were prospective buyers of the company's materials in bulk. The manager of materials sales pointed out that in the case of a recently developed improved material, on which the company enjoyed a high measure of market protection because of a secret process, management had refused to authorize its sale as a bulk material and had insisted that the entire output should be processed into consumers' goods and sold in that form. This meant that the firm's consumers' goods—which contained this material—were much better than those of its competitors, who were customers for materials. Some of them were very bitter about the matter and were threatening to withdraw their patronage.

According to the manager of materials sales this was not the first time this had happened, and this action seemed to represent a general policy of top management. He pointed out that this policy was not only costing his part of the business sales volume but was undermining the morale of his staff and of the materials account managers—who were forced to listen to the complaints of their customers, had few good new products to sell to kindle their enthusiasm, and were constantly in danger of losing large accounts on this issue. He also felt that the policy encouraged his customers to conduct research to develop their own materials, something that would ultimately cost the company its entire materials business, or reduce it to supplying only the smaller, weaker makers of consumer end products whose business was of doubtful profitability in any case.

Bill could see that this was a real danger to the company's business, but investigation soon disclosed that the margin of gross profit on materials was about 30 percent on sales, while that on consumers' goods was 50 to 60 percent of sales. Although the cost of marketing materials was between 5 and 10 percent of sales, while that of marketing consumers' goods ran around 30 percent, the profit differential in favor of consumers' goods was considerable, especially in view of the fact that the consumers' goods percentages were applied to a much higher selling price base than were those for materials.

On the other hand, the larger the number of firms selling goods made of a material, the larger the total volume of it marketed might be expected to be. Bill wondered if an acceptable and profitable compromise might be to confine the use of a promising new material to the consumers' goods part of the company's business for nine months to a year, thus giving it an opportunity to develop an advantageous position in the consumer market, then throw its sale open to all customers. If this policy were generally known, it might serve to soften the resentment of competitor-customers and give the materials account managers an occasional desirable new product to sell.

Bill saw very clearly that this problem would be aggravated if the new organization structure were adopted and the various customer group departments were made cost-profit centers. This plan would greatly increase the number of salesmen and executives whose livelihoods, positions, and futures depended entirely on the materials business.

In studying the sales records, Mr. Highman observed that a number of the products were sold in very small volume and were bought in very small orders. And the gross profit on some of these was very low. The same thing was true of a few of the items with larger sales volumes. He understood that a firm sometimes found it worthwhile, for production or marketing reasons, to deal in products on which it made no profit. But he also felt that in such cases management should know why it was doing so, and how much its losses were because of such a policy. Inquiry disclosed that his new company had no cost accounting system for marketing and hence no exact information as to profit or loss by products. Accounting work, however, was done by machine and the company had a computer installation on lease, which suggested that such figures could be obtained cheaply once the cost factors were worked out and a procedure set up. Bill also found that some years before there had been a vigorous pruning of the product line but that there was no procedure for continuous follow-up in product deletion work. He made two more entries in his notebook:

1. See the controller and explore with him the possibility of setting up a task force composed of an accountant and a marketing man to work out a system of getting net profit figures by products, by customers, by size of order, and by size of customer.

2. Have a procedure prepared for constant pruning of the product line by deletion.

At this point the new vice president's two weeks of office exploration had expired and he set out upon the second phase of his campaign of self-education about his new company. He took a "swing around the circle" visiting the district managers and meeting most of the account managers and a few of the combination salesmen. He also accompanied a few of them in calls on customers.

He came back with reinforced conviction that the proposed new organization structure would be a change in the right direction. But he was more than mildly disturbed by the problem of the firm's channels of marketing.

All materials were sold direct to users, many of whom were so small that the gross profit probably failed to cover the cost of calling on them and handling their orders. Many of these small customers were concentrated in certain industries and geographical districts. There were distributors who specialized in marketing materials and supplies to these industries, and in most areas of the country there were distributors who made a business of supplying materials, maintenance, repair, and operating items to all industrial firms, especially the smaller ones. Bill wondered if it would be possible, and more profitable, to sell direct to the big customers where the business was plentiful and to reach the smaller customers in thinner areas through distributors. Since distributors handled products made by many manufacturers in a number of lines, they were able on one order to serve a broad spectrum of the needs of the customer, with the result that the value of the order was greater. Also, they could profitably handle the needs of small buyers who could not possibly be served economically by the manufacturer.

This system would be hard to set up and administer and might reduce sales volume somewhat; but if it could be operated, it might increase profits. In order to analyze the problem intelligently, Bill felt he had to have some way of knowing which customers were unprofitable to the company. He decided that the development of a cost analysis system for marketing should claim high priority on his list of things to be done.

The consumers' goods line could be sold to ultimate consumers through about 75,000 retail outlets. About 500 wholesalers specialized in supplying these outlets. About 15,000 of the retail stores were units of chain systems that bought direct or were large enough to buy direct from the manufacturer. If a manufacturer tried to sell direct to the 60,000 independent stores, he would need about 600 salesmen. If he relied entirely on wholesalers, he would require about five men. Bill's company compromised by marketing through wholesalers but requiring each of its combination salesmen to make "missionary" calls on the retailers in his territory to take "turnover" orders, which were transmitted to the wholesaler to be filled at his regular gross profit margin; to arrange the stock; to try to enthuse the dealer to push the company's products, and to arrange and install point-of-sale promotional material. The general sales manager estimated that this "missionary" work required about 200 salesman man-years of work annually. This agreed pretty closely with the estimates Bill had got from a number of the district managers.

Two things seemed to be wrong with this procedure. Many wholesalers bought in very small lots—lots not much, if any, bigger than those which might be expected from retailers. They were not performing one of their primary functions, the carrying of adequate and representative stocks needed to serve their retail customers, but were depending on the company's excellent branch house and delivery system to perform this function for them.

Many of them also seemed to take the attitude that since the company had combination men making missionary calls on the retailers, these men could be relied on to do any constructive sales work which the company's products needed. They simply booked such orders as were offered and devoted their salesmen's time to selling their own private brands and other long profit items. There were a few who did a real selling job for the company's products and the volume they sold showed the benefits to be derived from such efforts.

Mr. Highman was not satisfied with this situation, although everybody assured him it was of long standing, but he didn't quite know what ought to be done about it. To sell direct to all retailers would increase marketing costs materially, although part of the increase would be covered by the wholesaler's gross profit margin which the company could keep under this system. To depend entirely on wholesalers and cut out "missionary" calls would cut selling expenses but might reduce sales volume more than proportionately. The company might pick out one or two of the best wholesalers in each market area and sell to them alone. Just what effect this might have on sales would be hard to predict.

Bill finally decided not to do anything for the present. If he got the new organization plan adopted and prevailed upon the general sales manager to head up the consumers' goods department, he could then dump the problem in that worthy's lap. He intended to push for some sort of action on it sooner or later.

At about this time Bill found on his desk a tentative budget for the marketing division for the coming year. This had been compiled by the manager of sales analysis and consisted of a series of estimates of sales by products in physical units and dollars (prepared as previously described) and estimates of costs of operation made by the district managers and department heads. An examination of the document suggested that most of his time during the next couple of months must inevitably be devoted to a series of conferences with his district managers and department heads, and with top management on this subject.

Internal evidence and comparison with tentative and approved budgets for previous years indicated that many of the unit heads had included pet items of expense—which apparently had been rejected previously and had now been exhumed and resubmitted on the theory that the new vice president might be more liberally inclined than his predecessor. Bill did not blame them for trying again and felt that each such budgetary item should be examined carefully and accepted or rejected on its merits rather than on the basis of previous executive action.

He knew that the most careful study and preparation must be given to every item in the final document so that he could defend it when the division heads met in the president's office to whip the company budget into final shape. He could see that for the next couple of months life for him would be pretty hectic and that he would have little time to work on reducing the number of items of unfinished business in his notebook. So he regretfully put it into the top drawer of his desk with a private promise to himself to return to it when the budget making storm had blown over.

We have now made you privy to most of the problems the new vice president for marketing discovered in his month-long study of his company's operations. Except for casual references, we have left out one very important problem: the people through whom he had to work. Due to the fact that creativity, enthusiasm, and the gift of pleasant personal relationships are so vital in marketing work, this may be viewed as a very serious omission. But the literary skill needed to put people on paper is so far beyond that of our somewhat prosaic pens that we will not attempt it.

We have not solved any of the problems Mr. Highman found. For a few of them possible solutions have been suggested, but our suggestions by no means represent all the alternatives or even the best ones. In this chapter we have shied away from solving the problems Bill discovered because our purpose here is to raise, not to solve, problems. The rest of the book is concerned with trying to present some possible solutions and with suggesting ways in which marketing problems may be solved.

Perhaps now we are in a position to draw a few summary statements about the extent and nature of the job of marketing management as illustrated by Mr. Highman's company.

1. It includes the organization, deployment, and supervision of all the facilities, people, and devices for personal selling, advertising, and sales promotion in the company.

2. It includes or is involved in the provision and direction of facilities for delivering the company's products to its customers.

3. It involves the selection of channels of distribution and the negotiation and management of the relations of the company with the outlets in the selected channel and of the outlets among themselves.

4. It involves the planning of marketing activities during each coming period, usually a year, although sometimes a number of years.

5. It involves the collection and analysis of all sorts of pertinent information about the present and possible future markets of the company and about performance in those markets.

6. Through forecasting or supplying basic information and analyses for forecasting, it plays a vital part in the production and financial planning of the firm.

7. It plays a highly significant, although not necessarily dominant, role in discovering possible new products, in evaluating them, and in introducing them to the market.

8. It is charged with collecting facts and making analyses of them which will guide in making pricing decisions and in preparing recommendations for such decisions. Sometimes it makes pricing decisions in conformity with company policy.

9. Its decisions and activities must be directed toward the achievement of profit and other objectives of the company, and not merely toward the increase of sales volume.

To Whom Can We Market?

CHAPTER 2

Studying the Market

The beginning and the end of profitable marketing work is the consumer or user. In making his plans and in almost every detail of carrying them out, the marketing manager must start with an understanding of the consuming or using group he serves, the things they want, how they want to buy them, how they use them and what for, how they think and feel about things, and what their objectives and primary motives are. He must think not so much in terms of "How can I sell to them?" as in terms of "What benefits or satisfactions can they get out of buying and using my goods or services?" He must not be content with a mere static look at these things but must make sure that he is aware of changes that are taking place in them and of the impact these trends are likely to have on the effectiveness of his own decisions and actions.

THE NATURE OF A MARKET

To the manufacturer a market is an opportunity to sell his goods or services. The Definitions committee of the American Marketing Association expresses it somewhat more eruditely:

1. The aggregate of forces or conditions within which buyers and sellers make decisions that result in the transfer of goods and services.
2. The aggregate demand of the buyers of a commodity or service.

The chief among these "forces or conditions" that comprise a market are people, money to spend, and willingness to spend it. The marketer may generate certain forces of his own that affect this complex but he can hope to modify only one part of it, the willingness to spend. The number of people and the money they have to spend are almost entirely beyond his individual control. By his efforts he may be able to stimulate or augment or channel willingness to spend, but there is considerable doubt about his ability to create it and, even if he can do so, the process is apt to be exceedingly expensive.

The businessman very often gives the term a geographical connotation, as the "New England Market" or the "Los Angeles Market." He is also apt to find it useful to think of people as groups distinguished by some common characteristic, such as the "college market," the "baby market," or the "suburbanite market."

The broadest distinction that can be made on this latter basis is between the ultimate *consumer* market and the *industrial or business* market. Ultimate consumers buy for personal or household use. In doing so they seek their own personal satisfaction, or the personal satisfaction of someone else for whom they buy. The industrial buyer purchases goods and services to be used in conducting his enterprise. His purchases may vary from lead pencils to gigantic electric generators. Many institutions, such as schools, churches, and hospitals, buy on much the same bases as do industrial or business firms. They are sometimes subclassified as the "institutional market." Typically, the industrial buyer is seeking benefits or functions performed in the conduct of his enterprise: in the final analysis, profit dollars in the bank.

We will be wise to examine these two types of markets separately. In doing so, though, we will also find it desirable to study each type in terms of the basic elements of a market, people, and the groups into which they associate themselves to buy; the amounts of money they have to spend; and the factors that influence their willingness to spend it.

Before we begin to discuss these elements that make up a market, perhaps it will be wise for us to note that in practically every market there are users, purchase influencers, deciders, and buyers, and that in the typical purchase transaction they are likely to be different people. For example, a cat is not a buyer or a decider in a purchase of cat food but she is certainly a user of the product, and undoubtedly influences its purchase by her feeding behavior. The woman in the household is usually the buyer of food and the users are all the members of her family. With respect to certain things, she may decide what to buy, subject to the influence of the other members of the family; with respect to other things, about which certain members have pronounced opinions, she may be merely the buyer of goods decided upon by others.

The housewife is apt to be both the decider and the buyer of draperies and hangings, but if her husband has pronounced color preferences, they may influence her choice. In the buying of goods and services for use in industry an official known as a purchasing agent does the buying, but he may or may not make the purchasing decision, and the decision-maker is almost certain to be influenced by a number of people, sometimes as many as six or seven, in the organization. The wise marketing manager seeks to discover which persons in the economic units that purchase his products fall into each of these categories and appeal to them accordingly. Different appeals may be effective for each group.

THE ULTIMATE CONSUMER MARKET

The domestic ultimate consumer market consists of the opportunity to sell goods and services to satisfy all personal or family wants manifested by all the people of the United States, every one of whom is a consumer. Every individual is a user of goods and services from the minute of his birth to the hour of his burial, and even thereafter if his family thinks enough of him to erect a monument in his memory. He selects from the vast array of articles offered to him by business those which he wishes and has funds to acquire, and passes by those that do not satisfy his desires or are beyond his means. The great problem of business is to produce and to offer for sale those commodities which the consumer is willing and able to purchase.

One of the chief problems of the marketing manager in the consumers' goods field is to determine the number of possible users who will be willing and able to buy a given article during a coming period and the amounts of it they are likely to purchase. Many items offered to consumers by business are able to satisfy a particular desire only partially. Insofar as they are purchased, they represent a compromise between what the consumer would like to have and what is available.

People

The first and most important dimension of a market for a consumers' good is people, for without people no market can exist. The first step, therefore, in the process of evaluating a market is to count the people in it. The Survey of Current Business reports that in November, 1963, the Bureau of the Census estimated that there were 190,000,000 people in the United States. These people are scattered unevenly over an area of some 3,600,000 square miles.

Throughout this whole area, movement of goods and people is practically free. Extensive rail, motor, air, and water transportation systems facilitate commerce and travel, while excellent communication systems, including mail, telephone, telegraph, radio, television, and national publications work to knit the entire population into a single economic and social unit. Vast and important improvements are occurring in these facilities and will probably continue to occur in the years to come.

There are, of course, local variations in climatic conditions, customs, and habits which affect the demand for particular types of goods. As a result of these differences, although the country seems to comprise a single market, it is really composed of a number of submarkets. For example, the people of New England have certain customs, preferences, and needs—such as baked beans and pie for breakfast—that are quite unlike those of the inhabitants of the Southern states who, for example, have a yen for hush puppies, hominy grits, and white cornmeal. These variations were far more important in the past than they are today. The leavening influence of motion pictures, the radio, television, extensive automobile travel, military service, and other forces has tended to eliminate some of them and to modify others.

For example, there was a time when manufacturers of style merchandise could count on a regular progression of fashions across the country from east to west, each vogue requiring a definite period to travel from the Atlantic to the Pacific seaboard. This is no longer true. The demand for a given new style of women's hats is likely to occur almost simultaneously on Fifth Avenue; in Tulsa, Oklahoma; Hastings, Nebraska; and Chico, California. This is due to a tremendous improvement in the speed and universality of communication media by which a new design is described over the radio and shown on national television, the motion picture screen, and in national advertising almost as soon as it appears. The dweller in the small town is almost as up-to-date in his or her demands as is the metropolitan consumer.

These influences will probably tend to increase rather than diminish in importance, and customs and markets are likely to become more uniform throughout the United States. It is said that the influence of television, radio, and the motion picture is leveling the distinctive peculiarities of speech in different sections of the country. The vast influence of television and radio, by which the words and ideas of a single speaker are conveyed simultaneously to millions of listeners in all parts of the nation, tends to direct their thinking into common channels. The progressive expansion of air travel is likely to carry this tendency still farther. All these changes vitally affect marketing problems, methods, and agencies.

There are, of course, still regional variations in market demand. These differences are to a certain extent determined by gradations in the buying power of the population in different territories and by climatic conditions which affect the need for or suitability of particular commodities. It is hopeless to try to sell rubber footwear extensively to the desert dwellers of southern Arizona, and the heavy winter clothing needed in New England finds little demand in Florida. These and other distinctive characteristics of demand in various parts of the country will remain, and must receive consideration by those who market commodities. But the tendency has been and will be toward greater uniformity in many other respects, although certain traditional traits or character or habits of thought or action, such as the conservatism of the native New Englander and the expansiveness of the sons of Texas and California, will probably die hard.

Population Trends

The marketing manager can not be content with knowing where his market is and how big; he must also try to determine where it is going and how fast, and how big it will be next year and ten years from now. The good marketing manager must pretty much leave to his subordinates the handling of the events of today and live his business life largely in building plans for the uncertain future. So trends which hint at the future are important, often more so than the actual current figures.

Increase in Total Population. Near the end of 1963 the Bureau of the Census estimated the population of the United States to be about 190,000,000. The figures for the last four census periods are shown in the accompanying table.

Census Year	Population	Population Increase	Percent of Population Increase from Previous Census
1930	122,775,000	17,064,000	16
1940	131,669,000	8,894,000	7
1950	150,697,000	19,028,000	14
1960	179,323,000	28,626,000	19

These figures might suggest that marketing managers of firms making consumers' goods can count on a fairly constant increase of between 1.5 and 2.0 percent a year in the total market. In fact, many of them, consciously or unconsciously do so, sometimes without being aware of the figures that seem to justify such reliance. Even if we disregard the influence of money to spend and willingness to spend it, and rely entirely on the number of persons in the population as a measure of the national market, this assumption may prove fallacious. The past history of our population growth discloses considerable variations in its rate, as is indicated by the precipitous decline during the decade of the 1930's and the pronounced bulge during the 1950's.

Population experts are by no means sure of the factors that influence rate of growth. So unsure are they, as a matter of fact, that they refuse to make hard and fast estimates of future population growth and instead offer a range of estimates, each based on a different set of assumptions. A set of these estimates made by the Census Bureau several years ago, is shown in Table 2–1.

TABLE 2–1

POPULATION ESTIMATES

(In Thousands)

	Estimate 1*	Estimate 2†	Estimate 3‡	Estimate 4§
1960	181,154	180,126	179,773	179,420
1965	198,950	195,747	193,643	191,517
1970	219,474	213,810	208,199	202,541
1975	243,880	235,246	225,552	215,790
1980	272,557	259,981	245,409	230,834

*On assumption of fertility rate 10 percent above 1955–1957.
†On assumption of fertility rate the same as 1955–1957.
‡On assumption of fertility rate declining from 1955–1957 rate to 1949–1951 rate by 1965.
§On assumption of fertility rate declining from 1955–1957 rate to 1942–1944 rate by 1965.

The manager engaged in marketing to ultimate consumers will be wise to keep informed as to rates of population growth and to note which of the experts' sets of assumptions seems to be working out in practice. This sort of information can be most useful in long-range forecasting and in planning five to ten years ahead, and is not to be entirely disregarded in preparing next year's marketing budget.

In the marketing of many kinds of goods the number of *households* is more important than the number of *people* as an element in determining demand. In this context a household is usually, but not always, a family. It may be composed of any small group of persons who live together and constitute an informal but fairly consistent buying unit, with a purchasing pattern much like that of a family. Furniture, household equipment and supplies, life insurance, and even automobiles are examples of goods and services which are customarily bought on a household rather than on an individual basis.

Changes in the number of household units tend to exercise a much greater and more immediate effect on the market for products whose demand they influence than changes in the number of people because the formation of a new household unit (especially if it be a family, and most of them are) immediately creates a need for a whole category of products to get the new menage equipped and in operation. Table 2–2 shows the number of households found by the Census Bureau and the Bureau's forecasts of changes in that number up to 1980.

TABLE 2–2

HOUSEHOLD FORMATION

Year	Estimate A*	Estimate B	Estimate C	Estimate D*
1960.		53,021,000 actual number		
1965.	57,517,000	56,076,000	55,311,000	54,565,000
1970.	62,933,000	61,094,000	59,689,000	58,814,000
1975.	69,318,000	67,003,000	64,906,000	63,900,000
1980.	76,006,000	73,085,000	70,544,000	69,382,000

*Estimate A is made on the most optimistic assumptions, and Estimate D is based on assumptions that on the whole are pessimistic.

A growing people tends to be an adventurous people, welcoming change, prodigal of the energies and lives of its members, imbued with confidence in its own future and what that future will bring in the form of expanding opportunities and purchasing power. A static or receding one, on the other hand, tends to be more conservative, fearful of the future, resistant to change, less willing to try new things. Thus a decline in the rate of population growth tends not only to cause a decrease in one of the chief elements that make up a market but to lessen somewhat the pressure for new and unique types of merchandise. This does not mean that a declining rate of growth inevitably causes a decrease in overall demand, for it may be offset by rising national income; nor does it preclude the introduction of new products, but it is likely to augment the difficulty and cost of popularizing them.

Geographical Shifts. The rate of population growth varies widely in different parts of the country. This is due in part to geographical variations in birth and death rates. But the movement of people from one place to another probably accounts for much more of the shift. Americans are a highly mobile people. A sample study by the Bureau of the Census in 1949 showed that in any one year about one person out of five changes his residence. About one out of every three persons who moves goes from one county into another. These figures vary considerably from one area to another, mobility being lowest (about 12 percent) in old, established states such as Massachusetts, New York, and Pennsylvania, and highest in relatively new states such as Nevada (31 percent) and Wyoming (29 percent), and states in which the nature of the social and economic structure is rapidly changing, such as Florida (about 29 percent). Table 2–3 shows the population growth rates between 1950 and 1960 for states at opposite ends of the scale.

The marketing manager should watch and adjust to these changes. But percentage figures alone can be misleading. For example, Illinois, with a growth rate of only 16 percent, increased as a market (measured by number of people alone) by 1,369,000—more than the combined increases of Nevada, Arizona, New Mexico, and Delaware with their much higher rates of growth. In general, population growth rates were high in the Pacific, Mountain, and South Atlantic states, and low in the East South Central, West North Central, New England, and Middle Atlantic states.

TABLE 2–3

EXTREME POPULATION CHANGES

State	Growth in People	Percentage Increase
Florida	2,181,000	79
Nevada	125,000	78
Arizona	552,000	74
California	5,131,000	48
New Mexico	270,000	40
Delaware	128,000	40
Arkansas	−124,000	−6
West Virginia	−146,000	−7

These shifts of population can be measured accurately only at ten-year census time intervals. But the trends are not apt to change quickly in direction or magnitude, and the Bureau of the Census makes sample estimates from time to time which may afford clues regarding them. *Sales Management* magazine in its annual supplement, "Survey of Buying Power," estimates population for counties and for many towns. These estimates have proved accurate enough to lead many firms to use them in making their geographical sales estimates. Then, too, any salesman worth his salt should be able to observe such changes as he moves through his territory by being alert to such things as the opening of new stores and changes in building activity. No manufacturer with a national sales force has any excuse for lacking at least some of this kind of current information to guide him in the geographical allocation of his marketing emphasis during the inter-census years.

Farm to City. The shift of population from rural to urban areas is a very long-continued one, having been under way for a century or more. Percentagewise, the relation of urban to rural population has been almost exactly reversed from 1880, when 28.6 percent of our people resided in urban and 71.4 percent in rural areas, to 1960, when

69.9 percent were urban dwellers and 30.1 percent lived in rural areas. The Bureau of the Census, which makes and reports these counts, does not confine the rural population to persons living on farms but also includes all persons living in places having a population of less than 2,500 and a population density of less than 1,500 per square mile. As Table 2–4 shows, the farm population proper has also been declining, both actually and relatively.

TABLE 2–4

URBAN, RURAL AND FARM POPULATION

Census Year	Urban		Rural		Farm	
1920	54,305,000	51.4%	51,406,000	48.6%	31,359,000	29.7%
1930	68,955,000	56.2	53,820,000	43.8	30,158,000	24.6
1940	74,424,000	56.5	57,246,000	43.5	30,216,000	22.9
1950	96,028,000	63.7	54,669,000	36.3	23,077,000	15.3
1960	125,347,000	69.9	53,976,000	30.1	13,449,000	7.5

The decline in farm population probably reflects the effect of the vast improvement in agricultural technology and the increased use of machinery which enables each farmer to cultivate a much larger acreage than he formerly did. Since this change has resulted in greatly increased income per farm dweller, there is some doubt that the decline in farm population reflects a decrease in the farm market for consumers' goods. Its net effect has certainly been a vast increase in the farm demand for such industrial goods as machinery, fertilizers, and prepared feeds, and perhaps for consumers' goods as well.

The concentration of people in large cities makes it easier for a manufacturer of consumers' goods to reach and market to them. His channels of marketing can be more direct. If he wishes to sell direct to retailers, for example, he will find that his typical urban salesman can make more calls per day than the man in a rural territory, for he wastes less time in travel. The sales per man are likely to be greater, and since the costs of "operating" a salesman do not vary much, the costs of selling (per dollar of sales) are apt to be less. Delivery distances are short, and while delivery is expensive per mile, the miles to be traveled are relatively few.

This effect is augmented by the fact that these centers of population make mass distribution possible. A department store, a supermarket, or a discount house must have a considerable population within a convenient radius to draw upon to be able to operate. The prevalence of these mass retailing units favors direct-to-retailer marketing, and may even make it necessary if the manufacturer is to get his fair share of the market.

Relationships are less personal in the city than in rural areas. The average farmer knows every other farmer for miles around and the dweller in a small town is apt to know most of the people living in the area. The typical apartment-dweller, however, neither knows nor cares to know his neighbors in the same building. This tends to magnify in rural areas what might be called the "bellwether effect" and to diminish its influence in the city: real leaders are easier to recognize when there aren't so many would-be leaders around. A common and effective device in marketing in a rural area is to pick out a person or family to whom the others in the community look up, sell him, and then use this sale as a lever on the others. The appeal is not so much "keeping up with the Joneses" as getting in on what is obviously a good thing. The same principle operates to some extent in the city—as the clustering of TV antennas and air conditioning "sweat boxes" indicated during the early development of those industries—but it is not nearly so powerful and the true leaders are harder to identify.

City to Suburb. Another important characteristic of population growth in recent decades has been the increase in suburban communities adjacent to the larger cities. This movement has been facilitated by the improvement of commuting services, railroads, highways, and other public transportation systems. In most metropolitan centers, however, this trend is more directly attributable to the extensive use of the automobile and the relatively larger incomes that have enabled the families of clerical and skilled workers to leave the crowded apartment house and tenement sections and to live in smaller communities of separate dwellings with yards and open spaces about them.

There are no accurate figures of the number of people living in suburbs. The estimates vary widely, according to how the estimator defines a suburb. Most of the estimates are probably too conservative, rather than too liberal, because most of those who make them tend to think in terms of the suburban cluster complex of the typical large city and to leave out of account the fact that smaller cities, even those with as few as 10,000 or 20,000 population, have their suburbs. They also tend to ignore what might be called the "string" residential areas, which are composed of individual residences strung for miles along the roads leading into even a moderate-sized city, and whose people tend to behave like suburbanites. So an estimate that one out of every four or five Americans is a suburbanite in his social and purchasing behavior is probably not unrealistic.

Nor does the number of people living in suburbs show a complete picture of the real importance of the suburban market. The incomes of these people are usually much higher than those of their city-dwelling brothers. For example, according to the 1962 County and City Data Book, published by the Bureau of the Census, the median family income in New York City was $6091, while in 15 suburban towns and cities in New Jersey, New York, and Connecticut the figure ranged from $7,829 (in Englewood, New Jersey) to $11,207 (in Ridgewood, New Jersey). The median for the 15 places was $8423.

The move from city to suburb causes highly significant changes in the family pattern of buying. It may be expected to create a family demand for such things as informal furniture, garden furniture, house paint, interior decorating materials, lawn and gardening tools, fertilizers, insecticides, station wagons, outdoor cooking equipment, basement workshop equipment and the dozens of other gadgets the new suburbanite soon feels are absolutely indispensable.

When the family moves to the suburb its relations with other people take on a more personal flavor. It can hardly avoid fairly close, although usually informal, relations with the neighbors. The kids usually set the pace with their gift for quick acquaintance around the block with others of their kind. Nor can the master of the house (without rudeness) avoid back-fence advice as to what to do about the bare spots on his lawn or the blight on his azalea bushes. These relationships assume the casual nature of the general informal living pattern which tends to characterize many, if not most, suburban communities.

In many suburbs, especially the newer ones, these neighborhood relationships tend to assume the form of "keeping up with the Joneses." My grass must be as lush as Joe's down the street; the car in my driveway must be as impressive as the one across the street; when the fellow down the block excavates for a swimming pool, I must begin to measure my backyard to find out where I can put a slightly bigger one—regardless of the amount of the mortgage on my house.

While the suburban market is lush and highly responsive to an imaginative approach, it is not easy for a manufacturer to reach as a unit. After the move from city to suburb, a family's buying tends for a time to be split between stores in the city and those in the new community. A gradual shift to local outlets may be expected and can be made less gradual by the development of shopping centers and the opening of branch stores. But these shifts create serious problems for the manufacturer in choosing his marketing channels and administering the relations among the outlets in them.

Population Density. The number of our people has grown, but the number of square miles in the continental United States has not. So the number of persons per square mile—population density—is constantly increasing. Population per square mile grew from 35.5 in 1920, to 41.2 in 1930, 44.2 in 1940, 50.7 in 1950, and to 60.1 (or, including Alaska and Hawaii, 50.5) in 1960.

Population density varies widely by states. It is highest in Rhode Island, which has 812.4 persons per square mile. New Jersey follows with 806.7, and Massachusetts comes next with 654.5. At the other end of the scale are Alaska with 0.4, Wyoming with 3.4, and Montana with 4.6. On Manhattan Island the density reaches the almost unbelievable figure of 77,195 persons per square mile. This means that if the land surface of the island were divided equally among the people living there, each person would have a space about 20 by 18 feet: he could shoot spitballs at his neighbor with a reasonable chance of scoring a hit. On the other hand, in Esmerelda County, Nevada, the density is only 0.2 persons per square mile: a man's nearest neighbor would be about two and a half miles away.

The densely populated areas are mainly those which are urban; the sparsely peopled ones are chiefly rural. There are three areas of heavy population concentration: (1) The Atlantic seaboard, from the north border of Massachusetts to somewhat below the mouth of the Potomac; (2) Along the Great Lakes, from about Rochester to somewhat north of Milwaukee; (3) The Pacific Coast, from slightly north of San Francisco almost to the Mexican border. Each of these areas is rapidly becoming one great metropolitan complex with little open land.

The marketing implications of density of population are just about the same as those of urbanization, which we examined earlier.

Age Shifts. The age distribution of a population exercises a significant effect on its importance and character as a market. This involves not only the kinds of things bought but the attitudes and habits that influence buying patterns. Changes in the age distribution, therefore, are of great importance to many manufacturers of consumers' goods. Such shifts also have the characteristics that, in large measure, they can be foreseen and their effects provided for.

Birth rates and death rates change slowly in the absence of widespread catastrophe. A large "baby crop" in any one year or succession of years can be relied on to cause a bulge through succeeding years in the demand for the goods and services peculiar to each age group as its members enter and pass through that age bracket. For example: toys and infant furniture and clothing during the early years; school books, school rooms, and bicycles during the grade and high school years; and household furniture and supplies when the population wave it causes hits the family formation age, about 20 to 25.

Pronounced changes are occurring in the age distribution of our population. Improvements in medical care have caused a long-run increase in the proportion of older persons in the population. This has been augmented by the spectacular "miracle" medicines developed and put into general use during recent decades. In addition, there has been an almost incredible "baby boom" that has added large increments at the other end of the age scale. Significant statistics from the reports of the Bureau of the Census (see Table 2–5) indicate these trends.

TABLE 2–5

POPULATION BY AGE SEGMENTS

	Number (in Thousands)			Percent of Total		
	1960	1950	1940	1960	1950	1940
Preschool (under 5)......	20,321	16,163	11,404	11.3	10.7	8.6
School (5–18)...........	48,684	34,941	34,764	27.2	23.2	26.3
Productive (19–59).......	86,616	81,306	72,616	48.3	54.0	54.7
Productive (19–64).......	93,758	87,404	77,345	52.3	58.0	58.3
Dependent (60 and over)..	23,701	18,294	13,746	13.2	12.1	10.4
Dependent (65 and over)..	16,559	12,196	9,017	9.2	8.1	6.8

The Bureau has made the following estimates (Table 2–6) of age shifts in the population between now and 1975. These estimates are based on the Bureau's most conservative assumptions as to the future behavior of the birth rate. They were made several years ago and although

TABLE 2–6

PROJECTED AGE SHIFTS

	Number (in Thousands)			Percent of Total		
	1965	1970	1975	1965	1970	1975
Dependent and School						
(below 20)...........	67,384	69,945	70,802	32.8	31.7	30.6
Productive (20–59).....	94,882	101,915	110,042	46.2	46.8	47.5
Old age dependent						
Over 60.............	25,106	27,470	30,053	12.5	12.7	13.0
Over 65.............	17,371	18,879	20,655	8.5	8.8	8.9

the birth rate dropped in 1962, its decline was less than had been assumed, and the beginning of the decline had already been delayed beyond that assumed in the system of estimates shown. This would tend to slow the percentage decline in the dependent school years and the percentage increase of the old age dependent group.

It is obvious that shifts in the age distribution of the population affect very considerably the sales forecasts and marketing plans of manufacturers of many kinds of goods used solely or especially by certain age groups, such as diapers, baby foods, and baby carriages at one end of the age scale, and hearing aids, horseshoes, and dentures at the other. And, to a very considerable extent, this effect can be foreseen. It is true that in planning next year's business a diaper manufacturer can not forecast the exact number of babies that will be born. But once a year's "baby crop" is here and its numbers are known, manufacturers of all sorts of articles its members will want and use (at various ages in their growth to maturity) can forecast with a high degree of accuracy how many of them will become of the age to demand his product and when they will do so.

Age distribution also influences the attitude and psychological climate of a population. Old age is a time of conservatism, not of adventure; it is a time of caution, when the yearning to try new things and experience new sensations has largely burned itself out. It is a time when peace and stability are more important than progress, for progress means change and the aged can not logically expect a change in position, physique, or purse to be other than for the worse. A large element of oldsters in a population thus seems likely to dampen its optimism and to make it more conservative and less receptive to new ideas and new products.

At the very least, the "senior citizens" constitute a bloc to whom the marketer will find it hard to sell new things. Perhaps, as they grow in number and in proportion, he will be wise to seek means of preventing them from infecting the entire population with their conservatism. Perhaps the shift of research emphasis their growing presence has forced on drug manufacturers—from seeking products to prolong life toward searching for drugs to make the added years more worthwhile—will in itself help to dissipate or at least contain the restrictive psychological effect of age on consumer demand. The whole subject deserves some careful thought by the generation of future business managers, some of whom may be laboring through this book.

Sex. The sex distribution of the population is changing. Before 1950 the number of men exceeded the number of women. In that year, though, the Bureau of the Census found 1,030,883 fewer men than women, a ratio of 99.2 men to 100 women. In 1960, there were 2,660,187 fewer men than women, and the ratio was 97.1 to 100. This trend seems to be continuing. It is especially characteristic of the older age groups. In 1960, males still predominated in the age groups under 18, while in the over-65 group, there were only 82.9 men to 100 women. These figures suggest that the shift is occurring primarily or entirely because women live longer than men.

Almost everyone agrees that this growing disparity has marketing implications but no one seems to know exactly what they are. Throughout much of our society the traditional division of labor between man, the breadwinner, and wife, the family purchasing agent, still persists in spite of a growing tendency of married women to hold jobs outside the home. The widespread demand for stores to stay open at night is probably one effect of this, but it is also highly probable that this demand is due fully as much to the growth of family shopping, made possible by the shorter workday, which leaves the husband a reserve of time and energy with which to do something during his evenings besides eat and sleep. This kind of shopping probably tends to subtract somewhat from the woman's purchasing agent function.

Certainly women dominate in the purchase of their own clothing, and if one can judge from masculine humor on the subject, men have little influence in the choice. Women probably make most of the decisions about purchases of children's goods, except perhaps for major items such as baby carriages, furniture, and mechanical toys, which Father often buys (fully as much for his own entertainment as for the joy of Junior). All but minor household items are probably usually bought by women. Major articles of this kind are apt to involve joint decision—although the wise man limits his participation chiefly to the matter of the amount of money to be spent for them. Most food is certainly bought by women, although their choices are heavily influenced by the tastes of the rest of the family. Things like automobiles are probably joint purchases, women being influenced heavily by appearance and ease of riding and handling, while the man is more likely to be interested in what is under the hood. Women buy a significant proportion of men's clothing and accessories, and probably the average man is more influenced than we think in his purchase of these articles by his ideas of how the "little woman" will feel about his choices.

While neither psychologists nor the more practical business managers who work with the raw materials of consumer demand entirely agree among themselves or with each other about the precise differences in mental behavior and emotional reactions that prevail between men and women, there are a few sex differences about which there is some approach to unanimity of opinion among the members of both groups. For example, the members of both sexes tend to act rather more on the basis of intuition and emotion than of logic. This trait of behavior is less persistent and less dominant among men than among women. The former are more often likely to be controlled, at least partially, by considerations of logic than are the latter.

In general, women react more slowly to outside stimuli than men do. This is a factor of vital importance in practically all attempts to manipulate consumer demand through personal selling and advertising. Most authorities seem to agree that women's dislikes are stronger and exercise more influence over their conduct than do their likes, while this trait is not so pronounced among men. This characteristic is apparent in their reactions toward persons, merchandise, ideas, and services. An appreciation of its existence should subtly but definitely color the nature of the selling appeals used by those who seek to exploit a consumer demand dominated by the reactions of women.

It is generally agreed that men are more conservative than women in the details of their ordinary daily lives. It is women who each season desire new styles of hats or shoes; men often can be separated from their old ones only by irresistible force or subtlest guile. The furniture in a woman's house must be shifted about from time to time to satisfy her wish for novelty; that in a man's office tends to remain fixed indefinitely, except for such changes as are necessary to impress customers, to improve efficiency, or to achieve greater convenience.

The average woman tends to be more interested in *what* things will do than *how* they do them. The reverse tends to be true of men. The vacuum cleaner salesman is more likely to interest the man than the woman of the house in a description of its mechanical construction and the principles on which it operates; the prospect's wife wants rather to see how effective it is in cleaning her living room rug or draperies or upholstery. The members of both sexes tend to be more interested in persons than in general propositions. This trait is probably somewhat more pronounced in women than in men, however. Women's conversation tends to run to superlatives; men talk in a more minor key, even to the point of seeking emphasis by understatement, a fact that writers of advertising copy are well aware of.

Most of these differences are slight, nor are they characteristic of all members of either sex. Men differ as individuals more than men as a group differ from women; the same is true of women. But the sex differences are sufficiently universal and pronounced to make it profitable for marketing managers, who must deal with people on a group basis, to give consideration to them in planning and conducting their operations.

Race. In 1960 the Census Bureau found there were 18,872,000

Negroes in the United States, 10.5 percent of the entire population. For a number of reasons they are highly concentrated geographically, about 11,500,000 of them, or over 60 percent, in the southern states. Then, in the communities in which they live, they are further concentrated in certain districts.

Whatever the social and moral implications of this concentration may be, it tends to intensify and perpetuate whatever differences may already exist in racial patterns of attitude, emotion, and behavior. These differences, whether acquired or inherent, serve to create the "negro market." And their numbers make it an important market.

Marketing managers are by no means of one mind as to whether the differences between white and colored are sharp enough or consistent enough to justify treating the negroes and whites in a trading area as two markets instead of one. Some firms have set up separate units, usually headed by negroes, to market to colored customers. Others regard negroes and whites as sufficiently homogeneous in buying behavior to constitute one market that can be served by one organizational unit. Certain it is that during recent years the negro people have developed their own magazines and, in many places, their own newspapers, which offer advertising media that are probably more effective in reaching and convincing them than are the general media that appeal primarily to whites.

A perceptive marketing manager will study his products to try to discern whether they are of such a nature that they are likely to be bought in different ways for different motives by the two races, and, if so, whether the differences are significant enough to make separate marketing methods worthwhile.

Money to Spend

It might be assumed that the amount of money a spending unit, either an individual or a family or household, has to spend within a period is its income during the period, plus all its assets that can be turned into cash. In emergencies this is true, but in his planning the marketing manager can not count on the emergency case being the usual one. He must base his plans on the customary behavior of the typical spending unit.

In the aggregate, Americans do not in any year draw from savings to buy consumers' goods except at the depths of a great depression, such as 1929 to 1933. Rather, they *add* to savings from current income. Therefore, income must be taken as the best index of money to spend. Even this is not all spent, but it *can* be used to buy goods and services if people are willing to do so. So expected savings are not subtracted from income in computing purchasing power and the total personal income is commonly used as the significant figure.

There are several basic concepts of income that must be distinguished if the student or the marketing manager is to understand its influence on purchasing power.

Total personal income embraces all payments received by persons from all sources, including transfers from government and business such as benefit payments received from social security and insurance sources. During recent years the amount which the federal, state, and local governments take from this total in personal taxes has grown

FIGURE 2–1

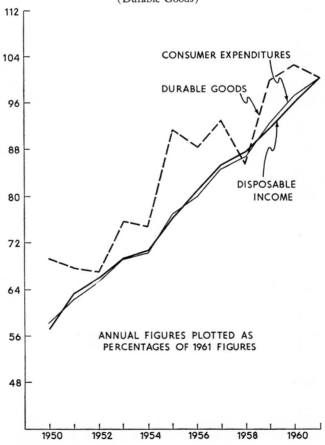

DISPOSABLE INCOME AND CONSUMER EXPENDITURES
(Durable Goods)

to such significant proportions that it is necessary to subtract them from total personal income in order to arrive at a figure that really represents what consumers have to spend or save.

Disposable income is the income people have left after government has taken its toll in personal taxes. It is the amount in the disposal of which consumers are free to exercise at least some measure of freedom of choice. Consumer purchases of many types of merchandise seem to follow a fairly regular pattern of behavior in response to changes in disposable income. Figures 2–1 and 2–2 illustrate this tendency.

As a practical matter, however, the consumer's choice with respect to

FIGURE 2–2

DISPOSABLE INCOME AND CONSUMER EXPENDITURES
(Non-Durable Goods)

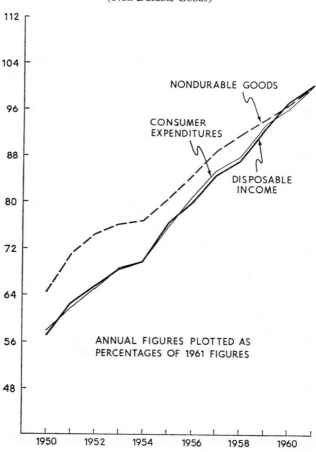

disposable income is not entirely free. A certain part of it must be devoted to the purpose of maintaining existence and working efficiency. Marketing managers who seek to sell what are called "deferrable purchase items," articles that may be bought now or later at the consumer's choice, must subtract the cost of basic living and maintenance necessities from disposable income to obtain the purchasing power available for the buying of their goods.

This residual fund has been called *discretionary spending power*. It is the amount available for the purchase of durable goods, appliances, luxury items, and other types of goods and services which may be bought or not, during any period, at the discretion of the family or other buying unit. It is sometimes argued that this fund can be considerably increased by the expansion of instalment credit. It is certainly true that by this means increments of discretionary spending power over a period may be mobilized and made available for expenditure early in the period without the laborious process of saving which many individuals will not undergo. It is highly probable, though, that the net effect of instalment selling is simply to make discretionary spending power available in more effective lumps at a somewhat earlier date than it would otherwise be.

Annual income statistics are reported in the July and August issues of the "Survey of Current Business" issued by the U.S. Department of Commerce. (All figures of personal and disposable income presented in our discussion are from this source unless otherwise indicated.) The same publication presents monthly estimates of these figures.

Two sources estimate discretionary income: the National Industrial Conference Board, which publishes its estimates in its monthly "Bulletin", and the Marketing Research Department of MacFadden Publications, which issues its estimates in its house organ, "Marketing Memos."

Over a long period of time the total personal income of the people of the United States has been increasing both in current dollars and in dollars of constant purchasing power. Table 2–7 shows for a number of years total personal and total disposable income in billions of current dollars and of 1947–49 dollars.

The increase in people has not kept up with the rise in income, with the result that income per capita has also risen during the 12-year period in terms of both current and constant dollars. It is important to note the behavior of per capita income in terms of a constant dollar not only because the result indicates changes in the physical volume of goods and services the consumer can buy, but because a price rise that outruns

TABLE 2–7

PERSONAL AND DISPOSABLE INCOME
(In Billions of Dollars)

	Personal Income		Disposable Income	
	Current Dollars	1947-49 Dollars*	Current Dollars	1947-49 Dollars*
1950...............	228.5	222.3	207.7	202.0
1951...............	256.7	231.3	227.5	204.9
1952...............	273.1	239.4	238.7	209.2
1953...............	288.3	252.0	252.5	220.7
1954...............	289.8	253.3	256.9	224.6
1955...............	310.2	279.7	274.4	239.7
1956...............	332.9	286.5	292.9	252.1
1957...............	351.4	292.3	308.8	256.9
1958...............	360.3	291.6	317.9	257.4
1959...............	383.9	308.9	337.1	270.6
1960...............	401.3	317.2	349.9	276.6
1961...............	417.4	329.0	364.4	287.2
1962...............	442.1	342.0	384.4	297.4

*The deflating factor used was the U.S. Bureau of Labor Statistics Index of Consumer Prices.

the current increase in income undermines confidence and engenders fears that adversely affect willingness to buy. The changes in per capita income, in terms of current and constant dollars for the most recent 12-year period, are shown in Table 2–8.

TABLE 2–8

PER CAPITA INCOME

	Current Dollars	1947-49 Dollars
1950.....................	1,491	1,450
1951.....................	1,649	1,482
1952.....................	1,727	1,514
1953.....................	1,788	1,563
1954.....................	1,770	1,547
1955.....................	1,866	1,630
1956.....................	1,975	1,701
1957.....................	2,048	1,704
1958.....................	2,064	1,671
1959.....................	2,163	1,736
1960.....................	2,217	1,752
1961.....................	2,267	1,787
1962.....................	2,366	1,830

Per capita income varies widely from state to state. In 1962 Nevada was highest with $3,278, followed by Delaware with $3,102, Connecticut with $3,089, and New York with $2,930. Mississippi held the dubious distinction of having the lowest per capita income, $1,285, while Arkansas with $1,504 and South Carolina with $1,545 vied for the honor. In general, the great industrial states, with their teeming populations, also rank high in per capita income—which makes them lush markets, demanding the best marketing efforts the consumers' goods manufacturer can spend in capturing them. For example, in 1962 people living in New York received 11.6 percent of the total national personal income; for California the figure was 11.2, followed by Illinois with 6.6 and by Pennsylvania with 6.1 percent. In spite of Nevada's high per capita income, it claims only 0.2 percent of the national total, while Delaware receives only 0.3 percent of the total.

The sources from which income is derived may have considerable significance to the marketing manager. Table 2–9 shows the percentages of the total personal income which have come from the six general sources during recent years.

TABLE 2–9

SOURCES OF PERSONAL INCOME

		Percent of Total from:				
	Wages and Salaries	*Proprietorships (including Farms)*	*Dividends*	*Rent*	*Interest*	*Transfer Payments*
1950........	64.9	16.2	4.0	3.9	4.4	6.5
1951........	68.0	16.2	3.5	3.6	4.3	4.8
1952........	68.7	15.2	3.2	3.7	4.4	4.8
1953........	69.8	13.9	3.1	3.6	4.6	4.9
1954........	68.9	13.7	3.3	3.7	5.0	5.5
1955........	69.2	13.3	3.6	3.4	5.0	5.6
1956........	69.5	12.9	3.6	3.2	5.2	5.6
1957........	69.4	12.5	3.5	3.3	5.5	6.1
1958........	67.8	12.5	3.4	3.3	5.7	7.2
1959........	68.5	11.9	3.5	3.0	6.0	7.0
1960........	68.9	11.3	3.5	2.9	6.3	7.2
1961........	68.1	11.2	3.5	2.9	6.4	7.9
1962........	68.3	11.0	3.7	2.6	6.6	7.7

These figures are significant to the marketing manager primarily because the source of income may afford some indication of the likelihood of its being spent. For example, the bulk of transfer payments, which includes money paid individuals by government or business and for which no services are currently rendered, is made up of pensions, annuities, and social security payments—which probably means that most of it will be spent. Rent, dividends, and interest are paid to people who have property or investments of one sort or another and are

TABLE 2-10

INCOME DISTRIBUTION

Income Receiving Groups	Percent of Consuming Units							Percent of Total Personal Income						
	1955	1956	1957	1958	1959	1960	1961	1955	1956	1957	1958	1959	1960	1961
Under $2,000	15.8	14.6	14.2	14.1	13.6	13.0	12.5	3.2	2.7	2.6	2.5	2.3	2.1	2.0
$2,000–2,999	11.3	10.2	10.0	10.1	9.6	9.2	9.0	5.1	4.3	4.0	4.0	3.6	3.4	3.3
$3,000–3,999	14.1	12.9	12.1	12.1	11.1	10.6	10.4	8.8	7.5	6.8	6.8	5.9	5.5	5.3
$4,000–4,999	14.0	14.0	12.7	12.5	11.4	11.0	11.0	11.2	10.5	9.1	8.9	7.8	7.3	7.1
$5,000–5,999	12.1	11.8	11.6	11.4	10.9	10.7	10.7	11.8	10.8	10.1	10.0	9.1	8.6	8.5
$6,000–7,499	13.3	13.6	14.1	13.9	14.1	14.3	14.4	15.8	15.2	15.1	14.8	14.4	14.1	14.0
$7,500–9,999	10.0	11.6	12.6	12.6	14.0	14.4	14.7	15.1	16.5	17.4	17.2	18.1	18.1	18.3
$10,000–14,999	5.9	7.2	8.0	8.5	9.5	10.6	11.0	12.5	14.4	15.5	16.3	17.3	18.6	18.9
$15,000–19,999	1.7	2.1	2.4	2.5	3.1	3.5	⎫	5.1	6.0	6.6	6.8	8.1	8.7	⎫
$20,000–24,999	0.7	0.8	0.9	0.9	1.1	1.2	6.3	2.8	3.0	3.3	3.4	3.6	3.8	22.6
$25,000–49,999	0.9	1.0	1.1	1.1	1.2	1.2	⎬	5.1	5.4	5.7	5.6	5.7	6.0	⎬
$50,000 plus	0.2	0.2	0.3	0.3	0.3	0.3	⎭	3.5	3.7	3.8	3.7	4.1	3.8	⎭

Source U.S. Department of Commerce, Survey of Current Business, April, 1963.

investment conscious. Except insofar as these payments go to retired people, who have previously built up the investments from which they come as a hedge against old age, they are very likely not to be spent but to be saved and reinvested. To a lesser degree this may be true of proprietorship and farm incomes. Except for people in the higher salary brackets, the bulk of wages and salaries is apt to be spent for goods and services.

Income Distribution. Not only have total income and per capita income been increasing but the distribution among the various income receiving groups has been shifting. The same sort of change is occurring in the number of consumer spending units in the several income receiving groups and in the percentage of total personal income received by the various groups. The shift has been away from the income levels below about $6,000 a year and toward the groups above that figure.

FIGURE 2–3

TRENDS IN INCOME DISTRIBUTION BY PERCENTAGE OF NUMBER OF CONSUMER UNITS

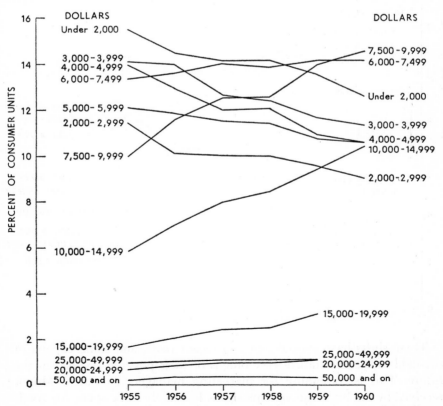

Table 2–10 shows this in terms of percentages; Figures 2–3 and 2–4 show it graphically. If the total personal income figures shown were reduced to the basis of disposable income, the effect would be to reduce considerably the relative purchasing power of the two or three highest income groups and to increase slightly that of the middle income groups.

FIGURE 2–4

Trends in Income Distribution by Percentage of Total Income

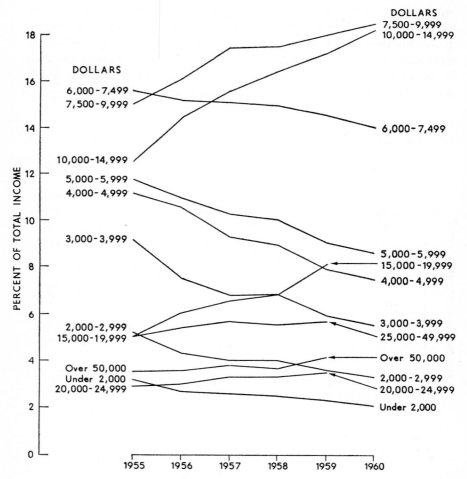

These shifts have slowed down in recent years, and some experts in the field of income statistics see omens of their possible reversal in the future. This is something for marketing managers to watch. Money received by the higher income groups is less likely to be spent for goods and services than that which goes to the groups farther down the scale. More of it is saved and less is spent. It is probable that the tremendous upward surge of consumer demand during the late 1940's and the 1950's was in no small measure due to this readjustment of income shares, which was to some extent obscured by the general increase at all levels. What we are really dealing with here is willingness to spend; so perhaps we should move on to that subject.

Willingness to Spend

Influence of Income Changes. The evidence as to what happens to the consumer spending pattern when income changes seems to be somewhat conflicting. Most discussions of this subject take as a point of departure the so-called "Engel's laws," as restated in the light of mid-twentieth century studies. This restatement is about as follows:

1. As income increases the percentage of it spent for food declines.
2. As income increases the percentage of it spent for housing and household operation remains about constant.
3. As income increases the percentage of it spent for clothing, transportation, recreation, health, education, and other non-necessity items increases, as does the percentage saved.

During the late 1950's, *Life* magazine conducted a study of the things for which households in seven income groups spent their money. The summary results of this study are shown in Table 2–11. Notice that while the families with the smaller incomes spent all they received—in some groups probably more than they took in—those at the higher levels spent less than their incomes and apparently made substantial savings. It is also worth noting that while the larger income groups spent more dollars for each product or service category than did those with the smaller incomes, the percentage they spent for food was less than that of their poorer neighbors, and the proportions of their income they spent for clothing, home furnishings and equipment, and automobiles were greater than those of the poorer groups.

The picture this study presents is in a sense a static one. It shows the spending patterns of families at different income levels as of a given time. But when a family moves from a lower into a higher income group (or the reverse) or when incomes increase or decrease all along the line, do the spending units involved in the change shift their spending pattern to conform to that of the new group they join? It is important for the marketing manager to have the static picture, but in a dynamic society it is even more important for him to be able to foresee the effects of change.

Some inkling of what happens to the spending patterns of a whole people when income rises or declines may be gleaned from a study of the behavior of overall consumer expenditures, reported each year by the Department of Commerce in the July issue of "Survey of Current Business." The surveys cover the long period of rising personal income we

TABLE 2–11

HOUSEHOLD INCOME AND EXPENDITURES
A. ANNUAL EXPENDITURES IN DOLLARS

		Annual Household Income						
	All House-holds	Under $2,000	$2,000-$2,999	$3,000-$3,999	$4,000-$4,999	$5,000-$6,999	$7,000-$9,999	$10,000 or More
All Goods and Services—Total....	*$4,110*	*$1,933*	*$2,924*	*$3,839*	*$4,363*	*$5,016*	*$6,063*	*$7,946*
Food, beverages, tobacco.....	1,203	689	976	1,167	1,271	1,417	1,622	1,913
Clothing, accessories.........	494	223	311	495	518	566	778	1,082
Medical and personal care....	222	139	153	209	225	262	286	444
Home operation and improve-ment....................	763	327	588	698	843	932	1,086	1,463
Home furnishings and equip-ment....................	346	132	229	286	354	458	523	809
Recreation and recreation equipment...............	215	98	138	192	233	256	322	513
Automotive................	591	206	375	554	621	797	925	1,156
Other goods and services.....	276	119	154	238	298	328	521	566

B. PERCENT SPENT FOR EACH TYPE OF GOODS OR SERVICES

		Annual Household Income						
	All House-holds	Under $2,000	$2,000-$2,999	$3,000-$3,999	$4,000-$4,999	$5,000-$6,999	$7,000-$9,999	$10,000 or More
All Goods and Services—Total...	*100%*	*100%*	*100%*	*100%*	*100%*	*100%*	*100%*	*100%*
Food, beverages, tobacco.....	29	36	33	30	29	28	26	24
Clothing, accessories.........	12	11	11	13	12	11	13	14
Medical and personal care....	5	7	5	5	5	5	5	6
Home operation and improve-ment....................	19	17	20	18	19	19	18	18
Home furnishings and equip-ment....................	9	7	8	8	8	9	9	10
Recreation and recreation equipment...............	5	5	5	5	6	5	5	6
Automotive................	14	11	13	15	14	16	15	15
Other goods and services.....	7	6	5	6	7	7	9	7

"A Study of Consumer Expenditures," *Life*, 1957. This study is based on a sample of 10,243 households.

have enjoyed. A summary of the percentage of total disposable income spent for several types of goods and services during a number of years is presented in Table 2–12. In addition to the decade of the 1950's, figures are shown for the year 1929, which was at the top of a boom, and 1933, which was at the bottom of the great depression. From 1929 to 1933 total disposable income was almost cut in half. During this

TABLE 2-12

Consumer Expenditures as a Percentage of Total Disposable Income

	1929	1933	1950	1951	1952	1953	1954	1955	1956	1957	1958	1959	1960	1961
Food, tobacco, beverages	25.5	27.9	30.7	31.6	31.7	30.7	30.9	30.1	30.1	26.1	26.0	25.1	24.8	24.4
Clothing	13.5	11.9	11.0	10.7	10.4	9.9	9.7	9.5	9.4	9.9	9.7	9.8	9.7	9.5
Personal care*	1.3	1.4	1.2	1.1	1.1	1.1	1.0	1.2	1.2	1.3	1.3	1.5	1.5	1.6
Housing	13.8	17.2	10.4	10.3	10.7	11.0	11.5	11.3	11.4	11.4	11.8	11.8	12.0	12.1
Household equipment, operation	12.9	14.1	13.3	12.6	12.1	12.0	12.2	12.5	12.6	13.0	13.0	13.1	13.2	13.0
Medical care	4.3	5.2	4.5	4.4	4.6	4.5	4.6	4.6	4.7	5.4	5.7	5.9	6.0	6.2
Personal business†	6.1	6.4	4.0	3.9	3.9	4.3	4.6	4.7	4.9	5.1	5.3	5.6	5.8	5.9
Transportation	9.2	8.7	11.3	10.1	9.8	10.1	10.6	12.0	10.5	11.8	10.6	11.6	11.8	11.0
Recreation	5.2	4.8	5.2	4.8	4.8	4.7	4.7	4.8	4.8	5.2	5.3	5.4	5.6	5.7
Private education	0.8	1.1	1.0	0.9	1.0	1.0	1.0	1.1	1.2	1.0	1.0	1.2	1.3	1.4
Religious and welfare	1.4	1.9	1.2	1.2	1.2	1.2	1.3	1.2	1.3	1.2	1.2	1.3	1.3	1.4
Foreign travel	1.0	0.8	0.5	0.6	0.7	0.8	0.9	0.9	0.8	0.8	0.8	0.8	0.9	0.8
Savings	5.0	−1.4	5.8	7.8	8.0	7.9	7.0	6.1	7.0	8.0	7.8	7.0	6.2	7.0
Increase of disposable income‡	....	−45.0	9.5	9.7	5.0	5.4	1.7	6.4	6.3	5.0	3.0	6.0	4.0	4.0

*Toilet articles, cosmetics, etc.
†Brokerage charges, bank, legal and insurance services, personal debt charges, etc.
‡Percent increase of each year over preceding year.

period of drastically declining income the following changes appear to have occurred in the consumer spending pattern:

  The percentage of disposable income spent for food increased.

  The percentage spent for clothing declined.

  The percentage spent for housing, household equipment, and operation went up.

  The percentage spent for recreation went down.

  The percentage spent for transportation declined, especially the expenditures for automobiles, which were cut to less than a third of their 1929 total.

From 1950 to 1961, total disposable income increased at an average rate of slightly more than five percent per year. During this period the consumer spending pattern seems to have undergone the following shifts:

  The food percentage declined. Some of this decline may have been due to dietary changes having nothing to do with shifts in disposable income.

  The percentage spent for clothing dropped. This change may have resulted from the pronounced trend toward informality in dress, which was very apparent during the period.

  The percentages spent for housing, household equipment and operation, medical care, personal business, recreation, private education, and religion and welfare all increased during the period.

For many kinds of products which, in contrast to food and housing,

TABLE 2–13

DISCRETIONARY INCOME AND DEFERRABLE PURCHASES

Year	Discretionary Income		Automobile Sales		Household Appliances Sales		Radio and TV Sales	
	In Billions of Dollars	Percent of Increase or Decrease*	Percent of Discretionary Income	Percent of Increase or Decrease*	Percent of Discretionary Income	Percent of Increase or Decrease*	Percent of Discretionary Income	Percent of Increase or Decrease*
1950.........	78.1	13.5	12.9	12.8	16.6	13.6	3.0	43.1
1951.........	80.9	3.5	10.8	−14.9	16.3	1.7	2.5	−9.4
1952.........	84.1	4.0	9.6	−6.9	15.2	−2.5	2.5	−2.6
1953.........	90.7	7.8	11.9	33.3	13.4	2.3	2.4	2.9
1954.........	87.5	−3.5	11.8	−4.6	15.0	−0.1	2.5	2.0
1955.........	97.2	11.0	14.8	39.8	14.9	10.6	2.4	6.1
1956.........	104.6	7.6	12.8	−7.0	16.5	18.7	2.7	22.8
1957.........	108.8	4.0	13.3	8.2	15.8	−0.4	2.8	4.5
1958.........	108.2	−0.6	10.6	−10.7	15.7	−0.9	2.8	2.2
1959.........	118.7	9.7	13.1	33.0	15.4	7.6	2.9	11.5
1960.........	123.2	3.8	12.8	3.3	15.0	0.9	2.9	5.7
1961.........	126.6	2.8	11.3	−10.0	14.7	0.5	3.0	5.5

*Percentages from preceding year.

SOURCE: Discretionary income from *Chartbook of Current Business Trends* and Issues of *Business Record,* National Industrial Conference Board; consumer purchase figures from July issues of *Survey of Current Business,* U.S. Department of Commerce.

are of such a nature that the consumer can buy them now or later—or not at all—at his option, shifts in total discretionary income would seem to exercise more influence on buying patterns than disposable income. Table 2–13 shows the fluctuations in discretionary income and in consumer purchases of several groups of deferrable purchase items. The use of correlation coefficients would probably have afforded a sounder

FIGURE 2–5

FLUCTUATIONS OF DISCRETIONARY INCOME AND PURCHASES OF AUTOMOBILES

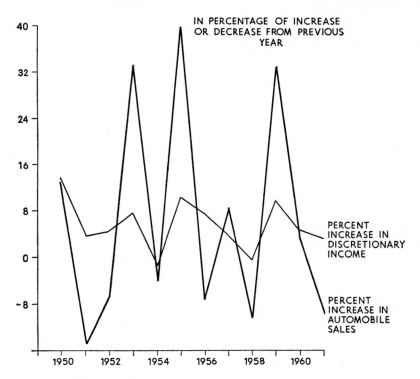

means of comparison. But 12 years is a rather small number of observations to which to apply the correlation coefficient technique, and any attempt to extend the period would encounter the distorting effects of World War II and the product shortages resulting from it. The figures shown seem to suggest that consumer purchases of automobiles, household appliances, and radio and TV equipment are at least somewhat sensitive to increases or decreases in discretionary income and even to changes in its rate of increase. Figures 2–5, 2–6, and 2–7 show this comparison in graphic form.

FIGURE 2–6

FLUCTUATIONS OF DISCRETIONARY INCOME AND PURCHASES OF
HOUSEHOLD APPLIANCES

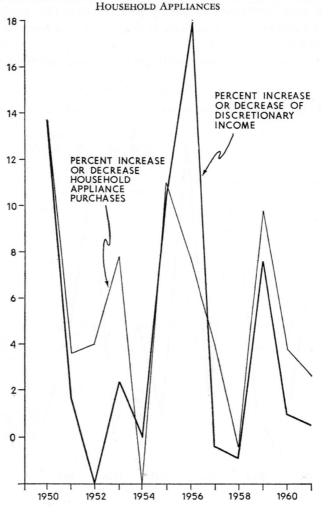

Standards of Living. The fact that consumer purchases do not fluctuate along with income more exactly than they do suggests that some other factor or factors exercise an influence on them. These factors are psychological. One of them, the standard of living, is more or less implicit in discretionary income, but probably exercises an influence on consumer purchases beyond its arithmetic effect on that figure.

It is hard to define a standard of living in the sense in which it is important to a marketing manager. In the economic sense it is the

complex of goods and services which the income of a society or a consuming unit enables it to buy. This projects the marketing manager
little farther in his planning than does a mere knowledge of income
trends and levels. The concept of standard of living that is of most

FIGURE 2–7

FLUCTUATIONS OF DISCRETIONARY INCOME AND
PURCHASES OF RADIOS AND T.V.'S

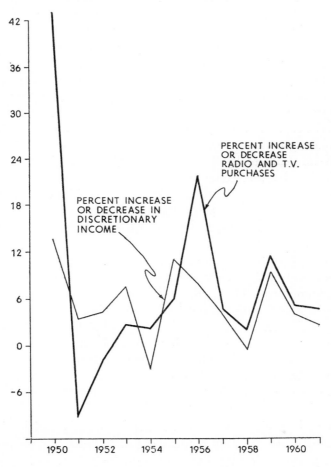

use to the manager is that of a complex of goods and services which
the typical spending unit regards as essential to its satisfaction and welfare. It is a bundle of goods and services which the family or other
consuming unit will not impair until after the practically complete
sacrifice of material satisfactions not in the bundle.

Each family or buying unit creates its own living standard, which changes as its economic or social circumstances change. Probably most marketing managers must plan on the basis of the average or typical standard of living; this too shifts as general economic conditions and social attitudes change. Other managers must relate their plans to probable or foreseeable variations that significant groups of consumers may make from the standard.

The history of civilization could be written around the motif of the struggle of humanity for higher standards of living. In its material aspect it is the story of man's eternal striving for things he does not have, and perhaps does not need. Under primitive conditions he sought the bare elements of existence, nor was his search always successful. In the twentieth century man's dream of a time when industry could provide something more than mere subsistence for the majority of the people seems no longer technically impossible of achievement; the increase in the capacity of the productive mechanism seems to have caught up with the growth of population in many of the countries of the world. If we could really find the proper basis on which to distribute purchasing power and create an efficient system for marketing goods and services, and if mankind could be dissuaded from wasting its substance in war, there is no reason why any sizable groups of persons in the more advanced countries of the world should suffer for lack of the elementary needs.

Climate. Climate exercises a profound influence upon peoples' willingness to buy. It is even sufficient to give rise to urgent needs for certain commodities. The civilized dweller in the northern portion of the country can hardly conceive of undergoing the rigors of winter without making heavy expenditures for heating his house and for the purchase of warm clothing—needs practically unknown to those living in the more southern states. In the North the consumption of gasoline increases in the summer and declines in the winter. In Florida and a few other southern states precisely the opposite seasonal variations are apparent.

The hot, blistering sun and the arctic blizzards which alternately parch and chill the Western plains make it necessary for the people living there to wear clothing quite different in texture and weave from that which suits the needs of the dweller along the eastern seaboard, which is often swathed in clouds and fog. The Southern summer heat induces among men a preference for light linens, seersuckers, gabardines, and crash materials, and so modifies the code of convention that even a banker may remove his coat in his office without forfeiting his status either as a businessman or as a gentleman.

The local and temporal miniature of climate is weather. Not only does it exercise an influence upon the emotional reactions of the average person, and thus modify his willingness to buy, but it affects his opportunities to purchase as well. Psychologists support the popular assumption that bad weather is emotionally depressing to many persons and so tends to dampen their willingness to purchase. A difference of a few degrees in the temperature of a summer day brings about a considerable variation in the total consumption of fluid milk in the average large city. When the weather is so rainy or cold that men prefer to keep their hands in their overcoat pockets when outdoors, their purchases of cigarettes are much less than when it is more clement. A cold, stormy, damp spring ruins the Easter-hat business, as well as the sale of all kinds of spring and early summer clothing. Rain at the wrong time in the afternoon keeps the "baby-carriage trade" off the streets, thus reducing the sales of cash-and-carry bakeries and bringing about corresponding increases in the business of competitive establishments that feature delivery service. The long-run weather forecasting techniques now being made available to business by the Weather Bureau are likely to be of great value in many types of endeavor to exploit consumer demand; for example, in the timing of production and various kinds of sales promotional effort.

Religion. Religion usually exercises a restrictive or negative rather than a positive or expansive influence upon the demand of the consumer group it affects. Its sumptuary admonitions tend to be couched in the "Thou shalt not" rather than in the "Thou canst" formula. The net effect of such a prohibition may occasionally be positive in character. The interdiction which the Roman Catholic Church places upon the consumption of meat on Friday has led Protestants and Catholics alike to adopt the practice of eating fish on that day of the week, probably because of the fact that dealers, in endeavoring to please their Catholic customers, offer on Friday unusually complete and attractive stocks of fish which appeal to Protestant buyers as well. The marketing managers of both fish companies and meat packers must accommodate their plans to this pattern of behavior.

The dietary restrictions of the Jewish religion, together with the concentration of people of that faith in New York City, have made the metropolis the greatest live poultry market in the country and have retained for it a thriving small-scale slaughtering industry.

The puritanical element which is present to a greater or less degree in most organized religious establishments, coupled with the emphasis they place upon the things of the next world in comparison with the delights of this, and their tendency to favor the mortification of the flesh for the benefit of the spirit, serve to limit the versatility of consumer demand and to dull and retard its response to new stimuli presented in the form of new satisfaction-giving commodities or services. At various times the church, through one or more of its sects, has set its face against the enjoyment of works of fiction, cosmetics, alcoholic liquors, tobacco, playing cards, musical instruments, buttons and all other forms of decoration on clothing, as well as many other goods and services. For example, several counties in Ohio and Pennsylvania, where members of the Amish and Mennonite sects constitute a considerable part of the population, are very poor markets for ordinary kinds of clothing and many mechanical products, such as automobiles, TV and radio sets, and various automatic kitchen equipment products.

Both the restrictions and the positive requirements which religion places upon its votaries are among the most powerful and persistent of the forces which influence consumer demand. The marketing manager can rely upon a market characteristic which results from them to change very slowly, if at all. He is liable to find it suicidal to attempt to bring about or to accelerate changes in such characteristics by means of the tools ordinarily used in manipulating consumer demand.

Habit and Custom. Habit exercises a powerful influence upon the purchasing behavior of the average individual. It almost surpasses the instincts in the insistence and pervasiveness with which it molds men's behavior. While in its essence it is an individual matter, it often assumes the aspect of a mass reaction. For example, a large number of people, each acting individually, form the habit of buying their newspapers or cigarettes at a certain point or of eating at a certain restaurant. Competitors of the favored dealers will usually find it costly, often commercially suicidal, to attempt to break this habit. On the other hand, the wise marketer does not hesitate to spend liberally to induce people's feet to form the habit of walking into his store or their minds that of thinking automatically of his brand or his service.

When it is translated into long-run terms, made characteristic of the group rather than of the individual, and embellished and fortified by the dictates of tradition and convention, habit becomes custom. It is not necessary here to attempt to explain the psychological background of men's conformance to custom, which in itself is often inconvenient, irrational, and sometimes positively harmful to those whose behavior it dictates. It is enough that we recognize it as <u>one of the most powerful forces determining consumer demand</u>. In some degree it probably influences the purchase of practically every type of merchandise and service. A few conspicuous examples should serve to illustrate the variety of consuming activities which it touches and, in touching, modifies: the wearing of evening clothes at certain conventional social functions, the eating of cereals for breakfast and not for other meals, the drinking of bock beer in the spring and not at other times of the year, the eating of cranberries and turkey as traditional features of the Thanksgiving dinner, the discharge of fireworks on the Fourth of July, the giving of presents at Christmas time, birthdays, and other anniversary occasions, the enthusiastic tolerance upon the bathing beach of a seminudity which elsewhere would be regarded as highly, although interestingly, inappropriate.

In general, it is liable to be very unprofitable for a marketer to attempt to oppose a custom. He will find it easier, less expensive, and more lucrative to plan his operations so that they conform to, and therefore are aided by customs, whenever it is possible to do so. A marketing decision which involves challenging custom is a matter of major significance to the manager who makes it.

Leadership. In their buying behavior, as in other segments of life, people tend to follow the leader. Probably the most widely known example of this tendency is to be found in the fashion goods industries. The dictum "They are wearing skirts longer this year," if it is pronounced by the right authority is apt to be accepted by women generally without too careful examination as to just who "they" may be. "They," the leaders of fashion, are women of position who make a career of being better than well dressed. While the real leaders are in the great centers of society and culture, each community has its replica, complete with local following.

But the force of the follow-the-leader principle is not confined to markets dominated by fashion. When air conditioning was done primarily on a single room basis and required a "sweat box" sticking out of the window, William Whyte observed the cluster pattern of such boxes in a neighborhood. This pattern suggested that at the center of each cluster was a leader whose neighbors could not ignore his acquisition. This process, often called "keeping up with the Joneses," is in essence a kind of imitation—and not only the sincerest form of flattery but the most convincing acknowledgement of leadership that can be made.

The marketing manager of a manufacturer of consumers' goods will not often find it possible or worthwhile to make direct contact with all the potential local consuming leaders in his market. But in many trades he will find it worthwhile to be aware of their existence, to try to reach them through advertising and sales promotional material, and to seek to induce his retail outlets to recognize them and try to capture their interest in his products. If such a leadership group can be recognized in a market, the manufacturer's marketing manager may be able to use them very effectively, through marketing research, as a source of information about possible new products, sales appeals, marketing channels, and various other matters vital to his planning.

Social Classes.   The social class to which an individual or family consuming unit belongs exerts considerable influence on the things it purchases and on the way in which it buys them.

Although in our society the lines between social classes are much less sharply drawn than in many other countries, and perhaps are less distinct than they used to be, class distinctions are nevertheless very real. They mark differences in norms of convention, codes of behavior, attitudes towards such things as education and occupation, political theories and loyalties; in short, people's patterns of thought, emotion, and behavior. Inevitably, their influence spills over into the field of consumer demand.

The Astors and the Vanderbilts are not supposed to eat sausages, munch hot dogs, or drink beer: these are prerogatives of more earthy mortals. The man who chews tobacco certainly does not belong to the socially elite, and there are still social clubs in which the smoking of a pipe sets off an epidemic of raised eyebrows. Sauerkraut and pig's knuckles is no dish for ladies and gentlemen, vitamin content notwithstanding.

We have cited these conspicuous examples to illustrate the point. But most of the influence which social class differences exert on consumer demand is almost certainly hidden and is often not identified or realized even by those it motivates. Probably it most often manifests itself as a vague but compelling feeling that certain things are done or certain attitudes are entertained by the "right people" and that, by the same token, certain other things are "common."

While class distinctions certainly influence the things people are willing to buy, their highest significance to the manager probably lies in their effect on the methods to be used in marketing. This involves such matters as the kinds of stores through which goods are sold at retail, pricing policies and practices, the buying appeals used, and the media and the language through which they are communicated. This works both ways. The members of the "great unwashed" are liable to be just as ill at ease in an upper class atmosphere as are their fellow mortals at the top of the social scale when forced to go "slumming." The classic example is supplied by the merchant who, having made a fortune in a poorly appointed, almost disreputable appearing store in a poor section of a city, decided that he would reward his faithful customers by building a beautifully equipped store for them to shop in—only to find when the new emporium opened that they stayed away from it enthusiastically. Probably their withdrawal of patronage was partly due to a suspicion that his prices had been increased to pay for the new store, but certainly many stayed away because they would have been uncomfortable in the atmosphere of elegance and culture characteristic of a class to which they did not belong.

In planning both his products and the methods to be used in marketing them, the wise manager will seek to define the social classes touched by his operations and to build his plans to conform to their peculiarities. This is easier said than done. The chief difficulty in doing it lies in defining the several social classes in terms sufficiently distinct so they can be counted and measured. Lloyd Warner and Paul S. Hunt, in *The Social Life of a Modern Community,* used an index, based on type of income, type of occupation, house type, and place of residence, with which they were able to segregate six classes:

Upper-upper: "old families"
Lower-upper: the newly "arrived"
Upper-middle: professional and business men
Lower-middle: white-collar salaried group
Upper-lower: skilled worker group
Lower-lower: unskilled labor

In studying almost 4000 households in Chicago, the *Chicago Tribune* developed an Index of Status Characteristics, based on three factors:

Occupation: 7 categories, weighted by 5
Sources of Income: 7 types, weighted by 4
Housing Type: 7 types, weighted by 3.

This is an area in which much additional work undoubtedly needs to be done to develop class limits and definitions that are meaningful in relation to marketing problems and readily usable on the basis of data not too difficult to obtain. Such studies will probably also show fundamental class differences in tastes, habits, and attitudes that affect marketing. Each marketing manager must interpret such general differences in relation to his specific problems. He will probably also be wise to seek differences which, while they may not be so basic or general, have specific significance in his particular situation. He may find that a review of his sociology will be helpful in this work; he can probably put himself on even sounder ground by retaining the consulting services of a professional sociologist.

Thought and Emotion. Theoretically, the consumer's act of choice should be an exercise of pure reason—at least that seems to be the opinion of many students of consumer problems. Even these savants, however, recognize that the greatest obstacle to the realization of this theoretical *desideratum* is the consumer himself, who insists on stirring all sorts of irrational and emotional attitudes and reactions, together with reasoned analyses, into the mixture out of which he distills his buying decision. The marketing manager is often accused of encouraging this process, and many times, certainly, he leaves few stones unturned in his attempt to do so.

But even without this outside encouragement, the very purpose for which the consumer makes a buying choice tends to force his decision process into the area of the emotions. The basic fact is that the consumer does not buy goods and services at all but the personal satisfaction that comes from having or using them. Much of this personal satisfaction is subjective and a thing of the emotions, often of emotions so deeply embedded in his personality that he does not know they are there.

A personal example may illustrate. For many years the writer has felt a vague but powerful disinclination to buy a certain brand of gasoline. Fancying himself a student of marketing, he soul-searched to try to find the reason why. His knowledge of the industry and his use experience on the few occasions when circumstances forced him to buy the disliked brand convinced him that this gasoline was just about as good as any other. He was embarrassed when his amateur self-analysis forced him to the conclusion that his antipathy to the product arose from the color of the paint used on the stations and their promotional embellishments. This understanding has not removed the antipathy, however, and in his gasoline purchases he still prefers to add to the surface satisfactions gained from the propulsive power of the fuel the subconscious satisfaction of buying it in a station with an attractive color decor. In spite of 40 years of studying marketing, or, perhaps, because of it, he thinks he is wise in catering to this emotion.

The classic case of such self-delusion was that of the housewives and Nescafe. When this product was first introduced on the market, it did not sell as well as expected. Conventional marketing research elicited the opinion of housewives that coffee made from Nescafe did not taste as good as the regular kind. Not satisfied, the marketing executives tried a psychological approach. To one half of a sample panel of housewives they showed a grocery list containing Nescafe and, to the other half, an identical grocery list—except that a well-known brand of regular coffee was substituted for Nescafe. Each group was asked to describe the housewife who prepared its list. It turned out that the lady who went to market to get the regular coffee was an exemplary housewife, while the Nescafe buyer was a careless housekeeper, indifferent to her family's welfare and her job; in short, no kind of material for membership in the Good Housewives' League.

The list of emotions that influence consumers' willingness to buy probably includes all those that man is heir to. Certainly powerful emotions such as fear, love, hate, desire for group approval, and desire for distinction belong near the top. But for the marketing manager to arrange such a list has little point. What he needs to know is what emotions are motivating significant numbers of people to purchase his product, or can be made to motivate them, and what hidden psychological reactions are restraining a worthwhile part of his market from buying.

The marketing manager's tool kit now contains implements for discovering these hidden motives and weighing their effects on his markets. These tools are the techniques of motivation research, which makes use of the methods and understanding of psychology, sociology, and anthropology in its search for marketing information about a specific situation or problem. We will look more carefully into this subject when we come to discuss marketing research.

The marketing manager's study of consumers' attitudes and reactions must be a continuing one, for they are constantly changing. The techniques of the attitude survey or public opinion poll, popularized by George Gallup and Elmo Roper, have opened the way for this sort of continuing study. Much pioneer work has been done by the Economic Behavior Program of the Survey Research Center of the University of Michigan, under the leadership of George Katona, in applying these techniques to discovering and measuring the changes in consumer's attitudes which affect their purchasing patterns. The Katona approach has dealt mainly with consumers' buying intentions and with expectations of changes in economic conditions that might influence their purchases. A wider use of the methods Katona has developed, with perhaps the addition of some features of the public opinion poll and motivation research approaches (applied to the marketing problems of the individual firm), may in the future enable the marketing manager to know a lot more about the waves of emotion and attitude that affect the results of his efforts and to draw his marketing plans so as to make use of them, rather than at times being their unknowing and unhappy plaything.

Much is still to be learned about the consumer and what makes him tick. The marketing manager will be wise to keep abreast of the developments in this relatively new field of study. In order to use the new tools that are being and will be developed in this area, the marketing manager need not be a motivation research expert, an opinion poll specialist, a psychologist, a sociologist, or an anthropologist. He needs only to have a general knowledge of how the tools work and the purposes for which they can be used, together with the imagination to visualize which of his problems they can be applied to helpfully and profitably. He can and should get specialists to do the work.

THE INDUSTRIAL MARKET

In the final analysis every manufacturer must look to ultimate consumer purchasers to provide a market for the products or services he makes. Some manufacturers make products or services that can be used by the ultimate consumer without further industrial processing, and we have just finished examining the nature of the consumer market in which they must operate. But other manufacturers produce materials, supplies, and equipment which all sorts of enterprises need to make the goods and services they market or furnish. This is known as the industrial market in spite of the fact that it contains elements that cannot accurately be described as industrial. The chief elements that compose this market are:

1. Manufacturing, mining, construction, and processing establishments which either make materials available, or fabricate them into products, or use them to create services such as power, communication, and transportation.

2. Farmers, who increasingly use machinery and buy materials they formerly made themselves. Statistically, they are generally classified as part of the consumer market, but more and more they tend to buy like industrial concerns.

3. Commercial concerns such as wholesalers and retailers, and intangible service units such as insurance companies and banks, which buy various kinds of supplies and equipment to facilitate their operations.

4. Institutions such as schools, hospitals, and churches, which purchase the same kinds of things with which to carry on their activities.

5. Governmental units, which are constantly increasing the portion they take of our total industrial output.

Although it is not possible to present a complete numerical picture of these elements of the industrial market, the following is a partial summary.

Manufacturing establishments 298,453
Mining establishments 36,394
Construction establishments 467,600
Farm units 2,416,017
Retailers and wholesalers 2,081,787
Service establishments 979,195
Institutions (The total is hard to compile; there are, for example, 6876 hospitals alone.)
Governmental units .... about 6000

In spite of their numbers the retail-wholesale group is probably the least important in terms of the volume of goods they buy; their purchases are largely confined to storage and display equipment, stationery and record-keeping equipment and materials, and packaging materials. The agricultural group buys in larger volume, chiefly machinery, fertilizers, and feeds, but in many respects the typical farmer's method of purchasing more nearly represents that of the ultimate consumer than that of the industrial buyer. There is a tendency, though, for farm operations, including buying, to be conducted more and more along industrial lines.

Many service businesses, such as beauty and barber shops, cleaning establishments, and repair shops, are very small concerns, and while their volume of industrial purchases is growing, they can not be said to constitute an important element in the total industrial market. The construction business is probably second to the manufacturing industry in the volume of its industrial purchases. In their buying behavior the two are very similar, often practically indistinguishable, but manufacturing establishments are responsible for the overwhelming bulk of the purchasing power that makes up the industrial market.

The industrial market is highly concentrated geographically. For example, in 1958 the Census Bureau found that seven states, New York, California, Pennsylvania, Illinois, Ohio, New Jersey, and Michigan, had within their borders 52.4 percent of the total number of manufacturing establishments in the nation. These enterprises employed 53.1 percent of the people working in the manufacturing industry and were responsible for 55.4 percent of the total value added by manufacture. Furthermore, firms in the states of New York, Pennsylvania, Ohio, California, Illinois, Texas, and Indiana bought 52.6 percent of the capital equipment installed by industry in that year.

This concentration is illustrated further by the fact that in the same year manufacturing establishments in 20 counties (out of the 3,000-odd in the nation) constituted 33.6 percent of the total number, employed 28.7 percent of the people working in industry, and turned out 29.9 percent of the value added by manufacture. Almost half of the total national manufacturing industry of the country was in 50 counties, which comprised 46.3 percent of the establishments, 44.1 percent of the employees, and 45.7 percent of value added by manufacture. Establishments in 12 counties bought 23.4 percent of the total capital equipment installed by the manufacturing industry of the nation, while those in 24 counties purchased 33.0 percent of it, and those in 50 counties, 46.1 percent.

The industrial market is characterized by another sort of concentration. In 1958 the 4,618 establishments (1.5 percent of the total number) which employed 500 people or more had on their payrolls 42.8 percent of the total number of persons working in the manufacturing industry; they created 48.4 percent of the value added by manufacture and made 51.6 percent of all the capital expenditures. If we include establishments with 250 employees and more, we have only 3.6 percent of the manufacturing units, but 56.7 percent of the employees, 62.1 percent of the value added by manufacture, and 64.0 percent of the capital expenditures.

Most of the other features of the industrial market seem to be of such a nature that they can be discussed more understandably in the setting of our treatment of types of goods than here. Then, too, this chapter is already long and you are probably tired reading it.

So we will add only one more thing—and that an observation which we will bring up again later—but it is something that cannot be repeated too often or emphasized too much: <u>The industrial buyer is seeking benefits, not satisfactions, and most of the benefits he seeks can</u> <u>have dollar signs put on them; they can be computed in terms of the sales-costs-profits equation. This is a fact that the marketing manager in the industrial market can never afford to forget.</u>

Product Management

The marketing manager of a manufacturing concern has a vital interest in the products his firm offers on the market. His interest in them is two-fold. In the first place, their nature and characteristics exercise a vital influence on the kind of job he has to do. In the second place, because of his position as his firm's chief point of contact with the market, he is apt to be expected to play an important part in determining changes in his company's product offering.

The marketing manager's job is very much influenced by the things he has to market. Their nature determines to a great extent such matters as the kind of marketing organization structure he needs, the sort of selling job he has to get done and the tools he can employ in doing it, the marketing outlets he can use and the problems he will face in managing their relationship with his firm and with each other, the factors that influence his pricing decisions, his difficulties of physical distribution, and many others—all problems he must solve in the process of managing the marketing operation. The product and its consumer are twin take-off points in the manufacturer's marketing management operation.

Under the theory of intrafirm functional management responsibilities that formerly prevailed, the marketing manager's relation to the product involved the adjustment of the firm's marketing facilities and efforts to the conditions under which the product was made. According to this theory it was the job of the marketing part of a manufacturing business to dispose of the products the company made by selling the quantities of them which cost factors and other production considerations indicated it was desirable to make.

A number of things have happened that tend to change this attitude. Rapid technological change has resulted in a proliferation of products and in the constant development of new products to better serve the purposes of old ones. Improvements in manufacturing processes and know-how have considerably increased the versatility of production and widened the variety of products the typical manufacturing unit can turn out. Improved communication methods and growing consumer sophistication have vastly increased the volatility of consumer demand. In addition, management has become increasingly aware of the extent to which the successful firm must be responsive to the market and its demands, and must suit its production activities to them.

These and other factors have undermined the old theory and led to widespread substitution of a new one: the function of the production part of a business is (more nearly) to make products the marketing department can sell in amounts that can be profitably disposed of. There are exceptions to this idea, both in the policies of individual companies and in the day-to-day administration of firms that in general accept it, but it is gaining ground nevertheless. As a result the marketing manager is expected to play an active role in the work of product management, such as discovering new product opportunities, helping to decide what products shall be added to the line, determining modifications to suit them more exactly to consumer wants and needs, and helping to decide which of them shall be deleted from the product mix and when deletion shall occur.

All of these activities, however, must take place within a general framework which has been established by basic variations in the characteristics and marketing behavior of different types or classes of goods and services. So in our study of the part that products play in the marketing manager's job, we will be wise to make it our first order of business to examine the different kinds of things he may have to market. We will then devote our attention to the tasks that are involved in managing the assortment of products a firm offers on the market and the part the marketing manager may be expected to play in this process.

CHAPTER 3

Types of Products

The things that are marketed differ widely in the way in which they must be manufactured, the way in which and purposes for which people use them, and in the way in which people want to buy them. These differences cause wide variations in the methods of marketing and create complex problems in the management of the marketing activity. The most important factors which generate these variations and problems are the purposes and methods of consumer use and the pattern of consumer buying habits or desires. It is primarily on these bases that our classification of products is set up.

The broadest classification of things that are marketed is (a) goods, or tangible things, and (b) services. The broad division of goods is consumers' goods and industrial goods, each of which falls into several natural subdivisions. The student should be warned that these classifications are not hard and fast and are useful solely to lend convenience in thinking about marketing problems. It is bootless to debate which class a given borderline product belongs to. With this reservation in mind, let us examine the typical characteristics and marketing behavior of the several classes into which products may fall.

SERVICES

Services have been defined as "activities, benefits, or satisfactions which are offered for sale or are provided in connection with the sale of goods."[1] This includes such things as amusements, hotel accommodations, electric and gas service, transportation, services of barber and beauty shops, repair and maintenance service. The term also embraces advice and help of sales people, credit extension, and delivery,

---

[1] From "Marketing Definitions," Report of Definitions Committee, American Marketing Association, Chicago, 1960. Unless otherwise indicated, all quoted definitions in this section are from this source.

by which a seller seeks to enhance the convenience of his customers; but since these activities will be described later in our discussion we will here confine ourselves to services that are sold as such.

The part of our economy that is engaged in supplying services has been constantly increasing. The movement of our population to the suburbs has vastly augmented the need for transportation services. The growing emphasis on security in consumers' thought patterns has expanded the market for such services as insurance, and the increase in the desire for convenience and the wish to enjoy the use of things while paying for them has augmented the demand for the services of banks and installment finance companies. Every time a woman buys a new automatic gadget for use around the house, she adds to her need for several kinds of service. Table 3–1, based upon estimates of the U.S. Department of Commerce, indicates the extent of this change.

TABLE 3–1

EXPENDITURES FOR SERVICES AS PERCENTAGES

	Of Total Consumer Income after Personal Taxes	Of Total Consumer Expenditures
1956	34.1	37.0
1957	34.7	37.6
1958	36.0	39.0
1959	36.5	39.2
1960	37.7	40.1
1961	37.9	41.0
1962	37.9	41.0

These figures include only services purchased by ultimate consumers, that is, buyers for personal or household use, and leave out those bought and used by business firms and institutions in running their enterprises. There is no official or accepted estimate of the amount or value of these industrial services.

Services possess a number of characteristic features which affect their marketing. Most of them are perishable. This is true to some extent of all those which are personal in nature: the facial or massage which the beauty specialist has time to give today, but fails to sell before the closing hour, can never be vended; the game of billiards which one could have played this evening, but did not buy, will probably never be sold; the audit that a public accountant can conduct today is lost if no client is willing to buy it. This factor makes timeliness vital in distributing many services.

A large number of services are peculiarly personal in character and may involve the most intimate likes and dislikes of the buyer. The quality of a haircut or a shave, the satisfaction derived from the manner in which a meal is served, even the poignant comfort of the ministrations of a mortician, all possess this characteristic. As a result, such services must be rendered in the presence of the buyer; they can be neither purchased nor delivered by proxy. This makes it necessary for the seller either to bring them to the purchaser, as in the case of electric light and telephone service, or to induce the buyer to go to the point where the service originates, as in the case of hospital beds, golf courses, theaters, and (usually) haircuts, shaves, and beauty treatments.

This characteristic is responsible for the fact that many services must be supplied in small units. It also tends to confine the operations of the supplying firms to a single community. The typical establishment rendering such services is apt, therefore, to be limited in size. This field seems to be one of the principal strongholds of the small, independent businessman. Obvious exceptions are the services of public utility companies and hotel chains.

GOODS

Most manufacturers primarily make and market goods rather than services. In the process of marketing, the marketer almost always must surround the sale of his goods with certain services that facilitate the operation. But his primary offering is goods: "Goods are those tangible things which are the objects of human desire and are sufficiently scarce to become the subjects of marketing activity." They fall into two great classes: consumers' goods and industrial goods.

Consumers' goods are those which are "destined for use by individual ultimate consumers or households and in such form that they can be used without commercial processing." Industrial goods are those which are "destined to be sold primarily for use in producing other goods or in rendering services, as contrasted with goods destined to be sold primarily to the ultimate consumer."

The distinction between them is based upon the divergent purposes for which they are to be used. The two groups are therefore not mutually exclusive. At one time a given article may be bought by an ultimate consumer for his personal use, and at another time it may be purchased by a firm for consumption in the conduct of its business. Both housewives and restaurants buy foodstuffs, and stationery and writing materials may be procured for the purpose of writing personal letters or for carrying on the correspondence and keeping the records of a business house, but most articles are characteristically bought for one or the other of the two kinds of use, and so, for all practical purposes, may be classified on the basis of their typical rather than their extraordinary usage.

Consumers' Goods

Amount of Consumers' Goods. Table 3–2 shows the Department of Commerce estimates for recent years of total consumer dollar expenditures for goods, and the percentages which they constitute of all consumer expenditures and of personal income after personal taxes. The percentages of durable and non-durable goods are shown separately. These figures suggest that while the importance of both durable and non-durable goods has been declining in the consumers' expenditure pattern, the significance of durables has dropped relatively, almost twice as much as that of nondurables.

TABLE 3–2

CONSUMER EXPENDITURES FOR GOODS

	Total Consumer Expenditures for Goods (in Billions of Dollars)	As Percentages of Total Consumer Expenditures			As Percentages of Total Income after Personal Taxes		
		All	Durable Goods	Non-durable Goods	All	Durable Goods	Non-durable Goods
1956.....	169.9	63.0	14.4	48.6	58.1	13.3	44.8
1957.....	178.1	62.5	14.2	48.3	57.7	13.1	44.6
1958.....	178.9	61.0	12.7	48.3	56.3	11.7	44.6
1959.....	190.7	60.8	13.9	46.9	56.6	12.9	43.7
1960.....	196.6	59.8	13.6	46.2	56.2	12.8	43.4
1961.....	198.9	58.8	12.9	45.9	54.7	12.0	42.7
1962.....	209.7	59.0	13.6	45.4	54.5	12.5	42.0

Nature of Consumers' Goods. The manufacturer of consumers' goods can never afford to forget that he is really marketing not goods but the satisfactions consumers can enjoy from having or using them. The product is merely the vehicle which carries the satisfaction. Even the consumer is not always aware of this and, with the surface of his mind, may think in terms of buying goods although the deeper motives that impel purchase or rejection are those that emanate from human satisfaction. It is never wise for the marketer to forget this.

The motives which influence the ultimate consumer in his buying are likely to be those which are commonly referred to as "emotional" rather than those we think of as "rational." The goods he purchases are apt to be chosen as the result of personal taste or whim or prejudice rather than on the basis of any careful, scientific analysis of their utilitarian qualities. For instance, the consumers in the New York market prefer eggs having white shells while those in the Boston area favor the brown-shelled variety, although there is no difference in the eating qualities of the two types.

Factors within the buyer, therefore, are sometimes more important than those within the merchandise in motivating a purchase. As a result, the consideration of prime importance in selling consumers' goods often is not what their characteristics actually are but what the prospective purchasers *think* they are. This opinion is not usually the result of any technical analysis of the physical properties of the merchandise, or of any systematic testing of its usefulness, but is likely to be the outcome of many influences that play on the consumer's psychology, including what he has been told about it.

Some of the satisfactions the consumer can get from the goods he buys are basic; some are, or seem to be, trivial; still others, while not basic, represent substantial additions to or modifications of those that are basic. For example, the basic satisfaction offered by an automobile is transportation, to carry one from where he is to where he wants to be. The old Model T Ford did just that, but almost nobody liked the possibility of a broken arm and the certainty of a frayed temper that were inherent in the process of starting the car by cranking. So when a manufacturer offered the motorist a car with a selfstarter that worked, it represented a substantial increment to the basic satisfaction users could enjoy from their cars. But when, at a later stage in the history of the automobile, a maker equipped his car with a pushbutton gadget to raise and lower the windows, it could hardly be said that by so doing he made an earthshaking contribution to consumer welfare and enjoyment. This is in spite of the fact that windows are sometimes hard to wind up and down and that many people dearly love to manipulate gadgets.

Many critics complain that most of the satisfactions which manufacturers seek to add to their products by modifications of them are of the trivial variety and really contribute very little, if anything, to the sum total of human satisfaction—all too often not enough to be worth the resources spent on them.

Consumer satisfaction is a subjective thing. It arises not from the satisfaction a user *should* get from a product, if he appraised his experience with it in the cold light of pure reason, but from the satisfaction he *thinks* or *feels* he will get, or *does* get, from using it. It is much easier to discover the amount of satisfaction a consumer should get from a product than to find out how much he thinks he will get from it. The former, involving primarily the physical properties of the article, can be achieved by applying the tools of logic and mathematics; the latter requires the use of the much less exact and much less reliable tools of psychology.

The subjective nature of consumer satisfaction affords grounds for severe criticism of manufacturers who base their producing and marketing decisions on it. Any attempt to manipulate the buyer's opinion of a product is bound to open the door to the charge that the manipulator is seeking to fool the consumer, especially if the manipulation does not involve any basic change in the product. Many critics are unwilling to recognize that satisfactions, which have little or nothing to do with the physical use of a product but proceed from the consumer's thinking or feeling about it, are real and worthwhile. They tend to view these satisfactions as flowing from desires that are unnatural and created by the marketer. The satisfaction arising from the style or fashion characteristic of products is an example.

As a result of these criticisms many crusaders have preached the gospel of specifications and exact technical descriptions for consumers' goods. Undoubtedly such things would be most useful, but in buying on the basis of his own personal and often emotional reactions the consumer may be wiser than the advocates of scientific purchasing know. The buyers of consumers' goods are interested primarily in obtaining not the tangible articles themselves, but the satisfactions to be enjoyed from their possession or use. Such satisfactions often have their origins fully as much in the character and emotions of the buyer of a commodity as in the inherent physical properties of the article itself. Satisfaction which is subjective, which has its origin in a whim or prejudice, is just as real and just as important as that which is objective and results from the mathematically measurable physical properties of a product. Intelligent buying of consumers' goods, therefore, may demand that so-called emotional considerations play an important part in their selection.

Consumers of many types of commodities justifiably tend to take it for granted that an article possesses the basic utilities it is supposed to supply and to look to peripheral qualities, such as convenience, prestige, attractiveness of appearance, the atmosphere in which it is sold, or novelty, to supply the intangible plus of satisfaction that distinguishes one maker's goods from another's. The manufacturer who neglects to build these intangibles into his product, and to make the consumer aware of them, is apt to miss a sizable part of his market.

Consumers' goods are commonly bought in small units. This is not true of all such articles, of course, but tends to be characteristic of most of them. No single purchase is usually very important from a monetary point of view. Therefore the typical seller must concentrate his efforts upon influencing large numbers of persons to favor his product rather than upon bringing heavy, concentrated sales pressure to bear upon a few small, selected groups of persons.

The market for this type of goods is very extensive. The prospective users of them are generally scattered from Maine to California and from Puget Sound to the Florida Strait, with overflows into Hawaii and Alaska. The number of possible consumers of many such articles is limited only by the total population. This emphasizes the producer's difficulty of getting in touch directly with all possible buyers of the merchandise he sells. He must depend upon indirect contact, achieved through many middlemen, to dispose of his goods. He is confronted with the extremely difficult task of inducing these middlemen to promote the sale of his products to ultimate consumers in the manner he desires.

This wide distribution of the users of consumers' goods also influences the type of publicity which must be employed by their marketers. It is usually not practical to advertise to so scattered and numerous a group of possible buyers on the individual basis that is often so effective with industrial goods. The media used must be many and diverse in character rather than few and specialized. The advertiser can not obey the perhaps apocryphal admonition of Colonel Prescott at Bunker Hill and "wait to see the whites of their eyes" before firing. He must launch broadsides of publicity in the general direction in which he thinks the customer target lies and trust to mathematical probability that some of his ammunition will find a profitable mark. Barrage rather than direct fire is indicated. This results in much heavier expenditures for advertising this type of merchandise than are necessary or profitable in industrial goods.

Consumers' goods are often classified into convenience goods, shopping goods, and specialties. These classes are set up on the basis of the manner in which the articles belonging to each are commonly bought. Since habits of purchase vary among individuals and groups of buyers, this classification is not all-inclusive, nor are the three types mutually exclusive. Many articles that normally are bought as convenience goods are purchased by some consumers in the same manner as that in which shopping goods or specialties are generally procured. This classification can be useful only if it is thoroughly understood that the class limits are in no sense hard and fast and that they are based upon the usual behavior of the average consumer in buying the commodities belonging to each group and not upon the inevitable conduct of every person in doing so. In practice, this limitation of the classification is not very serious because the manufacturer of consumers' goods usually must play the law of averages in marketing them whether he wishes to do so or not.

Convenience Goods. Convenience goods are "those consumers' goods which the customer usually desires to purchase frequently, immediately, and with the minimum of effort in comparison and buying." Typical examples of such articles are most tobacco products, soaps, most over-the-counter drug products, newspapers, magazines (with the exception of such publications as Fortune, The New Yorker, and Esquire), chewing gum, small packaged confections, and probably most food products. It is noticeable that most of these articles are of small unit value and are not bulky.

Goods of this class tend to be bought at points most convenient to the consumer. Habit plays a large part in their procurement. Since no one purchase of such goods is likely to loom very large in his budget, the consumer will not go far out of his way to procure them, nor is he willing to exert himself particularly in making investigations and comparisons in the process of selecting them. They are often purchased on impulse and without careful consideration.

Because of this characteristic and because convenience goods are bought by all classes and types of ultimate consumers, manufacturers of them must seek to achieve the widest possible distribution at retail. They must see to it that such goods are on sale in the largest possible number of retail establishments, which are located at points as convenient as possible to prospective purchasers, and available when they are in the buying mood. They must aim at blanket rather than selective distribution at retail. With some exceptions, they are apt to find it easier and cheaper to obtain such complete retail coverage by selling through wholesalers rather than by making direct contact with store operators. Such exceptions occur when a firm makes a considerable number of consumer items all sold through the same retail trade. The combined volume of sales may then be enough to support a salesforce to contact all retailers and a system of stock-carrying branch warehouses to service them.

Much of the work of promoting the sale of convenience goods at retail must be done by the firms that produce them. This may be accomplished in two ways. They may advertise extensively to ultimate consumers. Such publicity is likely to feature the names and brands under which the commodities are sold. Its purpose is not only to produce immediate sales but to induce general recognition of the article, and create good will for it among prospective buyers, or to confirm occasional users in the habit of purchasing it. Manufacturers of such goods also may attempt to induce retailers to display them prominently, placing them on the shelves so that they will stand out and attract the attention of customers.

Because of the expense the manufacturer incurs in this work and the rapid turnover which is characteristic of this type of goods, the margin of gross profit allowed the retailers and wholesalers handling them is apt to be small.

An extreme kind of convenience goods is impulse goods. These are articles customarily bought on impulse and without previous planning. The customer buys such a product because he happens to see it at a time when it seems a good idea to him to purchase it. The stick of chewing gum or small package of candy mints on the subway platform, the package of popcorn in the movie lobby, sun glasses on sale at a boat rental dock are examples.

Probably most consumers' products are occasionally bought on impulse, but very few are always bought that way. The compulsive gum-chewer is likely to buy his supply on plan by the carton; the inveterate muncher of candy mints is careful to buy a new packet before the old one is exhausted, but there is a large body of consumers who can take their gum and mints or let them alone. They will take them oftener if they see them for sale oftener. The manufacturers of these articles will miss a lot of sales if they fail to recognize that their products have impulse characteristics and fail to make their marketing plans accordingly. This means that they must seek out the largest possible number of places where consumers assemble or pass when they might be in the mood to buy these products and arrange to put them on sale there.

Shopping Goods. Shopping goods are "consumers' goods which the customer in the process of selection and purchase characteristically compares on such bases as suitability, quality, price, and style." Examples of articles usually bought as shopping goods are millinery, furniture, dress goods, men's and women's ready-to-wear, and women's shoes. Style or fashion is an important feature of most, although not all, of the products belonging to this class. According to P. H. Nystrom a style is a "characteristic or distinctive mode of expression or presentation in the field of some art." It is a design according to which a thing may be made. A fashion is a currently popular style.

Perhaps this is as good a place as any to comment on fashion as a merchandise characteristic. The central feature of the fashion characteristic is the ebb and flow of the popularity of a distinctive design or pattern of a thing. There are very few products or human activities that are not influenced by fashion in some degree. For example, the current school of philosophy is really a fashion in that branch of learning; the ranch-type house was a fashion in dwellings and is still a style, just as is the Cape Cod. But the fashion element exercises more influence on the demand for some products than for others, and for some it is a dominant influence in shaping consumers' buying behavior.

Once a style has been developed it continues to exist as long as there is a record of it. The toga is still a style but, fortunately for men and unfortunately for the textile business, it is not now the fashion. Incredible as it may seem, it is not impossible that togas may again become fashionable. Fashion is the style of the moment. It is "the thing" today. Tomorrow or the next day it will be relegated to the archives.

What has just been said illustrates a central feature of fashion behavior, the fashion cycle. A given style is introduced or revived. A few influential people conform to it. It gains in popularity. Shortly it becomes "the thing." Then its popularity begins to fade and in due course it passes into the limbo of things all but forgotten to await revival, probably in a slightly changed form but the same in its essential design. For instance, the Empress Eugenie hat has gone through at least two such cycles and the bustle has come back (pun unintended) at least once since originally developed.

Occasionally, a fashion develops into a fad which is distinguished chiefly by the greater speed with which its popularity grows and the abruptness with which it ends. Often the life of a fad is a few months or even a few weeks. A fad is also apt to be characterized by the fact that its design is more extreme and bizarre than that of a fashion.

The touchstone of success in making and marketing fashion merchandise is timing. The manufacturer must get into production and get his goods on the market while a fashion is in its early stages of growth. He must get his money out of the project and withdraw from it before its popularity has waned too much to permit him to dispose of his stocks. A stock of out-of-fashion merchandise is just about as salable as a last year's bird's nest.

Consumers buy shopping goods only after careful comparison. Before committing herself, the purchaser habitually examines a number of designs or the offerings of several stores in order to select the article that most exactly fits her wishes. In buying hangings for a room, for instance, a woman likes to compare various materials in order to choose one of a design and color which matches or supplements the color scheme and tone of the other decorations and furnishings of the room. She shops for merchandise that is precisely suitable for the particular purpose for which she intends to use it. She also wishes to select material that is in fashion, that is popularly regarded at the moment as "the thing" for the purpose. Its design must be that of today, not of yesterday, nor yet of tomorrow.

Shopping goods are also compared on the bases of price and quality, although the average person is prone to accept the former as an index of the latter. The quality of such goods is also very likely to be regarded as a function of style and suitability rather than of durability or usefulness. The importance of price comparisons in this field seems to be more apparent than real. The woman who sets out to buy a dress is apt to have determined upon a rather narrow range of prices within which the article must fall. If she can find none suitable within that range, her choice is likely to narrow down to the question of whether she shall buy at all. She usually does not attempt to choose among the articles offered at the several prices which she already has decided do not fit her purse.

The manufacturer may market an article of this type through a much smaller number of retail stores than are needed for convenience goods. Consumers will submit to considerable inconvenience in their pursuit of style and suitability. It is important that stores handling this kind of merchandise be located in the general shopping district, but precise location at a specific point is usually not particularly necessary. Department stores handle this type of goods extensively, although there are also many smaller shops which specialize in selling limited lines of style commodities.

The heavy congestion of traffic in the shopping centers of large cities has led many "downtown" shopping-goods stores to establish branches in outlying centers in which their suburban customers may buy less important shopping items. But these branches have not yet entirely supplanted the parent stores, with their more complete stocks and wider selections. One of the unsolved marketing problems of the manufacturers of shopping goods is to what extent to rely on the downtown stores as outlets and to what extent to shift to branches and the independent shops that spring up near them.

Most shopping is done by women. In consequence, stores selling this type of merchandise endeavor to surround the task of comparison and selection with the maximum of niceties and services, many of them apparently quite extraneous to the shopping process. This practice has been especially characteristic of department stores. They have operated lounging rooms, nurseries, postoffices, style shows, theaters, and concerts, to mention only a few items of a list that is almost endless. In some cases the policy of furnishing such free services has been extended to such lengths that the service tail seems to wag the product dog.

The contact between the producer and the retailer of shopping goods must be very close. Fashions change very quickly. Consumer demand for such articles is never stable. Therefore the manufacturer must produce most of them to order and not to stock. He must maintain sufficiently close connections with the consumer market to enable him to discover changes in demand at their inception. The retailer must shop the wholesale market with the utmost thoroughness to obtain exactly the merchandise his customers desire. In this field, therefore, the relations between manufacturer and retailer tend to be direct; either the producer sends his salesmen to make contact with the dealer, or the latter or his representative visits the market in which the producers are located in order to make first-hand comparison and observation of fashion trends.

Most of the advertising of shopping goods must be done locally and for immediate effect. Time is a vital element in their sale. The copy in this evening's paper is designed to sell dresses or hats tomorrow. If it does not do so, it is a failure. The bulk of the work of advertising such goods, therefore, falls upon the retailer and is done through newspapers. The dealer must actively promote the sale of such merchandise. To do the job successfully he must develop in the ultimate consumer a disposition to rely upon the advice and suggestions of his salespeople and the reputation of his store. This involves much more expert and costly selling work than is necessary in vending convenience goods. It also emphasizes the importance of the manufacturer's selection of exactly the right outlets to handle his merchandise.

For these reasons the expenses of stores selling these commodities are usually very heavy. In addition, the risk of handling them is great, owing to the rapid changes in consumer demand which are characteristic in the field. Therefore the manufacturer must accept the fact that retailers need a much larger gross margin than when they handle convenience goods.

Specialty Goods. Specialty goods are "those consumers' goods with unique characteristics and/or brand identification for which a significant group of buyers is habitually willing to make a special purchasing effort." Some articles that are usually bought in this manner are fancy groceries, high-grade watches, men's high-grade shoes, expensive pipes and tobaccos, and probably certain types of sporting and photographic equipment. The articles belonging to this group are neither so numerous nor so universally bought as shopping or convenience goods.

The most significant feature of the purchase of specialties is consumer insistence. In buying such an article the customer knows what he wants—or thinks he does—and is willing to go to considerable inconvenience and effort to procure it rather than to accept a substitute. Most of these goods are sold under brand. It does not follow, however, that all branded products belong to this class. Most manufacturers of trademarked articles would undoubtedly prefer their products to be in the specialty group, but in relatively few cases is it possible to put them there. Certain commodities have special characteristics which place them in this class whether they are branded or not.

The manufacturer's problem of selecting and managing a system of retail outlets for a specialty product is at once simplified and complicated by the fact that these goods are usually offered for sale in comparatively few retail stores. The establishments specializing in handling them are likely to be of a rather expensive type. Of course specialties are not all sold through stores confining their stocks to that class of merchandise, but they are apt to be vended rather more successfully through such outlets. Since the average consumer of specialty goods will go to considerable inconvenience in order to get the article that precisely fits his needs or wants, the exact location of the stores selling them is not usually so important as it is in the case of either convenience or shopping goods.

Since specialties have peculiar characteristics that distinguish them from other similar goods, extra sales effort must be expended in explaining, describing, and demonstrating these unusual features. Obviously most of this work can be done most effectively by the retailer and his salespeople. To assure their cooperation in the task, manufacturers of such articles usually endeavor to maintain very close and direct relations with the stores handling their products. These relations sometimes take the form of a franchise arrangement whereby the manufacturer designates a given retailer as the only one permitted to handle his product in a given area. This makes it worthwhile for the storekeeper to put behind the article the special sales effort that is necessary to stimulate the demand for it. Because of the unusual importance of the retailer and the extra effort required of him in handling these goods, his margin of gross profit on them must usually be quite large.

In some cases the manufacturer is not content to depend upon the retailer for this sales promotion work but, through his own sales-men engaged in house-to-house selling, endeavors to make contact with prospective buyers. This practice has been followed, for example, by concerns making vacuum cleaners and electric and gas refrigerators.

Commodities of this class are rather more suitable for sale by na-tional advertising than are shopping goods. But this must be extensively supplemented by local publicity which links the manufacturer's prod-uct with the individual dealer. As a general rule, the producer finds it necessary to aid in carrying on this publicity and to exercise some con-trol over it. Advertising of articles of this type must feature the special characteristics which distinguish them from the general run of com-modities that are similar but without their unusual qualities. Copy designed to sell decaffeinated coffee, for instance, must feature the facts that it has no unhealthful effects, does not disturb the sleep of its drinkers, and tastes just as good as regular coffee.

Durable and Nondurable. Some goods are consumed in one or a few uses. Others are more durable in that they give up their satisfac-tions over many uses. This difference exercises a considerable influ-ence on the problems of marketing them.

The consumer wishes to buy nondurable goods in relatively small quantities and usually at reasonably regular intervals. The retailers who sell them can count on a fairly even flow of demand and so of sales. This means that the manufacturer must make sure that re-tailers located conveniently to consumer buyers carry a stock of his products adequate to serve local demand. The relative regularity of the sales flow means that it is reasonably predictable, with the result that inventories can be more closely controlled and stock turnover can be more rapid; and retailers and wholesalers can use their dollars in-vested in inventory more often within any given time period. This in turn enables the manufacturer's outlets to operate profitably on a rela-tively narrow margin of gross and net profit.

Since the consumer is constantly buying and rebuying nondurables, he is quite likely to form buying habits. These habits apply not only to where he buys and how much, but to what he purchases and what brand. So brand loyalty is not only highly important but somewhat easier to achieve. It can also be more quickly destroyed by failures in quality.

When a consumer buys a durable good he expects to have it for a relatively long time. So he is apt to be willing to go to some trouble to get the right thing. This means that most, although not all, dur-ables are also shopping or specialty goods. Since it is a long time be-tween purchases, each sale is more important to the manufacturer. The atmosphere of the retail store, its displays, the product knowledge of its salespeople and their selling skill are more important than is the case with nondurable goods. This fact, plus the slower rate of stock turnover, makes necessary a wide margin of gross and net profit.

The effect of the long time intervening between purchases on brand loyalty is probably mixed. Between purchases the consumer has time to forget what brand he bought and perhaps even where he bought it. On the other hand, either an unpleasant or pleasant use experience with a brand of a durable good is apt to intensify a consumer's disloyalty or do much to cement his loyalty to the brand. Since the discriminating consumer expects constant improvement to be made in a durable good, a pleasant use-experience with a brand can be expected to insure that he will at least examine it before his next purchase and to predispose him to buy it unless someone can show him why he should not do so. The probable effect of an unpleasant use experience is illustrated by the case of a friend who bought a certain make of automobile and happened to get one of the "lemons" that even the most careful manufacturing controls can not prevent. Since that time, neither he nor any member of his family has ever visited the showroom of a car dealer handling that make.

Manufacturers of durables try to bridge the time gap between purchases by many methods, among which are franchising their dealers, attempting to maintain continuity of the franchise in each locality, trying to see to it that the dealer or some other authorized concern provides good repair and maintenance service, stimulating the dealer to maintain contact with consumers between purchases, and heavy advertising nationally and locally. In spite of all a manufacturer can do, the gap is usually imperfectly bridged. For example, how many automobile dealers operate a follow-up system by which they get in touch with customer-owners of their cars regularly to check on the satisfaction they are giving and to build a contact platform from which, at the right moment, to suggest that it is about time to buy a new car?

Many durable commodities have active secondhand markets. The sale of a new unit of such an article is apt to involve the granting of an allowance on an old one traded in by the buyer. The automobile industry is plagued by this problem, and it is perhaps more serious in that trade than in any other. It may well be taken as an example. Statistics and estimates indicate that for every new passenger automobile that is sold to an ultimate consumer in this country, between one and a half and two used cars must be disposed of by the dealers in the trade. Between 75 and 85 percent of all new car sales involve trade-ins of used cars.

Used car operations generally constitute a considerable drain on the motor vehicle retailing business. According to "Automobile Facts and Figures," published annually by the Automobile Manufacturers Association, the automobile dealer suffers a gross loss of several hundred dollars on each used car he handles. This loss must be made up out of his gross profit margin on his new car sales. This experience is doubtless duplicated on a smaller scale by many of the trades handling durable goods.

In industries vexed by this problem, secondhand goods usually constitute an active source of competition to the sale of new merchandise of the same kind. This competition is often so severe that retail concerns do not handle both new and used units of an article, or else they find it necessary to set up separate sales organizations. The presence of a secondhand market for a commodity limits the mobility of the prices of new units of the product. A reduction in the price of the new commodity at once causes a proportional cut in the trade-in values of all units of the article then in the hands of users, with consequent loss of good will.

From time to time the entire market for a durable product may be disrupted when the inventories of retailers become so loaded with secondhand units as to handicap them in disposing of the new ones. The pressure of these inventories may even force them to emphasize the sale of the used item at the expense of their selling emphasis on the new, with detrimental effects on the manufacturer's entire market. To forestall this some manufacturers hesitate to market through dealers who do a second-hand business, preferring those who turn it over to specialists, such as used-car lots.

Most durable goods which are mechanical in nature, and some which are not, require repair and maintenance service. Of course the manufacturer of such a product may take the attitude that his responsibility ceases when he has sold it, and that it becomes the job of the buyer to see that the machine continues to operate. If the producer acts on this theory, his sales are liable to suffer. Consumer goodwill toward such commodities depends to a great extent upon the availability of adequate repair and maintenance service for them. The wise manufacturer, therefore, will take steps to make sure that it is provided. This does not necessarily mean that the firm producing the article furnishes the service itself. When goods are sold to ultimate consumers through retail dealers, the manufacturer's participation in servicing them often consists in supervising, aiding, training, and encouraging the retailers in carrying on that activity.

The degree of satisfaction derived by the ultimate consumer from the repair and maintenance service he receives on a mechanical article depends primarily upon three things: (1) the presence of a conveniently located repair shop carrying an adequate supply of spare parts, (2) the assurance that a considerable measure of skill will be employed in the actual doing of the work, and (3) the charging of reasonable prices for it. In his attempt to make sure that retailers handling his product conform to these requirements in the service they offer, the manufacturer is likely to eliminate wholesalers and to sell direct to retail dealers. He is then in a much better position both to check the quality of the service they give and to apply pressure, training, and assistance toward its improvement.

Deferrable and Nondeferrable Purchase Goods. Some goods a consumer can buy at a time of his own choosing, others he must buy at once when the need or want arises. Food must be bought when the larder begins to get empty; cigarettes, when it becomes embarrassing to "bum" from a friend; drugs, when pain strikes or threatens; soap, when the cake gets too thin; and toothpaste, when the tube has been squeezed to the point of no return. To fail to rebuy is to cease being a consumer of the product (and in the case of food, to stop being at all). But in all but the rarest cases, the old car can be repaired to last another couple of months or half year; furniture or throw-rugs can be put over holes in the carpet; or a chair can be wired so it will hold together unless the sitter is too amply upholstered. In the meantime, the purchase of a new one is deferred. Most deferrable purchase items are also durables but not all of them are.

This difference becomes especially important during periods of business recession and boom. When conditions are bad and consumer attitudes become pessimistic, the demand for deferrable purchase items declines markedly. The tonnage of food eaten varies very little in good times and bad; its composition may change but its overall amount is remarkably stable. The purchase of drug products often actually increases during periods of recession. The quip about the relation between business headaches and aspirin and tranquilizers is not altogether a joke. The sales forecasting problems of a manufacturer of deferrable purchase goods are much more complex than those of the maker of nondeferrable items.

Manufacturers of deferrable purchase products have sought to overcome their handicap by at least three means. Some increase their advertising and selling efforts when a widespread consumer tendency to defer purchase begins to be felt, and to diminish them somewhat when orders flow freely. The automobile business offers an outstanding example of an attempt to meet the problem by making frequent changes in model, some of which represent improvements, and some merely surface modifications. The net effect is to "date" the old car in the consumer's driveway and to bring prestige pressure on him not to defer replacing it with a new one. Instalment selling has been widely used to help solve this problem. Its use enables the consumer to enjoy a product while he is paying for it and to reduce the financial pressures tending to force him to defer purchase. None of these devices has completely solved the problem but, almost certainly, they have helped.

Industrial Goods

Most people think of marketing exclusively in terms of trade in goods for personal consumption or use. But a tremendous amount of marketing activity must occur in order to provide the materials, facilities, and services needed to make the end products which are consumers' goods. Let us consider the automobile as perhaps the most characteristic consumer product of the modern age. The dealer who sells it must provide himself with office equipment and printed forms. The manufacturer must buy transportation service to carry it to the dealer; and he must buy paper, tarpaulins, loading blocks, etc., to prepare it for shipment, or trucks to carry it, and gasoline and oil to operate the trucks. To make his cars he must buy steel sheets, castings and forgings, upholstery fabrics, paint, and other materials. From accessory manufacturers he must buy such items as carburetors, radiators, bumpers, tires, and batteries. He needs machine tools of various types, and he needs equipment for power generation and transmission. To keep his plant going he must buy lubricants, floor-sweeping compounds, lighting, and a multitude of other items. To control his operations he must have automatic control equipment, accounting machinery, typewriters, desks, telephone service.

Each of the suppliers of these commodities and services must likewise buy materials and machinery and supplies, until each item is traced back to its constituent raw materials. Even the producers of these basic materials themselves use machines and supplies and services which they must buy from other suppliers. Hence we find an endless chain of industrial transactions involved in the production and sale of every item for personal consumption. The manufacturers of these industrial components, equipment, and supplies must market them to users.

Industrial goods and services may also be classified into a number of distinctive groups, each with its own peculiar characteristics.

Equipment. Equipment includes industrial goods that do not become part of the physical product and which are exhausted only after repeated use. Some of it is *major or installed equipment*, such as boilers, generators, stamping machines, presses, power lathes, bank vaults, big computing machines. It also includes *accessories* such as guages, meters, and control devices, most of which are designed either to control or to facilitate the operation of major equipment machines. A third distinguishable type is *auxiliary equipment*, trucks, typewriters, filing cases, shelving, and movable hoists. These three classes of equipment are not immutable or mutually exclusive. For example, trucks are major equipment for a trucking company.

The purchase of major or installed equipment items usually involves substantial capital commitments and is generally determined by basic policy decisions often made by the chief executives of the buying concerns. These decisions are grounded primarily on economic considerations. Their cost is usually charged to a capital account and must be amortized over a period of years out of the earnings made from their use. Marketing programs for such goods must be planned in the light of these purchasing considerations.

Such equipment is of two kinds. Some machines are *standard;* they are used in performing a certain operation or type of operation that is common to many firms and many industries. Others are *special-duty* machines; they are fitted to perform an operation that is peculiar to only one firm or only one industry. The demand for the former is flexible in that a change in any one firm or industry will not affect it too seriously. The demand for the latter tends to be rigid: a change in the operating conditions of a single firm may increase it greatly or cause its complete disappearance.

The cost of auxiliary equipment and accessories may be charged to operating expense, or, if capitalized, is usually written off in a short time. Purchases such as these are likely to be decided upon by departmental executives, with an eye to the operating efficiency of their departments. Many of these items, particularly those designed to facilitate executive control, find markets only in organizations of some size. The men making the buying decisions constitute for the most part a "horizontal" buying group; that is, they are mainly functional executives, having relatively similar problems in all industries. This is not always true of accessory control items which are often highly specialized and without which more expensive equipment is useless. These are likely to be chosen very carefully and their purchase dictated by the technical personnel of the buying firm.

Maintenance, Repair, and Operating Goods. These are often referred to as MRO items; they are relatively inexpensive and often short-lived articles that are necessary to the operation of a business. Some of them are accessory equipment, such as small tools, conveyors, small motors, and typewriters. Others are operating supplies, such as paints, oils and greases, towels, soaps, printed forms, and letterheads that are consumed in operating and maintaining a plant.

MRO items are the convenience goods of the industrial market. Their cost is usually charged to current operating expense and their purchasing is generally done as a matter of routine and often from the most convenient source. Many of these items have "horizontal" markets; that is they perform functions that are common to many industries and are bought very widely.

The manufacturer of an MRO item usually must see to it that his product is stocked and sold at many points convenient to the plants of its users. Often such items are not bought in large enough quantities in many industrial areas to support the cost of maintaining manufacturers' warehouses and salesforces there. As a result the maker must market them through industrial distributors who handle such articles produced by many manufacturers, thus gaining enough volume to justify facilities and staff to stock, sell, and deliver them.

Materials. These are goods that usually, but not always, enter into and form a part of the finished product. They may be *component parts,* such as batteries, ignition switches, lighting systems for automobiles, which are incorporated into the end product without change. Often they retain their identity and bear the maker's label, as is true of batteries and tires in automobiles, so that the buyer of the end product may know their source. This makes it possible for their manufacturer to advertise over the head of the industrial user to consumers of his end product and to bring customer pressure to bear on him to specify a component of a specific make.

Some of them are partially *fabricated* materials, such as steel sheets or textile fabrics, that undergo additional processing in the course of their incorporation into the end products. A few of these retain their identity sufficiently to enable the maker to advertise over the head of the industrial customer and thus build up a demand for them by the end product buyer. But most of them lose their identity in the process of fabrication.

Others are *process* materials that have been partially fabricated and undergo decided changes, usually chemical in nature, in the process of further fabrication so that they are not identifiable in the finished product. Examples are plastic molding materials, wood pulp, and dyestuffs and pigments. Some process materials, such as catalysts, simply facilitate production and form no part of the end product.

All sorts of materials are usually bought on definite standards or specifications, sometimes prepared by the buyer, and are subjected to qualitative tests before acceptance or use. In the interest of consistency of quality and delivery performance, many users wish to buy them on annual requirements contracts which specify that the buyer will purchase all or a stated part of his yearly needs from a given seller. In some cases when exact quality or technical precision or delivery is very important, the user is willing to commit his entire requirements to a carefully selected supplier. More often, though, he prefers not to put all his eggs in one procurement basket and seeks protection against disturbances of supply by such things as flood, fire, and strikes by dividing his requirements among several suppliers. When generally used standards for a product provide enough assurance of quality, and there is an active market for it, it is apt to be ordered when needed. But even then the number of suppliers is likely to be limited and orders are apt to be divided among them on a predetermined basis.

Marketing Characteristics. Industrial goods possess many marketing characteristics quite different from those of consumers' goods.

1. The demand for such products is rather inelastic in the sense that it often does not fluctuate sensitively or extensively in inverse response to changes in price. The demand for an industrial commodity arises from the demand for the article or articles which it is used to make. In the long run, a decline in the price of a material, through making possible a decrease in the price of the article it is used to make, may result in an increase in the amount of the end product consumers buy, and hence in the demand of its producers for the material. This occurs only as a result of long-continued changes in price and when the material in question is of considerable importance in the cost structure of the end product. This factor, plus the way in which a material is bought—alone or as a part of a "package" of materials from a single supplier—tends to determine the extent to which patronage is likely to shift from one supplier to another in response to price disparities. The package feature tends to cause patronage responses to price influence to be "sticky."

The short-run demand for an industrial good is apt even to be elastic in reverse in response to changes in price. When its price decreases, purchasing agents tend to suspect that the change is the beginning of a general decline in the market for the commodity, and they therefore reduce their stocks to the minimum by buying less of it. On the other hand, a slight price advance is often interpreted as an omen of a general and continued rise, and may result in substantial increases in demand.

START HERE   2. The demand for certain types of industrial goods tends to decline more rapidly and to revive more slowly during periods of industrial depression than does that for most consumers' goods. This is especially true of various types of equipment. The demand for such items is made up of two elements: replacements and new installations. The onset of recession tends to put an end to plant expansion and the building of new factories. Even replacements are often delayed, the existing equipment being repaired to serve the needs of the restricted operating schedules prevailing during periods of slow business, or out-worn machines being allowed to stand idle while the limited operations of the plant are carried on by those still in working condition.

While a few well-financed, well-managed concerns seize the opportunity afforded by the lower prices sometimes prevailing during a recession to bring their equipment up-to-date cheaply, most industrial firms are either not able or not courageous enough to do so. The optimism engendered by improving business conditions is necessary to induce the managements of most firms to make such expenditures. As a result, the demand for industrial equipment usually revives only after the market for consumers' goods has enjoyed substantial expansion. The demand for materials and supplies, of course, fluctuates roughly with that for the goods in the making of which they are used.

3. Industrial goods are usually bought by experts. A large percentage of the contracts for their procurement are negotiated by the specialized purchasing officers of the buying firms. Many of these men are engineers, and they usually have had long and varied experience in the work of procurement. In his negotiations such an official is likely to be assisted and advised by the engineering staff of his firm, its foremen and superintendents of production, and other members of its executive staff whose experience or training qualifies them to participate in the work. MRO items, materials of minor importance, and auxiliary equipment are usually bought by the purchasing department without much, if any, participation by other executives in the process. In the procuring of materials of prime importance and major installations, however, the chief executives of the company—sometimes even the members of the board of directors—are likely to take part. This means that very able salesmen must be used in selling such products, and that the information supplied to prospects by the sales force must be reliable, well organized, and well presented. This practice also makes it difficult to sell through middlemen.

4. A number of persons often participate in negotiating a purchase of an industrial good. Before a piece of expensive equipment can be sold to a firm, or its annual supply of a major material contracted for, not one but *at least* three executives of the buying house must be convinced of the desirability of making such a purchase and brought to the point of acting on that conviction. This makes it necessary for the salesmen to do a great deal of missionary work which may not be expected to result in sales immediately or even in the near future. It plays a definite part in shaping the sales organizations and methods of houses engaged in distributing industrial goods. This condition is less characteristic of the marketing of supplies and auxiliary equipment.

5. The possible purchasers of certain types of industrial goods are few. Industrial goods may be divided into two groups on this basis. Some of them can be sold only to the members of one or a few industries, and their market is said to be *vertical*. This is often the situation with materials and items of major equipment, particularly of the special-duty type. The prospective buyers of an article having a vertical market are apt to be very few. For example, four buyers habitually take more than 80 percent of the total volume of a certain material that is sold by a chemical company. This condition makes possible direct marketing in the distribution of a product of this type. Other industrial goods have *horizontal* markets; they are sold to members of many industries. Lubricating oil, hand trucks, cotton waste, and cleaning compounds are examples. These commodities are more likely to be marketed through middlemen, although not necessarily, since the number of possible buyers for even such a product is small compared with the number of those interested in the purchase of consumers' goods. The scarcity of prospective buyers vitally affects the methods and media used in advertising industrial commodities sold to many industries. It tends to emphasize the need for direct mail advertising as against the use of national media.

6. The units in which industrial goods are sold are usually large. A single purchase of major equipment may involve hundreds of thousands—on rare occasions millions—of dollars. A contract for the procurement of a prime material is apt to involve the buying firm's entire requirements for it during a period of six months or a year, and sometimes longer. Even commitments for supplies are likely to be made on a large scale. Partly as a result of this fact, many industrial goods are bought at infrequent intervals. Barring plant expansions, the purchase of a molding and pressing machine by a brickmaking plant is likely to remove that firm from the market until the machine becomes obsolete or wears out, a process which may require 10 or 20 years.

7. <u>The markets for industrial goods are generally concentrated geo-graphically</u>. We have shown the statistics indicating this concentration in the previous chapter. While there is a long-run tendency toward decentralization, a high degree of centralization is still characteristic of industry as a whole as well as of many specific trades. The localization of the automobile, specialty hardware, and textile industries is well known.

Most of the market for any particular industrial good usually consists of the demands of a comparatively small number of using concerns. The typical pattern of an American industry is a "big three" or "big four" distribution, with three or four firms controlling from 50 to 80 or 90 percent of the industry volume of sales and purchases. This factor, the importance of which has changed but little in the past decade and a half, added to the fact that <u>the total number of possible purchasers of many industrial products is small, means that much of the work of selling them can usually be organized and conducted on an individual</u> customer basis. The needs of each customer-firm can be analyzed with great care and detailed plans prepared for soliciting its business. The distribution of consumers' goods may be described as a "shotgun" or "area-bombing" process. Sales-promotional material and selling effort are distributed all over the market in broadsides in the hope that some units of them will come to the attention of and influence some prospective purchasers. The marketing of industrial goods more nearly resembles direct rifle fire or pin-point bombing in that each unit of sales promotional effort is directed toward a specific prospect or small group of prospects as a target.

8. <u>Many industrial goods are mechanical or technical in nature</u>. As a result, <u>considerable service must be rendered in the process of selling them and while they are in use</u>. Many machines used in industry are made to order according to plans and specifications prepared or approved by the buyer. In some trades a prospective purchaser expects each concern soliciting his business to prepare a set of specifications and plans to meet his requirements. He then combines the best features of all the proposals submitted, thereby apparently obtaining free engineering service. Whether or not such service is expected in a trade, most firms selling industrial goods, supplies, and materials, as well as equipment, must be prepared to furnish technical advice and information to their prospective customers concerning the use of their products.

Many manufacturers of highly complicated and technical machinery find it necessary to install their equipment in the plants of their customers, or to supervise its installation and train the buyers' personnel in its operation. They thereby attempt to make certain that their customers will receive the most satisfactory results from its use. This service is usually rendered free of charge.

No machine is perfect. From time to time all of them require repair and maintenance service. In some trades the users of equipment expect its makers to supply that service. Large users often operate their own repair service facilities, in which case the supplier must maintain a service to supply parts. This is often complicated by the activities of "pirate parts makers," who are in the business of manufacturing and marketing parts for standard machines in competition with the machine makers.

The maker of materials must often be prepared to supply technical advice as to their processing in the plants of buyers. The quality of this technical service tends to be a very significant factor in influencing customer patronage.

9. The problems involved in marketing many industrial goods are complicated by the prevalence of a policy known as "reciprocity." By this is meant the practice of buying from those who buy from you, or of soliciting patronage on the basis of a promise, explicit or implied, to purchase from your customer. For example, X Company, which manufactures trucks and tractors, might bring pressure to bear upon Y Company, from which it buys its steel, to induce the latter to purchase from X Company the trucks and tractors that it uses in its operations. This pressure involves the threat, overt or implied, to withdraw patronage from the steel company unless it becomes a customer of the truck concern. Very little can be said in favor of either the ethics or the economic desirability of reciprocity. It multiplies the difficulties of distributing many industrial products.

10. Some industrial products are leased instead of sold. This is especially true of machinery, although such items as heavy-duty tires have been distributed in this way. The outstanding examples of this method of distribution are shoe machinery and office machines. The user may pay the owner of the equipment a monthly rental, or a minimum monthly rental plus a fee, for each unit of product upon which the machine is used above a fixed minimum. For example, the shoe manufacturer using a certain type of machine must pay royalties ranging from 1/20 to 9/16 of a cent per pair for each of the six operations the machine can perform, provided that in case it is used in the making of less than 8,000 pairs a month, a monthly rental of four dollars is paid. This method of distribution affords the maker of the

machine some degree of control over the method of its use, a larger total income from the machine during its productive lifetime, a more stable income during periods of depression, and a considerable measure of aid in selling materials and supplies incidental to its use. The chief disadvantage is the heavy capital investment in machines on lease.

11. The motives which induce the purchase of industrial goods tend to be more rational than emotional in character. Emotional motives are likely to be much more significant in influencing the buying of consumers' than of industrial goods. The student should not assume that the hand with which the industrial purchasing agent signs orders is guided entirely by his brain and not at all by his feelings, but personal prejudices, fears, hates, likes, and dislikes probably play a much less significant role in shaping his official actions than they do in determining the buying practices of ultimate consumers.

The motives that influence buyers of industrial goods may be divided into two groups: those which affect the initial decision to buy a product, known as *buying motives,* and those which induce its purchase from one supplier rather than another, usually called *patronage motives.* The buying motives, one or more of which are most likely to be dominant in bringing about the procurement of industrial goods, are as follows:

a) *The reduction of the cost of operating the buyer's plant or turning out his product.* This may be achieved either by cutting his direct expense or by decreasing the amount of overhead cost which must be charged against each unit of output. This motive is especially influential during periods of recession, when a primary test of good management consists in the ability to reduce expenses.

b) *Increased productivity of the buyer's plant or labor force.* This usually, although not always, brings about cost reductions. As an inducement to buy it is much more important during periods of prosperity than of recession, because in good times the capacity of the average plant is often strained to the utmost to supply the demand, and an increase in productivity is eagerly sought.

c) *Flexibility in operation.* The machine that may be adjusted so that it can be used to manufacture a number of products, the material which can become a part of several finished articles, or a supply that will serve more than one purpose or that can be used under varying conditions, all meet this requirement.

d) *Protection.* The fact that a material, machine, or supply can be expected to reduce such risks as fire, accident, or theft constitutes a strong argument in favor of its purchase.

e) *Increase in the salability of the product.* Shirts made of material that does not have to be ironed, and cutlery manufactured of stainless steel are much more attractive to customers than are competing articles produced of substances lacking the special characteristics of these two widely advertised materials. A machine that can impart a superior finish to the industrial buyer's product or render it more useful will command his attention and careful study.

Among the rational considerations, or patronage motives, that are most likely to influence the purchase of industrial goods from one source rather than another are:

a) *Reliability.* The industrial buyer prefers to do business with a firm that keeps its promises; that makes deliveries at the times and places agreed upon; that always supplies goods of the precise quality described in its contracts of sale, and that can be relied upon to treat the customer fairly in every respect. Such reliability means money to the buying house, for, among other benefits, it enables it to reduce its stocks of materials and supplies; it decreases the losses from stoppages of production due to shortages of materials; it eliminates the costs of adjusting machinery and productive processes to make allowance for variations in the characteristics of materials; it cuts the cost of adjusting customers' claims arising from defective materials; it reduces the cost of inspection of materials and end products, and it goes far to assure uniformity of quality in the finished product.

b) *Service.* Industrial buyers are likely to be influenced not only by the quality and costliness of the repair and maintenance service rendered by a supplier, but by his willingness to render a variety of special services as well.

c) *Price.* Of course price is a consideration in practically every industrial purchase. In a surprisingly large number of cases, however, it is not the primary factor in influencing patronage. It is generally recognized that a very costly way to save money is to sacrifice quality for price in the procurement of equipment, materials, and certain supplies, such as lubricants, that are vital to proper maintenance. The price that is important in influencing purchase is not usually the quoted or invoiced figure but the amount which the material, supply, or equipment represents in the cost of making the end product. This may be affected by the flexibility of a machine in processing different materials, the way in which materials behave under processing by the machines commonly used, the speed with which machines or materials can be used to get work done, the number of people needed to service or control machines, and the amount of a supply, such as paper towels or lubricating oil, needed to perform its function. The analysis of price begins, rather than ends, with the figure billed in the invoice.

SEASONAL PRODUCTS

Certain goods are seasonal. Some are produced only during brief seasons but are used either constantly throughout the year or during periods which do not synchronize with production. For example, frozen foods must be packed when the fruits or vegetables are ripe. They are eaten throughout the year—probably less of them during the packing season than at any other time.

This lack of correlation between time of use and time of production of some commodities gives rise to the need for storage. It also tends to bring about a considerable degree of stabilization of price during certain periods of the year. The total potential supply becomes known shortly after production is completed, and price changes during the remainder of the consuming period depend primarily on variations in the demand for the article.

An equally intricate problem is presented by those products which are demanded only or mainly during certain seasons. If manufacturers make these goods only on order and at the time they are demanded, costs are unduly high because of overcapacity production during the season of great demand and of the excess productive equipment which must stand idle during much of the year. The alternative is to manufacture these goods at a fairly uniform rate throughout the year. If this is done and the goods are stored, the cost of storage, the interest on funds invested in stocks, and the risks involved in carrying them add so impressive an increment to the original cost of the merchandise as often to make this practice of doubtful profit.

A number of plans have been tried to overcome this difficulty. Some concerns have sought to solve the problem by diversifying the products or lines of products they make. A commodity selected for this purpose should have a seasonal demand which dovetails with that of the article it is used to supplement. It is desirable that it be made by the same machinery and workmen as the prime product, and that it be sold through the same outlets to the same ultimate purchasers. The fill-in should not be of such a nature that its production and sale damage the prestige of the prime product. For instance, a company making clinical thermometers, hypodermic syringes, and other instruments of precision for hospital use might find that to manufacture and sell such articles as automobile radiator thermometers and grease guns during the off-seasons would injure the reputation enjoyed by its medical instruments. This method of solving the problem is based on a change in production methods, but it has certain highly significant marketing features.

A few firms troubled by this difficulty have attacked it by varying their prices, increasing them during the period of heavy demand and lowering them in the off-season. A modification of this device consists of raising the quality of the product during the period of the year when demand is low, or adding accessories or services at that time which are not furnished at other times. While this latter variation is in all likelihood less effective than price adjustments, it is probably more generally employed. Neither of these methods has enjoyed very wide usage.

A common practice is that of applying greater sales pressure during the off-season than when the demand is brisk. This may be accomplished by adding to the amount of advertising during the poor season, by distributing more sales promotional material among dealers, by stimulating salesmen to greater efforts through contests, the payment of bonuses, or variations in commission rates, and by making their efforts more effective by increased supervision.

To aid their other efforts in this direction, concerns in many industries allow season datings, sometimes coupled with guarantees against price declines. For example, bills for stocks of paints and varnishes bought by retailers for resale during the spring, and delivered to them at any time after October 15, may be dated April 1; such stocks need not be paid for until such time after April 1 as the credit terms specify. The seller may also guarantee that his prices will not decline until after the date of the invoice. If they do so, he credits the account of the buyer with the amount of the decline. But if prices advance, the invoice remains unchanged. These devices may be used in seasonal industries to help the manufacturer move goods into the hands of wholesalers and retailers as they are produced; thus he avoids the need of storing them and finds it easier to finance their production and distribution since banks prefer to lend on accounts receivable rather than on stocks of goods in a warehouse.

HIGH UNIT VALUE

Many products are of high unit value. When the retail price of an article is more than $100, or thereabouts, many ultimate consumers are deterred from buying it because a sum must be accumulated which constitutes a sizable portion of a month's or a year's income. Sellers of such goods thus find themselves under a handicap. The most usual method of surmounting the difficulty is to sell them on the installment payment basis. While this practice is essentially financial in character, it has a number of interesting marketing aspects. In general the articles sold on such terms should be durable; they should not be too difficult to recapture from the buyer; and each of them should have an active secondhand market.

Since the amount of money involved in the purchase of a high unit value product is large, the buyer is apt to consider the transaction very carefully and to try to make sure that he gets exactly what he wants. As a result, the amount and quality of salesmanship needed at the point of sale is much greater than that required for articles of lesser unit value which are often bought on a routine basis. The high unit value characteristic makes it difficult for any one retailer to command the capital to carry an adequate stock of all competing makes of a product. For these reasons, manufacturers of such articles often make use of a retail "franchise" arrangement whereby they sell to only one or a few retailers in a local market who in turn stock and sell the product of only one maker.

The Nature of Costs

The marketing of a product is very much influenced by the costs generated by it or assigned to it. A firm's profit arises from the existence of a favorable differential between its costs and the prices at which it sells its goods. Of course, in the case of a firm making and marketing a line or mix of products this differential is not the same for all of them; for some of them it may not even be favorable. But its character and the nature of the cost items that influence it for a given product are certain to affect the marketing decisions and practices relating to that product.

Costs are usually divided into two great classes, *direct* and *overhead*. The direct costs per unit tend to remain the same regardless of the amount of output, with the result that their total for the firm or product tends to vary with the number of units produced. Overhead costs tend to remain constant in total regardless of variations in output, with the result that their amount per unit tends to fall as output rises and to increase as output declines. In practice such items as cost of materials and labor, applied directly to a product, are usually regarded as direct costs, while such categories as depreciation, service labor, supervision, research, and general administration are considered overhead.

This is apt to be misleading. For example, the costs of "clean-up and make ready time" in production run or batch operation, while classified as direct, tend to behave like overhead for they are the same regardless of the size of the batch or the number of units turned out in the run. The direct labor cost of a complex of production centers set up to carry on a factory process is apt to be the same, regardless of whether the complex is operating at 50, 75, or 100 percent of capacity. If marketing or product management decisions are influenced by cost information, and they should be, the decision makers should be careful to see to it that a much more sophisticated analysis of overhead and direct expenses is made than is ordinarily attempted.

With the increasing mechanization of industry, the growing application of automatic controls to machine operation, and the broadening application of technology and research in management, the importance of overhead costs in the total expense picture of the average firm has been increasing and may be expected to go on doing so.

When the overhead costs of a product, or line of products, are high, the tasks top management expects its marketing manager to perform become more complicated. The overhead expenses of a plant must be met, regardless of the amount of its output. The larger the number of units turned out within the limits of the plant capacity, the smaller are the indirect expenses per unit. These possible cost reductions are likely to loom large in the minds of those who must determine how much to make. Pressure is put on the selling machinery to dispose of an amount of output that will enable the production machinery to run at an optimum cost per unit. In the distribution of articles made by such a plant, unusual emphasis is apt to be put upon volume of sales as the ultimate *desideratum*.

This has two chief effects. First, it tends to stimulate advertising on a very extensive scale and use of the "go-getter" type of sales organization, personnel, and methods. This is often a short-sighted policy, to be sure, but it is apt to prevail under these conditions. Second, the dominance of overhead costs throws great emphasis on price as a competitive weapon. If, by lowering its prices and stepping up its sales promotion work, a firm can add enough volume to cut its overhead expenses per unit of goods sold by more than the total amount of the unit price reduction and the increased promotion costs per unit, its net profit is augmented. This opens the way to the control of a greater portion of the market through expanding productive capacity and increasing sales pressure. In the drama of wasteful competitive strife which American business has sometimes staged in the name of the great god Volume, overhead cost of production has played the stellar role, as well as written the lines and directed the piece.

As the deficiencies of high-pressure selling have become more and more apparent, marketing managers have grown more aware of the importance of careful product management. This, in part, involves study of consumer needs, and of the characteristics of merchandise itself, to suit the product precisely to consumer wants. Work of this kind should yield dividends, not only in the form of increased sales because of augmented consumer goodwill, but also in lowered selling costs due to the elimination of costly errors and waste motion in distribution.

The presence of heavy overhead expenses in a firm's cost structure is apt also to lead to top management pressure on marketing management to continue to expend marketing efforts and pressure on products that, in the light of their profit contribution, really no longer deserve such attention and should be deleted or deemphasized. This is done on the ground that such a product "sops up" a lot of overhead costs. Such a decision may be justified if no alternative products are available that promise adequate profits and in the market development of which the resources of the firm can be used. But it creates difficult problems for marketing management and is liable to preempt an amount of selling time and executive attention out of all proportion to its contribution to the long-run welfare of the company.

Joint Costs. It often happens that two or more commodities are associated in the course of their production, usually because they are made from the same raw material, the manufacture of each requiring the use of a separate element or portion of that material. Most people are familiar with the fact that the number of different finished articles derived by a meatpacking plant from the slaughtered animals runs into the thousands. A similarly extensive list of commodities is obtained by the by-product coke oven from the coal which forms its raw material.

Sometimes the same sort of situation arises when equipment is needed to make one product, the demand for which does not absorb all its capacity and the unneeded capacity can be used to make another product. Many of the costs of the equipment are then joint in nature. This probably happens more often than is generally recognized since it is likely to occur whenever a standard process or a materials mixing or chemical processing operation is involved.

The presence of joint cost products may have several marketing implications.

1. They are very frequently marketed together, even though no association exists between them in the matter of purpose or use. Insecticides often follow much the same marketing channels as paints and varnishes because many of them are by-products of the process of paint

manufacture. Sulphate of ammonia, used as a fertilizer, is sold by the same concern which vends certain tar products, used mainly for roofing and paving, because both are by-products of the process of making coke from coal. This feature of production often makes strange marketing bedfellows.

2. The supply of a by-product is usually controlled by the production schedule of the prime product. The number of hides turned out by the meatpackers, and the seasons when they are available for sale, depend upon the number of animals slaughtered during different periods of the year to satisfy the demand for meat—not upon any attempt to match the supply of hides to their market demand. The same is true of all the other groups of commodities which stem from common raw materials processed under such conditions.

This sometimes creates intriguing marketing problems. Some years ago it was found that a residue from the manufacture of certain antibiotics acted as a stimulant to growth when used as an additive to animal feeds. As the market developed, one company in the business found that the residue from the production of the antibiotics needed to supply its medical market profitably was not enough to satisfy the demand for the feed additive residue. The pure stuff could be used as an additive but would be prohibitively expensive if made for that purpose alone. So management had to decide whether to lose money on part of its additive business or to throw on the marketing manager the almost impossible task of trying to hold the patronage of additive customers while failing to supply their needs. It also might have cut antibiotic prices, at the risk of starting a price war and destroying a profitable market, without any real assurance of expanding its share of the antibiotic market—which it would have to do to solve the problem.

3. The price behavior of joint cost products is often very erratic. Their supply does not respond to changes in their prices to the same degree as other articles: often there is not even a trace of such response. This characteristic is especially disturbing to the prime producers of a commodity when part of its supply its made by firms that regard it as a by-product, and part by firms that make nothing else. The behavior of the by-product producers tends to disrupt the price structure of the entire industry.

CHAPTER 4

Managing the Product Mix

Products and product assortments are not static things. As has been pointed out, consumer products are for people and industrial products are for firms that use them in making things for people or for other firms. People are constantly changing their wants and desires, their standards of living, the conditions under which they live and the things they need and want to consume in order to get the most satisfaction out of living in those conditions. The technology of industry is rapidly changing with resulting modifications in the equipment and materials that business concerns need in order to utilize the new technologies. Their product needs are dynamic.

If a manufacturing firm is to be successful, both the products it makes and the methods it uses in marketing them must change to conform to changes in consumer wants and industrial needs as they occur. This gives rise to the necessity for a constant series of managerial decisions and activities centering around the product assortment the company offers. Few of these are entirely within the jurisdiction of the marketing manager. But all of them affect his job vitally, and in most of them he must play an important role. Therefore it seems wise at this point to examine the problems that are involved in the process of managing the product offering.

BACKGROUND MATERIAL

Perhaps it may be helpful to preface our examination with some background material in the form of definitions of certain terms commonly used in the field of product management, and a listing of the chief events in the life of a typical product.

Definitions

There are at least three, perhaps four, terms or concepts whose definitions will be helpful to us in our approach to this subject.

Product: a thing that affords a particular kind of satisfaction to the ultimate consumer or renders a particular kind of benefit to an industrial or business user.

Item: a variation of a product that is assigned a separate name or designation in a manufacturer's or marketer's catalog or product list. The manufacturer or marketer often refers to this as a *product* because the problems of managing an item are much the same as those involved in managing a product. To some extent this confusion of usage will inevitably characterize our discussion.

Product Line: a group of products that are associated together by reason of their use, their method of production, or the way they are marketed. Product line is sometimes loosely used to mean the same thing as *product mix.*

Product Mix: the group of products marketed by a particular manufacturer or marketer.

For example, an axe is a product. A double bitted axe of a certain weight is an item. Axes, saws, hammers, adzes, and other woodworking tools might make up a line of products. All the articles in the catalog or product list of a manufacturer, wholesaler, or retailer constitute his product mix. A product mix may consist of two products, a line or part of a line of products, or several, or parts of several lines of products. The existence of a product arises from a desire of the ultimate consumer or industrial user, or from the manufacturer's interpretation of that desire. A product line is determined primarily, or even entirely, by the way in which consumers want to buy or use the articles that make it up. A product mix is largely a creation of the marketer's decisions.

Stages in Product Life History

A few products are more or less timeless in the sense that they do not change much, if any. In our dynamic economy, though, it is rather difficult for a man of 70 to think of a single current consumer good that has not changed so materially in its form or in the precise desires or uses it serves as to be a different product from the one he knew in his youth. In some cases these changes represent new ways of satisfying continuing wants or needs; in other cases they involve the satisfaction of facets of want or need not served before. In most areas, existing products are constantly dying and new ones are constantly being born. An understanding of the most important events or stages that occur in the life of the typical product is therefore highly important in the study of the problems involved in product management, because the most serious managerial problems usually cluster around these events or around the point at which one stage ends and another begins. A useful list is the following:

1. *Idea.* The beginning of a product is an idea. At any one time a growing firm may have in its files many ideas for new products, some of them good and others impractical or unsuitable—the possibilities of all of them nebulous and uncertain.

2. *Screening.* Such ideas must be screened, those of doubtful promise winnowed out, and those worth spending money and resources on selected for development.

3. *Research Development.* This usually involves physical, chemical, engineering, biological, or other scientific research designed to convert the selected ideas into marketable products.

4. *Selection.* When the idea has been transformed into a tangible product whose precise properties can be explored and described, or which can be made available in the form of a prototype or sample, it must be tried out on an experimental basis, its production requirements and costs estimated, its market and profit probabilities forecasted, and a decision made whether to go ahead with it. This process may occur at some earlier stage of the development work, but it is almost inevitably repeated at the test tube, or drawing board, or prototype stage.

5. *Introduction.* During this stage plans must be made and carried out for making the product and introducing it on the market. Here also, the "bugs" that almost inevitably develop in making, marketing, and using a new product should be eliminated. As the process of introduction continues, almost imperceptibly the number and severity of managerial crises in making and marketing the successful product decrease, and it takes its place as an established member of the product mix.

6. *Maturity.* The story of the market life of a successful product can usually be described in the form of a curve that is roughly bell-shaped, perhaps somewhat flattened at the top (see Figure 4–1). During some or all of the introductory phase, sales are low and hard to

FIGURE 4–1

MARKET LIFE OF A SUCCESSFUL PRODUCT

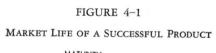

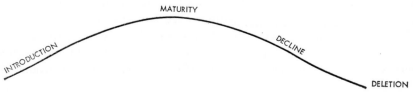

make, costs of both production and marketing are high, profits are low or nonexistent. If a product begins to catch on, sales increase and are easier to make, production costs typically decline because of both the economies of scale and improvements in process and know-how, and profits become more satisfactory. At some point in this process the product can be said to have "arrived," to have "matured." At some point, also, competition develops, and from then on the management problems of maturity tend to cluster around the making of marketing and price adjustments to meet competition.

7. *Decline.* Maturity tends to merge into decline. This may come slowly as the result of changing demand, the inroads of competition, the capture of parts of the market by other articles serving the same purpose (but slightly better suited to satisfy certain segments of demand) or by other erosive factors. Prices tend to draw nearer cost, and profit margin shrinks. Sometimes the onset of decline is spectacular when an entirely new product, much better suited to satisfy the need or want, appears on the market and is aggressively promoted.

8. *Deletion.* With most products the time eventually comes when their makers and marketers must face the decision whether or not it is worthwhile to continue them. When the decision is negative, they must be deleted.

This entire life process may extend over many years or it may be telescoped within a very short period. For example, the life cycle of a fad may cover only a few months. An article of clothing may come and go within a season or one or two years. On the other hand, the life cycle of a raw material, such as crude oil or copper ore, may extend almost indefinitely. The same is true of steel bars and sheets, although new forms of these are developed from time to time to suit new needs or to fit old needs more precisely.

MANAGEMENT PROBLEMS

The problems of managing the product mix tend to vary according to the stages of the product life cycle and to cluster around the points where one stage ends and another begins. They are especially numerous and difficult during the early stages of a product's life and near its end. So perhaps the best way to discuss them is in relation to these stages.

Getting Ideas for New Products

Few ideas for new products just happen. They must be induced and searched for, and the process of collecting them must be organized and managed. There are several common sources.

a) In most concerns the most prolific source of new product ideas is the firm's own research department. This division of the company is usually staffed with men of considerable originality and imagination. Some of this naturally tends to spill over from the projects they *are* presently working on into areas they *might* be working on. As a matter of fact, one of the problems in managing research is to prevent a scientist, whose job is to work toward a designated objective, from diverting his efforts into the exploration of interesting bypaths that open up in the course of his assigned project, although some of these may occasionally turn out to be more worthwhile than the initial objective.

Many of the ideas originating in the scientific area are impractical in the sense that it is not worthwhile to introduce them on the market. The men in the research area of a firm are usually more oriented toward scientific matters than toward the problems and possibilities of production, marketing, and profit. As a result, the process of screening is of particular importance with respect to ideas originating from this source.

b) Customers are also a prolific source of ideas for new products. This is more true in the case of industrial than of consumers' goods. The ultimate consumer is just as likely to feel the need or want for a new product as is his industrial counterpart. But he is prone to be much less exact and precise in defining it than the industrial buyer. As a matter of fact, such a want or need is apt to remain sunk in the unconscious or subconscious area of an a ultimate consumer's makeup until some manufacturer originates and offers him a product to satisfy it. Then too, the ultimate consumer is apt to be much less articulate about these wants than the industrial buyer, part of whose business it is to formulate the definition of his firm's needs and to hunt products to satisfy them.

Most makers of industrial goods find it worthwhile to study the operations of their customers to discover articles not now available that the customer firms could use with profit if they could be made. This work is often a part of the job of the salesmen. Some firms set up separate units to carry it on. Manufacturers of consumers' goods are likely to rely heavily on their wholesalers, retailers, and on marketing research for this purpose. This is an area of management in which organizational aspects have not yet been satisfactorily worked out.

c) Many new product ideas come from the marketing area. In the course of their work, salesmen are apt to have product shortcomings brought forcefully to their attention. They usually want new products because such a product gives them something new to talk about that may capture the customer's interest. If left to himself, though, the average salesman is not apt to think that it is any part of his job to be on the lookout for new product ideas or to report them. He must be trained and motivated to do so.

d) Some firms make very satisfactory profits by copying new products created by their competitors. To do this with products covered by patents is apt to come under the general heading of "living dangerously." But if the patent applies only to the process of making the product, which is usually the case in formulating and processing industries, such as food and chemicals, it is often possible to make the same product by a different process. In a number of industries it is common practice among competitors to cross-license their patents. Many industries are of such a nature that they operate entirely without patent protection. Competitors' product lists or the trade grapevine probably constitute one of the more fruitful sources of new product ideas for the average firm.

The firm that copies another's product has the advantage of knowing that there is a market for it. From the innovator's activities, also, a lot can be learned about how to make and market it. On the other hand, the copier has the sometimes difficult job of invading an area in which the innovator has an established market position, although the difficulty of doing this is diminished if he times his entry properly—after the innovator has established the existence of a market and before he has captured too large a part of it.

e) Product ideas often "walk in off the street" or come in by mail. These must be handled with extreme care. Many such ideas are ones that have already been examined and discarded, or laid by to await a more propitious moment for their development. Some very embarrassing lawsuits against highly reputable firms have resulted from careless handling of ideas of the latter type. The treatment of such "volunteer" ideas should be left in the hands of the firm's legal department or at least be prescribed by it.

Selection

The process of selection must occur at not less than two points in the early stages of a product's life cycle: when it moves from the idea stage into research and development, and when it is ready for market development. The nature of the selection process differs materially between these two points. In the idea stage it primarily takes the form of a screening operation designed to discover the ideas offering enough promise to justify the expenditure of research money, manpower, and facilities in trying to turn them into actual products. When a product has been created, and before resources are committed to making and marketing it, a decision must be made as to whether its promise of profit is sufficient to justify such expenditure. At the point of idea screening, the firm has very little costs invested in the project; when the production-marketing selection decision is made, it usually has heavy costs sunk in completed research. At the first point of decision, opportunity losses are at stake; at the second, *possible* opportunity losses tend to be offset to some extent by *certain* losses of sunk research costs if the project is abandoned.

Much the same factors govern both decisions. The data available about those factors tend to be much more extensive and reliable at the second decision point than at the first and they are susceptible of much more refined techniques of analysis.

The difficulties of the process of selection can be greatly reduced if the people who do the job have a clear notion of the product and market objectives or policies of the firm. Such knowledge of objectives arises as a result of a clear definition by top management of the kind of business the firm should be in. It might seem that this definition is made once and for all when the firm goes into business, but this is not true. The constant and rapid changes in technology and consumer demand tend to force a continuing re-examination of the definition. To dip into ancient history, Studebaker, once the outstanding maker of buggies and wagons, had to recognize that people were shifting to automobiles for personal transportation and carrying things in trucks instead of wagons. More recently, the Pullman Company had to deal with the fact that fewer people were riding in Pullman cars and that there was an increasing use of both house and truck trailers.

A clear, up-to-date definition by management of the kind of business a firm is in or should seek to be in is of great help to employes whose job includes the search for new product ideas; it is almost a must for the executives charged with the task of selecting ideas for research and nascent products for market development. Such a statement is apt to be influenced by most or all of the general factors mentioned below, along with others.

Factors in Selection

Production Facilities, Aptitude, and Know-how. Other things being equal, it is much wiser to seek to exploit new product ideas that involve the use of existing production facilities and techniques, or of facilities and methods similar to those currently used by the firm. This avoids the risks of mistake that occur when management must buy unfamiliar machinery, install it, and train workmen to use it. If the new product requires no change in production aptitudes and know-how, at either the workbench or supervisory level, the risks of mistakes and initial heavy costs are minimized. For example, a company that had been a low-cost operator in the general high-volume paper products business moved into the making of specialties which involve what is essentially a job-lot operation. It was a long time learning how to get its costs on the new line down to competitive levels.

Production factors are not usually the most decisive ones in product choice for new techniques can be learned and men with know-how can be recruited. But these factors may extend or shorten the period of development and increase or diminish its risks and costs.

Marketing Skills and Facilities. Much the same is true of marketing factors. Marketing know-how and skill become very important when the proposed new product must be sold in a market whose requirements are drastically different from those of the market the firm presently serves. For example, this occurs when a company in the industrial goods business attempts to market a consumers' good, since the entire spirit and nature of the operation must change; or when a firm skilled in marketing nontechnical products brings out an article that requires highly skilled technical service; or when the marketer of heavy specialized machinery tries to distribute a standardized industrial good with a horizontal market. In cases like these the risks and costs arise not so much from the need for the people in the marketing area to learn new skills, or to recruit people with those skills, as from the fact that the marketing managers must change the entire pattern of their thinking.

On the other hand, if a proposed new product finds its primary area of use in a market already served by the marketing department of the firm, its period of introduction will be shortened and the costs and risks of introducing it will tend to be diminished. Marketing considerations should not be allowed to dominate the process of product selection, for men with special marketing skills can be recruited and separate organizational units can be set up to market products requiring special skills and know-how. But the marketing requirements of a proposed new product should be a factor of some moment in the final decision with respect to it.

Financial Strength. Have we the financial resources to make and market the proposed new product successfully, or if not, can we get them on favorable terms? The introduction of a new product usually involves the commitment of capital funds in at least two forms: (1) investment in additional equipment and facilities, and additions to working capital that will be tied up mainly in inventories of the new product and the materials to make it, and (2) accounts receivable generated by its sale. These investments must come out of cash that is already in the business or cash that can be obtained from outside by the sale of securities or by borrowing.

The method of marketing the new product can have little effect on the amount of new capital for equipment and facilities needed to make it, but marketing decisions and action can influence the amount of additional working capital required. Crash programs of personal selling, advertising, and promoting the new product create heavy drains on working capital, while a more leisurely and less costly approach to its introduction tends to reduce the marketing demands for cash and may enable the firm to meet many of the demands with the cash inflow generated by sales. The selection of channels of distribution may diminish or augment the amount of inventory of the new product the firm must carry and the volume of accounts receivable it must finance. The method of marketing may make possible the manipulation of inventories so as to reduce both to the minimum.

Management Attitudes. Managerial ability is to a considerable extent interchangeable from one kind of industry to another, although the degree is still debatable, but managerial attitudes and habits of thought are hard to change. For example, a management that has grown up in an industrial goods business is apt to regard the high-pressure advertising that is characteristic of the consumers' goods business as "ballyhoo," and to be more than a little ashamed of engaging in it. A management that is accustomed to new products needing a two-year market development period before they begin to pay off is apt to find it hard to learn to think in terms of a new product requiring four or five years of market development expenditures before it begins to generate a net cash inflow. In the deliberations leading up to the final selection decision of a proposed product, the marketing executives will be wise to emphasize to top management the amount of money that must be spent on its market development and the length of time over which these expenditures must be made, as well as any changes in managerial thinking its introduction will entail.

Company Personality. This factor is closely akin to managerial attitude, which in part probably creates or influences it, and in part is created by it. It is the spirit of the "outfit" which extends down through all levels of the employee hierarchy and conditions the thinking of the individual, sometimes to such a point that he becomes a "company man"—as was exemplified in *Executive Suite,* a novel which appeared some years ago, and viewed with alarm by William Whyte in *The Organization Man.*

We need not argue whether this phenomenon of the company personality is a good or a bad thing. The important fact is that it exists, and that in selecting new products management must be aware that those which violate or challenge the company personality are much less likely to be successful than those which express or reflect it.

Promise of Profit. Theoretically, a firm should never put out a new product that does not promise to return a satisfactory profit. This concept is simple to express but difficult to apply in specific situations. Part of this difficulty centers around the question of what a profit is when applied to a specific product in a product mix. The concept of profit, however, is easy to define: income realized from sales, less all properly allocable costs. The complexity occurs in the area of costs.

Probable direct costs of material and labor are usually not too difficult to estimate. But when we consider *which* items of overhead should be allocated to a new product, and in what amounts, we meet such questions as:

Should the new product be charged with the costs of carrying and amortizing the funds spent on researching it?

Should it be charged an appropriate share of the expenses of research that produced no exploitable results?

Should it be charged with the costs of its own market development, and if so, should they be treated as current expenses, or as investment to be amortized over the product's expected life?

What share of general and administrative expenses should the new product be expected to pay?

These are only a few of the simpler cost questions that must be resolved, and the way they are resolved affects the profit that the new product may be expected to return.

How much profit is reasonable? Must the new product promise to return a percentage on investment equal to the average for the firm? Or must it promise *more* than that, so as to offset the lesser rate of return on waning products? Or is *any* contribution above costs, however small, desirable? Or, finally, should we be satisfied with any cash inflow in excess of direct expenses that may be applied against overhead?

Because of these and other complexities encountered in applying the profit concept in making new product selection decisions, some managements prefer to base such decisions on a forecast of the cash flow to be engendered by the presence of the proposed new product in the product mix. This involves setting down as cash outflow all payments made or forecasted in the interest of the new product, such as costs of research, costs of evaluation, money spent for equipment and facilities, expenditures for market testing and development, ordinary marketing and delivery costs, labor and material costs in manufacture, then balancing the cumulative running total of these estimated cash outflows against the coincident cumulative cash inflow from forecasted sales of the product.

This procedure introduces the time element into the selection analysis. Critical time points in such an analysis are (a) When expected cash inflow begins to offset, at least in part, the outflow drain on the cash position of the firm, (b) When the forecasted current cash inflow begins to exceed the current cash outflow, and the new product may be expected to start to replenish the financial reserves of the firm where hitherto it had been a drain, and (c) When the estimated cumulative cash inflow starts to exceed the cumulative cash outflow, at which time the product has fully restored its impairment of the firm's cash position and begins to improve that position. A discounting technique should be applied in these computations to get a clear picture. All of these estimates are, at best, educated guesses, but it is better to make the decision on the basis of educated guesses than to rely entirely on hunches or overall impressions, the only alternative.

Market Protection. This may result from the fact that the proposed new product may be patentable; from the likelihood that its production may require know-how that few, if any, competitors possess; from the fact that its marketing will require highly skilled technical service or other special know-how; or from the possibility of developing a marketing "franchise" or consumer preference through branding and heavy advertising.

Expected Volume. This factor is double-edged. Some large firms find it uneconomic to add to their product mix an article whose volume of sales is too small; it would tend to get lost in the shuffle and fail to receive the attention needed to exploit its profit possibilities. This opens a field of opportunity to the small or medium-sized concern which, by choosing products promising volumes too small to be attractive to its large competitors, can gain a measure of market protection from rivals whose superior resources it could not hope to match in a straight trial of strength. On the other hand, a small or medium-sized firm may not be wise to take on a product whose probable volume will be so great as to force it to outreach its financial resources, thus inviting the entry of bigger concerns whose competitive strength the small firm cannot match.

There are many other factors of selection that may be important to individual concerns. These arise out of the firm's individual strengths and weaknesses, its position in the market, its location, and other conditions peculiar to its makeup and character.

Attempts have been made to attach weights to the intangible factors mentioned above and to develop formulas to guide in product selection. Such formulas may be helpful, and at the same time dangerous, if they create in management the habit of relying on the formula and ignoring unusual but highly significant factors that may crop up in specific cases. When a decision-maker has a formula, he is apt to rely too heavily on it and to close his analytical eyes.

Development

Since development consists mainly of research or engineering design, its relations with marketing are apt to be tenuous. Probably they are usually not so close as they should be. After all, one of the primary business functions of research is to discover products that have commercial potentialities. The liaison between marketing and research, therefore, should be reasonably close if for no other reason than to prevent research funds and facilities from being wasted in projects without market promise. Just how this relationship can be worked out in organization structure is still a subject of debate. In any case, it is probably more a matter of personal contact and mutual understanding between the executives and workers in the two areas than of organization charts.

Introduction and Market Development

The planning and process of introducing a new product and building a market position for it are matters of infinite detail. Use tests, and perhaps marketing tests, must be arranged and conducted. Production equipment and facilities must be provided and production schedules prepared. Inventory requirements must be established and the location of inventory reserves determined. Advertising schedules must be arranged and sales promotion material must be prepared. Salesmen must be informed about the new product and trained to sell it. A price must be set. Channels of distribution must be selected and price relationships among them must be determined. Each of these jobs must be broken down into almost infinite detail and each detail planned separately. The end result of all this should be a schedule which sets forth who is to do what and when he is to do it.

In the consumers' goods field this work is usually done by the operating departments; production handles matters having to do with making the product and marketing plans and carries out the activities involved in its sale and distribution. Coordination may be provided by a product manager or a new products coordinator. In the industrial goods field, especially the chemical industry, it is apt to be in the hands of a market development department, which often operates a separate force of salesmen and handles the marketing of the product until it is an established member of the line.

This allocation of duties presents some difficulties. For one thing, who decides when a product is mature enough to be transferred to the marketing department? and what are the signs of such maturity? How can the know-how, expensively acquired during the introductory period, be transferred along with the responsibility for marketing the product? In some industrial goods firms the introductory work is planned and done by the operating departments, with a product development group providing coordination and guidance. In other cases this function is performed by a product manager.

The location of responsibility for product introduction is still a matter of debate among students of organization.

During the introductory period, management may also expect "bugs" to become apparent in the product. These are usually defects in its performance in use, which are disappointing and handicap its sales. Some of these are slight and easily remedied; others may be so vital to the satisfactory use of the product that, if not eliminated, they will compel its withdrawal from the market. Some of them stem from peripheral features of the product and can be gotten rid of by minor changes; others grow out of basic features that must be lived with, or that can be changed only after much additional research. Management must be alert to discover such "bugs" and quick to move to bring about their elimination, or to educate consumers to minimize their undesirable effects in use—preferably the former by all odds.

Often it is possible, by use tests or market tests, to discover most of these defects before the product is formally introduced. The use test is particularly effective with industrial goods. In this area it consists of arranging with selected customers to use sample lots of the product and carefully observing the results. Care must be taken in selecting such customers to include representatives of all significant stages of technology and types of operation in the customer industry, and in seeing to it that the test is conducted under the usual operating conditions.

In the consumers' goods field, preliminary use tests are often conducted among selected groups of possible users, such as employees of the company or their friends. The really significant use test in this area, however, is commonly provided in the course of test marketing. Certain typical small markets, usually medium-sized cities and their dependent environs, are selected. Within these areas the new product is sold with the employment of the marketing techniques planned for its general distribution. The results are carefully studied. If the test is properly done, the product's behavior in use often can be observed and checked, along with its general appeal and the effectiveness of the marketing plans used. The drawbacks of test marketing are chiefly two: (1) It delays the introduction of the new product, and (2) It is apt to be as carefully observed by competitors as by the innovator and may shorten the interval before rival products appear on the market.

Also, during the introductory period, management must be alert to discover and capitalize on the existence of uses of the new product not originally contemplated. This is especially important in the chemical industry and in other businesses making materials, nor is it unusual in the machinery industry and in the consumers' goods field. Often such uses require modifications in the product or its sale in different packages. (An example is the sale of a modified antifreeze solution, packaged in pressure cans to thaw out the frost on automobile windshields.) The marketing department bears the chief responsibility for searching out and promoting the exploitation of these unexpected uses. Such uses are especially likely to appear during the introductory period, but they may be discovered at almost any stage of a product's life.

During the process of introducing a product, two important kinds of decisions must be made which are primarily marketing in character and are highly significant in their influence on the work of winning a place for it in the market and developing its full demand possibilities. These are *branding* and *packaging*.

Branding

The practice of placing brands on merchandise is very old; evidences of it have been found in almost the earliest records of trade that have been preserved to us. But the device has never been so widely used as in the United States during the present century. This emphasis probably grew out of the economic forces unleashed by the industrial revolution, which so vastly increased the productivity of our industrial complex that it changed our market from one dominated by the seller into one controlled more largely by the interests and wishes of the buyer. Along with this came the separation between maker and user in time and space, and an intensification of competition among producers to capture a share of the market. The brand was found to be a highly effective weapon in this struggle.

A _brand_ is a "name, term, sign, symbol, design, or a combination of them which is intended to identify the goods or services of one seller or a group of sellers and to differentiate them from those of competitors."[1]

A _brand name_ is "a brand or part of a brand consisting of a word, letter, or group of words or letters comprising a name which is intended to identify the goods or services of a seller or a group of sellers and to differentiate them from those of competitors. The brand name is that part of a brand which can be vocalized."

A _trade mark_ is "a brand or part of a brand that is given legal protection because it is capable of exclusive appropriation; because it is used in a manner sufficiently fanciful, distinctive and arbitrary; because it is affixed to the product when sold, or because it otherwise satisfies the requirements set up by law."

Perhaps the relation of the three terms can best be illustrated by an example. The term Merck is a brand name. When presented in the following manner:

it is a brand and also a trademark because of the distinctive, somewhat fanciful way in which it appears and the symbol in which it is enclosed.

Purposes of Branding.   Brands serve numerous purposes in marketing. Probably the most important are those listed below.

1. _Identification._   For millions of Americans the name Abraham Lincoln stands for the combination of physical, mental, emotional and moral traits and behaviorisms that made up the complex personality of the best-loved of all our presidents. Likewise to those who know us, your name or my name denotes the combination of characteristics that distinguish you or me from other men. It is a sort of shorthand description. In the same way, a brand stands for, and describes for people

---

[1]These definitions are from "Marketing Definitions," American Marketing Association, Chicago, 1960.

who have heard about or used a product, all the things they have learned about it.

2. *Symbol for Goodwill.* Fifty years ago molasses was sold and delivered in a retail store by pouring or dipping it from a large container, usually unmarked, into the consumer's jug. If the consumer didn't like the taste when she got it home, she had no way of avoiding a repurchase. If she liked it, she had no way of making sure of repeating her satisfaction the next time she bought molasses. When syrup was branded Log Cabin, or Vermont Maid, the consumer acquired a visible or vocable symbol on which to hang the satisfactions she enjoyed from its use. The brand offers the manufacturer a convenient peg on which to hang consumer goodwill.

3. *Information.* Since the brand identifies a product and represents to people the things they know or feel about it, it serves as a quick and cheap way to inform possible buyers about it. Sampling, careful examination, lengthy description, are not necessary. The brand tells the story for better or for worse. Those who complain about branding sometimes fail to realize that the manufacturer who brands his merchandise runs the risk that the consumer who tries it will say "I'll never buy that again."

4. *Aid to Selling and Advertising.* This is probably a primary objective of most branding. All three of the uses already mentioned serve to make the job of personal and impersonal selling easier. If the brand itself has appeal, either visual or oral, it can be a powerful aid in the attempt to capture consumer patronage. One that is simple and easy to remember, flows easily and musically from the tongue, and has pleasant connotations, has an attraction all its own. The consumer has to decide *not* to buy the product it identifies—or a sale is made almost automatically.

Types of Brands. The *symbols* used as parts of brands are almost as varied as the imagination and designing ingenuity of those who create them. The variety of brand names is limited only by the scope of the pronounceable permutations and combinations of the letters in the language. However, most of them fall into certain classes.

1. *The Names of Persons.* The most common type of personal name used is that of the sponsor or someone closely associated with the sponsoring firm. Smith Brothers, Kellogg's, Post's, Westinghouse, Swift, Armour, are examples. This type of name has the advantage of close association with the sponsor. It is usually a word with which people are already familiar and know how to pronounce. It has the disadvantage that its use cannot be denied to another person having the

same name. Some of the most bitterly fought trademark cases have involved this kind of brand. The new user can be forced to indicate that his product is not the original article of its kind with which the brand was used, but this protection is sometimes more apparent than real. For example, who was the original Rogers in the silver business? or the Baker who first used his name in the marketing of chocolate? The name of a living person cannot be used in this manner without his consent.

2. _Place Names_. Examples are Elgin and Waltham, in the timepiece business. A place brand name has the advantage that it is likely to be known to consumers and they are apt to know how to pronounce it. It suffers from the fact that its use cannot be denied to other firms in the same place unless the name is used fancifully, for example the term Bermuda, applied to hot water-heaters.

3. _Descriptive Terms_. Descriptive terms, often with a quality connotation, such as Ivory, Royal, Regal, Evergrip, are widely used as brand names. If really descriptive of the essential qualities of the product, they are difficult to protect legally, but if the quality described is incidental or fanciful, as "ivory," applied to soap, they do not suffer this disadvantage. If the term used describes something that is attractive to most people, the product itself is apt to partake of this aura of approval.

4. _Coined Words_. Many brand names are words coined for the purpose. Among the well-known ones are Linoleum, Aspirin, Kodak, Sunoco, Esso, Jello. Sometimes these are put together from the names or parts of the names of the firms using them, sometimes they are completely original. A few firms have even used computing machines to put together extensive lists of combinations of the letters of the alphabet, according to prescribed patterns, so as to reduce the strain on human ingenuity and imagination.

Such words may possess a flow and singing quality which is lacking in most of those now is the language; Esso, Sunoco, and Jello, for example. In general, such a brand name is likely to be given legal protection without challenge unless it too closely resembles one already in use in trade. When applied to a completely new product, however, a coined name may be in danger of becoming generic in that people think of it as the name of all articles of the kind instead of only the product made by the original user: linoleum and aspirin, are examples. When this begins to happen, the originator is in the process of losing his brand unless he takes steps to forestall the loss by making the relation unmistakably clear. For many years the Eastman Company advertised "If it isn't an Eastman, it isn't a Kodak."

The use of a coined name in a brand throws a double task on the advertising of the firm. It must teach consumers a new word as well as the meaning of the word, while, if a word already in the language is used, the job is limited to teaching simply a new meaning for an old word. It must also be admitted that when people allow their imaginations free rein in coining words they sometimes come up with fearful and wonderful creations. One who reads the federal registration lists sometimes wonders what monstrosities, in the shape of products, some of the travesties of euphony can possibly fit.

Registration. Brands may be registered in the United States Patent Office. When this has been done the fact of registration becomes *prima facie* evidence that the firm which registered it owns it. This may be upset by evidence of prior use, but the burden of proof is on the user who has not registered. The marketing manager is wise to conduct his branding activities under legal guidance so as to be sure to adopt a mark that can be registered. A brand that is worth spending advertising money on is worth protecting, and developing protectable brands is not a job for a legal amateur.

National and Private Brands. The brands with which most people are familiar belong to manufacturers. They are sometimes called "manufacturer's brands" but more often "national brands." Those belonging to mercantile houses, wholesalers, and retailers are usually known as "private brands." There is no rhyme or reason to this nomenclature since many national brands are not distributed all over the nation, and many private brands, such as those of Sears, J. C. Penney, and Great Atlantic and Pacific Tea Company, are used in almost every state and are in no sense private.

In developing and using his private brands the wholesaler or retailer may be seeking a number of objectives. Not the least of these is a product or group of products over which he can exercise maximum control, within the limits of competition, with respect to quality, price, and promotion activities. He may achieve a measure of monopoly bounded by his ability to "sell" customers on the superior attractiveness of goods carrying his private brand. He may also wish to use the heavily advertised national brand, on which his margin of profit is narrow, as a "come-on" to attract customers into his store, hoping, once he gets them there, to sell them the higher profit private brand merchandise. On the other hand he may seek precisely the opposite end, to gain a product whose quality the customer trusts so that he can sell it at a price below those of its national brand competitors.

Usually the merchant does not produce his private brand merchandise; a large firm is quite likely to buy it from a manufacturer on a "specification contract." In such a contract the merchant usually specifies in great detail the quality of the product and commits himself to buy a designated amount of it within the contract period. The relations between the merchant and such a supplier are apt to extend over considerable periods of time. Many firms, usually small or medium-sized ones, make a business of supplying merchandise for private branding. On the other hand, some private branders obtain their merchandise from large manufacturers who also sell their own national brands. Sometimes the articles offered under the two types of brands come off the same production line and are identical in make and quality.

The reputable merchant is apt to exercise rigid control over the quality of the goods sold under his private brand, just as exacting as that of the manufacturer over the quality of the merchandise he makes for sale under his national brand. The less reputable merchants, of course, and those lacking the purchasing power to enforce exacting quality requirements are often content with poorer products.

Packaging

Most products are packaged for the market. Since goods began to move in trade, they have been packaged for shipment. At the beginning of the present century, however, very few of the articles sold through the average retail store were packaged for delivery to the consumer, except for paper bags or wrappings applied in the store. About 1912, for example, pickles and olives were dipped from a hogshead into a small waxed paper bucket for the customer; crackers came in a foot-square cannister; sugar and salt in barrels or 50-pound bags; cheese was cut from a giant roll about 6 inches high and 2 feet across; tea and coffee came in 100-pound bags or metal cannisters, molasses in a barrel, and kerosene in a metal drum—from which it was drawn off into the buyer's 5- or 10-gallon can and a potato jammed down over the spigot to plug it. Since then the grocery business has undergone a packaging revolution, and so have most other consumers' goods trades.

Several factors conspired to bring this about. The industrial revolution demonstrated the advantages of mass production, but, to attain its full development, mass production needed mass marketing. The essence of mass marketing at retail lies in speedy consumer selection and fast handling of merchandise, so that large volumes of goods may be sold to large numbers of people within a limited area of expensive store space. Packaging facilitated this. Then came the do-it-yourself attitude, of which retailers took advantage by developing and applying the self-service idea on a broad scale. In a self-service store the package and what is on the outside of it is the manufacturer's only salesman and the consumer's only source of information.

Functions of the Package

Basic economic factors largely determine the marketing purposes of packaging. They are:

1. *Convenience in Handling.* In a highly popular play of yesteryear a famous comedian, Frank Bacon, playing the part of an egregious but lovable liar, entertained with an unforgettable story of his adventures in herding a swarm of bees across the desert. If Frank had gotten his bees into a hive and plugged the hole, he would have had no trouble with them, and no story. Handling sugar or salt or eggs without a package may not be quite as frustrating, time-consuming, and wasteful as herding loose bees, but it has its difficulties, too. But all, fortunately, are largely eliminated by packaging. All retailing would be vastly more expensive and require infinitely more time and manpower without the package.

2. *Protection.* The package protects all kinds of products from dirt and contamination. Some products, such as drinks and most kinds of canned goods, need protection from the air to prevent deterioration or decay. For some types of products, candy, confectioners' sugar, and even cheese, the package affords protection against petty pilfering during the wholesaling and retailing process.

3. *Promotion.* During the last half-century, the use of the package as a means of advertising and sales promotion has increased tremendously; it has been pictured in advertising journals and shown on the television screen. On the shelves of a supermarket it must be relied on to capture the attention of the shopper and induce her to buy. The result has been a vast increase in the attention and effort manufacturers devote to the design, selection, and promotion of their packages.

4. *Use.* The package can be of great service to the consumer in storing and using a product. To serve this purpose a drug article must be in a package that will fit conveniently into the medicine chest and a food article onto the kitchen shelf. Closures that are easy to operate and that preserve the unused portion of the contents are highly important. Convenience in handling and pouring is a significant feature of this function of the package.

Features of the Package

The marketing manager who faces a packaging problem has several features or elements of the container that he may manipulate in order to achieve the effect he desires.

1. *Size.*   Probably the basic size unit of the package in which a product is sold should be that which will contain the amount of the product used by the average consuming unit between the time it is bought and the time it begins to deteriorate significantly. Some consuming units will, of course, wish to buy in larger and others in smaller containers. If these nonaverage groups are large enough, it may be profitable for the manufacturer to offer packages that satisfy them. The customers buying in larger containers may be offered a price advantage because the cost of making, filling, and handling a 10-pound package is by no means twice that of a 5-pound one. In determining the size of his package the manufacturer must make sure that it fits into the shelves on which the retailer wants to display it and into the space in which the user wants to store it in the home.

2. *Shape.*   The shape of the package is one of the chief ways in which it can attract the attention and capture the interest of the shopper in the store. The possible variations in shape and contour are almost infinite in number. In choosing among them, the package designer must bear several considerations in mind.

a) It is desirable that the retail container pack snugly into one or more of the standard shapes of shipping cartons without too much waste of space.

b) It should fit on the retailer's shelves or in his display cases, so as to make a striking and pleasing appearance, without serious waste of space.

c) It should fit in the spaces in which it is customarily kept in the user's home.

d) It should be easy and safe for the consumer to handle in use, and should afford a solid grip.

e) It should be capable of being piled or stacked in displays within the store so as to show to advantage.

f) It should not be too awkward or expensive to fill.

g) It should possess proper equilibrium and not be top-heavy.

3. *Closure and Reclosure.*   Few things about a package are so exasperating as the lack of any easy and obvious method of opening it. Not many consumers have missed the frustrating sensation of trying to "unscrew the inscrutable" in the form of seeking to open the containers in which some products are sold to them. This does not make for repeat purchases. Many marketing managers could profitably spend effort and ingenuity in making their packages easier and simpler to open.

Many products require packages that can be readily reclosed so as to preserve the unused portion of the contents. A primary requisite of a reclosure device is that it should be simple and obvious. By and large, women do not have the interest that men do in how things work. It is very difficult to get them to read the directions on the label for opening and reclosing a package before starting to open it. Such opening action is apt to be of a direct nature and may well destroy or nullify the usefulness of the reclosing mechanism. In marketing research surveys, made to find out what women do not like about packages, the complaint voiced most often and with the deepest feeling is directed against the difficulties of opening them and reclosing them. Some manufacturers have cut the Gordian knot and offered their consumer customers a service-plus by the use of the squeeze bottle or the aerosol package. This is not adapted to many products and is too expensive to be profitable for use in the marketing of many others.

4. *Color.* Color and shape are the package's two most effective features in attracting the shopper's attention and capturing her favorable interest as she moves through the retail store. In a book such as this we can not afford the space, nor have we the technical knowledge to discuss the psychology of color and its application to the problems of package design. The average marketing manager will probably be wise to admit that he is an amateur in this matter and to seek the guidance of professional package designers regarding it. Even the creations of these experts should not be adopted and incorporated into the marketing program without careful market testing to determine just how effective a package design is before the future of the product is confided to it.

5. *Material on the Label.* What the manufacturer says on his package label is apt to be very important. Some of this material may be determined for him. For example, the law requires the producer of a consumers' good drug product to show on the label a list of the active ingredients and the quantities in which they are present. If a product contains a poison, it must be so marked on the label. If any material in it is dangerous if overused, the safe dosage must be indicated. Food preparations must contain a list of ingredients, although the quantities present need not be indicated.

In general, it is probably good policy to devote the part of the label not pre-empted by the brand to conveying the sort of information about the product and its use that the buyer will want to know at the point of purchase. Many labels contain directions for the use of the contents of the package. Most of them should include directions for opening and reclosing it. Probably marketing research should be used more generally than it seems to be to find out just what information the buyer would like to find on the label.

Some years ago there was a strong movement in the direction of requiring by law the grade labeling of many products sold to the ultimate consumer. This seems to have subsided somewhat. An honest statement which describes the qualities of the contents and how they can be used with the greatest satisfaction is probably more useful than a grade, the precise definition of which can not always be kept in mind by the buyer.

Designing and Selecting Packages.   The marketing manager who has a packaging problem is apt to request his packaging department, if he has one, or a firm specializing in package design to prepare one or more designs for his proposed package. This will embrace the combination of shapes, sizes, materials, colors, closures, label material, and other features that seem to best fit his situation and needs. If more than one design is prepared, they are usually tested either by marketing research, or sometimes in market tests, to determine which meets most general consumer acceptance. Such tests may be expanded to compare the pulling power of the new package with that of competing packages on the market.

This is often a long, drawn-out process, especially when it involves the substitution of a new package for one long in use. This is sometimes necessary, for packages, like dresses, have a habit of getting out-of-date. It used to be the practice to make such changes slowly, a feature at a time, giving buyers an opportunity to get used to one small change before another was made. Over a period of time the entire face and form of the package might be changed. During recent years, the trend seems to be more in the direction of making the entire change in one operation. The announcement of the change is in and of itself news, and serves to call attention to the product and advertise it. Such a sudden change involves not only all the ordinary problems of preparing and putting on the market a new package, but the adjustment of inventories of the old package on the shelves and in the storerooms of wholesalers and retailers as well. It requires the utmost in careful planning, scheduling and management of relationships with the various units in the channel of distribution.

Shipping Containers.   Much has been done to decrease the weight and improve the containing properties of shipping cartons. Improvements are being made constantly and the wise marketing manager will take advantage of them.

Retail or use packages are usually packed in lots of dozens, or fractions, or multiples of a dozen to the carton. This practice is a venerable one. Attempts have been made to change to the decimal system but without conspicuous success. The decimal system has the advantage of making computations easier in reducing a price per case to a price per package. On the other hand, the figure 10 can be divided into whole numbers by only four numbers—one, two, five, and ten; twelve is divisible by one, two, three, four, six, and twelve. This means that in its most compact form a decimal carton must be long and thin, five by two, while a carton containing a dozen can be four one way by three the other, much more compact. In a trade that is committed to the dozen system, a marketing manager is probably wise not to try to buck so time-honored a convention.

Management during Maturity

The managerial problems that must be solved during the maturity of a product tend to center around competition. They involve chiefly the search for methods of cutting the cost of production, the development of more effective and less expensive methods of marketing, and the manipulation of price. Over the first of these the marketing manager has little control. The second and third are pretty much what the rest of this book is about, so we need not discuss them in detail here.

Decline and Deletion

At some stage in the life of the average product, sales volume or profit margins, or both, usually begin to decline. At some stage in this process of senescence management must face and decide the problem of whether to continue to make and sell the article or to drop it from the product mix. Because of this tendency of products to decline in profitableness or market appeal, a constant reexamination of each one is necessary, together with a policy or procedure for "pruning the line."

The first step in such a procedure is the selection of candidates for deletion. Typical symptoms of such candidacy are a falling profit level that approaches or passes below the rate of return considered by management to be desirable or minimum, a declining sales volume, or the appearance of a substitute with greater market appeal.

Simply because a product manifests any or all of these weaknesses, it does not follow that it should be deleted as a matter of course. By eliminating a product, management does not escape all the costs ordinarily charged against it. Such action causes no change in general and overhead charges and, when a product is deleted, their total must simply be redistributed over the articles remaining in the line. Very rarely will the deletion of one article in a product mix make possible a reduction in the number of salesmen on the force, the amount of warehouse space kept available, or the number of orders processed. A good device by which to study the financial effects of a deletion is to try to construct an operating statement of the firm with the product out of the picture and compare this statement with the current one.

The elimination of a product is likely to release capital formerly invested in its inventory, accounts receivable generated by its sale, inventories of materials needed to make it, and perhaps equipment used in its manufacture. Unless the firm has ready for development another project in which these funds can be used with greater return to the company, the firm will lose instead of gain by turning these assets into cash only to lie idle. This "opportunity cost" is usually a significant factor in a deletion decision.

Another most important consideration in a deletion decision is the probable effect of the dropping of one product on the sale of others in the product mix. This probability can be estimated by an analysis of the firm's entire sales to those customers who buy the questionable product. If all or most of them buy this product only, the volume lost by its deletion can be estimated with some exactness. If, on the other hand, those who buy the questionable article also purchase other profitable products from us, we run a more uncertain and much heavier risk in deleting it. If a customer has to turn to one of our competitors to buy something he needs and we no longer carry, the competitor's sales force is pretty poor if it cannot in the course of time take other business from us as well.

A classic example is that of a man who bought a drugstore in the Bronx. Examining the stock, he was just about to discard a small inventory of snuff, but luckily he thought to check the sales of the product. He found that all sales of snuff were made to one elderly dowager in the neighborhood, who also purchased about $50 of other products from the store each month. He decided to remain in the snuff business.

Product pruning is not a glamorous or exciting part of product management, but it is highly important. The firm that neglects to do it properly is likely to find that much of its capital and no small part of its manpower is tied down by products on which it makes little or no profit, and that this in turn handicaps it in exploiting product opportunities as they occur. Management must recognize and take advantage of the dynamic character of the product mix it handles.

PRODUCT DIFFERENTIATION AND MARKET SEGMENTATION

The economists who deal with monopolistic competition place a great deal of stress on product differentiation. Essentially, this involves an attempt by the marketer to endow his product with an individuality of its own that sets it off from those of other manufacturers or marketers which serve the same general purpose. By this means the marketer gains a species of monoply within a certain price range, limited by the value the average buyer attaches to this individuality.

Anyone who smokes cigarettes can measure these limits in his own case by seeking the answer to the question: How much of a price advantage would a brand other than the one I now smoke have to offer in order to induce me to change? On the basis of having asked this question of classes of beginning marketing students over a period of many years, I should say that the typical figure for students in a large university in a big city is somewhere around three or four cents a pack. It would probably be larger for their elders, whose pocketbooks are substantially deeper. Within this range each brand has a monopoly of the part of the cigarette market represented by the students who are devoted to it. Within that range competition has shifted from price to other factors.

Most nonmarketing people who have discussed this phenomenon have related it entirely to the activities of the seller, and many of them have seen in it nothing more than an attempt on his part to gain a semi-monopoly position. However they entirely miss the fact that if such an attempt on the part of the marketer is to succeed, there must be in the market a substantial group of people who regard as important the particular features, real or fancied, that his differentiation of the product offers.

The market for a product is not a monolithic thing, as it appears on the surface, but is made up of numerous segments, each defined by a desire for some particular feature or modification of the basic service the product provides. For example, the basic function of soap is to clean, but there are people who live in such circumstances that their only cleansing needs involve the removal of incidental surface dirt. Others need a soap that will remove grime, grease, or tar that is ground into their skins by the kinds of activities they carry on. Probably most people want lots of suds, but there are others who don't like suds. Most people do not like to use soap without scent, but preference as to the particular scent varies widely. Some like to use soap that is white, while others prefer green or yellow or pink or some shade of the basic colors. Some regard soap as nothing more than an agent for removing dirt; others can be persuaded that soap can feed the skin or perform other miracles of beautification.

Most of these preferences are inherent in the makeup of the people who compose the market. Most of them can be intensified and a few of them can be induced by the marketer, but the marketer who fails to base his product differentiation on a widely desired variation in its basic function faces an uphill fight in building profitable volume for it. The basis of product differentiation lies in market segmentation.

Market Segmentation. When a marketer practices market segmentation he simply takes advantage of these natural divisions in his general market, usually through some modification of the substance, form, appearance, or name of his product so as to increase its appeal to the chosen segment. Often he may seek to exploit the potential of several segments at the same time, varying his product and appeal to each one, or he may attack them one after the other.

There are many bases on which markets may be segmented. All have their roots in people, their backgrounds, their desires, their ambitions, the circumstances under which they live and work, and their relations with and attitudes toward other people. It may be worth our while to isolate and discuss several of the most common.

(*a*) *Geographic.* A market is often divided along geographic lines. Marketing executives recognize a phenomenon known as the New England market. They tend to look upon the Pacific Coast as a separate market empire. They know that the South needs and wants some products and marketing methods different from those popular in the North. To some extent these differences are matters of climate, predominant occupation, or the nature of the land, but some of them stem from pride of locality, tradition, and custom. Examples are Boston's preference for brown eggs as against the popularity of the white variety in New York, and the South's liking for hominy grits and beaten biscuits and its firm conviction that humans eat white corn meal while the yellow variety is "fit only for hogs and damyankees."

b) *Uses.* Practically every product has one basic use, but that basic use is apt to take many forms or it may be supplemented by auxiliary uses. Consider the family car. Its basic use is to carry people from where they are to where they want to be. But this takes many forms. Father may want to use the car to commute to work. If he drives by himself, it need provide only enough space for one man and his impedimenta; if he belongs to a driving club, it should seat five or six people without too much discomfort. But Junior may want to use it to take his girl for a ride, in which case the seating accommodations can be more than reasonably snug. Mother may use it to chauffeur the kids and then it needs a back seat into which they can be stowed without access to door handles. Dad may want it for carrying lumber and other materials for do-it-yourself projects, which means that it should have plenty of convenient luggage space. The family may want to use it for a Sunday afternoon spin, in which case it should look like something other than a second-hand truck and be able to withstand the assaults of other Sunday drivers. To large groups, one or the other of these specific uses may be dominant, and each of these groups forms a segment of the automobile market.

c) *Satisfactions.* Most products can be made to satisfy more than one desire. Let us again take the automobile as our example. Its primary satisfaction is that of movement, but it may offer others. It may gratify the driver's ego by supplying a sense of power and speed. It may be a thing of beauty. Its low cost of operation may gratify the owner whose budget is small or whose Scottish instincts of economy are highly developed. It may inflate the ego of its owner as a status symbol. But the same vehicle can not do all of these things, some of which are mutually contradictory. But an automobile manufacturer can design and build *different* cars, each emphasizing one or more of these satisfactions which segment the market.

d) *Group Association or Identity.* Manufacturers of many articles find it desirable to recognize and deal with "the college market," composed of students in institutions of higher learning and of a few old grads who never recover from being "college boys." There is probably a "country club" market, and almost certainly a "yacht club" market. These segments with the possible exception of the college market, are not so important in terms of total volume potential or in their influence on buying as are some of the other factors mentioned.

e) *Methods or Conditions of Buying.* A market may be segmented on the basis of the way in which the people in it want to buy. Many industrial buyers and some mercantile houses insist on buying direct from the manufacturer. In practically every community there is a group of women who "shop the specials." If the manufacturer wants their business he must plan his price and promotion program to enable his retail outlets to offer specials. Another consumer group wishes to buy in stores that emphasize quality and distinctiveness and they treat price as the "little dark sister" among patronage appeals. Then there is the not-to-be-ignored group who can barely bring themselves to buy even a stick of chewing gum that has no trading stamp attached.

In most cases this sort of market segmentation leads to differentiation in methods of marketing rather than of products. When product differentiation does occur as a result of it, it usually does not take the form of any change in the product itself but changes in such matters as packaging, branding, or details of appearance. For example, a slightly different package may be used for "specials" than for the usual run of business; different packages, carrying different brand names may be supplied to chain stores, department stores, mail order houses, or wholesalers who want to sell the product under their own private brands; or the product may be "dressed up" in various ways for sale through quality outlets.

f) Depth of Pocketbook. Income is perhaps the most universal basis upon which markets are segmented. No matter how enticing the appeal of a new Cadillac may be to a man whose income is low, he is not likely to be able to finance its purchase or operation. The iron rule of the pocketbook forces a high degree of uniformity in the buying patterns of people in the same income level. This uniformity is by no means absolute with all members of an income level over all product areas. For example, a family in the middle income group may shop for bargains in most of the things it buys, yet demand deluxe models of one or two items. In a new development suburb of New York, certain refugees from the cliff dwellings of Manhattan owned status-symbol cars and installed swimming pools at the expense of buying furniture for their living rooms. Anyone with a friend of moderate means who is a "camera bug" knows that while he may segment himself below his normal level for many of his purchases, he will place himself in or near the top segment in the photographic equipment and accessories market. By and large, though, income is probably the commonest basis of market segmentation.

Product Differentiation. Products may be differentiated in several ways.

a) Modification. Certain features may be added that enable the product to appeal to special segments of the market. This is the soundest method, especially if it is based on a careful analysis of the real needs and uses to which these market groups wish to put the product. Sometimes it is possible to present these modifications in the form of attachments, which some customers can buy and others can forego. For example, the buyer of an automobile can pay a little more and get automatic instead of manual gear shift, power steering, and special upholstery. The danger of this procedure is that the customer will lose confidence in the pricing system and come to regard the whole operation as a "gadget racket."

In other cases, versatility in use must be built into the product. In such cases the manufacturer must differentiate his product by making a number of models, each designed to serve one or more auxiliary or supplementary uses in addition to its basic function.

b) Quality. This is a broad term. In the industrial goods business it is apt to take the form of the exercise of great care in production and rigidity in inspection so that the buyer can be sure that every unit conforms exactly to the specifications. In the consumer goods business it is likely to consist in the use of the best materials, expert workmanship, and a willingness to insure the buyer against accidental failures of either by a liberal exchange or replacement policy.

c) *Appearance.* The automobile business supplies a good example of this. The liberal use of chrome, the exercise of the utmost ingenuity in the creation of tailfins and other decorative features, the design of body shapes that are unique but not too bizarre, the installation of whitewall tires and of bumpers that are fully as decorative as they are protective, are cases in point. Each model has its distinctive appearance that sets it off from every other.

d) *Packaging.* The package is probably fully as much a means of product differentiation as of product protection. The widespread development of self-service retailing, especially in supermarkets and discount houses, has thrown added emphasis on this function of the package. In a store of this kind the marketer must rely on the package to attract the buyer's attention to the product, to inform her about its characteristics, and to distinguish it from other products serving the same general purpose. The shopper finds it hard to ignore the presence of Mr. Clean on the supermarket shelf or to fail to realize what he is supposed to be able to do if she buys him.

e) *Branding and Advertising.* The name of a person identifies him to other people, and the identification is especially clear and sharp if the name connotes the flavor of the man's personality. Likewise, the brand is designed to identify the product, and its marketer hopes the brand will call up in the minds of possible users the image of usefulness or satisfaction-giving power they would like to enjoy. Through advertising and sales promotion the marketer seeks to make this hope come true by describing and emphasizing the product characteristics he wishes possible buyers to ascribe to it. The wise manager who wants to get the most mileage from his marketing dollar will go to great pains to see to it that his product actually has the satisfaction-giving features he wishes people to ascribe to it. His promotional efforts in the product's behalf are thus fortified by its performance in use.

This process of product differentiation has been severely criticized. It has been urged that much money and effort are spent to create trivial differences in products that have little or no relationship to the basic purposes they serve, and that expensive attempts are made to endow products in the minds of consumers with virtues they do not possess.

Both accusations are true to some extent. But the critic is not always justified in his assumption that it is unsound and wasteful for a customer to buy Brand A instead of Brand B of a product because he is convinced that the use of Brand A will afford him a minor satisfaction that may be entirely unrelated to the basic satisfaction both brands are designed to supply. Two brands of breakfast food may be equally tasty and nutritious, so both serve their basic purpose equally well, but one appears in the form of a flake, the other as small rings of doughnut shape. If I like the looks of the "sinker" type better than the flake, who is to say that the added satisfaction I get from eating the "sinkers" is not real or worthwhile? If there are enough people like me to form a significant segment of the market, who is to say that the effort spent in differentiating the "sinker" from the flake type is wasted simply because appearance has little or no relation to nutrition or eating qualities? The result has been an addition to the sum total of human satisfaction and that is one of the prime social purposes of business activity.

In general, the critic is probably correct in his contention that product differentiation without product differences that actually add to human satisfaction is wasteful. It is also probably not particularly good business management. The manager who spends enough money in developing his product to make reasonably sure that it actually does provide some added or distinctive consumer satisfaction will probably find that he gets it all back—and more—in the greater effectiveness of the dollar he spends on marketing it. To catch a new "sucker" every time you make a sale is an expensive marketing operation.

Product Rating Organizations

It is becoming increasingly difficult and costly for manufacturers of many kinds of consumers' goods to ignore the consumer-product rating organizations and their publications. The largest and most influential of these are Consumers' Union and Consumers' Research. In 1961 *Consumer Reports,* the publication of Consumer's Union, the larger of the two, enjoyed a circulation of about 850,000. It is probable that the combined circulation of these rating organizations does not exceed a million and a half. These organizations are financed by membership fees and subscriptions to their publications. In 1962 the budget of Consumers' Union was slightly under $4 million.

These are not large circulations when compared with the total number of consumers, nor are the budgets particularly impressive when matched against advertising expenditures in the consumers' goods field, but the ratings the organizations issue exercise an influence out of all proportion to the actual figures involved. Most of the subscriptions are family rather than individual in character, and the Bureau of the Census reports that the average family includes 3.65 persons. This means that the 850,000 subscriptions of Consumers' Union probably influence the buying habits of more than three million people. Many others are probably influenced indirectly by word of mouth. During recent years the number of subscriptions to such publications has been growing rapidly, and, with the resulting increase in the budgets of these nonprofit organizations, they have been improving the sophistication and reliability of their ratings, which in turn should enable them to further enlarge the sphere of their influence.

The facts just stated suggest that the manufacturer who makes products of the type now rated by these organizations, or in which they seem likely to interest themselves, would be wise to plan his product so as to gain a favorable rating. The history of the rating organizations indicates that the chance of achieving this through influence is very slim indeed. But it can be done by studying the product characteristics they attempt to measure and the types of tests they apply, and then building a product which these tests will disclose possess the chosen quality characteristics. A manufacturer may quarrel with the characteristics chosen as indicative of quality, and with the tests applied, but unless he can convince the managements of these organizations that his point of view is for the best interests of the consumer, he is stuck with them.

Right now the influence of these organizations is spotty. In a few lines, a low rating can be almost a deathblow for a product; in others, it is a handicap that can be overcome; in some it is of little influence. If the present trend continues, as it promises to do, the areas in which a proper rating is crucial may be expected to multiply, and its influence in other areas is likely to grow and expand.

Managing Marketing Channels

One of the most important things the manufacturer must do in marketing his products is to set up and manage his channels of distribution. A marketing channel or channel of distribution is the "structure of intra-company organization units and extra-company agents and dealers, wholesale and retail, through which a commodity, product or service is marketed."[1] It should be noted that this includes both (*a*) the establishments outside the manufacturing company—firms in business for themselves and connected with the company only by a contract or series of purchase and sale contracts through which the manufacturer's goods may reach the market, and (*b*) the units within the company whose chief task is to maintain contact with these outside units and endeavor to get them to market its products aggressively and effectively.

The management of marketing channels falls into three chief parts. First, the manager must determine the jobs that have to be done in marketing his products and the general type or kind of channel most suited to do these jobs. Second, he must choose the particular dealers and agents to be included in his distribution system. Finally, he must contact them, negotiate arrangements with them, and continuously manage his relationships with them, seeing to it that each conforms to a proper sphere of operations, providing incentives to enlist their best efforts on his behalf, and checking on their performance. The third of these general tasks involves a specialized type of personnel management and supervision.

If the marketing manager is to do these jobs effectively, he must know a great deal about the types of firms that specialize in wholesale and retail distribution. Such concerns are often called middlemen.

---

[1] "Marketing Definitions," Committee on Definitions of American Marketing Association, Chicago, 1960. All quoted definitions in this section are from this source.

Some of these are merchants who own the goods they resell; others are agents who arrange purchases and sales of merchandise belonging to others. Some of the merchants (the retailers) have as their main business selling directly to the ultimate consumer. Others, called wholesalers or distributors, buy merchandise and sell it to retailers and other merchants for resale, or to manufacturers and to institutions such as hospitals, schools, churches, and business concerns for use in running their enterprises. The merchant whose main business is in industrial goods is usually called a distributor or a supply house, although not all distributors are in the industrial goods business. The agents, who may be brokers, commission houses, manufacturer's agents, sales or selling agents, or auction companies, sell or buy goods for the account of their principals, receiving for their services a fee or a commission on the price at which the transaction takes place.

In order to use these middlemen effectively in getting his products to market the marketing manager must study their methods of operation, the kinds and quality of the services they render to their customers and to those whose goods they handle, their relations, competitive and otherwise, with each other, the managerial problems they encounter in operating their businesses, and the policies and practices by which they attempt to solve those problems.

For this reason, before we start to study the manufacturer's task of managing his distribution channels, we will find it profitable to examine in some detail the operations of each type of middleman, and to seek to understand the way in which he operates and some of the difficulties he encounters in conducting his business. In doing this we will try to look at each of them from the standpoint of the factors that determine the profitability of his business—because the manufacturer can get effective distribution service from a middleman only if he sets up an arrangement that contributes to the middleman's profit. He can no more build an effective channel of distribution out of weak, inefficient middlemen than he can create an effective working force in his factory out of poorly paid, inexpert weaklings.

CHAPTER 5

Retailers

Retailers are the most numerous type of business establishment. They number between 1,700,000 and 1,800,000 outlets. In their characteristics and operations they vary almost as widely as the men who manage them, but they have one thing in common that makes them retailers: the main business of every one of them is selling directly to the ultimate consumer. Most of them from time to time make sales to industrial or institutional users, but the bulk of their volume goes to buyers for personal or household use. Aside from this basic characteristic, their variation is almost infinite.

But neither their number nor their variety need be an insurmountable obstacle to either the student or the manufacturer who seeks to learn about their operations and gain a working understanding of their problems. In the first place, retailers tend to belong to groups, divided along the lines of product assortments carried, form of organization, scope of management control, method of operation, services rendered, and on other bases as well. In the second place, there are certain common functions that every retailer, from the corner peanut stand to the Great Atlantic and Pacific Tea Company, must perform. Likewise, there are several elements which determine the efficiency and success of retail establishments that are common to all types.

Therefore, we will organize our discussion of retailers around the following scheme: (a) Observing the different types or groups into which they naturally fall; (b) Studying the kinds of decisions and activities that are involved in managing any sort of retail store, and the peculiar forms these functions take in the different types or groups; and (c) Exploring the elements of efficiency that tend to determine success or failure, with some study of the extent to which these elements favor one type or another as outlets for the manufacturer.

Retailers may be classified on several bases, each of which involves some characteristic of organization, operation, or behavior. We will discuss those that are most important to the manufacturer in his choice of outlets.

PRODUCTS HANDLED

The most common and most obvious grouping of retailers is on the basis of the products they handle. Examples are foodstores, drugstores, hardware stores, and clothing stores. The Bureau of the Census distinguishes the following 10 general classifications:

Lumber, Building Materials, Hardware, and Farm Equipment	Apparel and Accessories
General Merchandise	Furniture and Home Furnishings
Food	Eating and Drinking Places
Automotive	Drug
Gasoline Service	Other Retail Stores

These classifications are too broad to be of much use either to the student seeking to understand the operations of retailers or to the manufacturer looking for guidance in setting up and administering his marketing channels system.

For example, the manufacturer of television sets is not interested in all the Lumber, Building Materials, Hardware and Farm Equipment (108,248 in 1958) or General Merchandise (86,644) and Furniture and Home Furnishings (103,417) stores. But he is interested in Hardware (34,670) and perhaps Electrical Supply (1,984) stores in the first group, Department stores (3,157) in the second, and Furniture (36,096), Household Appliance (24,224) and Radio and Television (16,761) stores in the third. (Within the 10 classifications listed above, the Census Bureau finds 95 more particularized groupings, most of which are narrow enough to give a manufacturer significant help in planning his marketing channels.)

These groupings of retailers and the kinds of products they handle are constantly changing. New products may trigger the development of new retailing groups. This happened, for example, as a result of the growth of radio and television. Where population is dense and purchasing power is high, retail stores can be specialized to a degree that is not possible in areas where demand is less concentrated. For example, in the average small town, with only a few thousand persons to draw patronage from, a camera and photographic equipment and supplies store can usually not develop enough sales volume to exist (although resort and tourist towns may provide exceptions to this rule). And a change in the density of population in an area, such as the growth of a suburban community, may change the kinds of retail outlets through which a manufacturer can most effectively market his products.

Retailers are like all humans in that the grass always looks greener on the other fellow's side of the fence. Merchants in one trade are under constant temptation to raid the offerings of stores in other trades by adding to their stocks long-profit items that are handled by such stores but which are not too foreign to the goods the raiders have traditionally carried. For a long time, drugstores were especially active in this practice, comedian-philosopher Will Rogers once remarking that "You can buy pretty much anything you want in a drugstore—even a few drugs." Druggists were rather bitter, though, when the process was reversed and supermarkets began to stock such items as aspirin, band-aids, and common laxative tablets. Supermarkets, which are traditionally food stores, have also moved into the nonfood, household articles business to such an extent that a group of wholesale distributors have found it profitable to specialize in supplying such items to them. The manufacturer who neglects to reexamine constantly his choice of retail outlets is apt to find that big chunks of his consumer market have slipped away from him through this process of product raiding among retailers.

SIZE

The average retail store is a small business. Its annual sales in 1958 were about $112,000, and are probably slightly more now; this was a little more than $370 for each business day. This average store employed about four and one-half people. Corresponding figures for 1954 were $99,000 for the year, $330 per day, and slightly more than four employees. These averages are interesting to the student or social scientist in that they show the extent to which the retailing trade is a stronghold of the small business man in our economic and social system. Both numerically and in terms of the influence he exercises, he is probably more important here than in any other significant segment of our economy, except perhaps in certain service trades.

But, from the standpoint of the manufacturer seeking a solution to his marketing channel problems, averages such as these are not highly significant. When a retailer's volume of a manufacturer's product grows great enough it becomes economic to market to him directly. The volume at which this occurs depends on the amount a retailer buys from a manufacturer on a single order and in the aggregate, and varies widely among products and types of retailers and with the width of the manufacturer's line. For a product with a high value unit of sale which the retailer buys at monthly or bimonthly intervals, with the result that the dollar amount of each delivery is high and salesmen's calls need not be frequent, the economical direct marketing volume can be less than for one bought in small sales units and at frequent intervals.

For example: there are about 35,000 hardware retailers in the United States. In 1958 only 1100-odd of them had an annual volume of more than $300,000 annually, and these stores made only 25 percent of total hardware store sales. Forty-two percent of the total volume of the trade was handled by retailers with annual sales of less than $100,000. It would probably not be economical for a manufacturer to try to sell direct to these small stores. Similar figures, for stores with sales of more than $300,000 in other trades, are:

> 28,000 out of 260,000 food stores handle 65 percent of the business.
> 2,500 out of 43,000 women's clothing stores make 47 percent of total trade sales.
> 750 out of 24,000 shoe stores sell 17 percent of total volume.
> 3300 out of 36,000 furniture stores handle 44 percent of total trade sales.
> 3400 out of 56,000 drug stores sell 27 percent of total volume.
> 2200 out of 37,000 liquor stores handle 33 percent of the total business.
> 325 of 9400 book and stationery stores sell 27 percent of the total volume.
> 750 of 23,751 jewelry stores make 29 percent of total jewelry store sales.

If in addition we note the percentage of the total sales volume of certain retail trades done by stores with annual sales of less than $100,000, the picture of the influence of store size on the manufacturer's marketing channel problem becomes even clearer. For selected trades these figures are

Hardware	42%	Household appliances	34%
Grocery	20	Variety	22
Women's clothing	28	Drugs	28
Shoes	41	Liquor	30
Sporting goods	49	Books and stationery	41
Cigars and tobacco	68	Jewelry	42
Furniture	22	Cameras and photographic supplies	30

The retailer with an annual volume of $100,000 sells about $1,925 worth of merchandise a week. If his gross profit is 30 percent, probably a conservative figure, he has to buy about $1,155 worth of stock each week. If he handles a very compact line that includes the products of only 10 manufacturers (a rather unusual situation), he can place an order totaling about $230 with each of them every two weeks, and most manufacturers would find it economic to handle orders of that size ($50 is probably about the break-even point). On the other hand, if the retailer carries the products of 50 to 100 manufacturers, which is probably a more realistic figure, he can hardly expect many of the producers to market directly to him.

A small store is much more apt to be intimately a part of the community than a big one. Of course some big stores, such as Marshall Fields, Macy's, and Neiman-Marcus, are so nearly synonymous with Chicago, New York, and Dallas that they seem to give the lie to this statement, but these are probably exceptions instead of the rule. The owner-manager of the small store is typically a local boy, who knows and is known by everybody in the neighborhood. His personality and his store tend to become merged and this composite, in turn, becomes a part of and helps shape the personality of the community. As a result, it has a powerful hold on the patronage of the consumers in its limited trading area.

The small store possesses a flexibility in its operations that the larger unit can not approach. Without a certain degree of standardization of stocks and activities the management of a large retail store becomes hopelessly bogged down in detail. Rules must be set up and enforced. Moreover, changing the managerial mind is something of a project, but the small store can add an item to stock, change its method of operating, or perform a special service or favor for a customer by the decision and action of one man who is on the spot, the owner-manager. So it is that, by and large, consumers have learned to look to the small store as a place to find "something a little different" or get a service not wanted by everybody. In the course of seeking these things in the small store, they buy many other things as well.

The size of the average retail store has been increasing. In 1958 average annual sales were about $112,000; in 1954 they were $99,000; and in 1948, $74,000: an increase of almost 50 percent in a decade. Part of this, of course, reflects an increase in prices, but not all of it, for the consumer cost-of-living index rose only about 25 percent during the 10-year period. In line with this change, the percentage of the total retail business handled by the larger stores has been increasing. For example, stores with annual sales of over $1 million, which in 1948 sold 19.8 percent of the total, in 1954 handled 26.4 percent, and in 1958 29.4 percent of all retail business. For stores selling a half a million or more, the same figures for 1948 were 31.2 percent, for 1954 38.7 percent, and for 1958 41.7 percent. The percentage of the business handled by stores selling less than $100,000 a year declined during the period. The indications are that this tendency is still continuing.

The trend toward larger stores is not uniform throughout all trades. In the grocery business, for example, the percentage of the business handled by stores selling a million or more annually increased from

11.1 in 1948 to 43.1 in 1958, and is still growing. This probably reflects the mounting importance of the supermarkets. In the hardware business there has been very little change. In the drug business there has been a pronounced shift in importance from stores selling *less* than $100,000 annually, the percentage falling from 49.7 in 1948 to 27.7 in 1958, and *toward* stores with annual sales between $100,000 and $1 million. There has been little change in the liquor trade and shoe trade, although shoe stores have tended to become smaller. The rapid increase in the overall importance of the bigger stores (selling $500,-000 and more annually), from 13.2 percent of total retail sales in 1948 to 25.1 percent in 1958, probably results, in part at least, from the growth of the discount house.

The size behavior of these individual trades has been pointed out not because it is important in itself, but because it emphasizes the necessity that the marketing manager must study shifts of this sort in those retail trades which are his natural outlets and adjust his operations to what is happening there.

Many retailing concerns are large enough that they can insist on buying direct from the manufacturer, and a few of them can afford to produce some of the things they sell. Both of these practices are made possible by the concentration in the hands of a single retail manager of purchasing power for a single product or for the products of a single manufacturer. This concentration may result from either the large size of the single establishment which the manager heads, or from the combined buying power of a number of smaller establishments through either common ownership and management or effective contractual arrangements.

Comparatively few of even the largest retailers have found it profitable to manufacture many of their own goods for resale, but many of them have found it very much worthwhile to engage in "contract buying." The general idea of this is that the big retailer contracts with a manufacturer, often a small one but sometimes a large one, to make a certain product, such as canned fruit juice, a TV set, or a washing machine, to designated specifications and at a specified price for a fixed period, usually a year. The retailer then resells this merchandise under his own brand, often in competition with the brand of the manufacturer.

DEPARTMENTATION

Practically all stores are departmentized to some extent. Even the "hole in the wall" stationery and cigar store has a section for magazines, another for newspapers, one for cigarettes, another for cigars, and probably a small packaged candy counter. Such departmentation is confined to merchandise and merely serves the ends of convenience in handling stock and serving customers. This is the primary purpose for which most stores are divided into departments.

The Department Store

The department store carries the principle much farther. A department store is defined as a "large retailing unit that handles a wide variety of shopping and specialty goods, including women's ready-to-wear and accessories, men's and boys' wear, piece goods, small wares, and home furnishings, and which is organized into separate departments for purposes of promotion, service and control." While the three elements, large size, wide variety of clothing and home furnishings assortments, and departmentation, are present in this definition, it is in its organization structure that the department store is really unique.

The department store was one of the earliest examples of the use of the principle of breaking down a large enterprise into a number of smaller pieces and setting up each piece as a cost-profit center under a departmental manager who exercised a high degree of autonomy within policies and objectives that were centrally established. The department store is divided into two kinds of departments: merchandise, and operating or service. Each merchandise department handles a particular kind or grouping of products, such as infants' wear, cosmetics, or gardening materials and equipment.

In any one store there may be few or many of these merchandise units (at one time Macy's of New York had 250). Each of them is managed by an executive who is known as a "buyer," a misleading title since the buyer has charge not only of purchasing merchandise for the department to resell but is responsible for getting the goods resold at a profit. When the number of departments in a store is great the buyers are usually grouped under several merchandise managers, who are in overall charge of a number of related departments; for example, all those handling women's apparel and accessories, or all those selling furniture and household furnishings and equipment.

The service departments, such as accounting, finance, advertising, delivery, and personnel, supply the services and facilities the buyers need in order to carry out their assignments. The costs of these units are allocated to the merchandise departments, usually in rough proportion to the extent to which each buyer uses each service. Some of the costs, such as product advertising, can usually be assigned directly; others, resulting from a single activity that serves several departments, must be allocated by a formula that may become highly complex and involve a number of debatable assumptions.

FIGURE 5–1

ORGANIZATIONAL STRUCTURE OF TYPICAL OLD-STYLE DEPARTMENT STORE

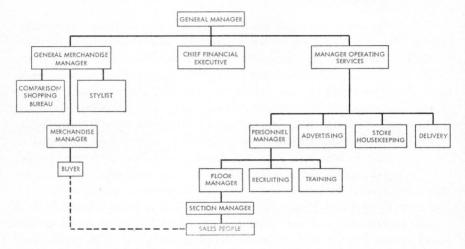

A typical old-style department store organization structure might look something like Figure 5–1. But, especially among the larger stores, there has been a trend toward either a four- or a five-part divisional structure according to the following pattern:

1. *Merchandising,* headed by a general merchandise manager to whom the divisional or group merchandise managers, who supervise the buyers, report. This area also includes such staff units as Fashion Coordination, Product Research, and Comparison Shopping. If there is no separate Sales Promotion division, the functions of advertising and sales promotion are apt to be performed here.

2. *Operations,* headed by a store superintendent or store manager who has charge of the housekeeping and physical facilities of the store. In addition to his general duties in operating the building facilities, he is apt to have charge of packing, workrooms, restaurants, and the purchase of non-resale materials and equipment.

3. *Finance and Control,* which supplies accounting, legal, and statistical analysis work, handles customer credit and prepares and administers the budget.

4. *Personnel,* which has charge of recruiting, selecting and training the employees, and, through its floor superintendents (with the section

managers under them), supervises the nonmerchandise activities of the sales people on the selling floor.

5. *Sales Promotion,* which supplies advertising service, displays, demonstrations, direct mail, and publicity (but is not always a separate divisional area).

One of the difficulties of this kind of organization lies in the fact that, while the buyer is held responsible for the profit or loss of her department, she does not have complete control over the chief tools—displays, advertising, and salespeople—by which she must resell the goods she buys. Advertising and displays are supplied by the Sales Promotion department, usually according to a budget on which the buyer does not have the last word, and the salespeople on the floor are subject to a dual supervision: by the buyer, with respect to merchandise matters, and by the section manager in all other matters. The trend in department store organization, however, has been away from the basic element of the form that originally distinguished it. The buyer's control over the profits of her department has been whittled away by limitations of the budget on how much she can buy and how much she can spend to resell it; by the standards set by the fashion coordinator; by the dictates of the merchandise manager; and by her lack of control over the people on the floor who sell her merchandise. So the manufacturer with goods to market through department stores can no longer assume that if he sells the buyer he has successfully opened this channel.

The department store is typically a large establishment. There are probably at least three or four with annual sales of more than $100 million. In 1958 the Bureau of the Census found 3,117 department stores. Of these, 2,128 had sales of more than $1 million dollars a year, and 2,891 sold more than $500,000 annually. This superiority in size is not as significant as it seems, however. Consider a department store with total sales of $10 million divided among 100 departments, each in competition with individual specialized stores handling the same line of merchandise. If the store's total volume is divided equally among its departments, each department is the substantial equivalent of an individual store with annual sales of $100,000, the general average for all stores.

Although the number of department stores is small, they control a share of the total retailing business (6.7 percent), that is out of all proportion to their numbers. In certain types of goods, particularly shopping merchandise, bought chiefly by women, the percentage is much greater than this, for the department store is primarily a shopping center that depends for its volume mainly on the patronage of women.

Because of the department store's size, and because of its unique position as a shopping institution in its trading area, the presence of a manufacturer's goods in its stocks often lends prestige much more valuable than the volume of them sold. In the case of some stores, such as Lord and Taylors, Marshall Fields, and Neiman-Marcus, this prestige may extend far beyond the community in which the store is located.

The department store is essentially a big-city phenomenon. The tremendous market represented by the concentration of population in the city and around it, coupled with the development of rapid transportation facilities within the city (and between the city and its satellite areas) made possible the volume of shopping goods sales that enabled the department store to exist. Since these transport facilities converged on the center of the city, that is where the department stores located. In 1958 the 760 department stores in the 21 largest cities in the country made just about half of the total sales of all such stores in the nation.

Two things happened to upset this situation. People moved from the city to the suburbs. They began to depend on private cars and buses instead of mass transportation facilities for local travel. The central downtown location of the department stores resulted in intolerable traffic congestion and impossible parking conditions if people tried to use the means of transportation they wanted in visiting these stores to shop. Many stores have sought to meet this situation by establishing branches in the suburbs. This helps to maintain the volume and market position of the department store, but it fails to touch the dilemma of its downtown unit. The pattern of the department store of the future is by no means clear and its development is something that the manufacturer with department stores in his marketing channels will be wise to watch carefully.

The relation between the main store and its branches is a matter of considerable importance to the manufacturer in planning and administering his marketing channels. Branches vary widely in size, merchandise offerings, and methods of operating. Usually, a branch is smaller than its parent main store and handles a narrower line of merchandise— although there are exceptions to both these generalizations. Its operations are likely to be geared somewhat to the shopping habits and preferences of the suburban area it serves. The branch is neither merely an extension of the main store nor a member of a chain, even when a single store operates a number of branches.

The personality or public image of the branch usually conforms roughly to that of the main store; the nature of its appeal is the same; and at least some coordination exists between the kinds of goods it carries and those stocked by the main store. In its top management group the main store is likely to have a manager of branches, one of whose duties is to assure correlation in these areas.

Each branch usually has its own manager and staff of buyers. In some cases these executives have wide autonomy, within central policy limitations, in selecting merchandise and determining operating methods. In other systems the branch executives are closely controlled by their opposite numbers in the main store. This variability in branch-main store relationships complicates the task of the manufacturer who proposes to include department stores in his marketing channels.

The department store leans very heavily on service as a means of attracting patronage, and formerly carried this appeal to even greater lengths than is now the case. Practically every form of service that managerial ingenuity could devise has at one time been offered by the department store to its customers. Even today it places more emphasis on this appeal than does any other kind of retailing unit.

The Leased Department

There are certain types of goods whose retailing requires special skills and experience, or the volume of whose purchase by the average department store is not large enough to earn any quantity price reductions. Examples are millinery, beauty parlor services and preparations, optical goods, photographic equipment and supplies, sewing machines, wallpaper, and books. In addition, it sometimes happens that a department store manager is unable to find or obtain the executive talent needed to make a go of a certain department, or he may feel that his store should have a certain department but he lacks the capital needed to finance it.

In any of these cases, the leased department may be the answer. Under this arrangement the department store leases certain space to a firm which specializes in operating leased departments of the kind desired; for example, optical goods. The tenant usually operates what amounts to a chain of leased departments. The lease may run from year to year or its duration may be indefinite, subject to termination by either party on proper notice.

Under the leasing arrangement the tenant pays the department store a flat annual fee, or an agreed percentage of sales or net profits, or a flat minimum fee plus a percentage of all sales or profits above an agreed minimum. The tenant then supplies the merchandise, pays the operating expenses he has agreed to undertake (which usually include wages of salespeople and service expenses), and keeps the remainder as profit. He may also agree that in operating the department he will conform to the general policies and market personality of the store, and that his salespeople will be subject to the overall discipline and procedural routines of the store even though their selling activities are controlled by the tenant.

The leased department chain offers manufacturers of certain types of goods a means of getting their merchandise into the stocks of many department stores through one contact. While leased departments are most common in the department store business, they—or some substantially equivalent operation—are to be found in other types of retail establishments.

OWNERSHIP AND MANAGERIAL CONTROL

The most commonly recognized groupings of stores, on the basis of ownership and managerial control, are the independents and the chains. There are several other groupings that can be distinguished under this basis of classification, but since they are much less important than the independent-chain groupings, we will deal with them later.

Independents and Chains

The independent store is one "which is controlled by its own individual ownership or management rather than from without, except insofar as its management is limited by voluntary group arrangements." This definition includes stores that belong to voluntary group organizations. In their relations with the manufacturers, whose goods they resell, the behavior of members of these groups is so distinctive that the manufacturer will be wise to study them carefully as a class, and often to market his goods to them differently from the way in which he manages his relationships with their brother independents who really "go it alone." Since independent stores possess certain characteristics as independents, whether or not they are members of a voluntary group, we will discuss them as a class and compare them with the chains. Then, in a separate section, we will describe the features that distinguish the voluntary group members as a class.

A chain store system is a "group of retail stores of essentially the same type, centrally owned and with some degree of centralized control of operation." The term *chain store* may have the same meaning or may refer to a single store unit of such a group. Obviously, two stores make a chain system even though their common ownership and management usually fails to afford them many of the advantages of chain operation: in many features of their behavior they conform to the chain pattern. The Bureau of the Census recognizes this and in its reports divides "multiunit" stores into seven classes, according to the number of units under one management, as follows:

2 or 3 stores	11 to 25 stores
4 or 5 stores	26 to 50 stores
6 to 10 stores	51 to 100 stores
Over 100 stores	

This breakdown is useful to the student and to the manufacturer in planning his marketing channels. Its usefulness, however, is limited by the fact that in the Bureau's attempt to prevent the disclosure of confidential information about individual chain systems, the figures it reported for geographical areas are often so fragmentary as to have little meaning.

Numerically, independent stores are much more important than the chains. In 1958 they constituted 89.9 percent of all stores; in 1954 the figure was 90.2 percent, and in 1948 it was 90.7 percent. In the matter of sales, however, they are much less significant. In 1958 they did 66.2 percent of total retail sales; in 1954, 70.0 percent, and in 1948 70.3 percent. While they lost ground to the chains on both bases of comparison during the decade, they are still numerous enough and control enough of the total retail volume to indicate definitely that the independent merchant faces no imminent prospect of disappearance from the retailing business. In certain trades, however, the chain systems have taken over a highly significant portion of the total sales volume. This is true of the general merchandise trade, where they have more than 55 percent of the total volume, the variety trade where they have about 85 percent, and the grocery business in which they sell over 52 percent of the total. Other similar percentages are:

Tires, batteries, and auto accessories	44%
Women's ready-to-wear	50
Millinery	48
Hosiery	52
Family clothing	51
Men's shoes	83
Women's shoes	72
Family shoes	53

The manufacturer who must reach the consuming public through these trades faces the difficult task of operating a marketing channel system that satisfies both chain managers and independent merchants. In many others he must include the chain outlets in his channel or forego a significant part of the total volume. The chains are still increasing their share of the market both by number of stores and by the percentage of the total sales volume they handle. This is a long-time trend. It shows no obvious tendency to level out although logically it may be expected to do so—as we shall see when we come to discuss the elements of strength and weakness possessed by the two types.

The independent store tends to be a smaller establishment than the chain store unit. The 1958 census showed that the average independent store had annual sales of $82,000, while the average chain unit sold $368,000 a year (and the sales volume of the average store belonging to a chain with more than 50 units was $534,000). This tendency for chain stores to have larger sales than independent stores, and for the units of larger chains to sell more than the units of the smaller chains, seems to be characteristic of most retail trades.

It is especially pronounced in the grocery business where the 1958 annual sales of the average independent unit were $88,000, while the average store belonging to a chain of more than 50 stores sold $1 million during that year. The figures in other selected trades are shown in Table 5–1.

TABLE 5–1

SINGLE AND MULTIUNIT STORE SALES IN 1958

	Single Stores	Multiunit Systems	
		All	More than 50 Stores
Variety.....................	$50,000	$321,000	$441,000
Tire, battery, accessories......	83,000	222,000	276,000
Shoes.......................	62,000	123,000	136,000
Eating places...............	43,000	106,000	105,000
Drug stores.................	98,000	272,000	414,000
Liquor......................	89,000	276,000	379,000
Cigar.......................	41,000	73,000	N.A.

The size of the individual store, either independent or chain, may be of considerable importance to the manufacturer in managing his channel relationships. In general, he is more likely to be able to afford to make direct contact with the larger store than with the small one. Many chain system managements want deliveries made directly to individual store units. On the other hand, many manufacturers are not content with making sales contacts simply with chain-wide or district buying offices but wish to get their salesmen into the individual stores to enlist the interest and support of the local store management and personnel for their merchandise.

The organization structure of the independent store varies according to its size, the kinds of merchandise it handles, its location, the kinds and amount of service it renders, and the composition and ideas of its ownership-management. One feature is unfailingly characteristic: the power of decision and action lodges within the organization structure of the store itself. This is true even when some managerial prerogatives have been delegated by contract to a voluntary group headquarters. At the end of the contract period, or after specified notice, the owner-manager may decide not to renew the contract or to withdraw from it.

The essential objective of the chain type of operation determines the kind of organization structure the chain system must have and imposes on it a certain degree of rigidity. The primary purpose of putting a chain system together is usually to gain the advantages flowing from operating a number of stores more or less as one. This means that the organization structure must provide for lodging in a central headquarters a large measure of control over the operations of the individual store units and for the performance by a central staff of many of the activities the independent owner-manager carries on within his own store. Some chain managements have sought in their organization structure some sort of workable compromise that provides enough centralized control and central performance of common functions to yield most of the advantages of chain operation and also allows enough autonomy to the unit store manager to enlist his originality and initiative. Most of them, however, put organizational emphasis on the uniformity of operation that comes from control at the top and seek to set up a structure that will assure that the store manager will do what he is told.

Two chief kinds of activity are necessary to keep a chain store system going. Goods must be bought and handled, and stores must be operated through which the goods are resold. The buying of goods can be concentrated at a central point. Each store must be managed where it is located. The specialization of knowledge and skill that makes for good buying runs along the lines of products or product groups. The activities of store management, while they involve a number of functional skills, must be applied on a geographical basis—to an individual store or to a group of stores in an area.

As a result of these factors the bulk of the personnel of the chain store system is usually to be found in two structural divisions: (*a*) *merchandising*, which has to do with getting goods and making them available to the stores, and (*b*) *operations*, which has charge of managing the stores. In the large system these divisions are likely to be supported by a number of staff units in the central office. There is almost certain to be a financial officer responsible for managing the flow of funds and for the keeping and analysis of records. There is very likely to be a personnel unit which supplies recruiting, training, salary administration, rating, employee relations, and other personnel services to all other units. A large chain system is also apt to recognize the need for a real estate unit, a research unit, legal staff, tax and insurance service, public relations, and other types of service that can be provided more effectively and at less cost by the central office than by any of the field units.

In a small chain the chief operations officer is likely to exercise direct authority over the store managers. In the larger system stores are apt to be grouped under division, district, or branch managers who report to the central operations officer. A very large system usually has several executive levels between the store manager and the chief of operations. In many chain systems the chief functions of these territorial executives are to channel central office orders and requirements to the store managers, to see to it that these directives are obeyed, and to channel information from the field to the central office.

In some chains the organizational structure is influenced by recognition of the fact that when the volume of goods bought passes beyond a certain point, no further advantages can be reaped from standardized, large-scale purchasing, and that in fact the buying procedure may become cumbersome, overly expensive, and may generate mistakes where mistakes are most costly to the retailer—in the selection and procurement of goods for resale. Other chain managements observe that bargains are often available locally and that localities vary enough in the products and product characteristics they demand so that it is profitable to allow, or even to encourage, flexibility in buying. In extreme cases these considerations result in at least part of the buying function being pushed down into the unit store. Other systems enlarge the functional scope of the division or district office by adding the buying activity and retaining in the central office only the purchasing work that can be done best there, such as procuring goods from abroad. A few chains, usually department stores or stores heavily involved in the marketing of shopping goods, set up a buying organization as a service unit in the central office and place in the hands of the store managers the power to order through it the goods they want.

It seems almost needless to say that a knowledge of chain system buying practices and the lodgment of power to buy (or buying influence) is highly important to the manufacturer who proposes to include chain stores in his marketing channel. It is probably worth while to point out, though, that there is no set of buying practices or standard pattern of buying power or influence common to all chain systems. The would-be manufacturer-supplier must study each chain system separately and seek to understand its buying machinery and how it operates. While this is liable to involve a lot of work, the volume of sales controlled by many chain systems makes it worth the expense.

Voluntary Groups

Many independent retailers, especially in the food business, belong to voluntary groups. Such an organization is "a group of retailers each of whom owns and operates his own store and is associated with a wholesale organization or a manufacturer to carry on joint merchandising activities, and who are characterized by some degree of group identity and uniformity of operation." Closely akin to this is a retailer cooperative, which is composed of a group of retailers who buy together either through a jointly owned wholesale warehouse or a buying club. They may also operate under a group name, advertise jointly, and perform certain managerial functions in common, such as layout and display.

While these two types of group organization have several characteristics that distinguish them from each other as general classes, they are enough alike so that the manufacturer meets approximately the same problems in including them in his marketing channel. So we can probably safely examine them together. This conclusion is fortified by the fact that voluntary groups differ from each other, and retailer cooperatives differ from other retailer cooperatives more widely than voluntary groups, as a class, differ from retailer cooperatives as a class. Both have one characteristic which inevitably dominates the manufacturer's relations with them: the principle of cooperative activity. Another common feature of all is that they suffer the weaknesses and enjoy the strengths inherent in all cooperative enterprises.

In 1954 the Bureau of the Census found 574 voluntary group grocery wholesalers and 193 retailer cooperatives in the food business. In the 1958 census report the Bureau failed to differentiate between the two types of groups and found 673 of both in the food business. In 1954 the voluntary groups sold 33.5 percent and the retailer cooperatives 17.7 percent of total general line grocery wholesale volume. Together they sold 51.2 percent of the total. In 1958 the sales of the two groups were 62.1 percent of all general line grocery wholesale sales. The census reports gave no indication of the number of retailers belonging to these groups or of their total sales.

Progressive Grocer, a leading trade journal of the retail food business estimated that in 1960 there were 351,050 retail food stores, with sales of $57,850 million. Of these, 91,000 with sales of $5,250 million were specialty stores; and 260,050, with an annual volume of $52,600 million, were general grocery and combination food stores. Of the grocery and combination stores 20,050 were chains with sales of $20,450 million, and 240,000 were independents with a sales volume of $32,150 million. Of the independent stores 84,000 belonged to voluntary and cooperative groups and sold $25,400 million; while 156,000, with sales of $6,750 million, were unaffiliated. Thus the voluntary groups and retailer cooperatives embraced about 24 percent of the retail food stores and sold about 44 percent of total retail food volume. *Progressive Grocer's* estimates are quite carefully done and are usually reasonably accurate.

Neither voluntary groups nor retailer cooperatives are very important outside the food business. They have minor significance in the variety trade, there are a few of them in the hardware trade; and they are probably slightly more important in the drug business than in either the variety or hardware fields.

A voluntary group is usually organized by and around a wholesaler or a number of wholesalers associated for the purpose, as is the case with the Independent Grocers Alliance. In a retailer cooperative the stores themselves take the initiative. In both, the relationship is formalized and expressed by a contract. This agreement usually specifies how the organization will be financed. Most of the retailer cooperatives require their members to contribute an initiation fee or to buy stock in the corporation, the customary form of organization. Others require each retailer member to make a (returnable) cash deposit when joining the organization. Most of them collect dues or fees on some regular basis, usually weekly. These may vary according to the amount and nature of the services rendered each store or they may take the form of a flat fee.

The contract also specifies what the retailer agrees to do for the group and what the group promises to do for the retailer-member. From the standpoint of the retailer-member the chief purpose of the group organization may be said to be to gain as many of the advantages of chain store management as possible without undue sacrifice of the freedom of independent operation. Two very obvious advantages of the chain system are its great purchasing power and the promotional value of the common name and uniform appearance of the stores belonging to it. So the things the retailer-members of the group agree to do jointly usually center around the achievement of these advantages.

In practically all of both types of groups the retailer-members agree to concentrate their purchases to some extent. In the retailer cooperatives this commitment is apt to cover all or most of the goods they buy. Some voluntary groups make the same requirement. Others commit their members to buy through the sponsoring wholesaler only certain kinds of goods (sometimes only the items to be resold as "specials"). The degree of concentration of purchases varies widely among the voluntary groups. The purpose of the concentration is to increase the purchasing power of the group sponsor or headquarters and to enable it to gain price concessions or other favorable arrangements from the manufacturer. What and how much a group headquarters can buy depends not only on the degree to which the members concentrate their purchases but on what they promote and how they promote it.

As a result, the group program usually includes a common schedule of "specials," uniform displays, point-of-sale promotional materials, cooperative advertising, and other forms of joint action to increase group sales and, consequently, group purchases of competitive products on which the independent store's prices must undergo intensive consumer comparison with the chains. Many groups develop their own brands, and membership involves common action in promoting their sale.

Some strong groups require all members to adopt a uniform store front, color scheme, store signs, and layout. When a new retailer joins one large group, employees of group headquarters descend on his store, redecorate it outside and inside, install a new layout with appropriate furniture and fixtures, fill the shelves with a standard inventory, and organize and conduct a "Grand Opening" of the store as a member of the group. The idea of all this is that the individual store thus draws promotional strength from the group and at the same time contributes to the promotional impact of the group on the market.

Many groups also provide accounting advice and services to retailer-members and supply various kinds of consultative help and advice with respect to store management.

Many of the groups find it necessary to maintain a force of supervisors or consultants who visit the individual members, much in the manner of salesmen, in order to explain the cooperative programs, sell the store manager on the benefits he may gain by supporting them, suggest and aid in installing improved methods of operation, and otherwise promote the loyalty and efficiency of the membership.

The manufacturer who proposes to market his products through these groups must be prepared to fit in with their methods of operation and contribute to the achievement of their objectives. He can enlist their cooperation in carrying out his marketing plans only by under-standing and cooperating in their programs. He can not do this by try-ing to set up a standard pattern of relationships with all these groups. Each group differs from every other, nor can the manufacturer always expect to receive the retailing services the group headquarters promises him. They suffer from the weaknesses of every organization that de-pends for its success on the uncoerced cooperation of a large number of small businessmen, many of whom are in competition with each other. These weaknesses center around the difficulty of holding the loyalty of the members in the face of the divisive pressures generated in the course of their daily operations. The value of the group members as outlets for the manufacturer depends very largely upon the extent to which the group executives are able to maintain this loyalty.

Consumers' Cooperatives

These are retail establishments owned and operated by ultimate con-sumers to purchase and distribute goods and services primarily to the membership.

Consumers' cooperatives are relatively unimportant in the United States but in many European countries they handle a highly significant part of the total retail trade. Here their share amounts to about one per-cent of the total. Most of this volume is in farm supplies and gasoline, both of which are bought by farmers primarily as industrial products for running their farms and not for personal or household consumption. The cooperative store's share of the true consumers' goods part of the retailing business is much less than one percent—only about one-half percent of food sales, for example—and for most other product groups much less than that.

There seems little likelihood that the consumer cooperatives' share of the total retailing business of the country will increase significantly in the immediate future. Our high standard of living has resulted in the absence of the intense pressure on the average family to make ends meet that stimulated the formation of cooperatives abroad. This pres-sure has further been relieved by the development in this country of retailing establishments, such as the chain store system, the supermar-ket, the mail-order house, and the discount house, that base their busi-ness on cutting costs and offering low prices. The mobility of the average American family makes it a poor prospect for membership in a cooperative retailing unit. All these factors are important in explain-ing the relative absence of consumers' cooperatives, but the most pow-erful deterrent is probably to be found in the temper and philosophy of our people—an individualism that disposes them to rely on individual enterprise instead of collective action as a means of getting the things they want. The net meaning of all this seems to be that if a manufacturer can now get along without the consumers' cooperative in his marketing channel, he can probably continue to do so.

If, on the other hand, he feels it desirable to use the cooperatives as outlets, there are a few things he should know about them. They are financed by membership fees or members' purchase of stock on a one-man-one-vote rather than a one-share-one-vote basis, by loans (preferably from members but sometimes from outsiders), or by the retention of earnings. The cooperative store usually tries to charge the same prices as those prevailing in other stores in its neighborhood, and in this way can sell to nonmembers as well as members without generating price wars. Part of its profits are paid to members as a patronage dividend in the form of a percentage, often about two percent, of the member's purchases.

The individual cooperative store usually belongs to a "wholesale" which services a number of stores. These wholesales are apt to be linked together in a regional organization for purposes of buying, providing managerial training, advice and counsel, and managerial services, such as accounting, to individual stores, and organizing and nurturing the development of new stores. These organizations develop and manage the merchandising and promotion of cooperative brands under which many types of goods are sold. These brands are not sold to the exclusion of manufacturers' brands but in addition to them. The inside of a cooperative grocery store looks much like that of any other grocery store—with the exception that many of the shelf goods bear the "Coop" brand.

The well-managed cooperative store fortifies its economic hold, through the patronage dividend, on the buying loyalty of its members, by a sense of "belonging," and by the feeling of contributing to a "movement." These appeals are effective in influencing comparatively few people, but they constitute a powerful hold on those few.

The manufacturer who wishes to include consumers' cooperative stores in his marketing channel must usually work through the wholesale or regional organization in doing so. He is not apt to have much success soliciting the patronage of individual stores.

Industrial Stores

These are stores owned and operated by a firm or a governmental unit to sell primarily to its own employees. Such stores are usually established only by firms that operate plants in remote locations not served adequately by ordinary retailers. Governmental stores of this type also are apt to be maintained to offset in some degree the general inadequacy of the wages paid by governmental units. In neither case is the store conducted for profit, and in both cases it is apt to be run by a special department of the firm or government unit. Some company stores confine their stocks to the products of the firm. These stores handle a very small percentage of the total retailing business.

Manufacturer's or Company Stores

A manufacturer may find it desirable to operate a store or a group of stores through which he sells his own products, sometimes together with complementary products of other manufacturers. One of the important chains, in the tire, battery, and auto accessories business, is of this type, as are a number of important chain systems in the shoe trade. Most manufacturers take a dim view of any extensive development of this type of outlet, feeling that the headaches inherent in getting their goods into the hands of the retailer are severe enough without incurring the additional pains involved in learning how to run a retail business. If done properly, however, it has proved to be a highly useful channel of distribution.

Many manufacturers operate experimental stores. The primary purpose of these outlets is to serve as a testing ground for new products and new methods of promoting the manufacturer's merchandise. Such a store may also serve as a showplace in a highly important market and play a key part in bringing the manufacturer's line to the attention of consumers in such a market. Manufacturer's stores, located in such places as New York, Chicago, Los Angeles, and Miami, are likely to be conducted for this purpose. Several wholesalers operate one or more stores retailing their line primarily or entirely to test out products, promotional devices, projects and methods, and store management aids and suggestions.

PATRONAGE AND APPEALS

We habitually think of a retail store as a place that sells merchandise. Too often the retailer *himself* thinks of his store that way. What he really has to sell is a package composed of merchandise, services, and a price or price level. The emphasis which he puts on each of these in his package determines the basis of his appeal for consumer patronage. He can not emphasize all three of them at the same time, for a high quality and wide assortment of merchandise and an extensive service pattern cost money, and the merchant who features them must set his prices at a high level or go without profit. He must put together a combination of the three which will be most effective in attracting patronage and returning profit in the market he serves and in the conditions under which he operates.

We will probably be wise to explore first the nature and dimensions of these bases of appeal and then examine several types of retailers whose operations illustrate distinctive patterns of appeal.

Merchandise

Store policies with respect to merchandise turn chiefly on two factors: quality and assortment.

Merchandise quality at retail is something like charm in a person, hard if not impossible to define but a highly potent force nevertheless. Certainly, it is not in all cases durability or usefulness, nor is it merely high fashion; but more nearly "right" fashion. It probably comes nearest to being the composite of characteristics that the average consumer thinks he would seek in a product if he had all the money he wanted to spend on it.

Store quality policy tends to fall into three patterns. In a retail market of significant size there are likely to be a few stores which make their appeal on the basis of top quality merchandise, a number that mainly offer goods at the low end of the quality scale, and a middle ground group whose merchandise offerings conform to Shakespeare's description "neat but not gaudy." Almost every sizable retail market has its Abercrombie and Fitch, its S. S. Pierce, and its Lord and Taylor. Along with these gradations in quality go differences in price, not only because of differences in cost but because consumers suspect that high quality merchandise offered at a low price is "phony" and because they will not knowingly buy low quality goods except at reduced prices.

A store's merchandise policy also involves the assortment it offers. Some stores make their appeal on the basis of a wide assortment of many different kinds of goods, hoping thereby to attract heavy consumer traffic and exploit the fact that a customer who comes into a store to buy one article may often be induced to purchase another. The department store probably offers the best example of this policy. At the other end of the scale is the specialty store, such as a photographic equipment and supply shop, which offers a very complete selection of items within a narrow line of merchandise. Many retailers, among them most of the chain systems, follow a policy of handling only items in their merchandise line for which there is a consumer demand large enough to enable them to achieve a standard rate of stock turnover while buying in the most economical quantities.

Service

The basic service of a retail store is to provide at a convenient spot a stock of the items of merchandise the consumer expects to find in that kind of store, and facilities that enable customers to get the merchandise handily. There are many gradations in the quality of these facilities, which may add to the pleasure and convenience of the customer's shopping. A second level of store service is the provision of salespeople whose primary functions, from the standpoint of the customer, are to supply information, provide a pleasant atmosphere for shopping, get desired merchandise off the shelves or from stock, help in fitting certain types of goods, offer advice in selection, see to the convenient packaging of the articles bought, and make arrangements for delivering them and paying for them. Other layers of service include delivery and credit, liberal return and adjustment arrangements, ready exchange of merchandise, layaways, shopping service, and numerous others associated more or less directly with the sales transaction. On top of these are such matters as lounging rooms, baby-watching, art exhibits, concerts, and other refinements whose relation to the actual exchange of merchandise is certainly tenuous.

The relationship between service and price is not so direct and consistent as that between quality and price. Many department stores that feature the low price appeal also offer extensive services, apparently on the theory that the combination will create large sales volume, thereby reducing overhead costs and augmenting profits, by increasing the number of sales dollars on which a profit is gleaned more than it reduces the amount of profit on each dollar. On the other hand, the self-service stores, especially the supermarket and the discount house, have cut services drastically in order to reduce costs and lower prices. In doing so, they have passed on to the consumer the performance of marketing functions that almost from time immemorial have been the task of the retailer.

Price

A few retailers largely deemphasize price as a patronage appeal. These are chiefly the ones who place very heavy emphasis on quality, completeness of assortment, service, or a combination of all three. Some of them even seem to use a very high price as a means of attracting customers. There is probably more than a little method in their madness, for in following this policy they rely on what seems to be a widespread consumer assumption that merchandise can't be good unless its price is high or, that when the price is high the merchandise must be good. Paying a high price for something that is conspicuous is also one way of keeping up with, or ahead of, the Joneses.

At the opposite end of the scale are stores that appeal for patronage almost entirely on the basis of price. Practically every city of any size has at least one department store that does this. Many of these firms, for example Macy's, maintain a high standard of merchandise quality; others adhere strictly to the policy "Let the buyer beware."

In between is the great body of the retail trade who follow a middle course, pricing most of their goods at what they feel is the market, but more or less constantly offering "specials" or conducting sales of selected articles to attract customer traffic into the store and to maintain its reputation as a place in which to get "good values."

During recent years the retailing business has been torn with dissension about the widespread revival and extension of a very old form of price appeal that is not always recognized as involving a cut in price: the trading stamp. The idea of something "thrown in" is perhaps as old as retailing. The baker's dozen, the free belt or pair of suspenders with a suit, the redeemable coupon in soap wrappers, are venerable price-cutting devices. The trading stamp itself is more than two thirds of a century old, although prior to the end of World War II it played no very significant part in the retailing picture. During the 1950's and early 1960's its use has become widespread, and even a firm of the stature of the Great Atlantic and Pacific Tea Company found it a tough competitive force to reckon with.

The mechanism of the use of trading stamps is simple. A stamp company sells stamps to retailers, usually only to one store in each trade in a community, but to stores in as many different trades as possible in each retail market. The retailer gives them to customers according to the amount purchased, usually one for every ten cents bought. The customer pastes them into books and redeems the books for merchandise premiums at premium outlets maintained by the stamp company. There are between 1,500 and 2,000 such outlets in the country. Some of the premium catalogues resemble those of small mail order houses. It is estimated that stamp sales to retailers total between two thirds of a billion and $1 billion dollars annually. Food stores account for more than half of this although the use of stamps is spreading rapidly into other trades.

It seems generally agreed that it costs the retailer two percent or more of sales to buy and handle the stamps. His benefit from their use consists entirely in added volume or volume held from loss to stamp-using competitors. This benefit is apt to be illusory unless a store's use of stamps increases its volume enough so that the spreading of overhead cost over the broader sales base reduces overhead charges per dollar of sales by two percent, or unless the smaller net profit per dollar of sales times the added sales dollars yields a larger total net profit than before. Several studies have been made of the effect of the use of stamps on retail prices and profits. They do not indicate that prices have been increased, or that stores have been put out of business because of the use of stamps. On the other hand, there is no clear indication that retail profits have been increased or prices reduced by it.

Trading stamps are not employed widely by stores using the high quality-high service-high price complex of appeals. Their use is quite general among stores emphasizing the low price appeal, those which aim to meet competition, and those to whom large volume operation is very important. It is probable that with many stores the motives leading to stamp usage were more defensive than aggressive, and Great Atlantic and Pacific Tea Company was a spectacular example.

While the manufacturer is not directly involved in the trading stamp fight, he must be aware of its implications and will be wise to study the effect, if any, which a store's use of stamps has on its value as an outlet for his products.

Examples of Appeals Complexes

Every retail store has its individual combination of appeals. Several groups of stores make use of characteristic appeal patterns. It was pointed out, for example, that the department store seeks to attract patronage on the basis of a wide assortment of merchandise with emphasis on shopping goods; but departmentation is the thing that makes it a department store. Certain stores are characterized more positively by their appeal pattern than by any other feature or combination of features.

The Supermarket. This large retailing unit "sells mainly food and grocery items on the basis of the low margin appeal, wide variety and assortments, self service and heavy emphasis on merchandise appeal," mainly the visual appeal of the goods themselves.

Since the Bureau of the Census makes no separate classification of supermarkets, there are no generally accepted figures as to their number or their volume of sales. Super Market Institute, the trade organization of the group, had in its membership in 1962 firms operating 16,900 stores which sold $21 billion dollars worth of goods a year, about 6 percent of all grocery stores in the country and about 38 percent of total grocery store sales. *Business Week* in its June 4, 1960, issue estimated that supermarkets accounted for almost 70 percent of all consumer grocery expenditures. One reason why estimates of supermarket volume vary widely probably lies in differences of definition. Some observers probably include the volume of what the trade calls "superettes," smaller stores that operate like supermarkets. Whatever their volume is, they constitute a highly significant element in the food business, and kindred forms of operation are making serious inroads into other trades as well.

If the sample of about 6,100 stores from which the institute received reports in 1962 was representative, the following facts are true of supermarkets:

About a third of them are single-store independents, about a third belong to two-, three-, four- and five-store chains, and a third belong to chain systems operating six or more stores.

The average supermarket has annual sales of $1,830,000.

The typical store in 1961 had a gross profit of 18.83 percent of sales; its operating expenses were 17.44 percent, and it made a net profit of 1.39 percent of sales. The gross profit and expense ratios have been increasing over a period of years.

The typical sale per customer transaction in 1961 was $4.88.

In 1961, 78 percent of the stores gave trading stamps (against 13 percent in 1954).

In 1960 the typical store made 5.4 percent of its sales in nonfood items, an increase from 3.5 percent in 1954. The items most often carried were health and beauty aids, housewares, women's hosiery, and stationery.

The supermarket's patronage appeal emphasizes merchandise and price more or less to the exclusion of service. There is reason to think, though, that the absence of service that is implicit in the self-service feature has in itself an appeal to the consumer, aside from its downward pressure on costs and prices. The housewife really likes to pick her own purchases off the shelf (her desire to handle merchandise before she buys it had always been a nuisance to the old-line retailer) and the supermarket has taken over this yen and put it to work for the store.

The freedom to compare, to choose this and to reject that, without the suggestions or advice or even the silently critical presence of a salesperson seems for many women to endow shopping with the atmosphere of an adventure or an excursion a little apart from the daily routine of living. And what mere man who has wandered into a well laid-out and well-managed supermarket or been sent there on family business fails to respond with a thrill and an open pocketbook to the wonderland of enticing products that unfolds before him as he blunders from aisle to aisle.

Because of its narrow profit margin, extensive floor space, and expensive parking facilities, the supermarket's management must be completely ruthless in weeding out products that do not pull their volume and profit weight in the boat. And because of the self-service feature, the product must sell itself—or be presold by the manufacturer before it appears on the shelves. Not only must the product itself be good but its package must attract attention and invite purchase. Supermarket chain managements do not hesitate to build private brands that meet their specifications if goods with the desired characteristics are not available on satisfactory terms under manufacturers' brands. Because of the paramount importance of sales volume the supermarket manager can not afford to allow his resale prices to be fixed by the manufacturer.

The Discount House. This retailing unit "features consumer durable items, competes on the basis of price appeal, and operates on a relatively low markup with a minimum of customer service."

The census reports contain no figures on discount houses, so we lack reliable statistical information about them. One estimate, probably as good as any, places the number of such stores at 3,000 and their sales at about 5 billion dollars a year. When discount houses began to be important, shortly after the end of World War II, the typical store was located in low-rent, unattractive quarters, usually on the low-grade edge of the retailing district. Its furniture and equipment was rudimentary and its service was practically confined to providing space for the goods and the customers' feet to rest on and to taking the buyer's money for the merchandise he carried away. Their expenses were reported to be all the way from 7 to 15 percent of sales. They featured nationally advertised brands of hard goods.

During the 1950's and early 1960's they moved into well laid-out, centrally located, well-equipped, attractive quarters. Their merchandise offerings have broadened to include soft goods; their merchandise emphasis is no longer so heavily on manufacturers' brands; their costs and their prices have gone up; and indeed many of them are now practically indistinguishable from low-price department stores. As a matter of fact, many of them *are* branches of department stores, started on the principle of "if you can't beat 'em, join 'em," and usually operated under a name other than that of the parent store. Some of the outstanding department stores of the country maintain such dubious offspring. Along with this upgrading in surroundings and facilities has gone an increase in costs, until the average is now probably near 16 or 17 percent of sales—but still a significant advantage when compared with the 35 percent or more of the department store or hardgoods specialty store.

Originally the discount house's chief—practically its only—appeal was a price below the standardized figure of the regular retailer. In the course of the developments sketched above the typical discount house has added many of the merchandise and self-service appeal techniques of the supermarket. In fact, some observers describe them as nonfood supermarkets. They have still retained their insistence on goods that can be handled at low enough costs to enable significant price reductions. But the cut-price sale of well-known brands advertised and sold through the regular outlets at uniform prices, set and policed by the manufacturer, is no longer so basic an element in discount house merchandising policy as it once was.

Vending Machines. In a vending machine operation at least two people are involved, the operator and the location owner. The location owner is the proprietor or the controller of any space suitable for a vending machine. The operator leases such space from the owner, buys or leases the machine from its producer, installs it on the location, usually buys the merchadise to go into it and keeps it stocked. For most location owners the income from the vending machine is incidental to that from some other operation. The management and servicing of vending machines is usually the main business of the operator. A few manufacturers whose goods are especially adapted to automatic selling function as operators.

In 1958 the Bureau of the Census found 8,152 vending machine operators with annual sales of about $842 million. Trade sources claim that in 1959 about 4 million machines sold over $2 billion worth of merchandise and services. Probably the discrepancy is due in part to the fact that the trade estimates include the sales of laundromat service, insurance, weighing machines, shoeshines, parcel locker service, subway tokens, and other services which the census omits from its retail count. It is quite certain that the volume of vending machine sales has grown rapidly. In 1954 the census reported that they made sales of about $640 million. The growth is probably due, in part at least, to mechanical improvements in the machines which made them more reliable and to imaginative experiments in their location and the products vended through them.

The chief patronage appeals of the vending machine seem to be convenience and timeliness—having the goods available for purchase where or near where the customer is when he wants to buy—and the unfailing interest in gadgetry. The stick of chewing gum or package of candy on the subway platform, the bottle of milk when all stores are closed, the cup of coffee or bottle or cup of soft drink or juice, or package of cigarettes in the waiting room, the novelty of buying from a machine that makes change, all illustrate these appeals. Some stores have experimented with outdoor or entryway automatic vending sections where customers may buy certain staple often-needed articles when the store is closed.

The census reports show that about 40 percent of total vending machine merchandise sales are of tobacco products and about 25 percent are candy, nuts, and confectionery. Ice cream, milk, and other beverages are also sold in considerable quantities. The fact that in 1958 these four groups of products were responsible for only 78 percent of total merchandise sales of vending machines, while in 1954 they accounted for 92 percent of the total, reflects the tendency to widen the merchandise categories offered for sale in this way.

It is highly probable that retail sales through vending machines will increase. But it hardly seems likely that the vending machine will become a very important outlet, except for a few products, until some means are found to overcome the limitations that now exist on the kinds of goods suitable for retailing in this manner. At present, in order to be sold successfully through vending machines, an article must be of relatively small bulk, small enough to be easily carried away, and of low unit price, probably some fraction of a dollar. It must be an article that is in fairly general demand and the characteristics of which are commonly known so that comparison and careful selection are not necessary. A final requirement, that the goods be packaged to facilitate handling by machines, is one which is in the hands of the manufacturer who wishes to market through this outlet.

The Mail Order House. This retail business "receives its orders primarily by mail or telephone and generally offers its goods and services for sale from a catalog or other printed material." Its appeal was originally based on low price and convenience to its chief customers, the farmers, who were often remote from most retail stores but were served by rural free delivery. It still emphasizes the price appeal, but with the improvement of country roads and automobiles it no longer has much, if anything, to offer in the way of convenience to most of its rural customers. It foregoes the appeal of the merchandise itself, although the larger mail order houses have established order and show rooms, where goods may be examined and ordered, in connection with their chain store units. For the farmer who is too far away from a city to shop in a department store the mail order catalog offers the convenience of a large assortment of merchandise that is listed in one document and can be ordered on one blank. The chief appeal of the mail order house probably lies in its catalog and the merchandise brochures it distributes to prospective customers. In 1962 Sears mailed to more than 9 million families copies of its 1,500-page, three-and-a-half-pound fall and winter catalog, listing over 140,000 items.[1] The descriptions of the articles included in mail order catalogs are among the most exact, complete, and convincing to be found in informational advertising literature.

In 1958 the Bureau of the Census found 2,550 mail order houses, with total annual sales of $1,986 million, about one percent of total retail sales. Thirty-five of these, offering general merchandise, sold $1,523 million or about 77 percent of the total. These percentage relationships are about the same as they were in 1954. Probably more than half of the general merchandise sales volume belongs to the three or four largest houses. In 1961 Sear's mail order operation alone made sales of about $700 million, about one sixth of the combined store, telephone, and mail order volume of the company.

There seems little likelihood that the mail order house's share of the retail trade will grow significantly in the near future. The portion of the population to which its appeals are apt to be convincing seems to be shrinking rather than increasing. Its expenses of operation are high; for example, in 1958 mail order payroll costs were 14 percent of sales as against about 11 percent for all retailing. Printing and distributing the catalog are highly expensive. The trend of postal charges threatens to make delivery impossibly costly. In spite of these handicaps the mail order house as a type has been able to appeal for customer patronage on the basis of lower price. Its large purchasing power and high sales volume have probably been the factors that enabled it to do this.

Some mail order operations are run by manufacturers. For example, the outstanding producers of garden seeds and bulbs and a large maker of men's shirts and underwear market in this manner. And many leading department and specialty stores operate mail order divisions.

These various types of retail establishments are in constant competition with each other as suppliers of consumer wants and as outlets for the manufacturer's goods. How well they perform these functions depends very largely upon their natural advantages and weaknesses and how well they are managed. So let us turn to an examination of these factors that govern retailing efficiency.

---

[1]*New York Times,* August 1, 1962.

CHAPTER 6

Retail Stores:
Management and Efficiency

The capacity of a retail business to survive and grow depends very largely on how well it is managed. Of course luck has something to do with it, but it takes a *lot* of good luck to offset poor management.

The process of managing any retail concern consists of making plans and decisions about certain activities that are necessary in retailing operations and in carrying on those activities or seeing to it that they are carried on. So in our attempt to study the survival and growth efficiency of the different types of retailers, we will look at each of the more important retailing activities and endeavor to isolate and appraise the factors that help or hinder the management of each type in planning and carrying them on. But in doing this we must bear in mind the fact that in any sort of enterprise good management starts with the quality of the managers it is able to obtain and keep, and the extent to which it can call out and use their talents. So we will probably be wise to start off by examining the factors that affect the kind of management a retail concern is able to attract.

FACTORS AFFECTING QUALITY OF MANAGEMENT

There seem to be three kinds of factors that determine the quality of the management of retail firms, along with all other types of business establishments. These are: the innate caliber and ability of the executive personnel whose services the firm is able to command, the setting in which the management group must work and the facilities it has to work with, and the incentives the concern can offer its executives to call forth their best efforts.

Innate Ability

While there are many individual exceptions, it is almost certainly true that the higher the remuneration a firm can pay its executives the abler is the leadership it can employ. In general, the greater the volume of sales a retail concern controls, the higher are the salaries and other money compensations it can pay to get good executives. A large volume of sales usually comes from offering a wide variety of different kinds of goods through one establishment, as the department store or the mail order house, or from linking together under one management a number of establishments each selling a narrower line, for example, the chain system. Sometimes the two are combined.

The annual compensation of the top executive of a leading department store in a city of 100,000 population or over is apt to approach the $100,000 mark. Recently the highest yearly compensation paid by a chain of general merchandise stores was $135,000: three of its executives received $100,000 or more, and all the directors and officers were paid a total of $1,600,000. But this was only .044 percent of the system's annual sales. Another chain system in the same field paid its chief executive $106,000, three of its officers received more than $100,000 each, and the entire official group was paid $823,000— or .056 percent of sales. The head of a regional food supermarket chain system received $102,250 a year (he was the only one at that lofty financial altitude) but all the directors and officers of the company received $433,000, which was .061 percent of sales.

These figures do not include payments to store managers, district managers, or to all the functional headquarters executives; nor do they include all "fringe benefits" received by the top managerial group. The three companies cited are not atypical. In thinking about these figures we should remember that since the Internal Revenue Bureau allows a man above the $100,000 income level to keep only about 10 cents out of every dollar he gets above that figure, differences in that area are more important as indices of status than for their monetary value.

Now let us examine the "take" of the top manager of a store with an average annual volume of $100,000. Dun and Bradstreet's "Operating Ratios of Retail Trades" indicate that his gross profit will be about 32 percent, or $32,000. The same authority suggests that he will have to pay about 22 percent, or $22,000, for expenses, leaving about $10,-000 for managerial salary and proprietorship profits. Not much managerial talent can be bought for that figure. The chances are that the small store group, which includes most of the independent and many of the specialty stores, can not command the quality of managerial ability that is available to the larger retail firms.

Working Environment

The quality of management enjoyed by a firm depends not only on the standard of managerial talent it is able to employ but on the conditions under which its executives must work. The manager of the small retail establishment works in the store where the things that matter happen. Only through blindness or the grossest inattention can he avoid being aware of most of the events that influence the welfare of his business. When opportunity knocks or crisis threatens, he can make an immediate decision and immediately start to carry it out. He can make his decisions and construct his pattern of action on the most intimate and personal knowledge of the details of his business.

But all this has its drawbacks. He is apt to be so absorbed in the care of individual trees that he can not see the configuration of the forest. To save time he tends, often unconsciously, to reduce to a routine matters that may require analysis and judgment of individual cases. He is likely to feel himself so pushed by the need to decide the clamorous issues of the moment that he fails to plan for the future. If facts must be gathered and analyzed, issues weighed, plans created and implemented, or procedures formulated, he must do it. If all sides of a problem must be looked at, he must do the looking.

On the other hand, the top management group of the big retailing firm can, if it wishes, operate in the relative calm of the higher levels of policy determination and overall planning. They are physically and to some extent mentally and emotionally removed from the organized madhouse that is the selling floor of the busy department store or supermarket. They have the support of specialized staffs to collect and analyze information about any phase of the firm's activities or any aspect of the environment in which it operates. Such a manager does not need to create policies and plans or to make decisions alone. It is true that somewhere around the place there must be a man who bears the responsibility of saying "yes" or "no" and of "pulling the switch." But the plans and policies and decisions with which he deals usually have been hammered out in the lower managerial levels and come to him as recommendations with reasons for and against. He can test the soundness of contemplated decisions against the opinions of others. His position is lonely but he is not a solo flyer, as is his counterpart in the smaller store.

But there is another side to the picture. Top management of the department store or the multiunit chain system is isolated from the places where the vital action occurs and from contact with the customers. As a result the manager may have the uncomfortable feeling that he is out of touch with reality and does not know what is happening, or, worse still, he may acquire the opinion that the figures, reports, and analyses that flow across his desk reflect the whole of the reality of his firm's operations and of its impact on the customers it serves and the people through whom it serves them. In other words, he loses the "feel" of the customers, of the store employees, and of the merchandise. Plans and decisions made by men without this "feel" are apt to lack something in realism.

In addition, the manager of a multi-unit retailing firm, regardless of how able he may be, cannot translate his plans and decisions into action at the point of sale with the same speed that the small store manager can achieve. Before these plans create action they must move down through the various levels of organization, and at each level must be translated in terms of the functions performed by the units at that level; and often something is missed or distorted in the translation. Action does not follow decision as night the day but more nearly as October follows May.

Both of these common handicaps of managing large-scale organizations are especially serious in a business as dynamic as retailing and as completely dependent on the shifts and turns of consumer whims and preferences—which often can be detected early enough to do something about them only by the "feel" that comes from close and constant contact with the market.

Personal Incentives

The third factor affecting the quality of retailing management consists in the incentives which the firm can offer the manager to call forth his best effort. By and large, the small store and, in general, the independent single-line store cannot begin to match the large department or multi-unit concern in the monetary inducements it can offer its executives. This has already been pretty well illustrated. In addition, the large retailing firm offers its top managers such intangible incentives as prestige, a sense of power, and the satisfaction of accomplishment that comes from handling big issues and making decisions of importance to many people. The president of Sears gets his name in the paper, his opinions are sought after and listened to, and people are aware that he "rolls big marbles." After a man's income becomes big enough so that the howls of the wolf can no longer be heard from his door except as a faint echo, these nonmonetary incentives gain tremendous importance, nor does their intangibility subtract from their power as motives for effort.

On the other hand, the small independent store offers its manager a different kind of "psychic income" to offset its weaker monetary incentive. The satisfaction of independence, the feeling that he "runs his own show," undoubtedly keeps many a retailer in business who could have made a surer and probably a better living working for someone else. The small independent store manager may not be a big man in the national or regional economy, but he can be and often is a respected man in his community. Often the identities of the store and the owner-manager become merged to such a point that his store is no longer a business but a way of life for him. He gives to it a devotion and subordination of self that money can neither buy nor adequately reward. Such a storekeeper often manages a lot better than he knows how to manage.

Summary Observations

This personal devotion of the independent owner-operator to the store he conducts and his close familiarity with all its details are probably more than offset as competitive advantages by the superior managerial ability usually possessed by the chief executives of the large-scale retailing concerns and by the greater precision with which they are able to apply specialized administrative skills to specific tasks. It is true that the officials of the multi-unit firm experience great difficulty in controlling the activities of the managers of its individual units. The chief executive of the department store often encounters almost insuperable obstacles in attempting to induce his department heads to carry out his plans and policies with any degree of precision, and chain headquarters finds it very difficult to get precise compliance with its orders by managers of widely scattered stores.

On the average, these junior executives are probably not superior in ability to the typical owner-operator of an independent store. But their hands are held up by the general managerial organizations behind them and their punches borrow effectiveness from the superior shrewdness and skill of the executive and supervisory staffs that plan and direct their battles.

The overall superiority of the management of the concerns engaged in mass distribution manifests itself at many points throughout the process of retailing, as in purchasing, control of stock, store housekeeping, location of individual stores, display of merchandise, alertness and skill in selling, and the use of accounting analysis. It results in a general tendency of the large organizations to perceive changing business conditions quickly and respond to them with intelligent changes in policy and methods. For instance, the executives of chain systems are likely to observe the existence of a falling price level and to adapt their operations to it more quickly than the managers of independent stores. They are more hospitable to new ideas and less unwilling to try new methods of retailing. Of course, the more able of the independent operators can beat them at this game, but the average individual storekeeper prefers to do a thing in the way in which it has always been done, nor is he likely to manifest a great deal of ingenuity in discovering or developing new techniques or selling devices.

On the other hand, the very size of the mass retailing firm tends to limit the extent to which it can make profitable use of its managerial talent, especially in the middle and lower executive echelons. The effective control of a large enterprise usually requires that its operation be standardized to a considerable degree. This is apt to hobble the initiative, ingenuity, and judgment of the store, department, or district manager. In addition, it subtracts substantially from the flexibility with which the mass retailing firm can adapt its operations to changes in local or trade conditions.

In spite of this handicap, the mass retailing concern has a built-in capacity to introduce new merchandise or operating methods with the minimum of risk to its existence or competitive position. The management of a chain system, for example, may wish to try out the sale of an article that seems foreign to its accepted line. It can place the item on sale in one store or one district, thus risking only the volume of that unit and leaving the rest of its business unaffected. Some years ago a chain system operating on a cash basis tried out instalment selling, first in one store, then in all the stores in one district, before putting it into effect throughout the system. To a lesser degree the department store and the mail order house can use the same device but, with only a slight change in his merchandise or his methods, the independent merchant may hazard his entire venture.

While for the several reasons outlined the management of the average independent store is apt to lack flexibility, the entire system of independent stores possesses a great measure of it. This arises from the fact that the vast body of independent store managers, actual and potential, always contains a group of imaginative, adventuresome individuals who are handicapped by neither custom, tradition, nor "top brass" rulings. They are free to start something new, something designed or adapted to meet a changed market situation, such as the supermarket or the discount house, both of which began as independent store operations.

The discount house illustrates adaptation very well. It is often regarded as a new type of retailing establishment. In fact, it is as old as the retailing business: in essence it is nothing other than a self-service, price-appeal store in a trade or group of trades whose members by "fair trade" and franchise arrangements sought to insulate themselves from price competition.

LOCATING THE STORE

One of the most important tasks a merchant must perform in starting a retail store is selecting a location for it. The factors affecting this decision depend upon the type of store he intends to operate, the line of goods he hopes to sell, and the classes of people to whom he desires to sell them.

In selecting a location for his store a merchant should consider the retail anatomy of the area in which it is to be situated. At least five general types of urban retail locations or areas can be distinguished:

1. *The Central or Downtown Shopping District.* This is the part of the city in which retail stores are concentrated and is usually convenient to all parts of the metropolitan area. All types of merchandise and services are sold here, although shopping and specialty goods predominate.

2. *The Subcenter, or Secondary Cluster.* This is a reproduction of the central shopping district on a smaller scale and serves only a portion or a subcommunity of the city. All types of merchandise are sold, although convenience goods predominate.

3. *The String-Street Location.* Stores are frequently scattered along a street for a number of blocks like beads strung on a string. This retail structure is most likely to be found on a radial street, but may occur on right-angled thoroughfares as well. Establishments so located are usually patronized both by nearby residents and by persons using the street's transportation facilities. All types of goods and services are generally sold by such stores, although there seems to be some tendency toward specialization; automobile dealers, for example, all tend to locate on the same street. A change in traffic regulations, or in the quality of the paving, or the opening of new subway facilities nearby, or new through streets may entirely change the character of the patronage available to stores in such a location.

In recent years a variation of the string-street location has developed in the form of stores clustered along main highways through suburban areas. Such locations have been found satisfactory for certain types of shopping and specialty goods outlets, such as furniture and electrical household appliance stores. These stores enjoy the benefit of much lower occupancy costs than their downtown competitors; they have ample parking facilities and they are able to bid for the patronage not only of people living nearby but of transients as well.

4. *The Neighborhood Location.* This is a small cluster of stores, usually grouped about the intersection of two through streets in a residential district and serving the people living in that district. Many such groups are scattered throughout the average city. These establishments sell mainly convenience goods and services (barbershops, beauty parlors, cleaning and dyeing firms). Practically their entire business comes from the persons living in the immediate neighborhood.

A modification of the neighborhood location which is developing many of the characteristics of the downtown shopping center is the suburban shopping center, such as the Shoppers' World outside of Boston, the Cross-County Shopping Center or the Bergen Mall near New York City. These are situated conveniently to main-travelled motor arteries and offer extensive parking facilities. Downtown stores are liberally represented by branches. Such a center attracts patronage from an extensive surrounding area, even from the parent city itself.

5. *The Nonconcentrated Location.* This is a retail site that, for some reason, stands alone and bears little if any relation to other stores. Examples are the drugstore or delicatessen shop serving a single apartment house, the confectionery store near a school, the newspaper stand near a bus or subway stop, and the motorists' store on a main traffic artery.

Choosing the Spot for the Store

The factors affecting store location in each of these types of sites or areas differ, and the retail manager will be wise to recognize these differences in choosing a place for his establishment.

The factors vary with the kind of goods sold. If the merchant's stock is to consist chiefly of shopping goods, he should locate in the shopping district of his trading area. The precise site that he selects is perhaps less important than it would be if he were selling convenience goods. The retailer of the latter type of merchandise must establish his store at a point that is most convenient to his prospective customers. If he plans to operate a downtown volume store he should select a site at which currents of pedestrian traffic cross one another or converge. If he intends to conduct a neighborhood store he will be wise to seek a location that can be most easily and conveniently reached by the majority of his prospective customers or to which they naturally or habitually come to shop.

The prospective retail merchant should analyze the market he seeks to serve and attempt to determine whether a need exists for a new store of the type he proposes to open: whether there are not already too many well-managed outlets bidding for the available business. The really efficient operator need not be unduly discouraged by the mere number of rivals in the market; there is almost always plenty of room for another *good* one. He should seek, rather, to analyze the quality of his prospective competition. A single, really good, ably managed competitive establishment is more dangerous than a dozen carelessly conducted, slovenly stores which fail to serve adequately the needs and wishes of the people of the community.

The traffic count is a device that is commonly used in selecting locations for stores selling convenience goods. It consists of counting the number of persons who pass by the site under consideration. In making this analysis, mere numbers are not particularly significant; the *character* of the passersby must be determined. Among other factors, the following are vital: the proportion of men, of women, and of children; where they are going (commuters moving from or to a train, for instance, are in the market for certain types of goods but not for others, while women wheeling baby carriages are better prospects for groceries than are high school girls on the way to or from school); and their purchasing power. The chain systems have used this device with unusual effectiveness, but it can be profitably employed by the independent merchant as well.

The merchant who is seeking a location for a store selling shopping merchandise should carefully study the transportation facilities serving the trading area from which he hopes to attract customers. He should seek a site that is conveniently located with respect to suburban streetcar or bus routes and stops, commuter stations of railroads, subway and elevated lines and stations, and parking space. The shrewd retail manager constantly studies the shifts in population and changes in traffic facilities which occur in his trading area and seeks to adjust his operations to them.

Certain types of stores gather strength from being located near one another, and some weaken one another in close proximity. For instance, the grouping of women's millinery shops, shoe shops, jewelry stores, and apparel stores near a common trading center facilitates shopping; the presence of each attracts trade for all the others. On the other hand, nearness to a meat store is likely to be very damaging to the trade of a millinery shop, and the proximity of an undertaking establishment is almost certain to be poisonous to practically every other type of retailing enterprise. Even funeral parlors, however, are preferable to a contiguous vacant building or storeroom or near-by wornout structure in obvious disrepair.

The rental demanded for a site should be a major consideration in selecting a retail location. In making his selection the retail manager must balance the rent that he must pay for a given site against the volume of sales he can probably make there and the net profit he will enjoy from them. The mere rental figure, in and of itself, means nothing except in relation to probable sales. In some parts of the country there is a growing tendency for the rental figure set in the retail lease to be a fixed percentage of the total gross sales of the store operated on the premises. This practice assures the retailer of a constant occupancy burden upon his sales, although at the same time it tends to deprive him of part of the benefits he might otherwise receive as a result of superior acumen in selecting his site or of persistence and skill in bargaining for it.

Store Types and Location

Since the department store is a shopping institution it must usually be situated at some point within the shopping district of the city it serves. Location at a precise point is generally not vitally important, although, since this type of store can use window displays with unusual effectiveness as a means of selling, it is highly desirable that it should have as much window space as possible facing main-travelled shopping streets, and proximity to parking space is of growing importance.

Because of its standardized stocks and methods of operation, the chain system is somewhat better adapted to function in "volume" (rather than "neighborhood") locations. The independent store, on the other hand, is usually well suited to serve the needs of a neighborhood trade. Its unstandardized stocks and operating practices enable it to cater to local and individual trading habits and peculiarities of demand. Each of these retailing institutions has its own natural locational stronghold from which it can cater to the class of consumer demand it is best adapted to serve. The mailorder house has some advantage in this regard in that it need not be located in a high-rent retail district but may set up its offices and warehouses at outlying points, so long as they are served by adequate transportation facilities.

The multi-unit system has certain advantages over the independent store in the matter of selecting locations. It can usually do the job in a much more systematic manner than the average independent merchant. In its records it has a fund of accumulated experience of the sales performance of various types of sites, upon which its managers may draw in considering each individual case. It is equipped to carry on much more careful and complete investigations and studies of specific locations than the independent merchant can attempt. It has the facilities with which to collect exact and detailed facts about local trends of business, to make traffic counts, and to observe shopping habits. On the other hand, it does not possess the intimate knowledge and "feel" of a neighborhood which comes from long residence in it. This advantage the prospective independent storekeeper is likely to have, although it seems to exercise less effect than might be expected because the performance of the chain systems in selecting sites appears to have been uniformly superior to that of the independent merchants.

Because of its greater volume of sales the typical multi-unit firm can afford to pay a higher rent for a given location than the average independent store. As a result, it usually outbids its smaller rivals in the competition for desirable sites.

The chain system is probably more flexible in the matter of location than the independent store. When a mistake is made in the selection of a specific site, the former can usually remedy it more quickly and with less loss than the latter. The proprietor of the independent store often owns the property in which his business is located. It is thus difficult for him to move, nor can he withdraw from business without serious loss in disposing of his furnishings, even if he does not own the building that houses his store. Typically, the chain system is a tenant. It paints, lays out, and decorates each of its units to look much like every other. When it moves, therefore, it does not suffer the lost patronage which the independent store usually sustains from presenting a changed appearance in a new location. When an independent merchant selects a location or moves from one site to another, he stakes his entire business future on the decision; in making a similar choice the chain system hazards only a small portion of its total business.

The larger chain systems maintain real estate departments which specialize in the work of negotiating leases or purchases of desirable sites. In general, therefore, their realty operations are conducted more efficiently than those of the average independent store. The presence of a unit of a well managed, aggressive chain system in a retail district tends to increase rentals in its immediate vicinity. This fact sometimes induces landlords to make concessions in order to obtain them as tenants. On the other hand, since property owners know that, because of its large volume of sales per outlet, the chain system is able to pay high rentals, they often demand more from it than they would from an independent merchant.

On the whole, however, the chain system possesses a distinct advantage over its independent competitor in the work of selecting and obtaining sites upon which to locate its units.

The supermarket manager faces a special problem in location. Because of the serve-yourself, carry-home nature of his operations, he must provide a place for his customers to park while they shop. This parking space must be adjacent to or very convenient to the store. The need for such space is one of the governing features in the location of a supermarket. For every square foot of store space the supermarket must provide from 2.3 to 4.4 square feet of parking space, depending on volume of sales.

This limits the locations open to supermarkets. They often find it impossible to obtain sites in the established business sections of cities and must locate in the outskirts or in newly developed or developing communities on the periphery. Only slightly more than 10 percent of the supermarket stores opened during the years of their peak growth were in large, long-established shopping centers. The need for parking space also tends to make occupancy cost a highly significant factor in the expense pattern of this type of store.

During the early years of the discount house, its manager had to find a location not too far away from the retailing center but where rents were low. As it has developed and become more like a cut-price hard goods store, or in some cases a department store featuring price appeal, it has had to be more selective in its location. Now such outlets are to be found in the recognized shopping areas of many cities and in some suburban shopping centers. If the discount house extends its merchandise offerings to include clothing and other soft goods items, as well as the hard goods with which it started, its managers will probably find that location in a desirable site in a shopping area is necessary and that the suburban shopping center with its ample parking space is pretty nearly ideal.

The quality store has location problems of its own. Not very many people in a given population have either the taste or the pocketbook to patronize such a store. The effect of this is reflected in the reply of the president of a New York quality department store to the question:

"Why don't you start a branch in Bergen County, New Jersey?"

"If you will suggest a spot in the area which has within a radius of X miles Y thousands of families with incomes of over Z dollars, we will put a store there."

PROVIDING BUILDING, FACILITIES, AND LAYOUT

The average retailer usually has little opportunity to determine the construction and layout of the space or building in which his store is located. Certain structures or spaces are available, and since he lacks the capital needed to erect his own, he leases the one he considers most desirable and does the best he can with it. The large department stores and the chain systems usually are able either to build structures to house their enterprises or induce property owners to build or remodel to fit their requirements. Outright ownership of a site is dangerous for the average retailer since it limits his flexibility and saddles his enterprise with a fixed occupancy charge regardless of volume. Since so few merchants can exercise any measure of control over this matter, we will not consider it in detail but will be content to mention a few of the more important factors involved in the work of equipping and furnishing the store space once it is acquired.

The shelving, counters, and other fixtures used must vary with the nature of the store, the merchandise it handles, and the character of the customers it serves. Refrigeration equipment excepted, much more expensive and impressive furniture and fixtures are necessary in a store that sells shopping or quality goods than in one which vends groceries or tobacco products or emphasizes the price appeal. A retail establishment that is too ornate and expensive looking scares away customers with modest pocketbooks, while a shabby, down-at-heels store is liable to have but little appeal for the "carriage" trade. The wise merchant seeks to appraise the character and background of his customers and to equip and furnish his store so as to serve their convenience and please their tastes.

There has been an almost universal tendency to increase the amount of merchandise on display and to make it convenient for the customers to handle and to examine the goods. This has been done by the use of glass display cases for perishable merchandise and by installing "island" display tables, bins, and platforms in what were formerly the aisles of the store. These changes have usually proved to be pleasing to the customers and profitable to the merchant. The popularity of quick-frozen

foods has resulted in material changes in the equipment of many grocery and meat stores and added greatly to the expense involved in
furnishing such establishments.

One of the most important physical features of the average retail
store is its lighting system. Proper lighting has been so largely reduced
to a science that there now exists no really valid excuse for its absence
in a retail store, except lack of capital.

The governing factors in equipping and furnishing a store are practically universal: the furniture and fixtures should suit the convenience
of customers; they should be attractive to prospective patrons of the
store and conform to their ideas of good taste and propriety; they should
aid in displaying the merchandise; and they should be of maximum
service to customers in their search for and selection of the commodities
they desire to purchase.

Layout

The layout of a store depends primarily upon the lines of merchandise it sells. The first task involved in laying out a store is to divide the
articles in its stock into groups or departments. The merchant must
also plan for housing the various special services he expects to offer
and the physical functions that are involved in conducting the enterprise. It is usually desirable to carry on these activities in a space that
is not particularly suitable for selling purposes. In general, the selling
value of space varies inversely with its distance from the main entrance,
the most valuable being the front windows and the area immediately
inside the entrance.

There are several bases upon which goods may be classified into
groups for purposes of layout. Articles which customers tend to buy
together should usually be stocked near one another; items that are of
the same general type (for instance, different varieties and brands of
breakfast foods in a grocery store) belong together; bulky articles often
are placed near one another; commodities that require the storekeeper
to render about the same type and amount of service in the process of
vending them to the customer (articles sold from the fountain as contrasted with those dispensed over the prescription counter of a drugstore, for example) are assigned to the same group; items that have
about the same rate of stock turnover or the same margin of gross profit
are often stocked together.

Several factors are usually considered in allocating space in a store
to the several groups or divisions of goods it stocks:

1. The sales and profit possibilities of an article or group of articles

usually influence its location. In general, the commodities having the greatest potential sales volume or promising the most net income to the business are placed in the most valuable or efficient selling spaces.

2. The merchandise should be so arranged as to make the entire store as attractive as possible to its customers. This means that articles having high display possibilities are placed in the most conspicuous spaces.

3. The merchandise should be so located on the selling floor as to minister to the convenience of the customers. To work out this principle it is necessary to study the natural flow of traffic within the store. The articles most frequently desired should be on sale where people expect to find them and in the spaces to which persons entering the store will naturally drift if left to themselves.

4. Goods should be so located as to facilitate and speed up the work of serving customers. This purpose is usually served by shelving near one another those articles that the average buyer tends to include in the same order.

5. It is usually wise to lay out a store so that joint-demand articles are near one another. The woman who buys a dress, for instance, may often be induced to buy certain accessory articles of apparel to go with it if they are on sale near the point where she purchases the garment. The store should be laid out to suit the convenience of customers and to conform to their habits.

Since the department store really consists of a group of stores, each dealing in a different line of merchandise and all using the same sort of equipment, and served by the same maintenance facilities and staff, it can afford a higher grade of equipment and select it more intelligently than the average limited-line store. This results partly from the specialized managerial talent which its larger volume of sales enables it to employ, and partly from the greater quantities in which it purchases furniture, fixtures, and other similar articles.

The chain system has a considerable advantage in this respect. Its managers can enforce a high degree of uniformity in the equipment of its different units. As a result it can buy furniture and fixtures in large quantities, and therefore at advantageous prices. The large scale of its operations enables it to conduct careful studies of such matters as store equipment and layout, and by trial-and-error tests to discover the most effective materials and plans for furnishing its units. It follows that the average chain store is equipped and laid out much more scientifically than the typical independent outlet, whose appointments and furnishings often depend upon the whim and taste (or lack of it) of the proprietor, or the persuasiveness of the salesmen of the supply houses from which he buys them.

The standardization of the equipment and layout of the several stores of the same chain system and the uniformity of their appearance constitute a tremendous advantage in metropolitan areas. The population in such districts is highly mobile. When a woman moves from one part of a city or from one suburb to another, practically the only familiar features of her new neighborhood shopping center are the storefront and interior layout of the local unit of the grocery, drug, or variety chain system she patronized in her old community. This is a very potent advantage in the struggle to gain and hold the patronage of a rapidly shifting population.

The chain systems have taught their independent competitors much about the promotional advantages of neatness, orderliness, and cleanliness in the layout and maintenance of retail stores. Throughout their history they have emphasized these features. Through their supervisory staffs they have enforced a fairly high standard with respect to all of them. Much of the chain stores' consumer patronage, especially that of women, was first enticed by the bait of their attractive appearance, resulting mainly from the neatness, care, and taste with which the furniture, fixtures, and stock were placed and arranged, and from their scrupulous cleanliness. While some independent merchants have learned to emulate them in this performance, all too many have remained blind to the promotional importance of these elementary features of store housekeeping.

The early supermarkets were equipped with the crudest and cheapest furniture and fixtures, shelving, tables, and display units often being constructed on the spot, and the customers being supplied with ordinary baskets in which to collect their purchases. The present units of this type of outlet must be well furnished and equipped with the most modern display cases. Since the supermarket operates on the basis of a large volume made up of a tremendous number of relatively small unit purchases made by people who serve themselves, a layout that facilitates the flow of customer traffic, fixtures that lend the maximum visibility to merchandise and add to the convenience of picking it off the shelf, and lighting that emphasizes the attractiveness of the goods are vital. The supermarket possesses no particular advantage over other types in the procurement of its equipment unless it is a member of a chain.

Much the same considerations apply to the discount house, and will become more important if its present trend in the direction of soft goods and house furnishings lines continues.

The independent stores that are members of strong voluntary or co-operative groups overcome most of their natural disadvantages in layout, furniture, and fixtures. Many such groups are equipped to supply their members advisory service fully as good as that of most chain systems, and, when they buy store facilities centrally, their purchases are in sufficient quantity to assure them the lowest prices.

The quality-service store must have a building, equipment, layout, and fixtures that create an atmosphere of quiet elegance. Its milieu must be rich but not ostentatiously so—and this is the kind that *really* costs money. On the other hand, the merchant who emphasizes price will usually find it desirable to avoid too rich an atmosphere; it is apt to scare his customers away or raise doubts as to his claims about price. Since he usually operates on a narrow margin and minimum service, and expects to make a small unit profit on a large volume of sales, he needs facilities that will help him get customers and their purchases through the store and out as fast as is consistent with exposing them to maximum amount of buying temptation in the form of merchandise.

PROVIDING CAPITAL

One of the most important functions which the retail merchant must perform is estimating the financial needs of his enterprise and providing funds to meet them. If it were possible to exhume and hold coroner's inquests upon the recorded remains of the occupants of retailing's "Boot Hill," one of the most frequent verdicts would probably be: "The deceased came to an untimely end by starvation through lack of adequate capital."

Providing funds is not a process that can be done once and for all when the store is started. It is a continuous process and becomes increasingly important and difficult as the business grows. The retailing business is especially susceptible to the disease of "over-trading"—trying to do a larger volume of business than the store's capital can safely support. When this happens, the capital is spread so thin that the least miscalculation or mistake in timing will throw the firm into bankruptcy.

A retail store needs two kinds of capital: that which remains permanently invested in the project and is used constantly by it, and that which is needed only during certain seasons and may be withdrawn and replaced from time to time. The person who proposes to start a retail business should own or be able to obtain through a long-time loan, on not-too-stringent terms, all the funds required to furnish the permanent capital needed for his enterprise. Its seasonal and emergency financial requirements may usually be satisfied safely by means of short-term loans, provided its operating record and condition justify such extensions of credit.

In computing the long-time capital needs of his establishment, the would-be retail merchant should include enough funds to pay for his furniture and fixtures. Many of the concerns that sell such equipment are willing to finance its purchase on the basis of open-book accounts, notes, or instalment contracts. The new storekeeper who takes advantage of these arrangements subjects his business to a constant drain upon its current income during the period of its initial development when every penny is badly needed in the struggle to grasp and to hold a share of the market.

He should also make sure that there is enough permanent capital in his business to pay for the basic stock of merchandise that he expects to carry. He can obtain much of this stock on credit from the wholesalers and manufacturers from whom he buys. In so doing, however, he limits the sources from which he can purchase and thereby restricts his selection of merchandise, forgoes the possibility of taking advantage of especially attractive cash bargains that may be offered by "distressed" sellers, and increases the delivered cost of his goods because of his inability to earn the cash discounts that may be allowed. When purchases are made on 2 percent 10 days; net 30 days terms,[1] it will be profitable for the purchaser to borrow money at any rate of interest less than 36 percent annually in order to pay within the 10-day period and thus deduct the 2 percent from the face of his bill. It is obvious that capital obtained in the form of credit from suppliers is often very expensive to the retail merchant. Even in securing the funds with which to purchase seasonal and emergency stocks, it is wiser for the storekeeper to borrow from a bank than to buy on credit when attractive cash discounts are allowed.

The new merchant's permanent capital should also be sufficient to pay all the operating expenses of his store for a period long enough to enable him to get under way and to build up a clientele for his establishment. The merchant who allows his optimism too free a rein in estimating this requirement is liable to find himself in financial difficulties almost before he opens the doors of his store to the public.

---

[1]Such terms authorize the buyer to deduct 2 percent of the total of the bill from the amount he pays, provided he pays within 10 days after the date of the invoice. The entire amount is due and payable 30 days after that date. This means that the buyer of goods priced at $100, who pays at the *end* of 30 days, pays $2 for the use of $98 for 20 days.

A merchant should also have enough permanent capital to enable his new retail business to finance all extensions of credit he expects to make to his customers. In computing his requirements for this purpose he should assume that many of his patrons will not pay within the credit period he designates. He must be prepared, therefore, to finance these additional involuntary credit extensions. Some retail establishments can obtain funds to finance credit extensions by borrowing from banks on the security of their accounts receivable. But a bank credit officer is likely to be more than usually dubious about the future prospects of a firm that finds it necessary to borrow on its accounts receivable too soon after it begins to do business.

The permanent capital of a new store should also be enough to enable it to meet any of the ordinary emergencies that are likely to arise, and to finance the sales-promotional work that must be done to build up a satisfactory and profitable patronage. The expenses involved in promotional work may include, among others, the costs of staging some sort of "opening event," of advertising and display, of prizes which may be offered in the course of conducting publicity campaigns, and the losses on merchandise that is sold at less than cost in order to attract patronage.

Some of the permanent capital of a new retail establishment may be borrowed on a long-time basis if the merchant can find a willing lender. He should understand, however, that by obtaining funds in this manner he saddles his business with a recurring interest and amortization expense which will be a continuous drain on his current income and handicap his every operation until it is paid off. It will probably be best for him to supply his seasonal capital requirements by means of bank loans, since any additions made to the permanent capital for this purpose must necessarily be idle much of the time.

The sources from which the small retail firm can draw capital funds are limited to the assets of the owner or owners, loans from acquaintances, and bank loans. To many small storekeepers the bank is not readily available as a source, either because they do not maintain accounting systems from which they can compile operating records to enable a banker to evaluate their credit, or, if they do have adequate accounts, the resulting operating statements are not such as a banker can view with enthusiasm.

The volume operation, whether it be an independent supermarket, a department store, a chain system, or a large specialty store, is able to make use of most of the capital sources supplied by the financial market. Such a firm is usually a corporation and has an accounting system designed to supply exhaustive operating statistics. It is thus able to raise funds by issuing stocks or bonds, borrowing from banks, or pledging accounts receivable or merchandise inventories with finance companies to obtain loans. The large concern can also afford to employ financial specialists to manage its funds.

Size and quality of management are the big factors that tip the competitive scales with respect to this factor.

MANAGING MERCHANDISE

For most retailers merchandise management consists in deciding what merchandise to buy for resale, and how much of it, and when. A few of the larger firms find it worthwhile, in addition, to carry on or arrange for research to originate products which they may produce or have produced for them to resell. Since this activity is rather unusual we will reserve its discussion until later and direct our attention first to the merchandising work of the ordinary retailer who must choose from among the articles offered to him.

What to Buy

In a sense, the manager of a retail store may be said to function as a purchasing agent for the ultimate consumer. His success or failure as a merchant will depend largely on the accuracy with which he senses and interprets the desires of his potential customers for merchandise and services and upon the resolution and skill he displays in acting on his interpretations. He has a number of sources from which he can get such information.

1. *Records.* In dealing with certain types of commodities he can safely rely on the theory that what people have bought in the past and are buying now they will want to buy in the future. In merchandising other products, such as style goods, precisely the opposite is apt to be true, although today's customer behavior may be indicative of tomorrow's—provided the "tomorrow" is not projected too far into the future. In observing and interpreting customer behavior toward merchandise the retail manager, even of a small store, can not safely rely on memory, for it is apt to be tricky and not always reliable. Accurate and detailed sales records are necessary in the use of this source of information.

2. *Customer Requests.* The requests of customers for articles not in stock are significant but not infallible indexes of consumer demand. Many managers of larger stores require their salespeople to fill out and submit "want slips" reporting such inquiries. Operators of small estab-

lishments, who themselves function as salespeople, often rely on memory for such information. Even in such cases some form of written record, however informal, is preferable because here, too, memory is notoriously tricky.

3. *Supplier's Advertising.* If a supplier plans a heavy, well prepared program of advertising of his product, the chances are that there will be an upward surge of demand, if the product is an old one, and some initial demand if it is new. The promotional plans of the manufacturer are worth study by the retailer handling his product.

4. *Marketing Research.* A few retailers, mainly large ones, use marketing research to discover the merchandise preferences of their customers. This is generally too expensive for the small merchant and has not been used very extensively by the big ones.

5. *Competitors' Experience.* If a retailer's competitor offers a product and seems to be selling it, it is likely that he should have it too, although it is rather unusual for a store to attain great success by being merely an expert follower and never a leader. The executives of large firms, especially department stores, rely on their "comparison" or "shopping" bureaus for information about the merchandise their competitors are offering and how it is selling. Comparison shopping of fashion merchandise may disclose styles that are growing in popularity and those whose demand is fading.

6. *Trial.* The best test of whether a product will sell is to try it. So many retailers follow the policy of buying trial lots (sometimes returnable) of new products and observing how they move off the shelves.

None of these methods is infallible. But the intelligent use of all of them, or such of them as fit the operating conditions of the individual store, is likely to improve the merchant's performance of the merchandise selection function.

How Much and When to Buy

This involves the management of inventory. In order to be in business at all the retailer has to have a certain basic stock——for each item the typical customer expects to find in such a store, there should be enough stock to supply the demands customers may reasonably be expected to make for it. Various factors, some of which the manager can control and some of which he cannot, may cause actual stock to fluctuate above and below this figure. The important facts regarding inventory are (*a*) *the amount on hand,* because this determines the amount of the retailer's capital that is tied up in stock, and (*b*) *the rate of flow-*

through, which determines how often he makes a profit or incurs a loss on the typical dollar invested in inventory. Without adequate records of stock all efforts to manage inventory are apt to be futile, for neither of the above basic facts can be known to the manager.

Three measures of flow-through are commonly applied to retail stocks.

1. *Stock Turnover.* When a merchant who has a dozen cans of Buster's Bullet-Baked Beans on his shelf sells them all and buys another dozen cans of the same indigestibles, he has enjoyed one turnover of his stock of Buster's Bullet-Baked Beans. Usually, however, this measure is computed in dollars instead of units of product. Two formulas may be used in computing it.

The Cost Formula: $\text{Stock Turnover} = \dfrac{\text{Cost of Goods Sold}}{\text{Average Inventory at Cost}}$

The Retail Formula: $\text{Stock Turnover} = \dfrac{\text{Net Sales}}{\text{Average Inventory at Selling Price}}$

Cost of goods sold for a period is *inventory at the beginning of the period, plus purchases during the period, minus inventory at the end of the period.* When stock turnover is computed on an annual basis, as is usually the case, *average inventory* for a small store is apt to be one half the sum of the Beginning Inventory and the Final Inventory; the big concern is apt to average 12 monthly or even 52 weekly inventories. The Retail Method of computing stock turnover is used mainly by department stores, which follow the practice of carrying merchandise in stock at the price at which they expect to sell it instead of at cost.

2. *Stock-Sales Ratio.* This ratio is computed, usually on a monthly basis, by dividing the value of either the beginning or the ending (preferably the beginning) inventory for the period by the sales during the period. It is used mainly by department stores and, since both their sales and their inventory figures are expressed at selling prices, it provides a fairly accurate measure of flow-through. If stocks are carried at cost, shifts in the items composing the inventory involving changes in gross margin are apt to cause the stock-sales ratio to present a distorted picture of what is happening to a store's inventory.

3. *Number of Days (Weeks) Stock.* This figure results from dividing the inventory (expressed either in dollars or units) by the average sales per day (week), expressed in the same terms. While stock turnover and the stock-sales ratio are almost always computed from dollars, and cover the entire inventory, number of days stock is apt to be figured on the basis of units and for individual items.

Two Examples of Stock
Flow-through Measures

A Small Store

Sales: $120,000 a year.
Initial inventory: $22,000 at cost.
Final inventory: $23,000 at cost.
Purchases during year: $91,000.
Cost of goods sold: $22,000   plus $91,000 = $113,000
                less $23,000 = $ 90,000
Average inventory: $22,500.
  $90,000 ÷ $22,500 = 4 stockturns (by Cost Formula).

Inventory April 1: $23,000 at cost.
Sales during April: $13,000.
  $23,000 ÷ $13,000 = 1.77 Stock-Sales Ratio.

Selling days during April: 26.
$13,000 ÷ 26 = $500 (sales per day).
Cost of goods sold per day: $375 (75% of $500).
Inventory April 30: $22,500.
  $22,500 ÷ $375 = 60 days stock.

A Department Store

Sales: $12,000,000.
Average of 12 monthly inventories: $2,000,000 at retail.
  $12,000,000 ÷ $2,000,000 = 6 stockturns (by Retail Method).

Sales during April: $1,200,000.
Inventory April 1: $2,600,000.
  $2,600,000 ÷ $1,200,000 = 2.17 (Stock-Sales Ratio).

Selling days in April: 26.
$1,200,000 ÷ 26 = $46,154 sales per day.
Inventory April 30: $2,400,000.
  $2,400,000 ÷ 46,154 = 52 days stock.

A series of annual or semi-annual stock turnover figures provides a good indication of the long-run trend of inventories and of the quality of inventory management. The trend of stock-sales ratios supplies the same thing on a short run basis. Number of days stock offers a very potent tool for making quantitative and timing decisions about buying. Neither stock turnover figures nor stock-sales ratios are of much use in maintaining a most important characteristic of a satisfactory inventory: balance. An inventory is out of balance when it contains more of one article than the store needs and less than it requires of another. If continued, such imbalance is likely to show up in an increase in the stock-sales ratio and a slowing of the stock turnover rate, but neither of these measures affords the manager any clues as to where the trouble is. A system of number of days stocks figures will be of great help in finding it.

Many, probably most, retailers buy an habitual amount of an item when its inventory drops to a predetermined figure. Both of these critical amounts are standards, however informally they may be arrived at, and they reflect the storekeeper's notion of what a standard inventory of the item should be. Other retail managers use an "open to buy" computation, generally on a monthly basis, that goes something like this:

What you expect to sell during the month, *plus* the inventory you want at the end of the month, *minus* what you have at the beginning of the month, *equals* open-to-buy: what you plan to buy during the month.

This computation can be made in dollars, or in units of product, or in both—which is probably the best way to do it.

All schemes of this sort depend on the establishment, either formally or informally, of standards of inventory and determinations of what inventory should be. Although very few retail managers employ mathematical formulas in computing inventory standards, they can be very useful for that purpose. Practically all the factors involved can be expressed in figures. These factors usually are:

1. *The cost of possession,* which includes the cost of storage space, interest, or other return on funds invested in stock, and losses from obsolesence.

2. *The cost of buying an order,* which includes the expense of time and materials used in negotiating and preparing it and all expenses involved in receiving a shipment and merging it with inventory.

3. *The effect of the size of the order* on the purchase price of the goods.

4. *The cost of business lost* because of merchandise shortages.

It does not require mathematical genius to prepare from these factors an equation or equations that will yield an economical inventory figure and an economical order quantity. The only one of the factors that is apt to be hard to quantify is the loss of business through stock shortages. Proper records should enable managemnet to set a minimum figure for this in the form of immediate losses of sales due to inability to meet requests for merchandise. Long-run losses due to damaged goodwill must probably be estimated.

Buying Merchandise

Too often the retailer regards the function of buying merchandise as a minor one, to be done at odd times when no really worthwhile work claims his attention. Too often it is performed by merely compiling and copying on an order blank a want-list of items, the stocks of which are low, or by checking with a supplier's salesman the goods on the shelves, authorizing him to enter in his order book the items that are running short, and refusing all his offers of new merchandise except those about which he is so unusually insistent that he wears down the merchant's resistance.

Merchandising and buying are two of the retailer's most important functions. Well-selected goods, well bought, are more than half sold. The store manager should conscientiously search out and cultivate every source of buying information and use every device by which his bargaining power may be increased and made more effective. The large retailing establishment recognizes the importance of this function by making a separate department responsible for it and assigning specialists to perform it. In the smaller store it is usually done on a part-time basis by the proprietor or by some employee designated for the task.

Many retailers are content to allow their sources to seek them out and make contact with them through salesmen. When the merchant practices this policy he should make every effort to maintain cordial relations with a sufficiently numerous and varied group of sources to be sure that he will receive an adequate offering of merchandise from which to make his selections and that there will be enough keen competition among them to enable him to obtain his goods at favorable prices. But he must also be careful not to buy from so many sources that he loses quantity discounts and his business is not worthwhile to any of them. Buying frequently and in small orders from too many sources tends to lose the retailer many valuable services which suppliers are prepared to render to profitable customers.

Retailing establishments that deal in fashion merchandise or certain types of perishable goods which must be examined in the process of appraisal usually send representatives to the market to do the work of buying. This facilitates the collection of fashion information, makes possible a detailed comparison of the offerings of different sources, enables the buyer to see fashion merchandise displayed on living models, and aids in playing one source against another in the attempt to obtain favorable prices and terms.

How Well They Merchandise

In theory the manager of the independent store is in an exceptionally favorable position from which to observe and capitalize upon the precise characteristics and dimensions of consumer demand in his market. He is usually a native of the community in which his store is located; he knows many of his prospective customers personally (often from childhood); he is a neighbor to them all and a friend and playfellow of many of them; and for a long time he has had the opportunity to observe their whims and peculiarities. He, if anyone, should be able to forecast the kinds of merchandise and the quantities of it they will wish to buy.

To a very considerable extent these theoretical advantages are realized in actual practice. The stocks of the independent store usually are more precisely suited to the requirements of its neighborhood than are those of the chain store, which must generally confine its inventory to a standard list of articles selected by an official or committee in the divisional or central headquarters of the system to which it belongs. But too often the benefits which might flow from this advantage are not realized or are dissipated by bad management. The average independent store operator is peculiarly susceptible to the wiles of the unscrupulous or unintelligent salesman who urges him to buy some plausible article which, since there is no real consumer demand for it, is doomed to gather dust on his shelves. Nor does he usually have the use of any of the supplementary aids to the work of demand and market analysis which mail order houses, department stores, and chain systems so liberally supply to their merchandising executives. He cannot afford a statistical bureau or stylist, nor does he generally operate an accounting system sufficiently detailed so that he can ascertain from it the previous selling performance of each item of merchandise. All too often, therefore, the merchandising history of the independent retailer is a story of unrealized opportunities and neglected advantages.

Since it is essentially a shopping institution, the department store faces a more difficult merchandising task than any other type of retailer. To be successful its manager must forecast the kaleidoscopic shifts of demand in the fast-changing lines of fashion goods. The department store has probably been the leader among retail institutions in developing machinery and techniques to carry on this function. It first placed the task of merchandising under the control of specialists; it developed and applied research techniques in collecting and analyzing information of aid in performing the task; it made use of the technical background, taste, and judgment of the professional fashion expert; it developed its comparison work for the purpose, among others, of keeping its merchandising information up to the minute; and it has installed and operated accounting systems designed to disclose almost hourly the selling experience and inventory position of each item in its stock.

In its merchandising work the management of the mail order house suffers from the difficulty that its decisions must be made a long time ahead of the date when goods are offered for sale. The nature and identity of the articles to be described in its catalog must be determined some months before publication. Nor can the firm's merchandise offerings be changed for from three to six months after copies of the catalog are distributed. It cannot adjust the goods it offers to changes in demand with the speed and accuracy its rivals can achieve. In order to offset this handicap it usually confines its stocks of fashion merchandise to semistandardized items, the demand for which changes slowly. It is practically debarred from handling numerous articles of exceptionally volatile demand.

The merchandising activities of the chain store system are largely conditioned by the fact that a considerable degree of standardization must exist in the goods offered for sale in its several units. This makes it impossible to adapt the stocks of each outlet with any degree of precision to the individual or local wants and needs of its potential customers.

The urge for standardization has sometimes led to results little short of ridiculous. There are hoary tales of a chain unit in the Deep South which was sent a stock of snowshoes; of plain white and conservatively colored handkerchiefs that were vainly displayed by a chain outlet to the negro trade of Harlem; of "specials" of canned fruit that were advertised futilely to the customers of a chain store located in a small town in a fruitgrowing and canning community; and of sugar offered for sale by another in 5-pound, 10-pound, and 15-pound packages to farmers accustomed to buy that product in 50-pound and 100-pound bags. In those sections of large cities which are predominantly foreign, chain stores can capture only a small portion of the total volume of sales because they cannot conform their stocks to the racial or national character of the merchandise demanded.

Most national or sectional chain systems suffer from a continuous conflict between the pressure of their local units for a great variety of special articles to satisfy consumer wants that are peculiar to their several communities, and the insistence of their buyers upon the standardization they need in order to purchase each article in sufficient quantities to earn and win price concessions from their suppliers. Some chain managements have sought to compromise these conflicting interests by requiring their buyers to display to the store managers samples of a great variety of the types of articles in which they deal. Each unit manager then chooses the numbers he wishes to stock. These selections are consolidated for central purchase. This device is especially useful to concerns dealing in merchandise that possesses the fashion element. In the final analysis, however, the conflict in chain merchandising between local peculiarities of demand and the need for standardization of stocks is an irreconcilable one. It may be reduced but not eliminated.

Many chain systems, particularly in the supermarket trade, use buying committees in their merchandising work. One such committee for a supermarket chain includes in its membership about a dozen headquarters buyers and about the same number of district supervisors. Thus, both the buyers' knowledge of the supplying market and the selling executives' feel of the consumer market are pooled. A buying committee makes decisions with respect to the addition of items to stock and deletions of articles from the line. The committee system has great significance to the manufacturer who tries to sell to firms that employ it. It means that his sales representative cannot be content with merely selling the buyer or with generating in the buyer a half-hearted acceptance for the product. He must arouse an enthusiasm that burns vigorously enough to stimulate the buyer to fight for the product in the committee. And he must also give the buyer facts and figures and reselling plans with which to fight for it.

The large retailing firm, whatever trade it may be in, is in a position to develop its own private brands and is apt to find it profitable to do so. Insofar as customers show a preference for goods under a retailer's private brand, he has a species of monopoly on their patronage. If a private brand is to capture the customer's preference, the merchandise sold under it must be good or its price must be low, or both. This means that the firms having such brands do a lot of specification buying; that is, they develop a set of specifications to which an article must be produced and contract with a manufacturer to make the article to those specifications at a specified price for a period agreed upon. The small store usually cannot afford a private brand, although many voluntary groups develop group brands for their members.

The store that features price appeal not only tends to be a close bargainer but places great emphasis on rapid inventory flow-through. Its gross margin is narrow and it must operate on the policy of making a very small profit on each of a large volume of sales dollars and of moving each inventory dollar through the purchase-inventory-sale cycle as often as possible within a period. For example, a store that nets one cent each time it sells a dollar's worth of merchandise must have a stockturn of six times a year to make a profit of 6 percent on money invested in inventory. The management of a price-appeal firm, therefore, is usually entirely ruthless about pruning from its line all items that do not turn rapidly and sell in large volume.

On the other hand, the quality store must work on the principle of making a substantial profit on each of a smaller number of sales dollars and can afford to turn less often its dollar invested in inventory. It is more interested in a wide margin of gross profit, and while not averse to a rapid rate of stock turnover, is not so insistent on it.

The ability to buy favorably is compounded of two elements: (1)

The amount of an article or group of closely related articles that a purchaser is in a position to buy from any one supplier at one time or over a given period, and (2) The skill and experience of the buyer in bargaining. It is generally true that the larger the quantities in which a retailer buys the goods he resells, the greater will be his purchasing power and the lower will be the prices he must pay. The more skillful, experienced, and adroit his buying representatives are and the more intelligently relentless they are in exploiting their bargaining advantages, the less he has to pay for his merchandise.

In the aggregate, the mail order house has tremendous purchasing power. The largest one probably buys annually, for resale by mail, merchandise costing in the neighborhood of two thirds to three quarters of a billion dollars. This total, however, is divided among a large number of items: as many as 140,000. While the bulk of the business of such an establishment probably involves comparatively few articles, its purchases of any one commodity or from any one manufacturer are not so great as they initially seem to be. Of course, in the case of articles that are handled by one of the two large houses in both its mail order and its chain store business, its purchases for these two purposes can be combined and its buying power augmented accordingly. Because of the large total quantities in which the mail order house purchases, it is able to departmentize the function and to effect a high degree of specialization in its performance. Not only are certain executives able to concentrate on the work of buying, but they can specialize by types or groups of articles bought. In their ability to procure merchandise on favorable terms mail order houses as a class probably exceed department stores and compare not unfavorably with the chain systems.

Superior purchasing power is often claimed to be one of the advantages of the department store. This is undoubtedly true of the larger establishments having annual sales of $20 million or more, but these are relatively few. As is the case with the mail order house, the apparently overwhelming buying power of the department store is considerably dissipated by the fact that its total purchases are divided among so many departments and lines of goods. This is much more significant in the case of the latter because of its smaller volume. For instance, during 1958 the average department store made sales amounting to $4,235,000, the average millinery store enjoyed a volume of only $37,000, and the typical shoe store sold only $87,000 worth of footwear and accessory items. The disparity in purchasing power seems to be tremendous.

But let us assume that the typical department store operates 50 merchandise divisions. Each of them has average sales of $84,700. If the volume of the millinery department is near the average, the department store enjoys an advantage in purchasing power of about 2.3 to 1 over its more specialized competitor, while if the sales of its footwear division are not too far from the average, the buying power of the individual shoe store is slightly more than that of its apparently larger rival.

The department store usually commands a considerable degree of skill and experience in those who perform the procurement function for it. Its buyers are or can be thoroughly familiar with the known indicators of consumer demand for the lines of merchandise in which they deal. By virtue of long experience many of them are past masters of all the tricks of bargaining. These qualifications are buttressed by the statistical information collected and analyzed by the store's research staff, by the observation and expert advice of the stylist, by the guidance and counsel of the merchandise manager (who is usually a graduate of the exacting school of experience in which the buyer is a student), and in many cases by the knowledge, skill, and contacts of the personnel of a New York or Paris office buying connection maintained to aid in performing the procurement function.

In its purchasing power the department store is usually equal to or somewhat superior to its independent, specialized store rival, and in the buying skill and experience it commands it is usually distinctly superior; but it does not compare so favorably with the large chain system or mail order house.

One of the chief advantages of the chain method of retail operation is the superior purchasing power it lends to the concerns using it. In the case of a smaller system, of course, this is not so significant, although the advantage begins to be apparent very early in the growth of a chain organization, since the entire volume of its purchases is usually concentrated upon comparatively few articles. The quantities in which some of the larger concerns buy certain articles, however, stagger the imagination. One hears of a chain system that in a single year purchased 45,000 tons of candy; of another which in one year bought 50 million pounds of coffee, 200 million pounds of sugar, and 200 million pounds of soap; of a third which contracted with a single manufacturer for 4,000 miles of lead pencils if laid end to end.

These fantastic figures, when translated into terms of the marketplace, mean lower prices, more favorable terms, special allowances, and other arrangements beneficial to the buyer. The restrictions of the Robinson-Patman Act reduced these advantages considerably. It is likely, however, that in many transactions, very considerable price allowances to the larger chain systems can be legally justified on the ground of the savings in costs of production, sale, or delivery enjoyed by the seller because of the quantity or method in which they purchase or by reason of the sales-promotional services that they are able to offer and that none of their smaller competitors can duplicate. In buying power the chain system clearly tops the retail field.

The chain system is also able to command very superior bargaining ability in the officials who have charge of its procurement work. The purchasing activities of the larger organizations are usually very highly specialized and systematized, and their buyers receive the benefit of every aid which research and science afford. Most of them are equipped for the task by long experience and training.

Due to differences in local demand, the chain system often faces the problem of reconciling the conflicting pressures of good merchandising and effective use of buying power and skill. Good merchandising dictates that the goods offered for sale in the several units of the system should vary to suit differences in demand in the communities where they are located. This requires either local purchasing or central buying of small quantities of many items. If maximum benefit is to be gained from buying power and skill the purchasing must be done at central or district headquarters, and the articles bought must be standardized so each can be purchased in economical quantities.

Some of the larger chain systems seek to reconcile these pressures to some degree by pushing all the buying work down into the regional offices, except that which can be done economically only at the headquarters level. Through its buying committee, a regional supermarket chain realizes some degree of local adaptation of stocks by allowing store managers facing the same peculiarities of demand to pool orders for items not needed by all stores. The actual purchases are then made by the central office. Other chain systems, especially in the department store trade, have the central buyers accumulate samples of merchandise to be shown to the unit store managers or buyers, who then place orders with the central buyers for items they want. These orders are consolidated by items or by suppliers to get as much of the effect of quantity purchasing as possible.

The voluntary and wholesale cooperative groups gain for their members a substantial part of the advantages of quantity buying. The larger ones can also command a high degree of buying skill. The degree to which either type of group can benefit the buying work of its members depends on the strength of the group leadership and the loyalty of its members, expressed in the consistency with which they purchase through the group instead of on their own and in their willingness to conform to the group promotional programs. The latter is important, first, because it tends to increase the group's purchases of the items promoted, and, second, because the manufacturer who grants allowances for store promotions is willing to grant them only for promotional work actually done, not merely promised. In fact, it is probably illegal for him to do otherwise.

The supermarket enjoys the buying advantage of a large volume mainly concentrated in the single product area of food. The average store belonging to the Super Market Institute has annual sales of about $1,851,000, all but about 5 percent of it in foods. However one looks at it, this is a whale of a lot of groceries and should give the unit that retails them considerable purchasing power. This is true of even the independent supermarket, if well managed. About two thirds of the supermarkets apparently belong to chain systems and enjoy the buying advantages of that form of operation as well.

During the period of rapid development of the discount house, when many manufacturers were still fighting to defend the uneconomical retail margins established under the "fair trade" laws, its manager had the double problem of getting merchandise and getting it at a price that enabled him to resell it at a discount. Often his buying had to be done more or less clandestinely to protect his sources from retaliation by the manufacturers.

Now that most manufacturers have become more or less reconciled to the activities of the discount house, its buying activities are becoming much like those of any other store emphasizing price appeal. It is not too hazardous to guess that as time goes on the operations of the discount house will resemble more and more those of the supermarket (with a flavor of the department store) and that its purchasing activities will tend to represent a more or less uneasy marriage of the buying methods of the two.

CHAPTER 7

Retail Stores: Management and Efficiency (Continued)

GETTING THE GOODS SOLD

Like every other marketing manager, the operator of a retail store must try to achieve the most effective mixture of personal selling, advertising, and sales promotion in order to get his goods resold. The usefulness of each of these tools varies between different trades, and different types of stores, and from store to store, according to the character of the community and the operating environment.

Personal Selling

In spite of the strong trend toward self-service, the salesperson still remains in many trades the most important factor determining success or failure. This is especially the case in the quality store, the store selling fashion goods, and the small one-man independent establishment. In a clothing store a good salesperson is almost sure to develop a "following" of customers who ask for him when they visit the store. The doctors are pretty uniformly convinced that entirely too many ailing people consult the local druggist and follow his prescriptions. The hardware store which has a "paint expert" whose advice commands respect can expect to capture more than its share of the community patronage.

Being a good retail salesperson is a harder job than it used to be. Merchandise is constantly becoming more complex and its technology harder to understand. A tremendous proliferation of varieties of the average product has occurred which makes it increasingly difficult to answer the question: "What's the difference between this and that?" A pleasant personality and the gift of "gabmanship" are not enough. In many trades a considerable knowledge about rather highly technical features of merchandise is necessary to enable one to be a good retail salesperson.

Retail salesmanship differs from field salesmanship. The field salesman must make the contact with the customer and impose his presence and his ideas on one who often is reluctant or feigns reluctance. The customer comes to the retail salesperson. Many people who "curl up inside" at the thought of pushing their way into a prospect's office or house can be good retail salespeople. Probably the primary characteristics needed are a sensitivity to the feelings of others and a desire to help, tempered with an appreciation of the boundaries within which helpfulness is economically feasible.

The management of personal selling in the retail business involves the same activities as sales management anywhere: selecting salespeople, training them, assigning their tasks, supervising them and appraising their performance, and providing incentives to induce them to improve performance. The tools for doing these things and the methods of doing them are the same as those used for field salesmen, except that supervision can be much closer and more constant and much more of the training can be done on the job.

How Personal Selling Activities Are Managed

In the small one-man store the management of personal selling activities consists of the attempts of the operator to improve his own selling technique. That this work is done neither conscientiously nor intelligently is evidenced by the fact that, on the average, the selling done in such stores is probably the least efficient of all saleswork in any type of retailing establishment.

In the larger enterprises the management of personal selling takes the form of an attempt by the manager to multiply his own selling ability, or that of his ablest salespeople by the total number of his selling employees through carefully training and supervising them. In the larger department stores and chain systems this work is highly specialized, often being performed by a separate division or department set up for the purpose. The training program is usually designed to impart the following kinds of information and skills: the proper methods of completing the various forms which the salesperson must execute in the course of serving customers, facts about the merchandise, the proper arrangement of stocks, selling technique, the relations of the salesperson with the customer, and the policies and ideals of the store. This training is sometimes carried on in formal classes. Much of it is done by means of individual conferences between the trainer and the salesperson.

The work of supervision in a large establishment is usually conducted, in the chain system, by the local managers, assisted by the supervisors, and in the department store by the floor manager or buyer, aided by the comparison shoppers. Two of its primary purposes are to induce the salespeople to make use of the aids which they are supplied and to determine the existence and the character of the need for additional training work.

The operator of the small store can employ no such elaborate machinery. His sales-management work must be done personally and individually on the job. He is usually his own shopping bureau, supervisor, trainer, and senior salesman. He must train his employees while they are working and whenever an opportunity presents itself. As a result this work is too often neglected, in spite of the fact that it is the essence of sales management.

A most important task involved in managing the sales activities of a retail business is the determination of the relative selling emphasis that shall be placed upon the different items in the stock and of the appeals that are to be used in promoting them. It may include not only the facts that are to be emphasized about the merchandise but even the preparation and prescription of the exact language which the salespeople are to use in presenting those facts to customers.

Ostensibly, the self-service stores make no formal use of personal selling. But whenever people belonging to the store come in contact with customers, a certain amount of selling, or unselling, will inevitably go on. In a supermarket, for example, the checkers and the men who keep stock on the shelves are certain to be asked questions by customers. The answers they give can do much to sell or unsell a store to the customer. A pleasant checker, who wins the liking of the customer, can do a lot to reduce the unpleasantness of the shock that inevitably occurs when the cash register has completed its computations and presents the summation of the bad news. About the only types of retail outlets that can really avoid some reliance on personal salesmanship to the consumer are the mail order house and the automatic vending company.

The manufacturer can often do much to improve the quality of the personal salesmanship applied to his goods in the retail store. His efforts can be especially helpful in the area of training and imparting facts about his merchandise. Manuals of product information, on-the-job training by the manufacturer's salesmen, in a few cases factory training courses available to retail salespeople, have all been used, along with many other devices to accomplish this purpose. By the use of PM's, premiums paid by the manufacturer to the salesperson for pushing the sales of his goods, the manufacturer may aid the retailer in providing performance incentives. The retail manager is apt to regard a PM program as a mixed blessing.

In their sales management work many of the larger retailing firms are handicapped by the unionization of their salespeople. The intervention of the union is apt to be a handicap to all their supervisory efforts and, in fact, to all control work—so far as its success depends on changing the behavior of people. But it is especially acute in the area of sales management. Good retail salesmanship is so much a matter of personality, of the heart instead of the hand, that the presence of the union as a sort of industrial go-between for a store and its salespeople is almost certain to detract from the spirit of service which is so necessary to an efficient retail selling performance. It is not an accident that consumers now complain more than ever before that retail salespeople simply "don't care." The small store with one or two employees is not likely to be unionized since it is too expensive for the union to get members one or two at a time.

Advertising and Sales Promotion

With the exception of the mail order house and the automatic vendor, a retailer can't sell a customer anything until that customer comes into his store. The building of store traffic is a matter of vital importance to the retail manager. His chief tools for this work are the location of his store, its appearance (really a type of advertising), the merchandise it sells and the service it gives, and advertising. Many small urban stores do practically no advertising in the ordinary sense of the word, depending for their traffic entirely on location, window and outside display, and word of mouth. Most stores, however, depend to some extent on advertising to bring in customers in a buying mood.

In managing his advertising, the store operator's first job is to decide how much to spend for it. This is very apt to be done either by formula, a certain percent of past or expected sales, or on a catch-as-catch-can basis: advertise whenever it seems to be needed, up to the point where the manager begins to feel that he has spent enough. Certainly this is an activity which should be planned ahead, probably six months to a year, with enough built-in flexibility to permit adjustments to meet all but the most drastic changes in market conditions.

In doing such planning the retail manager will probably be wise to decide what the job is that he wants his advertising to do, or may want it to do if the most likely shifts in market conditions occur. He then can plan to spend enough to do that job. Retail management is in a very good position to use this approach since so much of its advertising is designed to produce immediate or very short-run results. An advertisement of handbags in tonight's newspaper increases the sale of handbags tomorrow, or it probably does nothing. Therefore, the retail manager can check the effects of much of his advertising with considerable exactitude. On the basis of these checks, he is able to estimate ahead of time what the effect of a planned advertisement will be.

Most of the publicity work of retailers is local in character. It usually takes the form of advertising in newspapers, handbills, posters, and the like, broadcasts over local radio and TV stations, and window, counter, and shelf displays. The store manager's selection of media is therefore rather narrowly limited by the number and character of the publication agencies whose spheres of influence are confined to the community in which his customers live.

The selection of articles to be advertised usually presents numerous difficulties. Most store operators find it desirable to feature items on which they make price reductions. This is especially true of stores emphasizing the price appeal: the quality store is apt to select an article which exemplifies quality or exclusiveness to an unusual degree. The small merchant is likely to decide the question in favor of the goods sold by those manufacturers whose salesmen are most persistent in urging him to give their products publicity, who extend him the most aid in advertising work, grant him the most liberal advertising allowances, or supply the most attractive display material. This is especially likely to be the case with his window and counter displays.

Needless to say, this haphazard method of deciding so important a matter is not designed to bring about the maximum enhancement of the profits of the store. In choosing commodities to feature in his publicity the retailer should always consider the probable effect of such selection upon the profit of his entire establishment. The manufacturer will be wise to remember this in planning programs of cooperative advertising and promotion with his retail outlets.

Too many small merchants regard the work of preparing advertising copy and trimming windows as a necessary nuisance to be performed only when it can no longer be neglected. As a result, both tasks are done unintelligently and ineffectively, and their accomplishment has no beneficial effect on sales. When managed in this manner advertising is really a waste of time, energy, and money. The merchant is wise if he recognizes that his publicity work is an integral and important part of his job, which must be carried on according to a definite schedule and with the utmost care and skill of which he is capable.

The most important advertising work that the average small retail merchant can do is the arrangement of window and counter displays. They are undoubtedly the most effective publicity devices that he can use continuously to entice prospective customers into his store and to induce them to buy after he gets them there. Most independent retailers could profitably spend much more time and effort than they do in carrying on this work.

Many manufacturers offer their retailers a wide variety of aids to advertising and promotion work. This may include copy for local store advertisements featuring the manufacturer's products, the payment of part or all the cost of the space or time in which the copy is used, window display materials, racks and containers for use inside the store, shelf and counter displays, and an almost infinite variety of other point-of-sale promotional materials. The retailer must be careful to use this material to increase his own profits and serve his own customers, not merely to sell goods for the manufacturer. This suggests that the manufacturer is much more likely to get his promotional aids used if he builds them with the profit of the retailer and the interests of his customers in mind.

Ability to Use Advertising. Only a few retail concerns can make effective use of advertising in national media. In order to do so a firm must be prepared to sell to customers living in practically every part of the country. The large mail order houses and a few chain systems meet this requirement. The members of the entire group could almost certainly be numbered on the fingers of two hands. A few stores, usually selling very expensive quality merchandise and located in metropolitan centers that are likely to be visited by large numbers of people from all parts of the country, can afford to advertise in certain types of national media. Tiffany's, DePinna's, Saks Fifth Avenue, and Woodward and Lothrop supply examples with copy in The New Yorker. One or two of the voluntary chain groups have made use of national media in their publicity work.

If a retail establishment is to advertise profitably in a medium, its customers must be readers of the publication it selects. Since their patronage comes heavily from the farming districts, the mail-order houses find it good business to use magazines whose circulations are predominantly rural, such as the farm journals. If a chain system advertises in national media, it is obliged to pay for much waste circulation. Many readers of such publications live so far away from the nearest unit of the system that they cannot patronize it without great inconvenience. As a result of these and other factors, none of the mass retailing types has made as much use of national advertising as might theoretically be expected. Several chain systems have employed the national radio hookups, but on the whole they have made little use of this medium.

The department store is ideally adapted to advertise through the newspapers. Its natural trading area usually coincides more or less exactly with that from which the local newspaper draws its circulation. Practically every potential reader of a journal appealing to the strata of the population whose members a given retail establishment seeks to serve is a potential customer of the store. The advertiser need pay for very little waste circulation.

Most department store copy is designed to achieve immediate results in sales. This purpose fits in with the ephemeral nature of the appeal of any given piece of copy in such a publication. The store is also in a position to check immediately, directly, and with reasonable accuracy the effectiveness of each advertisement and of each journal. As a result of this exceptional adaptability of the newspaper to their purposes, department stores are among the chief users of its advertising space.

Department stores have also made extensive use of radio and television advertising media. The natural listening area of the average broadcasting station probably extends somewhat beyond that of the trading area of the department stores in the town or city in which both are located. The amount of this waste circulation, however, does not seem to be excessive.

The chain organizations have found that the newspaper is a profitable advertising medium. Like the department stores, they use it primarily to publicize specific offerings of merchandise. In most cities the units of the average chain system are scattered with sufficient uniformity over the circulation area of most local publications so that the system need pay for very little waste circulation when it uses them. Chain systems employ this medium far less than department stores.

The average independent merchant in a small town can profitably advertise in the local newspaper since practically all its prospective readers are possible customers of his store. In the larger town or city this is not the case. A few specialty houses, situated in the chief shopping district, attract trade from all parts of the city, but the trading area of the average independent store in such a place is within a radius of a few blocks from its site. Most of the money its manager might spend for advertising space in a newspaper with city-wide circulation would be wasted since most of the possible readers would not be prospective customers of the store. Some newspapers have tried issuing neighborhood editions but without conspicuous success. Those independent stores which belong to voluntary chain organizations have generally made excellent use of local newspaper advertising. Their publicity work in this medium has often equaled or surpassed that of the regular chain systems in aggressiveness and skill.

The mail order houses can make practically no use of the local newspaper as a medium for promoting their catalog business.

Window displays and counter displays are employed as advertising media by all the types of retailing establishments we have discussed except the mail order house and the vending machine operator. The displays of the department store are probably more spectacular and impressive than those of any other type. This is probably because the large size of the building required to house such an establishment usually results in its having extensive window space and because the shopping articles it features lend themselves especially to the building of attractive displays. The window display work of most department stores is supervised by specialists, often persons of considerable artistic ability.

The chain systems probably make more extensive and intelligent use of displays than the independent stores as a group. Many of them enforce a high degree of uniformity in the performance of this work by their individual units. Window or interior displays are planned, and samples of them are built by experts in the central or district headquarters. Photographs and drawings of these are furnished to the local managers, who are required to reproduce them in their stores. Other chain systems allow their local managers considerable discretion in this matter. In carrying on this activity they make extensive use of the display material prepared and furnished by the manufacturers of the goods they sell. By reason of the large number of outlets operated by the chain system it can afford to employ specialists of great skill to plan its displays. It is also able to train the managers of its local outlets in the methods of properly installing them.

The independent retailers who belong to voluntary group organizations can, if they will, use window and interior displays as effectively as the regular chains. The chief difficulty which the managers of these groups experience in attempting to achieve such efficiency on a widespread basis lies in the fact that the individual storeowner members are not always willing to cooperate in installing the displays that the central organization prepares and recommends. For this reason the manufacturer who grants an allowance to a chain system as part of a cooperative advertising or promotion deal can be much more confident that he will get his money's worth than when he makes a similar arrangement with a voluntary or cooperative group.

The independent merchant who is not a member of such a group must rely largely upon the manufacturers from whom he buys his merchandise for the material for his displays and upon his own ingenuity and industry for their installation. Too often the lack of these qualities results in his failure to make any real use of the promotional possibilities of his windows and counters. Of course it is absolutely out of the question for the average, nonaffiliated, independent small retailer, however intelligent and aggressive he may be, to employ an expert to supervise this work.

The department store usually makes comparatively little use of handbills, window stickers, and similar promotional devices. The expense of distributing "throwaways" to all its prospective customers is not small although it can distribute small promotion pieces to charge customers cheaply along with the monthly bills. The newspaper usually offers a more effective medium by which publicity may be carried to the customers in its territory, and the store finds it more profitable to use its window space for displaying actual merchandise rather than stickers.

The chain system can employ these selling devices cheaply and effectively. In doing so it enjoys a very distinct advantage over its independent competitor. The per unit cost of preparing a few hundred handbills or a single window sticker, for instance, is very high. When they are made by the thousand, however, the cost per unit approaches the vanishing point. In preparing such promotional material the voluntary group organizations serve their members very effectively.

On the whole the independent store, unless it belongs to a voluntary group, usually conducts its advertising activities at a relative disadvantage. Both the department store and the chain system can make effective use of most of the available advertising media with the possible exception of national magazines. The mail order house, aside from copy published in agricultural journals of national or seminational circulation, relies upon direct mail and makes the most extensive use of it of all types of retail outlets.

Because of its spectacular nature, the supermarket enjoys the advantage of being "news" in the struggle to obtain publicity. It is better able to use newspaper publicity than the average small food store because it usually draws its customers from a larger area of the community in which it is located, and therefore need buy little waste circulation when it purchases space in the local newspapers. Many supermarkets have carried the techniques of merchandise display to the level of a fine art.

PUBLIC ATTITUDE

During recent years much has been written about the public image or personality of a business. Perhaps the subject has been overemphasized. It would be difficult, however, to overemphasize its importance in the retail trade. The retail store is a local establishment. Its contact with the ultimate consumer-buyers who compose the market is direct and immediate. Community feeling toward a store exercises an immediate and decisive influence on its fortunes.

To the typical consumer a retail concern is usually one person, the person with whom he comes in contact when he enters the store. In the small store this is likely to be the owner-proprietor; in the chain store it may be the store manager or the clerk or the check-out girl; in the department store it is apt to be the salesperson. When the point of contact is an employee, the manager is almost certain to be the crucial factor, for his attitude and behavior tends to set the pattern for the store he operates.

An example or two may illustrate both the nature of this phenomenon and its importance. The owner-manager of a beautifuly laid-out, modern, and well stocked drugstore in a suburban town was an excellent pharmacist who taught in a nearby college of pharmacy; but he talked too much, volunteering much free advice to customers about their business and behavior while he served them. Within three months after he sold the business to a quiet, friendly pharmacist who would talk or remain silent—as the customer wished—the sales of the store increased 30 percent. The proprietor of the best hardware store in town, spacious, well arranged, completely stocked, was a "sourpuss' of the purest vintage, cold, supercilious, and sharp-tongued, although he always had what you wanted at a reasonable price. He was put out of business by Rudy who was as friendly and accommodating as a stray puppy with a genuine liking and respect for people—but whose stock was jammed into a space half as big as it should have been, poorly laid-out and unorganized. To the people of the town each of these stores was the man who ran it, and they reacted accordingly. There were plenty of people in town who would rather suffer their aches and pains than go into the store of the talkative druggist, and would rather allow the bugs to eat their flowers and vegetables than go to Mr. Sourpuss' store to buy insecticides.

Public opinion not only influences the patronage behavior of prospective customers of the individual retailing business but may exert
pressure to bring about restrictive legislation against certain types of
retailing outlets.

The large-scale retailing institutions work at a disadvantage in attempting to influence public opinion. Their top managers lack personal
touch even with their customers, not to mention the general public.
This is true of the mailorder house, the chain system, and, to a lesser
degree, the department store. This lack results in certain operating disadvantages. It tends to handicap the mass retailing enterprise in the
attempt to adapt its methods of operation to local peculiarities of behavior and trading practices, and to delay it in making such adjustments.

The process of making such local adjustments is especially difficult
for the management of a chain organization because, in making them,
it undermines the standardization of stocks and of methods of operation, usually a fundamental factor in the efficiency and control of the
system. The mailorder house can do very little in the direction of making such local adjustments. Since the department store usually seeks to
cultivate a market that is limited to the metropolitan area in which it
functions, it can adapt itself and its methods of operation with some
exactness to the peculiarities of its community. Often it succeeds in
taking on much local color and becomes the object of considerable
community pride and loyalty.[1] The independent merchant can and generally does conform his manner of conducting his store to his customers'
habits of living, working, and trading. He naturally tends to do so because he is one of them and accepts their peculiarities without question.

The mass retailing enterprises engender widespread public suspicion
and hostility simply because they are big. During recent years there has
been much anxiety about the welfare of the small businessman. There
has been a tendency among certain politically minded groups to extol
smallness as a virtue in itself and to frown upon size as such. The independent retail merchant is, beyond all others, the typical, small American businessman whom the professional worshipers of industrial and
commercial mediocrity seek to protect. His chief competitors and his
most striking antitheses in point of size, therefore—the department
store, the mail order house, and above all the chain store system—have
been the subjects of much vicious and unjustified propaganda.

The chain system, the mail order house, and, to a lesser extent, the
department store suffer from the fact that they are regarded as non-

---

[1]Marshall Field's in Chicago and Macy's in New York are cases in point.

community enterprises. In attempting to attract the patronage of the residents in the small suburbs and semirural communities on the periphery of its trading area, the department store suffers to a minor extent from the fact that it is a big-city institution. This disadvantage is even more damaging to the mail order house and the chain system. The people of small towns, especially in areas in which the population is predominantly agricultural, sometimes tend to be clannish and to look with rather active suspicion upon the "outlander." These two retailing institutions are definitely foreign to the local community. Both are operated from headquarters located in large cities, perhaps far away. Both are owned and their policies dictated mainly by persons living in great centers of population and finance. Even their local employees are less settled and stable and less a part of the community than those of the independent stores.

The chain systems and mail order houses are not warm, living, human beings, but cold, soulless, impersonal corporations. The provincial resident of the country town, like his equally provincial brother living in certain sections of a large city, feels that he is disloyal to his own kind if he trades with anyone other than the independent storekeeper with whom he grew up and whom he greets by nickname. When the competition of the chain store or of the mail order house threatens to put his old friend out of business, his attitude is liable to acquire an element of venom that does not allow him to be content with merely refusing his patronage to the alien retailing outlet but impels him to urge the adoption of legislation designed to eliminate it from the business structure.

This emotional antagonism is rationalized and implemented by a number of economic and social arguments directed against the chain and mail order forms of retailing. It is urged that they "take money out of town." All or practically all the merchandise they sell is bought from sources outside the town in which it is retailed. The daily money receipts of the local unit of the chain system are often dispatched to its central headquarters almost as soon as they are received. The people living in the community are said to get no further use from money after it falls into the chain store till. A dollar spent in an independent store, on the other hand, is supposed to continue to circulate in the neighborhood and to facilitate further exchanges of goods and services to the continuing benefit of all who live there.

As a matter of actual fact, there is little difference in the subsequent behavior or itineraries of the dollars spent by customers in chain and independent stores. For instance, in the food trade about 70 to 80 cents of every dollar received by each is used to buy the goods it resells. Except in the larger centers, the wholesaler from whom the independent merchant purchases is just as definitely "out of town" as the warehouse or headquarters of the chain system. About 5 cents of every dollar received by the independent store is used for salaries and wages as against about 7 cents of the chain dollar. All the employees of the former are usually local persons; the store employees of the chain are local while the warehouse and office people usually are not. Payments made for such items as rent, heat, light, and water, amounting in the case of the independent store to between 2 and 3 cents, and of the chain system to between 3 and 4 cents, per dollar of sales, remain in the community. Numerous other expenditures of the chain store, such as those for local advertising, taxes, and a portion of the miscellaneous outlays do not go out of the community in which it is located. Very little more of its dollar, as compared with its independent competitor, "goes out of town." The specious logic that lies at the base of this argument furnishes a justification for the sort of local trade barriers which, if generally adopted, would soon completely destroy our American economic system. Its advocates have no sound leg on which to stand, either in fact or in logic.

It is frequently argued that the mass retailing firms pay exceptionally low wages and require long hours of work from their employees. This charge is of doubtful validity. As a matter of fact there is pretty convincing evidence that, as far as wages are concerned, precisely the reverse is true. The following figures, computed from the reports of the 1958 Census of Business, indicate that the chains pay higher wages than the independents and that the bigger the chain, the higher is the wage.

TABLE 7–1

WAGES PER WEEK, 1958

	Independent Stores	All Multi-units Stores	Multi-unit Systems (50 Stores or More)
All stores................	$56.80	$62.70	$65.20
Department stores.......	53.90	63.80	73.10
Variety stores...........	37.00	43.40	44.10
Shoe stores.............	64.00	69.60	72.00
Grocery stores..........	52.80	75.40	79.70
Cigar, tobacco stores.....	45.00	47.70	48.80
Drugstores.............	54.40	58.60	64.20

It is not possible to compare the hours of labor in the two types of enterprise with any approach to exactness. The standardized hours of operation of the chain systems, however, give reasonable assurance that their employees do not work under conditions that compare too unfavorably with those prevailing in independent stores. The national wages and hours legislation undoubtedly falls more heavily upon the chain systems than upon the independents, since it will certainly be more rigidly enforced against the establishment with many employees. It is doubtful if it could be applied practically to the small, scattered, numerous independent establishments. Then too, more of the larger firms are unionized than of the smaller.

The opponents of the chain store also urge that it neither enters into nor contributes to the life of the community in which it is situated. Too often, neither its name nor that of its manager is found on the membership lists of local Chambers of Commerce and merchants' associations, or on the subscription lists of local Community Chest and Red Cross drives, Boy Scout or Girl Scout funds, church enterprises, relief contributions, and other community undertakings. In general, this accusation probably has some justification, although many of the better-managed chain systems have long since taken steps to overcome the difficulty by authorizing, sometimes requiring, their unit managers to take part in such community enterprises, usually according to previously prepared schedules, or by contributing directly when applications for funds for such contributions are approved by the district or home offices. But when the chain system makes donations to community enterprises, they are sometimes given in standard amounts and with an absence of warmth and personal interest which serve to infuriate rather than placate its enemies among the receivers.

Many chain systems have taken active and highly intelligent steps to overcome this handicap. For example, J. C. Penney Company strongly urges its store managers to identify themselves positively and intimately with the communities in which their stores are located and to participate actively in local civic projects. Sears, Roebuck and Company operates an elaborate and costly program throughout the farming areas to promote better farming. This is matched by a small-community program designed to put Sears influence and facilities behind local projects for community improvement. The chain store can become a part of the community if the management of the system is willing to encourage and support its local manager in making it so.

Much has been made of the claim that the chain stores and the mail order houses tend to put the independent merchant out of business and to create a monopoly in every field in which they operate. It is urged that in this way they undermine the economic independence of the small businessman, reduce the opportunities open to the youth of the country, and threaten the economic well-being of consumers who, eventually, will become entirely dependent upon them for the goods they must buy.

This is not a new accusation but a very venerable one; one that has been leveled repeatedly against new and more efficient business institutions.[2] The figures tend to give some support to this charge. During the decade 1948–1958 the number of independent stores declined slightly and the number of chain units increased a little. During this period also the single-store independent's share of the total retail sales volume fell from 70.4 percent in 1948 to 66.4 percent in 1958. But in many retail trades the figures indicate a tendency for the rate of change of this percentage to level off. Except in one or two lines of business, the available statistics give no indication that the chain systems are likely to crowd out their independent competitors completely.

There are sound bases upon which to conclude that, even in the absence of governmental interference, there would continue to be an important place for the independent retail merchant in the distributive system. Several serious elements of weakness in the chain form of organization and method of operation have been indicated in the course of our comparison of these types of retailing institutions. It is quite apparent that there are certain services that the independent store is better qualified to render the ultimate consumer than are its larger rivals, and that there are certain conditions under which it is better adapted to function than they. It seems safe to conclude that the chain systems constitute no very serious or imminent monopolistic menace. It is also probably not improper to remark that if, during the past couple of decades, the independent retailers as a group had expended the same amounts of energy and cash in improving themselves as merchants as they have poured out in public protest and in soliciting political action, they would have vastly improved their competitive position, even as compared with that which they now enjoy as a result of the various types of discriminating legislation they have succeeded in having written upon the statute books.

---

[2] "This type of institution will result in oppression of the public by suppressing competition and causing the consumer in the end to pay higher prices and ultimately create a monopoly. It will close to thousands of young men who lack great capital the avenues of business which they should find open to them." (Excerpt from a resolution against the department store adopted by a convention of retailers in 1895.)

"It is repugnant to the democratic spirit. But is no more than what the independent worker has been subjected to in the last 50 years. One by one and hundreds by hundreds have been dragged from self-employment over the ruins of an independent business into the narrow dependency of corporate employment. Meantime the ranks of Socialism grow and the end is not yet." (Excerpt from an editorial on the department store appearing in the *Springfield Republican* in 1895.)

As a result of the natural antagonism of the people of the less thickly populated communities toward the alien chain store and of the criticisms of the chain method of retailing just outlined, and as the outcome of a constant campaign of propaganda maintained by certain groups of independent retail merchants and wholesalers, a considerable body of legislation has been adopted designed to handicap chain systems or to eliminate them from the retailing field. The Robinson-Patman Act was intended to achieve this purpose by limiting their buying advantages. The so-called "fair trade" laws have handicapped the chain system in its use of the price appeal as a competitive weapon. About a dozen states have discriminatory taxes on chain stores, designed to drive them out of business.

These levies are all in the nature of annual license fees, graduated on the basis of the number of stores operated by a given system within the state or within the United States. The most onerous of them, that of Texas, at one time reached a maximum of $750 for each store belonging to systems operating more than 50 outlets each within the state. The average chain grocery store in the United States enjoyed total sales of $782,000 in 1958. The license fee for such a unit operated by a firm maintaining 50 or more stores in the state would amount to less than 0.1 percent of its total sales. This is a handicap of about 10 percent for an enterprise that is accustomed to operate on 1.0 to 1.5 percent net profit. The license type of tax has repeatedly received the approval of the United States Supreme Court.[3] A number of such laws have been repealed by state legislatures. Others have been invalidated by the decisions of state courts.

By propaganda prepared by and issued through several associations, by contesting the validity of these laws in the courts, by lobbying activities, and by direct political action, the chain organizations have sought to combat such legislation. They have succeeded to the extent that they have limited the application of antichain laws to about a fourth of the states in the Union; through court decisions they have reduced or eliminated the nuisance features of many of the statutes and have limited the method and scope of application of the taxes. The pressure for the passage of such laws seems to be somewhat less insistent now than it was several years ago.

A number of chain organizations have sought to reduce the tax handicap to a minimum by increasing the size of the average outlet. In the food business this has involved the closing of numerous small stores and

---

[3]Indiana law, 283 U.S. 527; Florida law, in part, 288 U.S. 517; Louisiana law, 301 U.S. 402.

the opening of a much smaller number of large combination markets. This change was also due in part to economic considerations and changes in shopping habits. This protective measure is not possible in many trades.

Approximately the same pressure groups that have sought to have the chain method of distribution legislated out of existence have attacked the supermarket. Their efforts have resulted in a few scattered municipal ordinances imposing discriminatory license fees upon this type of retailer and establishing handicapping regulations of its methods of operation. The movement has largely died down since the supermarket is often a local enterprise and is not generally found in the smaller rural communities, which are most characterized by the provincialism that constitutes the emotional basis of the movement.

The attack against the discount house has been two-pronged. It has involved active propaganda to the effect that the discount house is a "cheap, illegitimate" establishment which sells second-rate goods and outdated models. The opponents of the discount house have also sought to handicap it by legal means. They have invoked the restrictions of the Robinson-Patman law to eliminate any advantage to the discount house in the prices at which it can buy merchandise, and they have brought the heaviest possible pressure upon the manufacturer to force him to use the so-called fair trade laws to prevent it from selling at reduced prices.

In the face of consumer preferences and the basic economic factors involved, these attempts have not been notably successful. To make its price reductions possible the discount house does not depend primarily on buying at lower prices than the conventional retailer but on operating at a lower cost. The pressure on manufacturers to enforce fair trade contracts has forced many of them into an agonizing reappraisal of the economic and commercial validity of such contracts with a result that more than a few of them have to all intents and purposes abandoned these arrangements.

What has happened in the course of attempts by traditional retailing groups to use special interest legislation to destroy or handicap the department store, the mailorder house, the chain system, the supermarket, and now the discount house simply illustrates the basic truth that under our economic system, if consumers want to buy certain goods in a certain way, some businessmen will find a way to sell them those goods in that way, legally if possible, extra-legally if necessary. Special interest laws have proved a weak crutch indeed alongside intelligent, aggressive competition that is directed to the end of selling the consumer what he wants, in the way he wants to buy it, and at the lowest possible price yielding a reasonable profit. That is the best way for a retailer to create a favorable public image of his business.

MANAGING OPERATING EXPENSES

A very important part of the job of the retail store operator is the management of expenses. Many retailers act on the theory that the essence of this activity is to reduce operating costs and that the way to manage expenses is to cut them or eliminate them. This is not true. To make money the business man must *spend* money. The essence of expense management is more nearly to direct expenditures upon those activities that will increase profits most and to control the amounts spent on each of the several cost generating factors so that each dollar spent will return the largest volume of profits.

Thus it comes about that the total dollar volume of a retailer's expenses is not particularly important. The important things are what the dollars are spent for, and their relation to total sales and to total gross profits. The beginning of wisdom in expense management lies in knowing when to spend money, what for, and how much.

Retailing expenses possess two characteristics that are of prime importance in their management:

a) They arise mainly from activities that are carried on and facilities that are provided to render various services to consumer customers and to attract and keep their patronage. The retail manager can't cut out the cost of a service and still give the service, and if his customers want the service he can't eliminate it and keep his customers.

b) A large part of the expenses of the average retail store behave like overhead. The space, facilities, and people needed to handle a given volume of business will often serve to handle half again as much, or twice as much. Within these volume limits most of the expenses of the store behave like overhead. This throws tremendous emphasis on the importance of volume of sales in achieving the optimal relationship between retailing expenses and gross profits.

These observations as to the nature of retailing expenses suggest the chief ways in which the merchant may approach the job of managing them.

1. He may reorganize the activities and facilities involved in rendering a consumer service so as to use less of them or a less expensive kind and still furnish the service satisfactorily. In using this approach the

manager is apt to be wise to devote his attention first to the activity or service that generates the heaviest costs. This approach has definite limitations in that it cannot be pushed very far without impairing the quality of customer service and endangering customer patronage. The most expensive customer services are those that involve personal contact between the customer and a representative of the store. If the number of such representatives is reduced the customer service contacts are apt to be delayed: "You can't get a clerk to wait on you"; if they are paid less they are apt to be disgruntled or lower calibre people, and service contacts are less pleasant and helpful.

2.   He can follow the venerable practice of "watching the corners"; that is, rigidly hunting down minor leaks of expense money wastefully used and stopping them. This too is self limiting, for the manager is likely soon to find himself spending more to stop an expense leak than the loss than escapes through it.

3.   He can increase sales volume. This usually involves spending more money instead of less, but if the rise in sales is large enough, the total expense per dollar of sales is reduced, and more of the gross profit sticks in the till as net income. The "razzle-dazzle" promotions that are so characteristic of discount house operations represent an increase in total expenses in order to get a more than proportionate increase in sales, thereby reducing the expense per dollar of sales and taking the same net profit from a larger number of sales dollars—or even a lesser net profit from each of a more than proportionately increased number of sales dollars. This approach to the problem of managing expenses is characteristic of most types of retailing establishments, although perhaps less so of the quality store, the high fashion store, and the neighborhood convenience outlet than of most others.

4.   He can eliminate or reduce activities. These may be of two kinds; activities that aid in management and those that are needed in providing customer service. Dropping either kind is a touchy matter. If a small retailer fires his part-time accountant or cuts down the accounting service he buys, he will know less about his business and make more of his decisions without a proper basis of fact and analysis. The same is true of the chain system manager who closes out his marketing research unit, or of the department store merchandise director who decides to get along without his stylist. When a retailer decides to discontinue a customer service he always runs the chance that he will lose so much patronage by doing so that the latter state of his business will be worse than the former. On the other hand, the supermarket and the discount house have proved that, if conditions are right, con-

sumers actually prefer to do without the clerk, delivery, and credit services, although a parking space service must be provided instead.

The average expense-sales ratio of department stores is about the highest of any type of retailer; it is between 30 and 35 percent. This reflects primarily the wide assortments of merchandise they carry, their heavy reliance on the fashion appeal, and the extensive services they render. In response to the pressures of discount house competition, many of them have sought to diminish this handicap, usually by setting up special departments or branches which render little service and whose stocks are limited to fast-moving items. But as the discount house develops, it seems to be moving as much or more in the direction of the traditional department store position with respect to these matters than the department store has moved toward the discount house.

So far as reported figures show, there seems to be little difference in costs between the independent store and the chain. Any attempt at exact comparison is doomed to frustration because of differences in the method of keeping accounts and because of the failure of many independents to recognize and record all their costs. For example, many small merchants fail to include as costs depreciation on facilities and equipment used and salaries to owner-managers. On the other hand, many of them include profits as owner-manager salaries. The chain figures are blurred by the allocation of central office and warehouse costs, some of which represent the expenses of performing wholesale functions. The available figures seem to suggest that the chain system has some (but very little) cost advantage over the independent and that its slightly lower prices are made possible by lower merchandise costs earned through quantity buying.

The voluntary and cooperative groups are usually to be found somewhere between the chains and the unaffiliated independents in operating expenses, merchandise costs, and prices.

The operating expenses of the supermarket, as reported by Super Market Institute, were 17.44 percent of sales in 1961; those of the ordinary grocery store are probably between 20 and 25 percent. In 1954 the supermarkets expenses were under 15 percent of sales. This upward tendency has been characteristic of the entire history of this type of retailer. During the early years of supermarket development one heard rumors of operating expenses of 7 or 8 percent, and price differentials offered evidence to support the rumors.

The upward trend in supermarket operating expense-sales ratios is probably due to the restoration of consumer services formerly withheld, the addition of lines of merchandise that are more expensive to handle, and above all the approaching saturation of the market with supermarket units which makes it more expensive to capture the volume needed to keep costs down.

Very little is known about the expenses of discount houses. It may be presumed that they are as low as (probably well below) those of supermarkets because both types operate on the basis of withholding the same customer services, and the supermarkets, being older, have had longer to edge away from their original position of stark austerity with respect to services and resulting expenses. A leading New York discount house several years ago announced a merchandising policy which indicated that its operating expenses were less than eleven percent of sales. Probably this figure is now much below the average. It may be expected to increase as discount houses move into more expensive quarters, widen their assortments of merchandise, and increase in numbers, so that they must compete with each other for sales volume instead of with the much more vulnerable high-cost, high price department and specialty stores.

The store emphasizing the quality or fashion appeal must almost inevitably face high operating expenses. Its furniture and fixtures must create an atmosphere of quiet elegance that costs money. Its salespeople must be numerous, expensive, and well trained. It is precluded from bidding for volume with the flamboyant devices available to its fellows emphasizing price appeal. Its services must usually be extensive and expensive.

CONTROLLING OPERATIONS

To be effective the retail manager must know what is happening in his store or stores, compare it with what he thinks should happen or would like to have happen, try to rectify or offset the effects of unfavorable discrepancies between the two, and plan methods of preventing the repetition of mistakes and failures. Some retail managers may be able to do much of this work by direct observation. Others must rely on reports, records, and analyses. All of them can do it better if personal observation is fortified by records and statistical analysis of the facts they disclose. The basic records needed by managers of all types and sizes of stores are those showing sales, prices, stocks, costs of merchandise, and operating expenses.

In theory the manager of the independent store should have all the best of it on this basis of comparison. He has only a small establishment to supervise. All parts of it are immediately and constantly under his eye. Nothing of significance can happen without practically forcing itself upon his attention. Over the activities carried on in his store he should be able to exercise a control more detailed and exact than any his mass distribution competitors could be expected to rival.

In practice, these advantages are often not completely realized. The things right under one's nose are often the hardest to see. Statistical conclusions reached through repeated observations, unrecorded and uncounted, are not always accurate. And all too often the small store's record-keeping system leaves much to be desired. The accounting system of the small independent retailer is often not far removed from the traditional two boxes: one for bills payable and the other for accounts receivable—and a pocket for cash. Rarely does it serve either the purpose of preserving a record of the past performance of the business or the infinitely more important one of aiding in managing its present activities and planning its future.

The average small retailer knows very little about either the technique or the uses of accounting and statistical analysis. He is not qualified to develop or to install a set of books that will meet his needs. There are several sources from which he can obtain help in this work if he is willing to make use of them. Several retail trade associations have prepared standard systems of accounts for use by firms operating in their respective fields. Many progressive wholesalers have developed accounting methods and forms adapted to use by their customers. Some wholesalers are prepared to aid the individual storekeeper in installing such a set of accounts and to teach him to operate it, sometimes even to help him adapt it to the peculiar needs of his enterprise. A few manufacturers offer the same kind of service to retailers handling their products. Several collegiate bureaus of business research have prepared model systems of accounts for different types of stores. It is often possible for a retailer to make arrangements with an accountant living or practicing in his vicinity, in consideration of a reasonable fee, to install and, by periodic visits, supervise the operation of a set of records and reports that will serve his needs.

The merchant should seek to use his accounting system not merely as a record of the past history of his business but as a means of determining the profitability of his current activities and of discovering the directions in which, and the extent to which, he should modify each of his operations. Many small retailers who maintain adequate accounting systems do so merely for income tax purposes, or because they regard it as the businesslike thing to do, and totally fail to reap the real benefits to be derived from the information thus made available.

Many voluntary and cooperative groups provide accounting, record systems, and forms for their members. This service usually includes in-struction in operating the system and in using its results. Occasional groups provide a complete record keeping service for their members.

The mass retailing establishments, the chain system, the department store, the mailorder house, the large supermarket or discount house, can afford to use the most refined methods and equipment for keeping and analyzing records. For example, their managers can learn at any time the inventory and order position of almost any article the store handles, at what rate it flows through stock, how much of it is being sold, how much net profit or loss is made on each dollar of its sales, and the cost of performing each major function involved in handling it. These facts are only the beginning of the information and control results of its analysis that the executives of the large retailing establishment are able to use in making decisions and supervising their execution.

Let us take a look at how management may use this kind of infor-mation. Suppose the buying committee of a chain of supermarkets considers a certain product that has been in the line for some time and is up for review. The committee has before it, among other facts, the sales of the article through each store in the chain, the trend of its sales, the profit per unit and per dollar sold, the number of units and the dollars they represent that must be carried in stock, the annual profit enjoyed on a dollar invested in the article, and, if it seems desirable, some indication of the effect its sales have on the volume of other related products. The decision to delete the product or retain it can be made in the light of the most complete analysis of the facts about it and in relation to all the considerations involved. As another example, the merchandise manager of a department store observes from the reports crossing his desk that stocks of a certain article are high in relation to sales and that it is not moving according to plan. If he knows his job he will move to find out why things are going wrong and what can be done to remedy the situation.

The mass retailing manager can also make use of the most advanced and complex tools of control. Insofar as control involves influencing the behavior of people, and it usually does, the manager of mass retailing is at something of a disadvantage compared to the owner-manager of the small store. The control the latter exercises over his people is per-sonal, simple, and direct. He is on the spot to see that his suggestions or directions are understood and carried out.

On the other hand, in a chain system, a department store, a mail order house, or even a large supermarket, discount house or specialty store, the chain of command is apt to be long and to pass through many levels. The manager must work through merchandise managers, buyers, floor managers, district superintendents, store managers, personnel managers, and numerous other specialized intermediary executives. In the process of transmission, his ideas are liable to become warped and twisted and his plans sadly altered.

His plans and policies must of necessity be general and cover the behavior of organizational units operating under varying conditions. When the performance of a unit varies from plan or policy, therefore, the control process must involve a decision as to whether (*a*) if unintentional, the variance was the fault of the unit manager or was due to local conditions he could not be expected to overcome, or (*b*) if intentional, the departure from plan or policy was justified by the unusual operating conditions faced by the unit manager.

The problems of control faced by the management of the voluntary or cooperative group are much the same as those observed in the mass retailing organizations, with the added complication that the manager of the headquarters of such a group must depend for his results on the cooperation of his store-owner-managers, that flows from free contact and persuasion, instead of on that to be gained from the somewhat more rigid employer-employee relationship.

We hope we have said enough to give you some background from which to consider the problems the marketing manager must meet in choosing retail outlets as members of his channel system and in managing his relations with them. He must recognize that retailers are not all alike but vary widely in size, control, methods of operation, and areas of strength and weakness. All of these things vitally affect a store's suitability as a channel member, the marketing services the manufacturer can expect to get from it as an outlet, and the way in which he must manage his relations with it—and its relation to other stores—with respect to his goods.

A further complicating factor in the manufacturer's problems of managing his relations with his retail outlets lies in the fact that often those relations can not be direct but must be second-hand and achieved through wholesale intermediaries. So we may be wise to examine these intermediaries and try to see how they operate and what their elements of strength and weakness are as avenues of contact with their customers.

CHAPTER 8

Wholesale Outlets

In the last three chapters we have examined the various types of retail outlets which sell to ultimate consumers, and have sought to explore and understand the kinds of management problems they face and the more important factors that influence their success or failure. This has been necessary in order to enable us to study intelligently the manufacturer's problems in selecting and managing marketing channels. He can not manage these relationships skillfully without understanding the different types of retailers, how they operate, and the problems they face.

We must now seek the same understanding of the wholesale trade, which is composed of firms that sell to retailers or other wholesale firms for resale, and to institutional, industrial, or business buyers for use in their operations. These firms fall into several important types, each of which we will treat separately. With respect to each we will try to give some indication of its importance in the wholesale area, to describe how it operates, the services it offers its suppliers and its customers, and to outline some of the problems its managers must meet and try to solve.

Some wholesale outlets are merchants in that they buy and own the goods in which they deal and look for their income to the profit they hope to make by selling at a price high enough to cover purchase price and operating expenses with something left over. Others are agents. An agent does not take ownership responsibility for the goods (although he may have them in his custody) but negotiates or arranges for their purchase or sale and depends for his income on a commission or fee paid by the seller or buyer he represents.

THE WHOLESALER

Not every firm in the wholesale trade is a wholesaler. The use of the term is reserved for "a business unit which buys and resells merchandise to retailers and other merchants and/or to industrial, institutional and commercial users but which does not sell in significant amounts to ultimate consumers."[1]

Functions or Services

In the process of wholesaling there are certain marketing functions that must be carried on or services that must be supplied both to the manufacturer and to the buyer. Not all wholesalers perform all of these functions or perform them in the same manner or to the same degree. In fact, wholesalers fall into groups that are distinguished by the services they perform and the way in which they render them. Before we study these groups, however, we will be wise to examine the wholesale functions or services and try to understand some of their implications.

Merchandising. The wholesaler helps both the producer and the retailer to perform the merchandising or product management function. The characteristics of the article the manufacturer makes, the amount of it he turns out, and the time at which he puts it on the market, all depend heavily upon consumer demand and the buying habits of users and retailers. On these matters the wholesaler can supply information to the producer who sells through him. But the data that he furnishes are likely to be much less complete and satisfactory than those that could be obtained from retailers or from consumers themselves. The wholesaler performs the function of supplying information about the market much less effectively, although usually somewhat less expensively, than the manufacturer himself can do it through marketing research or constant direct contact with retailers and users of his products.

The wholesaler may supply the retailer with several aids in making his merchandising decisions. He can inform the dealer about new products that come on the market. Manufacturers, of course, through salesmen, advertising, or by mail, can furnish this information. In most cases, however, it is doubtful whether the producer is able to perform this service as cheaply as the jobber. Especially is this true when the maker of a new commodity has a small output, is poorly financed, or manufactures a narrow line of goods. The same considerations apply to the process of informing the retailer about changes in the manufacturer's plans for future production.

The wholesaler is sometimes able to advise his retailer-customers about probable future changes in the prices of the goods he handles.

---

[1] Unless otherwise indicated, all quoted definitions in this chapter are from Marketing Definitions, Report of Definitions Committee, American Marketing Association, Chicago, 1960.

He is often in a position to observe the imminence of such changes before they occur, and such information is likely to be of great use to the retailer in planning his purchases.

The storekeeper can glean from his wholesalers or their salesmen much valuable information about the demand for specific products in other localities and the methods employed by other retail stores, not necessarily competitors, in handling and promoting the sale of certain articles. He may be able to use such knowledge effectively in planning his own buying and promotion work.

Practically all these items of information can be furnished much more satisfactorily by the jobber than by the manufacturer. The data supplied by the latter are almost always certain to be fragmentary and to apply to only a small part of the retailer's stocks. If he works at the task, the wholesaler can present a much more complete and well-rounded picture of the market than the manufacturer can attempt.

Buying. The wholesaler offers the retailer very important help in the work of buying and assembling his stock. In fact, this constitutes one of the chief justifications for his existence in the economic system.

Goods of many kinds are made in many places and by many producers. For the convenience of his customers each retailer must collect from among the welter of products a stock of more or less homogeneous articles which the consumer expects or wishes to buy in that particular type of retail establishment. Much of this work is done for him by the jobber. The wholesaler assembles in one stock a much larger number of items of merchandise presenting a much wider selection than is likely to be found on the shelves or in the storerooms of any of his customers. The average retail drugstore is reported to carry from 10,000 to 15,000 items, while the wholesale druggist stocks upwards of 40,000 items. The hardware jobber's catalog contains from 20,000 to as many as 75,000 items, while the average retail hardware store carries only 9,000 to 10,000 items.

The retailer could buy direct from the manufacturer and thus perform this assembling function himself. Many manufacturers send salesmen to call on retailers and are prepared to make deliveries, either from branch houses or from the factory direct. But if the retailer tried to buy all his goods direct, and all manufacturers provided facilities for him to do so, the effect on both parties would be devastating. For example, there are about 700 manufacturers of drugs and medicines. Suppose that 500 of them regard a given retail druggist as a desirable outlet for their products, and each sends a salesman to make a 15-minute call on him once every two weeks. The harassed storekeeper would be obliged to spend 62 hours a week in interviewing them all, not to mention the time and energy needed to handle the multitude of orders to be placed; deliveries to be received, unpacked, checked and merged into stock; invoices to be checked; and drafts to be drawn in payment. On the other hand, he may buy from a wholesaler who lists in one catalog practically all the articles he needs and is prepared to sell them in one order, taken by one salesman, during a single call; to ship them in one consignment, bill them on one invoice, and accept payment for them by one check.

Carrying Inventory. In our discussion of the retailer we indicated something of the importance to him of a rapid flow-through of merchandise. One of the basic jobs of the marketing system is to have available the merchandise consumers want, where and when they want it, and in the amounts in which they want to buy it. Almost always this task is divided among the firms at the several levels of distribution, manufacturing, wholesaling, and retailing. In most trades the lion's share of it probably falls on the retailer. This throws considerable pressure on him to look for some means to shift the burden. The wholesaler offers a way to do this in part.

In seeking to reduce his inventory the retailer runs the risk of loss of business because of stock shortages. He can shrink his stocks without increasing unduly the risk of disappointing customers if (*a*) his supplier maintains adequate stocks within convenient delivery distance of his store, (*b*) his supplier makes fast delivery, and (*c*) his supplier's delivery is certain and accurate; that is, he can always count on getting exactly the goods ordered within a constant time period after placing an order. To be adequate a supplier's stock must contain all the items the retailer may want to order and in sufficient quantity so that he can fill all orders for each item that customers may reasonably be expected to place.

The manufacturer can and sometimes does supply this service through systems of branch warehouses. The number of such storage points any one manufacturer can maintain is limited. The warehousing function is subject to very definite economies of scale, and if a producer attempts to operate too many branch houses he finds most of them too small to be economical. The wholesaler, by adding together the stocks he needs to service sales of the products of a number of manufacturers, can get a total inventory which affords him the economies of scale, even though he serves a relatively small area containing relatively few retailers.

For example, in 1958 there were 311 general-line drug wholesalers and 2731 wholesale firms specializing in certain types of drug items.

In the same year there were 393 manufacturers' stockcarrying branch houses in the drug industry, but these were divided among at least 20 to 30 manufacturers, no one of whom could afford more than perhaps 30 warehouses. The wholesalers' storage points thus blanket the country with a thoroughness no one manufacturer can approach. The situation in the drug business is typical of that in many trades. The stocks of the manufacturers' branches are nowhere near so heavy as those of wholesalers. In 1958 all wholesalers' inventories were 9.7 percent of their sales; the same figure for stockcarrying manufacturers' branches was 4.9 percent. Table 8–1 indicates the situation in several trades as computed from material in the 1958 Census of Business.

TABLE 8–1

INVENTORIES AS PERCENT OF SALES

	Wholesalers		Manufacturers' Stockcarrying Branches
	(General)	(Specialty)	
Drug....................	13.7	10.3	3.8
Dry goods..............	14.3	11.7	7.4
Grocery...............	6.4	4.9	1.9
Electrical.............	10.6	11.2	4.9
Hardware..............	17.6	15.2	3.3
Tobacco...............	4.3	——	1.4

These figures indicate the extent to which the wholesaler can and does perform the stockcarrying function for the manufacturer. For some products that require special handling or equipment, such as meat and glass, the manufacturer can perform this function better than the wholesaler. In the case of merchandise that must be produced seasonally, such as canned goods, or that can be manufactured most efficiently at a constant rate but suffers from a highly seasonal consumer demand, such as paint, the wholesaler can and does relieve the producer of much of the unusual stockcarrying burden that results from these peculiarities.

Delivery. The same factors that enhance the importance of the stockkeeping function in wholesaling tend also to emphasize the significance of the delivery service. A retailer can safely reduce his stocks to the minimum only if he is able to rely on his sources to deliver with exactness, speed, and certainty the orders he places with them. Notice that not only the speed with which orders are delivered is important but also the consistency with which that speed is maintained. If Wholesaler A can be counted on as surely as death and taxes to deliver within 3 days after the order is placed, the retailer must carry 3 days' stock

plus a reserve for unexpected demand, say another 4 days', plus a reserve to cover an order that might go wrong because of circumstances
Wholesaler A can not control—about 4 days: or a total of 11 days. If
Wholesaler B usually delivers within one day, but occasionally takes
as long as 5 days, his retailer-customer must carry 5 days' stock plus his
emergency demand reserve of 4 days—plus another 5 or 6 days' reserve
against unavoidable failures of delivery: a total of 14 or 15 days inventory. Inconsistency of performance makes the difference.

The excellence of the wholesaler's delivery service depends on (1)
the distance to be traveled in making deliveries, (2) the speed with
which it is traversed, (3) the rapidity with which the clerical work of
handling orders and the manual labor of preparing them for shipment
or delivery is done, and (4) the care with which the whole operation is
supervised to prevent failures or mistakes.

Three factors tend to complicate the wholesaler's delivery operations:

1. Many of the orders he receives are small indeed. In every wholesale trade, managers complain of the large proportion of orders that
are for less than $5 or $10—in general for amounts so small that the
cost of handling and delivery far exceeds the gross profit. This is often
due to the kindheartedness of the independent retail owner-manager,
who can't bear to send a salesman away disappointed, and so gives each
of them a tiny order his house would be better off without. In part it
arises from poor stock control, which results in many emergency orders.
It may also occur because the retailer fails to understand the real costs
he incurs by ordering too often and in too small quantities.

2. Many retailers order in broken-package lots. Many products are
packed in cartons containing a dozen, or some multiple of a dozen, consumer packages. When a retailer orders a fraction of a dozen of such
a product, his wholesale supplier must break open a carton and repack
the number ordered for delivery to the customer. This is especially
likely to happen in the case of products for which there is little demand
and which consumers want infrequently. Many drug products are of
this type, but they are to be found in almost every wholesale trade
from groceries to industrial supplies.

Wholesalers have tried all sorts of methods to overcome these two
difficulties. Most of them are modifications of three or four devices: refusal to handle broken-package orders or orders of less than a certain
value, for example $25; a service charge for small or broken-package
orders; a quantity discount for full package orders or orders above a
certain value; and sales campaigns to inform the retailer about the

cost to him of small and broken-package orders. None of these are ever completely successful or satisfactory.

3. Many wholesalers operate far outside their economical delivery areas. The fact that many of the operating expenses of the wholesaler behave like overhead (within fairly wide limits) brings heavy pressure on him to reach for all the sales volume he thinks he can get. For example, the staff needed to operate an order-handling routine that is economical for a 100 order per day burden can probably also handle 150 or 175 orders per day. If a truck has to go 30 miles out to make a delivery on the periphery of a wholesaler's territory, the direct costs of its going 2 more miles to deliver another order may be surprisingly small: all the expense of getting it 30 miles out tend to behave like overhead. One of the most obvious ways for the wholesaler to get added sales volume over which to spread this overhead is to expand his territory.

In certain wholesale trades, firms located in Chicago make free de-

FIGURE 8–1

How Deliveries Are Made

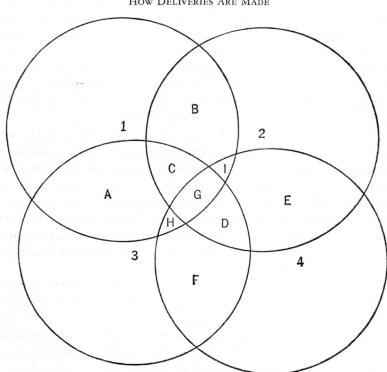

liveries in St. Louis in competition with St. Louis houses, which reciprocate the favor by shipping orders into the Windy City without charge for transportation. New York jobbers deliver in Philadelphia in competition with firms in that center, which, in turn, compete for a share of the New York market.

Often truck deliveries are made far beyond the economical limits of such service. Figure 8–1 illustrates what happens as jobbers in several contiguous wholesaling centers, or markets, extend the areas over which they make deliveries. The territory served from such a center tends to be roughly circular in form. In this figure the numbers 1, 2, 3, and 4 designate the locations of such trading centers. As jobbers at these points extend their deliveries outward, they begin to overlap the areas naturally belonging to other markets.

In the figure such overlapping occurs in areas A, B, C, D, E, F, G, H,

FIGURE 8–2

Zoned Deliveries

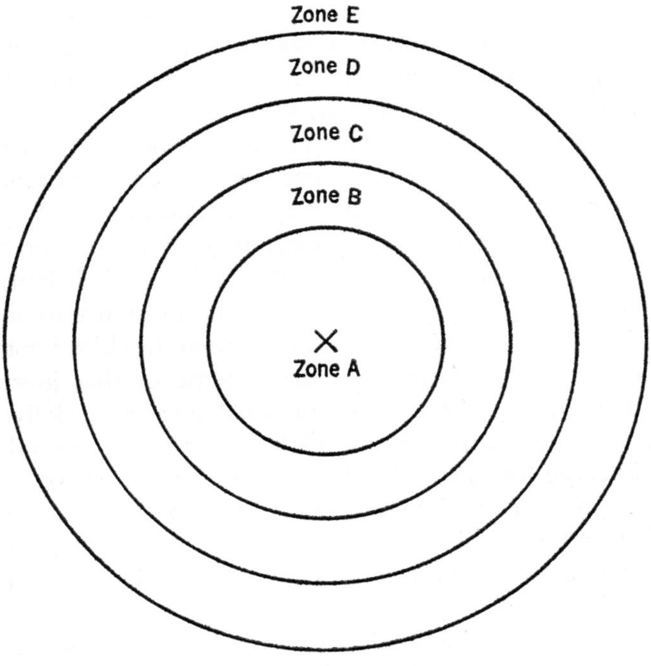

Zone E
Zone D
Zone C
Zone B
×
Zone A

Zone A: Gets deliveries every day
Zone B: Gets deliveries every other day
Zone C: Gets deliveries every third day
Zone D: Gets deliveries every fourth day
Zone E: Gets deliveries once a week

and I. Buyers in C, D, H, and I may receive deliveries from three centers, while all four give this service to firms located in area G. This is likely to mean that the business in these areas is divided among these centers and the share of each market, in turn, is subdivided among the wholesalers in it.

Since overextension of the delivery service tends to reduce the number of deliveries made by any one jobber's truck in certain areas, it increases the cost of delivering the average order there. Many jobbers have sought to limit the cost of this service by establishing zones that are bounded roughly by concentric circles around their warehouses. They deliver daily to customers within the inside circle; less frequent deliveries are made to those in the outside circles; and the most remote zones may receive deliveries only once a week. This practice limits the use of the delivery service as a competitive device in the outlying zones. It is illustrated in Fig. 8–2.

From the economic standpoint, the wholesaler's participation in the performance of the delivery service often makes possible very substantial savings in the total cost of the physical movement of merchandise from producer to consumer. Goods can be transported at much less expense per unit in large quantities than in small. The jobber very often buys and takes delivery in carload or truckload lots. As was indicated above, his warehouse is likely to be located much nearer the stores of his retailer-customers than is the producer's factory or branch house.

The presence of the jobber in the distribution system, therefore, makes it possible for goods to be transported in carload or truckload lots at lower freight rates, over the longer portion of their journey from factory to consumer, and leaves a relatively short distance to be traveled in the more costly less-than-carload or less-than-truckload lots. In the interest of achieving reductions in the expense of that journey, it is desirable that the distance traveled in small lots or by delivery truck should be reduced to a minimum, while the part of the total distance traversed in large lots and by rail or by overland truck should be increased. The presence of wholesalers in the system facilitates this process since their warehouses blanket the country more completely than it is possible for manufacturers' branch houses to do. However, the overlapping of trading areas, the indiscriminate use of free deliveries as a competitive device, and the tendency of wholesalers to cluster in large cities tend to detract from the social economy of the jobber's performance of this function. But still it remains one of the chief economic reasons for the wholesaler's existence.

As we have indicated, some manufacturers perform this function through their own system of branch warehouses, sometimes supplemented by stocks carried in commercial warehouses. But the demand for a manufacturer's goods within economical delivery distance of a market center must be great enough to justify a warehouse of economical size and to enable him to ship to it in carload or truckload lots before he can profitably operate a branch there. This tends to put narrow limits on the number of branch warehouses a manufacturer can maintain. The use of stocks carried in commercial warehouses suffers from the drawback that the producer loses some of his control over stocks and most of his control over customer service.

Financing. The wholesaler plays an important role in financing distribution. Jobbers occasionally make loans to small producers to finance their production operations. Wholesalers usually pay their bills more promptly than retailers, thereby reducing the amount of operating capital needed by the manufacturer who sells through them. There seems to be no precise knowledge of the degree to which they do this. It is commonly supposed that producers find it necessary to extend longer credit terms to retailers than to wholesalers. The assumption is of doubtful validity. The customary credit terms reported by Dun and Bradstreet for various trades from which they gather data indicate that wholesalers usually receive smaller cash discounts but are allowed credit periods that are as long as those granted to retailers, and often longer.

The manufacturer of seasonal goods often finds the wholesaler useful in financing both his production and his distribution activities. The jobber may be induced to place advance orders for such merchandise and to take delivery of it during the slack season. In a few cases such goods are paid for when delivered. More frequently, however, the wholesaler demands and the seller allows a "deferred" or "season" dating on such orders. For instance, on orders of golf clubs and balls shipped by the maker after November 1, the buyer may be allowed until April 10 to pay, and still take his cash discount. If a wholesaler buys on such terms, he does not reduce the manufacturer's seasonal requirements for working capital, but he does make it easier for the maker to obtain such funds. Banks prefer to lend money on merchandise which customers of the borrower have displayed a willingness to buy. For this reason, loans may be obtained more advantageously on accounts receivable than on stocks in the manufacturer's warehouse. In this way the jobber may help producers of seasonal goods to solve their financial problems.

Even though the manufacturer must grant considerable amounts of credit to wholesalers, he may well find it less costly and hazardous to do so than to sell an equal volume to retailers on account. The number of customers he must carry on his books, and upon whose financial standing he must check, is much smaller. If, for instance, the producer of an article distributed through drugstores wishes to sell direct to retailers and to give them the credit service, he will find that to obtain complete coverage of the market he must maintain a record of about 56,000 retailer customers. But if he sells to wholesalers only his books need contain no more than 400 or 500 accounts. The difference in the clerical costs is obvious.

The same is true of the outlay for gathering credit information about his customers. On the average, wholesalers have more capital than retail merchants. The credit rating bureaus give a large percentage of the latter no ratings at all, or ratings so low as to supply little indication of their ability to pay. Most wholesalers enjoy ratings sufficiently high to give some indication of their financial soundness. Credit information about retailers is likely to cost more and be less complete and satisfactory than that with respect to wholesalers.

The wholesaler finances the retailer by selling him merchandise on open-book account. As a general rule, the jobber is very liberal in rendering this credit service. His liberality consists not so much in the actual terms allowed as in laxness in enforcing them. In the grocery trade, for instance, at a time when 38 percent of wholesalers' sales on credit were for 10 days or less, and 85 percent of credit sales were for 30 days or less, outstandings were 113 percent of credit sales, or about 34 days' credit sales. The average retailer was thus taking a longer credit period than the terms allowed him. The terms most commonly used by wholesalers are 1 or 2 percent 10 days, E.O.M.,[2] or 1 or 2 percent 10 days, net 30 days.

Theoretically, the wholesaler might be expected to grant more credit and on more liberal terms than the manufacturer finds it possible to allow through his branch houses. The existence of very close relations between the firm granting credit and the one receiving it should result in more liberal terms. Since the wholesaler is characteristically more local in nature and in closer contact with his customers than the manufacturer's branch house, he should have the advantage in this respect. For the same reason, he should be able to adapt his credit policies and practices more precisely to local and trade needs and habits than can the manufacturer's branch house, whose financial activities, in

---

[2] The buyer is allowed 1 or 2 percent off the face of the bill if he pays on or before the tenth day of the month following the date thereof. The account becomes delinquent if it remains unpaid after the eleventh day of that month.

the interest of safety, must be controlled from a central office. The figures reported by the Census Bureau seem to indicate that these assumptions are not realized in actual practice, and that the manufacturers, through their branches, really make about the same percentage of their total sales on account as do wholesale merchants.

Selling. The wholesaler participates in the performance of the selling function. Formerly, selling was regarded as an activity that was entirely individual to each successive agent in the marketing process. When the manufacturer got an order from a wholesaler or retailer he felt that he had completed his part of the sales task. When the jobber sold to a retailer he flattered himself that he had done all the selling he could be expected to undertake. But all parties have come to understand that the selling process is not complete until the merchandise involved has been moved into the hands of the ultimate consumer: goods are not really sold to the retailer until a customer has taken them off his shelves. From a selling standpoint, the most significant moment between the manufacture and the use of an article occurs when a consumer who is or may become interested in buying it is face to face with its retailer, or with the product on a retailer's shelf. At that moment occurs the selling which really counts. This fact must be kept constantly in mind in any discussion of the selling function.

The manufacturer who distributes to retailers through wholesalers will almost certainly find that his selling expenses are considerably less than they would be if he solicited them directly through his own salesmen. Consider a producer of a drug item who seeks complete retail coverage. To attain it he must maintain touch with some 56,000 stores. Let us assume that each of his salesmen can call on an average of 20 customers a day and that he wishes to make contact with his trade twice each month. If the salesmen work 5 days a week, he will need 280 of them to do the job. Most direct-selling drug manufacturers operate sales forces of 600 or more men, who also call on physicians.

Suppose, on the other hand, that he decides to sell through wholesalers whom he wishes to solicit once every two weeks. Assume further that each of his salesmen can average only four calls a day on this type of customer. In 1958 there were 311 general-line wholesalers of drugs and drug sundries in the country. He might wish to call on another 100 or 200 specialty houses which handle his products. To keep in proper touch with them our producer will require a force of 10 men. One drug manufacturer, who relies entirely on wholesalers to distribute his line, has for several years used only 6 salesmen.

Of course, not all manufacturers will wish to sell to all existing firms in either the wholesale or the retail trade, but the salesmen needed ratio between the two groups will tend to remain about the same, regardless of what the precise coverage policy of the producer may be. The total expense involved in making contacts with wholesalers remains much smaller than that of selling to retailers, even when we take account of the fact that higher wages must be paid and more liberal expense accounts allowed to salesmen selling to jobbers than to those calling on retail stores.

The total expenditures of all parties in making contacts with the retailers are likely to be less per dollar of sales if the task is done by wholesalers than if it is performed directly by manufacturers. We can assume that it costs just as much for a jobber, through one of his salesmen, to complete a call on a given retailer as for a producer to do the same thing. When the manufacturer does this job, however, the entire cost of it must fall on the one line of goods he makes. The wholesaler, on the other hand, can spread it over the entire list of articles he carries. Thus the amount of it that must be allocated to the average dollar of his sales is usually substantially smaller since the average order is bigger.

But mere comparative costs do not tell the entire story of the wholesaler's discharge of the selling function. The matter of the quality of the sales service rendered is equally significant from the standpoint of the manufacturer, perhaps more so. The producer is often inclined to feel that the wholesaler serves merely as a conduit through which goods may flow to market, and that he possesses none of the properties of a pressure pump to force them into consumption. In general, this opinion is not without justification. To a considerable extent the weaknesses of the wholesaler as a selling unit result from the very nature of his operations. We have noted the large number of items of merchandise offered for sale by the average wholesale house.

There are about 700 manufacturers of druggists' preparations, proprietary medicines, and toilet preparations. Suppose that a jobber handles the products of only 500 of them. The calls of his salesmen on retailers probably average 20 minutes (about 2.4 seconds per manufacturer) or less in length. The manufacturer in this trade, which is fairly typical in this respect, can logically expect very little real selling service from his wholesalers or their salesmen. Nor can we overlook the natural tendency of the jobber's salesmen to push those goods that are easy to dispose of and to neglect those more difficult to sell.

Under certain conditions the jobber may supply reasonably satisfactory selling service to the producer. If because of the liberality of a manufacturer's price policy or favorable market conditions the wholesaler enjoys a "long" margin of gross profit on an item or a line, he is likely to try to induce his salesmen to promote its sales to their customers. Thus, they may do a real job of selling for the manufacturer. Since this sort of price structure tends to result in price-cutting, however, it is likely to be only temporary in character.

A wholesaler may be stimulated to push the sale of the merchandise of a manufacturer who grants him an exclusive dealing franchise or privilege. In such a case the producer usually agrees with the jobber that he will sell to no other wholesaler distributor in the territory. In turn, the jobber contracts to expend special effort in actively promoting the sale of the merchandise to which he has exclusive rights.

This policy has several drawbacks from the standpoint of the producer. By adopting it he limits his retail outlets in an area to the customers of one wholesaler. The results he obtains in each trading area depend upon the caliber of the house he is able to induce to handle his goods therein. In general, this method may be expected to work best for manufacturers of specialty products, articles requiring the repair and maintenance service, and, possibly, perishable goods. To be legal, the franchise arrangement must be a one-sided affair: the manufacturer agrees not to sell to any other wholesaler in the market area, but, under the anti-trust laws, he can not prevent the wholesaler from handling the goods of competing manufacturers. In some trades practical considerations may limit the wholesaler to one line, but they are few.

The exclusive dealing arrangement is not always entirely satisfactory to the wholesaler since he has no assurance of its permanence. He may be able to make such a contract covering a period as long as three, or even five, years, although usually not more than one year. Even when the arrangement is most favorable to the wholesaler, the manufacturer has frequent opportunities to terminate the contract. In case he does so, the wholesaler finds that he has spent time and money in developing business for the competitor to whom the franchise is next granted—or for all his competitors if the producer chooses to abandon the exclusive policy. In spite of these objections, a number of very successful and mutually satisfactory relationships of this character have existed over considerable periods of time.

The existence of the conditions just described has been one of the principal factors motivating wholesalers to develop and attempt to popularize their own brands. In carrying out this policy a jobber purchases anonymous merchandise, attaches to it his own "private" label or brand, advertises the brand, and promotes the sale of goods bearing this label to his customers, and usually to the ultimate consumers in his market. Additional reasons for this practice are to be found in the fact that many manufacturers who sell branded goods to wholesalers compete with them by selling those same brands directly to the wholesaler's retailer-customers and to chain stores which resell them at reduced prices in competition with his customers.

If a wholesaler develops in his territory a consumer demand for goods bearing his own label, he thereby makes it possible to offer his retailer-customers merchandise that cannot be handled by chain stores, and, in selling which, they are to some extent free from the necessity of meeting the price competition of these mass retailing units. The wholesaler also can maintain a more satisfactory margin of gross profit on such noncompetitive goods than is possible on widely advertised articles sold under the makers' brands. Probably a majority of the food wholesalers sell at least a few products under their own labels. The same is true of the more important concerns in the hardware, drug, and stationery trades.

Although the tendency of jobbers to sell under their own brands resulted, to a considerable extent, from the direct-to-retailer distribution activities of manufacturers, the development of private brand marketing, in turn, serves to stimulate the growth of direct-to-retailer marketing among producers. It considerably reduces the effectiveness of the wholesaler as a selling agency for the manufacturer's goods. Undoubtedly it has been both a primary cause and a significant result of the trend toward the use of manufacturer-to-retailer marketing channels.

As has been indicated, the work of selling merchandise is not complete until the retailer has disposed of it to an ultimate consumer. This transaction is the focal point of the sales process. But the retailer is not only the most significant link in the selling chain, he is often the weakest one as well. This is true on the basis both of natural aptitude and of training. A large percentage of the independent retailers entering business each year have had no previous experience or training that in any way fits them to engage in it. Many of them do not remain in business long enough to learn their jobs. Various studies indicate that about 10 or 15 percent of all independent retailers go out of business each year. There is thus a vast floating element in the personnel of the retail trade composed of proprietors who never develop any real proficiency in the technique of retail salesmanship and management.

If the wholesaler is to do a real job of selling, therefore, he must train, stimulate, and aid his customers in their sales promotion efforts. It is not always easy to do this. His salesmen, through whom most of this work must be done, are usually not enthusiastic about it. It requires much intelligence, knowledge, patience, finesse, and tact. The results are rarely immediate or tangible. Many retailers resent such activities on the wholesaler's part unless they are carried on with a great deal of tact and circumlocution.

As a group, wholesalers are in a much better position to train independent retailers in selling than are manufacturers. Any given producer is able to sell to a dealer only a small portion of the items in the latter's stock. His training efforts are likely to be confined to an attempt to build up the retailer as a sales outlet for the specific goods he, the manufacturer, sells. On the other hand, the wholesaler is equipped to supply the storekeeper with practically all the articles he resells. The jobber, therefore, is interested in building him up as a *merchant*. Any improvement in the retailer's general sales performance is likely to benefit the wholesaler. His efforts in this direction can be rounded and complete, if he chooses to make them so, while those of the manufacturer are almost certain to be one-sided and deficient.

The wholesaler's performance of the selling function has not been all that it might have been. Many have done little or nothing in this direction. Perhaps this group failure is primarily due to the fact that they have attacked individually a task that is essentially collective. The individual wholesaler who attempts this work is liable to find that he is training his customers to sell his rival's goods as well as his own— sometimes *instead* of his own. He may also discover that his efforts are being duplicated or his suggestions contradicted by those of a competitor. The task demands a type of cooperative action in which very few groups of wholesalers seem willing to participate.

Importance as Retail Supplier

At one time the wholesalers of the country supplied the retailers with practically all the goods they resold except small amounts bought locally. Gradually this relationship has been changed by a long-time decline in the importance of the wholesaler as a supplier of the retail trade. There are no figures from which to measure this trend with any pretense of accuracy. From the reports of the Census of Business we can compute some very rough indicators. They are shown in Table 8–2. These figures suffer from the fact that we do not know the average percentage of gross profit for retailers. The ratio, wholesalers' sales to retailers divided by total retail sales, ignores this percentage, and if the percentage has changed during the 30-year period, the ratio is proportionately inaccurate. The same thing may be said of the cost-of-

TABLE 8–2

SALES MADE BY WHOLESALERS TO RETAILERS AS PERCENT OF
TOTAL RETAIL SALES AND RETAIL COST OF GOODS

	Total Retail Sales	Retail Cost of Goods (at 30% Gross Profit)
1929...................	40.1	53.4
1939...................	39.8	42.5
1948...................	33.1	41.0
1954...................	26.9	38.1
1958...................	27.9	40.0

goods-sold ratio, which is based on the assumption that the gross profit margin of retailers was 30 percent throughout the period. This assumption is probably inaccurate because, with the growth of chain systems, supermarkets, and discount houses, gross profit has probably declined. This would tend to decrease the importance of the wholesaler below that indicated by the gross profit ratios shown above for the most recent years. The figures probably indicate the trend in the wholesaler's importance as a supplier of the retailer more accurately than they reflect its order of magnitude. The trend is certainly down despite a slight recovery from 1954 to 1958.

How They Perform These Functions

Wholesalers vary considerably in the services they render and the extent to which they render them. On this basis they may be separated into a number of groups.

Service Wholesalers. The largest and most important of these groups perform all or practically all the functions that must be carried on at the wholesale level of distribution and are known as service or full-function wholesalers. In 1958, the census reports showed that there were slightly more than 171,000 of them and their annual sales were almost $103 billion, about 40 percent of which was made to retailers and about 32 percent to industrial and business users. In that year the average service wholesaler had sales of slightly more than $600,000, his operating expenses were 14.4 percent of his sales, he carried stocks to service sales for almost a month and a half, and he had about 10 employees.

Service wholesalers vary widely in size, and size seems to exercise a considerable influence on their internal operating relationships. For example, the stockcarrying function is much less burdensome for the big house than for the small one. For the average small house selling less than $100,000 a year in 1958, inventory investment was 13.4

percent of sales; for the large firm with annual sales of more than $10 million the figure was 8.0 percent. This is in spite of the fact that the stocks of the large house are probably more complete and adequate than those of the smaller one. Operating expenses also seem to be a function of size. The average firm selling $10 million or more a year had operating expenses of 6.4 percent of sales; a typical firm with less than $100,000 annual sales had an expense percentage of 29.2.

In most trades the big firms capture the lion's share of the business. In 1958, 3,088 wholesalers made 31.0 percent of the total sales of all wholesalers; 10,866 of them did 50.4 percent of the total business; 25,250 had 67.0 percent of the total, and 48,795 of them sold 80.8 percent of the total volume of all wholesalers. Table 8–3 shows similar figures for a few selected trades. The figures show for each trade (*a*) How many wholesalers have about one third, one half, two thirds, three fourths of all the business in the trade, (*b*) The percent of the total business they have, and (c) The operating expense as a percent of sales of the size classification having the highest expense ratio.

Table 8–3, computed from the 1958 Census of Business, suggests that a manufacturer of grocery products who is content with a chance at his share of two thirds of the volume of his type of goods sold through general line grocery wholesalers, can get it by calling on 354 firms and giving them a price that allows a gross profit of 7 percent of sales plus a satisfactory net profit to the wholesaler. If he wants a chance at all the business he must call on 2,703 customers and price his goods so as to allow the wholesaler something more than 14.6 percent gross profit. If he wants his goods handled by wholesalers handling 85 percent of the total business done by general line grocery houses, he needs to call on only 870 firms and establish prices that will allow them a gross profit of 7.5 percent of sales, plus a reasonable net profit.

The organization structure of the service wholesale house varies with size and with the types of goods it handles. The small firm is apt to be a one- or two-man affair. If it is a partnership, there is likely to be some division of managerial functions between the partners. This is likely to take the form of one specializing in the sales work of the firm and the other managing its merchandising activities, including warehousing, order handling, and delivery, with both participating in major decisions in each area.

In the large firm, the management of the selling work is usually specialized. Merchandising decisions may be made by a committee and carried out by buyers whose work consists mainly of collecting information about products and suppliers, perhaps making buying recommenda-

TABLE 8-3

CONCENTRATION OF SALES

Trade	About 1/3 of Total Trade Sales			About 1/2 of Total Trade Sales			About 2/3 of Total Trade Sales			About 3/4 of Total Trade Sales			All the Business	
	Number	Percent of Total Trade Sales	Highest Expense (as Percent of Sales)	Number	Percent of Total Trade Sales	Highest Expense (as Percent of Sales)	Number	Percent of Total Trade Sales	Highest Expense (as Percent of Sales)	Number	Percent of Total Trade Sales	Highest Expense (as Percent of Sales)	Number	Expense (as Percent of Sales)
General line groceries...	—	—	—	163	49	5.1	354	66	7.0	870	85	7.5	2703	14.6
TV-Radio............	118	26	12.7	156	45	12.7	475	74	13.8	807	88	14.6	2403	19.6
Hardware............	73	36	17.2	236	58	17.6	—	—	—	492	74	20.1	2628	28.0
Drugs...............	135	39	12.8	—	—	—	405	71	13.6	630	82	14.7	3042	27.0
Tobacco.............	—	—	—	494	52	5.3	—	—	—	1167	78	5.8	2759	6.9
Wines and spirits......	54	31	9.8	170	54	9.8	—	—	—	489	82	9.9	1289	15.5
Cameras and photographic supplies......	34	33	17.7	94	54	20.0	—	70	—	212	77	20.3	776	26.2
Sporting goods.........	31	32	17.5	87	51	17.5	193	70	18.0	306	81	19.6	948	24.7
Jewelry, general line.....	27	22	19.2	35	40	19.2	83	60	19.7	132	72	21.9	534	22.3

tions, and negotiating purchases. In other firms the merchandising and buying activities are in the hands of buyers who are likely to specialize by types of products. For example, a large grocery house is apt to have a buyer for canned goods, one for spices, condiments, etc., one for coffees and teas, one for cereals, and perhaps others. These men are likely to have the power to make merchandising and purchasing decisions, subject, perhaps, to the approval of a chief buyer or a member of top management. Many wholesalers organize the power and responsibility of the buyer into much the same structure as that found in the department store. The buyer thus becomes responsible for the profit performance of his merchandise although he has even less control over the salesforce than does his opposite number in the department store.

A primary requisite of successful marketing through wholesalers is a knowledge of the structure of each customer firm so as to locate the persons who influence merchandising and buying decisions or have the power to make them.

Order handling is apt to be under the direction of an office manager. If delivery is made by the firm's own trucks it is likely to be managed by a separate executive. Since these two activities are so important to the success of the firm and since they are so closely associated, perhaps more firms should place them, as some do, under the direction of a manager of customer service.

There are five unusual types of service wholesalers who deserve special mention.

1. A rack jobber "markets specialized lines of merchandise to certain types of retail stores and provides the special services of selective brand and item merchandising and arrangement, maintenance and stocking of display racks."

In 1958 the Census Bureau reported 1,508 rack jobbers. Their average annual sales volume was $423,000. Their investment in inventory was 8.9 percent of annual volume, or about two thirds of a month's sales. Their operating expenses were high, 18.3 percent of sales, over half of it in payroll. They employed an average of 11 persons.

Although they deal with other retailers, rack jobbers mainly service supermarkets and chiefly handle items that are not in the regular line of the stores they serve. For example, they are very important in the non-food business of the supermarkets, particularly stationery, toys, housewares, health and beauty aids, hosiery, lingerie and other accessory soft goods, records, and magazines.

The rack jobber contracts with the retail store to keep certain shelf or rack space stocked with specified merchandise, usually on a "guaranteed" sale basis; that is, if merchandise does not sell within a reasonable time, the jobber removes it and credits the retailer with its purchase price. The jobber renders this service through a force of sales-service-men, each of whom operates a service truck stocked daily from a central warehouse. The serviceman visits the retailer once or twice a week, removes obsolete, damaged or slow moving items from the rack and stocks it with fresh merchandise. He makes 8 to 10 calls a day and handles a total of 40 to 70 retail customers. A serviceman averages between $600 and $800 in sales daily.

The rack jobber buys direct from the manufacturer. For an item expected to be sold to the consumer—customer at $1.00, he pays the manufacturer from 45 to 60 cents, varying with the article. For such an item his price to the retailer varies from 59 to 74 cents. His gross profit varies from 18 to 30 percent of his sales price. A mass retailer, buying in quantity, can purchase most of these articles at less than he has to pay the rack jobber.

The question may be raised, why is the retail manager willing to pay more to the rack jobber? The rack jobber performs the warehousing function, delivers the goods to the store, places them on the shelf or rack, and housekeeps the space. As a result of the guaranteed sale arrangement, the retailer pays only for merchandise he is able to resell. Many of the items handled by the rack jobber move in such small quantity through the retail unit that even the mass operator can not afford specialized buying and merchandising talent to handle them. Since the rack jobber serves a number of firms, he can supply this talent.

There seems to be evidence that some of the very large supermarket chains use rack jobbers to introduce new items outside the lines they normally handle and, when and if sufficient volume is built up, change to direct purchase and handling. This suggests that at least some of the recent growth of the rack jobbers' business may be temporary since supermarkets and other mass retailing units have been expanding their lines rapidly during recent years. In spite of these factors, the services which the rack jobber is equipped to supply seem to be sufficiently needed and valuable to assure him a continuing place in the distributive system.[3]

2. Many of the firms we have been discussing as service wholesale merchants would not readily recognize themselves by that name; they

---

[3]Much of the material in this discussion is from J. J. Sheeran, "The Role of the Rack Jobber," *Journal of Marketing,* July, 1961.

are usually designated "industrial distributors." Such a house sells the bulk of its volume to commercial, industrial, institutional, or professional buyers for use in conducting their enterprises.

These firms fall into groups on two bases. Some of them, such as electrical equipment distributors, office machines distributors, and abrasives and abrasive materials distributors, specialize in handling particular kinds of products. Others confine themselves to servicing certain groups of buyers; for example: oilwell supply houses, beauty and barber supply firms, and janitors' supply houses.

Industrial supply houses are highly concentrated geographically. For example, 57 percent of the chemical supply houses, selling 67 percent of the total volume are in 6 states: New York, Massachusetts, California, Illinois, New Jersey, and Texas. Forty-four percent of the iron and steel products distributors, with 57 percent of the sales, are in 5 states: New York, Pennsylvania, Illinois, Texas, and California. And 48 percent of the nonferrous metals distributors, making 78 percent of the sales, are in New York, Illinois, and Pennsylvania.

These firms are heavily concentrated in and around the large cities. For example, 53 percent of the distributors of industrial chemicals, with 65 percent of the sales, are in the metropolitan areas of cities of one million population or more; 54 percent of the stationery and office supply houses, with 63 percent of the sales, are in such areas; and 57 percent of the metals and metal work distributors, making 73 percent of the sales, are in or near such cities.

The typical industrial distributor is a small operation, a surprising number of them having sales of less than $200,000 annually. On the other hand, here as elsewhere, the lion's share of the business belongs to the larger firms. Operating expenses as a percent of sales in almost all distributor groups tend to decrease significantly as distributor size increases. This is a factor of great importance to the manufacturer and has probably exercised strong pressure toward the granting of exclusive franchises to industrial distributors. For example, a manufacturer of electric wiring supplies, who limits his distributor outlets to firms selling a million dollars or more per year, can base his price structure on a gross profit providing for distributor operating expenses of about 15 to 16 percent instead of the more than 30 percent he will need if he tries to include all distributor outlets in this trade. Other trades show the same characteristics of size differential.

The general mill supply house serving a horizontal market may carry 15,000 to 20,000 items in 600 or 700 product lines, while an electrical supply firm may handle as many as 60,000 electrical items made by 200 or 300 manufacturers. The large house is apt to operate a number of field salesmen, each of whom services about 135 accounts, averages 8 calls a day, and sells over $200,000 worth of goods a year. The salesman is apt to be a man of some technical training and considerable knowledge of factory operation.

In general, industrial buyers prefer to purchase direct from the manufacturer. This is not usually possible for the small house, which can not place orders big enough to make it worthwhile for the maker to sell him direct. Even the larger industrial buyer often finds it desirable to purchase some items from the distributor. The chief factors that influence him in this direction are:

a) Delivery is apt to be speedier. For example, an aircraft manufacturer found that he could get one-day delivery of valves from the distributor, while it took 4 to 6 weeks to get them from the manufacturer —an average saving of about 35 days. Similar time saving on other items ran from 3 days to 29 days.

b) The cost of buying may be less. By combining a number of items on one order to the industrial supply house the buyer may cut the number of orders placed and thereby reduce his clerical costs.

c) The price may be less. By buying in carload or truckload lots the distributor may enjoy freight savings that enable him to make a lower price to the buyer than the manufacturer can allow when he pays a higher unit freight charge on smaller quantities.

d) Adjustments may be made more easily and conveniently because the distributor is a local concern.

e) The distributor is often able to offer information about products and the market which the manufacturer can not supply.

f) Since the distributor is on the spot, he can often give the buyer emergency help which the manufacturer can not duplicate. The prompt handling of one emergency order that prevents a shutdown may be worth a considerable price differential on many orders.

3. In some trades there are super wholesalers: firms that buy from the manufacturer and sell mainly to other wholesalers. Examples are piece goods wholesalers, who sell 55.8 percent of their volume to other wholesalers; specialty dry goods houses, 52 percent; sugar, 51 percent; rope and cordage, 49 percent; precious stones, 48 percent; and textile bags and bagging, 40 percent. In some cases, such as precious stones, the intervention of this added intermediary in the chain of distribution is probably due to the need for special knowledge or skill—which the ordinary wholesaler can not afford to employ on his staff and for which

he is willing to rely on the super wholesaler. In the majority of cases it probably arises from the fact that the ordinary wholesaler can not buy in the quantities that the manufacturer regards as economical, and so the super wholesaler intervenes to perform the service of breaking transaction quantities (that are economical at the manufacturer's level) into lots that can be economically bought by the ordinary wholesaler.

4. There are at least three types of cooperative establishments that perform all or most of the functions of the service wholesaler.

a) The wholesale arm of consumers' cooperative stores. Most consumers' cooperative associations belong to regional "cooperative wholesales" that perform for them all the services which the service wholesaler renders his retailer-customers. Most of these establishments are to be found in the food business, although, since many of the cooperative stores are of the supermarket type, they have followed the supermarket's lead in moving into a number of nonfood merchandise fields. The manufacturer who sells to these wholesales may expect them to buy his goods in lots that are economical to him, but once his products get into the cooperative retail stores they are apt to encounter vigorous competition from the coop private brand which many dedicated consumer-members buy almost exclusively. He may also expect to lose some of his popularity with his regular wholesaler and retailer customers.

b) The cooperative wholesaler. This is a firm set up and operated by the retailers who buy through it. These establishments are to be found mainly in the food and drug trades. In their purchases the retailer-members usually manifest a fairly high degree of loyalty to the organization. They generally receive their membership benefits in the form of dividends, based on patronage, or of prices, based on cost from the manufacturer plus a handling charge to cover operating expenses. Many cooperative wholesalers have their own private brands which they often promote very aggressively.

These wholesalers are not a dominant element in either the grocery or the drug trade, but the manufacturer who ignores them is missing a considerable block of business.

c) Farmers' cooperatives. Most cooperative associations of farmers were organized to sell the products of their members, but many of them purchase fertilizer, insecticides, feeds, and other farm supplies and equipment for their members. Since farmers buy these things to use in carrying on their business, their marketing follows the pattern of industrial goods, and the cooperative that handles them performs many (if not all) of the functions of the service wholesaler or industrial distributor. Grange and Farm Bureau federations are also active in buying farm supplies and equipment.

Many of these cooperatives are associated on the basis of region, or crop produced, or both. Some of the regional groups control large blocks of sales of farm supplies and certain types of equipment. The coop usually buys the merchandise and resells it to farmer-members either at market price, in which case it pays a patronage dividend, or at cost price plus a handling charge.

A manufacturer who markets products sold to farmers for use in running their farms can hardly afford to ignore the farmers' cooperative as a possible outlet. And he must know and conform to their philosophy and methods of operation.

5. Mutual houses, another type of service wholesale firm, should also be mentioned. A mutual wholesaler may be either a cooperative or a private enterprise run for profit. Its characteristic feature is that the retailers who patronize it pay a yearly, monthly, or weekly fee for the privilege of buying from it at cost. The mutual house thus earns no gross profit but pays its operating costs and gets its profit, if any, out of the fees paid by patrons. There are a number of these firms in the drug trade. They are almost unknown elsewhere.

CHAPTER 9

Limited Function Wholesalers and Agents

We have been discussing types of firms which in some degree render all or nearly all the services involved in wholesaling. There are at least three groups of wholesale merchants which do business on the basis of limiting the extent to which they perform certain of these services, or of withholding them altogether.

LIMITED FUNCTION OR LIMITED SERVICE WHOLESALERS

The Cash and Carry Wholesaler

This type of house renders neither the credit nor the delivery service. The retailer-buyer picks up the merchandise in his own truck or car and pays cash for it.

Cash and carry wholesalers are most numerous in the food business although there are a few of them in trades such as hardware, feed, and farm supplies. Many service wholesalers operate cash-and-carry divisions either within their regular warehouses or as separate depots.

In 1958 the Census Bureau reported 1,860 cash-and-carry wholesalers, of whom 371 were in the food business. While the food group constitutes only about one fifth of the total number, their sales were about one third of all cash-and-carry wholesale sales. Between 1954 and 1958 they slightly more than doubled in number, and their sales increased a little more than that. Most of the growth, in both numbers and sales, was not in the food business.

Table 9–1 was compiled and computed from the 1958 Business Census and shows several significant operating figures of cash-and-carry wholesalers in 1954 and 1958 compared with service wholesalers, and, in the food business, with those service wholesalers who operate voluntary groups and those who do not. During the four-year period the cash-and-carries lost a significant part of their lower operating cost advantage. It appears likely that this was due to a significant increase

245

TABLE 9–1

WHOLESALE OPERATING FACTORS

	A. All Trades			
	1954		1958	
	Cash & Carry	All-Service Wholesalers	Cash & Carry	All-Service Wholesalers
Average annual sales........	$302,000	$572,000	$312,000	$601,000
Average number employees...	3.7	10.4	4.1	10.0
Number weeks stock........	3.9	6.0	3.3	5.9
Operating cost as percent of sales....................	8.8	14.0	10.9	14.4

	B. Food Trades					
	1954			1958		
		Service Wholesalers			All-Service Wholesalers	
	Cash & Carry	Voluntary Groups	Inde-pendents	Cash & Carry	Operating Voluntary Groups	Not Oper-ating Vol-untary Groups
Average annual sales........	$481,000	$4,292,000	$1,526,000	$511,000	$7,780,000	$2,484,000
Average number employees....	3.1	45.4	21.1	3.7	53.2	28.2
Number weeks stock........	3.1	4.1	4.7	3.8	3.2	4.2
Operating cost as percent of sales........	4.2	7.4	8.9	6.0	5.3	8.4

in the number of employees per establishment without a corresponding increase in sales volume. The chief patronage appeals of the cash-and-carry wholesaler have always been a lower price, made possible by lower operating costs and the possibility of inspecting merchandise before purchase—especially when it was perishable. The first of these seems to be in the process of being lost.

Drop-Shipment Wholesalers

A drop-shipper does not perform the stockkeeping function. He solicits orders from his customers, just as his full-service competitors do, but he transmits these orders to the manufacturers of the goods ordered, and they drop-ship them directly to the buyers: the wholesaler never has physical custody of the merchandise. Goods handled in this way must be sold in orders of sufficient size so that the manufacturer will not find it unprofitable to ship each order separately. Legally, the goods are sold by the producer to the jobber who, in turn, sells to the retailer or industrial buyer. The shipper looks to the wholesaler for payment, while the buyer holds him responsible for delays and mistakes in delivery.

This method of operation, in comparison with that of the service wholesaler, effects a considerable reduction in cost and hence in prices charged. The drop-shipper's establishment can be of the most rudimentary type. He is often known as a "desk jobber" or a "hat jobber," not to mention other less flattering epithets sometimes applied to him by unsympathetic competing service wholesalers. In spite of this hostile attitude most regular jobbers from time to time arrange drop-shipments for certain of their customers and in handling certain types of goods. While this is a service to the buyer in the immediate transaction, it is probably a dangerous practice for the wholesaler because it tends to get the customer out of the habit of depending upon his stockkeeping and delivery services and is apt to stimulate direct-from-manufacturer-to-retailer dealing.

Since 1949 the Bureau of the Census has not classified drop-shippers separately, so we have no accurate statistics of them. But we do know that they are most numerous in the lumber and building materials and coal trades. Although statistically insignificant in the aggregate in such trades as dry goods and drugs, in certain metropolitan markets they constitute at times a highly disturbing element in the business of the service wholesalers.

Drop-shipment wholesalers seem to be especially well suited to handle articles that are bulky. Such commodities are generally bought by users or retailers in quantities so large that very little, if any, saving in transportation costs may be made by distributing them through wholesalers' warehouses. Their entire journey to the retailer or user is generally made in carload or truckload lots, regardless of who ships them, and the service wholesaler must make his appeal largely on the basis of speed and certainty of delivery, factors that are not always of great importance in the handling of these products.

Wagon Jobbers, or Truck Wholesalers

These firms usually perform, in some degree, all wholesaling functions except that of credit extension, and some of them even offer that service. The wagon jobber differs from the service wholesaler in that he performs in one operation the functions of selling and delivering; he usually confines his stocks to limited assortments of fast-moving items, or perishable or semiperishable goods, and he generally sells for cash and in original packages.

Truck jobbers usually operate only in densely populated areas. The typical truck wholesaler maintains an office and warehouse and operates a fleet of trucks. Many small, one-man firms use garages or sheds as combination warehouses and offices, and employ one or two trucks each.

Before each trip the truck is loaded with a stock of the goods the wholesaler has for sale. The driver acts as salesman, delivery man or porter, and, usually, collection agent. Each day he travels a predetermined route, laid out for him at the central headquarters. If he sells certain types of goods, he may canvass the same customers every day. In the food business he generally traverses each route at least once in 10 days. In this trade the salesman-driver usually averages about 50 calls a day, and in making them he travels between 50 and 100 miles. The larger organizations employ route foreman or supervisors to train, discipline, and manage the truck salesmen.

The stock of goods carried by truck jobbers is usually rather limited, consisting mainly of perishable or semiperishable products and of specialty items requiring unusual sales effort. In the food field many of these wholesalers operate as exclusive outlets for the manufacturers whose products they handle. In such a case the affiliation between the manufacturer and the jobber is likely to be rather close.

By his method of operation the truck jobber might be expected to effect certain economies in rendering the wholesaling services. The selling, delivery, and collection functions are performed by one man operating one vehicle, and during the course of a single call. There should be considerable savings in the costs of those activities as compared with the expenses sustained by the regular wholesaler in carrying on the same operations. The latter transports a salesman and a truck separately to the buyer's store and handles each order twice— from warehouse to truck and from the truck into the buyer's store. The wagon jobber completes only one handling, since goods are moved into the vehicle in bulk. The immediate delivery feature, coupled with the usual practice of selling for cash, effects considerable reduction in accounting costs.

On the other hand, a truck is expensive transportation to use in making calls that do not result in sales. When a shortage occurs in a truck's stock, which is inevitable and frequent, two calls are needed to complete a transaction (one of them off the regular route and out of the usual routine) or a sale is lost and a customer disappointed. Not all the stock in a truck is sold during any given day. The excess is carted over the entire route at heavy expense. Because of the combination of the selling and delivery functions, one man must act as salesman, truck driver, order filler and porter. If the wholesaler pays him on the basis of his manual functions, no very high type of salesman can be obtained. If his wage rate is set at the level of his selling function, much of the time for which he is paid is spent doing less expensive tasks. The result is liable to be either poor salesmanship or high selling expenses.

The operating statistics of truck wholesalers (Table 9–2) were computed from the 1954 and 1958 reports of the Census of Business. While the number of truck wholesalers grew considerably during the four year period (45 percent) their total sales increased very little,

TABLE 9–2

TRUCK AND SERVICE WHOLESALER OPERATING STATISTICS

	1954		1958	
	Truck Whole-salers	*Service Whole-salers*	*Truck Whole-salers*	*Service Whole-salers*
Average annual sales...............	$275,000	$572,000	$209,000	$601,000
Average number of employees......	4.9	10.4	3.5	10.0
Average number of weeks' stock....	2.0	6.1	2.2	5.9
Average operating expenses (as percent of sales)................	14.2	14.0	14.7	14.4

with the result that the average establishment became smaller. Probably more truck wholesalers are to be found in the food business than in any other trade.

The truck distributor may be said to be adapted to the wholesale marketing of the following types of products and to the following kinds of customers:

a) Perishable or semiperishable goods. He can handle them with the requisite speed.

b) Goods the demand for which is readily and rather accurately predictable. Such predictability reduces the stock shortages and overages which are so costly to this kind of distributor.

c) The products of manufacturers operating on a small scale and selling in a local market.

d) Small customers, such as keepers of roadside stands and other little retailers not adequately served by regular wholesalers.

e) Stores in thickly populated urban areas where customers are not far apart.

Types by Goods Handled

Like retailers, wholesalers fall into classes or groups according to the products they handle, or perhaps (more exactly) according to the customers they supply. Their precise operating area is sometimes hard to define. When codes were being prepared under the National Recovery Act, a group composed of trade members and government representatives worked almost all of one day trying to define a wholesale stationery house and were able to come up with nothing better than the formula that it was a firm that bought and resold to retail stationery stores the articles a retail stationery merchant wished to buy from his supplier.

The types of goods handled by a wholesale trade change along with shifts in the merchandise stocked by its retail customers. The articles stocked and sold by a drug wholesaler, for example, have changed materially as retail druggists have shifted the lines they handle. The same thing is true, perhaps even to a greater extent, of the hardware wholesaler.

The industrial supply house offers an example of the two-fold trade division. As a general class, it is characterized by the fact that it sells to industrial users. An oilwell supply house sells to a certain kind of industrial user, but a machine tool house or an abrasives and abrasive materials supplier is distinguished by the added fact that it sells only a certain kind of goods.

In almost every wholesale trade there are general line houses and specialty firms. For example, in the food business we find general line grocery wholesalers who handle a complete assortment of grocery

TABLE 9–3

DISTRIBUTION OF TRADE SALES BETWEEN GENERAL LINE AND SPECIALTY HOUSES IN PERCENT OF TOTAL

	Groceries		Drugs		Dry Goods		Hardware		Jewelry		Electrical Goods	
	General	Specialty	General	Specialty	General	Specialty	General	Specialty	General	Specialty	General	Specialty
1929......	69.3	30.7	76.1	23.9	38.0	62.0	87.8	12.2	29.2	70.8	48.2	51.8
1939......	69.2	30.8	69.8	30.2	27.1	72.9	89.4	10.6	26.6	73.4	47.1	52.9
1948......	67.5	32.5	61.9	38.1	19.0	81.0	84.3	15.7	25.6	74.4	42.7	57.3
1954......	55.4	44.6	58.5	41.5	16.7	83.3	78.5	21.5	17.4	82.6	35.8	64.2
1958......	62.6	37.4	51.1	48.9	7.4	92.6	68.0	32.0	20.0	80.0	39.1	60.9

SOURCE: 1958 Census of Business.

products except the more highly perishable items, such as meats, fish, fresh fruits, and vegetables. In addition, the Bureau of the Census finds in the trade dairy products distributors, poultry products distributors, confectionery wholesalers, fish and seafood distributors, meat wholesalers; restaurant, bakery and hotel supply houses; bread and bakery goods distributors, canned goods wholesalers, flour wholesalers; frozen food houses, soft drink distributors, and sugar jobbers, as well as numerous other groups so finely particularized that the Bureau did not feel it worthwhile to classify them separately.

Table 9–3 shows for several wholesale trades over a number of years the division of trade sales volume between general line and specialty houses in percentage of the total. These figures show that in these key wholesale trades there has been a long-run trend away from the general house and in the direction of the specialty wholesaler, although in groceries, jewelry, and electrical goods there seems some tendency for the trend to flatten out, perhaps even reverse itself. Table 9–4 compares certain operating statistics of general and specialty houses in these trades in 1958.

TABLE 9–4

SOME GENERAL AND SPECIALTY HOUSE OPERATING STATISTICS

	Average Sales per Establishment ($1,000s)		Inventory Investment as Percent of Sales		Expenses as Percent of Sales		Average Employees per Establishment	
	Gen.	Spec.	Gen.	Spec.	Gen.	Spec.	Gen.	Spec.
Drugs.........	$4,647	$506	13.7%	10.3%	12.8%	16.0%	75	10
Dry goods......	1,459	747	14.3	11.7	13.8	12.4	22	8
Groceries.......	3,741	617	6.4	4.9	6.4	10.7	32	8
Electrical goods.	1,376	675	10.6	11.2	11.5	14.6	18	11
Hardware......	3,605	328	17.6	15.2	17.5	20.4	83	8
Jewelry........	318	322	16.8	16.0	19.8	18.1	7	6

SOURCE: 1958 Census of Business.

The specialty house is often able to carry a more complete selection of types, sizes, and varieties of the relatively few commodities it stocks than is profitable for the general firm with its much more varied line. The manager of the former concern is likely to be more familiar with the detailed conditions of the part of the trade in which he operates, with resulting savings in purchases. He is also likely to be more exact and speedy in conformance to trends, and to have superior capacity to give valuable advice and suggestions to customers. Since he carries relatively fewer articles he can train his salesmen so that they have a more intimate and exact knowledge of them than the representatives of the general house can be expected to possess concerning the much more numerous items of the more varied line they sell. All these factors enable the specialty house in spite of its smaller sales force, to do a much more effective job of selling than its full-line competitor, and this in turn makes it a much better outlet for the manufacturer's goods.

On the other hand, the general wholesaler can, through one call, by one salesman, in one order—and by one delivery—supply practically all the needs of the retailer. This makes it easier for the storekeeper to do his buying and enables him to carry on his purchasing work more economically. The full-line house may find it possible to enjoy many of the advantages of specialty wholesaling by departmentizing its operations along the lines of types of merchandise. The process cannot be carried too far, however, without the danger of losing other advantages.

From the standpoint of the manufacturer the general line house is likely to offer complete coverage of the market with fewer wholesale outlets to service than the use of the specialty firm requires. On the other hand, since the specialty house carries fewer products, its salesmen can do a more aggressive job of selling each one than is possible for the general line salesman. The manufacturer who markets through specialty houses must set up his price structure so as to allow a little more margin to the wholesaler than is needed for the general line firm. The specialty house often offers a means of bidding for the business of the large retail and industrial customers in a trade with relatively few wholesale contacts. If a manufacturer is willing to take advantage of the 30-70 principle (30 percent of the customers take 70 percent of the volume) and forget about the business of smaller retailers and smaller industrial buyers, he can usually do so fairly effectively through specialty wholesalers.

Geographical Types

Very few wholesalers are national in the sense that they operate in every state or nearly every state in the union. A much larger number are regional and market in several states or in parts of several states. By far the largest number are local in that they confine their activities to the natural wholesale market of a particular city or metropolitan area. These wholesale market areas are generally recognized and are a very influential factor in the trade. But when one attempts to set up boundaries for them on a map, the process becomes almost impossibly complex. The trade associations and the Department of Commerce have prepared wholesale trading areas for the grocery, drug, hardware, and dry goods trades. But, in practice, these are honored in the breach. Probably the most accurate way to describe the local wholesaler is to say that he trades within his concept of the trading area of the place where his warehouse is located.

Many national and regional wholesalers operate branches at strategic points throughout their markets, hoping by this means to offset the delivery advantage enjoyed by the local house. But this also exposes them to many of the managerial problems inherent in any chain operation.

From the standpoint of the manufacturer the national or regional house seems to offer an opportunity to achieve countrywide or regional coverage by one contact. This may be illusory, for such a firm often allows its branch managers a high degree of autonomy in both their selling and buying activities. This means that the manufacturer must maintain sales contact with each branch as well as with the central headquarters, and it may have the effect of actually increasing the selling work to be done over that necessary to market through an equivalent number of independent wholesale houses scattered over the same area.

AGENTS

So far we have been discussing the merchant types that function at the wholesale marketing level. These all have one thing in common; they take ownership responsibility for the goods they handle. Let us now turn our attention to the several kinds of agents which perform some of the wholesaling functions.

Agents have two essential features: (1) They do not take title to the goods they handle, and (2) They do not themselves buy and sell for their own account, but merely negotiate such transactions for others. Since by their method of operation they avoid in large measure the gravest and most unpredictable risk in the marketing process, that of demand fluctuations, they need much less capital to finance their activities than do merchants. The expense of the space, equipment, and labor necessary for storing and handling merchandise is dispensed with or kept at a minimum. Of course this relative lack of expense is accompanied by a lack in the number and extent of the wholesaling functions they perform.

There are four principal types of agents or agent middlemen: brokers, commission houses, selling or sales agents, and manufacturer's agents. It is a mistake to assume that in actual operation these four groups are sharply or completely segregated; here, as elsewhere, we find the overlapping of functions and the baffling confusion of nomenclature that are so characteristic of all phases of marketing. The fact that an operator calls himself a broker is no indication that he does not act as a commission firm as well. Selling agents shade by almost imperceptible degrees into manufacturer's agents, and vice versa. It is doubtful if there is a commission house in business which does not upon occasion function as a broker. In spite of this general vagueness and overlapping, it is useful to try to effect some degree of segregation in our discussion of these groups and to describe separately the operations that are typical of each of them.

The Broker

The broker performs only a few of the marketing functions. As a matter of fact, he generally concentrates upon but two of them, buying and selling. Even these he does not render in their entirety. He does not himself purchase or vend, but merely negotiates and facilitates the making of contracts of exchange. He may be defined as "an agent who does not have direct physical control of the goods in which he deals but represents either buyer or seller in negotiating purchases or sales for his principal."

He may represent either a buyer or a seller. Today he may act for a principal who wishes to sell, and tomorrow he may represent one who wants to purchase. As a general rule he does not formally act for both buyer and seller in the same transaction. Cases of such double representation are not unheard-of, and there may be rare trades or localities in which it is the accepted practice. But it is usually regarded as unethical on the part of the broker and poor policy from the standpoint of those for whom he acts. As a matter of actual fact, however, in a transaction in which only one of the parties is represented by a broker, the agent is apt to distribute his services to some extent between the two of them. He gets no fee unless an exchange is made. If he technically represents the buyer, therefore, he may serve his own interests better by inducing his principal to increase slightly the price offered than he would by seeking only to bring about a reduction in that demanded by the would-be seller. By trying to influence both parties he may increase his chance of receiving a fee, while, by bringing influence to bear upon only one, he would run the risk of failing to enjoy any remuneration.

Some brokers concentrate on representing buyers; a larger number habitually act for sellers. Regardless of the direction of a firm's concentration, however, it is not apt to turn down a possible fee to be made by departing from it.

Brokers' principals are usually producers, wholesalers, or retailers. Firms making industrial materials may use these middlemen either to sell their output or buy materials for them. The broker's relations with his principals are not necessarily continuous. Of course, any individual agent of this type may contract to act for certain firms continuously over a given period. In the absence of formal agreement, continuity of relationship may result from habit, personal liking, the quality of the services rendered, or some other similar consideration. But the nature of the broker's operations tends to make him a free-lance, acting for a succession of different principals.

Typically, the broker exercises no physical control over the goods whose purchase or sale he negotiates. He does not have them in his custody. Often he never sees them. He bears no responsibility for them unless in his descriptions of them he exceeds the truth or the powers granted him by his principal.

There are several relations which an agent may bear to the prices and terms of sale involved in the transactions in which he participates:

1. He may act as a go-between, carrying information from one party to the other and giving advice to his client. This is the position the broker most often occupies.

2. He may be directed by his principal to buy or sell "at the market." This means that he is obligated to bind his principal to pay or accept whatever price prevails on the market within a reasonable or specified period of time after he has received such instructions. The broker sometimes operates on this basis, but not usually.

3. The agent may be given a maximum or minimum price, above or below which he may not commit his principal to buy or sell. Such limits are often placed upon the broker's operations.

4. An agent may be directed to buy or sell at a price subject to confirmation by his principal. This is a modified form of (1) and is generally used when the agent is acting at a distance from his client. This arrangement is rather prevalent in the relations between brokers and those whom they represent.

The broker is paid a commission or fee. The former is a percentage of the price of the goods bought or sold; the latter is a definite sum per unit dealt in. Payment by commission tends to put a premium on increases in the price to be agreed upon. Its use is somewhat to the advantage of a principal who is selling through a broker, but tends to work against the buyer who employs this type of agent. This tendency is somewhat offset by the fact that the agent gets no pay unless an exchange occurs. To effect a sale means more to him than to increase the price by a few dollars.

The remuneration received by brokers varies with the trade they are in and the goods they handle. In some cases it is a fraction of 1 percent of sales; in others it may amount to several percent of the price. The Bureau of the Census reported that in 1958 the operating expenses of brokers representing sellers were 2.4 percent of sales; in 1954 the figure was 2.2 percent. This increase represents a continuation of a long-time trend.

Brokers apparently sell about one third of their volume to industrial buyers, although the proportion varies widely for different products. About half of their sales are made to wholesalers. Most of the remainder of their volume goes to retailers. Their sales to ultimate consumers are so small as to be insignificant.

In 1958 the average broker representing sellers mainly negotiated sales amounting to $2,263,000 annually and, he had about three employees. The typical brokerage house is not a large establishment, nor is the broker, as such, a dominating figure in wholesale distribution. His main stock in trade is an up-to-the-minute knowledge of his market and of the firms and people in it. He has been very aptly called "the eyes, the ears and the feet" of his principal. While it may appear to be a mark of laziness for a businessman endowed with organs of perception and locomotion to employ another for these purposes, his action in so doing may be justified if by this means he achieves for his firm a greater and less costly keenness of managerial perception, a more thorough understanding of market conditions, or more speed in the execution of marketing plans.

A manufacturer may find a broker a useful outlet under a number of conditions, some of which are:

a) An overstock can often be disposed of quickly and inexpensively through a broker. The danger is that the broker will sell to the manufacturer's own customers or to firms which will resell to them.

b) An industrial goods manufacturer may sometimes, as a result of his regular operations, have a one-time supply of a by-product material for which the broker can find a buyer.

c) If a manufacturer's output is small and he can not afford a salesforce, the broker may supply an outlet.

d) For the maker of a product that is highly standardized and traded in a localized or fairly well organized market, the broker may supply the low cost means of selling that such a situation usually demands.

The manufacturer who needs to use a broker in one or more of the temporary situations mentioned above will find it worthwhile to give him a certain amount of business constantly so as to keep contact with him and retain his goodwill.

The Commission House

While the broker and the commission house are in many respects much alike, there are certain pronounced differences between them. The commission operator may be defined as "an agent who usually exercises physical control over and negotiates the sale of the goods he handles." Although an agent of this type does not own the goods in which he deals, he has them in his physical custody during the process of selling and delivering them. His principals are commonly located at points remote from the place of sale. They consign merchandise to him; he cares for it while conducting selling negotiations, and, if his promotional efforts are successful, he delivers it to the buyers and collects for it, remitting the proceeds, less his fees and charges, to the shipper.

Legally, the commission house is obligated to exercise the same degree of care of the merchandise in its custody as that which a reasonably careful man would bestow upon goods that he owned. The amount of clerical work and physical handling involved in its operations is often considerable.

Commission agents in practically every trade perform an extensive series of physical services in handling the products they sell. In doing this work they take the place of the owners. The commission agent does not represent buyers. His principals are usually country assemblers or large producers of the goods he handles. In the grain trade he receives consignments chiefly from country elevators and from large grain owners. Livestock commission men represent mainly country traders and large ranchers and feeders. Long-time contracts usually do not exist between the agents and their principals, although in some cases, especially when the agents finance the shippers, arrangements are made covering an entire season's business.

The representation of the principal by the agent is not so direct in the case of the commission concern as it is in that of the broker. The former does business in its own name. The buyer does not necessarily know the identity of the owner from whom he purchases, but looks to the agent for the fulfillment of the terms of the contract.

The commission agent is rather more likely to be instructed to sell at the market than to be bound by restrictions as to the price he may accept. Much of the merchandise he handles is either perishable or in freight cars at the time of sale. Delay in vending or delivery is likely to result in its decay in the first case and in heavy demurrage charges in the second. To set a price below which the agent may not sell, or to require him to sell subject to price confirmation, is very likely to result in delay in the disposal of the goods consigned to him. Then, too, since the shipper is usually a considerable distance away from the market in which the sale is made, he cannot be familiar with the conditions prevailing there. For these reasons the commission house is apt to be allowed considerable discretion with respect to prices and terms of sale.

The commission house may perform the financing function by giving credit to the buyer, and this transaction is strictly his own affair: the shipper does not share in it and expects to receive a check for his merchandise immediately after it is sold, just as if the sale had been for cash. In some trades the commission house may finance the shipper. This process may involve merely the provision of the funds needed to move the goods from the country to the terminal market. It may include the furnishing of credit for the purchase and handling of the commodity at points of origin as well, or it may even extend to the making of loans to producers during the growing period.

When a transaction is completed, the commission agent prepares and sends to the shipper an "account sales," in which he sets forth the amount received for the goods, an itemization of his expenses in caring for them, his commission, any other authorized deductions, and the balance due his client. This document is usually accompanied by a check for the net proceeds of the transaction. The commission may be in the form of a percentage of the price received for the goods or of a stated amount per unit handled. The remuneration of the commission agent is usually somewhat higher than that of the broker, commensurate with his greater responsibility and services. Its precise amount varies with the trade and the market.

In 1958 the average commission agent negotiated sales amounting to $1,692,000. His organization consisted of about 6 employees and his expenses were 2.2 percent of sales.

Commission agents are not of great importance as outlets to the manufacturer. The nature of their operations especially suits them to the work of assembling; that is bringing together numbers of small lots of a product from scattered areas and making them available in a central market. This is peculiarly the marketing problem of agricultural producers. The manufacturer's problem is precisely the reverse, breaking down his total output into lots suitable for limited areas and individual customers. This is not to say that commission houses are *never* found in the manufacturer's marketing channels, but they are generally not as useful to him as other types of agent outlets. The student should be warned that in reading trade literature he must be on the lookout for a tendency of businessmen to use the term "commission merchant" or "commission house" to mean the manufacturer's agent and the sales or selling agent as well as the true commission firm as we have defined it here.

Sales or Selling Agent

This is "an agent who operates on an extended contractual basis; sells all of a specified line of merchandise for his principal or the principal's entire output; and usually has full authority with regard to prices, terms and other conditions of sale."

The Bureau of the Census reports that in 1958 the average selling agent negotiated sales amounting to $3,324,000 at a cost of 3.5 percent on sales and employed about 9 people. In 1954 his sales were $2,634,-000, his operating costs 3.6 percent, and he employed about 7 people. Sales agents are heavily concentrated in the textile industry.

A sales agent is usually unrestricted as to area and the customers to whom he sells. He really constitutes a sales department for each of the firms he represents, leaving their managers free to devote their primary attention to production activities. The agent does not necessarily concentrate on handling the goods of one producer but may represent competing concerns. In the cotton textile business one such firm sometimes acts for as many as 30 mills. The contract between a sales agent and his principal usually extends over a period of a year, or a selling season, although it may go on indefinitely, subject to cancellation by either party.

Sales agents are sometimes interested financially in the firms they represent. Less frequently the reverse is true; the principal has a financial interest in the agent. As a general rule, the former relationship is due to one of two causes. The agent may have financed the entrance of the manufacturer into business in order to build up his own volume of sales (not a few of the mills in the textile business were started in this manner). In the second place, the agent sometimes finances the operations of the producer by buying, loaning on, or guaranteeing his accounts receivable, by making advances on his inventories of unsold merchandise, or by endorsing his notes. Any of these temporary financial arrangements may readily be transmuted into a more permanent partial or complete ownership relation as a result of bad judgment or misfortune.

Many selling agents in the textile and clothing fields maintain designing departments and advise their principals as to the types of articles to be produced. Often an agent sells for future delivery goods to be made according to such designs and then turns the orders over to a client for manufacture. Except in the case of staple articles the agent usually plays a considerable part in the mill's performance of the merchandising or product-planning function.

Practice varies with respect to the degree of control exercised by the selling agent over the amount of merchandise produced or stocked. In the case of goods that are made to order, of course, it is very great. The mill can safely make only enough to fill the orders the agent secures for it. The latter usually allocates the business he obtains to the several plants he represents, in accordance with the amount and type of goods each is equipped to manufacture (although, without doubt, more personal considerations sometimes affect his performance of this allotment function). In other cases, involving staple merchandise, the agent agrees to sell the entire output of a mill although he apparently gives no guarantee to do so. Under this arrangement also he allocates the orders received among the concerns that he represents.

There is no uniformity with respect to the matter of control over price. Some principals allow their agents practically complete power to fix prices. When this is the case the mill usually furnishes its representative with operating cost information. It then becomes the agent's job, through his cost-accounting staff, to compute a selling price that will net the principal a satisfactory profit and, through his sales force, to sell its output at that price. This practice tends to stack the cards in the hand of the agent. In order to effect sales upon which he can realize commissions, he may be under some pressure to cut prices to such a point that very little, if any, profit may remain for the principal. It is easier and less costly for him to sell goods by price reductions than by applying additional sales pressure to prospective buyers.

Other manufacturers specify the prices at which their representatives shall sell. Agents whose clients have followed this policy have been known, at times when the market was weak, to undersell their clients for future delivery. If the market declined and the principals were forced to lower their prices, the agents turned such orders over to them to be filled. Otherwise they had to sustain the losses on them, amounting to the differentials between the mills' prices and those at which they had sold. The net effect of such a procedure is that the agent works against the interest of his principal by engaging in price competition with him.

Some mills allow their sales agents a measure of control over the stocks which the mills carry. When the principal must look to the representative to finance his inventory, of course, such control actually exists without its being formally conferred in the contract. When the financing service is not rendered, the grant of this power must be included in the agreement setting up the agency relation.

Although selling agents are heavily concentrated in the textile and dry goods trade, they are also found in machinery and equipment, clothing and furnishings, plumbing and heating equipment, furniture and house furnishings, industrial chemical and grocery businesses. In none of these fields, except perhaps the textile trade, are selling agents particularly significant in terms of the portion of the total sales volumes they handle.

The weaknesses of the selling agent as an outlet for the manufacturer arise very largely from the fact that if he does not have control over the price of the merchandise, his effectiveness in bargaining is limited, whereas if he does have such control, he is in a position, by cutting prices, to adversely affect the welfare of the mill without being himself seriously damaged by doing so. As a matter of fact, action contrary to the interests of his principal actually may be beneficial to the agent, since it may increase the volume of sales on which he collects commissions and tend to keep his selling-cost ratio at a minimum.

When he represents a number of competing concerns, the agent can hardly be said to be in a position to give wholehearted selling service to any one of them. His presence in a trade means that the business of producing the article he handles and that of distributing it are divorced from each other, or at least maintain separate managerial establishments. This is contrary to the whole trend of our economic system, which constantly throws more emphasis on the close coordination of production and marketing and the dependence of both on the wishes of the consumer. The amazing thing is not that the sales agent has given a selling service somewhat less than completely satisfactory, but that he has done as well as he has.

The Manufacturer's Agent

This agent "generally operates on an extended contractual basis; often sells within an exclusive territory; handles non-competing but related lines of goods; and possesses limited authority with regard to prices and terms of sale." He differs from the selling agent in that (a) He usually sells only part instead of all the output of his manufacturer principal, (b) He usually operates within a limited territory, (c) He does not handle competitive products but complementary, noncompeting ones, and (d) He usually lacks the selling agent's control over prices. About a fourth of the manufacturer's agents carry stocks on consignment. Since these inventories represent only about half a week's sales, the agents' performance of the stockcarrying function is rudimentary.

The student who reads trade literature should bear in mind the fact that manufacturer's agents are not always called by that name, but may be referred to as "manufacturer's representatives," a term that is also sometimes applied to salaried or commission salesmen, "commission men," and, in the food business, food brokers. The important thing is not what an agent is called but what he does.

According to the census reports there were, in 1958, 9,983 manufacturer's agents and 2,069 selling agents. Their sales were about $9.7 billion and the selling agents' volume was $6.9 billion. The average manufacturer's agent had annual sales of $970,000; his operating costs were 5.9 percent of sales, and he employed about 4 persons. In 1954 the Bureau of the Census reported statistics (Table 9–5) for both stock-carrying and nonstockcarrying houses.

TABLE 9–5

SELLING AGENTS' STATISTICS FOR 1954

	With Stocks	Without Stocks
Number.	2482	6238
Average annual sales.	$686,000	$874,000
Operating costs (in percentage of sales).	6.9	5.3
Number of employees.	4.3	3.0

Manufacturer's agents are quite common in the industrial goods field, particularly in handling certain types of equipment, and in the food business. They are also to be found in the textile, clothing, electrical goods, plumbing equipment and materials, and metals trades.

While he represents a number of principals, the manufacturer's agent does not usually handle goods of competing houses. But the articles he sells are apt to be related to one another in use or sale. Such an agent, operating in the field of industrial goods, for example, may sell a line of belting, belt dressing, pulleys, and lubricating compounds, each made by a different manufacturer. He usually exercises no more than advisory influence over prices, terms, or amounts produced. In an industry such as furniture and house furnishings, he often maintains a designing department to serve his clients.

The manufacturer's agent usually sells for shipment direct to the purchaser by the manufacturer, who generally bills the buyer direct. About one out of every four carries a stock of goods owned by the manufacturer and consigned to the agent. This ratio runs as high as one in three in the machinery, equipment, and supplies trade, and as low as one in eleven in the dry goods business. The stocks carried by these houses are very small and are probably used chiefly to fill emergency orders, or are carried by agents located at some distance from the factories of their principals.

Ordinarily a principal grants to each of his manufacturer's agents a definite territory, within which the agent is the sole distributor. The territories allocated to any particular agent by the several firms he represents often do not coincide exactly but, in general, are likely to tend to do so. To get complete countrywide representation for his product a manufacturer must make arrangements with several agents, each operating within a particular district.

The greatest variation exists in the commissions charged by manufacturer's agents. Some are reported to be as low as 1 or 2 percent on fast-moving bulk merchandise; others as high as 20 percent on highly technical industrial goods. Some agents are paid an annual fee, although this is not the usual practice.

Manufacturer's agents apparently sell to retailers for resale and to industrial buyers in about equal proportions. In the following trades most of their sales are made to retailers: furniture and house furnishings, clothing and furnishings, plumbing and heating equipment and supplies, lumber and building materials, and groceries and foods. Their sales to industrial buyers are most important in the following types of goods: machinery, equipment and supplies, chemicals, metals, automotive products, and textiles. They distribute most of the remainder of their volume to wholesalers. Sales to these customers are most significant in the following lines of merchandise: groceries and foods, hardware, paper and its products, and metals.

There are several conditions which tend to make the manufacturer's agent a significant part of the distribution systems of many manufacturers.

1. In certain lines of business he is useful in introducing new products. This is the case with groceries and foods, in which trade he handles mainly specialties and novelties. He is often employed for this purpose in the distribution of industrial goods. In this field the agent is likely to have the contacts which a new firm lacks entirely, or which an old firm lacks in a new field, and which are so necessary in introducing a new product.

2. He furnishes an outlet in areas where there is not sufficient demand to justify the maintenance of the manufacturer's own salesforce, but in which the producer wishes more individual representation than a wholesaler or industrial distributor can or will give him. By spreading his costs over a number of items the manufacturer's agent is able to reduce them to a reasonable figure on each item. Because he does not sell competing articles or very many noncompeting ones, he tends to give an individualized sales promotion service.

3. For the same reasons he is especially adapted to handle the output of small, highly specialized manufacturers, each producing one or two items of a general line. He is frequently used under these conditions to distribute machinery, equipment, supplies, and certain types of furniture.

4. If a manufacturer is poorly financed he can escape the expense of paying a sales force by using manufacturer's agents. He pays only for sales actually made, and then only after the transaction has been consummated—and often after he has received payment for the goods.

The manufacturer's agent has the advantage of economy as compared with the producer's own sales force. He can offer a more individualized selling service than the wholesaler can usually achieve. In comparison with the sales agent he is superior in that he confines his efforts to the products of one competitor and thus gives more particularized sales representation. As a result of these advantages he has been gaining in number and importance. On the other hand, in order to get complete coverage of the country through manufacturer's agents, the manufacturer must put together a sort of patchwork quilt of a number of agents with attending problems of overlapping and uncovered areas. In addition, the manufacturer's agent shares with the selling agent the drawback that his enterprise is usually an individual proprietorship, or a partnership, and hence lacks continuity. The producer who uses either of them as outlets must expect constant problems of replacing agents who have gone out of business.

Purchasing Agents

There are a few firms which are known as purchasing agents and which specialize in buying for wholesalers and large retailers. This type is not to be confused with the industrial purchasing agent who is a salaried employee of an industrial firm, charged with the task of buying the goods it uses in conducting its business.

These firms are situated in or near central markets to which their clients, usually because of location, do not have ready access. They tend to specialize by types of products: hardware, for example. While they may be fairly important outlets for manufacturers in a few trades, they have no widespread significance.

Resident Buyers

The resident buyer is closely akin to the purchasing agent, but is much more important numerically and probably in sales volume handled. He may be defined as "an agent who specializes in buying, on a fee or commission basis, chiefly for retailers." His customers are mainly department stores, although many specialty stores, especially those retailing fashion merchandise, make use of his services.

Most of the resident buying houses are located in central markets, chiefly New York, Chicago, and Los Angeles. Some large department stores and chain store systems own and maintain buying offices in one or more of these centers, and these are sometimes referred to as resident buyers, although more often they are called "private offices." Others, sometimes called "associated offices," are owned cooperatively by groups of stores. The latter often function in much the same manner as the true resident buying house.

The client store looks to its resident buying house (*a*) to purchase any merchandise the client may request, (*b*) to keep the client informed about conditions in the market, (*c*) to assist store buyers in selecting merchandise, (*d*) to organize and facilitate joint buying activities among its clients, and (*e*) sometimes to conduct research work of benefit to all client stores.

Two Forms of Pay for Resident Buying Houses. The "salaried house" receives payment from its clients in the form of an annual fee. The precise amount of this payment is often the result of bargaining, although in a few cases it is set as a fixed percentage of the purchases made through the agency, or is graduated according to the total annual sales of the client stores. These offices usually represent the larger stores.

The "commission house" is paid by the manufacturers whose goods it sells to its clients. Its remuneration is received in the form of a commission of from 3 to 5 percent of the sales price. Such offices seem best adapted to serve the smaller stores since their fees vary according to the services they render and do not constitute a burden of overhead costs upon the stores using them. Their clients can shift from one office to another at will.

Much jealousy exists between the two groups. The advocates of the salaried houses contend that since they are paid by the client stores, they more truly represent the retailers' interests than the commission houses are apt to do. In their choice of sources they are not limited to those that allow commissions; nor are they under pressure to place orders with any one supplier because of the unusually high commissions he may allow. The friends of the commission firm point out that the retailer has the advantage of its services at no cost to him, and that, since its income depends upon the amount of its purchases, it is apt to be more alert to discover and take advantage of buying opportunities than is the salaried house. The most potent argument against the commission house lies in the fact that although it is supposed to be employed by one party to a bargain, it receives its pay from the other party to that same transaction. It is argued that the hand that writes the paychecks usually rules the conduct of those who receive them.

The cooperative or associated resident buying house is owned and controlled by the member stores. Its expenses are commonly allocated among these stores on the basis of sales volume, although sometimes according to the amount each buys through the office. The largest organizations of this type are the Associated Merchandising Corporation, the Cavendish Trading Corporation, and the Specialty Stores Association. The membership of most of these groups is composed of large stores.

Some of the advantages claimed for this type are the facts that, owing to the intimate relationship among the members, cooperative research concerning store operations can be conducted; the stores have complete control over its activities; and the members' contributions contain no element of profit to the buying office.

Some of the services that a resident buying house usually performs for its clients are as follows.

1. By constantly shopping the market its buyers can furnish the store buyer much more complete information as to market conditions than the latter can acquire in the time he is able to spend there.

2. It can discover new sources and develop cordial relations with them.

3. When the store buyer comes to the market, the buying office publishes the fact, furnishes him office space, and sometimes arranges interviews for him with selected sources.

4. It maintains and makes available to the store buyer a resource, or vendor file, listing the names of all worthwhile sources and including pertinent information about their offerings and operating methods.

5. It maintains display rooms where especially interesting merchandise may be examined, and sample rooms in which salesmen may display their wares to store buyers requesting such service.

6. Its buyers may accompany the store buyers in the market and aid them.

7. It places orders or reorders for the store upon request by telephone, wire, or letter.

8. It seeks to discover job lots at attractive prices, and will arrange for their purchase by a client or group of clients.

9. It may consolidate the orders of several of its client stores, and thereby obtain reduced prices.

10. It may send samples of new types of merchandise to its clients. On the basis of an examination of such a sample, or of testing its attractiveness to customers on the selling floor, a store may authorize the buying office to place an order for the article.

11. It may consolidate several orders of the same store, each for a different kind of merchandise, into one shipment, thereby speeding transportation and sometimes cutting the cost of it.

12. It follows up orders for future delivery and makes sure that the sources ship them when specified. In case the goods delivered are not satisfactory, it may represent the client in making adjustments.

13. It furnishes market and fashion information, mainly through the bulletins and style reports which it sends regularly and frequently to its clients.

14. It may conduct research activities into the organization and management of its client stores, thereby making possible an interchange of information as to operating methods. The associated groups have been especially active in developing this service. In some cases it has taken the form of a sort of clinic by means of which a number of successful heads of departments of member stores study a weak department of another member and make recommendations for its improvement.

15. A resident buying house may be influential in organizing and carrying out plans for "group buying." In conducting this practice a representative of the office usually scouts the market, gathering samples of a particular article: house dresses, for instance. The store buyers then attend a meeting at which these garments, with the manufacturers' labels removed, are displayed and discussed. Certain numbers are then selected for group purchase through the buying office. Individual stores often obligate themselves to take a certain number of units of each item selected.

The advantages of this procedure are twofold. First, the merchandising knowledge and experience of all the buyers in the group are pooled. This is almost certain to result in some improvement in selection. Second, lower prices are obtained on the larger amounts of goods bought. This type of activity is especially characteristic of the associated offices. Although it is often carried on by groups not connected with any sort of resident buyer, the most successful examples of it are to be found among such organizations.

The resident buyer ordinarily assumes no responsibility for payment for the goods he purchases for his clients. The seller usually must ship separately to each store, and bill and collect from each individually.

A number of resident buying houses conduct jobbing businesses on the side. The stocks carried are usually limited in both amount and variety. From such inventories they can quickly fill emergency orders for staple merchandise.

The manufacturer who makes merchandise that must be sold through department stores and specialty stores in the fashion or semi-fashion field can hardly afford to ignore the facilities and services offered by the resident buying house. Its use forces him to do the selling job in two stages. First, he must sell the buyer for the resident house, and only then does he have the chance to sell to the store buyer, but in doing the second job he has the help of the resident house buyer. In dealing with the resident house he finds himself up against the combined purchasing power of all the client stores with consequent pressures on prices and terms. On the other hand, the resident house offers him a means by which to reach all the stores that use its services. Probably the advantages and disadvantages balance out pretty evenly. The small or even the medium-sized manufacturer can not reach all the client stores economically in any other way.

Auction Companies

The auction company is not a very important element in the marketing of manufactured goods. A few items, such as certain types of jewelry, are sold to consumer buyers at auction. Other types of manufacturers may use it occasionally as an outlet at the retail or wholesale level. It is important in the fruit and vegetable trade, the raw tobacco trade, and in the sale of skins and furs.

The auction company is prepared

a) To receive merchandise and divide it into auctionable lots, and otherwise prepare it for sale.

b) To arrange a sale and advertise it.

c) To prepare and distribute a catalog of the goods and lots offered for sale.

d) To provide an auctioneer and the various clerical services involved in completing the sale.

e) To collect from buyers and remit to the sellers.
f) To arrange for delivery.

The auction company is paid a commission, based on the selling price, or a fee per unit sold. In 1958 its expenses averaged 2.5 percent of sales.

The auction company is a quick way of selling large amounts of merchandise. It also provides assurance that the price will be the best that market conditions permit at the moment of sale. Theoretically, the auction company sells goods "as is," with no assurances as to quality; the buyer is supposed to be entirely on his own. But in actual practice the management of an auction company finds it highly desirable to see to it that when goods are sold by sample the sample accurately represents the quality of the whole lot. Otherwise buyers will discount their bids and the auction will lose its effectiveness.

CHAPTER 10

Channel Management

We are now ready to consider the major problems involved in managing marketing channels. This is one of the most crucial areas in marketing management and, in the solution of these problems, the intangible elements are highly important. So managerial judgment looms very large.

Common Misconceptions

There are several misconceptions or gaps in management thinking about the channel problem that often confuse the student and impair the soundness of executive decisions. One of these is the idea that a channel of marketing includes only business units external to the producing firm. This is not true. A marketing channel or channel of distribution embraces both intracompany organization units and extra-company agents and dealers.

Another way to look at it is that a firm's marketing organization consists of (*a*) one or more organization units within the firm, and (*b*) a system of business units outside the firm, both of which it uses in its marketing work. If a company's marketing program is to be effective, the activities of the inside units and those of the outside units must be closely coordinated so as to make a single, forceful impact on the market. A manager who thinks of the inside organization units in one frame of reference and of the extra-firm units in another is likely to be handicapped in achieving such coordination.

Most of the problems we will deal with in this chapter center around this task of fitting together the activities of the outside and the inside marketing channel units so as to achieve a common impact on the market. We will defer to the next section the discussion of the problems involved in managing the marketing channel units that are inside the firm.

A *second* misconception is the notion that the really big problem in managing channels is that of selection. There is no denying the importance of choosing the most effective channels and the best operating units in the channels. This is basic to good marketing management, just as careful choice is basic to good personnel management in any functional area of business. But the act of selection opens the door to a whole series of executive decisions and actions involved in administering the relationships of the manufacturer to the units in the channel, and of those units to each other. The most careful and intelligent selection work may be undone if lax administration of day-to-day relationships generates dissatisfaction, with resulting loss of individual outlets and overlapping or conflicting activities of various units. The work of outside independent units in the channel must be managed in much the same way as the work of the company salesmen is managed.

What has just been said gives the lie to a *third* misconception: that channel management is a one-shot affair. The marketing manager who completes a job of organizing or reorganizing his channels cannot heave a sigh of relief and relax in the confidence that his channel problems have been solved for a while. For the unit membership in a channel is constantly changing; some firms go out of business or, for reasons of their own, drop out of the channel, and the managerial personnel of an outlet changes with the result that its performance is improved or worsened.

The very nature of the outlets in a trade may change over a period of years, as is exemplified by the growth of the suburban shopping center store, the supermarket, and the discount house. The manufacturer who delays too long in shifting his channel in response to such changes may find their opportunities closed to him when he finally gets around to capitalizing on them. Managing channels is a constant, day-to-day process.

Nature of Channel Relationships

All human relationships, except perhaps that of outright warfare, are a mixture of conflict *and* cooperation. Consider the ordinary employer-employee relationship. The employer has certain objectives he can achieve by hiring the employee; usually he wants to get certain work done that he can't or doesn't want to do himself. The employee has certain objectives that he can gain by accepting the job. He wants to earn a living, but he may also want to earn it with the least exertion, pleasant or otherwise. He may wish to work under the most pleasant surroundings or to work at a job that will afford him a sense of personal accomplishment or subject him to the least rigid discipline. On the other hand, the employer has such objectives as high quality of product which requires meticulous and exacting workmanship, low costs of operation, or conscientious service to customers which demands that the employee be pleasant even when his head aches or his feet hurt.

Some of these objectives of the two parties coincide and can be achieved by the same activities; others are in conflict. Good management consists in so arranging matters as to bring about the greatest area of coincidence, and in working out some mutually acceptable reconciliation of the objectives that conflict.

In managing his channel relationships the manufacturer must work with two kinds of sanctions. In the part of his channel that is inside his own organization he can depend on the sanctions that arise from the contract of employment. He can do a certain amount of ordering and expect his orders to be carried out. In dealing with the outside units in his channel he must rely on the sanctions that are implicit in the contract of purchase and sale of either goods or services, or both. These units are usually independent concerns engaged in business to make a profit. The manufacturer's ostensible sanction, therefore, lies in the amount of profit that these firms can make in marketing his products.

Really, the difference between the two is not so marked as it appears at first examination. Both relationships can be terminated at the will of either party, subject to union pressures in the case of the employee, and to pressures of the market in that of the outside unit. In both cases the final sanction lies in the interests of the two parties and in the extent to which they coincide and to which adjustments minimize the impact of their conflict. They differ in the fact that, in dealing with the independent businessmen who make up the outside part of his channel, the manufacturer faces a group of managers who are independent-minded and used to making their own decisions. It is also true that a termination or impairment of the relationship will usually have a less damaging impact on them than on the hired employee. The retailer who drops a manufacturer's line often stands to lose only the profit he made from handling it; the salesman who quits or loses his job foregoes his entire livelihood unless he has another waiting for him. The fact remains that the marketing executive of a manufacturing firm who tackles the job of managing his channels without an acute awareness of the coincidence-conflict mixture of interests characteristic of the supplier-outlet relationship is headed for serious trouble.

KINDS OF CHANNELS

Perhaps, before we go farther into the specifics of channel management, we should examine briefly the kinds of channels typically available to the manufacturer's marketing executive. Each of the channels we will describe is a type. Several of them are subject to considerable variation in relationships within the typical pattern. The following are the most common patterns.

1. *Manufacturer to Consumer.* This is usually implemented through the manufacturer's own salesforce, often supplemented by a system of branch houses through which physical distribution is effected.

(This type of channel is rather rare in the consumers' goods business, although isolated instances exist. For example, a maker of men's shirts and other accessories sells direct to consumers by mail, and in the shoe industry several manufacturers market direct to users through their own chain store outlets.)

The direct channel is widely used in the marketing of industrial goods for reasons that will be developed in the following discussion. In this field, also, a modification of the direct channel is found in the form of an agent, either selling or manufacturer's, through whom sales contact is made with users—to be followed by factory shipment if orders are received, or by contacts of salaried experts if precontract technical service is needed. In the marketing of highly standardized industrial materials brokers are often used to make initial contacts and assist in contract negotiations. Perhaps the use of some form of agent is prevalent enough in the industrial goods business so that it should be regarded as a separate type of channel.

2. *Manufacturer to Distributor to User.* This is a very common pattern in the marketing of industrial goods. The distributor involved is commonly classed as a kind of wholesaler. He buys the goods outright and resells them to industrial consumers. This channel is especially fitted for the marketing of supplies, materials, and auxiliary equipment that have a horizontal demand; that is, they are used by many industries. Some makers of major or sub-major equipment, especially small or highly specialized houses, make use of this channel. In the industrial goods business this is regarded as an indirect channel.

3. *Manufacturer to Retailer to Consumer.* The use of this channel is practically confined to the consumers' goods business. Sales are usually made by the manufacturer's own salesforce calling on the retailer, although in the fashion goods business the retailer may visit the producer to purchase, or a resident buyer may intervene. Except in the case of bulky items, such as furniture and automobiles which are shipped from the factory or assembly plants, delivery is usually made to the retailer from the manufacturer's branch house or from a commercial warehouse in which he maintains stocks. This is generally regarded as a direct marketing channel.

4. *Manufacturer to Wholesaler to Retailer to Consumer.* This used to be the dominant channel in the marketing of consumers' goods, but its importance has been declining steadily for a long time, although it has enjoyed a slight recovery in recent years. The manufacturer sells to the wholesaler through a small force of salesmen, and usually ships to him in quantity lots from the factory or a branch house or commercial warehouse stock in a central wholesale market. In a few trades, in which drop-shipment wholesalers operate, goods are shipped direct from the factory to the retailer. Many manufacturers complain that some wholesalers dilute the benefits of this system by ordering in very small quantities, often not much (if any) larger than those which might be expected from retailers.

In some trades, manufacturers using this channel have found it worthwhile to operate forces of detail men or "missionary salesmen" who visit retailers much less frequently than they would have to do if they were charged with the entire selling job. Any orders they take from the retailer are usually turned over to the wholesaler of his choice. On such orders the wholesaler receives his usual margin of gross profit. The detailers also are generally charged with the job of informing the retailer and his salespeople about the manufacturer's products, stimulating them to promote the sale of his merchandise and working with them in carrying out his local and point-of-sale promotional campaigns. They may also be expected to travel with the wholesaler's salesmen and train and stimulate them to sell the manufacturer's products. In the drug business they spend much of their time calling on doctors, explaining their employer's products, and distributing samples and printed material descriptive of them. The use of these salesmen represents an attempt by the manufacturer to enjoy some of the benefits of direct marketing without incurring all its costs.

This channel is generally regarded as indirect.

5. *Manufacturer to Agent to Wholesaler (or Distributor) to Retailer (or Industrial User) to Consumer.* This channel is not widely used for manufactured goods, although in some trades it is highly important. The agent involved is usually a broker, a manufacturer's agent, a sales agent or a specialized type of resident buyer. The food broker, really a manufacturer's or sales agent, often operates in this manner, although he is likely to sell to large retailer buyers as well as wholesalers. In a few trades a super-jobber, who buys outright the goods he handles, takes the place of the agent in selling to ordinary wholesalers. Obviously, this channel is indirect.

6. *Mixed Channels.* As was pointed out, each of these channels is a type, and manufacturers create many variations within each type.

Many of them also find it profitable to mix one or more types in their channel systems. For example, a manufacturer may use one channel for one product or product line and another for a different product group, or he may service one customer group through one type of channel and use an entirely different avenue to reach another class of customers. He may sell direct to customers who are large, or potentially so, and use wholesalers (distributors) or agents to reach smaller buyers. In areas where customers are concentrated and potential volume is heavy, he may market direct, and rely on agents or wholesalers (distributors) in regions where potential buyers are few and scattered.

We have described these typical channels for purposes of simplicity and ease in studying the problems of channel management. The marketing executive is wise not to go strictly by the book in this work but to set up a channel pattern that fits the special needs of his particular marketing problem.

ESTABLISHING CHANNEL RELATIONSHIPS

Comparatively few marketing managers ever face the task of setting up marketing channels from scratch. This problem arises when a new firm starts in business or when an existing firm moves into a new market or launches a new product that must be sold to a group of customers not previously served. Almost every one of them, though, must constantly reexamine, reappraise, modify, and reorganize existing channels. Much the same things need to be done in both these situations. First, the manager should study his company, its products, and the market it wants to serve to determine what marketing tasks he must get done through the outlets in the marketing channel he chooses. Second, he should study the kinds of outlets available and the pattern of their activities to determine which of them are best suited to do these tasks. In the course of this study he will almost inevitably perform entirely or in part the third and fourth steps in the planning and selection process, choosing the most desirable individual firms within type groups and negotiating working relationships with them.

Factors Affecting Jobs to Be Done

The jobs the marketing manager needs to have done by his channels depend on three kinds of factors: those arising from the nature of the product or products he has to market, those imposed by the character of the market in which he wishes to sell, and those resulting from the strengths and weaknesses of his own company.

Product Factors. The list of product characteristics that influence the nature and dimensions of the job the marketing manager must depend on his channel outlets to do is very long and it varies with each product. We can not discuss them all. The most we can do is to examine the ones that are most common and indicate the nature of the influence exercised by each.

1. *Unit Value.* If the unit value of a product is high, it is feasible for the manufacturer to sell direct either to the user or to the retailer if it is a consumer's good. This characteristic does not always demand direct sale but it does tend to make it economical because, since the number of dollars involved in each transaction is high, the heavy costs of making a direct sale can be spread over more sales dollars and so be smaller for each sales dollar. If the unit value of an article is low, the amount involved in each sales transaction is apt to be small, with the result that it can not economically be sold direct by itself but must be grouped with other products into an assortment or line with a resulting increase in the size of the average sales transaction and reduction in marketing costs per unit and per sales dollar. Retailers, wholesalers, and agents are specialists in the business of assembling and handling assortments, which means that small unit value indicates the desirability of indirect channels.

2. *Bulk and Weight.* If a product is so bulky or heavy that the typical purchase constitutes a carlot or truckload shipment, two of the chief factors that justify the stock carrying channel outlet are lacking: local stock carrying and economies in transportation. If other factors are favorable, the manufacturer can sell direct, or if his own sales-force is not economical, he can market through agents for factory shipment.

If, on the other hand, a product's bulk and weight are such that neither the user nor the retailer can buy it in carload or truckload lots, the manufacturer is apt to find that he can reduce the costs of marketing it by including the wholesaler or industrial distributor in his marketing channel. This does not follow inevitably, for wholesalers and distributors may refuse to buy in economical shipping lots—in which case the manufacturer's marketing manager will be wise to question the validity of their inclusion in his channel. Bulk and weight must usually be considered in relation to unit value rather than as entirely separate factors.

3. *Technical Nature.* In general, the more highly technical a product is the more direct should be its channels of distribution. In the industrial goods field this characteristic may give rise to the need for the manufacturer to offer the buyer technical advice and help in designing the product, preparing specifications for it, installing it, and using it.

Many makers of industrial goods find it necessary to maintain staffs of highly skilled experts to provide these services. There are not many consumers' goods products that require this kind of service. When it is needed for any kind of product, this means that there must be direct contact between the maker and user and that contact should usually begin at the selling level.

Many technical and semi-technical products require repair and maintenance service. This is more apt to be important to the maker of consumers' goods than of industrial products because many users of the latter maintain machine shops or maintenance staffs to provide such service, while the ultimate consumer is apt to be relatively innocent of technical or mechanical knowledge and ability. This means that the industrial goods maker's interest in the repair and maintenance service is often confined to the provision of repair parts, which does not require direct contact.

On the other hand, if a consumers' good that is technical or mechanical in nature is to give satisfaction to its users, the repair and maintenance service at the local level must be good and reasonably priced. Automobile owners, and ladies who preside over automated kitchens and laundries, are well aware of this. If the manufacturer of such equipment wants to retain their patronage he must endeavor to at least equal the quality of maintenance service offered by his competitors. Other factors usually prevent him from doing this by direct consumer contact, but this characteristic of his product often puts him under considerable pressure to make his marketing channels as direct as possible. He is apt to seek to do this by selling through selected retail outlets, with whom he maintains contact by either (*a*) his own salesmen, (*b*) exclusive wholesalers, or (*c*) "tame-cat," or owned, wholesale outlets.

4. *Perishability.* If a manufacturer's product is highly perishable he will usually find it desirable to choose channels that will (*a*) move it into use as fast as possible and (*b*) provide facilities and care to prevent or delay its deterioration. In the industrial goods field this may involve marketing direct to the user, although it may also take the form of the use of agents who sell for factory delivery, which gives the maker an opportunity to control the speed with which the product moves and the care that is taken of it during its movement to the buyer.

In the consumers' goods field, perishability is apt to cause the manufacturer to market direct to the retailer through his own branch houses, as is the practice in the meat packing industry, or to distribute through specialized wholesalers equipped to care for the product, as is true in the frozen foods business.

5. *Fashion.* If a product is characterized by the style element and subject to rapid changes in fashion, the marketing channel to retailers must be direct. Interestingly enough in this kind of business, it is the retailer who seeks out the manufacturer, or at least the wholesale market in which the manufacturer operates, and not the other way round as is usually the case. This occurs for several reasons:

a) The store buyer wants to compare the offerings of a number of manufacturers. In order to be most effective this process of comparison must take place within a short period of time, usually a few days. This can be accomplished when the buyer visits the market—while it would hardly be possible if salesmen of manufacturers visited buyers in their stores and showed samples. Many buyers wish to make their comparison by viewing garments on living models. It would be a bit expensive and cumbersome for the manufacturer's salesman to dash about the country shepherding a bevy of models.

b) By visiting a wholesale market the store buyer is able to gather information and impressions about fashion trends. She does this by talking with other buyers (most of them visit the market at about the same time each season), by consulting her store's resident buying organization if it has one, and by "shopping" the stores in the fashion centers, such as New York, Los Angeles, or Chicago, where the wholesale markets are located.

c) By being in the market the buyer for a big store can play one manufacturer off against another, and the small store buyer may be able to pick up merchandise bargain crumbs she would miss if not there in person.

While these are the chief reasons for this reversal of the usual procedure, there are others.

In this situation, the manufacturer's channel decisions consist largely in trying to make sure that his offerings are brought to the attention of the resident buying houses serving the stores likely to sell most effectively the kinds of merchandise he makes, and, when the store buyers come to town, in making direct contacts with them, ranging from merchandise displays to highly expensive wining and dining.

Not all style goods are handled in this manner. It is characteristic mainly of those whose fashion cycle is short and whose changes are fast-moving. For example, men's clothing tends to be marketed more like other goods, with the manufacturer seeking out the retailers, sometimes through wholesale intermediaries, instead of the latter visiting the central markets. The same thing is true of many other types of goods that have the style element to a minor degree.

6. *Standardization.* Goods that are standardized can move through indirect channels with outlets at several levels. But if each buyer wishes a product that is made to suit his needs, the manufacturer must usually deal with the prospective customer directly, although the initial contact

may be through an agent. This situation rarely occurs in the consumers' goods field. It is quite common in the marketing of industrial goods, especially equipment and technical materials such as chemicals. For them the buyer often prepares his own specifications and sometimes expects the supplier to offer technical help in doing so. When this is the situation the supplying manufacturer had just as well set up his marketing channel on a direct basis since he will have to make direct contact eventually in any case.

When a product is standardized in the sense (*a*) that all units of it, regardless of who makes them, are of substantially uniform characteristics and quality, or (*b*) that all units sold under one brand are identical or practically so, there is no compelling need for direct contact between the maker and the user every time a sale is made. Such a product can be marketed through indirect channels, with several intermediaries between the manufacturer and the consumer. Whether it is done that way by any specific firm depends on other factors in the company situation.

7. *Stage of Market Development.* When a product is new its properties and uses are largely unknown to consumers and, since it lacks wide acceptance in the market, its manufacturer must seek outlets that are willing to give it special attention by bringing it to the notice of prospective buyers, explaining and possibly demonstrating its usefulness, participating in the work of advertising it, and in general putting a lot of sales effort behind it. The marketing manager is apt to feel that these things can be done best by his own salesforce calling directly on retailers or users. This is not always economically feasible. In this case, he may find it desirable to seek outlets, like manufacturer's agents, who specialize in handling new products, or to try through franchise arrangements to limit the number of competing items his outlets handle or to commit them to devote special selling and promotional effort to his product.

As a product becomes known and gains wide market acceptance and preference its maker may find that his interests are best served by more general distribution by a larger number and variety of outlets who function more as *conduits* and less as *pumps*. At this stage he is apt to rely heavily on advertising to pull his merchandise through these relatively undynamic channels.

8. *Length of Line.* If a manufacturer makes a long line containing many products sold in the same market, to the same types of customers, and in large volume, he is in a better position to use direct marketing channels than when he confines his efforts to one or two products or to

a variety of articles marketed to several types of consumers. The economics involved here have already been discussed.

Nature of the Market. The characteristics of the market in which a manufacturer must distribute his goods creates its own set of factors which influence his choice of channels. Like the product characteristics just described, these market factors are very numerous and varied. We will describe only those which are most common.

1. *Number of Customers.* If the number of potential customers for a product or a line of products is small, the cost of a direct sales force is apt to be low, the orders that must be handled relatively few, and the number of shipments small. All of these things tend to make it possible for the manufacturer to use direct marketing channels.

For example, it would have been foolish for a firm that developed and made silicon transistor material (for which there were less than 50 customers, three or four of whom bought 80 percent of the total volume) to market any other way than through its own salesmen. The whole selling job could be done by one or two men; orders were few and big and so were shipments. On the other hand, it would be hopelessly expensive for the maker of an ascorbic acid preparation to help preserve home-frozen fruits and improve the taste of frozen citrus concentrates to try to sell the product direct to all the grocery stores and many of the drugstores of the country in which people expect to be able to buy it. The price of the average order would probably not be enough to pay the cost of the call of the salesman who made it. Indirect channels, including wholesalers and probably agents, are necessary.

2. *Where the Customers Are.* When possible customers are concentrated in certain reasonably small areas, the cost per call of a manufacturer's direct salesman is apt to be relatively low; the number of branch warehouses needed to service the trade directly is limited, and the cost per delivery is less than it would be if they were scattered. But if prospective buyers are widely scattered over the whole country, the average manufacturer's line can not be sold in sufficient volume in most areas to pay the costs of direct marketing. A wholesaler or distributor must combine it with other products to gain the volume necessary to cover the expenses of selling, handling, and delivery. When customers are scattered thinly over most of the market, with concentrations in certain limited areas, the manufacturer may find it profitable to use mixed channels of distribution.

3. *Customers' Buying Habits and Preferences.* The manufacturer who chooses to ignore the preferences of his customers and to try to change their buying habits faces a difficult and highly expensive job.

He is much wiser if he tries to find out where and how often they want to and usually do buy, how much they want to buy at a time, and the circumstances under which they want to buy, and then chooses channels and outlets that fit into this pattern. The maker of the ascorbic acid preparation mentioned above first tried to market it through drug wholesalers and retailers because, in another form, ascorbic acid is a medicinal item. But he found that housewives regarded its new form as a food and were loath to go to a drugstore to buy it. When he started selling it through grocery stores, particularly supermarkets, a meager and bitterly disappointing sales volume was turned into a profitable one. The consumer buyer is a good place to start in planning marketing channels.

If consumers want to buy a product often, in small quantities, and at the most convenient places, its manufacturer will be wise to try to achieve as nearly complete coverage as possible; that is to have it offered for sale in every suitable outlet. This will tend to mean marketing through wholesalers, if it is a consumers' good, and through distributors if an industrial good. If, on the other hand, users are choosy and want to shop around and compare, a system of franchise or exclusive outlets, one or two in each market area, may be feasible, and this in turn may make it possible to market direct to these selected customers.

4. *Importance of Quality.* In the industrial goods field the need for precise and consistent quality in a product, and for variations in the characteristics that make up quality, tends to point in the direction of direct marketing channels so that the manufacturer may at all times keep on top of the quality situation and have a clear and precise knowledge of the quality needs of the users of his product. If he markets an article that is standardized, with reasonably wide quality tolerances, he can and probably will find it profitable to market through indirect channels.

The maker of a consumers' good which leans heavily on quality as a patronage motive will find it worthwhile to make sure that it is sold only by outlets that cater to the "limousine" trade and that endow their facilities and activities with an atmosphere that connotes quality to the consumer. This is apt to mean that he can choose these outlets and manage his relations better if he establishes and maintains direct contact with them than if he tries to work through intermediaries.

5. *Nature of Use.* The *purpose* for which the typical customer wants to use a product and the *way* in which he wants to use it greatly influence the way in which he wants to *buy* it—and the appeals that will capture his patronage. Its manufacturer must choose marketing channels that conform to these wants and that can effectively present the convincing appeals.

A common example is the company that makes both consumers' goods and industrial goods. Most of the oil companies use different sales and delivery channels to handle gasoline and motor oils to ultimate consumers from those they employ to market industrial lubricants, fuel oil and derivative materials. A type of channel, different from either of these, is utilized to market fuel oil for household consumption. The ascorbic acid preparation for household use (mentioned above) is moved through an entirely different channel than Vitamin C, which is the same thing in bulk form and is marketed as a material to pharmaceutical manufacturers for use in making vitamin tablets. Often the maker of an industrial good that is used by several industries for different purposes must employ different channels in marketing it to each customer trade.

6. *Horizontal versus Vertical Markets.* If an industrial good is sold to only one industry or homogeneous group of users its maker is apt to find it possible and profitable to use a direct channel. In such a case four or five prospective customers are likely to control the lion's share of the demand, and a few dozen often take 90 percent or more of the industry's requirements. Each purchase involves a large quantity, and customer-supplier relationships tend to continue over long periods. If, on the other hand, a product, such as an abrasive, is used by many industries, its manufacturer is likely to find it more economical to use indirect channels. Purchases are apt to be made in relatively small quantities and by a relatively large number of buying units.

7. *Volatility of Price.* When a manufacturer uses an indirect channel which includes, for example, wholesalers and several kinds of retailers, he must establish a system of price relationships between outlets at different levels and between different kinds of outlets at the same level. Whenever prices change these relationships are likely to be disturbed. A change in the manufacturer's price is apt to cause all outlets at all levels in the channel either to suffer losses or enjoy unusual profits on the stocks they hold when the change occurs. If the manufacturer fails to protect his outlets against losses of this kind they are liable to become disgruntled and withhold the cooperation he wishes and needs from the units in his marketing channel. Such adjustments are always cumbersome, difficult, and expensive. The more direct the channels are the less difficult are the adjustments. So, when price is volatile, direct channels are desirable. While price stability does not demand indirect channels, it does make them feasible.

8. *Price Spread Margin.* The spread which cost and the market allow between the manufacturer's price and the final price to the ultimate consumer or industrial user has a great deal to do with the feasibility

of direct marketing channels. We have pointed out several times that a direct marketing operation is highly expensive, and to point it out again is not to over-emphasize its importance. The forces of the market, represented by his competitors and customers, determine the price at which the manufacturer can sell his product. The same forces, in the form of competitors and user-buyers, fix the price at which it is finally sold to the ultimate consumer or industrial user. The differential between the two is available to pay for the marketing process. If the differential on a product is great, expensive direct marketing methods can be used and the product can bear all their costs alone. If the margin on a product is narrow, the work of marketing it must be performed jointly with other products so that the cost can be spread over them all and thus be less for each.

We have somewhat oversimplified the situation in trying to make the principle clear. For example, if a product sells in large volume direct marketing may be economical, even though the price spread is small. Marketing cost must always be related to both the number of units sold and the price spread on each unit, and not to either one of them alone. The marketing channel that costs the greatest total number of dollars may cost the least per unit of product that moves through it.

9. *Channels Used by Competitors.* The manager who is trying to break into a market should view with respect the channels used by the firms already in it. This does not mean that he should slavishly follow their example, but it does mean that he should have a good reason for *not* doing so.

To an outsider the marketing channel relationships prevalent in a trade may appear illogical. Sometimes they are. But usually there is (or once was) a good reason for them. If that reason still exists, to run counter to it is liable to prove very costly. If the original reason has long since been lost in the mists of time, defiance of it is apt to be even more expensive. There are few things men cling to and defend more fiercely than ways of doing things that are illogical and outworn but to which they are accustomed by long usage. On the other hand, many marketing managers have won brilliant success by breaking away from generally accepted methods and relationships at the right time. The key phrase here is "at the right time."

So the marketing manager who considers breaking away from customary channel relationships will be wise to ask himself two questions: Are they really illogical and ineffective? Is this the right time to make the break? Of these two questions the second is often the more important and almost always the harder to answer.

Company Factors. In choosing his marketing channels the manufacturer needs to take account of the characteristics of his company and its management. Again, these are many and varied, but certain ones are almost always important.

1. *Financial Strength.* This is especially important in the case of a firm that is new, or of one that is moving into a new market. If such a company is strong, and well financed with a deep warchest, it can afford to spend considerable sums over a number of years (without offsetting return from sales) to develop from scratch the kind of channel that the marketing manager believes he will eventually need when established in the market. If, on the other hand, the finances of his firm are weak, he must use channels that will bring in cash most quickly with the least cash outflow. This may mean that he must market through agents whose fees or commissions need not be paid until after the goods are sold and the money is received for them. If his finances are a little less tight, he may be able to market through wholesalers or distributors who reduce his inventory requirements by carrying stocks. He has to spend money to sell to them before he gets any cash inflow, but they usually discount their bills with the result that he has less working capital tied up in outstandings than he would if he marketed direct to retailers or industrial users.

A poorly financed company whose sales volume is subject to wide fluctuations, either seasonal or cyclical, is likely to be forced to use agents because, during periods of poor business, it has no marketing expenses (except perhaps advertising) unless sales are made and the cash flows in to pay marketing outlays. Such a firm may also market through wholesalers or distributors, for the expense of selling them is low and they tend to provide a quick cash flow by discounting their bills, or, if they do not, their relatively strong financial position enables the manufacturer to borrow on accounts receivable on favorable terms.

2. *Reputation and Market Standing.* If a company is well known and has won for itself a high standing and strong position in the market it is likely to be able to be very choosy in selecting its outlets. This is especially important if the nature of the product or the market indicates the use of a franchise or exclusive channel of distribution. A firm in such a position can attract and sew up the strongest and most aggressive outlets in most of its trading areas. The marketing manager must be careful not to push this advantage too far, for the Department of Justice tends to take a dim view of it, feeling that it holds within it the power of monopoly.

The firm that is new to a market, or has a weak market position, and wishes to use the franchise or exclusive channel relationship is liable to find that it must take the outlets that its stronger competitors have passed over. A powerful newcomer may not be willing to accept this situation and may prefer to build his own system of outlets by helping promising dealers to start in business. This is a fairly common practice among the oil companies who, by a complicated leasing and franchise-dealing system, effectively guarantee the credit of a promising filling station operator, enabling him to build and equip a station and begin its operation.

Market standing may endow a manufacturer with another kind of power in the channel relationship. If through advertising and aggressive marketing practices he has developed a strong consumer demand for his brands, retailers and wholesalers are almost compelled to handle them. There is a rather long list of branded products which a retail grocer practically has to handle if he is to be in the business at all. If the wholesaler wants the retailer's business, he must supply these products. This means that the manufacturers who own these brands can, if they wish, be more than a bit dictatorial in their dealings with both wholesalers and retailers. They can't afford to carry this attitude too far because even the most powerful producers need some cooperation from their outlets. But they are not under the necessity of the careful management of their channel relationships that weaker firms must practice constantly.

3. *Market Contacts.* When a manufacturer enters a new market one of the most important things he lacks is market contacts. He has no established relationships, either business or personal, with the important firms in the trade. He may know their names, but he is not likely to know the people within each firm who make buying decisions or exercise buying influence. Even less likely is he to know what manner of person each of them is and what approaches or appeals are apt to influence him favorably, irritate him, or leave him cold. In this situation the marketing manager has the choice of using direct channels to build these contacts slowly and expensively, or of seeking the services of outlets which already have them. In many businesses market contacts are the chief stock in trade of brokers, sales agents, and manufacturer's agents. The wholesaler or distributor and his salesmen are also likely to have entre into the offices, and often into the confidence of the executives who influence the buying decisions of customer firms.

For example, a maker of industrial materials brought out a small consumers' goods product suitable for sale through supermarkets. Wisely, the marketing manager sought the services of a number of rack jobbers who, within a remarkably short time, achieved widespread distribution for it through these outlets. Another materials manufacturer developed an article suitable for sale through all types of grocery stores. Through a half a dozen food brokers (manufacturer's agents) he was able to get his product fairly quickly on the shelves of many chain super-markets and into the inventories of grocery wholesalers and, through them, into the stocks of retail food stores generally. For both of these manufacturers the cost of developing direct contacts in this new and un-known market would probably have precluded the marketing of these products.

4. *Marketing Objectives.* The manufacturer's marketing manager must make his channel decisions in the light of the marketing objectives of his firm. If his company is out to increase its share of the market, he will need to choose his outlets on a different basis and establish a different set of relationships with them and between them than he can be satisfied with if the objective is merely to maintain a market share already achieved. The latter objective may not seem to be a very healthy one, but it must be remembered that beyond a certain point the cost of capturing an additional share of a market may be more than it is worth, and that the larger a firm's market share is, the more closely and critically its activities will be watched by the Federal Trade Com-mission and the Department of Justice.

Some years ago each of the three leading manufacturing firms in a certain industry had a different marketing objective. One was com-mitted to having the largest volume of sales of any firm in the industry. Another sought the highest margin of net profit on sales. And the third had as its goal to be Number Two in both volume and net profit rate. As a result of these company objectives the marketing manager of the first concern was forced to look for the most aggressive outlets and could not afford to ignore any outlet in the search for sales dollars. The second needed to be very selective in his choice of outlets and to control their activities closely, and finally found a chain of company-owned and operated retail stores helpful in achieving the firm's objective. The third could afford to be more catholic in his choice of outlets.

General Observations. In a few cases, one of the factors we have been discussing is decisive in determining a firm's choice of marketing channels. Usually, though, the process of selection is one of balancing out a number of the factors to arrive at a channel pattern suited to the particular situation and aspirations of the company and its management. You have doubtless observed that many of these factors are intangible and hard to measure, which makes this decision a very difficult one.

When a marketing manager has developed a reasonably clear and detailed picture of the job he wishes his channel outlets to do he should be in a position to determine the general type of channel he needs: direct to user, or to retailer, wholesaler-retailer, distributor-user, agent; and the retail, wholesale, or agent trade group, such as grocery, drug, equipment, etc. Having made this decision he must determine the extent of coverage he will attempt to achieve within the selected channel groups. Within this framework there are at least three patterns of relationship open to his choice.

Extent of Channel Coverage

General or Complete Coverage. A manufacturer may decide to try to market through every outlet in a channel whose credit is satisfactory. When he adopts this policy he is apt to find that no matter how aggressively he may sell he can rarely, if ever, achieve complete coverage in the sense of getting his product on sale by every outlet in the chosen channel. He must be both very aggressive and very lucky to get his goods into the stocks of more than about 80 percent of the outlets in a channel.

The manufacturer who seeks general coverage works on the theory of not passing up a single chance of making a sale to an ultimate consumer or industrial user. If he advertises heavily and widely, the complete coverage policy minimizes the possibility of waste advertising that convinces consumers who, once in a buying mood, cannot find his product in the outlets they patronize. He also achieves greater security and stability in his sales volume since the loss of one of several outlets in a market is not so serious as would be the loss of his only outlet there or one of a selected few.

On the other hand this policy is liable to be expensive, for it involves getting and keeping his product in the stocks of small outlets as well as large. The little merchant buys in small quantities that are expensive to sell and deliver. On his business with many of them the manufacturer or his wholesale distributor is likely to lose money. This can be avoided by not soliciting the business of loss customers, although this too entails its own expense in the form of a cost accounting system detailed enough to disclose the profitability of individual customers and in the form of careful supervision of salesmen's activities involved in carrying out the policy.

General channel coverage also tends to result in a loosening of the manufacturer's control over the methods of handling and selling his product at the lower channel levels. For the manufacturer of very high quality products this is apt to be intolerable. It creates difficult problems for the producer of perishable articles and for the manufacturer who is committed to a policy of price maintenance—fixing the price at which his product is resold. This practice also means that the manufacturer's contact with the market is remote and tenuous, with the result that he gets little market information from his outlets and must rely on expensive marketing research to obtain it. In addition, since his contact with the point of final sale is second-hand and since the individual merchant who handles his product has little competitive advantage to gain by promoting its sale (because most of his competitors also offer it), the manufacturer is at a disadvantage in trying to win and keep the dealer cooperation that is necessary to any hard hitting point-of-sale promotional program.

Exclusive Franchise Arrangements. Some manufacturers find it profitable to go to the opposite extreme and market through only one outlet in each trading area. This sort of arrangement is known as an exclusive franchise. (It should be pointed out that in this usage the word "franchise" has no legal significance but is merely a trade expression.) This policy prevails in the automobile business, for example. This is a one-sided deal because, while a manufacturer can agree with a wholesaler or retailer not to sell through any other dealer in a specified area, he cannot legally bind the dealer to an agreement not to handle any product which competes with his own. To try to do so is a violation of the antitrust laws. Of course, as a practical matter, if a product promises enough possibilities of profit to a merchant to make its franchise an attractive property, its manufacturer may be able to effect a large measure of exclusive dealing among his outlets as a result of their fear of losing the franchise if they handle competitive products.

The oil companies get substantially universal exclusive dealing performance from their filling stations by supplying on favorable terms pumps with the manufacturer's brand on them with the perfectly legal understanding that no competing product shall be delivered through them. Legally, the station operator can if he wishes, stud his premises with a forest of competing pumps (and occasionally one does so), but considerations of space and the heavy inventory requirements of this method of operation compel almost uniform dealer compliance with the exclusive principle—not to mention the effect of the operator's knowledge that the oil company does not approve any such promiscuous associations of its pumps.

Even when a manufacturer has to be content with a one-sided deal in which he can get no better commitment from the merchant than a promise of special marketing services, the exclusive franchise arrangement may be of advantage in several ways.

a) The manufacturer may expect the merchant to push the sale of his product more aggressively than he would under a general coverage system. The merchant knows that any demand he creates can be satisfied only by him. For this reason he may be willing to cooperate in the manufacturer's local and point-of-sale promotional programs and even occasionally to originate promotions of his own. In order to win this sort of outlet cooperation the manufacturer must convince his dealers that the exclusive arrangement is a continuing one and that he is not using it merely as a means of building up demand to a point where it will be profitable to revert to a general coverage system. When this is done, as it often is, the merchant may find that he has spent money to build up demand for later capture by his competitors. The best assurance a manufacturer can give for the continuity of his exclusive policy is a record of honest dealing and assumption of ethical obligations.

b) As part of the exclusive franchise contract the outlet may agree to carry complete and adequate stocks. A usual arrangement is that he starts with a stock suitable to his expected volume of sales to be adjusted later in accordance with the standard inventory found desirable for the sales volume he actually achieves. This must sometimes be adjusted to suit local peculiarities of demand.

c) The exclusive franchise arrangement is especially useful to makers of products requiring considerable service either in the process of selling or during use. If all a manufacturer's business in a trading area is in the hands of a single outlet, it can afford to set up facilities and train personnel to make demonstrations, supply at least rudimentary technical service, do installation work, and provide repair and maintenance service.

d) This system also tends to reduce the manufacturer's costs of selling, orderhandling, and delivery. Sales calls are fewer although longer, orders are fewer and larger, and advantage can often be taken of carload or truckload transport rates.

e) The manufacturer who wishes to control the resale price of his product is apt to find that the exclusive franchise helps a lot. The outlet is under no great competitive pressure to cut prices. If price cutting occurs, the culprit is easy to spot and a penalty is ready to hand in the form of cancellation of the franchise.

f) This arrangement simplifies the manufacturer's credit problems.

He can pick outlets of high credit standing to begin with, maintain closer contact with them, and follow the fluctuations of their businesses more closely than is possible when he markets to all outlets.

g) The franchise system can be of help to the manufacturer in planning his marketing activities. His close relations with his outlets enable him to enlist their aid in forecasting sales and to build reasonably accurate estimates of future sales volume. Since he can usually count on a high degree of cooperation in his promotional programs he can check their effects with reasonable accuracy, and so can make fairly reliable forecasts of the benefits of the promotions he plans.

In spite of all these advantages, the exclusive franchise is not always the answer to the marketing manager's prayer. It has several serious drawbacks.

1. He may not be able to get the best outlets in every trading area; other manufacturers may have been there first and tied up the best ones. If his product is superior and his terms more attractive, he may be able to win or build satisfactory outlets, but this is likely to be an expensive process. Then too, once a manufacturer is tied up with a poor outlet in an area he may encounter considerable difficulty in shedding it, and even more in dissipating the bad reputation acquired by having been associated with it. As a result of this drawback the exclusive franchise system is apt to cause the manufacturer's marketing performance to be spotty and not uniform throughout the market. If he seeks general coverage he benefits from the fact that there are good outlets and poor ones in every trading area, and his goods are sold by all of them.

2. Customer coverage is liable to be spotty. Arranging the trading areas assigned to outlets so as to avoid overlaps and uncovered areas is a sort of jig-saw puzzle and may result in possible user-buyers in certain areas being inconveniently located with respect to the outlets designated to serve them. Then too, in every trading area there are some possible buyers who are bound to be lost because, for personal reasons, they would not purchase from the chosen outlet if it were the last one on earth.

Many industrial buyers do not like to purchase without competition among suppliers and will go to considerable lengths to avoid doing so. Competitive quotations are often the purchasing agent's best protection against top management criticism.

In addition, it is hard to keep a franchise system fully staffed. Merchants constantly go out of business or change franchises or change managements, so that the manufacturer must constantly make adjustments to maintain complete coverage by satisfactory outlets.

3. The system denies the manufacturer the advantage of the principle that "competition is the life of trade." The merchant who knows that he has the business in a product sewed up in his area is apt to become lazy and indifferent and not do as good a job as he is capable of. Cases are not wanting of merchants who took the franchise for a particular brand simply to keep competitors from getting it and then merely went through the motions of carrying out the obligations involved while devoting their real efforts to promoting a competing brand.

This difficulty may be offset somewhat by careful supervision and by assigning a sales quota to each outlet. To be effective a quota must be realistic. It is not easy for the manufacturer to make it so. If it is too small, it does not stimulate; if it is too large, it may force the outlet to cut prices and engage in promotional activities not in keeping with the manufacturer's marketing policies.

There are a number of conditions that indicate the use of the exclusive franchise arrangement. The following are the most common.

a) *New Products*. When a product is new to a market it requires description, explanation, display, and sometimes demonstration at the point of final sale or during the process of final sale. If all outlets in a trading area handle such a product no one of them is apt to be willing to make possible business for a competitor by doing these things. On the other hand, if a merchant knows that any customers he makes by these expensive activities are his alone, he is more likely to be willing to carry them on.

Some manufacturers make use of this situation in a way that merchants in their marketing channels are likely to regard as unfair. When they bring out a new product they introduce it on an exclusive franchise basis—which they discard as soon as enough market acceptance is built up for it to make possible more general outlet coverage. Such a policy is liable to be self-defeating since merchants soon become aware of the manufacturer's pattern of behavior and become hard to snare in his franchise net. To recognize when a manufacturer is playing this game is not too difficult: when a product or a situation has none of the characteristics indicating the use of the franchise arrangement *except* its newness, the assumption is that the arrangement will be of short duration. Agents are much more likely than merchants to accept such behavior as one of the facts of business life and to be willing to live with it.

b) *Technical Products*. These usually require special service during the process of final sale and after they are in use. Their final sale also requires well trained personnel. These things are expensive for the outlet. But the need for them is apt to continue throughout the life of the product. To get them, the manufacturer often must offer an exclusive franchise as an inducement.

c) *High Quality.* A product that is sold on the basis of the high quality appeal usually also carries the implication of exclusiveness. This implication is enhanced if it is sold by exclusive franchise dealers. Such a product usually has a low rate of stock turnover. The facilities, equipment, and personnel of the merchant selling it must be such as to create an atmosphere of elegance and quality. Such an atmosphere costs money. All these factors point strongly toward the use of the exclusive franchise arrangement.

d) *High Unit Price.* When the unit price of an article is several hundreds or thousands of dollars it is apt to be impossible for a merchant to carry a stock of the products of a number of competing manufacturers. Consider what would be the inventory investment of the automobile dealer who handled the cars of all major manufacturers. There are few retail merchants in the country with that kind of capital structure.

e) *Special Sales Effort.* You will probably have observed that a number of the factors mentioned involve special effort during the process of sale. There are other conditions which render such effort necessary, and whenever they exist the exclusive franchise arrangement is indicated.

Limited Franchise. The manufacturer may be unwilling to rely on only one outlet in each trading area but may choose to grant a limited franchise to a few (usually two or three) merchants in each market area. This is an attempt to compromise between general coverage and the exclusive arrangement, and it suffers the usual weaknesses of a compromise policy.

It offers the manufacturer most of the advantages of the exclusive arrangement but in a watered-down form. For example, it affords the outlet some incentive to push the manufacturer's product—over what he would have if every outlet in the trading area handled it—but the merchant knows that at least one competitor is likely to share the rewards of such effort. The security he would enjoy under the exclusive arrangement is somewhat dissipated and his enthusiasm is apt to be dampened accordingly. Much the same effect occurs with respect to the other advantages of the franchise method.

All but one of the disadvantages of the exclusive franchise arrangement also apply to the limited franchise. The danger that the franchise merchant will become lazy is largely eliminated, for now he has competition. It *is* limited, to be sure, but it often happens that competition between two rivals is more vigorous than among many.

The limited franchise arrangement is not usually applied to manufacturer's agents or sales agents, who almost always operate on an exclusive basis. It is sometimes used with brokers.

SELECTION OF OUTLETS

Once a manufacturer's marketing manager has selected the type of channel to use and the extent of coverage which will best suit his needs, he must choose individual outlets. If he seeks general coverage, this is no problem. He simply sells to every outlet that will buy and is limited only by considerations of credit standing, cost of selling, order handling, and delivery.

But if he elects to use either the exclusive or limited arrangement, the choice of specific outlets becomes important. The process of selection usually involves an analysis of individual outlet firms on the basis of a number of factors that indicate their suitability to the manufacturer's needs. Some of these are general in that they apply to practically every situation. Some of them may be peculiar to the situation and marketing problems of the individual manufacturer. We can discuss only those of general application. In turn, some of these apply to all kinds of outlets: wholesalers, distributors, retailers, and agents. A few are peculiar to merchants.

Selection Factors

Promise of Continuity. If a manufacturer is to have his goods constantly available for purchase throughout the market he must at all times have an outlet in each trading area. To do this is one of the chief problems of marketing through the franchise system. Merchants and agents go out of business; the quality of their management changes; they shift their franchise relationships. Whenever one of these things happens, the manufacturer has the job of replacing an outlet. This is expensive and, while he is doing so, his goods are not being sold in the trading area involved, which adds to the naturally spotty performance of this system of channel management.

Therefore, in picking a franchise outlet the manufacturer usually finds it desirable to examine its survival probabilities. A one-man firm promises less continuity than a partnership and neither holds as much promise as a corporation. An outlet management that is obviously planning for continuity by getting, holding, and training young men with managerial talent provides the best kind of assurance of continuity, pretty much regardless of other factors. A well financed firm is less likely to succumb to unexpected adversity than one on or near the ragged financial edge. The very worst continuity risk is a well-run firm owned and managed by an aging man who built the business himself and who has not learned to delegate. Another poor bet is the firm with a record of shifting franchises frequently.

Trading Area. The trading area covered by an agent or merchant is a matter of prime importance to the manufacturer who is trying to piece together a mosaic of such areas so as to cover the country. Very often a strong outlet in a marketing center demands an exclusive territory that encroaches on an adjoining trading area, or that includes certain lush segments of it. If the manufacturer bows to this demand, he is apt to find it impossible to get a good outlet to handle his product in the invaded trading area. On the other hand, if he can find a good outlet willing to supply complete coverage in two or more recognized trading areas, his problem of selection and administration is simplified.

Trade Standing and Reputation. What a merchant's or agent's competitors and customers think of him is important to the manufacturer in his work of outlet selection. If competitors look upon an outlet with respect (and just a touch of trepidation) and if customers rely on his knowledge and are confident of his fairness and honesty, he is worth very careful consideration. Such an outlet gains a certain amount of patronage merely by reason of his good repute. The fact that such an outlet handles a manufacturer's product goes far to establish the assumption of its quality in the trading area. "It must be good or Lord and Taylor's wouldn't handle it." This factor is very important in selecting outlets for a product to be sold on a high quality basis.

In the case of an agent, the matter of trade contacts is of primary significance. He should know and be known by the most important prospective customers and have entre into the offices of the executives who exercise buying influence and make patronage decisions. In the case of new products this is usually the most important thing he has to sell to the manufacturers he represents.

Other Products Handled. This factor is closely akin to the matter of trade standing and reputation. A good outlet usually handles good products. The fact that a merchant or agent sells the related but noncompeting products of several manufacturers of high repute is pretty convincing evidence of his own standing and reputation and of his ability to market the kind of products they make. It also means that in his line our high quality product will be in good company and will enjoy some of the sales momentum that comes from such association. It is highly desirable that the other products handled by an outlet not be competitive to ours but be complementary in that they are sold to the same kinds of consumers, are used in association with our product, or are customarily bought together with ours.

Selling Personnel and Methods. How good are the outlet's salespeople and how well informed are they about the products they sell? What patronage appeals does the outlet management use in its selling work? Of course, when a merchant or agent takes on a product he has not handled before, his salespeople can not be expected to know all about it. But he can be willing to see to it that they learn by taking advantage of the training programs and facilities the manufacturer may provide. If he is not willing to do this, the chances are that his field representation will not be too good. If a product is technical, the technical training and background of the outlet's selling personnel is usually a reliable tip-off.

The marketing policies and practices of the outlet should conform to those desired by the manufacturer. For example, if the latter makes a quality product or one with special use features, or if he wishes to control the resale price, he will not be wise to select an outlet that habitually cuts prices or emphasizes high-pressure selling tactics.

Outlet's Objectives. Why is the outlet willing to add the manufacturer's product to his line? This question is not applicable to the selection of manufacturer's agents who do not handle competing products. Merchants and sales agents do not always follow this policy. In dealing with them the manufacturer must be alert to the danger that the outlet management may take on his product for the purpose of keeping it out of the hands of competition and with no notion of giving it the attention and marketing service desired. The products already in the merchant's or agent's line may provide a clue to his intentions with respect to a new product.

Stock Carrying Performance. This factor applies chiefly to merchants, although a few manufacturer's agents offer the stock carrying service. An outlet's probable performance of this service can be forecast by an examination of the representativeness and adequacy of his stocks of products already in his line and by his willingness to agree to carry the standard inventory if one has been set up by the manufacturer. Makers of complementary products in the merchant's line may be willing to comment on his inventory performance.

Financial Position. This factor also is important in the selection of merchant outlets. Its significance as an indicator of continuity has already been mentioned. If a merchant is not well financed, he may not be able to do the stock-carrying job desired, to handle his accounts receivable commitments, and to keep down the manufacturer's working capital requirements by discounting his bills at the same time.

Facilities. If a merchant is to carry adequate stocks and provide proper delivery service, he must have the facilities to do so or be able and willing to get them.

Selection Aids

In the process of making his final choice, the manufacturer's marketing manager may make use of a number of aids. A *Dun and Bradstreet* report may disclose useful information about an outlet, particularly at the wholesale level. *Trade directories and trade journal files* may provide lists of candidates and information about their trading area coverage and operating methods. *Visits or inquiries* addressed to noncompetitive firms, sometimes even to competitors, may afford useful information. *Interviews with customers* of an outlet may furnish clues as to its standing in the trade and the degree of customer confidence and loyalty it enjoys. But these interviews must be conducted with great circumspection to avoid damaging the very assets they are designed to check upon.

Some marketing managers visit prospective outlets to inspect their facilities, their methods of doing business, and the quality of their management. A few even send men to travel with their salesmen to check on the quality of the selling service to be expected and on their relations with customers.

Once the critical factors have been decided on and pertinent information obtained about them, the process of final decision may be facilitated by the use of semi-mathematical tools. This involves assigning weights to the several factors and attempting to reduce the findings with regard to each factor to numerical terms. Thus, it may be decided that the "ability of the sales force" is twice as important as "other products carried"; so it may be assigned a numerical value of 20 points as tops as against 10 points for "other products carried." Each candidate outlet can then be graded on each factor against these standard figures. Thus outlet X might receive 17 points on its sales force and 5 on the other products it carries, indicating that its salesforce was reasonably strong but that its product line left much to be desired. The ratings assigned to all the intangible factors can then be totaled to obtain a summary figure.

The marketing manager must be careful not to use such a mathematical analysis as a crutch but merely as an aid. The process of reducing intangibles to numerical terms is a tricky one, and often a marketing manager's feeling about a prospective outlet may be more reliable than the most elaborate formula analysis. The mathematical method may be very helpful, though, in eliminating prospective outlets and reducing the field to one or two candidates from whom the choice can be made on other bases with greatly reduced chance of error.

ADMINISTERING CHANNEL RELATIONSHIPS

The channel relationship is established by a contract. This may consist merely of the placing and acceptance of an order, in which case the continuance of the relation is provided by a series of orders given and received or of agency transactions consummated. This is the usual type of contract when the manufacturer seeks general channel coverage.

In some cases the agreement takes the form of a blanket order or contract in which the channel member agrees to buy a fixed amount of a manufacturer's product or a specified portion of his own requirements during a coming period. When the manufacturer uses a franchise arrangement, its terms are usually set out in a formal contract covering a future period (such as a year) which may be renewed either formally or at will, or for an indefinite period but subject to termination by either party after proper notice of intention to do so.

Many manufacturers of industrial supplies and minor equipment reinforce these arrangements with statements of company marketing policy which afford distributors some additional assurance of the continuity of the relationship so long as both parties remain satisfied. Such a statement is apt to be published from time to time in the firm's advertising. Similar statements of policy are not unknown in the consumers' goods field even among manufacturers operating on the general coverage basis.

The Contract

At a minimum the contract is apt to establish relationships with respect to the following matters:

Protection. The general coverage arrangement usually provides no protection for the channel member against the competition of his fellows although it often, either directly or by implication, assures protection for wholesalers or industrial distributors against the manufacturer's own acts in the understanding that any sales made by his missionary men will be turned over to the merchant for delivery.

The franchise contract, by its very nature, either limits the number of competitors of the channel member or eliminates his competition entirely. It should also clearly set forth the circumstances under which and the degree to which he will be subject to the competition of the manufacturer in the form of sales to "house accounts," those large buyers to whom the manufacturer proposes to sell direct. Many industrial buyers, chain store systems, and large department stores want to buy direct from the manufacturer.

The manufacturer usually is not willing to leave any stone unturned in seeking to get the business of such an account and is prone to believe that "if you want a thing well done, do it yourself." Sometimes he is willing to allow the outlet a portion of the margin on house account business; sometimes he wants the outlet to make deliveries, for which he grants an allowance; sometimes the channel member is excluded from participation in this business altogether. The house account is always an irritant in channel relationships. It is likely to be less so if the management of the outlet knows exactly who the house accounts in his trading area will be and where he will stand with relation to their business.

Inventory Requirements. Under the general coverage system the outlet is free to carry whatever stocks he wishes subject to the pressures of the manufacturer's salesmen. The franchise agreement should include a statement of all obligations the outlet assumes with respect to the inventory he carries.

Price. If the manufacturer wishes to control the resale price of his product, he may do it by suggestion or by taking advantage of the provisions of the Fair Trade laws. Such a suggestion usually takes the form of a "list price" which, by implication, is the resale price with a discount to the channel outlet. For example:

List Price	$5.00 (retailer's selling price)
Retailer's Discount 30% ($1.50)	3.50 (price to retailer)
Wholesaler's Discount 30% and 15% ($0.53)	2.97 (price to wholesaler)

If the product is "fair-traded," the designated resale price becomes legally enforceable in many states, although not as a part of the contract. Since the courts take a dim view of resale price maintenance, the price arrangements described above are rarely, if ever, included in channel contracts, although the manufacturer's desires with respect to it are almost certain to be implicit in them.

Helps to Outlets. The manufacturer often does not obligate himself in the channel contract to supply all the helps to the outlet that he is actually prepared to give. We will discuss these later in some detail.

Outlet's Obligations. Under the complete coverage system the outlet usually assumes no obligations with respect to the manufacturer's promotion program beyond participating in whatever portion of it he may want to at the moment. A franchise contract usually imposes on the franchise holder some obligations of this nature. Often they are stated so broadly as to be not much more than a pious profession of purpose. Now and then they are quite specific.

Areas of Supervision

The work of supervising channel relations and activities is quite varied. For purposes of discussion we will probably not be too unrealistic in classifying them into three groups: promotional helps, incentives, and training.

1. *Promotional Helps.* Almost every tool in the kit of the advertiser and sales promotion expert has been used in this work. By a bit of classification legerdemain we can fit them into four groups.

a) Pull-Through Devices. Most merchants and agents want to handle products that are not too hard to resell. Therefore the manufacturer who creates a powerful suction to pull his products through his marketing channel is apt to be able to place them in the listings or stocks of most of the outlets he wishes to have and to enjoy a reasonably satisfactory sales volume per outlet. He has two chief tools with which to accomplish this. *One is a heavy advertising campaign and the other is a force of missionary salesmen.* When a retailer is asked to buy a product he is very much influenced by the advertising its manufacturer does, or proposes to do, to pull it off his shelves into the hands of ultimate consumers. In a like position the wholesaler wants assurance that the manufacturer will create suction, either by depletion of the retailers' stocks through advertising or by missionary pressure on the retailers, to pull the product out of his warehouse and into the hands of retailers. Of these two tools, merchants prefer advertising for reasons described in a previous chapter.

b) Local Advertising. This may be of several types. Probably the least popular is "boiler plate" advertisements: copy prepared by the manufacturer which the wholesaler or retailer can insert in local media. This suffers from the drawback that the retailer has to pay the cost of the space. A much more popular plan is for the manufacturer to pay part or all the cost of advertisements placed by the retailer that feature the manufacturer's product and that are either prepared by him or meet specifications he sets. This is usually called "cooperative advertising." Its advantage over the manufacturer's placing the advertising himself is that the retailer gets "local" rates, which are much lower than the "national" rates the manufacturer would have to pay.

Makers of industrial goods sometimes list the names and addresses of their outlets in their advertisements in trade journals, or use as a copy theme the services the distributor or agent renders to the buyer. Many manufacturers also provide various types of printed material, descriptive of their products, to be mailed or handed out by retailers or distributors to their customers. Classified telephone listings constitute another type of local advertising help.

c) *Point-of-Purchase Material.* Examples of this sort of material are store signs, counter and floor display and sales equipment, interior displays, display cards, brochures, and pamphlets. This is by no means a complete list. Point-of-purchase material has gained vastly in importance as a result of the growth of self-service retailing. Aside from the product itself, or its package, such material is the only selling influence on the floor of many retail stores.

It is not always easy to get these things used. Retailers in many trades get them almost by the ton. Competition to have them used is hot and sometimes vicious. A primary task of the missionary salesman is often to dig them out of the backroom or the basement and set them up on the selling floor. Probably the most effective means to secure their use is to make them so that they really sell goods and fit the retailer's needs. This is certainly a *sine qua non* to the success of any other method of inducing their use.

d) *Demonstrators.* Makers of mechanical goods often supply their retail outlets with representatives who demonstrate their use and effectiveness.

The Robinson-Patman amendment to the Clayton Act requires that all these helps be available to all outlets on proportionally equal terms. Precisely what this means has not yet been entirely determined. The wise marketing manager will submit any proposed program of outlet helps to legal opinion before putting it into effect.

2. *Incentives.* The chief incentives the manufacturer can offer to stimulate the performance of his outlets are almost certainly financial. The marketing manager will be wise to remember, though, that the effectiveness of financial incentives can be greatly enhanced by a reputation for fair dealing and consideration of the outlet's interest. Much depends on the financial incentives given, but much also depends on the way in which they are given. The best way for a manufacturer to get a reputation for fair dealing is to deal fairly, and the best way for him to convince outlets of his consideration for their interests is to be actually concerned about them. Lip service is not enough.

The chief financial incentive for an agent is his fee or commission on the sales of a product; for a merchant it is the net profit he can make from handling it. Since such a large part of the total operating expense of a mercantile business is overhead, or behaves like overhead, many such operators, finding it unprofitable or almost impossible to compute costs by individual products, simply use an average cost per dollar of sales in making operating decisions. This has the effect of making gross profit the decisive criterion by which the relative profitability of a product is judged. Obviously, the manufacturer is not entirely a free agent in determining the margin between the price at which he sells to an outlet and the price at which the outlet can resell. His own costs provide a floor below which his selling price should not go, without very good reason, while the price prevailing in the outlet's market more or less fixes the upper point of the margin.

Insofar as a manufacturer has freedom to manipulate his outlet's margin, he should probably seek one that will provide a net profit that the outlet management regards as adequate and try to avoid one that may be regarded as either narrow or lush. A margin that is too narrow is apt to dampen or extinguish agents' or merchants' enthusiasm for a product; one that is too generous is liable to invite price cutting or to induce complacency: "We are making a very nice profit on this item; why wear ourselves out trying to sell more?" Here, as in so many human relationships, balance is the crucial factor. If the manufacturer builds an active demand by heavy advertising, so that the outlet enjoys a satisfactory volume of sales without promotional effort, the gross profit margin can be much narrower than would be necessary otherwise. This is especially apt to be true with the larger, better managed outlets which are likely to have adequate cost analyses by products.

Many manufacturers find it desirable to keep enough "fat" in their margins to enable them from time to time to offer special deals to their outlets in the nature of temporary price cuts for "deal" quantities. These are usually coupled with some sort of special advertising or point-of-sale promotion campaign. The price reduction often takes the form of merchandise premiums, special packages, the traditional "baker's dozen," or some other similar device.

Some manufacturers offer "PM's," variously interpreted as premiums or "push money," to the outlet's salespeople. These are usually offered at the retail level, although they are not unknown in the wholesale trade. The wise manufacturer will never offer these without the consent of the outlet's management for many merchants prefer not to have their employees receive payments from outsiders.

Various forcing methods may be used as incentives. The franchise agreement often includes the setting of quotas for the outlets. This carries the implication that the continuance of the franchise depends, at least to some degree, upon the fulfillment of the quota. Sometimes these arrangements can become rather arbitrary. For many years the franchise agreements between the automobile makers and their dealers provided that the manufacturer could ship a dealer cars up to his quota, with sight drafts attached to the bills of lading. This meant that the dealer had to raise the money to pay the drafts—and had to take the cars regardless of the condition of his stock and finances at the moment.

Some manufacturers of heavily advertised products sold on a complete coverage basis follow a consistent policy of trying to overstock retail dealers on the double-barrelled theory that the more of a product a dealer has displayed on his shelves, the more of it he will sell and the harder he will try to sell it. In most situations this is a dubious incentive but it has been used effectively by some concerns, especially in the grocery business.

Many manufacturers try to win the loyalty of their outlets and thus stimulate their performance by making inventory adjustments. If an outlet becomes overstocked the manufacturer takes back the excess and credits the account with its cost, sometimes but not always with the deduction of a handling charge. When goods deteriorate in the outlet's stocks, this policy is almost a must; otherwise consumers are liable to be sold merchandise that is shopworn or otherwise unsatisfactory—to the damage of the maker's brand reputation. In general, there is room for considerable doubt whether the outlet loyalty generated by this practice offsets the effect of the decrease it brings about in the pressure on the merchant to sell.

Not only is the level of the manufacturer's prices an important factor in securing outlet loyalty and cooperation but the way in which prices are administered is also highly important. In many trades it has been customary to quote prices in the form of a string or chain of discounts from a list price, as, for example, 50, 30, 25, 15, and 10% off list, each percentage figure applying to the price remaining after the deduction of the previous one. Thus if list is $1.00, the application of the above chain discount results in an actual price of 20 cents. This makes prices hard to figure and complicates the outlet's work of pricing for resale. The practice of quoting actual sales prices may be a boon deeply appreciated by the outlet.

The way a manufacturer administers price changes may be important to outlet loyalty: when he changes his price, the wholesalers and retailers handling his product must also change theirs. When such a change occurs, the outlets are almost certain to have stock on hand bought at the old price. They thus make an extra profit or sustain a loss on these stocks. They are not averse to taking the added profit but are apt to be acutely unhappy about suffering the loss. The manufacturer may seek to diminish the loss by announcing a price reduction some time before its effective date, thus enabling his outlets to reduce their inventories to the minimum when the change takes effect. But this has the effect of drying up his demand in the interim and causing a rush of orders too big to handle right after the effective date. It also tips off his competitors and may prevent his gaining even a temporary advantage from his pricing action.

A much more common practice is that of guaranteeing floor stocks. Under this system the manufacturer changes his price without previous warning but allows the outlet a rebate amounting to the difference between the old and new prices on all his goods in the outlet's stock. Often the merchant's word is taken as to the amount of inventory he holds. The practical effect of this is to antedate price reductions. Adjustments are rarely made on price advances.

3. *Training.* In administering outlet relationships the manufacturer often faces a two-pronged training problem. He must train the manager or managers of many outlets and the salespeople of almost all of them are apt to need training. The manufacturer who seeks complete coverage may profit from the expenditure of some effort and money on outlet training, although it is obvious that his competitors may benefit from it almost as much as he. When a franchise system is used, outlets are apt to be more receptive to the manufacturer's training efforts, and his competitors can gain none of the benefits. Many makers of industrial goods regard a distributor's willingness to accept and even pay part of the cost of training for himself and his salesmen as a very important factor in judging his fitness for a franchise.

The subject matter of training directed at outlet managers varies considerably, but it almost always includes information about the manufacturer's product and his marketing policies. The central theme of this is likely to be how the outlet can make more money by the resale of the manufacturer's products. Sometimes carefully worked out promotional programs are presented and the manufacturer's representative is prepared to help the merchant set up their operation (the Armstrong Cork Company has been unusually successful in this sort of work). This type of training is usually imparted by the manufacturer's salesmen who are sometimes prepared to act almost as consultants to their customers in profitable methods of reselling his merchandise.

Many manufacturers are prepared to offer their outlets training in such matters as the development and operation of proper accounting systems, the installation and conduct of effective systems of stock control, the principles of store layout and merchandise arrangement and display, and methods to improve overall selling efficiency. The manufacturer is not in as good a position to profit from this training of retail outlets in overall store performance as is the wholesaler because the manufacturer can benefit from it only insofar as it affects his product (which is one out of many) while the wholesaler, who sells all the items his retailer customer handles, can benefit from its effect on all of them.

The manufacturer's training of his outlet's salesforce usually is centered around product information and methods of selling. Sometimes this training is imparted on the job by the manufacturer's salesmen or special training representatives who travel with the wholesaler's or distributor's salesmen, or visit the retailer's store to do this work. These men may be expected to hold meetings of the outlet's salespeople for this purpose. In the industrial goods field this sort of training is apt to be administered in factory schools operated by the manufacturer who often pays all its expense except the salaries of salesmen while in attendance.

Control of Channel Operations

A manufacturer's channel arrangements need constant reexamination. Markets are always changing: new ones are developing and old ones are waning. New types of outlets, such as discount houses and shopping centers, are continually coming into existence, and the influence of old ones is diminishing. The nature of the channel job constantly changes. For example, when electrical household appliances were new, heavy reliance had to be placed on the retail dealer to demonstrate them, explain them, and build a market for them; so the retail gross profit margin had to be large. The discount house has proved that this is no longer true.

Unrealized pressures and sources of discontent have a way of building up in marketing channels and, unless perceived and checked, eventually reach the point of explosion. Some years ago a combination of enforced expensive showrooms, a toughening of the selling situation, the multiplication of bootleg used car dealers, and a too rigid quota system, which automobile manufacturers allowed to develop and grow without remedial measures, resulted in a congressional investigation (provoked by the dealers) and the passage of the so-called "good-faith law" which, while it doesn't mean much, is a threat to manufacturers' operations and an enduring reminder of the arbitrary and inconsiderate way in which they once administered their channel relationships—and might do so again unless held in check. It is not a memento that breeds an atmosphere of confidence and trust within the automobile marketing channels.

What has just been said points the need for the manufacturer to have some sort of feedback from the outlets in his marketing channel and, if possible, from consumer or user customers of his outlets from whom he can glean some idea of what is happening in the market, how his outlets feel about his policies, and how ultimate consumer or industrial user customers of his outlets feel about their performance. It is hard to believe that there was no indication of the profound changes taking place in the electrical appliance market until the sudden outburst of the discount house. Nor can one easily accept the notion that, until the automobile dealers appealed to Congress, there was no indication of the disaffection among them that could have been picked up by a manufacturer who was interested in knowing about such matters, or even by one alert enough to see the signs and listen to the rumblings.

A feedback of control information about channel outlets can be obtained in several ways. Dealer or wholesaler complaints provide a source that the manufacturer has only to use without any cost of development. Of course, not all complaints are significant; in any group there are chronic grumblers. But when a number of outlets complain about the same thing, it will bear looking into.

The correspondence of outlets—the letters they write to the manufacturer—may afford tip-offs as to the state of mind that prevails among them. When warmth departs and is replaced by politeness or silence, something is wrong. This reaction usually does not indicate what the trouble is, but it shows pretty clearly that there is trouble and that somebody should start trying to locate it.

By an observant attendance at dealer meetings and discerning study of dealer trade journals, a manufacturer can often gain clues as to the attitude of his outlets and the state of their morale. Clues from these sources are likely to be specific and to indicate pretty clearly what the nature of the trouble is.

Marketing research attitude surveys among outlets and customers of outlets should provide the manufacturer with reasonably reliable feedback information about the morale of his channel members and about their performance in servicing the final buyers of his product. Such surveys are expensive but often well worth their cost. In this area their conduct is a very delicate operation and should be carried on by experts. Great care must be exercised to avoid generating the very reactions we fear to find already in existence.

Finally, the manufacturer who cultivates a climate of cooperation and willingness to listen is apt to find that it is at once a highly effective invitation to the flowback he wants and a most efficient tool for use in remedying the difficulties the flowback may disclose. This climate is a very delicate thing to maintain, and the clues and hints of information it brings must be carefully and quickly analyzed and acted upon, for if the gathering storms they disclose are long ignored they are liable to destroy it.

A Possible New Look at Channel Management

In spite of all that manufacturers can do, wholesalers and retailers, by and large, are apt to cooperate imperfectly. This results from the very nature of their operations. Their interests are divided among many products. A particular manufacturer's interest is only one of many and, at best, can receive only the partial attention of his outlets. In many trades the situation is compounded by the practice among wholesalers and large retailers of building up their own brands, competing with those of the manufacturer. These private brands have first call on the outlet's promotional efforts. Manufacturers' complaints are constant and bitter that their outlets fail to do a good job of helping to market their products.

This situation has led to the suggestion that the traditional flat gross profit margin to all outlets be abandoned and that a three-step system of paying by the service-piece rendered be substituted. This scheme might work something like this.

1. The manufacturer prepares a list of the marketing services he wishes his outlets to perform. Such a list might include

Carrying adequate and representative stocks.
Ordering in economic quantities.
Using promotional materials.
Training salespeople in selling manufacturer's product.
Making demonstrations of manufacturer's product.
Using manufacturer's advertising pieces.
Making sales presentations of manufacturer's products.

2. A method or system for checking the performance of each of these tasks is developed. This should not be too difficult for any item on the list except the making of sales presentations.

3. The outlet is paid a fee or allowed a percentage of gross profit for each service performed, perhaps graduated according to the excellence of its performance.

Fragments of this plan are now in use in a number of trades. For example, this is the basic principle on which many cooperative advertising programs work, and in some trades special allowances are given for the use of certain readily checked types of promotional material. In some cases these allowances are on the basis of a fixed amount per piece used. This system would seem to have the advantage that it conforms to the spirit and the letter of the Robinson-Patman Act while general percentage promotional allowances, with no checks of performance, are certainly of dubious legality.

Many manufacturers may yet be forced to an agonizing reappraisal of their relationships with merchant outlets in their marketing channels.

Managing Selling and Customer Services

In the previous section we discussed the general subject of marketing channels and the problems of managing them. In it we focused our attention mainly on the channel units outside the firm and on their relations with the operating divisions inside the company which are charged with its marketing work.

The day-to-day work of the marketing division of a firm is usually of two kinds: it tries to sell the products or services of the company, and it renders the customer services which are needed to facilitate the selling work and to consummate sales transactions. The nature and extent of these activities, and of the staff and informational services that are needed to help plan them and carry them on, usually dictate the form of the organizational units inside the firm that belong to a company's marketing channels.

The making of a sale is a crucial point in the marketing process: without it nothing much can happen. Therefore it is a matter of absorbing interest to the marketing manager. The process of trying to effect sales transactions is selling. A more formal definition of it, suggested by the Definitions Committee of the American Marketing Association, is "the personal or impersonal process of assisting and/or persuading a prospective customer to buy a commodity or a service or to act favorably upon an idea that has commercial significance to the seller."

Selling work is of two kinds, *personal* and *impersonal*. Personal selling is carried on by representatives of the marketing firm, usually salesmen, who seek to establish personal contact with prospective buyers. In impersonal selling the marketer tries to achieve contact with the prospective customer through various communication media used in advertising and sales promotion. As was indicated in our earlier discussion, some manufacturers attempt to make this contact directly with ultimate consumers or industrial users through their own salesmen and through advertising and promotion materials that go direct to the final buyer. Others find it more desirable to carry the direct personal contact only to the agent or merchant, although in such cases they usually attempt to establish and maintain impersonal contact with ultimate buyers through advertising and sales promotion.

In studying the management of the internal marketing operations of the firm we will probably be wise to examine (1) the problems centering around organizational structure; (2) those involved in managing the work of personal selling; (3) those which arise in managing advertising and sales promotion activities, and (4) those having to do with providing the most profitable customer service.

CHAPTER 11

Marketing Organization

The manager's work of organizing consists of visualizing the various functions which an enterprise must carry on to realize its objectives; classifying them into groups which are related or fit together, setting up administrative centers to supervise them, and establishing lines of authority, responsibility, and relationship between those centers. A cardinal rule of good organization structure is that lines of authority and lines of responsibility should coincide, so that a man is not held responsible for something he has not the authority to do or get done.

This is especially important and difficult in marketing organization and the temptation to violate the rule is more than ordinarily enticing. Most units of a firm deal with tangible things. For example, production involves the manipulation of materials and parts, finance requires the handling of money, and even the statistical compilations issued by the accounting division result from the processing of figures which are definitive enough to assume at least the appearance of tangibility. When a thing is being processed, authority over it and responsibility for it can readily be shifted at the point where it passes from the possession of one man to that of another.

But the process of marketing is essentially one of mobilizing, deploying, and applying intangibles such as ideas, attitudes, emotions, enthusiasms, only the factual bases of which have any semblance of tangibility. The point of division between organizational units of the marketing area must be fixed, therefore, primarily on the basis of what each unit is supposed to do with an intangible; the intangible itself remains in the possession of all units that use it. This tends to cloud the boundaries between units, but it also serves to enhance the need for special effort to give them all the clarity and sharpness careful planning can achieve.

The success of marketing work depends heavily upon the enthusiasms and morale of the people who do it and upon teamwork among them. Nothing is quite so dampening to a man's enthusiasm and morale as to be saddled with the blame for a failure to do something he did not have authority to do. Nor is there any much more potent generator of the jealousy and bickering that kill teamwork than uncertainty as to where one man's authority and responsibility end and another's begin.

It is not always easy for the marketing manager to enforce sharp divisions of power among his subordinates or strict coincidence of authority and responsibility. Customers respond differently to various methods of approach and cultivation, and the pressure is very great to leave no sales tool untried regardless of who tries it. The manager may find it hard to reprove a subordinate for an act outside the scope of his authority when it resulted in an order. Often he is not himself entirely innocent of encroaching upon the area of authority he has delegated.

Very few marketing managers ever have the opportunity to organize a marketing department from scratch. The job is usually that of reorganizing an existing set-up to conform to changed conditions. This throws upon the manager not only the obligation of working out the kind of organizational structure that he thinks should exist but also the task of accomplishing this without disrupting existing relationships and channels of communication, and without creating personal hardships or upsetting the morale of the existing executive and operating personnel any more than is absolutely necessary. This is especially important in the marketing area because the success of marketing work depends so much on teamwork among the people in it and on their enthusiasm and initiative, all of which is easily dissipated by an unnecessarily drastic reorganization. The difficulties of the job resemble those of rebuilding a boat while sailing in it at sea.

The process of reorganization is also complicated by people. The planner of a completely new organization can set it up exactly as he thinks it should be and then seek people to fit into the work positions he has created. The reorganizer has most of his people already in the company employ. The temptation is almost overwhelming to build a job for "Old Joe," a faithful who has been with the firm for a long time, or for "Young Bill," who is a comer. The question "Should we set up our structure around *activities* or around *people?*" becomes acute.

Probably a viable compromise is, first, to build the organization structure as it should be, and then to "cut and piece" to fit jobs to key people. This has the big advantage that in the course of tailoring his ideal structure to provide places for Old Joe and Young Bill, the planner is forced to ask himself, "Is the company's obligation to Old Joe great enough, and is Young Bill's probable future contribution valuable enough to outweigh the weaknesses I'm building into the organization structure?" Otherwise, this question is likely never to be asked.

BASES FOR ORGANIZATION

In any organization problem the organizer has a choice of several factors around which to group operating, service, and staff units. The factor or combination of factors which he uses as a basis for his structure should depend primarily upon such circumstances as the kind of product to be marketed, the nature of the market, the strengths, weaknesses, and objectives of his firm, and the nature and intensity of competition, all of which condition the kind of marketing job the organization he builds will have to do. The chief factors around which a marketing organization structure can be built are the functions to be performed, the geographical areas within which they are to be carried on, the products to be marketed, and the customer groups to be served.

Functional Organization

The broadest functional classification that can be used as a basis for organization is that of planning and doing. A marketing department

FIGURE 11-1

MARKETING DEPARTMENT ORGANIZED ON A "PLANNING AND DOING" BASIS

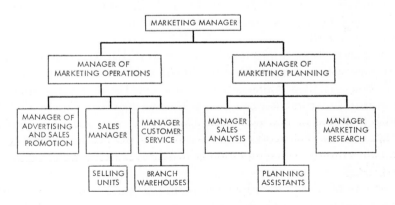

set up on this basis might look something like Figure 11-1. The advantages of this form of organization are that it makes it possible for the planning of marketing activities to be done by people who, through specializing in it, develop a certain degree of expertness and that it enables them to do this work without the disturbing effects of the pressures engendered by the constant crises, major and minor, which preempt so large a part of the working day of the operating executive. But perhaps its greatest advantage is that it assures that the planning work gets done —because it is in the hands of a group of people whose *first* order of business is to do it, rather than in the hands of operating executives who are almost bound to look on it as an incidental part of their duties.

On the other hand, this structure may result in plans that lack something in realism since they are drawn by persons not intimately aware of all the field conditions that affect the success or failure of marketing operations. This, in turn, may cause the members of the operating group to bestow something less than their complete confidence upon plans which they are apt to regard as "blue sky stuff."

The manager of such a functional marketing organization may be able to offset this weakness to some extent by seeing to it that there is a constant exchange of personnel between the planning and operating units. He may expect this to be vigorously resisted by the heads of the two units. An operating executive will be highly unhappy about losing one of his good performers while the latter does a stint in planning— and the reverse will be true of the leader of the planning group. More- over, a man who is good at getting things done is not always a good planner, and it is even less likely that a skillful planner is equally effec- tive as an operator. As an added touch, the constant shifting of jobs this scheme entails tends to dilute or inhibit the growth in expertise which is necessary to top-notch performance in both fields. The manager who uses it may have to be content with something less than the best per- formance in both.

He may seek a compromise by seeing to it that the men in his plan- ning unit spend considerable time in the field traveling with salesmen and observing their contacts with customers. He may supplement this by insisting that in the process of preparing marketing plans the plan- ners consult constantly with the operating executives to make sure that their plans are realistic. Of course, this costs money, but probably it is less expensive than to try to operate with plans that ignore the facts of the market.

In spite of these limitations the planning-operations axis of market- ing organization can be very useful. It has been employed with con- siderable success by the military services under field conditions much more fluid than any the marketing manager is likely to encounter.

A second type of functional organization is illustrated in Figure 11-2. In this type of structure the planning work is done by the heads of the operating and staff groups, under the direction of the marketing manager. One of its chief drawbacks lies in the fact that if the marketing operation is complex and requires highly specialized staff and service units, the marketing manager's span of control tends to become too wide, with the result that in trying to supply personal supervision to all the executives under him he provides adequate supervision to none.

The functional element is to be found in practically all marketing organization structures; the sole question is at what level. It may occur near the top, as shown above, in which case it is the dominant factor, or it may be shoved down into the geographic, product, or customer units, thus assuming a minor role.

FIGURE 11–2

MARKETING DEPARTMENT ORGANIZATION ON BASIS
OF TRADITIONAL FUNCTIONS

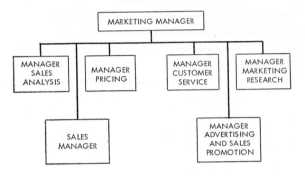

The role it should play in marketing organization structure probably depends on the kinds of products marketed, the kinds of customers who can buy them, and the relative importance of the several functions in the process. If a firm sells one product to a homogeneous group of customers, and if advertising, personal selling, and customer service are of relatively equal importance in the marketing process, a predominantly functional structure will probably prove very satisfactory. If it markets a number of products which are highly technical and differ markedly in their properties and uses, this kind of organization is not likely to operate very effectively. Regardless of what kinds of products a firm may sell, if it markets them to different groups of customers who use them for different purposes or who want to buy them in distinctly different ways, the marketing functions are not apt to offer the best basis for organization. If either advertising, or personal selling, or customer service is of overwhelming importance in the marketing process, so that it dwarfs the other two (which is the case with advertising in the sale of most cosmetics), the top marketing executive is apt to want to keep that function immediately under his eye. So he is likely to keep them *all* there, and to set up a functional structure.

Geographical Organization

A dominantly geographical type of organization would look some-

FIGURE 11–3

MARKETING DEPARTMENT ORGANIZATION ESTABLISHED ON A
GEOGRAPHIC BASIS

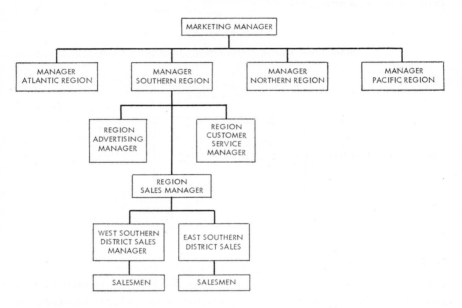

thing like that represented in Figure 11-3. Here some of the functional units have been pushed down into the regional areas. Usually it is desirable to retain in the central office such staff or service units as marketing research, sales analysis, and pricing. Marketing research requires people who are skilled in statistics, questionnaire construction, interviewing and analysis, and, like sales analysis, its effective and economical conduct often depends on the use of expensive computers. It would be wasteful to maintain a staff of experts and a computer installation at each regional office when a central unit can do all the work needed.

One of the regular functions of sales analysis, checking on the performance of the operating units, lies in the area of control. Marketing research is also often looked to for this kind of work, and it is not too good to have it done in the units being checked. If pricing is done in the regional offices, the firm incurs the risk of violating the Robinson-Patman Act by selling at different prices to competing customers. Since several top executives went to jail a few years ago for violations of the anti-trust laws, marketing executives prefer to keep the pricing function in the central office.

The geographical basis is present in the marketing organization structure of practically all companies. In many it is the dominant element. It is especially suitable when considerable differences exist between regions in the way in which customers buy or use the company's products. It may be the dominant structural element when the items in the product mix are homogeneous, or when the firm sells only one product and the customers are all of one kind.

The management of the personal selling force must almost always be organized on a geographical basis. When customer service is a very important patronage influence its management is likely to be more efficient if pushed out into the regions, so that those who are in charge of it are in close contact with customers and can readily learn their special service needs. If advertising must be done in national media, it obviously must be managed centrally. If, on the other hand, the impersonal selling work consists mainly of local advertising (sponsored jointly by the manufacturer and the dealer) and of point-of-sale promotion, it can often be managed best in the regional offices. Even in such cases, however, advertising and promotional materials can be most economically and effectively prepared in the central office.

Product Organization

If a firm markets a few products that exhibit pronounced differences in their marketing characteristics or require important variations in marketing methods and services, a structure that is divided predominantly along product lines (as in Figure 11–4) is indicated. In such a structure marketing research and sales analysis are likely to be retained at the staff level for the reasons outlined in our discussion of the geographical basis of organization. But the case for doing so is not so strong here because the product marketing managers are usually all housed in the same office as the marketing director, and their subordinates can make use of common computing equipment. On the other hand, the marketing managers each handle separate products or groups of products, so their exercise of the pricing function is not fraught with the danger of customer discrimination which exists when the power to determine prices of common products is placed in the hands of regional managers.

Probably the product type of marketing organization occurs most often in firms which are broken into general operating divisions on the basis of products. Each division in making and marketing its own product or products operates more or less like a separate business. Such firms sometimes have a small high-powered marketing department in the central office which makes general marketing policy for all divisions of the firm, checks on divisional marketing performance, and sometimes supplies certain marketing services that can be furnished most economically by a central unit.

FIGURE 11–4

MARKETING DEPARTMENT ORGANIZED ON PRODUCT LINE BASIS

At the other extreme are the firms whose salesmen are specialized by products but are supervised by executives who are not. This is not a common type of formal organization, although the salesmen of any multi-product company are apt to specialize to some extent on pet products without the blessing of the organization chart.

Many firms seek to compromise by setting up their marketing structure predominantly on some basis other than products, and superimposing upon it a group of product managers or specialists, each of whom operates in a staff capacity to gather information, recommend plans, check performance, and generally provide a focal point for all matters affecting the product or products assigned to him.

These product managers present one of the most difficult problems in organization, not only as it applies to the marketing area, but to the entire structure of the firm. Some companies try to make them responsible for the profit and growth of their respective products. Unless this is accompanied with power to make decisions and to administer their execution, the product manager is saddled with responsibility for something over which he may have some influence but no authority. If he is granted these powers his authority is apt to collide with that of the operating executives with resulting confusion and frustration. If he is a mere staff officer with power only to recommend, it is difficult to get a good man to take the job. Some firms further compound the natural confusion by making the product managers responsible to some executive outside the marketing and production departments, while placing upon them the responsibility of preparing plans and offering suggestions and recommendations with respect to making and marketing their products. To make this kind of a system work smoothly management must staff it with men of such goodwill and cooperativeness that they are almost impossible to find.

Many firms feel the need of product managers, but none has found an ideal spot for them in the organization structure.

Customer Organization

When a firm's market consists of a number of submarkets or customer groups that differ sharply in the services they require and in

FIGURE 11-5

MARKETING DEPARTMENT ORGANIZED ON "CUSTOMER GROUP" BASIS

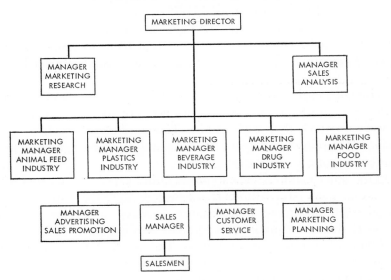

their methods of buying and product use, a structure based primarily on customer groups may be desirable. It might look something like the situation represented in Figure 11-5.

This company markets its products to five industries. Its business with each of them is under the direction of a separate marketing manager who has his own salesforce, advertising staff, and customer service units. If the principle is carried to the extreme even general staff and service functions, such as marketing research and sales analysis, may be pushed down under the customer group marketing managers. In many cases it will be more economical to concentrate these functions, and perhaps even advertising and customer service, in specialized units. The customer group managers then negotiate for the services of these central units much as though they were buying them from outside firms. For example, one firm with this organizational structure maintains a central sales promotion section which has in it a man who is highly skilled in building and installing displays for trade shows and conventions. A customer group marketing manager who wants such a display hires the services of this man in much the same way he would employ an outside specialist, except that the price is fixed by the marketing manager.

The customer group structure offers several advantages, not the least of which lies in its tendency to emphasize the importance of the customer in the thinking of all personnel throughout the firm. No small part of the function of each operating marketing unit is to interpret and represent the interests of its special customer group in its contacts with all other elements in the company organization, such as production and research. This form of organization tends to result in a high degree of customer orientation throughout the entire personnel of the firm.

It also enables the salesmen and those who supervise them to become really expert in the product and service needs of their customers and in the ways in which they wish to buy. This is likely to result in a very precise adaptation of the firm's products and marketing services to the requirements of the customers.

On the other hand, it is apt to prove rather expensive in areas where business is sparse and customers are widely scattered with the result that salesmen must travel long distances between calls. Some firms seek to obviate this by maintaining a force of combination salesmen to sell to all types of customers in such areas. The use of this device is limited by the fact that what is a sparse area for one kind of customer may be richly endowed with another type of customer.

Customers whose operations are diversified offer another drawback. For example, food manufacturers in our chart are apt to make and market animal feeds as well, and to use much the same kind of ingredients in each operation. Disputes are therefore apt to arise between customer group marketing managers as to which of them shall be responsible for the business of such customers. If the food business of such a customer is allocated to one operating unit of the marketing firm and its feed business to another, duplication of salesmen's calls is apt to result, with attending extra expense and exasperation of customers. Such disputes can usually be ironed out unless the occasions are too numerous, and the extra sales calls may pay for themselves in the more expert and fruitful selling services rendered. And the customer's exasperation may be reduced to a minimum, or be nonexistent, if different units within his purchasing department buy the same ingredient for different operations, such as food and feed, as is often the case.

The marketing manager who is contemplating the customer type of structure can probably sharpen his decision and lend soundness to it by implementing it on paper to the point where he can tell how many salesmen he will need, about how much extra travel it will entail, which customers will present problems of overlap, what their buying organizations are, and how important their business is. Such a study will not make the decision for him but it may bring out the factors involved and enable him to roughly quantify their importance.

General Considerations

It should be borne in mind that the organization charts we have just examined were shown for purposes of illustration only. Very rarely, if ever, will one of them be found in its pure form. The typical marketing organization structure is a combination of two or more forms constructed to suit the needs of the company and the conditions under which it operates. Usually, though, one of the four bases mentioned is dominant in determining the form the structure will take. No one of them can be said always or even generally to be more desirable than the others. It is pretty generally true, however, that the marketing organization planner is wise always to keep in mind that the customer is the most important person who has anything to do with a firm and that the organization structure can do much to create and maintain, throughout the marketing personnel, an acute consciousness of the customer's needs and wishes.

Decentralization. The problem of centralization versus decentralization is especially important in marketing organization. The problems of marketing a product or group of products are apt to vary widely in different geographical areas. Different groups of products, made by the same firm, may present highly discrete marketing problems. Different types of customers for a single product often vary widely in their uses of it and so in the manner in which they buy it. The supplier's marketing problems vary accordingly. For example, the food manufacturer is apt to find that the tasks of selling his product to hotels, restaurants, and institutions are entirely different from those of marketing through the retail trade, and that these, in turn, vary widely between chain systems and independents, big stores and little ones, and supermarkets and more orthodox outlets.

Then too, the characteristics of a market are usually fluid and its condition changes rapidly. Nor do these changes always occur in different markets according to any common pattern. The only element of change they all have in common is change itself.

These facts tend to emphasize the need for decisions to be made as near the market as possible. But they also stress the importance of coordinating the various marketing activities with each other and with other functions of the firm, especially production and finance.

In a centralized form of organization all major decisions and many minor ones are made at and administered from the top. The regional, functional, product, or customer group structural units serve merely as links in the chain of command or, to mix metaphors with abandon, as relay stations to transmit orders from central management to the operating units.

In a decentralized organization as much as possible of the power of decision and of the authority and responsibility for administration is shoved down into the subordinate units. Under such a system the regional manager is "Mr. Company" in his area, and even the salesman has wide discretion in planning and carrying on his work. The central management contents itself with setting objectives, determining general policies, making budgets and long range plans, coordinating the activities of subordinate units, and checking on their effectiveness.

In general, the decentralized method lends itself well to the purposes of marketing. When it is employed, the local, product, or customer group manager can make use of his close contact with his market and his greater sensitivity to its shifts to fit the operations of his unit as exactly as possible to the changing needs and wants of his customers.

In addition, the effectiveness of marketing work depends heavily upon the enthusiasm and morale of those who carry it on. Both of these tend to be enhanced when the subordinate has a lot to say about how he does his job. This privilege also tends to build in him a sense of responsibility for doing it as well as he can.

In some cases the decentralized form makes it possible to establish cost-profit centers in the middle or even the lower levels of the market-ing structure. For example, a regional manager may be made respon-sible for the costs of his operation and for the profit resulting from it. His performance is then judged largely on the basis of his profit con-tribution. The same thing may be true to an even greater extent of product or customer group marketing managers. The beneficial effect of such a set-up on marketing costs and results is sometimes startling.

On the other hand, decentralization presents the top marketing man-ager with serious problems of control and information. In seeing to it that things go right he must rely very largely on the use of objectives, policies, budgets, plans and reports, in the preparation of which his subordinates play a major part. He is apt to feel that he is "out of things" and that he does not know what is going on. He must rigorously ignore Benjamin Franklin's dictum that "If you want a thing well done, do it yourself." In spite of these drawbacks, the marketing manager is probably wise to build into his organization structure as much decen-tralization of authority and responsibility as the circumstances will permit.

Importance of Objectives. All marketing organization work should start with a thorough understanding of the overall objectives of the firm and the conditions under which they must be achieved. For example, if a company's prime objective is gaining a dominant share of the market, it is apt to need an entirely different marketing organization structure than would be required if its objective were to reap a high rate of profit on a smaller volume. If a dominant overall objective is diversification, the marketing organization must have a large measure of built-in flex-ibility in the sense that it is possible to add new units to exploit new markets without upsetting the whole structure in the process. The char-acteristics of the customers and the nature of the competition markedly affect the amount and kinds of supervision and supporting services that need to be provided in the marketing organization and the levels at which they must be available.

Making Jobs Clear. In the actual doing of all organizational work the mere construction of charts showing lines of authority and responsi-bility is not enough. This must be implemented by various devices de-signed to make unmistakably clear who is responsible for what and who is delegated power to do what. The tools most commonly used for this purpose are (*a*) a position description for each significant job, which lists and describes the activities into which the job may be divided (and which grants corresponding powers), and (*b*) a procedure which deals with each important operation in which several structural units must cooperate and which presents a description of each step in the process, indicating who is to do it and when. These devices may be supplemented by a chart something like that shown in Figure 11–6.

FIGURE 11–6

ORGANIZATIONAL BREAKDOWN OF AN ADVERTISING OPERATION

ACTIVITY	MARKETING VICE PRESIDENT	MARKETING MANAGER	PRODUCT MANAGER	SALES MANAGER	ADVERTISING MANAGER
Advertising Budget	Decides	Supervises Preparations and Recommends	Originates Advertising Plan	Consults with Product Manager	Assists Product Manager and Estimates Cost of Plan
Determining Appeals		Decides	Recommends	Approves	Consults and Implements in Copy
Contacts with Agency					
Selecting Media					
Other Activities					

The textual material in each of the boxes in the above chart should be brief but long enough to be unmistakably clear. The chart has the advantage that each man involved can, by reading down his column, get a complete idea of everything he is supposed to do in planning and carrying out the advertising function and, by reading across, can gain an understanding of where his activities must fit into those of other executives.

Whatever device is used, every new marketing organizational structure should be implemented as completely as possible on paper before it is adopted and promulgated. If this is done conscientiously and carefully, many weaknesses will be discovered and remedied and many mistakes avoided. Then too, the "shakedown" period is apt to be shorter and less painful because the people who man the positions in the new organization have a source or sources from which they can learn what their new duties and relationships are, and where and how their new jobs fit into the structure.

A good organization structure, manned by people who believe in it and like it, is a highly effective combination. But even a mediocre structure which the company personnel like and believe in is apt to be much more effective than an ideal one which they do not like or whose basic concepts they do not understand or accept. The reorganization planner therefore will be wise to sound out the ideas of the people who will man at least the upper and middle level positions in the new structure. Of course, he must confine his explorations to basic concepts; to raise questions about specific jobs would be to create and maintain more than the usual atmosphere of fear and uncertainty during the reorganization planning period.

The fact that marketing work so largely involves the manipulation of intangibles—ideas, emotions, attitudes, enthusiasms, and biases—and must be accomplished by the closely coordinated efforts of different organizational units using different tools causes this element of belief in and acceptance of the departmental organization structure to be more than usually important in the marketing area. It is hard to arouse and maintain enthusiasm or to achieve cooperation for channels of communication, authority and responsibility that the people manning them do not feel are right to begin with. They tend to get the feeling that they are being made to do it the "hard way," and resentment further dampens morale. No effort to get an acceptable organization structure in the first place, or to "sell" it to the people in it (both before and after it is promulgated) will be entirely wasted.

CHAPTER 12

Managing the Sales Force

Salesmen are important people, and the salesforce is the cutting edge of the marketing effort of the typical firm. Personal salesmanship plays a vital part in maintaining the health and promoting the growth of a free enterprise economy.

THE SALESMAN'S PLACE IN THE PICTURE

The Firm

The salesman is much more than merely a means of personal contact between the firm and its customers. If a company markets through middlemen, his job is not only to sell to them but to manage the company's relations with its outlets and to stimulate and supervise their efforts to resell its merchandise. He is his firm's chief tool in channel management. If, on the other hand, the firm markets direct to users, its salesmen collectively are its marketing channel and have the responsibility of managing its relations with the consumers of its products or services.

All too often the salesman is looked upon as someone who cannot get a really worthwhile job elsewhere. He is assayed at about 40 parts brass, 40 parts wind, and the remainder vacuum. Arthur Miller's characterization of salesman Willy Loman at the end of his career, beat up physically and emotionally, without achievement to remember or security to look forward to, bankrupt of human dignity, is accepted by many people as the norm instead of the caricature it actually was. Let us examine some of the elements in the job of a salesman. Perhaps then we can understand a little better how important his function is and the kind of person he must be to perform it.

1. *He must collect and supply information.* From the standpoint of the customer, this is usually the salesman's most important job; this is especially true in the industrial goods business. The purchasing

officer looks to the salesman to supply technical information about the product and its uses. All industrial and commercial customers rely to some extent on their suppliers' salesmen to inform them about changes in the market.

The salesman is expected to supply information to his own firm about his customers and prospects, the activities of competitors, shifts in the market, new methods of using or reselling the product, and any other pertinent facts he may be able to collect by keeping his eyes and ears open or by asking the right questions. In spite of all the solid achievements of marketing research the average management probably depends on its salesmen for the bulk of the information needed to guide its daily operations and much of its forward planning.

2. *He must manage service relations.* If the salesman has done his contact work well and built customer confidence, he is the natural person to whom the customer will look when trouble is encountered in using or reselling the product. While the salesman may not always be able to solve these problems himself, he is expected to mobilize the technical or promotional service facilities of his company to get them solved. This go-between function is exceedingly important in the industrial goods field. In the consumer goods area, since the problems are usually essentially commercial in nature, the salesman can handle more of them himself.

3. *He must discover new customers.* The salesman is usually responsible for his own territory and for the business in it. It is up to him to search out all firms in his area that can use or resell his products and to endeavor to persuade them to do so. If his company follows a policy of selective marketing he is expected to study prospective customers and to be prepared to supply information and advice in the work of selecting outlets.

4. *He must administer company policies.* The reasons for a firm's policies are not always readily apparent to its customers. It is up to the salesman to understand policies that affect customer interests and to explain them and justify them. This is not always easy, for policies are sometimes made without complete knowledge of the detailed facts of the market and must always be expressed in general terms which may have some weird interpretations when the attempt is made to apply them to specific situations.

5. *He must build the company image.* To the customer the salesman *is* the company. His statements are regarded as those of the company; the promises he makes are made by the company; his personal behavior is the behavior of the company: he offers the only means by

which the average customer can make personal contact with the company.

"The XYZ Company is a pretty conservative outfit," a purchasing executive commented about one of his potential suppliers. "Their salesman is a good, sound guy, but something of a stuffed shirt." The image a firm has in the eye of its highly important customer-public is shaped largely by its salesmen.

6. *He must represent customer interest to the firm.* To some extent at least, the salesman must sell in two directions. For example, when delayed deliveries handicap or irritate a customer, a good salesman will apply whatever influence and pressure he can exert to get his firm to meet its obligations. When a good customer needs an emergency delivery the salesman is apt to leave no stone unturned to induce his firm to shortcut its normal order handling routine and get the stuff to the buyer as fast as possible. If a good customer needs special promotional aids, or wants some minor modification of the product or its packaging, or desires some sort of joint research, an alert salesman usually tries to see to it that these matters receive careful consideration by the proper persons in his company.

7. *He must build customer enthusiasm for the firm and its products.* The satisfactory performance of this part of the salesman's task depends to a very great extent on how well he does all the others. But in addition to doing what he can to make his company's products and services as good as they can be, his job also certainly includes pointing out and emphasizing the strong points of the firm's product-service package and trying to convince the customer of their superior significance. To what extent it is good salesmanship or good ethics for him to cover up or try to explain away or minimize product or service weaknesses is an open question.

8. *He must carry out marketing programs.* The marketing plans and programs of a firm almost always involve action by its salesmen. This action is usually essential to their achievement. It is the salesman's duty, therefore, to understand the part he is expected to play in the marketing plan and to do his best to make it work. This may not be easy. He may feel that the plan is not the best for the purpose; some of its details are almost certain not to fit the conditions peculiar to his territory; compliance with it may cost him immediate commissions or sales credits. Good management will see to it that these discrepancies are not too numerous or too sharp. But the salesman must realize that managers, like salesmen, make mistakes and that each must live with the errors of the other.

9. *He must take orders or make sales contracts.* This is generally regarded as the only element of the salesman's job. Actually, it is often merely the end result of his other activities. In some cases, such as the textbook trade and some industrial goods businesses, the salesman rarely if ever enjoys the satisfaction of taking an order. In general, though, the culmination of his efforts is the customer signature on the dotted line at the crucial time, and all his skills are focused on the achievement of that end. No small part of his skill lies in the knowledge of just how and when to approach this culminating act of "closing," of putting the customer in a position where he must place an order or say "no."

The real nature of a salesman's job is conditioned by the relative emphasis which the conditions of the market and the objectives of his management put on the several parts of his task as we have described them. If primary emphasis is placed on getting immediate orders and maintaining constant contact with customers, his job is largely one of routine selling. The results he gets will vary roughly with the number of calls he makes: the more calls the greater the sales volume. On the other hand, if great importance is attached to his management of service relationships and to helping the customer solve problems of product use, or to build resale promotional programs, his job lies in the area of what may be called "creative" selling. The number of calls he makes is less important, but what he says and does during each call is of vital significance.

A typical example of *routine* selling is the work of the house-to-house salesman; another is that of the man who calls on small retail stores. Examples of creative salesmanship are supplied by the salesmen of heavy, expensive machinery or of highly technical chemical materials, and the man who handles the accounts of large department stores, supermarkets, or chain store systems. Obviously, there are all sorts of gradations between these extremes, although the trend seems to be in the direction of the more creative type.

From this brief description we can glean some idea of the importance of the salesman's work to the firm that employs him. His are the efforts that keep its products from piling up in its warehouses, that enable its production facilities to be operated at optimum levels of cost and efficiency, that make it possible for management to assure some degree of continuity of employment to nonselling workers, and that create an inflow of cash to pay wages and other bills and perhaps to provide profits. Upon him depends much of the success of new products and upon him falls the often distasteful and always difficult task of disposing of overstocks and inventories resulting from merchandising mistakes. The growth of a company depends in no small degree upon the skill and devotion of its salesmen. Its ability to maintain its share of a competitive market lies largely in their persuasive hands and voices.

The Economy

Our economy is essentially a competitive one. During most of its history it has been characterized by the intensive use of machinery that has constantly become more highly specialized and complex, by operations on an ever-increasing scale, and by heavy investments in research which engender constant changes in products, techniques, and production processes.

These things can not be supported without a large volume of sales for each firm and for each industry as a whole. They are economical only if sales volume enjoys a considerable measure of consistency, for they result in high overhead costs, the total of which remains about the same regardless of sales volume. Ours has therefore been a selling economy, and the salesman has been a highly important artificer in its construction and maintenance.

It is fashionable among armchair observers to disparage the salesman and his work and to regard him as an excrescence on the body economic instead of as a vital part of it. This is not hard to do, for the salesman in his effort to do his job has often been guilty of excesses, some of which violate good taste and some of which can hardly be regarded as ethical. Then too, the improvements in manufacturing efficiency have been so vast that it is easy to conclude that the problems of production have largely been solved. On the other hand, personal selling appears still to be done, as it was originally, by the salesman seeking out and canvassing one customer at a time with none of the efficiencies of mass operation.

This is not always a true picture. In most firms management has done much through research to locate customers and appraise their potentialities, thus making it possible to deploy salesmen where the business is; and through advertising and sales promotion, which are mass media, to open customers' doors to the salesman and render each minute of his call more productive. But the business of personal selling is still a man-to-man affair, and the casual or biased observer finds it easy to compare the obvious triumphs of production technology with the apparent backwardness of the art of selling.

These observers fail to grasp the fact that the combination of mass promotion and personal selling effort that blankets the market has supplied the sales volume from which flowed the financial resources to make possible improvements in production efficiency. They also fail to understand that the salesman is the cutting edge of competition which supplies what is by all odds the most powerful incentive to improvement in efficiency. Finally, they neglect to note that the salesman is far and away the most fruitful avenue of communication between management and the market, and that the news which he gathers and reports about customer reactions to products and services and buyers' wants and preferences has been a powerful stimulant and usually a reliable guide to the improvement and development of product and service offerings to suit them more exactly to the market. This factor has played a stellar role in the mechanization of our industry and in increasing the scale on which it operates.

The salesman, like the advertiser, has sold us practically everything except himself—and the part he really plays in our economy.

The Salesman Himself

Before we start to examine the problems of sales management we might be wise to look at the conditions under which the salesman works and to try to visualize what manner of man he must be to function in the environment these problems create.

1. *He must be able to work alone.* When he is on the job he has no one at his shoulder to whom he can look for support and encouragement. When the going gets tough, he is denied the accretions to morale and inner strength which come from belonging to a group. He must, to an extraordinary extent, be an individualist, willing and wanting to stand on his own feet. This is apt to mean that he is a man of strong opinions and that he does not respond gracefully to attempts to order him around. He is likely to do better when he is led than when he is bossed.

2. *He must be able to work in a hostile atmosphere.* It is true that many of his customers are his friends, at least off-the-job friends. But when a salesman calls on a customer the customer is apt to have in mind certain concessions or special favors he would like to get. He may be ready to place an order or sign a contract but he is not likely to divulge that fact to the salesman until he has tried every approach he has been able to devise to get the concessions or favors desired. One tried and true approach is to complain about products and services; another is to extol the virtues of the salesman's competitor. Until the climax of the interview is reached, and passed, the salesman and the customer are antagonists in a sort of poker game that is serious business.

As soon as that climax is passed the salesman is on his way to see the next customer.

This means that the salesman must have tight control of his temper and be able to ignore remarks that other men are free to resent. The average seasoned salesman is more or less impervious to insults because he has been insulted by experts. To rise above the atmosphere of hostility in which he works, he needs to be a man who really likes people and enjoys dealing with them, or who reaps a real satisfaction from inducing cantankerous, critical, privilege-seeking customers to sign on the dotted line. He must also have an ego that is self replenishing.

3. *He must be able to stand disappointment.* Not all calls result in sales. In many lines of business, as a matter of fact, very few calls culminate in orders or contracts. In many fields the typical customer must be cultivated over months or years before he yields a dollar's worth of business. There was the salesman for ceramic kilns who worked from January through November without making a single sale but was rewarded during the first two weeks of December with five contracts which aggregated the largest annual volume he had ever enjoyed. The salesman must have the dogged courage to keep going on even when the process does not seem worthwhile.

4. *The salesman must usually be a person of ready enthusiasms.* The "You've gotta show me" type of individual generally does not make a good salesman. A veteran sales manager once remarked that if he had the task of selling the Brooklyn Bridge he'd rather have a prospect list made up entirely of salesmen and ex-salesmen than of any other group. This does not necessarily mean that salesmen as a group are completely gullible and without critical judgment, but it does mean that their enthusiasms about people and things tend to be much less inhibited than those of the rest of us.

5. *The salesman needs a positive personality, preferably one that attracts people and captures their liking.* This is not to say that most sales are made on the basis of personality. They are not. Almost invariably, over half of a manufacturer's sales are made to a few large customers, who are represented by professional buyers. These people are not paid to buy from a supplier because they like his salesman. But if a buyer likes a salesman, his liking assures that the salesman will get an opportunity to present his case and that his presentation will receive a sympathetic hearing. This gives him a tremendous advantage over the man whose story is heard reluctantly or not at all. Moreover, even the most rigidly impartial buyer is apt to be influenced more than he realizes by his likes and dislikes of the men who try to sell things

to him. Nor can it be denied that some patronage is influenced heavily and consciously by the buyer's personal feelings toward the seller.

6. *The salesman should invite the confidence of other men.* This is especially important in the industrial goods business, although it is also highly significant in many parts of the consumers' goods area. Obviously, the best way to capture other men's confidence is to be absolutely honest with them.

These remarks appear contradictory in the light of the salesman's reputation for exaggeration. Actually the average buyer, professional or nonprofessional, is prepared to discount and forgive a salesman for a certain amount of "puffing" about the peripheral features of a product and to vest complete confidence in what he says about product or service features that *really* count. For instance, when a salesman says "This is the most closely woven material I've ever seen," the buyer reaches for the salt container; but when he says "This material contains not less than 150 threads per inch," the buyer expects to be able to count 150 threads or more in any inch he may sample. "Our delivery service is unexcelled" is apt to be taken by the buyer as nothing more than an expression of the salesman's enthusiasm, but if the salesman says "We deliver within 10 days after we receive the order," he had better mean exactly what he says if he wants to retain the customer's confidence. Customer confidence is generated by specific claims that are provable and by specific promises that are kept.

PROBLEMS OF SALES MANAGEMENT

Managing the personal selling work of a firm is a specialized form of personnel administration. In many ways, though, it is much more difficult than ordinary personnel administration. Due to the intangible nature of selling work and to the extent to which its success depends on a man's use of such endowments as enthusiasm, tact, and finesse in dealing with people and of skills which are not readily measurable, the tasks involved in sales management are usually much more complex than those encountered in the administration of factory or clerical employees whose required skills are much more measurable and the results of whose performance can usually be much more immediately and accurately observed.

The elements of the sales management function are essentially the same as those of any other personnel administration activity. Various classifications of them have been made. For convenience we will use the following: (*a*) selection, (*b*) training, (*c*) assignment, (*d*) supervision, (*e*) providing incentives, and (*f*) control.

The background of all good sales administration work is a thorough knowledge of the selling job which the firm needs to have done. It may require salesmen whose primary function is to get orders, as is the case with house-to-house canvassers and, usually, with men selling for firms that market direct to retailers. It may need men who rarely, if ever, get orders, as, for example, a college textbook salesman or a building materials man calling on architects. A study of this kind should be designed to provide a clear understanding not only of the primary activities the firm wants the salesman to carry on but of the subsidiary functions it expects of him as well. The end result should be a job description which is a listing of the sub-tasks desired and a short but clear explanation of each. It should also probably include some indication of their relative importance.

From this may be drawn a specification of the kind of man needed to do the job. This should include not only natural endowments of character, physical attributes, mental ability and personality, but also such matters as knowledge, skills, and techniques. While this sort of information is most important in the work of selection, it should also serve to guide the planning and carrying on of the function of training. It is apt to be of aid in assigning salesmen's tasks, for different types of customers or territories may need different talents in the men serving them. It should serve a useful purpose in supervision by providing a background against which to view a man's actual behavior and may supply clues pointing to the real causes of difficulty in problem situations. Two of the primary functions of an incentive system are to attract and hold the kind of salesmen needed, and to stimulate them to do the things the company wants done. So a job specification can provide a guide to developing systems of remuneration and, for control work, it may provide at least the rudiments of a standard against which to measure actual performance. A clear understanding of the salesman's job is vital to good sales management.

Selection of Salesmen

The old adage "You can't make a silk purse out of a sow's ear" applies with full force to the work of sales administration. A sales force can be no better than the raw manpower material from which it is built. This is not to say that proper training and supervision are not worthwhile, and do not make performance better than it would be without them, but that the quality of the manpower to which they are applied sets definite limits on the results management can expect from them.

The quality of the manpower recruited depends very largely on the methods of selection employed.

Candidates. The first step in selecting salesmen is getting candidates for selling positions. The average firm has several sources it may tap to replenish its candidate pool. For many firms the schools and colleges offer a fruitful source. This is especially true if the selling job requires technical training or if the stakes of each sales contact are large and the job requires a high degree of imagination and intelligence. It may also be a worthwhile source for salesmen whose job is of a more routine nature, provided the opportunities for promotion to managerial positions are numerous and attractive.

For the firm whose selling is of the routine type, newspaper advertising may be fruitful. Firms which need salesmen of considerable ability may find advertisements in the want ad columns of publications such as the *New York Times* worthwhile. Trade journals are often a fruitful source. A man who reads the trade journal of his industry is apt to be one who takes his job seriously and is well informed about it.

Many firms find good candidates among their own clerical, warehouse, and production employees. These persons have the advantage that they know the product and the company. In some trades customers and their employees offer the same advantage. This source must be handled with care to avoid creating customer ill will. Competitors may sometimes be made to contribute unwillingly to the candidate pool. But a salesman hired away from a competitor can also usually be hired away by a competitor just as easily, and he brings along a ready-made set of working habits, some of which may not fit the needs of his new employer.

Sometimes employment agencies are worth contacting, although, since the agency gets no fee unless its candidate gets a job, they are apt to lack discrimination in their recommendations, and the new salesman comes to his employer with a mortgage on his earnings during the early months of his employment. Finally, many candidates just "walk in off the street." While many sales managers frown on this source, the job hunter has at least shown enough gumption to go after a job instead of waiting for one to come to him.

Tools of Choice. The two tools most widely used in choosing salesmen are the application blank and the interview. Other aids often used are references, physical examinations, and tests.

Usually the application blank is designed to present a fairly complete picture of the background and career history of the candidate. From it the sales manager can discover whether the applicant has the more objective qualifications, such as education, technical training, or work, or other experience which have been set up as requirements for the job. The information it contains is usually very carefully studied, some firms even applying statistical methods to its analysis.

Most firms probably require sales candidates to undergo a physical examination. Selling on the road is not an easy job or one that can be well done by a man who is sick or suffering from physical infirmities. And, while references are generally required, they are usually not weighted very heavily. Respondents, even those mildly hostile to a candidate, are prone to tell the best and not the worst about him. If a form is used which requires the respondent to answer specific questions, useful information can often be obtained, especially from former employers. Respondents will lie by omission but usually not by positive statements.

Tests may be of several kinds. For example, a firm hiring men to sell automatic accounting equipment may submit its candidates to a test designed to show understanding of accounting principles and methods. General intelligence tests have been found useful. Psychological tests designed to disclose a man's emotional balance may prevent the employment of persons who cannot stand the frustrations and emotional pressures of selling work. The most widely used is the aptitude test, which is designed to show whether a man has the interests and attitudes that have been or are supposed to be characteristic of a good salesmen. There is much controversy about tests, although many firms use them extensively. They are probably more useful in eliminating unfit candidates from a group than in spotting the man who will do the best job.

The interview is generally employed at two points in the selection process: the beginning and the end. Often an initial interview is used to prevent obviously unfit candidates from applying. When the field has been reduced by one means or another to several candidates, the choice of no one of whom would seem to be a serious mistake, the final selection is often made largely on the basis of interview. For this purpose the jury method, in which each candidate is interviewed by several executives who then discuss and compare them all, is very useful. The interview results may be made specific by requiring each interviewer to fill out a form for each candidate on which he records his observations of a list of characteristics regarded as indicative of the man's ability to do a good selling job for the company.

Training

The management of training is largely a matter of deciding and implementing answers to the questions *what, how, where,* and *when.*

What. The training process usually deals mainly with information and techniques. In order to do a good job a salesman must know a lot about his company, its history, its methods of doing business, its objectives, its policies, its procedures in handling customer business, and the men in it. He must have a working knowledge of the products he is to sell, how they are made, what they are used for, and how they operate. He should know as much as possible about customers and prospective customers. The rudiments of this he can learn in training; the details can come only as the result of contact and experience. He must also have a working knowledge of competitors, their products, their methods of doing business, and their strengths and weaknesses. Finally, he needs to be trained in the techniques of selling which promise to be most effective for him and most suitable for the firm.

How. If salesmen can be trained in groups, at least the basic information they need can be imparted most quickly and cheaply through more or less formal instruction, by methods closely akin to those used in any school. For product information, factory experience may be most effective. Experience probably affords the best means by which a man can acquire detailed information and absorb it so completely that he does not know he has it until an occasion arises when he has to use it. In formal instruction, techniques can be explained and illustrated and a certain amount of practice gained by their use in simulated situations. It is probably difficult for them to become second nature to a man without their repeated use in actual selling situations under fire. It is best that such experience be gained under the close direction of a trainer or a field supervisor who can observe, criticize, suggest, and demonstrate.

Where. Many firms feel that formal informational instruction, especially when given on a group basis, can be carried on best in the home office. When it has to be given on an individual basis, as is apt to be the case with a small company or one with a very low salesman turnover rate, it may be carried on either in the home office while the trainee is ostensibly working at a clerical or staff job or a series of such jobs, or in the same manner in a regional office if some executive there is a good trainer. If possible, the jobs to which the trainee is assigned should be ones in the doing of which he will unconsciously absorb the kinds of information he needs in his selling work.

Training in the techniques of selling can usually be done best in the field. This should be carried on under the general supervision of a training specialist in the home office or under the field supervisor who will have charge of the new salesman when he is assigned a territory, provided the supervisor is reasonably skilled in the work of training.

When. There is a difference of opinion as to when training should be given. Some managers feel that a man's instruction should be as complete as possible before he faces a customer. This makes sense when customers are few and each one's business is highly important to the firm. Others are of the opinion that a trainee will learn more and faster if he is given only the rudiments of what he needs to know, put out on a selling job long enough to learn its difficulties, and then brought in for thorough training. The theory is that the trainee's brief selling experience will impress him with the importance of learning and give him some background from which to understand the significance of what he is taught. This method can be used safely only when customers are small enough and numerous enough so that the loss of an order or even a customer is not vital.

Training Old Salesmen. The work of training is never complete. Old salesmen must be taught new tricks, informed about new products, corrected in selling faults they unconsciously develop, and instructed in carrying out new company policies and procedures. Much of this work can best be done in the course of the routine process of supervision. Some of it can be done through conventions and conferences. Some firms even operate schools for the purpose, and most firms with large sales forces have, in the headquarters office, a unit which plans training programs and either administers them or aids the field managers in carrying them out.

Assignment

The salesman's job is usually assigned on a territorial basis. As a general rule the limits of sales territories are drawn along the boundary lines of political units, such as wards, townships, counties, or states because they are generally known and easily recognized. The sales manager is wise to try to equalize territories in terms of sales opportunities and travel difficulties even though he can never approach complete equality in these matters.

It is usually desirable to try to administer the salesman's relations with the company and his territory so that he develops a proprietary attitude toward the territory and feels that in it he is "Mr. Company." This attitude can not be generated without the solid substance of actual delegation to him of final authority and responsibility for customer contacts within his area. Many marketing managers insist that company executives, even the most exalted, refrain from making customer contacts unless accompanied by the salesman or after clearance by him.

Some firms assign salesmen's tasks by means of customer or prospect lists. This is usually the case with men who handle house accounts. The method may also be used by firms whose customers are few in number and not widely scattered. Other concerns give their salesmen no assignments except to go out and sell. This method is often followed by small firms making industrial materials or equipment, the precise uses of which are not completely known, which thus need a lot of "birddog" selling to explore the market. It is also used by insurance companies and investment houses.

Supervision

Sales supervision is a mixture of a variety of activities. It includes a considerable amount of training work, the exercise of discipline, the application of nonmonetary stimulants to performance, and the provision of field leadership. The good supervisor must be a happy mixture of practical psychologist, flag waver, and sympathetic confidant with somewhat more than a touch of Simon Legree thrown in. A good salesman is apt to be more than a little temperamental, a characteristic which tends to be emphasized by the fact that he works alone and by the inevitable frustrations that attend his job. As a result his field manager needs rather more than the usual supervisory skill in human relations.

In his capacity as trainer the supervisor is usually expected to correct errors in the selling techniques of the men under him, to make sure that they understand changes in company policy and procedure (and know how to act in conformance with them), to observe especially effective selling methods used by one man and pass them on to others in his charge, and to advise and counsel his men with respect to difficult selling situations. Some sales managers rely on the field supervisor almost entirely to train older salesmen, but whether or not this is true he probably does the lion's share of that kind of work.

In general, salesmen want to behave in the manner expected of them. But, being human, they occasionally become careless or lazy, and now and then intentionally contemptuous of the instructions of the management. Salesmen are somewhat more ingenious than other employees in devising ways to circumvent the rules and much more imaginative in manufacturing excuses for such infractions. In this area lies the disciplinary function of the supervisor. In applying discipline, he must be careful to stop short of dampening a man's enthusiasm or damaging his self-confidence since these are two of the most effective tools of the salesman's trade.

Sometimes infractions of the code of good behavior reflect a deep-seated resentment against some feature of the company's attitude or behavior or a lack of understanding of the reasons why things should be done as required. Sometimes they grow out of personal problems. It is part of the supervisor's job to ferret out such difficulties and correct them or, if correction lies beyond his powers, to report them to his superiors who may be able to do so. The sales supervisor should not apply discipline in bulk lots but rather in carefully compounded and measured individual doses.

The supervisor should be the source of many of the nonmonetary and informal incentives to good performance, such as a feeling of self-importance, a sense of personal prestige, the comfort of belonging, and the conviction that the company is a "good outfit to work for." To the salesman his immediate supervisor *is* the company: because of the salesman's isolation, this is much more true of the field supervisor than of his approximate counterpart, the foreman in the factory. His ability to build morale by judicious praise is fully as important as criticism or correction. He must be very careful not to impair but instead to build the self-respect which is a man's chief buckler when he faces a customer. Above all, the supervisor must seek to impress upon the salesman an understanding of the importance of his work to himself, his family, his company, and the society of which he is a part. The beaten, dejected, frustrated, and pitiable Willy Loman in Arthur Miller's play, "The Death of a Salesman," was probably fully as much the product of bungling, unfeeling, and inept supervision as of Willy's own inadequacies or of the failures of the society to which he belonged.

Leadership defies description. It assumes so many forms that those who try to describe it almost inevitably wind up describing its effects or manifestations instead of the quality that creates those effects. In the sales supervisor it is probably most of the things we have been talking about, plus whatever other qualities a man has that causes other men to trust him, to believe in him, and to follow him. Outstanding field leaders are few and hard to come by. So in most of his supervisors the sales manager must be content with a partial equipment of the traits of leadership or with the highly diluted essence of it. Because of the nature of their jobs and the conditions under which they work, salesmen have a more compelling need for leadership than workers in any part of the enterprise. Management has not yet solved the problem of how to get it and keep it at the field level.

Providing Incentives

In seeking to stimulate his salesforce to maximum achievement the sales manager has two kinds of incentives with which to work. Some of them are monetary; others are subjective or psychological. Most men are willing to struggle for money with which to buy the good things that make up the "more abundant life" for themselves and their families. But most men also want other, less tangible things, such as prestige, a sense of accomplishment, the joy of combat and of winning, a feeling of realizing oneself and making full use of one's powers. The successful manager must use both types of motivation in a well coordinated system of incentives.

The sales manager probably has a greater than ordinary need of a proper combination of them because of the type of men he manages and the kind of work they do. Their business is to sell goods and services for dollars, so they are apt to be more conscious of the importance of dollars than other workers. They are constantly engaged in trying to impose their own ideas on other men and to move them to favorable action. To do this successfully they must have the intangibles mentioned above in abundant measure.

There are at least three, possibly four, types of compensation through which management may provide monetary incentives to salesmen. They are salary; commission, with or without drawing account; bonus; and the point system of payment. Very often two or more of these are combined in the compensation system of a firm. The possible number of such combinations, including variations in detail, is almost limitless. Success in constructing a compensation scheme depends largely on a clear understanding of the uses and weaknesses of each of the basic types of payment and skill in fitting one or several of them into the operating situation of the firm so as to preserve the strengths and minimize the weaknesses of each.

Commission. In its usual form the commission is expressed as a percentage of the dollars sold, which percentage is paid the salesman. In a few cases it is a fee per unit of goods sold. The commission is often supplemented by a drawing account. The combination then might work something like this:

Salesman receives 5 percent commission on sales;

Salesman draws $200 in cash on the 1st and 15th of each month;

During the month his sales are $13,000, on which he is entitled to 5 percent, or $650.

At the end of the month, the company subtracts from the $650 commissions he has earned the $400 he has drawn during the month and pays him the remainder, $250.

The commission provides a powerful incentive to the salesman to bring in sales during the pay period but it does not offer him much inducement to do anything else. In the process of selling, many firms must have a great deal of customer service and development work done that may not bear sales fruit for months, sometimes years. Take, for example, a company making heavy equipment, technical materials, or bridge steel, or a food firm which wishes to market through large chain systems. For such concerns, the commission is not an adequate compensation incentive.

Suppose, furthermore, that a firm markets a line of products with varying rates of gross and net profit. Obviously, a straight commission brings pressure on the salesman to push the sale of the items that are easiest to sell in quantity and defeats the objective of the firm to put sales emphasis on the high-profit items. This defect may be offset by a system of commission rates varied from product to product according to their profit rates. Then too, the sales manager who pays his salesmen entirely by commission can expect to have trouble getting them to submit reports other than expense accounts, nor can he rely on them to do much of the information gathering and reporting that is so helpful in the work of management.

On the other hand, the pressure toward large sales volume is powerful. Moreover, the firm using this system pays only for sales made, and its selling cost remains about the same percentage of sales whether volume is high or low.

Salary.   Most of the advantages of the salary grow from the fact that with it the firm buys the salesman's time and can expect less resistance when it asks him to do work that does not result in immediate sales or that may not be directly connected with selling at all. When a firm's sales are made in big lumps at long, irregular time intervals, payment by commission is almost impossible because the salesman's income must be reasonably regular and must be in amounts that are manageable by him. These requirements are met by the salary system. There is often no other way by which to pay for missionary work, customer service, development work, and the gathering and reporting of market information.

Bonus.   The bonus is generally used in combination with one of the other methods. In sales management the bonus is almost always paid for specific performance of some sort and not, as is so often true in other functional areas, in the form of a handout based on profits or the whim of the manager.

It may be used as an adjunct to salary as an inducement to perform certain reasonably measurable activities not likely to result in immediate sales. It may be tied in with either the salary or the commission as a payment for doing an exceptionally good selling job during a period. It may be given as an incentive to and reward for any performance "above and beyond the strict call of duty."

The bonus should be paid as a regular part of the compensation system and for the doing of specific things. If it is to be a useful part of the incentive compensation system every salesman should be able to earn a bonus and should understand clearly what he must do to earn it.

Point Systems. A few firms use some sort of point system which, in general, works somewhat as follows:

Management divides the salesman's job into a number of sub-tasks, such as volume of sales made, demonstrations, point-of-sale material installed, or new customers gained.

The manager then assigns points to each of these sub-tasks according to his appraisal of its importance.

Points are recorded during the pay period.

At the end of the pay period a man's point score is totalled and points are translated into pay dollars according to a predetermined ratio.

This scheme looks better on paper than it works in practice. Its use is indicated only when the salesman's job involves a number of important activities that do not produce immediate sales. But if very many such activities are included in a point system it becomes so complicated that the salesman finds it hard to compute his earnings, and arguments between him and the office as to the amount of them are liable to ensue. And, unless all important sales activities are included, the system fails to do what it is designed to do.

Quotas. A quota is an amount of sales assigned to a salesman or selling unit during a coming period. It is used very widely as an incentive device. The incentive provided may be monetary in that the quota is a part of the compensation system. For example, a salesman's commission rate may increase as his sales volume approaches or exceeds his quota, or a bonus may be paid to the man who makes or betters his quota.

The quota may also be used as a nonmonetary incentive, something akin to par or a handicap system in golf. For example, one firm sets a sales objective for each man. His achievement, or failure to achieve his objective, has no effect on his pay but, since each salesman helps set his own objective, the typical man displays considerable emotional commitment to its achievement.

Anyone who has ever observed or participated in setting up a system of handicaps for a golfing foursome will appreciate the chief drawback of the quota. Unless each salesman who does a good selling job has a reasonable and substantially equal chance of achieving his quota its use may not only fail to provide an incentive, it may actually dampen his working ardor. And this is not a planning balance that is easy for management to achieve, depending as it does on the ability of the man, the potential of his territory, the intensity and quality of local competition, and any local conditions that may temporarily disturb any of these factors in the territory.

Nonmonetary Incentives.   Probably the most generally used of these is the contest. Managing a contest is a highly complicated task and requires very careful planning and supervision. It must be planned so that every man has, by working hard, a chance to win, and so that in winning or trying to win he helps achieve the firm's objective in holding the contest. The contest also involves certain dangers. The excitement and tension it generates may be followed by a slump, or dealers may be overstocked. Used too often, contests may lose their charm and, in doing so, may dull the effectiveness of other incentives.

Awards and prizes are another type of nonmonetary incentive. They may be so classed because so many managements have found that the cash value of the award has little relation to the stimulus it provides. The amount of recognition or prestige it carries is a much more potent measure of its effectiveness. The same requirements for success apply in the use of awards and prizes as in the management of contests.

The conditions under which many firms operate—for example, almost all industrial goods houses—preclude the use of contests and narrowly limit the effectiveness of awards and prizes. Probably, in the final analysis, the most effective nonmonetary incentives are those mentioned at the beginning of our discussion of incentives: the day-to-day treatment of the salesman which is designed to impress upon him the importance of his work, to build his own confidence and self-reliance, to convince him of the firm's and his manager's confidence in him, and, in short, to create and maintain in him a feeling of being recognized and valued. All the rest is frosting on the cake.

Control

Since we will later devote a chapter to the general subject of control of marketing operations, we will now merely touch upon several of the problems of controlling the activities of field salesmen.

The work of compiling records of the salesman's performance and comparing it with standards in the form of past sales, potentials, planned sales, planned calls, quotas, or objectives can usually be done most cheaply and effectively by a sales analysis unit in the central office.

How well a salesman shows up in such a comparison depends not alone on his own ability and devotion to his job but on the subtler forms of day-to-day control work carried on by his field supervisor. This consists of reviewing his selling plans, observing his selling performance on the job, and pointing out and trying to correct defects and mistakes. It is not necessary to stress the importance of this sort of grass roots control work, but the field supervisor can not be expected to do it effectively unless he thoroughly understands its importance and is well trained in doing it.

A type of control work that applies especially to the salesman is that involved in keeping his expenses within reasonable bounds. Some firms seek to do this by allowing each man a daily expense stipend. The problem here is to set the proper amount. To be fair it may have to be varied according to the cost of travelling the several territories. The Bureau of Internal Revenue seems to view this with reservations, preferring itemized expense accounts. Many firms prefer such itemized expense accounts. The canny salesman knows that these will not always be checked and that only a sample of them is likely to be examined from time to time. Probably only a corporal's guard of all salesmen can truthfully say that they have never "doctored" an expense account, nor is the doctoring process without justification. Any one who has traveled on an expense account knows how hard it is to include in it all the costs of living away from home.

A rigid control of expenses tends to defeat its own purpose. It presents a challenge to "beat" it and a justification for doing so. If the company insists on being "small" about the matter, why shouldn't the salesman follow suit? The result is that a lot of imagination, heavy thought, and valuable time are expended on fancy expense account juggling, time that could much more profitably be spent on planning sales and making them. Probably the best managerial policy is to be reasonably liberal in what is allowed and to merely keep the total within the bounds of good sense and propriety.

The work of personal selling must be directed within the framework of the general marketing objectives and plans of the firm. It must be coordinated with the other activities designed to attract and hold the patronage of possible buyers. One of the most important of these is advertising, and another is sales promotion. To do this successfully the manager must understand the uses and techniques of these activities and the problems of managing them.

CHAPTER 13

Management of Advertising and Sales Promotion

INTRODUCTION

Advertising and Sales Promotion Defined

Advertising, as defined by the American Marketing Association, is "any paid form of non-personal presentation and promotion of ideas, goods, or services by an identified sponsor." Advertising differs from publicity in that publicity is not paid for by the sponsor, and from propaganda in that propaganda deals only with ideas and the sponsor is often unidentified.

Sales promotion refers to those marketing activities, other than personal selling, advertising, and publicity, that stimulate consumer purchasing and dealer effectiveness, such as displays, shows and exhibitions, demonstrations, and various nonrecurrent selling efforts not in the ordinary routine. Sales promotion activities supplement, extend, and function as a link between personal selling and advertising in the overall selling mix. This chapter and the next will focus on the management of advertising, with secondary attention to sales promotion.

Advertising is a large and growing part of marketing. According to *Advertising Age* magazine, total U. S. advertising expenditures amounted to $12.5 billion in 1962. This represented a 240-fold increase over 1865 and more than a four-fold increase over 1945 outlays. Advertising expenditures amounted to 2.3 percent of gross national product in 1962. In that same year our top 100 national advertisers spent a record $2.66 billion on advertising. Most of this money went into newspaper ads, magazines, radio and television programs and commercials, business paper advertising, direct mail promotions, outdoor ads, and similar media.

Advertising, of course, is not equally important to all manufacturers. On the average 1.13 percent of the sales dollar was said to have been invested in advertising in 1962. Such an average, however, conceals as much as it reveals. Large companies like General Motors, Proctor & Gamble, and General Foods each spend well in excess of $100 million in advertising every year; a producer of branded drugs or cosmetics may budget as much as 40–50 percent of sales for advertising. Other large firms, like Hershey Chocolate Corporation and countless small and medium sized companies, invest little or nothing in this form of selling. Clearly then, advertising is a dominant marketing force in certain companies and totally insignificant in others. One of the aims of this chapter is to clarify why this is so.[1]

First, however, a few general remarks are needed about what advertising is and is not, and about what it can and cannot do, for the role of advertising has often been misunderstood by both laymen and business executives. Some overzealous champions of advertising invest in it with a blind and childlike faith. They are overawed by its mystique and ascribe far more power to it than is usually warranted. Others may be unnecessarily fearful of advertising as a social and economic force, or unduly skeptical about the practical results it can produce. Eldridge Peterson has helped to cut through a fog of misunderstanding and frustration with these words:

Here are a few simple statements of fact about what advertising can do, and what it can't do that may help to clear the air. Basically, though with some oversimplification, advertising *can:*

Build a brand name that will create consumer acceptance, perhaps even consumer demand, for your product or products.

Introduce new products, new improvements, and new ideas to the public and to the trade almost overnight.

Create an "image" of your company valuable in attracting good personnel and investment capital, in creating good public relations for your company in your plant community and in other circles of influence, such as government and labor.

Obtain distribution for new products and widen distribution for older items.

By doing these things, it can assume part of the sales load. The dollars spent on advertising are not an "extra" expenditure, but money that would otherwise have to be spent on other phases of marketing.

Advertising *cannot:*

Be expected to do a *precise* job and produce a *precise* result—at least, at this stage of its development.

Produce miracles—it cannot enable you to buck a basic customer trend.

---

[1]Students wishing to explore specific cases to learn why some companies rely heavily on advertising, while others eschew it, might explore articles such as (1) "P&G: What Explains Its Success?" *Printers' Ink,* September 28, 1962, pp. 29ff., and (2) "How Is Hershey Doing—Without Advertising?" *Sales Management,* May 20, 1960, pp. 33ff.

Put over an inferior product by sheer quantity and quality of verbiage, no matter how much money you spend.

Work effectively if management makes the advertising budget a catch-all for every expense it can't charge elsewhere.

Function efficiently if used for vanity purposes—mere self-glorification, or providing management with opportunities to mingle with top TV personalities, for example.

. . . . Some of the mystery of advertising evaporates if we consider it in elementary terms. If a company has only one large customer, it can reach him most effectively by calling on him personally. If the company has 50 to 100 customers, it can still reach them individually, if not by personal calls, at least by telephone. If it has more than 100, it can, perhaps, write each one a personal letter. But as the number of customers and prospects increases to the point where all these methods become impractical, the company turns to advertising.[2]

Thus it is well to recognize at the outset, and to keep clearly in mind at all times, that advertising is simply a method of selling—nothing more and nothing less. In intent and results, although not in method, it potentially has all the good and bad features and is subject to the same social, economic, and commercial uses and abuses as any other type of salesmanship. It can be tasteful or blatant, attractive or repulsive, truthful or deceptive, costly or cheap, effective or ineffective. Advertising, therefore, needs to be viewed as both an alternative and a complement to personal salesmanship. It is but a part of the total selling effort, and other elements of the sales mix can be of equal or greater importance.

Advertising and Personal Selling Related

In the late 1950's and early 1960's the McGraw-Hill Publishing Company ran an ad repeatedly and without change in its business publications. It was a widely read and noted advertisement for it dramatically depicted how very closely advertising must be keyed to personal selling. The illustration showed a stony-faced buyer leaning forward in his swivel chair. Beside his photograph were the following words, directed at business readers and including company salesmen.

I don't know who you are.
I don't know your company.
I don't know your company's product.
I don't know what your company stands for.
I don't know your company's customers.
I don't know your company's record.
I don't know your company's reputation.
Now—what was it you wanted to sell me?

---

[2]Eldridge Peterson, "Why Management Is Reappraising Advertising," *Dun's Review and Modern Industry,* October, 1958, pp. 49 and 58.

The moral, of course, is that the selling process is often started before the salesman calls—with advertising. Advertising has a pre-selling, a selling, and a post-selling role to play in many companies. It can pave the way for the salesman by opening the door of the buyer. It can reach buying influences unknown to the field salesman or difficult for him to contact. It can back up the salesman during his call, help to speed up the selling process, represent him between sales calls, and reduce field costs. Because of inflation, rising salaries, hiked travel costs and field expenses, a severe shortage of good salesmen and the need for costly training or retraining, the cost per personal sales call has soared in recent years in both industrial and consumer markets. It is not surprising, therefore, that many companies are using advertising to make impersonal sales calls for them. Television, newspapers, and other advertising media function as a substitute salesforce, if not entirely, at least in part.

Nonpersonal sales calls through advertising are often much less expensive than personal visits. Spot TV commercials, for instance, may be used at a "cost-per-thousand" of perhaps 3 dollars. By contrast, when personal sales calls cost $25 each (and they are often much more expensive), the cost-per-thousand is $25,000. Obviously, however, nonpersonal sales calls may be *less effective* than the personal variety, and they are not always made on the right prospects.

Steps in the Selling Process

Let's take a closer look at the nature of the selling process. Whether personal or impersonal in nature, selling is essentially a communications problem. Advertising, sales promotion, and personal selling are alternative and complementary ways of communicating information about an idea, product, or service. The purpose is to educate, inform, remind, or persuade a potential buyer. We can best analyze the selling process by breaking it down into its elements. Different analysts have used different breakdowns. One defines selling as a four-step process of getting attention, holding interest, arousing desire, and obtaining action. The IBM Corporation describes selling as a process of progressively moving a prospect from a state of unawareness of the product or his need for it to awareness, comprehension, conviction, and ordering. McGraw-Hill discusses selling in six phases: making contact, arousing interest, creating preference, making a proposal, closing the order, and keeping the customer sold.

The particular breakdown used is not especially important for our purposes. That may vary from one selling situation to another. What is important is that advertising and personal selling have different roles to play at each step in the process. It is useful to relate our choice of selling methods to particular steps in order to arrive at the best mixture of personal selling and advertising in the total sales program, in terms of both cost and effectiveness.

Sometimes the entire process is carried out by only one agent of demand creation. The selling of heavy industrial equipment, for instance, may rest almost entirely on the personal efforts of highly trained sales engineers. Advertising, on the other hand, may shoulder the lion's share of the sales burden for such products as cigarettes, packaged food products, drugs, and cosmetics. For many types of commodities, however, the selling load is shared by personal and impersonal selling methods.

Vigorous personal selling is perhaps more effective than advertising at all steps in the selling process, but it may not be the more efficient procedure. If not, advertising can be called upon to help the salesman perform part of the selling job. Although advertising may not be particularly powerful at such critical selling stages as making complex proposals, closing a sale, or servicing an account, it can often be effective (at low cost) in making initial contacts, arousing interest in a product, creating customer preference, and keeping customers sold on a previous purchase. Advertising can often perform these functions more efficiently than the salesman. By using it at these stages we can release a salesman's time for increased attention to the really critical selling steps. Thus, by dividing the selling task up and assigning it appropriately we may end up with more advertising at some stages in the process to permit more attention to personal selling at others.

If we understand that advertising is simply a method of selling we will find it easier to examine some of the more intricate aspects of its management. How is advertising actually planned? What is involved in executing these plans? How do companies organize to get advertising work performed? What controls are employed in advertising? The remainder of this chapter and the next will be directed toward answering such questions.

ADVERTISING PLANNING

The advertising and sales promotion plan is part of the overall marketing program. It consists of a formal, written document which is usually prepared annually by the advertising department of the seller's organization, by an outside advertising agency, or by the agency and its client in cooperation.

In practice, such plans appear in many forms, with the basic format and detailed contents varying widely from one company to another.

No two plans are exactly alike and there is no universally applicable formula or procedure for planning that will fit the advertising needs of all firms in all situations. Nevertheless, we shall discuss advertising planning in terms of a broad three-step procedure which is adaptable for use in most situations.

The three phases of advertising planning, each of which will be broken down for further discussion, are (*a*) preliminary fact-gathering and analysis, (*b*) establishing a control plan, the basic strategic framework consisting of a clear statement of advertising objectives, the setting of the budget, and related matters, and (*c*) campaign planning, which gets us into the development of the actual advertising copy or message, media scheduling, and supplementary sales promotion activities.

Preliminary Fact-Gathering and Analysis

The logical starting point in advertising planning is to develop a statement of the concrete facts from which specific plans will evolve. These facts must then be analyzed to yield a picture of the problems and opportunities in the selling situation toward which advertising efforts can be profitably directed.

Although advertising is undeniably a highly creative function requiring a good deal of imagination and ingenuity on the part of copywriters and others, the creative work is likely to be of higher quality if it rests upon a foundation of sound factual premises. Advertising based upon too many unknowns or upon flimsy assumptions is unnecessarily risky and uncertain. Of course, there are situations (such as the case in which a producer is attempting to promote a new product in an unfamiliar market area) where it may be impossible to get all desired factual information before advertising is released. Even in such circumstances, however, the assumptions on which plans rest should be clearly and explicitly defined so as to permit testing and double-checking as soon as operating experience can provide the factual references.

One of the hallmarks of a good advertising plan is objectivity. What facts are needed to achieve it? The variables which influence advertising activity and plans are virtually infinite. The task, therefore, is to identify at least those which are of major importance. Enough data must be gathered to provide an understanding of how advertising is to be tied in with other marketing efforts. Thus, all major facts about the market— competitive advertising, company resource, product attributes, product-mix charateristics, distribution channels, price policies and price structures, organization and methods for personal selling, existing advertising and sales promotion policy, philosophy and attitude of top mangement toward advertising, and similar items—all need to be collected and summarized for analysis as a prelude to planning.

FIGURE 13–1

HOW BBDO REVIEWS CLIENT MARKETING

Here is BBDO's "suggested outline" for reviewing the marketing of client products. It serves as a pattern for the agency's client presentations

1. Statement of facts

A. Sales history
Should be defined year by year for a sufficient number of years to be significant in terms of dollars, units and share of market.

B. Price history by years
This should include deals, other promotions.

C. Product history
This covers quality problems that may have been encountered; product improvements; any swings in consumer preference between client's product and competitive products; the package, and changes that have been made.

D. Competition
Principal competitive brands, nationally and locally; competitors' business in terms of volume and trends; advantages of the competitors vs. the client.

E. The market
Is it growing, declining or static? Who uses the product? Who makes buying decisions among retailers and wholesalers? What changes are taking place in consumer income, population, distribution patterns?

F. Consumer attitudes
What do consumers like or dislike about client's and competitors' products and why?

G. Distribution
The distribution picture at all levels; the strong and weak markets and the reasons.

H. Advertising expenditures
A history by years; cost per unit; % of sales.

I. Selling expenditures
A history by years; cost per unit, % of sales.

J. Promotion expenditures
A history by years; cost per unit, % of sales.

K. History of advertising
Media strategy; copy philosophy and themes; can ad effectiveness be pinned down?

L. Summary of product facts

2. Problems and opportunities

The identification of problems and opportunities comes from an analysis of the facts as outlined, in the section above.

3. Objectives

This involves enumerating all the objectives toward which future planning should be directed.

4. Outline of future planning

A. Advertising plan
Copy: basic copy policy; examples of the basic copy idea; copy themes directed to special groups or areas; possible copy tests.
Media: specific media recommended; the cost, amount and schedule of advertising in each medium; possible media tests.
Trade advertising: basic copy policy; examples of the basic copy idea; copy themes directed to special groups or areas; possible copy testing; specific media recommended; cost, amount and schedule of advertising in each medium; possible media tests.

B. Promotion
This covers specific dealer promotions; specific consumer promotions; timing of promotions; possible promotion tests.

C. Selling activity
This includes the amount and type of sales work.

D. Special activities
These are to meet problems or exploit opportunities in media, promotion and/or sales.

E. Possible product changes

F. Possible package changes

G. Possible pricing changes

H. Possible research projects

I. Establish overall timetable

J. Summary of expenditures
In total dollars related to projected production and as % of net sales; broken down by media, promotion, testing, by sales areas, etc.

5. Summary

A. Significant facts
B. Problems and opportunities
C. Major objectives
D. Recommended plan

SOURCE: *Sponsor,* September 20, 1958, p. 39.

Figure 13–1 supplies some idea of the variety of information needed to develop a sound advertising plan. It represents a checklist used by Batten, Barton, Durstine and Osborn, one of our largest advertising agencies, to guide them in ensuring a comprehensive review of all factors affecting the advertising needs and plans of their clients. Whether such information is gathered by the agency or by the seller himself, it is often summarized in the form of an opening section or as an appendix to the written advertising plan. The summary of facts forms the basis for rational decision-making and double-checking in advertising planning.

Conclusions and constructive inferences drawn from the data help to pinpoint specific problems and opportunities in the advertising area. Study of the facts helps to crystallize marketing objectives and to clarify the obstacles which must be overcome through advertising efforts in order to achieve them. Further analysis clarifies the financial constraints and other limiting factors or boundary conditions within which the advertising manager must make his plans. Criteria for weighing and choosing between alternative advertising approaches and methods are also revealed by the data. In fact, the early collection and analysis of basic data is critical to all stages of advertising planning and decision-making, from diagnosis and prescription to implementation and follow-through.

Reliable information, therefore, is the keystone in generating sensible advertising plans. Having first assembled the facts, we are then in a position to put together an overall advertising strategy. In the interest of making the final stage of campaign planning progressively easier and less risky, our next step after the preliminary fact-gathering and analysis phase is to prepare a broad control plan. Further research, of course, may be needed in the control planning and campaign planning stages to fill gaps and supplement the facts gathered in the earlier pre-planning phase.

The Advertising Control Plan

The purpose of an advertising control plan is to clarify and communicate our reasons for advertising, to determine how much money we are willing or able to spend on advertising and sales promotion, and to resolve other issues so as to provide a positive set of guidelines for the actual campaign planning which is to follow. Thus, elements of an advertising control plan which are typically of greatest importance are (1) a statement of objectives, (2) a financial framework within which advertising will be required to function, and (3) a resolution of any special strategic considerations which may be important in the specific company situation and relevant for purposes of advertising planning.

1. *Setting Advertising Objectives.* The major problems in setting advertising objectives center around (*a*) establishing an appropriate planning period, (*b*) gearing advertising to company needs, (*c*) setting up promotional targets, and (*d*) pinpointing the concrete advertising and sales promotion goals needed to support the marketing program.

a) The Advertising Planning Period. Most advertising plans are one-year programs. They are usually prepared in the fall of the year to cover the twelve-month period just ahead—or at other times when fiscal periods other than calendar years are used as the basis for company planning. The long, steady-pull techniques used by many advertisers of well established products may require only modest year-to-year refinements to achieve a balance between short-term and long-range advertising objectives and activities.

Special advertising situations, however, may call for different time dimensions in planning. Manufacturers of products with seasonal demand characteristics, for example, may actively engage in advertising for only three or four months each year, and their planning horizons are correspondingly shortened. Start-and-stop advertisers, such as seasonal promoters, also have to take special pains to ensure sound timing for the commencement of promotional efforts and to allow enough lead-time to plan, prepare, and place the advertising so it is ready to go on introduction day. Sellers of products heavily affected by the business cycle sometimes extend the advertising planning period to cover the forecasted interval between peaks of the cycle. They may then engage in contra-cyclical advertising within this time framework.

New products present a special problem as far as time planning is concerned. While the initial planning period may be as short as three months or as long as five years, depending on the estimated lifespan of the product, perhaps most companies still make definite plans to cover a period six months to one year beyond the beginning of test marketing. Later on, revised plans may be issued as market penetration and expansion is achieved. In some cases the horizon for promotion planning can be geared to distribution expansion plans. In any event, the advertising and sales promotion plan must be forward looking enough to fully cover the introductory phases, and should embrace a sufficiently long additional period to establish a pattern of sustained market performance for the new product.

Although the time period over which advertising is planned ahead is contingent upon the particular problem faced, we must establish a time framework for planning with as much clarity as possible. Advertising is a dynamic activity. It plays a shifting role over time, as a product moves from one stage of the product life-cycle to another or from one market situation to another. Time-planning helps us to anticipate changes in advertising requirements which may develop within the planning period established.

b) Gearing Advertising to Company Needs. Advertising objectives derive from general marketing objectives which, in turn, grow from broad company goals. Advertising managers sometimes complain that it is difficult for them to get approval for creative advertising programs from their superiors. A major reason is that advertising managers often fail to communicate how advertising fits into the total business effort. To correct the situation and win approval for his plans the advertising manager must assure appropriate support for companywide operations by reviewing broad company aims and policies very early in the planning process.

The broad company objectives relating to growth, profitability, and other key areas which help shape the advertising task are typically set by higher management and handed down to subordinate managers. The advertising manager must analyze advertising's role in the achievement of these corporate goals and communicate his interpretation to his superiors for endorsement or modification. This step prevents the advertising department from defining its tasks too narrowly in terms of short-run departmental interests only.

Through consultation with the marketing director, the advertising manager must also attempt to gear his operations to other areas of the marketing mix. The chief problem is to determine how sales and advertising together are expected to contribute to marketing objectives. Then the division of responsibilities between advertising and sales can be made and plans laid for coordinating the separate efforts. Specific sales objectives, problems, and plans with which advertising is to be intergrated can be procured from the sales manager. Joint discussions may reveal the means by which advertising can increase sales or contribute other business values. An evaluation of the basic "advertisability" of the products to be sold must be made in terms of a product-market analysis designed to reveal whether sales volume is likely to be more, or less, responsive to advertising efforts than to personal selling.

Many promotional decisions will hinge on sales volume and market share estimates. To justify any advertising or sales promotion at all there must be a certain minimum sales volume available. Probable maximum and minimum volume estimates can be forecast and, within this range, volume goals must be set high enough to support minimal advertising. If the advertising manager knows that our sales target, at a planned price of one dollar per unit, is to be 150,000 units in the coming year, he has a basis for planning his own operations more wisely. In introducing a new dentifrice the advertising manager will be helped by a concrete statement such as this: "The product is to be established by September 1 with a market share somewhere between 15 and 30 percent."

With sales goals and volume estimates made, the sales manager and the advertising manager are ready to resolve the question of how much personal sales effort, advertising, and sales promotion are to go into the promotional mix and in what proportions. Basically, this can be resolved by discussion and negotiation. Whether demand is likely to be relatively more, or less, responsive to advertising than to personal selling; what the opportunity costs are (a dollar spent on advertising, of course, represents a foregone opportunity to spend that dollar for sales promotion or personal selling); whether personal or impersonal selling is likely to present the strongest appeals to particular promotional targets, and similar issues, can be discussed.

This helps to ensure effective integration of sales and advertising plans, for the negotiation process moves toward what may be regarded as an exchange of commitments. By committing their respective organizational components to achieve concrete goals, or to contribute in some predesignated way toward achieving them, the sales manager and the advertising manager each has a basis for claiming financial and other resources to support his respective plans. They have also taken a step toward establishing the standards of performance by which their superiors will judge and reward them. Objectives defined in advance of the budgeting procedure help to determine how corporate funds are to be spent and, specifically, whether the dollars are best spent on advertising or on something else.

c) Promotional Targets. Whom do we want to reach with our advertising? This raises one of the most critical issues in advance planning. The answer will greatly affect the specific details of campaign plans. For instance, corporation advertising, or institutional advertising as it is sometimes called, may be directed at stockholders, employees, labor unions, competitors, suppliers, bankers, trade associations, governments, leaders in a local community, or other publics with whom the company must maintain harmonious business relations. The purpose of corporation advertising is to sell the company rather than the company's products. It may, for example, attempt to create an image of the firm as being a nice place in which to work, or an attractive one in which to invest. Different advertising messages and different means for conveying them may be required for each promotional target.

Whether advertising seeks to sell the company that makes the product or the products that the company makes, it must be beamed specifically at the kinds of people who can do something about it or at least influence others to take action. A first requisite for product advertising, therefore, is to correlate promotional targets with our general market segmentation strategy.[3] Obviously media planning and copy strategy will vary greatly between high income groups and low, between one ethnic group and another, and so on. Promotional targets, however, must often be defined in more precise terms than those in which the general market targets are typically expressed.

Although advertising is sometimes viewed as *mass* selling, in contrast with personal salesmanship directed toward individuals, few of our national sellers are truly mass advertisers in the strict sense of the word. Many find it necessary to take selective geographic approaches to local markets because market strength varies so much from area to area. Explicit decisions must be made as to whether the advertising is to be national, regional, or local in the scope of its coverage, and as to whether the advertising impact is to be blanketed evenly over this territory or directed at particular sales soft spots or at areas of unusually high potential. Thus the question "Where are they?" is a natural extension to the query "Whom do we want to reach with our advertising?"

Individuals, as well as groups of people, must often be pinpointed as promotional targets. Once you have determined customer groups in such terms as locality, age, income, and sex, you may have to focus your sights on the most logical prospects within these target areas. The purpose of advertising is to get somebody to do something. Who is that somebody? Suspect→Prospect→Customer has long been respected as a formula for direct mail advertising and personal selling. The man who doesn't own a horse is not a logical promotional target when advertising buggy whips, and a woman who has just purchased a new toaster is likely to be an indifferent reader of some promotional flyer featuring toasters.

In some cases promotional targets extend beyond potential buyers to include the individuals who influence buying decisions, even though they do not make the final decisions nor place the orders themselves.

---

[3]Students may wish to review the discussion of market segmentation and product differentiation in Chapter 4.

In industrial marketing, for example, the purchasing agent or product buyer may make the final decision to purchase an item and actually sign the order for it. Yet, if designers, quality control people, production engineers, shop supervisors, or others in the plant exert a significant influence on the decision to buy or on the act of buying, they must be staked out as promotional targets. Often the industrial salesman must rely on advertising to reach the purchase-influence that he doesn't have the time or capacity to reach himself. Similarly, a toy manfacturer might decide to appeal directly to children through comic book advertising or television in the belief that the kids will more forcefully influence their parents or relatives to purchase the plaything than if the ads were aimed at mom or dad. In the ethical drug field personal sales calls may be made on druggists, while direct mail and other promotional efforts are aimed at doctors who influence the pharmacists' buying behavior via the prescriptions they write for their patients. New product advertising may be directed toward so-called "tastemakers"—the experimentally inclined style- and taste-setters whose canons serve as consumption cues for the mass market.

Another problem is to determine at what points in the distribution system we will aim our advertising. Certain classes of dealers or key accounts may be singled out for promotional attention. Promotional targets may also be set in terms of trade level, with special attention devoted to the advertising, display, and other requirements at each link in the marketing chain. Company salesmen, the distributor or his personnel, the dealer and his facilities, and each end use market may be individually examined to identify the pressure points where promotional effort can best be applied.

Basically, we have to choose between "push" and "pull" strategies. The first is aimed at resellers, who in turn are expected to advertise to their customers to force distribution of goods through marketing channels. "Pull" promotion reaches over the heads of the channel members and it is aimed at our customers' customers. The idea is that the ultimate customer can be appealed to directly, can become "pre-sold" on our product, and will insist on it when he enters a store to buy such a product. This leaves the retailer no real alternative but to stock the item and make it available to his customers. Large manufacturers with strong national brands in the convenience goods field tend to stress this "pull" or pre-selling approach. Producers with less well-known brands, limited financial resources, or excellent channel relationships may favor the "push" strategy. Generally, however, a balanced treatment with a blend of push-pull elements is required in most marketing situations. Both end users and middlemen may be established as promotional targets, although one may receive higher priority than the other.

Having established promotional targets, the advertising manager already has some idea of what kinds of advertising or sales promotion to employ in his marketing program. Market research, of course, may be needed to supplement personal judgments in staking out promotional targets and choosing the most suitable methods for reaching them.

d) Pinpointing Advertising Objectives. Many advertisers never make their objectives explicit. Some state goals in very general terms, such as increased sales, augmented profits, or assisting the salesforce. These high-sounding promises cannot be checked very closely, for we can seldom trace advertising's contribution to such goals with any degree of accuracy. The key to successful advertising lies in making our objectives as explicit as possible.

Advertising efforts should achieve precise aims which form a part of the total marketing function. Once we have determined whom we want to reach with our advertising and where they are, we must decide what we want to tell them. Table 13–1 lists some examples of possible general advertising objectives. When we have goals like these we not only have a key to copy and media strategy but we make it easier to evaluate our progress after the advertising program has run its course.

Goal formulation is a process of successive refinement. Once company goals have been established, subgoals for the marketing division and the advertising department can then be defined. Each advertising campaign and every advertisement in each campaign should also have a specific objective so that the time, talent, and money invested in it will be a positive contribution to broader objectives. Precision in committing resources is contingent on having clear objectives. The diagram sketched below indicates the sequence in which goals are derived.

Company Objectives
↓
Marketing Objectives
↓
Advertising Objectives
↓
Campaign Objectives
↓
Objectives for Individual Advertisements

The objectives at any level should be consistent with those above and below it, and the objectives should become progressively more precise

TABLE 13-1

EXAMPLES OF ADVERTISING OBJECTIVES

Advertising Objectives with Corporate Publics

1. To gain government contracts
2. To bring about favorable government legislation
3. To overcome public prejudices or mistaken impressions
4. To create goodwill by informing the public about company contributions to general welfare
5. To reduce employee turnover, attract labor, or reduce union difficulties
6. To obtain the support and goodwill of the investing public and bring about a wider diffusion of stock ownership
7. To build company acceptance and recognition among commercial and investment bankers
8. To solidify relationships with suppliers and subcontractors

Advertising Objectives Related to Stages in the Product Life Cycle

1. To overcome buyer resistance against new products
2. To secure trial purchase or promote demonstrations for new items
3. To familiarize potential customers with uses of new products
4. To inform the public about the availability of new products
5. To test consumer reactions to new products
6. To uncover customer dissatisfactions with existing products
7. To promote new uses and applications for mature products
8. To arrest the decline of a dying product

Advertising Objectives Relating to the Competitive Situation

1. To engender competitive goodwill
2. To discourage new rivals from entering the field
3. To prevent further loss of markets to competitors
4. To offset sales gains made by rivals in outlets not used by us
5. To emphasize product attributes and features which are superior to competitive offerings
6. To counter competitive reactions to our sales strategies
7. To prevent the substitution of our products by competitive items

Advertising Objectives Relating to Salesforce and Trade Channels

1. To make it easier for salesmen to establish working contacts with wholesalers, retailers, and industrial buyers
2. To provide supporting sales-aid programs for salesmen
3. To produce leads for salesmen
4. To motivate dealers and improve trade relations
5. To boost sales from supermarkets by at least 15% next year
6. To regain lost retail accounts
7. To increase size of orders
8. To get distributors to push the full line
9. To stimulate window and interior displays and cooperative advertising to tie in with our national program
10. To educate wholesale and retail sales personnel
11. To bring traffic into the stores

Advertising Objectives for End Markets

1. To get buyers to mail in an order
2. To solicit customer requests for the name of the nearest dealer
3. To persuade buyers to insist on our brand
4. To uncover and attract new users
5. To reach individuals inaccessible to the salesman
6. To overcome seasonal slumps by promoting early buying
7. To induce present customers to use more of our product
8. To create new buying habits
9. To trade-up the consumer to a more expensive item
10. To resell lost customers
11. To combat unfavorable consumer attitudes that hinder the sale of the product
12. To build sales of related items in special market areas
13. To make it possible to obtain a price premium from the buyer
14. To persuade at least 40 housewives per dealer to visit each of our dealers during the month of January

Miscellaneous Advertising Objectives

1. To help level out production peaks and valleys
2. To reduce storage costs
3. To close out old merchandise

and measurable as we move down the hierarchy. A specific ad campaign may have one or more objectives, although it is often sound to limit the number as we move down the ladder of goals. Once all the advertising aims have been pinpointed, we can analyze each one to determine the nature, magnitude, and importance of its advertising task. This will enable us to resolve questions of advertisement expenditure planning on rational grounds.

2. *The Financial Framework for Advertising Planning.* The second major step in creating an advertising control plan is to develop the financial framework within which advertising will be required to function. This involves such things as determining the advertising budget and formulating payout policies.

a) Establishing the Advertising Budget. There are several methods used in determining the size of the advertising appropriation.[4] One list covers no less than 24 different approaches. The more important types, however, can be summarized under two broad headings. The first class of budgeting methods may be called the *breakdown methods.* Here the total lump sum is determined and this figure is then broken down and allocated into subcategories of advertising expenditure. The second class can be termed the *buildup methods*, in which appropriations for individual programs are added up to produce the overall budget figure.

Among the more common approaches for establishing the lump sums used under breakdown methods are the following:

1) *The fixed percentage or unit method.* This is a widely used technique and there are many variations on the theme. The total appropriation can be set at so much per ton, per case, per customer, or other physical unit of sales. It can also be fixed on the basis of some percentage of past, present, or expected future dollar sales or profits.

Many objections have been leveled at this method. It is difficult to defend on logical grounds, especially when past sales is used as the base figure, because the method merely perpetuates the historical pattern of the business, erroneously treating advertising as a result instead of a cause of sales volume.

The practice of using a percentage of expected or intended sales as a basis for fixing the appropriation has more to recommend it, especially in stable marketing situations where there is little variation in advertising tasks from year to year. It is certainly a simple method to use. In many industries the ad-sales ratios of all companies are published. These

---

[4]While we have consulted several sources in preparing this section, we are most indebted to Joel Dean's "How Much to Spend on Advertising," *Harvard Business Review,* January, 1951, pp. 65-74.

figures serve as a basis for making interindustry and interfirm comparisons.

2) *Matching competition.* The amount to be spent for advertising may be set at enough to keep up with rivals. Although this policy marks the company practicing it as a follower instead of a leader, it at least gives some protection against being outgunned by competitive advertising efforts. A company in the aspirin business, for instance, cannot expect to buy a large segment of the market with a $5 million advertising budget when strongly entrenched opponents are spending $8 million or $10 million.[5]

The aim of this method is to offset or neutralize a competitive advantage. It is a purely defensive approach with many limitations. No two firms in the same industry are likely to have the same advertising objectives or needs, and their required outlays are therefore likely to differ.

3) *Plow-in methods.* All available funds may be designated for advertising. This may be good policy in introducing a new product on limited capital but it is hardly desirable over the long pull. At some point the cost of advertising inevitably exceeds the gross income (or the dollar value of other business benefits) derived from it. Choice of the method reflects a strong faith in the power of advertising and a management philosophy viewing advertising as a long-term investment rather than a current expense.

It can be argued that this method results in the government paying a substantial part of the outlay in a tax situation where expense dollars "really only cost 50 cents." There are dangers in following this policy, however, since periods of low capital liquidity may be precisely the moments when advertising support is most needed. The method also ignores alternative uses for available funds and may put the company in financial straits when unexpected emergencies arise.

Although several other techniques could be discussed, these three illustrate the basic nature of breakdown methods for setting the advertising budget figure. All of the specific techniques in this category are somewhat artificial and arbitrary for they attempt no clearly rational matching of advertising costs and benefits. The result is likely to be overspending or underspending, neither of which is desirable.

Furthermore, these methods merely fix the *scale* of the overall advertising investment. They tell us nothing about how the lump sum is

---

[5]"Ad Dollar Pressure is Vital," *Advertising Age,* September 21, 1959, p. 1.

to be broken down and distributed over time, to market segments or regions, to alternative media, to products in the line, to various advertising messages, to different distribution channels, or to other segments of advertising effort. The problem of allocation—the relative effectiveness of different ways of spending the same total amount of advertising money—is typically resolved by highly arbitrary and mechanical methods. This sometimes breeds an unhealthy political climate within the company. Each person with a real or imagined claim to advertising funds clamors for his piece of the advertising pie, and the biggest slice usually goes to the man that shouts the loudest or is the most persuasive instead of to the man who can put the money to its most productive use.

Dissatisfaction with breakdown methods has led many companies to turn to other techniques for establishing the advertising budget. Let us take a closer look at how one large corporation goes about setting the annual advertising appropriation.

The General Foods Corporation recorded net sales of more than a billion dollars in the fiscal year 1959, derived from 81 principal consumer-advertised grocery products and supported by a $96 million advertising budget. While most of the money went into television, magazine, and newspaper advertising, a sizable proportion was spent on radio and poster advertising, display materials for use in retail stores, package premiums, prize contests, coupons, and various consumer deal promotions. How is a budget so large and so complex actually established?

When General Foods starts to make up an annual marketing plan they do not say: "We will spend so-and-so-much for advertising." Rather, the budget is put together in a step-by-step additive fashion. For each individual product they ask themselves what it will take in advertising and sales stimulating inducements, first, to maintain the market position of the product and, second, to increase its volume of sales (if that seems possible).

For a relatively new product they may ask themselves how fast it is feasible to build volume and what such a growth rate will call for in terms of advertising and sales promotion. These calculations, based on a weighted estimate of present volume and future potential for each product, result in an appropriation of so many cents per case. Carefully worked out budgets for each of the 81 brand names and their large number of varieties are then added up to get the total figure, which turned out to be $96 million in 1959.[6]

---

[6]For further details on this case see "Underspending on Ads Is Wasteful," *Advertising Age*, July 27, 1959, pp. 1 and 44.

The General Foods procedure is an example of a <u>buildup method</u> for establishing the advertising budget. In this category, as was also true for the breakdown approaches, there are several specific procedures, of which the following are best known:

1) *The objective-and-task method.* This approach is based on the explicit doctrine that the <u>nature of the advertising job to be done in-fluences the size of the investment</u>. It inquires as to how much money is needed to accomplish predetermined advertising objectives, such as those outlined in Figure 13–1. Certainly it is the results reflected in the objectives that management is really paying for.

The actual method is based on finding the answers to four questions: (1) <u>What do we want to accomplish, and what is the dollar value of</u> each of our advertising objectives? (2) <u>What tasks must be performed by advertising and sales promotion to achieve each objective</u>? (3) <u>What will it cost to perform these tasks</u>? (4) <u>Are these costs less than the esti-mated value of the objectives to which they relate, and do we have</u> sufficient money to cover them?

The steps toward the objective may, of course, be altered to fit the funds available, but if the answer to the fourth question is affirmative, the money to cover these costs is appropriated as a part of the budget. Separate budgets, in effect, are established for each objective, for each product, for each market, and so on. The total budget is the sum of the individual ones.

This is an intelligent approach to the problem. Although many advantages might be cited, its primary value lies in the fact that it requires well defined objectives and brings all contributing factors under careful scrutiny. It is a particularly effective approach where there are marked differences in advertising requirements from market to market, as in overseas selling, because it necessitates close study of each individual area. It cannot always be followed, however, because it is not always possible to visualize exactly what the task of advertising must be during a coming period, especially when conditions are disturbed and competition is in a state of flux. There are problems in measuring the value of objectives even when they are explicitly stated, and the cost of performing the associated tasks depends upon the particular forms of advertising employed to perform them. Nevertheless, the method at least forces the budgeter to attach rough priorities to his advertising goals and to weigh the cost and effectiveness of various media as an integral step in the budgeting process.

2) *Budget models.* Mathematicians and operations research experts have recently been attracted toward improving the accuracy of budget-

making procedures for advertising. While budget-setting is coming to be more scientific in some companies (with the aid of electronic computers and other sophisticated and refined analytical tools), the help of the model builders has been slowly accepted. One expert claims that he can program a computer to determine how much a company must spend on advertising to achieve a given market share and what share of market will produce maximum profits for the company. He has devised a series of mathematical equations which relate various marketing factors to each other. These equations reveal relationships between sales volume and advertising expenditures of the company and its competitors. Changes in proposed outlays by the company can be projected into the future and an estimate of future sales and market share mathematically computed.

It is also claimed that if a rival changes his expenditure strategy, this too can be projected. Theoretically, the computer could run through thousands of such possible situations in a few minutes and pick out the most profitable advertising expenditure patterns. While not yet in widespread use, we shall undoubtedly be hearing more about mathematical advertising budget models in the years ahead.[7]

Buildup methods such as those just discussed clearly recognize that advertising does not become operational until it is fully integrated into the marketing program. An advertising appropriation can and should be as carefully engineered as an appropriation for new plant facilities, and should be subject to the same critical analysis. The buildup methods take us in the right direction. They ensure built-in justifications for all outlays and avoid the risks and problems associated with arbitrary allocations. The scale problem and the allocation problem are simultaneously resolved in the buildup methods. How we vary advertising weight from product to product or market to market of course can be as strategically significant as the size of the overall advertising appropriation.

Although the buildup methods seem to offer more guidance than the breakdown methods, they should not be rigidly viewed as alternatives. Sometimes we may need to use a combination of methods. In planning the promotion of a new product, for instance, we might use the objective-and-task method in combination with some percentage-of-expected-sales figure. The basic budget might be set to reach the desired sales volume within some stated period, but a percentage-of-sales figure

[7]For a nontechnical discussion of budget models see "Planning Ad Budgets: A New Model," *Printers' Ink,* June 17, 1960, pp. 67-69, and "Ad Budgets: A Growing Science," *Printers' Ink,* December 16, 1960, p. 16ff.

could be used as a limiting or control factor rather than as the determining factor for establishing the appropriation. This would provide some insurance against overspending on advertising in the event that sales forecasts later prove to have been overly optimistic. If advertising of new products is controlled at some pre-set ratio of expected sales, a higher-than-normal percentage figure might be used to reflect the fact that the new product may require a greater per-unit promotional punch than established items.

Regardless of how the budget is set the advertising manager is expected to operate within the budget once it has been approved. The budget functions as a control tool as well as a planning document, so periodic checks of actual outlays against the budget figures must be made. Of course, budgets may need to be revised from time to time. If current experience shows a previous forecast to be in error the budget can be modified to reflect this. Budgetary revision is a simple matter, of course, if the original appropriation was based on so many cents per case or on some percentage of expected sales. So-called "flexible budgets" can also be employed in managing advertising appropriations.

b) Payout Planning. "Payout" refers to the investment needed to attain advertising objectives, and "payout period" is the estimated time it will take to recapture that investment and begin to make a profit. In formulating policies on payout periods we make an explicit decision whether to view promotional spending as an investment to achieve long-range goals by sacrificing short-term gains, or as a current expense intended to produce immediate profits.

Payout policies are especially important in promoting new products. Some firms have to invest millions of dollars in a new product before it begins to make money. The payout periods vary widely from company to company and industry to industry. Some large firms use a pay-as-you-go policy. Others try to key investments to the product life cycle as an aid in determining when a new product will reach its maximum profit or volume.

In recent years there has probably been a departure from the long-steady-pull techniques and a new emphasis on short-term, high horsepower campaigns for products that are here today and gone tomorrow —due to diminished brand loyalty, cascading new product entries of competitors, and shorter product life cycles. This refers most appropriately to articles like toiletries, which are often short-lived, ranging from a few years for toothpastes to a few months for some cosmetics.

"Investment spending tactics, by which advertisers poured back all profits on a new product into additional advertising over a period of years, are being carefully reconsidered. At one time P&G allowed as much as a three-year payout on a new product before expecting profits. Nowadays payouts must be shorter or the competition will kill you."[8]

At some point we must get our bait back. Payout policies directly affect the choice of promotional media; for example, pay-as-you-go tactics may call for self-liquidating premium offers in preference to high-cost free sampling. The period is influenced by fear of competitive retaliation (which shortens the payout period), by patent protection (permitting longer periods), by the rate of new product development to be financed by the company (a high rate requiring shorter payout periods for individual products), and by similar factors.

c) Reserve for Contingencies.   The advertising budget must be made flexible in order to meet unusual conditions or overcome special unforeseen problems which may arise during the planning period. New products still in the laboratory may be released ahead of schedule; or unexpected weather conditions or competitive inroads may develop and adversely affect sales. Unless a reserve is established these unusual conditions, which demand extra advertising expenditures, will throw the budget out of line and reduce its value as a control tool. Therefore some portion of the total advertising budget should be set aside during advance planning in the form of a contingency account from which funds can be drawn to carry out special advertising as conditions dictate.

d) Expenses Charged to the Advertising Budget.   The size of the budget depends on what goes into it, and the question of which expenses are rightly chargeable to the advertising account is a critical issue in many companies. If the advertising budget is padded or deflated by arbitrary bookkeeping it is difficult to determine the true effect of advertising or to clarify its association with sales. Since the sales manager and the advertising manager must compete for funds, conflict can be minimized if there is a clear understanding of who gets charged with what expenses at the time the budgets are approved.

Printers' Ink has studied this problem over the years and has separated expenses into three groups. The "white list" includes those charges which definitely belong in the advertising account. The "black list" contains charges which do not rightfully belong to the advertising account, even though they are often put there in actual practice. The "gray list" includes borderline charges, sometimes belonging in the advertising account and sometimes elsewhere, depending on the circumstances.

---

[8] "Avalanche of New Products Changes Ad Tactics," *Sponsor*, September 20, 1958, pp. 34–35.

FIGURE 13-2

Expenses Chargeable to Advertising

Ad department charges in descending order	Window display installation costs	Product publicity
	Charges for services performed by other departments	Factory signs
Space and time costs in regular media	Catalogs for dealers	House organs for salesmen
Advertising consultants	Test-marketing programs	Signs on company-owned vehicles
Ad-pretesting services	Sample requests generated by advertising	Instruction enclosures
Institutional advertising	Costs of exhibits except personnel	Press clipping services
Industry directory listings	Ad department share of overhead	Market research (outside produced)
Readership or audience research	House organs for customers and dealers	Sample of middlemen
Media costs for consumer contests, premium and sampling promotions	Cost of cash value or sampling coupons	Recruitment advertising
Ad department travel and entertainment expenses	Cost of contest entry blanks	Price sheets
	Cross-advertising enclosures	Public relations consultants
Ad department salaries	Contest judging and handling fees	Coupon redemption costs
Advertising association dues	Depreciation of ad department equipment	Corporate publicity
Local cooperative advertising	Mobile exhibits	Market research (company produced)
Direct mail to consumers	Employee fringe benefits	Exhibit personnel
Subscriptions to periodicals and services for ad department	Catalogs for salesmen	Gifts of company products
Storage of advertising materials	Packaging consultants	Cost of deal merchandise
	Consumer contest awards	Share of corporate salaries
		Cost of guarantee refunds
Catalogs for consumers	Premium handling charges	Share of legal expenses
Classified telephone directories	House-to-house sample distribution	Cost of detail or missionary men
Space in irregular publications	Packaging charges for premium promotions	Sponsoring recreational activities
Advertising aids for salesmen	Cost of merchandise for tie-in promotions	Product research
Financial advertising	Product tags	House organs for employees
Dealer help literature	Showrooms	Entertaining customers and prospects
Contributions to industry ad funds	Testing new labels and packages	Scholarships
Direct mail to dealers and jobbers	Package design and artwork	Plant tours
Office supplies	Cost of non-self-liquidating premiums	Annual reports
Point-of-sale materials	Consumer education programs	Outright charity donations

Source: Printers' Ink.

In 1960 *Printers' Ink* surveyed a sample of national advertisers to determine which charges should be included in each list. Figure 13—2 shows the results. Promotional items were arranged in descending order, according to the percentage of companies that charged the item to the advertising budget. The white area includes those charges that were considered advertising expenses by two-thirds or more companies. The gray areas, split at 50 percent, includes those items that fell into the advertising budget of one- to two-thirds of the companies responding. The black area shows those charges that were considered advertising costs by one-third or less of the companies.[9]

The advertising control plan covering the elements discussed above, plus whatever special strategic planning considerations might be deemed important and relevant for advertising planning in a specific company situation, provides a promotion planning framework serving several purposes. It clarifies basic promotional objectives, shapes the scale on which promotion is to be conducted, provides some broad criteria for selecting particular promotional alternatives, and serves as a set of standards for measuring advertising performance. The control plan thus contains many clues for campaign planning, to which we now direct our attention.

---

[9]"Is Your Ad Budget Up To Date?" *Printers' Ink,* December 16, 1960, pp. 26–27.

CHAPTER 14

Campaign Planning and Advertising Organization

CAMPAIGN PLANNING

Advertising programs usually contain one or more advertising campaigns. While small companies may conduct only one campaign at a time, many large firms have several running simultaneously.

A campaign consists of an organized series of advertising messages appearing in one or more media. The usual unifying element in a campaign is a single central theme or keynote idea directed at a single advertising objective for a designated promotional target. Individual advertisements in a campaign may appear self-contained and independent, but they are actually planned to tie together and reinforce each other. All ads in a given campaign are usually designed to resemble one another in at least some respects. "Thus, a unified theme or content provides *psychological* continuity throughout the campaign while visual and oral similarity provide *physical* continuity."[1]

How does the campaign plan relate to the advertising control plan? The campaign plan can be viewed as a tactical counterpart to the more strategic control plan. Advertising media and appeals in a campaign plan are determined by the choice of advertising objectives and limited by the financial framework set forth in the control plan. Whereas the control plan stresses the *why,* the *when,* and the *where* of advertising, the campaign plan focuses on the *what* and the *how.* Thus the campaign plan is a natural extension of the control plan.

The task of blueprinting an advertising campaign consists of generating substrategies meshed in with the control plan. More specifically,

---

[1] C. A. Kirkpatrick, *Advertising* (Boston: Houghton Mifflin Co., 1959), p. 409.

it involves the creation of (1) copy strategy, (2) media strategy, and (3) supplemental sales promotion strategy.

Copy Strategy

What must be communicated to our promotional target to realize the campaign objective? And how is this selling message to be formulated? The advertising message consists of both the promotional copy and the way in which that copy is laid out and presented. To crystallize messages most sharply, copy is usually determined before layout. Pictures, headlines, and other elements of an advertisement are later designed to make readers, listeners, or viewers aware of the copy and to hold their attention long enough for the message to achieve its aim. A sound advertising idea or theme often succeeds despite poor technique in layout or typography, but a poor copy idea will probably fail even with excellent technical treatment. The task of creating an advertising message begins with uncovering a basic copy approach.

The Central Theme or Keynote Idea. The central theme or keynote idea is the integrating device which wraps up all elements of the advertising campaign into one unified package. It summarizes in a nutshell what the advertiser really wishes to communicate. Its function is to achieve simplicity in message development, consistency of viewpoint throughout the campaign, and continuity and repetition aimed at promoting recognition and recall of the message. Thus it serves as a guide for copy strategists in helping them increase message impact by developing greater audience awareness and understanding.

The central theme is usually built around one or more fundamental human wants or needs closely associated with the product. Its value is dependent on the strength of the appeal it carries in terms of its ability to motivate buyers, and upon the size and other characteristics of the buyer group susceptible to the appeal.

This suggests that we must be very familiar with the psychological make-up of our market or promotional target. In developing our theme, we are drawn into the murky waters of human motivation where we find no pat answers even to simple questions. Psychologists, sociologists, and other behavioral scientists have yet to supply the advertiser with a unified theory of human motivation.

However, we should certainly draw upon whatever guidance we can get from the behavioral sciences. For instance, many psychologists have prepared lists of major motives which purport to cover the common denominators of human activity most useful to copy strategists. One such list has been prepared by Dr. Melvin S. Hattwick. He has suggested that people have eight basic wants in life: food and drink, comfort, freedom from fear and danger, to be superior, to attract the opposite sex, welfare of loved ones, social approval, and to live longer. Hattwick urges the advertiser to study such basic wants and the psychological drives behind them. They may be used as basic appeals because they are quickly aroused, are usually wanted at once, are vigorous and strong, and are practically universal.

In addition, according to Hattwick, people have nine other secondary or learned wants, which appear in life as we grow older. They are: bargains, information, cleanliness, efficiency, convenience, dependability or quality, style and beauty, economy or profit, and curiosity. These secondary wants are usually less effective as central themes in copy strategy but may function as effective keynote ideas in certain situations.[2]

Automotive seat belts provide an interesting illustration of the care and imagination needed in selecting basic appeals for a central theme. For years advertisers of these safety devices were met with a curious public apathy and low sales. Indeed, some marketers felt the seat belt was a "nonsalable" product. But a manufacturer of automotive parts, the Midas Company, thought the product could be sold with a fresh appeal. According to Mr. Gordon Sherman, the company president,

> Social consciousness can play a larger role than self-preservation in the sale of a product primarily designed to save lives. At first glance, seat belts seem to have their strongest selling point in simple self-preservation. In the field, however, we found this sales message working against us. There is a naive bravado on the part of the man in the street that leads him to give more consideration to what his fellow man thinks than to the basic safety offered to him and his family.[3]

When the copy slant was shifted to emphasize children and families, and when nonsafety social appeals were stressed, sales of seat belts increased. The copy read "Let seat belts do the baby-sitting for you" and "Their use eases fatigue, helps the driver remain more alert, and controls the effect of centrifugal force on turns." Because they were more positive in tone and approach, in terms of supplying socially acceptable reasons for buying a seat belt, these appeared to be stronger than self-centered safety appeals.

Advertising literature abounds with rules of thumb for selecting basic appeals to be developed into central themes for advertising campaigns. Here are some typical examples:

---

[2]Melvin S. Hattwick, *How to Use Psychology for Better Advertising* (New York: Prentice-Hall, Inc., 1950), pp. 25–26.

[3]"Selling a 'Nonsalable' Product," *Sales Management,* February 2, 1962, pp. 75–78.

1. Rational appeals are more effective in industrial markets where purchasing is done by professionals; more emotional appeals can be used if the housewife is the promotional target.

2. Basic appeals are stronger than secondary appeals, so we must choose an appeal which strikes deep.

3. Positive appeals, such as promoting the welfare of loved ones, are stronger than negative appeals, such as the "scare copy" used in some advertisements for automobile insurance.

4. Since a filled need is no longer a motivator, appeals should be aimed at future needs and hopes rather than past pleasures.

5. One specific, concrete theme is better than several broad or generalized themes.

6. New products require a more dramatic, shocking, or jolting theme than do established products.

7. Appeals which create deep and lasting impressions and which will not "wear out" quickly are to be preferred since they are consistent with such tested advertising principles as repetition, frequency, and continuity.

Although useful to the copy strategist, such propositions must be tempered with judgment and used with discretion. Human motives are subtle and often hidden, and they change over time. Research should be used to test the specific validity of such rules whenever there is much at stake in advertising.

The Purchase Proposition. The choice of appeals, and the copywriter's amplification of them, depends as much on product analysis as it does on market analysis. The central theme must precisely identify the product with some habit, feeling, want, or emotion of prospective buyers. Thus the selected theme must be consistent with the product image and user benefits the product is capable of delivering. Whether we begin with the product and evaluate its uses, benefits, and applications, or with the promotional target with its needs, wants, and problems is of no great consequence. The two steps must interact. The key questions are: "What does the consumer really need or want?" and "Can my product supply this at a price the consumer is able and willing to pay?"

The product is a means to some end valued by the customer; it represents a solution to either a latent or manifest consumption problem. Thus the product must be promoted in terms of what it will do for people. This can be done in either factual or imaginative terms. One seller of diamonds, for example, promotes on the basis of such product attributes as size, color, clarity, and cutting, and on the reliability of his franchised jewelers in helping the buyer to evaluate these tangible attributes. Another has developed a series of "product romance" stories. Diamonds are associated with "the magic of yesterday" to promote diamonds as anniversary gifts, and with "the miracle of Springtime" when young love blossoms into a market for engagement rings. The latter approach seeks to interpret a physical product, diamonds, in terms of some human experience meaningfully related to it instead of in functional terms. Any appeal which attempts to promote a generic product class, like diamonds, is referred to as a primary appeal. Selective appeals, designed to promote one brand over another and induce a buyer to select one specific product from a class, must also be chosen. A standard question posed by advertisers in one large corporation is: "What is there about this product that will get the most customers to buy in the face of competitive claims and pressures?" The answer they come up with is called "the purchase proposition."

The customer must be supplied with reasons why he should part with his money. These reasons, of course, must be realistic, truthful, unique, persuasive, and believable, and they must be stronger than competitive counterclaims. If there are known dissatisfactions with substitute products not present in our item, these "plus features" can serve as major sales points to be exploited in copy. The results of technical product testing and consumer use-testing establish proof of product performance. Once such selling points are identified and developed they are segregated by the strength of the purchase proposition for each promotional target before finished copy is attempted. Sometimes the chief selling point can be boiled down to an effective slogan, such as Gleem toothpaste's "For People Who Can't Brush After Every Meal."

The purchase proposition, then, is the sales story you wish to tell. Its creation depends on translating product benefits into promises which tie in closely with basic human motives and appeal strongly enough to get the prospect to take some desired action. In summary form, the purchase proposition functions as the central theme for the advertising campaign.

Developing the Copy. The effectiveness of the selected theme will vary with the manner of its presentation; that is, by variations in copy style and the illustrations shown with it.

Copywriting is highly creative work and it is impossible even to describe what good copy is. Advertising copywriting is much like any other creative writing, and it is almost as difficult to convert a poor copywriter into a good one as it is to transform a hack writer into a prize-winning novelist.

There are few reliable rules for good copywriting. Human interest and reading ease are certainly desirable aims. Truthfulness, simplicity, clarity, freshness, humanness, realism, and economy in the use of words are attributes of effective copy, as they are of all writing. Some companies have prepared written policy statements on copy development for the guidance of their copywriters. And there are research techniques for testing copy, once it has been produced, to measure its effectiveness. But there is no real formula to guide the copywriter.

There are, however, several checklists to which he can turn for stimulation. One of the more famous ones, prepared two decades ago by Victor O. Schwab, proposed five basic guides to good copy:

1. Get attention.
2. Show people an advantage.
3. Prove it.
4. Persuade people to grasp this advantage.
5. Ask for action.

Such checklists, in essence, are nothing more than lists of steps in the selling process, such as were discussed in Chapter 13. For that is what good copywriting really consists of: a solid sales message effectively communicated.

Media Strategy

Advertising media are the tangible vehicles for delivering a promotional message; for example, newspaper pages, outdoor billboards, and television shows. To formulate a media strategy is to determine how and when we intend to reach our promotional targets with such media. This requires an awareness of the available media alternatives, a consideration of the factors involved in evaluating media, the task of composing a media mix, and questions of timing and frequency to ensure proper scheduling of the selected media.

Media Alternatives. Inexperienced advertisers often think too narrowly in terms of a restricted range of media alternatives. Newspapers, magazines, radio, television, and handbills may come quickly to mind, and the thought process stops there. Actually, the advertiser usually has available a very large number of media through which his message can be transmitted. These differ widely in their characteristics and their fields of effectiveness. Wise advertisers recognize this diversity of media and consider all alternatives when developing media strategies. It is as important to choose the right medium, or combination of media, as it is to choose the right advertising message, and an overlooked alternative may be a lost opportunity. It is impossible here to list all advertising media; however, the more commonly used types are—

1. *Publications*
   a) Newspapers

b) Magazines
   General
   Class
   Women's service
   Farm
c) Business papers or trade journals
d) Miscellaneous
   Consolidated catalogs
   Year books
   Directories
   Bulletins
   Programs
   House magazines

2. *Outdoor and Transportation*
   a) Billboards or posters
   b) Electric displays
   c) Painted bulletins and signs
   d) Wall space
   e) Airplanes, balloons, trucks, and floats
   f) Streamers, banners, and pennants
   g) Car, bus, and taxi space
   h) Passenger station and subway space

3. *Entertainment*
   a) Radio
   b) Television
   c) Motion pictures ("Minute Movies")
   d) Slides (projector, reflectoscope, and magic lantern)

4. *Direct Advertising*
   a) Catalogs
   b) Folders, stuffers, and circulars
   c) Broadsides
   d) Booklets
   e) Letters, cards, business forms, and tags
   f) Special bulletins
   g) Instruction and data books and sheets
   h) Samples and models
   i) Price and discount sheets
   j) Labels, packages, wrappers, and inserts
   k) Calendars, novelties, and souvenirs

5. *Point-of-Purchase and Merchandising Aids (Relate promotion and merchandising to other media.)*
   a) Sales portfolios and kits
   b) Window and wall space
   c) Display racks
   d) Counter and showcase displays

e) Floor space

f) Dealer signs and helps

g) Demonstrations and exhibitions

h) Premiums, deals, and samples

i) Vending machines.[4]

In addition to considering such *types of media*, the advertiser must be aware of the *individual media* within each class. Although both are daily newspapers, the *New York Daily News* is quite different as an advertising medium from the *New York Times*. In some of the more specialized types of media, such as business, trade, and technical magazines, there are names and titles which often surprise the student of advertising when he meets them for the first time. The first step in media strategy, then is to be sure we have all of the alternatives before us: both broad types of media and the individual media in each class.

Evaluating Media. The advertising control plan imposes strict limitations on media choices. It functions as a rough screen to reduce the range of alternatives open for consideration. Extremely expensive media may be ruled out on budgetary grounds. Small budgeters might be attracted to such special budget stretchers as free publicity and cooperative advertising with dealers. Since some media will produce results more quickly than others, selection of the most responsive medium may be dictated by short payout policies. In short, the promotional targets, advertising objectives, budgetary limits, payout policies, and other elements in the advertising control plan, together with the copy strategy, serve as a kind of job description for advertising media. These factors set forth the functions to be performed by advertising media, and the limits upon that performance, in the form of a set of media specifications. The task of selection is to evaluate individual media against these benchmarks.

Each medium has its own values and requires certain conditions for its most effective use. The core problem is to match markets and media. We must decide which media will reach designated markets (or other promotional targets) most effectively and cheaply. The decisions hinge on detailed information about the market and the media themselves. Coverage, effectiveness, and costs are the three chief criteria to be weighed in assessing the relative merits of each medium.

If the geographic reach of a medium extends too far beyond the marketer's area of distribution, it cannot be efficiently employed because it results in paying for costly "spill-over" coverage. Distribution and

---

[4]Paul H. Nystrom (ed.), *Marketing Handbook* (New York: The Ronald Press, 1954), pp. 397–400.

media coverage patterns can be classified as local, regional, or national. A local operator has a more limited range of media which he can use efficiently than either a regional or national marketer. Local campaigns may be built around newspapers, local spot TV or radio commercials, billboards, car cards, and similar community media. Media with national coverage, such as network radio and television, would be out of the question.

As geographical market coverage is expanded, the number of feasible media alternatives is increased. One of the most significant advertising developments of the 1950's occurred when several national magazines, such as *Look, Life,* and *Reader's Digest,* began to offer special regional issues to advertisers. This was a real boon to regional marketers and to national marketers whose products had regional or seasonal demand characteristics. Until then they could not efficiently use magazines with full national coverage. For the first time they could match "national" media to regional distribution patterns without excessive overlapping.

The next issue is whether the medium can reach designated market segments within the desired geographic area. Each market segment, whether defined in terms of age, occupation, income, social class, or other variables, has its own set of attributes. Similarly, each medium has its own audience profile. The readers, listeners, or viewers for one medium may differ sharply from those of another. Careful analysis of circulation statistics and audience data is therefore necessary to determine whether the audience profile meshes properly with our market targets.[5]

Statistical breakdowns are supplied by most media. In many cases the medium's audience is audited, measured, and certified by an independent bureau or rating agency. Our interest attaches to both the number of people in the available audience of each medium who can be exposed to our message and to all relevant characteristics which describe the composition of that audience. Daytime radio and confession-type magazines, for instance, penetrate low-income groups more deeply than many other media.

The effectiveness of each medium in influencing its audience to take action must also be estimated. Television, for instance, is usually regarded as a powerful medium because it can influence the audience both visually and orally. The editorial policies of print media can be examined to see if they are consistent with our product image. News-

---

[5]For a more detailed discussion of matching market segments and media profiles see Sidney W. Dean, Jr., "Fission in Markets: It Calls for a New Strategy in Media Buying," *Sales Management,* November 10, 1959, pp. 58–62.

papers may be favored because of their flexibility and selectivity in delivering specially prepared copy to local markets if we have varying requirements from one community to another. Print media usually offer more merchandising and promotional possibilities than other vehicles.

Media effectiveness by type may also vary widely from market to market. New York City, for instance, is much more of a "print media market" than Los Angeles. This is partly because New York has more commuters on public transportation systems who read magazines, newspapers, and car cards on the way to work or recreation. The Los Angeleno is more likely to be reached effectively by the radio in his car or the one on his backyard patio. Attitude surveys and rating devices have been used to assess the influence of a particular medium on its audience. Both qualitative and quantitative information and a high order of executive judgment are needed in assessing the relative effectiveness of various media.

Efficiency, rather than mere effectiveness, is ultimately the chief concern in media evaluations. Thus cost factors become vital. In principle, if we were choosing between two media of equivalent coverage and effectiveness, we would pick the one which was available at the lower cost. But media economics and cost calculations are not quite that simple. Costs, for example, are expressed in many different ways.

Media rates are usually expressed in terms of space or time costs. Print media may be priced at so much per line, per column inch, per page, or per fractional page. Radio and television may be priced at so much per second, per minute, or per hour. But there are also qualitative factors which affect these unit prices. Television prime time, such as the Sunday evening period, is priced higher than nonprime time of the same duration. The position of a printed advertisement will also influence media costs; full page back covers on magazines, for instance, may come dearer than full pages between the covers. Thus, both the quantity and the quality of space and time have a bearing on media costs.

Media costs are sometimes reckoned on the basis of some "cost-per-thousand" figure. This usually refers to the dollar cost required to reach a thousand readers, subscribers, viewers, or listeners. But every member of the audience obviously does not often see each and every advertisement in a given medium, and the medium's audience is rarely precisely matched with the advertiser's promotional target. Therefore attempts are sometimes made to refine and express the cost-per-thousand in terms of logical prospects or customers (instead of readers or subscribers), or in terms of actually delivered printed, auditory, or audio-visual impressions.

Yet it is further clear that the impressions created by one medium may differ qualitatively from those of another. We have no economical and effective techniques for measuring the true depth and intensity of psychological impressions. For such reasons the least costly media are not always the wisest purchases. A higher rate may be warranted if a medium makes truly powerful selling impressions on logical prospects.

A further factor complicating the media cost picture is creeping inflation. Media costs have drifted upward over the past several years, but the rise has occurred at a faster rate in certain media than in others. Thus, while we would ideally like to make media decisions in terms of precise unit costs, this proves to be impossible because both the units in which costs are expressed and the cost figures themselves are elastic and changeable. They require subtle interpretations by management. Even the hard dollar-and-cents yardstick has to be wielded with judgment when evaluating media.

The Media Mix. No medium is intrinsically better than another except in relation to a specific situation. Given that situation, however, we might at least subjectively rank media in terms of their relative desirability as determined by cost, coverage, and effectiveness. But even if we have the media listed on a rough ladder, from best to poorest, we should not conclude that the choice is limited to the one best medium. Advertising media are complementary as well as competitive message carriers; one can often reinforce and extend the influence of another.

A medium such as direct mail may be judged unsuitable as the mainstay of a media plan, yet it might function beautifully in a supplementary role. Therefore several kinds of media are usually required in a well balanced plan. This combination problem further complicates the media selector's task. It should be clear that the generation of media strategy demands just as much creativity, originality, and imagination as does copy strategy. The media planner, however, has more precise tools at his disposal than the copywriter. Since many of the variables involved in media planning are susceptible to symbolic and mathematical expression, executives have been turning more and more to the electronic computer for decision making assistance.

The Media Schedule. The final step in media planning is to resolve questions of timing and sequencing and prepare a media schedule. The first step is to determine the overall "time-shape" of the campaign. Basically, there are three alternatives to choose from, each plan reflecting how funds appropriated for the campaign are to be distributed over time. The choices are:

1. *Level expenditure method.* Under this plan funds are spent at a uniform rate for the duration of the campaign. Equal amounts of money are spent for each month or other equivalent time period. Individual advertisements in the campaign are likely to be uniform in size and copy treatment, and a fixed list of media may be used throughout the campaign. This pattern is often followed when the planned campaign merely represents a continuation of past and present campaigns, as in the case of mature, established products backed with steady-pull advertisements and a "keep on sawing wood" strategy.

2. *Concentrate the bulk of the budget early in the campaign.* This method, sometimes referred to as the "smash and follow-up" approach, devotes the lion's share of the budget to the opening days or weeks of the campaign. Expenditures slowly taper off while the campaign runs its course. Advertising may initially break with ads of larger than normal size and the use of dramatic copy; later the size of the ads may be reduced and the copy toned down. This approach is often used for products which are dramatically new and for which a ready and eager demand is known to exist.

3. *The snowballing, or rolling thunder, method.* Here, small expenditures are made early in the campaign but are consciously built up until a peak is reached at some predesignated time. This method is useful as a "save your gunpowder" strategy, when advertising under conditions of high uncertainty, for it preserves funds and permits more flexibility if later adjustments in the media schedule become necessary. It is also associated with the early "teaser" advertising and the subsequent build-up of an advertising crescendo often associated with certain new product promotions or new market invasions. The three methods are illustrated in Figure 14–1.

The choice of campaign time-shape depends on many factors. In advertising a new product, for example, the campaign should be timed to mesh with forecasted sales volume at both introductory and sustaining levels, and with initial programs for pricing and distribution. A smash send-off may be used to get the jump on rivals—or to discourage them altogether. Plans for rapid distribution, especially when coupled with penetration pricing strategies, may call for explosive promotion with large initial advertising outlays, high-impact media, and eye-stopping copy and layouts.

By way of contrast a slower, market-by-market approach may be taken. Some firms, having gone overboard on new products—only to find out later, to their chagrin that they had greatly underestimated promotional costs—now resist the natural temptation to move too quickly in gaining market coverage. A slow, intensive approach in one zone, before moving on to another area, permits the marketer to gather information as he feels his way, allows time for testing to uncover and correct flaws in promotion planning, and encourages timely adjustments to plans as needed. Slow penetration permits better geographical maneuvering. Some companies invade each local market with almost battle-plan precision and attention to detail, each market being thoroughly softened up by promotional bombardment prior to entry.

FIGURE 14–1

BASIC TIMING AND SEQUENCING ALTERNATIVES IN PREPARATION OF MEDIA SCHEDULES

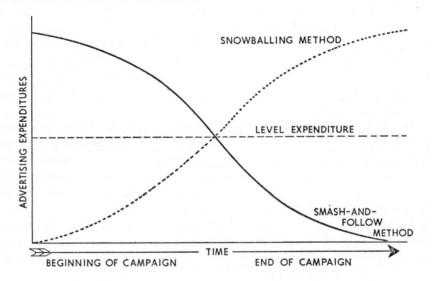

Less explosive promotion is needed with skimming price policies and highly selective trade channel policies. Such patterns may be called for if the company or brand name is not well known and respected in the markets selected for entry, or if the product is so radically new as to require a long time for it to be worked into new consumption patterns, or if the item is so superficially new as to invite buyer skepticism.

Level expenditure or snowballing advertising schedules typically permit more attention to synchronizing advertising with other aspects of marketing. Peak advertising and promotion must "break" at precisely the right time, and not *before* the product is physically available to consumers in the marketplace. In recent years a leading beauty aid and a candy bar were both heavily promoted to consumers before distribution pipelines could be adequately stocked. The net results were disgruntled buyers who found they couldn't actually get the things which advertising had pre-sold them on, unhappy dealers, and wasted advertising impact.

Advertising intended to help secure dealer representation and pipeline inventories may of course be released ahead of consumer copy. Trade ads, for instance, may be used early to produce inquiries leading to trade prospect lists. Advertising may also be keyed to trade shows or exhibits with fixed dates, timed to coincide with seasonal deadlines, or otherwise paced to get maximum mileage from the advertising dollar.

Production considerations may also influence the campaign time-shape. If the plant can supply only 15 percent of the total market, then only 15 percent of the market can be penetrated, and this forces a consideration of the sequence in which local or regional markets are to be entered. Which area is to be first and which is to follow, which outlets are to be opened first and which are to be next and similar priorities and schedules influence the timing of advertising and sales promotion. Delivery problems may also impose limits. One company, for instance, found that in order to guarantee quick delivery on a new product, precedence had to be given to only ten prime markets before national distribution and advertising could follow.

Payout policies and other elements of the advertising control plan also affect the campaign time-shape. For instance, a snowballing ad expenditure geared to market-by-market distribution may be dictated by the need to finance marketing from current revenue, even though advertising-minded executives might personally prefer a smash-and-follow or level expenditure strategy. In short, consideration of the time-shape of an advertising campaign forces us to reassess the associated issues of *when* to break the advertising and in *what sequence* markets are to be covered.

There are still other questions, relating to *flexibility, duplication, frequency,* and *continuity,* which must be taken up before the schedule can be set.

Some *flexibility* must be built into the media schedule. A new product may turn out to be "hotter" than expected, for example, and production capacity may become overtaxed to the point where out-of-stock conditions call for temporary cutbacks in advertising. The reverse, of course, may be true for a new item that ends up "colder" than forecasted. While media plans may be projected quite far ahead in some cases, actual commitments should be deferred as long as possible to ensure needed flexibility.

Duplication refers to the fact that media audiences sometimes overlap: two media reaching the same person are said to duplicate each other. In designing the media mix to be incorporated in the schedule, the advertiser must determine how much duplication, if any, is desired. While duplication reduces the total audience available for a given budget, the message repetition resulting from it helps to expose more readers of a publication to a particular advertisement and to reinforce awareness of it.

Frequency refers to the number of ads of a similar variety used in a given time period during the campaign; for example, one advertisement in *Business Week* each month, or two 20-second television commercials per day. The question of whether or not there are to be periods of advertising inactivity during the campaign brings up the issue of *continuity*. Continuity and high frequency are desirable because advertising involves a learning process. Repetition of message exposures helps the audience learn the advertising message. The cumulative impact of many messages, issued frequently and continuously, helps to reinforce awareness, understanding, memory, recall, believability, conviction, and related aspects of learning.

Because the time dimensions of advertising's impact follow the learning curve, sales generated by it often show a lagged response: *today's* advertising will help produce *tomorrow's* sales. Thus information suggesting that current advertising is not producing current results should not necessarily lead to stopping the campaign. Ideally, both continuity and high frequency should be assured ahead of time. There may be many exceptions to this generalization, however. As the size of advertisements in the schedule is increased, frequency or continuity may be sacrificed. If four-color ads are used instead of black-and-white, this will increase production costs and may force a cutback in frequency or a loss of continuity. Budgetary controls may also, of course, reflect continuity objectives. To avoid "hand-to-mouth" administration of the budget, initial outlays may be intentionally held down in order to establish a rate of expenditure which can be consistently maintained for the course of the campaign.

Thus, media planning requires the calculation of time, space, and production costs by type of media and by individual vehicles in the media mix. A chronological listing of all media to be used during the campaign, together with data on their coverage, the size and characteristics of the advertisements planned for each medium, the number of times each ad is to appear and when it is to appear, and other such information is then assembled. This data is consolidated in the form of a written media schedule summarizing the timing and sequences for executing copy and media strategies.

Supplementary Sales Promotion Strategy

The generation of sales promotion plans to supplement, extend, or reinforce other forms of personal and nonpersonal selling involves essentially the same steps and considerations as copy and media strategies. However, sales promotion methods and media assume different physical forms. Sales promotion at the store level may involve the preparation and placement of signs, decals, window displays and streamers, manuals, folders, point-of-purchase placards, merchandising racks, and other tangible in-store sales aids or dealer helps. Participation in local cooperative advertising programs, conventions, and distributor incentive contests may also be included under the heading of sales promotion.

At the consumer level coupons, free samples, two-for-the-price-of-one deals, and other familiar marketing "gimmicks" are examples of sales promotion devices. In some cases sales promotion is regarded as even more important than personal selling or advertising in the marketing mix. On the whole, however, there is a temptation to over-rely upon these devices.

Sales promotion plans bring the details of national sales and advertising programs down to the local level. The objectives of sales promotion can be many and varied. Consumer deals, for instance, may be used to introduce a new product or to induce brand switching on an established item to produce short-term increases in market share. Sales promotion within trade channels may be aimed at obtaining proper inventory levels, gaining enthusiastic dealer acceptance of a product, securing favored display and shelf positions, or some other desirable distribution aim. In most cases the objectives of sales promotion are of a short-range nature, and its effects are typically short-lived.

Sales promotion strategy or tactics must be planned and executed with the same care and attention to detail as we have suggested for advertising. Sales promotion targets, objectives, and budgets must first be set; then the specific forms or types must be decided upon, procured, and distributed. There is such a variety of sales promotion methods in common use today that it is impossible even to list them all. However, some insight into sales promotion strategy may be gained by taking a look at a typical situation where it is heavily used: the introduction of a new product to the consumer market.

Despite sound scheduling of effective messages in appropriate media, advertising may not produce sales of a new product. This may be true simply because it fails to overcome the consumer's natural reluctance to part with his money for something he has never bought or used before. Therefore sales promotion devices may be called upon to reduce or eliminate any risk to buyers of the new product, or to offer special inducements to achieve the sampling and first product trials that the marketer hopes will lead to subsequent repurchase of the new product by the consumer.

The major sales promotion techniques employed in such a role might be visualized as occupying different rungs on a ladder of increasingly strong incentives. First are the simple confidence-builders. Testimonials, seals of approval from respected testing laboratories, guarantees and warranties, return privileges, combination offers whereby the new item rides the coattails of a well-established complementary product, and similar techniques may provide sufficient extra incentive to move the less timid prospects to act.

Next in increasing strength of inducement is the "extra value," or bargain. Coupons, stamps, premiums, trade-in offers, outright price reductions, and special deal packs—two products banded together for the price of one, 1-cent sales, one case free when you buy five—are representative of this group.

Third, there are the no-charge alternatives. Free goods given to dealers for their own use, free samples delivered by mail or crew to prospects, and free trials for limited periods are strong inducements to product sampling since they require no cash outlay or risk-taking by the trier. The strongest motivation of all is to actually pay the customer to try the new product. Cash or merchandise awards attached to free samples, dealer "push money," and the giving of free resalable goods to storekeepers are examples of this extreme form of inducement.

Many factors influence the choice of such specific techniques. Among the major criteria are:

1. *Cash Outlay Required of the Seller.*   Free samples, for instance, can only be distributed in the case of rather inexpensive items, and the cost of distributing free samples by crews in rural markets may be prohibitive.

2. Legality.   Some forms of sales promotion are taxed, licensed, restricted, or forbidden in certain states and localities.

3. Flexibility, Selectivity, and Control.   It is usually easier to shut off a

special pack or deal after the introductory period than it is to increase price. Coupon offers can be made with definite expiration dates. Field crews can control the distribution of free samples to correlate with retail store coverage patterns.

4. Product Characteristics. Products appealing to the basic senses of sight, touch, taste, and smell are most suitable for physical sampling. Thus toothpaste, which can be quickly judged on the basis of flavor, feel, sudsing action, and aftertaste, is an ideal product for small quantity sampling, as are many food products. When product performance or reliability cannot be quickly assessed by the consumer, some form of guarantee technique may be called for.

5. Impact on the Trade. Coupons are difficult to store and count at retail levels; they slow the check-out procedure and they invite misredemption. Special-deal packs compound the stock carrying problems of both wholesalers and retailers. Dealer preferences, administrative headaches, and the ease of merchandising the promotion to the trade in a manner that will ensure enthusiastic dealer and jobber cooperation are important factors.

6. Possibility of Repeat Purchase. Sales promotion devices to induce new product sampling are most suitable for items which are rapidly consumed and replaced by the buyer. Overly large free samples keep users out of the market too long. Special devices to stimulate repurchase, such as the "repurchase value offer" whereby the customer uses the boxtop or label of his first package as part payment on the second, may be used. The greater the cash outlay required by customers after the product trial, the greater customer involvement in a near-normal buying process is likely to be. Deals are said to produce a substantially lower repeat rate than other sales promotion devices because they attract the more fickle, bargain-hunting members of the market to try the brand. Coupons probably accelerate sampling and speed up customer responses more than outright price reductions.

Of course we may employ two or more of these sales promotion devices in combination; that is, we may need a sales promotion mixture for the same reasons we need an advertising media mix.

Sales promotion strategy is sometimes formulated as a step distinct from advertising copy and media strategy. However, since they are so closely related, copy, media, and the supplementary sales promotion should usually be viewed as integral components of the campaign plan.

One or more advertising and sales promotion campaign plans, together with the master advertising control plan to which they relate, make up the advertising program for the manufacturer. This program, as a whole, should be reexamined in detail and checked for internal consistencies before it is approved for implementation. This advertising program is the heart of advertising management.

ADVERTISING ORGANIZATION AND OPERATIONS

The planning of advertising and sales promotion is only part of the total managerial job. The other major functions are organizing, executing, and controlling.

Organizing for Advertising

An organization structure to coordinate the efforts of all members of the promotion team is a prerequisite to success. Although top management, the corporate marketing staff, the sales manager, the field salesforce, members of the dealer and distributor network, and others might also be regarded as members of the advertising team, we will focus on the advertising department itself and its relationships with advertising agencies and other outside service organizations.

The Advertising Department.[6]   Advertising departments range widely in size, scope, position in the corporate hierarchy, and internal structure. The size of the advertising department depends on the size of the company, the nature of the firm's advertising objectives and requirements, and on concepts of how advertising tasks can best be carried out: whether the company will turn to outside agencies for the creation and production of advertising and sales promotion or whether these tasks . are to be performed inside the firm.

Many industrial companies maintain large advertising departments and produce much of their own material. Eastman Kodak has more than 400 persons in its advertising department, as does General Electric Company in its central department at Schenectady, New York. Most advertising departments, however, are quite small. The median number of people is reported to be three, and advertisers spending over a million dollars per year report a median number of ten in the advertising department.

This staff is usually hired, assigned, and supervised by an advertising manager or director. The advertising manager himself may report to the chief executive of the company, the top marketing officer, the sales manager, or to some other executive. In a multi-division company advertising can be either centralized at the top or decentralized to the division level, depending upon the economics of specialization and scale and upon how widely advertising needs vary from division to division.

The advertising director is charged with a wide range of duties, again depending upon company requirements and organizational philosophies. Typically, however, his main responsibilities are to prepare the advertising program and present it for approval or modification, to supervise the creative functions and the actual production or procurement of advertising and sales promotion materials, to interpret the company to its advertising agency, to supervise the agency and evaluate its

---

[6]In preparing this section we have drawn heavily from (1) "The World of Advertising," *Advertising Age,* January 15, 1963, pp. 25-34, and (2) "What's the Matter with Industrial Advertising Departments?" *Industrial Marketing,* February, 1958.

services, and to appraise the overall results of advertising. In order to carry out such functions he must see to it that his own internal department is efficiently organized.

The advertising department itself can be organized in several ways. Project teams, task forces, brand managers, product sponsor groups, and other organizational approaches may be adopted. Basically, however, there are six distinguishable methods for organizing the department.

1. By Type of Work. Here the departmental work is broken down by subfunction of advertising: copywriting, art, photography, media, production, distribution, accounting, and control. Separate sections or individuals may be assigned one or more of these tasks.

2. By Type of Media. Separate units may be set up for print media, broadcast media, outdoor advertising, point-of-purchase, displays and exhibits, and so on.

3. By Product or Product Group. Brand managers, for instance, may be assigned to provide advertising and sales promotion support for designated products or lines. This has become a very popular type of organization for many companies, especially large advertisers of consumer products such as foods, drugs, cleansers, and cosmetics. The approach helps to ensure that each product in a multi-product firm receives the attention it needs.

4. By Promotional Target. Because each end-use market, trade channel, or other promotional target may have unique advertising requirements, the advertising department may be divided into such patterns as ultimate consumer-industrial-institutional, trade-consumer, or baby-teenage market breakdowns.

5. By Geographical Division: National, Regional, State or Local. This is popular with brewers and other advertisers who face widely varying local patterns of legal restrictions on advertising and sales promotion. It may also be used where seasonal or other advertising requirements vary sharply from one area to another.

6. Combination Methods. Perhaps most large advertising departments employ a combination of one or more of these breakdowns. For example, both functional specialists and product sponsors may be used in the same department.

An organizational pattern should be developed so as to take maximum advantage of specialization, to facilitate control and coordination, and to assure adequate attention to variations in the advertising task between products, customers, areas, functions, and media. The pattern should be aimed at insuring advertising efficiency through achieving objectives and keeping costs down. The principles and practices of advertising organization are fundamentally no different than those applying to other elements of marketing management, except that the corporate advertising department must often be structured to provide sound working relationships with outside agencies.

Advertising Agencies. Most large advertisers work through one or more advertising agencies. Those who use national media almost invariably do, while many of those who limit themselves to local newspaper advertising and sales promotion devices make little or no use of agencies.

Historically, the advertising agency began as a seller of white space for the publishers of print media. For this selling service the agency received a commission, sometimes as much as 25 percent (although tradition later came to fix the figure at 15 percent) of the price charged by the medium for its advertising space. This fee was paid by the medium. Thus, the early advertising agency functioned as a space retailer.

Through experience the agency found that the difficulty of selling space to an advertiser could be reduced considerably by supplying the client with advertising materials to be placed in that space. If this material actually sold goods or helped to achieve other goals for the advertiser, he would naturally become less reluctant to buy space. So the agency went into the business of producing advertising materials and supplying advertising services to its clients, the advertisers. Somewhere in the process the agency came to look upon the advertiser as its principal or client, even though it still received its fee from the publishers.

Since the advertiser paid the same price for space whether he bought directly from the medium or through the agency, and in addition often found it difficult or impossible to procure space directly from the media, the agency enjoyed a very well protected position in the advertising system. This position was long under attack by advertisers and was examined from time to time with a conspicuous lack of sympathy and enthusiasm by government authorities. The matter came to a head in the middle and late 1950's when a consent decree officially frowned upon the uniform 15 percent commission system—although most media continue to pay it. But there has been a notable tendency among agencies to reexamine their commission structures and the services they render to advertiser clients to make sure that they earn their compensation. Basically, the modern agency

1. Prepares the advertisements, including the writing of copy; provides the illustrations; plans the layout; and in general prepares the message to be distributed through print, broadcast, or other media.
2. Selects and contracts for media time and space.
3. Puts the message in mechanical form for reproduction by the medium, and gives instructions to assure proper reproduction.
4. Checks and verifies the publication, broadcast, or placement of the message by the medium.
5. Audits, bills, and pays for the cost of services, space or time, and preparation of the advertising.

As a background for rendering these services the agency finds it necessary to perform several other functions. It may help its client plan his marketing activities. For example, it can give valuable advice as to the role advertising should play in attaining overall objectives and what the cost will be. It can be of great use in determining appeals and media schedules. In fact, through advice and suggestion it can be of great aid in almost all stages of planning.

Take the case of new products as an illustration. Close cooperation with the advertising agency helps to clarify the promotional requirements for the new product and translate them into creative copy and media plans. The agency, in fact, is usually appointed prior to test marketing and may even be designated at the inception of the new product idea. When the Colgate-Palmolive Company decided to bring out Baggies, clear plastic bags on a tear-off roll, used as food wraps, it appointed Street and Finney of New York as the agency.

Nineteen different agency staff members helped Colgate in a number of ways. They offered suggestions on the physical nature of the product itself and its possible uses, and contributed to decisions on its name, box size, design, price, quantity of bags per box, size of bags, ease of handling, potential customers, and protective qualities. They gathered marketing information on both Baggies and competitive products, retail attitudes, allowances and discounts, price-off deals, displays, spot advertising, salesforce materials, shelf facings and positions, and promotions. They developed a complete advertising, sales promotion, and publicity campaign, including the creation and production of six TV commercials, and offered suggestions to Colgate's own advertising production department on supporting sales promotion material.[7]

While media commissions—the embattled and battered 15 percent kind—are still likely to form the chief basis of compensation to advertising agencies for their services, many are modifying their rate structures to encompass cost-plus pricing, special service charges, and other fee systems which reflect payment for specific job performance. It would appear that a gradual transition away from the straight media commission has gotten underway.

Among the chief considerations in managing the agency relationship are careful selection, close supervision of the agency (along with a refusal to abdicate to it), and problems associated with switching agencies.

Advertising agencies are commonly evaluated and appointed on the basis of an "account presentation." Theoretically, the agency presenting

[7]"Partners: Agencies, New Products," *Printers' Ink,* April 13, 1962, pp. 31–32.

the best advertising program for a product or a company is awarded the account. Unfortunately, too many advertisers do this on a cursory basis. The agency that has as much as an hour in which to make its presentation and bid for an account often regards itself as fortunate. Sometimes the selection is made on a personal basis, such as friendship, or even relationship of executives.

Since large advertising budgets are usually at stake, more time and more care needs to be devoted to agency selection. Figure 14–2 highlights some of the factors to be considered in evaluating agencies. Agencies should first be screened, and those passing this initial screen should then be invited to make their presentations—and should be given enough time to provide a basis for rational choice.

There is a tendency among some marketing managers to regard the agency as the expert in advertising and to turn over to it all of the planning and execution of the mass advertising part of the marketing program. In doing this the manager should take care not to sidestep one of his major responsibilities. It may be sound to *delegate* responsibilities to an agency, but it is dangerous to *abdicate* authority to it. It has long been a management principle that delegation without control is really abdication. Thus two of the prime responsibilities of the advertising manager are to supervise the agency closely and to change agencies promptly if the circumstances warrant it. However it should be observed that in recent years there have perhaps been far too many capricious changes of ad agencies. These arbitrary account switches inhibit long-term agency cooperation; and they can be reduced with careful initial selection and closer subsequent supervision.

The advertiser may also have important relationships with other outside service firms: graphic arts specialists, printers, point-of-sale supply firms, advertising specialty houses, direct mail concerns, sales incentive agencies, and other advertising and sales promotion specialists. These external organizations must be hired and supervised with the same degree of care exercised in the case of advertising agencies.

Before this discussion of advertising organization is concluded, a brief comment on joint ventures may be appropriate. Many advertisers cash in on the potentials which lie in tie-in promotions with producers of complementary but noncompeting products. For instance, producers of frankfurters, buns, catsup, and soft drinks may join forces on a special summer picnic promotion. Manufacturers of basic steel and producers of household appliances have teamed up with electric utility firms to jointly promote electrical appliances to the mutual benefit of all. Such joint ventures can function as budget stretchers in achieving many specific campaign objectives.

FIGURE 14–2

BASIC FACTORS IN EVALUATING AND SELECTING ADVERTISING AGENCIES

How to Judge an Agency

The Management

What you primarily "hire" in an agency is its management; and if your agency relationship is to be an important one, you should apply the same critical standards to its top people that you would apply to any other important business associates:

1. Do they have the character of people with whom you want to do business?

2. Are they sufficiently able, and has this been demonstrated by their record of success with other clients?

3. Do they have broad experience in all the phases of modern advertising that are important to your account?

4. Are they really interested in your business?

5. How well do they (or will they) service your account? What manpower, talent, and facilities will the agency provide?

The Basic Product

The basic product of an agency is, of course, the advertising it produces. To evaluate its effectiveness in today's crowded marketing and advertising world, you must look well below the surface of the message. You must check:

1. The *basic strategy* of the campaign.

● This is always a marketing decision. It is the strategic choice of the strongest selling appeal of the product for your best prospects, aimed at the right markets, at the right time.

● It is the selling strategy on which the advertising is based—and only this determines how much impact the message can have on a consumer.

2. The *selling creativity* of the message.

● This is the measure of how ingeniously and creatively the advertising *sells*. It is distinctly different from its "surface creativity" (see below).

● It is the skill with which a product's selling points are converted into *convincing* words and pictures, rather than merely "tricky" ones.

3. The *surface creativity* of the message.

● This is the power of the message to call attention to itself, to stop the consumer with the vitality and originality of its appearance.

● In essence, it is always the combination of an advertisement's ability to "stop" and "sell" that determines how well it works for you.

The Basic Operations

To keep ahead of the technological advances in advertising and the complexities of modern marketing the agency must continuously update its services. You must check these areas as they apply to your particular needs:

1. *Manpower:* Are you getting the caliber and depth of management and staff work that you need?

2. *Planning:* Does the agency plan thoroughly enough to meet all your requirements, today and tomorrow?

3. *Research:* Does the agency use research effectively to improve its own products? Does it have research facilities available, in scope and depth, to serve your marketing requirements?

4. *Media:* Are the agency's media operations strong enough to insure you the best media values? Does the agency introduce new and more efficient media patterns for your advertising?

5. *Television and radio:* Is the agency's programming operation effective in finding and keeping the right programs on the air for your company?

The "Marketing Services"

The degree to which any company uses the marketing services of an agency depends not only on the nature of its business but also on its traditional approach to the agency relationship. Some clients encourage a close working partnership with the agency in all phases of marketing, others do not, and there is every shading in between. The unmistakable trend, however, is toward increased participation by the agency.

Here is a list of the marketing services you may want from your agency now or later—whether in the form of agency recommendations or field activities and finished product:

● Comprehensive marketing plans and forecasts
● Pricing and sizing polices
● Product innovations
● Package designs
● Collateral material for consumers and trade
● Promotion programs for consumer and trade
● Salesmen's meetings and material
● Distributor and dealer meetings and contact, and so on.

SOURCE: *Dun's Review and Modern Industry,* October, 1958, p. 64.

Executing the Advertising Program

A modest but well-executed advertising program is often more effective than a poorly conducted large-scale effort. Thus the advertiser must carry out his plans with great care. The chief considerations are those of advertising testing, getting the enthusiastic backing of top management and the sales organization, and merchandising the advertising to the salesmen and the trade.

Advertising can be pretested in several ways. For example, television commercials are often previewed by selected audiences as a check before broadcasting them. Individual magazine ads are tested in the field by personal interviewers to determine reader reactions before a campaign begins. The relative merits of two different layouts for a magazine campaign can be tested by split-run methods, whereby one layout is presented to a controlled portion of the magazine's readership and the other layout goes to the remaining readers of the medium. Entire campaigns can be tested and evaluated in small test markets before they are released for national use. Testing of these types is a form of insurance that reduces the risk of launching ill-conceived advertisements or campaigns.

Support for the program must be generated at all organizational and trade levels to assure enthusiasm, acceptance, and effective use of advertising and sales promotion materials. The place to start is inside the company. Top management must first be sold on the program; then the support of the field salesforce must be won. Close coordination between sales and advertising is as crucial at the field execution stage as it is in the planning stage. Salesmen must be adequately supplied with promotion materials and trained to use them properly. Salesmen often fail to support advertising and sales promotion programs because they do not understand how nonpersonal selling affects their day-to-day work. This calls for training aimed at convincing them that advertising and sales promotion will actually help them in face-to-face selling situations, for a few Doubting Thomases in the salesforce can severely blunt the cutting edge of otherwise sound advertising and sales promotion programs. The salesforce not only needs to be persuaded to use promotional materials but should be trained in how to employ them most effectively in the field.

Much advertising is wasted in trade channels. Materials are often sent to dealers or distributors without warning, explanation, or regard to timing. Middlemen need time, assistance, and instruction if they are to tie in effectively at the local level with advertising and point-of-sale activities to support the national programs of their suppliers. The supplier's program must be strongly merchandised—or sold—to resellers, and this calls for dramatization all the way down the line.

The dealer must also be told by the salesman how best to use advertising, displays, and other materials in the local setting. By notifying the trade well in advance of proposed advertising plans, and supplying them with media schedules and sample layouts and materials, we can trim waste, improve advertising effectiveness throughout our marketing channels, and help to ensure an integrated total pattern of advertising activity. It must always be remembered that the beginning of good performance in getting salesmen and dealers to use advertising and promotional materials is preparing such materials so they will help sell goods.

Advertising Control

The problem of advertising control can be divided into two parts, internal and external. Internal control is the administrative function of assuring that advertising performs according to plan. External control refers to the legal and other restrictions on advertising imposed by society.

Managerial Control over Advertising. Part of the waste and ineffectiveness in advertising is due to inadequate managerial controls and a lack of evaluation and follow-through. The advertising control plan discussed in Chapter 13, containing objectives, budgets, and other planning elements, is the chief control tool at the advertiser's disposal. It serves as a set of standards and guidelines for top-level advertising appraisal and action.

However, the plan must be supplemented by policies, procedures, and organizational arrangements to achieve a close control over detailed advertising activities. A system of priorities and schedules, together with estimates on time, cost, and manpower requirements, is essential to the control of individual projects. Deadlines and target dates signal the need to ride herd on lagging suppliers and get the work out. Inventory control procedures must be developed to cover sales promotion stocks. In fact, the day-to-day work of the advertising department is chiefly devoted to various steps in a complex acquisition-storage-distribution-utilization process.

This work can be accomplished more efficiently if the work flow, paper flow, information flow, and cash flow associated with the process are administered under a set of policies and procedures—procedures to facilitate field requisitioning of advertising supplies and to allocate materials to sales territories and local markets, and policies for controlling dealer cooperative advertising, backed up with valid means for establishing proof of performance, and so on. Most textbooks deal only with the glamorous and highly strategic aspects of advertising and fail to point out that the grand strategies are doomed to fail if the daily nuts-and-bolts activity of the advertising department is not rationalized and closely controlled.

Social Control of Advertising. Advertising has always been subjected to social criticism. Many attacks upon it have been totally unjustified and reflect an abysmal ignorance of its functions. Other criticisms, however, have certainly been warranted. More than a few ignoble advertisers have misrepresented their wares or used extremely poor taste in concocting their messages.

To protect the public from potential advertising abuses at least 21 federal government agencies have been given regulatory authority over advertising. Most of these have to do with isolated single issues. The six chief agencies that enforce laws affecting advertising are the Federal Trade Commission, the Post Office Department, the Internal Revenue Service, the Food and Drug Administration, the Federal Communications Commission, and the Alcohol and Tobacco Tax Division of the Treasury Department.[8]

The principal federal laws are the Federal Trade Commission Act, the Whealer-Lea Act, the Robinson-Patman Act, the Food, Drug and Cosmetic Act, and the Communications Act of 1934. These laws are designed to ensure truth and taste in advertising and to prohibit misleading (even though technically truthful) advertising claims. They also forbid the advertiser to grant his customers any advertising allowances and promotional services which are not available on "proportionally equal terms" to all customers who sell the same product in competition with each other. Mislabeling, abuse of certain terminology, untruthful claims of product ingredients, sending advertising or sales promotion materials through the mails for purposes of a lottery or in order to perpetrate a fraud, and "payola" schemes are other examples of prohibited practices.[9]

There are also countless state and local ordinances which tax, license, restrict, or ban certain advertising and sales promotion materials and practices. Better Business Bureaus and other local groups likewise function as watchdogs over the consumers' advertising interests. And pro-

---

[8] "Federal Laws Affecting Advertising," *Advertisers' Guide to Marketing for 1957, Printers' Ink,* p. 389.

[9] For a brief summary of the powers, procedures, organization, and resources of federal agencies in the field of advertising see "The World of Advertising," *Advertising Age,* January 15, 1963, pp. 185–88.

fessional advertising associations and media groups have prepared ethical codes to guide their membership.

The advertiser, with the guidance of legal counsel, must comply with all laws affecting him and must adapt to the prevailing social and political climate surrounding current advertising issues. Since the flaunting of established canons of taste and the violation of established laws only serves to undermine customers' confidence in the seller, it is clearly in the advertiser's own best interest to comply with all these restrictions. The only alternative to self-regulation in advertising lies in regulation by the government. For all of these reasons, it is wise for the marketing manager to submit sales promotion plans to the scrutiny of the company attorney.

To summarize our discussion of the management of advertising and sales promotion:

We have said that the first task of the marketing manager is to grasp how advertising, sales promotion, and personal selling are interrelated.

Sound advertising plans—grounded in fact and analysis and based upon the notion that campaigns and strategies can best be generated within the context of a broad control plan—must then be created.

The advertising manager must see to it that his own department and all outside agencies and suppliers are welded together into an effective advertising team, and he must take pains to ensure that the efforts of this group are executed and controlled, according to plan, within the letter of the law and in keeping with the spirit of social custom and good taste.

CHAPTER 15

Managing Customer Service

In the previous three chapters we have discussed two parts of the internal marketing organization which are designed to make and maintain contact with customers and the market. In doing so they render prospective buyers and users of the company's products the service of informing them about the company and the things it markets.

The informational picture they provide is not always a balanced or complete one since advertising and personal selling activities are certain to be designed more to convey reasons why people should buy the firm's products than reasons why they should not buy them. In spite of this limitation, and of the fact that these activities are designed primarily to make sales for the marketer, they perform a service to the customer and the market of which he is a part.

But the manufacturer usually finds it necessary to render a number of services which are designed primarily to satisfy the needs of the customer or user, and which exercise an influence on sales that is only secondary (although often highly important) as a selling tool. Some of these, such as stock carrying, order handling and delivery, are necessary to carry out the sales agreement. Others, such as credit, are designed to make it easier for the customer to buy. Still others, such as technical and maintenance service, enable the customer to get more benefit or satisfaction from the use of the product.

In this chapter we will discuss only those services which the manufacturer most often provides. Some firms set up a division of the marketing department, often called the Customer Service unit, which has charge of all of them. In other companies they are scattered among various arms of the marketing department or even among other organizational units of the firm. Perhaps you can get a better idea of their nature and of their relationship to the marketing effort if we describe several of them in some detail.

DELIVERY SERVICE

This discussion will be confined to delivery service provided by manufacturers to retailers, wholesalers and other middlemen, and to industrial customers. In providing the physical delivery service to his customers the manufacturer must manage two types of operations: the actual movement of goods to the point designated by the customer, and the maintenance of stocks at points from which such movement can originate. He must balance out the often conflicting objectives of getting the goods to the customer exactly when and where the customer wants them delivered, and of doing this with the least expenditure of his and his customer's money. For a large company it often involves not only arranging for the movement of goods but managing inventories in company operated branch warehouses and commercial warehouses, as well as reserve stocks usually held at the factory.

The physical distribution decisions and activities involved in delivery service should be built on a foundation of carefully formulated management policy regarding the level of service which best meets company objectives. This level may well vary between high volume and low volume products, between geographical areas, and between types and sizes of customers.

Management requires a detailed knowledge of customers' needs and desires regarding speed of delivery after orders are placed. Certainty of delivery is also vital, as many outlets plan closely timed promotions for which shipments must be on hand before a definite date and, because of limited storage space, no earlier than necessary. Industrial customers are also interested in reliable performance of delivery promises, especially for materials or components used in the production process. With increasing mechanization and automation of production the need for precise schedules becomes more rigorous. Some industrial buyers seek sources of supply that are sufficiently reliable so they can avoid all except emergency in-plant stocks by feeding the deliveries directly from the receiving platform into the production process. Needless to say, the delivery service acceptable to customers can be substantially affected by the level of service provided by a seller's direct competitors. Knowledge of competitor performance and capacity to perform is therefore essential.

Although in theory the facts required to assess customer needs for delivery service should be available in full detail from the manufacturer's marketing department, some managements express a measure of skepticism in evaluating information from this source. The marketing manager is well aware that he is being judged largely on sales results, and that delivery service is often a powerful selling weapon. As a result, his interpretation of customer needs and competitor performance may well be exaggerated.

It cannot be overlooked that the purpose of finished goods stocks is to service sales, and that improvement in such service can be used to increase sales. But management must consider the economics of such use. For example, suppose that a firm's annual sales are $100,000; its average inventory is $10,000; and the annual cost of carrying inventory is 25 percent of the value of the stocks, or $2,500. The cost of inventory carrying is thus 2.5 percent of sales. This means that every dollar which management adds to stocks in order to increase volume must add $10 to sales in order to pay for itself. This relationship is apt to be overlooked unless decisions with respect to finished goods inventories are tied closely to considerations of profit rather than to sales volume alone. The conscientious marketing manager should be careful not to insist on delivery standards that are higher, and therefore more costly, than are really necessary.

A starting point, of course, should be to define the exact delivery performance of the company over an adequate period of time and adequate sampling of territories, and to collect such reliable information as can be gathered regarding competitors' delivery performance. Such information may be developed by the company's marketing research department, assuming that it is free to operate in an objective manner, or by a consulting organization. Such research may be extended further with the objective of finding out the nature and extent of customers' real needs and wishes for delivery service, and the degree to which this service influences patronage.

Once management has determined upon appropriate levels of delivery service to customers it is ready to begin to plan how to render this standard of service at the lowest cost. There are several major opportunities to be explored in seeking to reduce costs. These include the following:

1. Reducing the amount of inventory in factory stocks, in transit stocks, and in field or branch warehouse stocks.

2. Reducing transportation costs by better utilization of equipment and by more efficient equipment, if goods are moved in company owned carriers.

3. Increasing efficiency in materials handling—especially loading and unloading of trucks, containers, and railroad cars.

4. Faster transportation movement.

5. Better coordination between trucks and railroads through the use of piggyback movements and containerization.

6. Better handling of information throughout the whole physical distribution range of activities.

Inventory costs per year, including such elements as interest, warehouse charges, handling expenses, insurance, obsolescence and deterioration, range in amount from 20 to 30 percent of inventory value. Progressive managements are becoming increasingly aware of the benefits of viewing physical distribution as a total system, operating as a part of the overall company system of activities. In some cases this has taken the form of setting up a specialized organization unit which is charged with managing all kinds of inventory, materials, in-process and finished goods, and directing its flow into the plant and out to the customer.

One reason for delay in sensing the potentialities of this approach is that various portions of the activity have traditionally been assigned to executives in different company departments who could not have an overall view of the flow of goods and the cost implications of the various practices followed. Each of these executives tends to manage his part of the process in ways he thinks are most acceptable to his superior. The production manager, for example, is primarily interested in achieving low unit costs through long uninterrupted runs, and is not particularly concerned at the size of the inventory which this generates. The comptroller, on the other hand, might be very conscious of inventory costs and attempt to cut them to the bone without due regard to customer delivery service needs. The traffic manager may seek a low shipping cost per ton-mile without fully recognizing the cost results of increased inventory in transit—as well as the patronage losses due to reduced flexibility in making rapid adjustments to changes in customer requirements. Theoretically, a specialized unit can seek to reconcile all these conflicting interests.

The Systems Approach to Physical Distribution

Operations research personnel at Arthur D. Little, Inc., were early workers in developing the systems approach to physical distribution problems, and the following discussion is largely based on an article by John F. Magee of that organization.[1] The starting point is to recognize that products which are slow movers require more inventory, relative to sales, than fast-moving products.

This is illustrated in Figure 15–1, where the product line is broadened by replacing item A with items B, C, and D. If total sales are the same as those previously generated by item A, and the division between B, C, and D is as shown by the bar lengths, inventory requirements in-

[1] John F. Magee, "The Logistics of Distribution," *Harvard Business Review*, July-August, 1960. The exhibits are shown as they appeared when this article was reprinted in Charles J. Dirksen, Arthur Kroeger, and Lawrence C. Lockley, *Readings in Marketing* (Homewood, Ill.: Richard D. Irwin, Inc., 1963), p. 328.

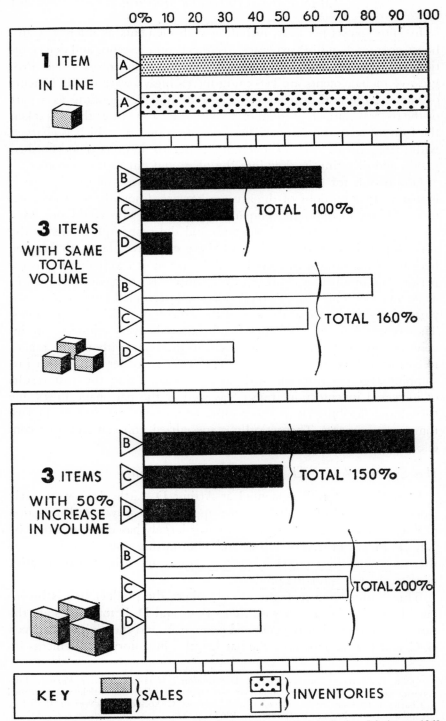

FIGURE 15–1

WHAT HAPPENS TO INVENTORIES WHEN THE PRODUCT LINE IS BROADENED?

SOURCE: John F. Magee's "Logistics of Distribution," *Harvard Business Review*, July-August, 1960.

crease by 160 percent. If sales increase to 150 percent of the former level, inventory requirements go up by 200 percent. This occurs basically because there is usually more variability in actual day-to-day sales of low volume items as compared with average daily sales, over a period of time, for high volume items. The extent of this variation from the average has an important bearing on the level of inventory required to cover replenishment lead time. The higher the variability, the larger will be the inventory needed to assure a desired level of customer service for the particular item.

The degree of correlation between successive time periods for these variability patterns is also important in its effect on inventory levels. If sales variability patterns are highly consistent from one time period to the next, this means that the full effect of the variability upon inventory will be continuously present. If, however, correlation is low over a given time, indicating that in one time period variability may be high while in another period it may be low, this introduces an offsetting effect which enables inventories to be smaller and still give the same service.

A similar analysis should be made of sales correlation between geographical areas. If this is low, it would favor the use of a limited number of regional warehouses; while if it is high, reducing the number of points at which stocks are carried would cause little inventory savings to offset the greater transportation charges.

The relatively higher inventory requirements of low sales volume items become more dramatic when it is recognized that from 10 to 20 percent of the products in the mix of the typical manufacturer represent 80 percent or more of his total sales, while half of the items represent about 4 percent of the sales. This is illustrated in Figure 15–2.

The situation is likely to get worse rather than better as more products are generated by increasing technology as well as increasing competitive pressures. If stock is maintained at local points for many small volume items, a substantial inventory must be kept to service sales of these items. Inventory control techniques usually allot some "safety stock" to provide for this. A characteristic pattern of stocks on hand over three reorder cycles is shown in Figure 15–3. One way to approach this kind of problem is to consider centralizing stocks of the slower moving items at a limited number of regional warehouses and using faster transportation methods, including air cargo. In many situations the higher transportation cost could be more than offset by inventory savings.

In a study of possible cost savings in physical distribution, market

FIGURE 15–2

WHAT FRACTION OF TOTAL SALES IS ACCOUNTED FOR BY WHAT FRACTIONS
OF TOTAL ITEMS IN THE PRODUCT LINE?

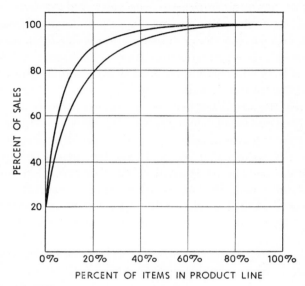

SOURCE: Magee, *op. cit.*

FIGURE 15–3

WHAT IS THE CHARACTERISTIC INVENTORY PATTERN OF STOCKS ON HAND
IN THE TYPICAL COMPANY?

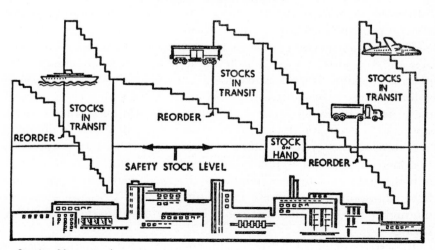

SOURCE: Magee, *op. cit.*

patterns of past sales by customer types and sizes must be known in detail. It is of particular importance to know whether different types of customers have different delivery service needs and different buying practices. The product assortments purchased by large customers can be especially revealing as they often represent 80 percent or more of total sales volume. If this purchase mix regularly contains both fast and slow moving products, that fact throws light on the feasibility of downgrading delivery for slow moving items, as would happen if they were centralized in regional warehouses and no particular effort were made to substitute faster transportation methods. Often the downgrading of service can be small enough (and the markets affected also small enough) for substantial savings to be made without serious loss of sales. Magee cites a case in which the reduction of stock carrying points from 50 to 25 increased total transportation costs 7 percent but cut inventories by 20 percent, and total physical distribution costs by 8 percent, the equivalent of 1 percent of the delivered product cost. Delivery time was set back from first to second day after receipt of order for only 5 percent of the markets served.

Another example of the systems approach is the Hypo Company, an imaginary firm devised by General Electric's marketing services staff.[2] On sales of 500,000 units of a $100 product distributed to 10,000 customers scattered throughout the United States, savings of nearly $3 million were calculated. The actions suggested to achieve this result included reducing the number of distribution points from 100 to 25, cutting warehouse replenishment time from 25 days to 10 days, stocking slowest moving items in only 5 key warehouses, and stepping up the manufacturing cycle from 3 weeks to one week. A summary of the savings is shown in Table 15–1.

TABLE 15–1

SUMMARY OF HYPO COMPANY DISTRIBUTION COST SAVINGS

	Savings
Reducing distribution points from 100 to 25.............	$1,460,000
Reducing warehouse replenishment time from 25 days to 10 days..	811,000
Stocking slowest moving items in only 5 key warehouses....	146,000
Stepping up manufacturing cycle from 3 weeks to 1 week (achieving reduction in in-process inventory)...........	506,000
Total Savings.................................	$2,923,000

---

[2] "The Case for 90% Satisfaction," *Business Week*, January 14, 1961, pp. 82–85.

The Manufacturer and His Distributors' Stocks

The discussion so far has dealt with delivering manufacturers' products to customers, and the application of systems-type thinking to this general problem. The marketing manager, however, is very much concerned with the activities of his distributors and customers in handling and using his company's products. He wants to be sure that distributors carry sufficient stock to serve the needs of their customers, provide good delivery service, and do both of these at the lowest possible cost. The ultimate resellers of the manufacturers' products may face serious inventory problems both in terms of having enough of the right products available in stock or immediately accessible through other channels, and of avoiding excessive stocks with high carriage and obsolescence costs.

Although inventory levels throughout the manufacturer-distributor-user, or retailer, complex are a pervasive factor contributing to high distribution costs, there are other aspects of wholesaler and user behavior of importance to the manufacturer. One of these is the practice of many customers of ordering in uneconomic quantities. At times this may be unavoidable if unpredictable demands require a fill-in type order. At other times it is due to a failure to recognize that a small order represents almost as much paperwork and handling costs as a larger order, and thus is very costly to both buyer and seller. Industrial users may be just as guilty as wholesalers or retailers in this regard since the purchasing department often seems much more interested in bargaining for a lower unit price than in minimizing the total acquisition and use cost of the purchased products.

The Gates Rubber Company made a comprehensive study of its distribution system.[3] It showed that distributors' purchase orders ranged from $51 to $860 per order. It also indicated that there was an excessive number of back-orders or "referrals" (orders they did not have stock to fill) by Gates' own branches. One wholesaler, purchasing about $100,000 worth of products annually, had been issued 804 invoices by the company—one for each shipment—but had placed only 208 orders and thus had received an average of 3.87 invoices per order. This resulted from the branch offices being out of stock, which caused extensive back-ordering. Furthermore, this customer had received shipments not only from the warehouse which normally serviced his needs, but from 15 additional company warehouses at various locations in the country.

---

[3]Walter F. Crowder, "Innovation in Industrial Distribution," speech before the Second Annual Industrial Distribution Conference, Cincinnati, September 18, 1962 (pp. 10–13). Mr. Crowder is editor and publisher of *Industrial Distribution*.

As a result of this study the company worked with the distributors to encourage them to increase order size. It was found that the factory branches had been carrying too much of the fast moving lines and too little of the slow moving lines, and steps were taken to make adequate stocks of the latter available. Changes in company operations resulted in fewer major branches, better placed small service centers, regular truck routes from the factory, and new production schedules tied closer to actual field needs. The results of this major overhaul of the physical distribution system were reductions in inventory (amounting to several million dollars), a cut of 52 percent in warehouse personnel, a 26 percent decrease in communication costs, the reduction of back-orders and interbranch referrals by 39 and 74 percent respectively, a decline in stock replacement time in branches from 22 days to 9 days maximum, and many operating cost savings for distributors cooperating in the program.

This sort of problem faces many makers of consumers' goods products and the application of the same techniques may often achieve similar results. The small order problem is apt to be even more pervasive and costly in this field than in the marketing of industrial goods.

Improved integration of physical distribution activities between wholesalers and distributors and their customers has been growing during the past few years. In the industrial goods field this has been applied especially to industrial supplies used for plant maintenance, repairs, and operations. The essential elements of this arrangement, which has been termed "stockless purchasing,"[4] are

1. A large part of the stock carrying function and paperwork is shifted from the buying plant to distributors.
2. Items are carefully classified and, in each major class, one distributor is selected as a primary supplier
3. Standardization of items is aggressively sought, using the full knowledge of both the customer and distributors.
4. The extent of reimbursibility of distributors for obsolescence of nonstandard items kept in stock at customers' request is agreed upon in advance.
5. Prices are negotiated for three to six month periods, and sometimes longer.
6. Shipments are made by distributors against requisitions rather than normal purchase orders. Some arrangements permit telephone releases or make use of prepunched cards which the customer transmits by wire to the distributor's data processing system.
7. Billing is on a monthly basis.

---

[4] Van Ness Philip, "Stockless Purchasing at Viscose," *Industrial Distribution,* December, 1961; Don Winston, "Stockless Purchasing for Smaller Plants Pays Off in Sales," *Industrial Distribution,* January, 1962; and Van Ness Philip, "Automatic Purchasing Succeeds," *Industrial Distribution,* October 1961.

The American Viscose Company, facing high inventories of materials and supplies, and with many duplications, excessive storeroom areas, and much spot ordering paperwork, took the initiative in working out an arrangement of this sort with several distributors who supplied them. After three years of experience it was reported that a number of benefits[5] had developed.

33 percent less inventory in all MRO supplies: shelf items reduced by one-third, machine parts by one-fifth.

5,000 bins eliminated in plant stores.

30 percent reduction in the payroll of the staffs of the company's central buying and plant stores departments (14 fewer employees at the central buying office, 20 fewer in the plants).

52 percent reduction in the number of purchase orders for suppliers.

Substantial progress in a "clean sweep" removal of inactive items: of 4,176 items in 10 product classes, investigation showed that 2,353 had not turned over in one year.

To date, 900 items have been removed through standardization.

The company believed that it could continue progress along these lines by substituting planned materials management for unplanned purchasing, coupled with long-term working agreements with a carefully selected group of industrial distributors. Although the first examples of these stockless purchasing arrangements resulted from initiative taken by industrial customers, some of the more progressive industrial distributors have been promoting the idea among other customers with some success.

For such arrangements to be put into effect, and to operate satisfactorily, it is necessary that there be actual benefits to the industrial customer and to the distributors (which arise through improved efficiency of the joint operation) and that both parties believe that such benefits will materialize. A common source of resistance on the part of the distributor is the fear that the benefits of being able to concentrate substantial sales with one customer will be more than offset by the customer's insistence on a low price. Where distributors know their costs, or are willing by accepted distribution cost accounting methods to determine costs of handling individual accounts, price negotiation should not prove to be an insurmountable obstacle.

The industrial customer's resistance frequently comes from the purchasing department, where the buying staff may consider reduced paperwork as a threat to their jobs. Although some personnel reduction may result when the volume of spot ordering is dramatically reduced, the

---

[5]V. N. Philip, "Stockless Purchasing at Viscose," *op. cit.*

time freed for doing a broader gauged purchasing job was welcomed by many purchasing departments. Where real problems of resistance exist it may well be because not enough attention is being given to the total cost of acquisition and use of supplies, as compared with seeking the lowest possible price as each individual order is negotiated. Also it must be remembered that, since the buying company has shifted back to the distributor a large portion of the stock-carrying function (and some of the record keeping as well), the distributor may well be entitled to a higher price than formerly because of the extra services he is providing. The customer, because he has reduced his materials management costs within the plan, should find that total acquisition and use costs are reduced.

The manufacturer who is aware of this sort of activity on the part of distributors may find that he can provide better and more economical inventory and delivery service by marketing through indirect channels than by selling direct. In doing so he must adjust his standard stock requirements for his distributors and his own reserve inventories to the problem this method of operations creates. While this plan was developed and is mainly used in the industrial goods field, there is no reason why some modification of it should not prove useful to such retailers of consumers' goods as supermarkets, discount houses, and many department stores.

Materials Handling Improvements

Substantial improvements have been made in material handling methods for both bulk and packaged products over recent years. Mechanization of loading and unloading has advanced farthest (as might be expected) for heavy bulk products where the substantial costs of such equipment can be offset by very significant savings. Progress has also been made in mechanizing the handling of packaged merchandise, and manufacturers of lift-trucks have been ingenious in their designs to permit ease of handling and maximum utilization of warehouse space. The "grab" design of lift-trucks has been helpful for some kinds of loading and unloading operations, as contrasted with the fork-lift design.

There is also a trend toward mechanization of warehouses, not only in the inward and outward movement of goods but in the assembly and flow of goods in response to orders. Efforts have been made to achieve a high degree of automation in the warehouse operation.[6] Interest in

[6] Melvin Mandell, "Should the Warehouse Be Automated?" *Dun's Review and Modern Industry,* October, 1961.

total or near-total mechanization of order filling at warehouses will undoubtedly continue. The record to date contains both successes and failures. One of the difficulties is that a highly automated system has less flexibility for easy adjustment to changing market conditions than one which is semi-automated. The costs are high, and such warehouses are usually owned by manufacturing organizations. Over a period of time means will undoubtedly be found to build more flexibility into the systems and thus lessen the impact of market changes.

One reason for part of the difficulties has been that some companies moved into a highly mechanized warehousing approach before having made a basic study and rearrangement of their total physical distribution systems. Without a well-thought-out total physical distribution system, the use of an automated warehouse is almost foredoomed to failure. For example, high volume operation is necessary to justify the costs of highly mechanized systems in warehouses. Thus local warehouses might not be able to support the cost, whereas if regional warehouses are feasible in terms of the total physical distribution system, there would be an opportunity at least to consider the desirability of automation. Furthermore, the location of such regional warehouses would have to be right for the foreseeable future because the cost of making a mistake would be very high indeed.

Recent Developments in Transportation

Significant changes have occurred and are occurring in the physical delivery facilities with which the manufacturer must work in marketing his products. Some of these represent improvements while others complicate his problems.

The railroads have lost business to both common carrier and privately operated motor trucks, a trend which started in the 1940's. Table 15–2 shows the total traffic in millions of ton-miles for railroad, motor vehicle, inland waterway, oil pipeline, and air freight for selected years, as well as the percentage in each year carried by different methods of transportation. In 1945 the railroads had slightly over two thirds of the domestic intercity freight traffic, and motor vehicles only 6 percent. In 1960 this percentage had dropped to 44 for railroads and increased to 22 percent for motor vehicles.

The United States is confronted with a transportation problem of major importance in which a key factor is the difficulties encountered by railroads in remaining competitive and solvent and in earning sufficient profit to attract capital investment. Railroad management has complained that the regulatory policies pursued by the Interstate Commerce Commission are now outmoded by the growth of new competition, and that difficulties in getting various types of rate changes approved have placed them under a severe competitive disadvantage.

There have been a number of attempts to secure approval for rates which would place the railroads on a more competitive basis with trucking, but it has proved difficult to get approval for many of these proposals. Legislation is currently before Congress, known as "minimum rates" legislation, which if passed, would give all common carriers freedom to reduce rates on agricultural products and bulk commodities. Another burden of the railroads is strong unions which have aggressively sought to protect jobs, even though the need for some of these positions has largely disappeared. While it is widely recognized that the national transportation problem is serious, and comprehensive studies have been made,[7] there does not seem to be any realistic effort to take constructive steps in a well-thought-out overall plan of action.

TABLE 15–2

VOLUME OF DOMESTIC INTERCITY FREIGHT TRAFFIC

	Total Traffic (millions of ton-miles)	Percent by Type of Transportation				
		Railroad	Motor Vehicle	Inland Water	Pipeline	Air
1945	1,072,490.........	68.6	6.2	13.3	11.8	.008
1950	1,094,160.........	57.4	15.8	14.9	11.8	.029
1955	1,298,060.........	50.4	17.2	16.7	15.7	.037
1958	1,231,184.........	46.7	20.8	15.4	17.2	.048
1960	1,346,650.........	44.2	22.2	16.6	17.0	.058

SOURCE: *Statistical Abstract of the United States*, 1962, p. 570.

Although the share of intercity freight carried by motor vehicles has increased sharply over the last 17 years, companies offering common carrier truck service operate only about one quarter of the total motor trucks in use. The remainder are owned and operated by private industry.

There are many reasons why a manufacturing firm may prefer to operate its own trucks. Sometimes the nature of the product may require

---

[7]"National Transportation Policy," Preliminary Draft of a Report Prepared for the Committee on Interstate and Foreign Commerce, United States Senate, by the Special Group on Transportation Policies in the United States, U. S. Government Printing Office, 1961.

special equipment and handling; for example, plate glass and chemicals. Also, when the manufacturer operates his own trucks he may be in a position to give somewhat more flexible service to customers, and if volume is heavy enough it may be cheaper to operate company owned vehicles than to use common carrier truckers. However, some evidence suggests that the advantages may at times be illusory. Costs of ownership and operation may be underestimated and some of the true costs may never actually be charged to the operation. Furthermore, there is the problem of empty return trips—unless deliveries to customers can be matched with pickups of materials or other products being purchased by the company. There is also the possibility of hauling loads for others on an individually negotiated basis; but no published statistics are available on the extent of this practice.

A number of innovations in freight car design have been adopted by the railroads. Box-cars are designed so that there will be less damage in transit and they now permit much greater ease of loading and unloading. Oversize tank cars have been made available for more economical hauling of bulk liquids, thus permitting lower rates for shippers.

The railroads have instituted a new method of train operation to help coal companies sell more effectively to the utility market. This has been called the "unitized train," consisting of 100 or more cars that shuttle back and forth between the mine and the utility. This train is a special-purpose operation, carries no other kind of cargo, and never stops at yards for switching. It costs less to run and provides the customers with better service.

The Gulf, Mobile, and Ohio Railroad recently established rates of $1.30 per ton for two unitized trains of 125 cars operating between a coal mine in Percy, Illinois, and an electric utility near Joliet, Illinois. This compared to $3.17 a ton for smaller shipments. Similarly, the New York Central Railroad started an operation between a coal mine at Lynnville, Indiana, and a utility at Hammondville, Indiana, in which the rate is $1.45 per ton—against $3.42 per ton in single car shipments.[8] These are types of contract rates which, historically, have not been favored by the Interstate Commerce Commission because they give preferential treatment to the big shipper and thus work a hardship on small businessmen. Despite opposition by another railroad to the New York Central operation, the Interstate Commerce Commission did not investigate or suspend the rate. Other railroads have petitioned for similar rates, and they may spread to other types of products.

---

[8]Railroads Give Coal Buyers a Break," *Business Week,* March 9, 1963, p. 34.

By operating more cars to a train and running trains on faster, more precise schedules, the railroads have materially improved the speed and certainty of the delivery service manufacturers are able to offer through their use.

Piggyback. Piggyback service consists of moving truck trailers on railroad flatcars. The trailer is pulled by the usual truck tractor during the course of collecting a load of freight and is then driven to a terminal where it is loaded on a flatcar, usually by driving it up a movable ramp. The tractor is driven away and the trailer body (with its wheels) is secured to the flatcar. Two truck bodies can be carried on each flatcar. When the piggyback car arrives at its destination the trailer is moved off the flatcar and another tractor and driver make delivery of the contents. There are, altogether, five main plans under which piggyback operations are carried out.

1. Railroads and Motor Common Carriers. Railroads carry trailers owned by motor common carriers, making a flat charge per trailer based on weight and distance, regardless of commodity. The trucker performs the entire transportation service except for the piggyback journey.

2. A Railroad Operation: Door-to-Door. Railroads carry their own trailers under their own tariffs. Usually this service is confined to established territories contiguous to rail terminals.

3. Shipper Trailers, Railroad Cars. The railroads carry trailers owned or leased by shippers at a flat rate per mile. The shipper delivers the trailers to the railhead and picks them up at the rail terminal.

4. Shipper Trailers and Shipper Cars. Railroads carry trailers owned or leased by shippers on flatcars which are also owned or leased by shippers. A flat charge is made per car. The shipper takes the trailer to and from the rail terminal and loads and unloads cars.

5. Joint Rates: Truck-Rail-Truck. Railroads carry their own trailers, or common carrier truck trailers, under joint rail-truck rates on an end-to-end basis. Although somewhat similar to Plan 1, this is a true joint operation which, in effect, extends the territory of each participating carrier into that served by the other; permits each participant to handle shipments originating in or destined to the other's territory, and allows each to sell service for the other.[9]

TABLE 15–3

PIGGYBACK CAR LOADINGS FROM 1955 THROUGH 1962

Year	Loadings	Year	Loadings
1955	168,150	1959	416,499
1956	207,783	1960	554,212
1957	249,083	1961	591,246
1958	276,767	1962	707,000

SOURCE: American Association of Railroads.

[9] Material adapted from *Railway Age*, March 28, 1960.

Late in 1962 the Interstate Commerce Commission began an investigation of various piggyback plans, which was still underway in the spring of 1963. Piggyback car loadings have grown at a rate of about 23 percent a year from 1955 through 1962, as shown in Table 15–3.

Although the number of car loadings represented by piggyback cars was only about 2.5 percent of the total in 1962, these cars had higher average loadings per car and therefore contributed a higher percent of total revenue.[10]

An obvious saving available in piggyback is the elimination of a driver and operating expenses for the rail haul portion of the trip. The rates charged vary because of the variety of arrangements of ownership of equipment. Piggyback provides faster delivery service than boxcar shipment because one loading and unloading is eliminated. Also, the trailer can be driven to the customer destination as soon as it is unloaded from the flatcar, thus lessening the delay at the terminal. There is less damage to goods and less danger of pilferage.

Among the disadvantages of piggyback is the freight charge for the weight of the trailer and its wheels, and the added height, represented by the wheels, which at times causes problems with bridges and other overhead structures, as well as making a higher center of gravity. A further objection is that there is waste space underneath the truck and that if containers were used, which could be nested tightly, 50 percent more cubage would be available for freight.

Although it is expected that piggyback will continue to grow—one railroad executive estimated a 17 percent increase for 1964 and another a 30 percent increase—it seems likely that, over a long period, containers which can equally well be put on flatcars or trucks will provide a more flexible means and a more efficient one. There will be some problems in this development as overhead unloading methods will probably be needed at terminal yards. There are, further, indications that Plan 5 arrangements, involving joint rates of truck-rail-truck service, are beginning to be established in many areas of the country. This will undoubtedly lead to further rates of this kind and should make the piggyback operation more widely available.

Second Thoughts on Distribution Responsibility

As was indicated earlier, the chief marketing executive does not always have charge of the physical distribution service. In some companies the production department is charged with delivering merchan-

---

[10]Raymond E. Clancy, "Growth, Economics and Future of Piggybacking," unpublished Master's thesis submitted to the School of Industrial Management, M.I.T., June, 1963.

dise where and when and in the quantities designated by the marketing unit. Sometimes this obligation extends only to the branch warehouses, which are under the management of marketing and from which marketing arranges for delivery to customers. In other cases marketing has entire responsibility for the job, subject to advice and help from the traffic department and to top management rulings as to how much of the company funds shall be tied up in finished goods inventories.

There is a growing school of managerial thought which suggests that the administration of all kinds of inventories, materials and components, goods in process, and finished goods, is one job and that a lot of money can be saved by coordinating it properly under one executive. When control of inventories is thus centralized, control of most of the physical delivery service almost inevitably goes with it.

While this proposal has much to commend it, there are some disquieting features. Inventories are not all one piece, but are carried for different purposes. Stocks of materials and components are held to insure against production stoppages resulting from shortages. Finished products inventories are maintained to service sales. They have one feature in common: the smaller they can be and still serve the purpose, the less they will cost.

There is, however, more than a trace of danger that an executive in charge of both kinds will be tempted to concentrate on this common feature and perhaps overlook their basic purposes. In the case of materials and components, the penalty for this is immediate and spectacular, for a shutdown and its cause is known to everybody in the plant. But who can prove that a customer quit buying because he had to wait two days for a delivery? Or that a prospect refuses to buy from us because our reputation for prompt deliveries is not good?

Perhaps a compromise might lie in making the marketing manager responsible for profit from his operations—not merely for volume— and in including among his duties the administration of finished goods inventories and delivery. This is almost certain to make him cost conscious and to lead him into serious thought about the proper balance between cost generating stocks and the added volume (and possibly lower selling costs) resulting from superlative physical delivery service.

ORDER HANDLING

There is no romance in order handling. It is definitely a nuts and bolts part of the marketing process, but it is a very important part; and one that merits the manager's careful attention in its planning and administration. How well it is done plays a central role in determining the speed, certainty, and accuracy of a firm's delivery service to its customers. The costs it generates often constitute a highly significant part of total marketing expenses.

When goods are ordered from stock the management of order handling consists of organizing, staffing, and supervising a procedure or routine designed to make sure that exactly the items and amounts called for on each order are made ready for transport to the customer as speedily as possible. Three characteristics are important here: accuracy, certainty, and speed. When orders are for future delivery, or must be made to specification, the essence of the function lies in following up to make sure that production is scheduled so as to enable delivery to be made on the promised date; that exactly the right thing is being produced; that the various critical dates in the production schedule are met; and that the goods are shipped or delivered on the specified date.

Not all of these activities are always under the direction of the marketing manager, but they are of vital import to him and can add impact to his selling efforts, or largely nullify his work, according to how well they are done. So he must interest himself in them and seek to improve their efficiency whether he wishes to or not, and regardless of where final responsibility for them rests.

Orders for Future Delivery

When orders are for future delivery, and each must be produced between the time when it is received and the specified delivery date, a fairly common procedure is to designate certain employees as customers' representatives. Each representative is assigned a number of customer orders. It is his job to represent the customer within the company and to do all he can to see that each of his orders is made and delivered as promised in the contract. In doing so he is privileged to make a nuisance of himself to the production planning, the materials procurement, and the several processing units in the interest of the customers whose orders he handles. He usually has little, if any, real authority. He is supposed to gain his ends by persuasion, admonition, pleading, and pestering, sometimes fortified by implied threats when he operates, as he sometimes does, out of the office of the chief executive.

The customers' representative is usually a part of the marketing organization although, as noted, he sometimes reports to a top executive. Such representatives are often young men in training for sales positions or minor executive jobs. These gentlemen are almost invariably an annoyance to the production and procurement people, but as a result the latter often get orders out faster than they otherwise would, just to keep the customers' representatives out of their hair.

Orders to Stock

When, as is usually the case, a company can fill its orders from stock, the order handling operation is apt to be more elaborate and more routinized. It is also likely to be complicated by the presence of branch warehouses scattered through the market area. These branches are sometimes entirely concerned with the physical distribution of the company's products to customers. When this is the case the branch manager is likely to report to a Manager of Branches or a Manager of Customer Service in the central office, and the operations of all branches are apt to be highly standardized. Sometimes the branch is a combined selling and physical distribution unit, in which case the branch manager may be delegated very wide authority and may have under him all kinds of customer service. In such a case the order handling operations are likely to be less completely standardized.

Whatever the nature of the branch or delivery unit may be, the tasks that have to be done in handling orders are about the same. They fall into two classes: paperwork, and physical order filling and preparation for transport.

Paperwork. When an order comes into a house a number of clerical operations must be performed on it. The following is a partial list:

a) The name and address of the customer must be checked for accuracy.

b) The shipping terms and directions must be checked or specified.

c) The credit standing of the customer must be verified.

d) The items ordered must be edited to the end that orderpickers will know exactly what is ordered.

e) The order pattern must be checked for internal consistency. For example, there was the 1,000-case order from the customer who usually bought in 10-case lots. Not wishing to offend him by seeming to question whether he knew what he was doing, the salesmanager telephoned to thank him for the large order. With considerable excitement, the customer admitted that two extra ciphers must have crept in somehow.

f) Unit prices must be checked and extensions made and totalled.

g) Discounts must be entered.

h) Often an invoice must be prepared and a copy of it transmitted to the customer with the order. Sometimes the order itself is duplicated and a copy of it is sent along instead.

In an organization of any size these operations are joined into several groups, each of which is performed by one person or several people who specialize in handling it. This increases the efficiency of the operation but it means that the wages of these people behave like overhead cost in that their total amount remains the same in the face of wide variations in the number of orders handled and sales dollar volume. And, within any one day or week or month, pronounced variations are bound to occur in the number of orders received, with the result that even the most efficiently organized order handling crew is almost certain to be idle a significant part of the time. Measures can be taken to diminish this but it can't be eliminated. One of the problems of managing this activity is to maintain a proper balance between the advantages of division of labor and those of flexibility.

Along with this work must go that of keeping records of additions to and withdrawals from stock to the end that management may know at all times the amount of inventory on hand, and when and by how much to replenish it. Much of this work as well as some of the order handling paperwork can now be done by business machines and computers. The area of use of such equipment may be expected to broaden continually and a wise management will be constantly on the alert to increase the efficiency of this work and reduce its costs.

Order Filling.   This consists of removing from storage the items specified on the order and preparing them for transport. If delivery is to be made by company trucks and personnel and over short distances, the shipping containers can be rudimentary. If shipments must be made over long distances and by public carrier, goods must be carefully packed.

The difficulty and cost of order filling varies considerably, according to the size and nature of the order. Some goods, if ordered in sufficient quantity, can be shipped in bulk. This may mean that they are transported in tank cars or trucks or gondolas, or in containers such as hogsheads or carboys, designed primarily or entirely to facilitate handling without regard to promotional usage. Other products may be handled by the case. Many orders call for some fraction of a case. Most goods can be handled most efficiently in bulk lots, although the practice of palletizing has reduced (and for many products practically eliminated) the differential between bulk and case lot handling. Firms that receive orders of all three types, bulk, case lot, and loose pieces, sometimes find it desirable to develop and staff an order filling routine for each. A relatively small volume of loose piece or broken package business makes a separate unit to handle it worthwhile.

Order filling work has been mechanized by means of traveling belts, overhead carriers, lift-trucks, and other devices. All these carry the goods after they have been selected from stock. A few warehouses have been mechanized to the point where selection is also done by machine. The marketing manager must be alert to developments in this field and to their possible application in his own operations.

General Considerations

Order handling routines vary widely. No two firms organize the operation in precisely the same way. Whatever the details of the procedure may be its objectives should almost invariably be the same: it should be designed to get orders through the house and ready for delivery as speedily as possible. It should include every usable safeguard to assure accuracy in sending the customer exactly what he ordered and the amount of it he specified. It should do both of these things consistently and with the fewest possible failures. And it should do them at the lowest possible cost.

COMPLAINTS AND ADJUSTMENTS

Regardless of the excellence of a manufacturer's order handling procedure, orders have a way of "going haywire." Not even the most meticulous inspection system will prevent imperfect units of product from occasionally getting into the channels of trade and the hands of users. When either of these things happens the customer is likely to complain or to demand that his supplier do something about it.

Handling these complaints is always a nuisance; but it is an expensive nuisance to ignore. For the customer with a complaint is a customer who is in the process of being lost. Proper handling may preserve him; careless treatment will often alienate him completely.

Many firms find that the cheapest and best way to handle complaints is simply to assume that the customer is always right. This usually involves replacing merchandise complained of as speedily as possible, or reshipping the order, or granting an adjustment if one is requested.

The administration of this policy is complicated by the fact that some customers are chronic complainers. The unearthing of such a buyer leaves the supplier with two alternatives: to suffer with him or to refuse to do business with him. In some trades it is complicated, if not made impossible, by a widespread practice among dealers of sending back merchandise they can't sell, claiming that it is defective. Sometimes they even *render* it defective before returning it. This is especially apt to happen in seasonal trades. It reflects careless or inefficient buying on the part of the dealer, or undue pressure applied by the supplier's salesmen. Something can be done to mitigate the difficulty by training salesmen not to oversell their customers and by using a compensation system that discourages them from doing so, but it is highly improbable that the practice can be completely eliminated.

When the stakes of each transaction are high, each complaint is likely to be the subject of a separate negotiation. Some firms make it so anyway.

Some firms delegate the handling of complaints to their field offices; some place it in the hands of their salesmen. More commonly the salesman is charged with the job of investigating the complaint, recommending how it shall be disposed of, and informing the customer of the action decided upon. When such decisions are made in the home office it is highly desirable that such tasks be delegated to a single person or unit so that they will be handled promptly and according to a common pattern.

Often much can be learned by an analysis of complaints and adjustment claims. For example, persistent failures or mistakes in delivery indicate the presence of some defect in the order handling or delivery procedure. Close study of them may suggest the location or nature of the defect. Too many returns in a territory may be a symptom of overselling and, if they are general, may indicate that the system of salesmen's compensation is not what it should be. Persistent complaints about product quality may point the finger at failures in inspection or improper production methods.

MANAGING THE CREDIT SERVICE

One of the commonest excuses of customers for not buying is, "I haven't got the money." This is true not only of the ultimate consumer buyer but of the industrial buyer and wholesale and retail dealer as well. The marketer may seek to overcome this objection the hard way by trying to persuade the buyer that his product is amply worth foregoing the satisfaction of some other current need in order to purchase it. But the marketer is likely to find it easier to convince the customer that he will be wise to buy the article now and pay for it bit by bit as he gets the money. This involves credit.

The manufacturer would undoubtedly rather stay out of the whole matter of credit and leave it to those who specialize in finance. Sometimes he is able to avoid it or to limit the extent of his participation in it. But when he is marketing an article of high unit value, in relation to the purchasing power of the buyer (as is the case with an automobile in the consumers' goods field, or a tanker ship in the industrial goods business), he can't avoid it.

Then too, in the consumers' goods trade and to a lesser extent in some parts of the industrial goods business, credit is a matter of convenience. The user who buys many small purchases finds it convenient or less costly to allow them to accumulate during a fortnight or a month and then be billed for them on one invoice and make one payment. Such extensions of credit are apt to strain the financial resources of the retailer or the wholesaler or distributor to the point where he looks to the manufacturer to relieve the burden. So the latter often finds himself in the credit business whether he wishes to be or not.

Since the need for credit permeates all marketing levels and since the attractiveness of the idea of getting something for nothing, even though for only a little while, is so strong and so universal that the temptation to sell credit terms first and foremost, and the merchandise to which they apply only as a poor second, assails almost every marketing manager. This is probably less true of the executive handling industrial goods than of his consumers' goods fellow.

Leasing

In the industrial equipment industry the leasing contract is sometimes used to enable the buyer to avoid the need for credit. When this arrangement exists directly between the manufacturer and the user, the maker of a machine leases it to a user; for example, a shoe manufacturer who pays either a flat fee per time period (per month or year) or a fee per unit of use (as per pair of shoes processed), or a combination of the two. The machine maker thus relieves the user of any financial commitment for the equipment except for an installation fee which is often nominal. Because of this, many small firms, which would otherwise never get started, are able to get into the shoe making business.

Third parties sometimes get into the act. For example, a construction contractor often has need, over short periods of time, for heavy expensive equipment that he can't afford to buy for such limited use. Certain firms specialize in owning such equipment and leasing it to contractors, thus achieving enough usage to make the investment pay. Or an oil company may have more profitable use for its capital than to invest it in tanker ships. A three-way system of contracts is drawn whereby an insurance firm or a commercial finance house buys a tanker from the ship manufacturer and leases it to the oil company on a long-time rental contract at a fee high enough to amortize the investment and return a satisfactory interest rate.

The oil companies use the same device to facilitate the opening of new gasoline stations. The company and a would-be station operator spot and option an attractive location. They then execute a contract whereby the oil company leases the location and a station to be built on it from the expectant operator at an annual rental rate that is high enough to pay amortization and interest on the investment. On the basis of this the operator borrows money from a bank to buy the location and build a station. The oil company re-leases the completed property back to the operator, who then goes into the business of handling the company's products.

The leasing arrangement may be useful for several nonfinancial purposes:

1. By leasing machines on which he has a patent a machine maker may help to either lease or sell other machines used in connection with it (on which he has no market protection) if the user needs the patented machine and feels that his operating problems will be eased by having his entire shop or processing line equipped with tools produced by the same maker.

2. The lease enables the equipment maker to get at his machines and keep them in repair so that users will get the most satisfactory service from them.

3. If the maker of a machine also markets materials processed by it, such as shoe findings, the leasing arrangement may facilitate the sale of these materials.

Types of Credit

When a seller extends credit to a buyer he usually does it on either an *installment contract* or an *open book account* basis. Loans are also a source of both mercantile and consumer credit. Of the total average monthly consumer credit outstanding in 1962 about 76 percent was installment, about 9 percent open book account, and about 9 percent loans. These relationships are fairly typical of those during recent years. In 1962, also, the average monthly consumer credit outstandings represented 3.2 months' retail sales. Installment outstandings originating from automobile sales were about 40 percent of all installment outstandings and represented 5.8 months' automobile sales.

Aside from the automobile trade the bulk of the mercantile credit—that extended by manufacturers to wholesalers and retailers, and by wholesalers to retailers—probably is of the open book variety. Typically, the merchant's inventories are sold and his receivables liquidated within a relatively brief period so that, in theory, there is no need for long continued credit. Sometimes this is wishful thinking and the merchant is constantly in debt to his supplier, paying something on account from time to time but with no more real intent of liquidating the obligation than the federal government has of paying the national debt.

Most suppliers, both manufacturers and merchants, take steps to discourage this. The most usual step is the allowance of a discount to the customer who pays cash. The discount terms most widely used are "2% 10, net 30," and "2% 10, end of the month." The first of these means that the buyer who pays within 10 days after the date of the invoice may deduct 2 percent from the face of the bill, which becomes overdue 31 days after its date. This is equal to an annual interest rate of about 36 percent. The second term means that the buyer who, on or before April 10, for example, pays all bills dated during March, may deduct 2 percent. In spite of the fantastic interest rates involved, many merchants fail to take their discounts.

The administration of an open book account system for customers is an expensive, often exasperating operation. While the marketing manager often does not set or administer credit standards, he is usually very much involved in the process. If credit standards are too rigid or harshly enforced, sales are apt to be lost.

Installment credit has been the subject of hot controversy. In comparatively few trades does the manufacturer have to take the lead in extending it. Historically, this was not true. For example, fairly early in the history of the automobile trade the manufacturers found it necessary to set up finance houses or departments to discount consumer installment paper originated by their dealers in selling cars. These establishments are now divorced from their parent firms and, to a considerable extent, their functions have been assumed by banks and consumer finance houses which handle all kinds of consumer credit.

The controversy has centered around two aspects of installment financing: the amount of it and the terms in which it is explained to consumer users. Often the charge made for it was stated in terms which suggested an interest rate. Since this rate continued to apply to the original amount throughout the life of the loan—even while the original amount was gradually being paid off—the net effect was apt to be misleading to the customer although the amount charged often was not exorbitant. The cost of recording, computing, and administering installment credit is very high and must be included in the rate. The Federal Trade Commission has battled against the misleading features of this procedure with the result that most statements of installment contracts are now put in terms of how much the consumer owes, how much per month he will have to pay, and how long it will take to pay the loan off.

Many people are disturbed by the amounts of goods consumers buy on credit, especially on installments, feeling that many of them mortgage their financial future to such an extent that they can no longer buy the things they need and that the mountain of debt hanging over the market constitutes a serious threat to the stability of the economy. This is true if credit is unwisely extended in the first place. But if it is based on a proper analysis of the buyer's ability to pay and represents a sound financial investment on the part of the firm extending it, these fears hardly seem well grounded. Insofar as installment credit is handled by financial concerns, this requirement is likely to be met. The danger occurs when the credit is extended and carried by the seller whose financial judgment is liable to be warped by his desire to sell goods. He may, and sometimes does, advertise and sell low down-payments and long payout periods instead of merchandise. When this becomes general, the situation is dangerous.

How Much Credit Service?

If the marketing manager's job is defined as one of making sales, he is justified in using credit service more or less indiscriminately to that end. If, on the other hand, his function is that of selling the firm's products profitably, he must weigh the cost of the credit service against the return from the goods it helps to sell and try to strike the most profitable balance for the firm. Often this is not done, nor is it easy to do.

On one side of the balance are the costs of credit. The most obvious of these is the loss from bad debts. Another is the cost of administration made up mainly of record keeping, correspondence, and collection work. The cost of funds tied up in outstandings is a hidden expense that is often disregarded. Many firms treat discounts taken by customers as a marketing cost instead of deducting their amount from gross sales to get net sales. This is probably sound because it forces recognition of the fact that the basic managerial purpose of granting credit is to help make sales.

On the other side of the scale is the increase in gross profit realized from the added sales made through the use of the credit service. Reasonable or liberal credit may also reduce the costs of advertising and personal selling per dollar of sales by making these activities more productive through minimizing the force of the "I haven't got the money" objection to buying.

Most of these factors can be quantified. This means that mathematical methods can often be used to aid managerial decisions about credit policy. However he does it, it is the job of the marketing manager to balance the credit service factors out to get the most profitable net result for his firm,

MAINTENANCE SERVICE

In a previous chapter we discussed the need for providing repair and maintenance service in marketing certain kinds of durable goods. This involves the furnishing of replacement parts and the performance of mechanical service.

When a maker of industrial goods markets direct to users he might be expected to supply the repair and maintenance service himself, and he often does. But this sometimes does not work out as well as desired because his marketing organization is apt to be preoccupied with making sales of the equipment and to neglect the much less glamorous parts-and-service end of the business. Then too, since many users maintain shops to do their own repair work, their need is mainly or entirely for parts and they want to buy these at the most convenient points, which makes it necessary to market them through distributors. The result sometimes is that the manufacturer markets equipment through one salesforce and replacement items through another. When it is the custom of the trade for the manufacturer to supply both parts and service he is likely to maintain a service unit which may be an arm of the marketing department or may belong to the production area.

The practice also varies in the consumers' goods business. For example, automobile companies rely on their retail franchise dealers to supply both parts and repair service. A number of them seek to maintain this service at a high level; (*a*) by including in the franchise contract standards as to the stocks of parts dealers are to carry and the quality of the mechanical work done in their shops, and (*b*) by operating training schools and programs for the dealers' service managers and mechanics.

One of the large electrical appliance firms maintains service units in the chief consumer market centers, out of which they operate mechanics who handle service calls throughout the tributary area. The makers of certain small consumer items rely on their dealers to make simple repairs and maintain factory or branch shops to which dealers can send their products for major difficulties.

Maintenance service is always an unglamorous and often exasperating part of any business, but much of the consumer's satisfaction from a product depends on it. The wise manager takes an active interest in it. Whether it should be controlled by the marketing manager or by a production executive is a matter of some discussion. Since, in its essence, it is a reproduction operation, a production executive might be expected to manage it better. But marketing management is almost certain to be more acutely aware of its importance in the making of sales and thus more vitally interested in maintaining its excellence and consistency. The important thing is that the management of the work be confided to an executive of considerable ability whose heart is in it.

TECHNICAL SERVICE

In an earlier chapter we pointed out that many marketers of industrial goods find it necessary or desirable to provide technical service for their customers. This may include such activities as preparing plans and specifications for special equipment, installing or helping install such equipment, training the customer's employees in using it, conducting applications research to develop special materials suited precisely to the customer's needs, and advising the customer about how to use materials or equipment to get the best results.

The work of preparing plans and specifications for equipment is pretty certain to be done by the engineering unit or by a special engineering research staff. The marketing group is apt to be involved in it to the extent that it uncovers the customer need or desire for such work, explores the project to the point where its feasibility becomes apparent, keeps in touch with the customer and the firm's engineers while it is going on, and cooperates in trying to complete the deal when the proposal is submitted. It also acts as a go-between in arranging the details of installation and in providing training in the use of the machines after they are installed. In some firms the marketing area maintains a small unit to do this training work, although the usual procedure seems to be to have it done by an arm of the engineering department.

Much the same relationship exists between the marketing and research groups in developing special formulas of materials to suit the particular needs of customers. The actual work is done by an applications group in the research department, while the marketing staff acts as an originator of the projects, as a coordinator and, in finally closing the deal, as a follow-up unit.

Practice seems to be divided in the provision of advisory service with respect to the proper use of materials. In some firms the marketing department contains a small technical unit which handles all needs for this kind of service which do not require special research. When this unit receives a request that can be satisfied only after specific research, it turns it over to the research group, follows it up, and usually transmits the results to the customer. Needless to say, in this situation mutual confidence and cordial working relationships between marketing and research are vital to good performance. Other firms have this work done by the research department on request of the marketing department. The important thing is not who does the work but that some group is clearly charged with the job of doing it.

INFORMATION SERVICE

A part of customer service that often is not recognized as such is the providing of information. All firms do a certain amount, whether or not they operate a special unit. Much of the information involved is transmitted through salesmen, or by letter, telegraph, or telephone. A company that has much of this to do will probably be wise to set up a separate marketing area unit to handle it.

Many kinds of information are involved in this service but most fit into the following groups.

1. *Products.* The customer looks to his supplier for information about the latter's products. This is especially true of new products. Of course, this sort of data will be communicated in the selling process, but, especially in the technical goods field, the customer is likely to want more detail than the salesman can impart in the relatively short period of his call—and to want it in permanent or semi-permanent form for constant reference.

This service is often extended to include information, imparted informally, about complementary products of other manufacturers that may be useful to the customer. This is likely to be especially appreciated in the industrial goods field. But how much and what kinds of information a manufacturer should supply about his competitor's goods is a moot question. A fairly solid precept is to volunteer no evil about them, but direct questions probably must be answered.

2. *Prices and the Market.* Certainly we should inform customers of changes in our prices. News of impending price changes probably should be transmitted at the earliest time possible without risk of losing the competitive advantage the change was designed to gain. Such warnings, however, may be selective, going only to especially valuable customers, sometimes by routes that approach the grapevine in informality.

General information that we have picked up about the market may be of value to our customers. We should be the experts in our market and know more about its overall aspects than our customer. This information may be of great value to him and we can do much to cement our relations by supplying it.

3. *Processes.*   Through our salesmen and other sources we are likely to pick up information about new or improved processes used in customer industries or about new methods of operating in a customer retail trade; the customer is apt to be grateful for such news. This sort of thing must be handled with great discretion so as to avoid disclosing to one competitor confidential information about another.

4. *Orders and Contracts.*   When a firm sells orders for future delivery, or on customer requirements contracts, it is highly desirable that the customer be kept informed at all times about the status of such transactions. The stage of production reached in making goods ordered to specification, any unexpected difficulties in procurement or production, and changes in the amount or location of stocks needed to fulfill a requirements contract are examples of such information. If voluntary and currently supplied, such news items relieve the customer of much worry and correspondence and, upon occasion, may enable him to revise his own plans to avoid or minimize losses resulting from otherwise unexpected failures or delays in delivery.

5. *Company Policy.*   Changes in company policy that affect customer relations should be broadcast to customers in a form that can be kept for future reference. This applies (among others) to policies about products, credit or shipment terms, channels of marketing, and services.

As has been pointed out, this work may be scattered through a number of units in the marketing area. But it will probably be done better if a small organization unit is established as a sort of clearing house and is charged with the task of collecting and organizing customer information, supplying it to other units of the firm, answering customer inquiries, and handling information releases initiated by the company.

Management of Pricing

Profits arise as a result of the difference between costs incurred and prices received. So it is not surprising that management takes an active interest in both; nor is it to be wondered at, since the final testing of the validity of all decisions occurs in the market, that the marketing manager is usually deeply involved in pricing decisions.

People too often regard price and cost as entirely independent factors. This is not true; each acts upon and is influenced by the other. By spending more in making its product, a firm may improve the article's quality and increase the price at which it can be sold. By offering his product at a lower price, a manager may increase the amount of it sold and thereby gain the advantages of volume production, which often manifest themselves in lower unit costs. This interaction marks out one area of pricing management.

The price a marketer can get for his product is determined by what prospective buyers will pay for it. The management of pricing therefore might seem to be quite simple—and it *would* be so if the marketer had a monopoly and could read the minds and emotions of prospective buyers. Neither of these things is usually true. Few firms possess monopoly power, and buyers as a group are not prone to reveal their market intentions to suppliers except when they express them through the act of purchase or refusal to do so. So the marketer must deal with a group of prospective customers of uncertain intentions while keeping a weather eye on competitors of whose plans he has little knowledge, except that they do not propose to be helpful. This outlines a second area of pricing management.

A lot has been written about the forces that determine prices. This, in fact, is the central theme of much of the body of economic theory. The theorist approaches the subject from the overall basis: the complex of forces that influence prices generally and over the long run. The marketing manager must deal with it specifically for his company, for his product at an instant point of time, in his market, and under the special conditions prevailing there at that time.

It seems sensible, therefore, for us to take two bites at the subject. First we will examine the background factors that affect pricing and will endeavor to determine how and to what extent the theories that have been developed about them can be useful to the marketing manager in his pricing work. Then, in a subsequent chapter, we will examine some of the specific problems that must be solved in managing the pricing activities of a firm, and the policies and practices that have been developed to help solve them.

CHAPTER 16

Pricing: Basic Factors

The student generally comes to the study of marketing with some background knowledge of economic theory. The latter subject is seriously concerned with prices in the process of exchange. Its major objective is that of developing a body of theory with respect to the price aspect of market behavior, a subject also of vital interest to those engaged in marketing practice.

RELATION BETWEEN ECONOMICS AND MARKETING

Both general economics and marketing, then, are primarily concerned with markets and the competitive efforts of businessmen to exploit them. The two approaches to the subject display several important points of contrast. Perhaps the most significant difference lies in the fact that economics, seeking general explanations of business activity, considers competition in a general way and without immediate regard to its implications with respect to any specific individual or set of individuals. Marketing, on the other hand, aims at the very practical objectives of aiding the businessman in meeting competition, or avoiding its more sinister effects. But although they represent very different points of view, the two ways of looking at markets are not necessarily in conflict with each other. The detailed information gathered by marketing men for strictly limited individual purposes can be used by the economist to enrich the body of data from which he draws his generalizations. On the other hand, the broad background of economic thinking may be of aid to the practicing specialist in marketing if he knows how to make use of it.

One purpose of this chapter is to show the marketing student how the method learned in his courses in general economics may be brought to bear upon his study of the more practical subject and upon the analysis of pricing problems. The first requirement for making effective use of economic analysis in the work of making pricing decisions is to realize that it cannot be applied in detail to each concrete marketing situation. In many purely theoretical phases of economics, such as the mathematical analysis of the laws of supply and demand, all the multitudinous, diverse, confusing, qualifying conditions, which are almost always a part of the episodes of actual business life, are excluded from consideration. Economic laws are meant to describe tendencies inherent in every market situation rather than to predict the outcome in each specific instance. At the very start, then, the marketing manager must forbear attempting to draw on his knowledge of economics and its techniques of analysis for a type of help they cannot possibly render.

The real value of a knowledge of economic thought to the manager is that it provides him a background for the analysis of actual situations. But an acquaintance with economic theory, however intimate or profound, cannot enable him to foresee or understand many of the details usually involved in a practical problem. So far as it goes, however, a knowledge of economics may be of use in identifying the really important elements that are common to practically all pricing situations, and the marketing man who makes intelligent use of the methodology and concepts of economics is often well on the way toward a satisfactory solution of his problems.

The accomplished chess player knows the proper sequence of moves that follow a particular opening. But after a certain point is reached in a game, he is thrown on his own resources, and he can never hope to win without using his own capacity for analysis and judgment. So it may be said that a background of economic thinking provides the marketing manager with a series of "opening gambits," but that when he reaches the stage of "end play," in which the game is won or lost, he has no choice but to rely on his own reasoning powers and soundness of judgment to reach a solution.

The essence of the service which the theoretical method of attack can render to the marketing manager lies in the fact that it aids him in his work of analysis by isolating the issues and suggesting the questions that must be asked. The answers to these questions must be found in a maze of marketing facts, many of which cannot be neatly fitted into the ordinary economic concepts. But the mere act of asking the right questions about supply and demand, mobility of capital, and other aspects of competition serves to indicate which items in the welter of fact are of real significance.

SUPPLY AND DEMAND

Economic theory, with respect to price, begins with a discussion of supply and demand and may be said to end with the price equilibrium existing between the two. Economic thinking from Ricardo to the present day has placed its chief emphasis upon supply as the most potent factor which controls pricing, along with other aspects of economic life. A basic principle that has been accepted in practically all such thinking is the varying effectiveness of different sources of supply, for example, the marked variation in the fertility of land. Thus economic analysis has from the first assumed that because of their great fertility some acres would be among the first to be used and the last to be removed from use, while other acres, at the margin of productivity, would be cultivated only in cases of unusual demand for the product. The cost of production of the marginal, or least efficient, producer has been assumed to be the final determinant of supply and hence of price.

Supply

But in considering supply in any actual situation the marketing manager must ask many questions of a much more detailed character. Do the additional units, which may be produced at the margin of efficiency, really show a decrease in quality or an increase in unavoidable or undeferrable cost per unit? Is the supply subject to marked, unforeseeable and uncontrollable variations, both in quantity and in quality, over a period of time, as in the case of some staple farm crops? Are there technical limitations, such as the lack of trained workers or "know-how" that will restrict production, even though the needed raw materials are abundant and the demand for the product is constantly growing? What effect is the availability of component parts—or the lack of them— likely to have on the supply of an assembled product? In the case of a highly fabricated product, what is the maximum output that can be expected from present capacity when the growth of the demand is outstripping the increase in capacity? Or if demand drops off, to what alternative uses can the equipment be put? What scale of production, in relation to capacity, would actually be most favorable for present equipment, as measured by the point of lowest unit costs? While these questions about supply naturally pertain primarly to production, they and many other questions of like nature usually must be answered before the manager of marketing can plan his distribution program.

Demand

Economists have never given demand the comprehensive analytical treatment they have devoted to supply. One key demand concept they have emphasized is the notion of diminishing utility: the idea that the satisfaction a consumer derives from any one unit of a product grows less and less as successive units are consumed or made available to him. Upon this tendency and upon the resultant theory of marginal utility the economist grounds most of his conclusions respecting demand. These theories are supplemented by the doctrine of the elasticity of demand, the idea that the amount of an article people will buy tends to vary inversely with its price. But the marketing man must go much farther than this in his analysis and seek to find out just which sections of the general population provide the active market for his product and what motives influence them to buy it.

Further than that, he must search for the answers to many questions. To what extent is the price at which I offer my product a major factor in limiting its sale? Just how and why does the individual consumer come to be a user of my commodity in the first place, and to what extent can my market be expanded by means of advertising and other channels of consumer influence? Is the type of satisfaction that the user derives from the article a relatively stable one, or will the desire for it presently pall, with the result that it will have to be changed merely for the sake of change? Is the commodity which I handle a vital part of the standard of living of those who use it, or does it belong in the class of articles which consumers can and do get along without—or defer buying—when disturbed economic conditions bring about uncertainty or a decrease in their purchasing power? If the product is a durable one and therefore constitutes a sort of reservoir of a given form of satisfaction, for how long can the period of use of any given unit be stretched beyond what is normal, and for how long can its replacement be postponed? To what extent is the demand for my commodity dependent upon fashion movements? What motives cause people to buy my merchandise and thus constitute the wellsprings from which flow its utility and its demand?

The marketing manager cannot be content, as the economist can, with merely explaining the mechanism by which supply and demand come into equilibrium. In attempting to bring a given lot of supply into the market and to effect its sale on profitable terms, he must answer all these questions and many more. During recent years marketing research has sought to answer many of these questions by the use of the techniques of psychological and mathematical analysis.

LIMITATIONS ON THEORETICAL CONCEPTS

Let us examine the nature of the competitive relationships that exist in the market and influence the marketing manager's efforts to attain his objective. One of the ends that competition serves, in the opinion of the typical economic theorist, is to maintain the level of business efficiency in terms of costs. He reasons that only the efficient competitor with low costs can survive the constant pressure of the unremitting struggle. Those with high costs are eliminated because they continually lose money on their operations. Those who endure must be constantly introducing new cost-reducing improvements in equipment or in managerial technique in order to continue to exist and to excel.

But in any actual field and in any given business situation the relations that really exist between cost efficiency and survival are usually exceedingly complicated, and sometimes in conflict. This is partly because of a lack of precision in the definition of efficiency. The economist often does not distinguish clearly between survival power and operating efficiency. The business which is most likely to outlast an industrial reverse is apt to be the one that is built for survival rather than for operating efficiency. The two are not necessarily coincident, since to achieve the latter often involves greater risk or greater rigidity than is compatible with safety.

Survival Efficiency

Efficient production, from a purely technical and cost standpoint, may call for the highest degree of specialization in productive equipment. For example, the most efficient spinning mill, from an operating standpoint, would probably be one that was designed to turn out a single count of yarn day in and day out. Every piece of equipment in the place would then be selected to fit the production of that single size of yarn, and would be automatically fed and controlled. The whole mill would be in balance from the standpoint of that narrow production objective, with just the right number of beaters and carders to prepare the needed cotton for the spinning process. But such a complex might prove disastrous if demand were to shift so that the given count of yarn was no longer needed or so that the factory could no longer operate at or near optimum capacity. The millowner who wishes to be on the safe side will build a certain amount of versatility into his plant so that it will be capable of making reasonable adjustments in production to meet changes in the character or amount of market demand, even at some sacrifice of technical efficiency.

The two principles were given a thorough and dramatic test many years ago in the automobile industry. The Ford plant was set up to achieve the maximum production efficiency on a single model, and its managers clung to that policy long after the nature of demand began to change. By contrast, the General Motors plan was to keep productive capacity sufficiently flexible so that it could be used to make a variety of models. Under the latter plan equipment could be changed gradually, in line with new technical developments and market trends. The Ford Company, sacrificing versatility for maximum cost efficiency, underwent a terrific strain when its standard model was finally acknowledged to be obsolete; and its plant had to be shut down for months to undergo complete retooling. Only the tremendous financial resources of the Ford family enabled it to survive.

Survival or growth demands that a relatively large portion of the assets of a company be kept in a liquid state so that they can readily be turned into cash in case of need generated by either new opportunities or changes in demand. Considerations of productive or profit-making efficiency frequently require that practically all of a company's total assets be kept at work in the specialized form of equipment or materials needed to produce and market its output. Many of the hazards the operators of highly specialized and efficient plants ordinarily assume are in the nature of bets against possible contingencies which could be completely provided against if management were willing to accept the lower earnings resulting from some idle capital, or the higher current expense of operating inefficiencies due to the use of less highly specialized equipment.

The marketing manager must consider the risks and the elements of efficiency in his field, and weigh the effect of each factor upon his survival ability and upon immediate and long-run prospects of growth and profits. He must recognize that the relation between efficiency and survival is not always clean-cut and must rid his mind of preconceived notions of what constitutes efficiency in his business.

Profits and Survival

The economist assumes that profits are the mainspring of business activity, but in practically every business there are competitors who make no profits, or only meagre profits, and who have little or no promise of more but who hang on like grim death to their precarious positions. Apparently many of these firms have other than profit reasons for staying in business. This fact must be considered most carefully by one who plans to enter a new field that is cluttered with many such apparently inefficient operators.

To develop a business at the expense of such rivals is liable to be an uphill job. The true reasons for their survival, the average age of firms now occupying the field, and the current rate of increase or decrease among them are factors that must be considered, as well as the basic character of the hold they have upon the market, which enables them to hang on. The progressive new enterpriser, with improved equipment and the most up-to-date, efficient management, may be put out of business by a group of competitors who run their businesses without profit and are constantly being eliminated by failure. Yet their number is somewhow renewed from year to year; they continually absorb a significant portion of the volume of business available and exercise a depressing influence on price.

Relative Immobility of Capital

A central assumption in economic theory is that of the mobility of capital. When funds can no longer be employed profitably in one field it is assumed that they will be transferred to another, where greater returns are possible. Thus capital is directed to the enterprises in which it is needed and forced out of those in which there is relatively less need for it. By this means, supposedly, capital is automatically apportioned to furnishing the satisfactions that are most desired by consumers and that set the objectives of production.

While there is much truth in this analysis, there are serious limitations upon its applicability to any specific situation or in any given field of economic activity. There are several considerations that may cause an enterpriser who is not making a profit to continue in his chosen field indefinitely rather than attempt to transfer his investment to another. A very large part of his capital is liable to be tied up in highly specialized equipment which cannot be used in any other line of production.

One hope of getting back his investment lies in the prospect of making an outright sale of his plant to someone else. But prospective purchasers are liable to be willing to pay only a price that is based on the plant's earning capacity, as revealed by an examination of the owner's operating records, and such a sale will probably yield only a fraction of the original investment to be transferred to other fields of enterprise. If the plant is sold on this basis it remains in the industry, with its capacity and equipment but with much lower fixed costs. All capital costs being much smaller (interest on money invested, insurance, and depreciation), owing to the lower base upon which they may now be computed, the plant as a competitive factor is even more dangerous than before.

Rather than take his losses all at one time, the owner of such an enterprise may prefer to hang on to the last, running the business at an actual, though not necessarily an apparent, loss. As long as its operation yields anything at all above current outlays, that yield may be set off against the fixed investment. Such a program of operating a plan at a loss as long as it hangs together and does not involve too much in the way of maintenance costs is, in effect, a slow process of turning into cash the original amount invested in it. A firm that is operating on this basis is likely to fix its prices without regard for costs other than the out-of-pocket type.

Nonprofit Motives for Capital Flow

Economic theory is based on the assumption that profit is the only motive causing capital to flow into or remain in an industry. Over the long run it is true that profit is the primary inducement for the creation and maintenance of production capacity, and thus of supply. But it is also true that once capital is invested in a business it tends to find non-profit reasons for staying there. Managerial inertia often has the effect of keeping a company in a business, or causing it to make and market certain products in a multi-product line on which profits are unsatisfactory or nonexistent.

Management's fear of the unknown tends to bring about the same result, because when capital is withdrawn from one product or project it must be invested in another; and the new item is apt to be one with which management is unfamiliar. The manager's pride may be involved. To withdraw from a business, or from making and vending a product, may be viewed as a confession of failure. A variation of this is the prestige that is supposed to attach to making and marketing a full line. All of these nonprofit motives may cause the supply of an article to change very slowly in response to shifts in demand and price and may minimize the influence of the marginal concept.

Role of Overhead Costs

The theorist's conclusions with respect to the influence of cost on price are further undermined by the fact that overhead expenses play a much more important and influential role in the cost behavior of the typical American firm than is generally assumed. Minute division of labor and automation in production, the organization of production and physical distribution on a process line basis, together with the inherent joint-cost nature of most marketing and many production activities cause much of the expense, even that of direct labor, to behave like overhead cost.

This brings the marketing manager and his chiefs in general management face to face with some difficult decisions, decisions that they often make in direct contradiction of the assumptions of economic theory. For example, when competition forces the price of one item in a firm's line down to the point of loss or unsatisfactory profit, theory assumes that the firm will withdraw from making and selling that item, thus reducing the supply of it. Sound management principles, however, dictate that the executives of the firm attempt to picture what the entire direct and overhead cost structure of the firm will be without the item, and that they attempt to compare that picture with the existing company cost structure rather than base the decision entirely on the relation between the product's price and the costs presently resulting from it and allocated to it. A firm may even find itself worse off without a losing product than with one because of the effect the reallocation of overhead costs (after its deletion) will have on the profitability of the remaining products.

The decision is also complicated by the principle of opportunity costs —the availability of profitable uses to which capital and facilities released by dropping the item can be put. The net result of all this is that the supply of many articles does not behave as the theory assumes it should in response to the relationship between cost and price.

Overhead costs also play a part in determining the position of so-called "garage" or "quonset hut" operators in many industries. In the chemical industry, for example, these are small concerns, usually with one-man management, which conduct their operations in small quarters (often *literally* quonset huts or reconditioned garages), and make products requiring no great amount of production know-how or capital investment in expensive equipment. They are often family affairs and have little or no overhead expense. They conduct no research, or very little, and make products developed and pioneered by larger concerns liberally endowed with overhead costs. They sell almost entirely on the basis of price.

There is little the large firm can do about them pricewise. If it cuts price to drive them out, legally it must extend its price reductions to all customers in the quonset hut operator's trading area. If it succeeds in liquidating one, another is likely to take his place. It also runs the risk of incurring suits under antitrust laws on the ground that it is trying to obtain or maintain a monopoly or to suppress competition. Most large concerns tend to accept this kind of competition as one of the facts of business life and make no attempt to meet its prices, knowing that if this kind of operator grows big enough to be more than a mere nuisance, he too will learn the meaning of the nasty word "overhead."

Static Nature of Demand Concept

The economist's concept of demand is essentially a static one. The typical demand and supply schedule he uses in constructing his theory looks something like this:

Number of Units That Would Be Bought at the Price	Price	Number of Units That Would Be Offered for Sale at the Price
1,000,000	$0.50	300,000
800,000	0.75	500,000
700,000	1.00	700,000
550,000	1.25	1,000,000
400,000	1.50	1,500,000

This is assumed to mean that if the price were $1.00, buyers would purchase 700,000 units, while if it were 75¢ they would buy 800,000. The assumption is that when price changes from $1.00 to 75¢ a unit, the amount demanded at any given price does not change. The demand for 800,000 units at 75¢ was there all the time. The price simply moves into a range that enables the larger demand to express itself in purchases.

This assumption fails to recognize that the mere fact that a shift in price occurs is likely to *change* this latent demand, and it makes no attempt to ascertain what would be the change in the number of units taken as a result of the fact that price *was changed* from $1.00 to 75¢ a unit. A price change does things to peoples' thoughts and feelings that may increase or decrease the 800,000 units set opposite the 75¢ figure in the economist's static demand schedule.

The mere fact of price change has an effect on buyers' thinking and emotional patterns, and causes them to be willing to buy sometimes more, sometimes less, at the new price than they thought they would before the price change occurred. Nor does a given price change in a given direction always produce an effect in the same direction or of the same force.

Demand is especially dynamic in response to price change in the trading in goods sold to mercantile houses for resale and to industrial buyers for use. When the price of a material falls, the industrial buyer at once wonders whether the drop is the first step in a general decline or merely a temporary dip. He will buy only what he absolutely must get, until he studies the matter further and decides which assumption is true. If he concludes that the price cut is the forerunner of a general decline, he will hold his purchases to the irreducible minimum, riding the decline down on a policy of hand-to-mouth buying. The same pattern of behavior tends to characterize the mercantile buyer. Together, these two types of buyers are responsible for about 60 percent of the total dollar volume of transactions of purchase and sale.

The marketing manager who is fortunate enough to be able to construct a demand schedule for his product must realize that a change in price is apt to cause a change in the demand figures on the schedule.

Effects of Product Line Marketing

In spinning his theory, the economist usually thinks in terms of a group of sellers each making and vending a single product to a group of buyers, each interested in purchasing a single article. This is not the way of the marketplace.

The typical marketer offers for sale a line of products or a product mix composed of a number of articles, ranging from two or three to thousands. While it is an ideal policy for such a marketer to price each item in his line so that it carries its own costs and returns its appropriate share of net profit, competitive forces almost always bear unequally on the several products and render this impossible. As a practical matter, the marketing manager is forced into the policy of developing and trying to maintain a pattern of prices for all the products in his mix which will pay the costs of, and return a satisfactory profit on, the entire operation, varying the prices of individual items to suit the exigencies of the competitive situation.

The result is that some items are usually priced below the satisfactory profit margin level, while others are sold well above that level. It would probably not be easy to find a firm with an extensive product mix which does not sell some items at prices that yield an unsatisfactory profit or none at all.

A natural question is, Why should they do this? Some firms do so because of a desire for the costly luxury of prestige, the reputation of "carrying a full line." A much sounder motive is that of preempting a customer's patronage so as to make it difficult for a competitor to get his head into the tent. For example, if the Smith Company does not sell Products X, Y and Z, which are "dogs" in the line, and its customer, the Jones Company, must buy them from the Brown Company, the Smith people are in due course liable to find that the Jones Company is also buying from the Brown people all or part of its necessary supply of Products A, B and C, long-profit items which the Smith Company *formerly* sold to the Jones Company. It might have been profitable for the Smith Company to have lost money on the dog items and to have kept the Brown people out of the Jones business in the first place.

This tendency toward product line or product mix marketing has the effect of nullifying much of the economist's theory of the influence of cost on price—or of rendering it so unrealistic that it has little practical value in making business decisions or in forecasting business events.

COMPETITION

Let us now examine competition, in its theoretical role, as an ideal basis of organization of economic activity which compels businessmen to work in the public interest. Many economists base their discussion of this phase upon a highly specialized (and fictionalized) definition of economic freedom or free competition. Competition, under these terms exists in a given field only if the market is altogether without restraint or control on the part of any supplier or organized group of suppliers. Many of the incidents of daily business routine may be regarded as limitations upon this concept of the term, or even as denials of it. The marketing manager usually depends upon a body of regular customers instead of selling today to one set of buyers and tomorrow to another, the members of both chosen at random. Thus the actual condition falls somewhat short of being one of free competition, which requires, according to the theory, that the pairing of buyers and sellers occur on a wholly random basis. But practically all actual business is conducted on the basis of a fixed routine of some sort, and routine demands that the list of customers of a firm should be of stable composition, changing but slowly. This usually works out in actual practice.

Theoretical Limitations: Monopoly

Theoretical economists have concerned themselves with a variety of limitations on free competition. The most frequently considered of these is monopoly. The word monopolist has the literal meaning of a single seller and, in this sense, refers to a market situation in which the sole supply of some wanted article is in the hands of a single selling unit. Under such conditions the seller can exact a higher price for his product than the buyer would be obliged to pay if there were other sources available. The power of the monopolist is limited only by the degree to which purchasers may be able to get along without his product or to find acceptable substitutes.

The price he will actually charge, however, is determined by considerations of his own profit. It will generally be fixed at a figure somewhat higher than that established under competition, but self-interest will restrain him from advancing it to a point where his volume of sales falls off to such an extent that the gain in margin from the higher price is more than offset by the loss of sales in physical units. There are very few products or services which lend themselves to the establishment of complete monopoly. The nearest approach to it is probably found in such utilities as light and power, vended by companies operating under exclusive franchises granted by states or municipalities, or a product on which a firm has an unassailable patent.

From the marketing viewpoint the matter of chief interest in the theory of monopoly is the recognition that the monopolist is free to pursue a conscious policy concerning price. A firm operating under free competition would, theoretically, have no alternative but to be guided wholly by the competitive price established by the uncontrolled interactions of buyers and sellers. But if any given concern seeks to exercise any degree of control over its own price policy, the most convenient point of departure in considering its possibilities of success is probably the theory of monopoly as taught by the economists, even though the firm in question is far from being free from competitive pressure.

Imperfect Competition

Conditions resembling monopoly exist when the bulk of the market is divided among only a few sellers: the "Big Three" or the "Big Four." Theoretically, the price is apt to be fixed somewhere *between* the competitive and monopoly levels. As a matter of fact, the fiercest competition often exists among a small number of large concerns that have preempted a given field. The very fact that the executives of a big firm feel they have obtained full control of a market, except for the presence of one or two important competitors, may cause the rivalry to be more embittered and particularized than it might be if its opponents remained numerous and hence largely unidentified. This situation has given rise to some of the outstanding instances of price wars and cutthroat competition. Price reductions made by one rival must be matched by another if it wishes to avoid loss of market position. This in turn provokes further cuts by the first, and so on, in a seemingly endless downward spiral, until the situation becomes intolerable to all.

The aptness of the adjective *imperfect* in this situation is emphasized when each of the limited number of competitors differentiates his output of the product by special features or brand names in an attempt to endow it in the buyer's mind with an identity that sets it apart as a separate product. Economists have developed a "theory of imperfect competition" to describe what the behavior of price will be under these circumstances.

This theory continues to assume the primacy of price as a basis of competition, even though a chief objective of differentiation is to shift competitive emphasis from price to other factors. It also assumes that all competitors entertain the common dominating objective of maximizing profits. This assumption may be sound in the long run, but at the time of any particular pricing decision one or more competitors may be putting primary emphasis on other goals.

In such a market the probable reaction of individual leading competitors is a vital consideration in the making of any pricing decision. Under such conditions pricing becomes much like a poker game, or an exercise in military strategy. It often pays off to react to a rival's move in a way contrary to that prescribed in the theory because the competitor will not be expecting it. Robert E. Lee won most of his victories by violating the accepted military theory that the commander of an inferior force should never divide that force in the presence of an enemy. It may be good *long-run* policy to behave according to the theory, but it may also be necessary to make specific decisions in violation of it in order to stay alive and strong enough to capitalize on the theory and to reap its long-run benefits. Shrewd judgment of the probable reaction of a dangerous competitor to a pricing move is apt to be more important in pricing decisions than knowledge of the general theory of price behavior.

The marketing manager will find it profitable to study these theories since they may conceivably suggest pricing methods that will prove sounder in the long run than those currently in use in his trade. But prudence dictates that he avoid diverging too suddenly or too sharply from established practices, since there is probably a practical logic behind them based on long experience.

Monopoly in Buying

The firm that is the sole or most significant buyer of a product or service constitutes another limitation on competition. We need not labor to develop artificial or farfetched illustrations of this condition. The relations existing between large department stores, chain store systems, mail order houses or buying syndicates and the small manufacturers who are in the business of supplying them furnish ready-made examples. Although such suppliers are able to reduce their costs materially by having assured markets for their output, thus stabilizing production and avoiding selling expenses, they cannot ordinarily apply these savings entirely to increasing their profits because the powerful buyer is usually in a position to force the acceptance of his price.

Nor does the stability of operations, which provides another motive for giving up the chance for greater profits in the open market, always prove dependable. The buyer may find more satisfactory sources of supply, or for other reasons may cease to take the output of the small producer who has built his entire business to fit the needs of such a closed market. The fear that his business may be wrecked by the loss of one customer causes many a small manufacturer to look askance upon the opportunity to find a mass outlet in the purchases of a single large customer. He endeavors instead to build his business upon orders from smaller and more numerous buyers. These are policy decisions that marketing managers must make under actual conditions, in the making of which the analysis must be carried far beyond the unrealistic treatment of competition offered by the theoreticians.

Price Leadership

A situation known as price leadership is characteristic of several major fields of enterprise. The price leader is the large firm that exercises such influence upon its smaller rivals that, in effect, it sets the prices of its own and competitive products, even though it does not control the entire output. The small firm stays in line probably because of fear of reprisals should it break the price, and because it secures enough volume at the established figure to give it a satisfactory profit on its operations. Leadership entails risks and responsibilities as well as opportunities since, in maintaining prices and standards of competition, the dominant concern makes it easier for potential rivals to gain a foothold in the field and to claim growing shares of the market.

No small part of the cost of price leadership arises from the fact that the leader must be prepared to enforce his leadership by winning price wars against any competitor who challenges him. This requires low production costs and a deep war chest. In general, the price leader, once he establishes himself in that position, suffers a gradual decrease in importance in terms of the percentage of the total volume of sales that he is able to retain for himself.[1]

Price Discrimination

The seller who enjoys some degree of monopoly advantage is in an unusually good position to practice price discrimination. It is generally assumed that he will charge all the traffic will bear. Price discrimina-

---

[1] During much of its history United States Steel Corporation has occupied the position of a price leader. Throughout most of that time its percentage of total volume has declined. A condition of *sectional* price leadership exists in the oil and the commercial fertilizer industries.

tion introduces a refinement of the traditional theory of monopoly under which he charges different prices to different customers or groups of customers, in each case collecting all that buyers in that segment of the market can be made to pay. Unless this practice can be kept wholly secret, it ordinarily involves grave hazards, for customers who have been discriminated against are liable to offer stubborn resistance to all efforts to sell them the same merchandise again—or they are liable to seek some even more effective way to retaliate against the seller who has been guilty of the practice.

In past years independent retailers and wholesalers in many lines of business attributed a large part of their difficulties to the fact that some of their competitors, notably chain store systems, were presumably favored by price discriminations on the part of the manufacturers who also sold to the independents. This feeling undoubtedly furnished much of the drive necessary to place the Robinson-Patman Act on the statute books, which is an effort to curb such favoritism. When a company markets substantially the same product to two or more noncompeting industries; for example, an antibiotic to the drug trade as a human medication and to the animal feed trade as a growth-stimulating additive, price discrimination can be and is commonly practiced.

Basis of Competition

The economist generally assumes that the primary focus of competition is upon price. This is not always true. To the buyers of many kinds of goods the first consideration is quality or, more exactly, suitability. A woman buying a dress or a hat or a pair of shoes looks first for an item of apparel that fits her idea of what she wants in the way of an ensemble. If the price is too high, she compromises her notion of what she would like to have with what she feels she can afford to pay so as to arrive at the most satisfactory combination of price and suitability.

The industrial buyer's first requirement is almost always suitability for the purpose for which the purchase is being made. Firms making highly technical products, or articles in the use of which safety is a primary factor, often buy on the premise that quality or precise suitability is the only factor that should influence their choice and that "price is no object." The wise industrial buyer turns a deaf ear to price appeals until assured that the product is suitable for his purpose.

The mercantile buyer is primarily interested in getting goods that he can resell to his customers. To him resalability equals suitability. He habitually seeks to answer three questions about a piece of merchandise: (1) Will my customers buy it? (2) If so, what price can I get them to pay? (3) Is the difference between what I can sell it for and what I must pay for it enough to cover my expense margin and expected profit?

A second basis of competition, other than price, is service. This may mean a variety of things in addition to the usual ingredients of delivery and credit. It may involve technical advice and help, maintenance and repair, help in planning facilities or equipment, cooperation in research programs or use-test projects, help in handling emergency needs, and a variety of other things. In the industrial and mercantile fields and in certain areas of the consumers' goods market, such as cars or TV sets, service is (within limits) more important than price. Merchandise or materials at any price are of little or no good to the mercantile or industrial buyer if not delivered when needed, or if not suitable when delivered.

A third nonprice basis of competition is personal relationship. In the retail trade this factor is often much more important than price. Innumerable cases could be cited of retail stores whose volume of sales changed by a third or a half as a result of a change of owner-manager or a shift in managers with no change in merchandise, service, or pricing policy. This factor is less important in the industrial and wholesale trades, but the confidence engendered by personal relationship exercises a powerful although sometimes unrecognized influence on the patronage of mercantile and industrial buyers. Every sales manager can tell stories of orders lost because of wrong selling contacts, or of contracts won because of personal confidence or friendship.

One very capable industrial purchasing officer, when asked what was the most important factor that influenced his patronage of a supplier, replied "Confidence." His appraisal is not unique. To the buyer, the integrity and reliability of the salesman reflects the integrity and reliability of the firm he represents. Often the salesman's character and personality speak louder than his price book.

By these observations we do not mean to indicate that price is not an important basis of competition. Even after all our subtractions it remains a vital factor. These limitations are outlined merely to warn against too great reliance in managerial thinking on the overemphasis which the theoretical economist accords price as a basis of competition. Price is an important member of a *family* of bases; it is not *the* basis.

In summary it may be said that while economic theory provides an opening approach to the study of competition, the marketing manager needs to consider the whole question in terms of the individual enterprise he is attempting to guide, in adjusting itself to competition, and in making the most of its opportunities in doing so. But in making this approach it is not sufficient to consider the matter *solely* on the basis of the theory of monopoly or of completely free competition. There are many other phases of the process of adjusting the individual establishment to competition besides that of price manipulation.

Furthermore, the questions which confront the manager in the field of price policy alone are commonly far more complicated than that of merely determining what the traffic will bear in terms of the usual theories of price.

CHAPTER 17

Pricing: Policy and Practice

Pricing is one of the most important and difficult areas of managerial decision. We might expect, therefore, that pricing decisions would be reserved to top management. This is almost always true in the small firm, but as a concern grows larger and its product mix expands and becomes more varied, the chief executive is apt to find that if he retains all pricing decisions in his own hands he lacks time to make them properly and still handle all the other matters demanding his attention. In spite of this, some top managers of fairly large business concerns continue to make practically all pricing decisions personally. Others delegate this work, or most of it, usually to the marketing executives, and take little or no part in it.

Probably both these courses of action are wrong. While each pricing decision is a distinct problem set in conditions different from every other, and so must be handled on its own merits, certain general principles apply to all pricing problems. This means that pricing is an activity that usually can be managed, to some extent, by policy.

In a company of any size it is the task of top management to set up policies with respect to pricing and to delegate to subordinates the work of carrying them out in specific instances. The chief executive of such a firm should probably take part personally in making only the more important specific pricing decisions which affect significant parts of the total annual volume of sales.

The establishment of pricing policies tends to remove the setting of prices from the area of "management by emergency"—where it is otherwise almost bound to be, since competitive action tends to create crises that must be handled quickly if offsetting reaction is to be effective. Such emergency decision is liable to be especially disastrous in the area of price management because pricing situations are usually highly complicated and obscure, and because mistakes are apt to be costly. The establishment of pricing policy enables management to devote careful thought to the kind and extent of reaction that is for the best interest of the company under each of a series of situation patterns. The result is likely to be that most of the pricing decisions of the firm are made on the basis of careful reasoning and deliberate judgment, which would otherwise not be the case.

In actual practice, who really manages the pricing work of the average firm?

Most companies apparently rely on the chief marketing executive to study prices constantly and to keep abreast of all conditions affecting pricing policy and action. Some firms place this responsibility upon the executive vice president or general manager.

Somewhat under half of all concerns apparently place the determination of price-cost relationships in the hands of the marketing manager. About half of them put this responsibility on the executive vice president. A few assign it to a committee.

The pricing officer most often reports to the chief executive of the company. Somewhat less frequently he reports to the director of marketing. In a few firms he is responsible to a committee. The person to whom the pricing officer reports is likely to be the man who really makes the pricing decisions because in all probability he must approve them before they are put into effect.[1]

HOW ARE PRICES DETERMINED?

While each pricing situation presents a separate and distinct problem to be solved in its own setting, the fact that pricing decisions must be made constantly causes the average firm to develop a pattern to be followed in making them, even though the pricing officer may not realize that he follows any set routine. Such patterns fall into several types.

1. *Formula.* Most pricing decisions are made with the use of a formula. The formula employed most commonly is cost plus a set figure, or a set percentage on cost or selling price. Most retail and wholesale prices are set in this manner. For example, if an article costs $1.00 a unit and a 33—⅓ percent gross profit is desired, its selling price will be fixed at $1.50. Or it may be the practice of the merchant to charge 50¢ a unit for handling the article, in which case the selling price also will be $1.50.

The percentage method is probably used more generally. By the use of a conversion table any desired gross profit or margin percentage on

---

[1] *Current Pricing Practice,* Dartnell Corporation, Chicago, 1957.

selling price may be translated into a percentage on cost. Sometimes it is referred to as markup or markon. Thus, 33–⅓ percent on selling price equals 50 percent on cost, and 25 percent on selling price is 33–⅓ percent on cost.

In his pricing work the manufacturer is likely to start with factory cost. He knows, for example, that his marketing costs and general and administrative costs are a certain average percentage of sales, say 15 percent, and he wants to make a profit of 10 percent on sales. His pricing formula is

$$\text{Factory Cost divided by (100 minus 25) times 100}$$

Formula pricing is simple and easy and lends an air of precision to the operation. Its chief difficulty lies in the fact that the buyer knows nothing and cares less about the formula. He is interested only in what he has to pay for what he gets, and if he thinks the formula price is too much its beautiful precision exerts no influence on him to buy.

A formula may be used as the basis for pricing practice, but the formula, or the result of its application, may be modified in the light of competitive conditions. Thus a retailer may work on the basis of a system of markups on cost, for example, 25, 33–⅓, and 50 percent; the one he applies in a specific situation depending on the nature of the product, the difficulty of selling it, its rate of stock turnover, and the way competitors are pricing it. A manufacturer may start with factory cost and add a percentage markup; then he modifies the resulting figure in the light of competitive conditions and his estimate of the probable reactions of buyers to it.

2. *Competitors' Prices.* Some firms set their prices entirely or chiefly on the basis of competitors' pricing action. Such a concern may follow a policy of always meeting competing prices exactly, or of pricing a fixed percentage below any reputable rival—like Macy's in New York—or of setting its prices above those of competition and depending on factors such as service, convenience, or prestige to attract volume.

3. *Hunch.* Some firms price by hunch. One who has been long in a business develops a "feel" for the right price for an article. This is especially true in the retailing business, where the store operator is in constant close touch with his trade.

4. *Trial and Error.* This is probably the oldest method of pricing and is involved to some degree in all the others. No matter what method a pricer may use, he may be wrong in the figure he sets. When this happens the best he can do is to try again. When his mistake is in the upward direction, it is not too difficult to rectify. But when his

initial figure is too low, he often cannot increase it without alienating customer loyalty and opening the door to competitive inroads on his volume.

5. *Scientific Methods.* The chief methods in this category are marketing research and test marketing, described elsewhere in this chapter.

ESTIMATING THE EFFECTS OF PRICE ON SALES VOLUME

Several methods have been used to estimate the effect of different prices on the physical volume of a product that will be sold.[2] None of them is entirely reliable, but the proper one, applied under the right conditions, offers a much better basis for pricing than pure guess.

1. *Value Analysis.* This method is generally useful only in pricing industrial goods. Value analysis involves an attempt to compute the dollar value of the benefit the industrial buyer will enjoy from using the product. This benefit may appear in the form of a reduction in the cost of the customer's end product or as an increase in its salability. The dollar value of the benefit afforded by an industrial product fixes the maximum premium that can be charged for it over the price of the best competing industrial materials or equipment.

2. *Test Marketing.* A seller may test the effect of different prices on sales volume by trying them out in a series of test markets selected so as to be as nearly comparable as possible. These tests should be conducted under carefully controlled conditions so that the chief volume-influencing factors, other than price, are as nearly equal as possible in all the test areas. A different price is set in each area and area sales volumes are carefully observed. Great skill is needed in planning and conducting test marketing operations and in interpreting their results. It is never possible to hold constant all volume-influencing factors other than price; the unskilled or careless observer is likely to draw conclusions not justified by the results. Price test-marketing is not a game for amateurs.

3. *Historical Analogy.* Sometimes a new product closely resembles an old one in its marketing characteristics. If the price and volume behavior of the old product are known, valuable conclusions can often be drawn as to how to price the new one. The method may also be applied to products already in the line. The probable volume response to a proposed price change can sometimes be forecast from the past volume behavior of the same article or other articles after past price changes of like magnitude and direction.

---

[2] This discussion follows Joel Dean's "Pricing from the Seller's Standpoint" (privately mimeographed, 1949).

This method also must be used with great care since conditions other than price are never the same now as they were when the past price changes were made. Careful analysis may serve to isolate the chief nonprice factors that affect volume and disclose the degree and probable effects of shifts that have occurred in them.

4. *Field Research.* The techniques of marketing research can sometimes be applied to the problem of forecasting the effects of contemplated prices or price changes on sales volume. This involves asking possible users what their reactions will be to such prices or price changes. This may be done by personal interview or, less effectively, by mail questionnaire. For example, consumers may be asked how much extra they would be willing to pay for an additional feature in a mechanical product, such as an automobile; or they may be queried as to how much they would be willing to pay for a new product; or how a shift in the price of an existing product would affect the amount of it they would buy.

This method may work well in some cases. Its use is subject to serious hazards, however. What a person says he will do in a hypothetical situation often bears little resemblance to what he actually does when the situation arises.

5. *Executive Judgment.* The judgment of a seasoned executive as to the volume effect of pricing decisions may produce estimates fully as realistic, sometimes more so, than the use of more refined methods. An able man of long experience may develop a feel as to what is the right price in a situation.

But before an executive relies too heavily on this sense or feel, he should examine his record of pricing decisions carefully and make sure that his batting average really is satisfactory. Memory alone is not enough in this analysis. A man tends to remember his successes and forget or discount his failures, and unless he makes a systematic examination of his performance from the record he is apt to entertain somewhat inaccurate notions about its excellence.

TYPES OF PRICING SITUATIONS

The need for making pricing decisions arises usually from one of three situations. When a firm puts a new product on the market a price must be set for it. When a competitor changes his price, the decision must be made to sit tight or to follow suit, and, if the latter, how far to follow. A firm may itself initiate a price change as a matter of strategy or as a result of shifts in cost, unsatisfactory volume, inadequate profit results, an overstock, or some other adjustment of intra-firm conditions or policy. Perhaps our discussion will be easier to follow if we center it around each of these situations in turn.

Pricing a New Product

When a firm puts a new product on the market its managers usually face a very difficult job of balancing quality, cost, and price so as to arrive at the most profitable combination. In the sense in which we use it here quality means those characteristics that make a product attractive to customers and increase its salability. The addition of such characteristics to a commodity generally increases its cost. Thus, as a product is made more salable its cost tends to go up, and its price will be higher or its gross profit must shrink. Up to a certain point the cost of a product usually falls as sales volume and along with it volume of production increases. The pricing executive must work out the compromise of these three factors that will achieve the optimum result for his firm.

In most cases the best combination for the short run is the one that will bring into the company treasury the largest number of gross profit dollars during the early stages of the product's market life. By the time a firm gets ready to put a new product on the market it usually has a considerable investment in it. It has spent money in researching and developing the product; additional sums may have been spent in use tests, market research, and perhaps in test marketing operations; new equipment may have been bought or existing machinery modified in preparation for its production; stocks of the commodity have been produced and money has been spent in getting them into the hands of distributors and dealers.

Before the new product is put on the market, heavy expenditures for advertising and selling it have probably been made. These will be continued and perhaps increased during the early stages of its market life. It often takes a year, sometimes three to five years, of expensive marketing effort before a product reaches its maximum sales volume.

All this may represent a considerable drain on a firm's finances. In the short run, therefore, management's first objective might logically be to get back its "seed corn and fertilizer"—to recapture its investment. This must come out of the gross profit, the difference between selling price and factory cost of the product. This is why the quality-cost-price combination that brings in the largest number of gross profit dollars during the early stages of a product's market life is often the one that is to the best short-run interest of the firm.

The methods already suggested for judging the effect of price on volume may be helpful in determining this combination also. Since three factors are involved, each partly independent and partly dependent on one or more of the others, mathematical techniques may be helpful.

A firm may be in a position to ignore short-run considerations and act entirely on the basis of its optimum long-run interest. It can then plan to recapture its capital investment more slowly and make its pricing decisions with the idea of assuring the greatest long-run profit during the entire market life of the product. This is a much more complicated problem than pricing to achieve the short-run objective, and one that throws much greater emphasis on managerial know-how and experience. It also emphasizes the marketing strategy elements in the situation.

Whether long-run or short-run objectives should dominate in pricing a new product depends largely on three factors: the expected life of the product, the financial position of the firm, and the degree of market protection it may expect its product to enjoy. If the expected life of a new product is short its innovator must get into the market fast, "clean up," and get out in a hurry. This means that he must price to get the largest possible number of gross profit dollars within the short life of the product. If a company's funds are limited, it must work toward the short-run objective of getting its investment back as fast as possible. If it is well financed, it can follow a longer-range strategy.

The matter of market protection is rather complicated and deserves careful attention. A product may gain market protection through a valid patent, a successful campaign of product differentiation, or through the possession of production or marketing know-how, the lack of which excludes or handicaps competitors. Regardless of the presence or absence of these, a firm may usually expect that during the early stages of a product's life, from a few months to as much as two years, it will enjoy a degree of market protection approaching temporary monopoly. This is because in most industries a considerable period of time must elapse after a new product makes its market debut while competitors appraise its possibilities, decide whether to duplicate it or to put out one similar to it, and do the research and development work involved in getting a rival product on the market before it suffers real competition.

A patent gives its holder a degree of monopoly ranging from practically complete, if there is no acceptable substitute commodity, to merely a more than ordinarily effective product differentiation if there are substitute commodities, or if the patent is not basic but covers only a modification or special feature of the article. In many industries the holder of a patent is faced with the decision as to whether he shall license others to use it on a royalty basis, thus inviting competition, or refuse to license and retain its privileges for himself. If he does the former he may practically, although not by contract, control the prices at which licensed competitors sell, but he cannot control the prices at which their distributors or dealers vend the product.

If the holder of a patent is well financed, he is probably wise to price the product with the long-run objective of getting the largest net dollar return during the life of the product—with due regard to the unfavorable effects too high a price will have on public relations and to the fact that an unusually large profit will stimulate competitor research to discover a way to circumvent the patent or to develop a substitute product that is more salable. The techniques that have been developed for attacking the measurable elements of this problem have been suggested. In the final analysis, though, the fixing of a price on such a product leans heavily on executive analysis and appraisal of the intangibles.

When a firm brings out a new product on which it can expect market protection only during the limited period required for competitors to study it, appraise its possibilities, and prepare to make it and sell it, the innovator has a difficult problem to solve. Shall he price it at all the traffic will bear during the period of market protection, and try to get back his investment and as much profit as possible before competition develops? Or shall he price it at a figure somewhere near where its price may be expected to settle when competition becomes active?

The first policy, a "skimming price," invites competitors to enter the field, but if the innovator succeeds in accomplishing his initial objective of recapturing his investment, it puts him in a strong position costwise because he can regard his capital overhead costs as practically nonexistent when competition becomes active. This policy may also have the effect of alienating customers who may feel that they were overcharged during the initial stages.

The manager who follows this policy and prices his product very high during its stage of market protection must decide when to cut his price, and by how much. The ideal time to cut is when his most aggressive competitor is just about to decide whether to invade the field. The ideal cut at this point, or for that matter at any other point, is probably one substantial enough to warn the competitor that he faces a real struggle in any proposed invasion. Market information is not always sufficient to make this possible, and to do it requires considerable managerial courage.

While the second policy, "penetration pricing," tends to discourage the entry of competition, it delays the payback of initial investment, defers the beginning of profit enjoyment, and may leave the innovator saddled with considerable capital overhead when competition develops. Moreover, if a new product is really good it is very doubtful if any sort of price manipulation will seriously discourage competitors from making and selling it. On the other hand, this policy enables the originator of a new product, before competitors start to handle it, to establish a market position from which it may be hard to dislodge him.

Some of the factors that are influential in guiding the choice between these two policies are as follows. If the new product is one for which there seems likely to be an immediate demand, or which seems likely to be short-lived, or to become highly competitive quickly, or one that has heavy development costs, the policy of a high initial price seems to be indicated. If the product holds promise of a long life or of attracting only mild competition, or enjoys valid patent protection, a lower price policy may be more desirable.

When a new commodity is of such a nature that its sponsor may expect to be able to build a measure of market protection by product differentiation, through branding and other promotional devices, his problem of pricing policy is of a somewhat different nature than either of those described. It might be expected that price would be a useful tool in achieving such differentiation. Strangely enough, a high price is often more useful than a low one for this purpose. If the promotional appeal rests on high quality or distinctiveness, a noticeably high price fits in with and supports the general impression the promotion is designed to create.

If, on the other hand, the product is intended for wide sale in the general market, price manipulation is apt to be much less useful. In such a case an unexpectedly low initial price, even at the expense of gross and net profit, may be highly effective in capturing consumer acceptance and loyalty. But it may also have precisely the opposite effect through raising doubts in the consumer's mind as to the quality of the product. Moreover, once a price is established in the market it is harder to raise than to lower it. The most effective policy is usually to set the price that is expected to prevail in the long run, after the new product is in quantity production, and to offer various kinds of special deals and inducements that are generally understood to be temporary in nature.

Figure 17–1 shows the kinds of information one company seeks to obtain and analyze in setting the price for a new product.

FIGURE 17-1

FACTORS TO BE CONSIDERED IN PRICING NEW INDUSTRIAL PRODUCTS

THE PRODUCT:

1. How much of the product are we prepared to produce?
2. What is the maximum price at which we can sell this amount?
3. What is the probable life of the product?
4. What is the projection of cost, volume, and price across this probable life span?
5. What are the product advantages and disadvantages that must be considered in making price comparisons?
6. Do we have product or process patents, or does our patent situation put us in a strong defensive position, or are we likely to be able to secure a strong position in the future?
7. How much will the cost of goods sold vary with volume of sales and hence of production?
8. How much will the costs of selling and distribution vary because of varying price levels?
9. What are the incremental costs of the product?
10. How much will dollar sales vary with changes in price?

COMPETITION:

1. What are the competitive or industry factors that affect our ability to sell at the price that will bring the maximum gross and net profit?
2. How much will it cost competition to get into production?
3. How long will it take competition to get into production?
4. What are the customary pricing practices of competitors in selling to the trade channels to be served in marketing the product?
5. What are the prices of existing products that are comparable or closely related to the new product in use?
6. If the product is a substitute for an existing product of a competitor:
   a) How much of our new product must customers use to replace the competitor's old one?
   b) What price on our new product will have the same effect as the price of competitor's existing product on the cost structure of the customer's end product?
   c) What is the competitor's probable cost on his existing product?
   d) How important is the competitor's existing product in his volume and profit structure?
   e) What is the competitor's pricing policy? Is this policy that of the firm or of a dominating personality in it?

CUSTOMER CONSIDERATIONS:

1. If the product is a substitute for an existing product of ours:
   a) How much of the new product must customers use to replace the old one?

    b) How much must the price be to bring in the same or greater gross or net profit than the old one?

    c) Will the use of the new material make the customer's end product more or less valuable to its buyers, and how much?

    d) What will be the effect of a price on the new product on the cost structure of the customer's end product?

2. How important will the price of the new product be in the cost structure of the customer's end product?

3. How much does this importance vary among the several types of customers and end products?

4. What will be the effect of the price on our relations with important customers?

5. How does the proposed price fit in with the other elements of the marketing plan for the new product?

When a Competitor Initiates a Price Change

When a competitor changes his price how should we go about deciding what to do about it? If the change is a reduction, the need for fast decision and action is usually more urgent than when it involves an increase in a competitor's price. Failure to adjust to the latter is likely to mean, at the most, merely the sacrifice of additional profits. If the rival's action is not well founded, inaction on our part may mean the protection of our existing market position and profits, or their enhancement. On the other hand, delay or failure to act in response to a competitor's price reduction may endanger both our market and profit positions.

The first step in deciding what to do in response to a rival's price change is to try to determine why he made it. This should tell us whether it is likely to be a short-run or a continued shift. He may be seeking to dispose of an overstock, distress merchandise, or goods not well suited to the market, or he may need ready cash and be trying to squeeze it out of inventory. On the other hand, his action may be a harbinger of a general market decline or he may be out to increase his share of the market. If the latter is his intent, we probably will not wish to be a complacent contributor to his plan.

We must decide whether the product whose price is cut is one on which we are compelled to be price competitive. This is apt to depend on such factors as the following:

How important a segment does it represent in our total volume and profit structure?

How price conscious is the trade with respect to the product?

Is the product regarded as an important or an incidental element in the total competitive picture? If customers regard it as highly important, we are liable to lose standing in the trade if we allow ourselves to be long under-priced. This customer attitude is also likely to mean that patronage will shift quickly in response to price change and that delay on our part will cost us heavily in sales volume.

We must analyze the relation of the price-cut product to other com-modities in our line. If important customers buy it in conjunction with other profitable products in our mix, and its price constitutes an impor-tant element in their total purchases, we run the chance of losing their patronage on these other products if we fail to act promptly to meet the price reduction.

And what is the cost behavior pattern of the price-cut product? If we fail to meet the cut and lose physical volume, will the ensuing cut in production increase its unit cost materially and further damage our competitive position? If this is the case, speedy decision is necessary and we are practically compelled to meet the cut.

If we act in response to a competitor's price cut, should we meet it only partially, meet it exactly, or undercut it? If our product has features that render it more attractive to customers than our rival's, we may be safe in ignoring the reduction or meeting it only partially. In general, though, it is desirable to go all the way. If we view the competitor's action as an invitation to a price war and are willing to accept his challenge, we will undercut his price sharply. It may be good policy to develop an understanding in the trade that when we accept the challenge of a price cut, we mean business and will consistently under-price all the way down. Such a policy may be costly in specific instances, but it is apt to discourage irresponsible price reductions.

When We Initiate a Price Change

What are the reasons that may cause a firm to initiate a price change? Such action may be triggered by a variety of motives, ranging from those that are purely logical to some that are quite emotional. Space will not permit us to discuss them all, so we will limit ourselves to pointing out those that are most common.

1. *Cost Changes.* A change in the cost of a product should lead to an examination of its price. A shift in cost sets up an entirely new pat-tern of relationship between price, cost, physical volume, and gross profit dollars brought in. If cost increases, management has to decide whether an offsetting rise in price will reduce physical volume, and if so whether the shrunken physical volume, multiplied by the existing gross profit per unit, will be larger or smaller than the existing physical

volume, multiplied by the shrunken gross profit per unit, if price remains unchanged. If cost declines, management must determine whether the greatest number of gross profit dollars is to be gained by holding price constant and taking a larger gross profit per unit on the present physical volume, or by reducing price to offset the shift in cost, thereby realizing the same gross profit per unit on the higher volume likely to result from the reduced price.

Then, too, the managers of the firm must consider whether the factors that caused the shift in their cost are also operative on those of their competitors, and if so what their rivals will do about it. Mathematical analysis and the theory of games may sometimes be useful in making such estimates.

We may occasionally initiate a price change, usually a reduction, in order to increase our sales of a product and thus the amount of it we make. We thereby reduce our cost of production or enjoy a discount for quantity purchasing. This will work only if our competitors are not in a position to follow suit, and if our price reduction will bring about an increase in the total amount bought sufficient to entitle us to the discount, or to enable us to make the expected reduction in production cost.

2. *Change in Market Position.* A firm may lose market position for a number of reasons; among them are mistakes in marketing policy, an unusually attractive or effective promotional program of a competitor, or a shift in consumer preferences. Its management may become dissatisfied with its market share and decide to try to increase it. Or management may decide to use price as an instrument of strategy to remedy its unfavorable position, or to achieve its objective of market expansion.

3. *A Change in Business Conditions.* When business conditions shift it is sometimes good policy to lower price in an attempt to escape the worst results of recession, or to raise it to enhance the benefits of a period of prosperity. Price changes are an almost inevitable feature of shifting business conditions.

4. *Change in Competing Product.* If our rival succeeds in improving his product and we can find no way to better ours, we find ourselves at a competitive disadvantage. We may turn to price reductions as a weapon with which to equalize our positions in the market. We will probably be wise to look upon this as a holding action, to gain time to find ways to improve our own product, rather than as a policy of long-run effectiveness.

5. *Temporary Conditions.* A number of temporary situations may

cause a firm to initiate a change in price, usually a reduction. A mercantile house may have bought more of an article than its market will absorb at the usual price, or a manufacturer may have overproduced. A wholesaler or retailer may have bought or a manufacturer may have made a stock of a product that is not readily salable. A firm may be caught short of cash but with a stock of salable merchandise on its shelves or in its warehouse. In any of these cases, a temporary cut in price may prove an effective remedy.

6. *Promotional Strategy.* Mercantile firms, especially retailers, customarily use price as a weapon of promotional strategy. A temporary cut in price is apt to be tied into an advertising or point-of-sale promotional campaign. The idea behind such a campaign is apt to be to use the advertised price as an inducement to attract customers into the store with the notion that either they will buy other products, the prices of which have not been cut, or that they can be turned into regular patrons of the store. A manufacturer may use the same device, working through his retail dealers. Here the price cut is apt to take the form of some sort of special deal.

7. *Personal Reasons.* A wide variety of personal factors are influential in triggering price changes. These are most common in the retail trade, although even executives of manufacturing firms have emotions and sometimes allow them to erupt in their pricing decisions. Needless to say, such decisions are not always consistent with the accepted canons of proper pricing policy.

When the management of a firm contemplates initiating a change in its price, it should do several things.

First, it should seek the answer to the question, Is price such a major factor in influencing patronage or consumption that an increase or a reduction in it will cause a considerable shift in the physical volume of sales? Sometimes the conditions are such that a price change will bring about very little change in the amount bought.

For example, some years ago a firm making and selling prescription chemicals to wholesalers found that it was losing money on the business. It increased the prices at which it sold them. Its management was pleasantly surprised to find that wholesalers welcomed the change and retailers did not object to it. The wholesalers had also been losing money on the business and found that by applying their regular markon percentage to a higher base they got enough gross profit dollars to enable them to enjoy a net profit. The retail druggists did not object because the cost of materials constituted so small a part of the prices they charged for the prescriptions they compounded that the change made no significant difference in their profits. Many of them also applied their regular markons to the higher base and actually were better off after the change than before.

On the other hand, a reduction in the price of an industrial good often has little effect on the amount bought since its demand depends on the demand for the end product it is used to make. So unless its price is an important enough element in the cost of the end product to make possible a significant cut in the price of the end product, and induce an increase in its volume, a reduction in the price of the material has little effect on the amount of it sold. If the price of the material constitutes an insignificant portion of the cost of the end product, and the material is bought as a part of a package transaction involving several other materials, a change in its price, unless very drastic, is apt to cause no serious shift in patronage.

Second, before a management initiates a price change it must consider what the reaction of its competitors is likely to be. Will they retaliate with equal or deeper price cuts or will they sit tight? If they retaliate, how quickly will they react? If we cut price, and our competitor hesitates long enough to allow us to capture significant volume at the lower level, we may be able to hold enough of it to make the maneuver worthwhile. The reverse is true if we increase our price and competitors fail to follow or are slow in doing so: we may suffer a crippling permanent loss in volume.

This suggests that an executive in charge of pricing will be wise to study his opposite numbers in competing firms and the pricing policies they operate under so as to be able to make an intelligent guess as to what they will do in any given pricing situation. Thus several years ago a well known oil company was known to follow the policy of being Number Three among the companies (operating in the markets where it was not price leader) in making any price change. A pricing executive in another industry was known to be very combative and often to react to competitive price moves without adequate reflection.

Third, what effect will a change in the price of one product have on the sales of another sold by the same firm? Sometimes a cut in the price of a relatively low-volume item may help bring added sales of a companion high-volume or high-profit article. Sometimes an advance in the price of one article may lose the firm that sells it a substantial volume of business in a high profit companion item.

Fourth, before initiating a change in price, management should assure itself that the proposed action is consistent with its established policies, long-run objectives, and standing in the trade.

PRICE STRUCTURE AND STRATEGY

By "price structure" is meant the relation that all the prices at which the same product is simultaneously sold at various levels and at different stages in the marketing process bear to one another. This includes the prices at which it is offered to the consumer by various types of retail stores and in different communities, as well as those at which it is bought and sold by the various intermediaries who function between the manufacturer and the retailer or the industrial or commercial consumer. A price structure is more than a simple list of quotations, since each figure set has an intimate influence on the others. They form a web of relationships and are so closely knit together that a change in one part of the system is likely to have far-reaching and not always predictable effects upon every other part of it.

Example of Price Structure

As an illustration, let us consider the price structure of a well-known oral antiseptic as it was disclosed by a detailed study some years ago. The large size was marked 75¢, which was called the "consumer list price." At the time of the survey this figure had come to be scarcely more than a convenient point of departure from which to compute and with which to compare the actual prices at which the product was being sold. In each of the cities studied there were some stores that actually disposed of the article for 75¢, but in only one was that the prevailing price. In another community the most usual figure was 63¢, and in still another it was 59¢. But in each of these cities the selling prices of individual dealers varied all the way from 50¢ to $1.00, according to the intensity of the competition faced by each retailer and the nature and extent of the services he gave his customers.

There was also a variation in the prices at which different retailers bought the product, although this was not as great as that existing in their selling prices. The nominal wholesale price to the retailer was $6.00 a dozen, which represented a discount of 33⅓ percent from the consumer's list. Some dealers, however, who were able to buy the product direct from the manufacturer, received an additional 5 or 10 percent discount, according to the quantity purchased. Thus the quoted wholesale price per dozen was reduced in some cases to $5.70 or $5.40.

The price per unit to the retailer was thus either 50¢, 47¢ or 45¢ for a product marked to sell to consumers for 75¢ but actually offered to them at practically every whole-number price between 50¢ and $1.00. But these quoted figures still exceeded those at which the commodity could actually be obtained from the wholesaler. Some jobbers allowed as much as 10 percent off their announced prices as quantity induce-ments, while practically all of them gave cash discounts in varying amounts. Some storekeepers bought through retailer-owned coopera-tives, from which they received patronage dividends on their pur-chases, with the result that the net price they paid for this commodity really remained an indeterminate amount until the end of the dividend period.

A further complication in the wholesale price structure of this article arose from the manufacturer's practice of giving "deals" to induce the retailers to spend more promotional effort upon the sale of it. Thus any dealer might have an opportunity, once or twice a year, to purchase the article direct from the manufacturer if he was willing and able to take the "deal" quantity and to undertake the display work or other promotional effort the manufacturer required as part of the deal. There are many types of such arrangements, but one of the simplest is the "free-goods deal" in which the nominal list price remains unchanged but the buyer is given from one to three packages free with each dozen he pays for. Thus, if the list price were $6.00 a dozen, or 50¢ a pack-age, a "deal" might entitle the buyer to 15 packages at an actual price of $4.80 a dozen, or 40¢ a bottle.

The manufacturer nominally sold the article to the jobber at the wholesale list price of $6.00 a dozen less 16⅔ percent. Thus the regu-lar price to him was $5.00 a dozen, or 41⅔¢ a package. There were, in addition, a few variations in the net prices paid by various buyers, resulting from the manufacturer's compensation for certain special sell-ing services that these purchasers promised to render. The actual net figures per unit paid by large chain store organizations were (for some articles) less than those paid by any other type of buyer, wholesale or retail.

The price structure sketched above is one of no more than average complexity. While the price structures of some articles are somewhat simpler, those of others possess many more refinements and complica-tions than are found in that of the oral hygiene product which we have used as an example. Nearly 200 separate and distinct sets of rela-tionships were at one time used in the sale of various kinds of electrical merchandise alone. The pricing system in the copper and brass industry includes a bewildering complex of "offs" and "ons" from basic list prices that make the computation of any specific price almost an exer-cise in higher mathematics. Nevertheless, there are a few major ele-ments of such systems which are essentially the same for practically all types of goods. These features that are common to most price structures may be taken to represent efforts to make allowances for the major elements of cost in handling different products or in serving different classes of customers. The effect of the Robinson-Patman Act has undoubtedly been in the direction of uniformity in price relationships. The degree to which such uniformity has *actually* been achieved still leaves plenty of room for improvement.

Price Lines

A firm usually does not put all its eggs in one price-quality basket. Whether a seller is a manufacturer or a mercantile house, he generally finds it desirable to offer his product at several different prices, each of which is likely to apply to a product modification that represents a variation in quality or attractiveness to the customer. Each such price-quality combination is known as a *price line.*

Examples of this practice may be found in the clothing departments of practically every department store. A firm like General Motors offers a spectacular example. Not only does it divide its market offerings into such broad price-quality lines as Cadillac, Buick, Oldsmobile and Chevrolet, but within each of these it has subsidiary *narrow price lines.*

The chief advantage of price-lining flows from the natural segmentation of most markets. The people who want to buy clothing or automobiles vary widely in their tastes and in the depth of their pocketbooks. The same thing is true to a greater or lesser extent of all products. These variations in consumer purchasing power tend to fall roughly into layers. Price-lining constitutes an attempt on the part of the marketer to offer to each income or demand layer or range the most attractive quality variation of his product that can be profitably made and sold at a price within the means and wishes of the consumers in that range. It is based on the idea that variety of consumer choice, both as to price and product features, increases sales volume.

The drawbacks of price-lining are matters of both production and marketing and have to do mainly with cost. It tends to reduce the quantities in which a product is manufactured because each model must usually be made by a separate process. This tends to limit the savings resulting from volume production. This tendency can sometimes be diminished by using certain common components in several models. This is especially feasible in the case of mechanical goods, such as automobiles.

Price-lining tends to increase marketing costs also. It may be necessary to sell each line through a separate group of wholesale or retail outlets—as is the case with the broad lines in the automobile business—

with resulting increased costs of selling and advertising. If several price lines are marketed through the same outlet, each outlet must carry adequate stocks of each model or line, with resulting increased inventory costs. These stocks must also be backed up by reserve stocks held by the manufacturer. The total of these will be greater than the reserve needed for a one-line offering. In addition to the costs of carrying inventory, this situation tends to cause a slower rate of stock turnover for the product throughout the distribution structure, with a corresponding increase in the amount of working capital needed by all the elements in it.

Quantity-Price Variations

The quantity purchased is a factor that is involved in almost all price structures. It generally costs less per unit to distribute 100 units of an article at one time and in one lot than it does to complete a transaction involving a single unit. It does not usually cost twice as much of a salesman's time and effort to sell a $100 order as it does to dispose of a $50 one. As a matter of fact, the selling cost is likely to be about the same for one of these orders as for the other. The clerical expenses involved in checking the larger order, in recording it, in preparing and submitting an invoice for it, and in collecting for it are not much (if any) greater than are those which result from performing the same functions for the smaller transaction.

Since the $100 order is likely to be composed of full cases of the same articles which are included in the smaller one in broken-case lots, the total cost of the work of preparing the smaller may actually exceed that of handling the larger purchase. One trip of the delivery equipment, one stop of the truck, and one load carried by the driver or porter into the place of business of the buyer are probably necessary to deliver each order, regardless of the size. The cost of performing these services in connection with the larger transaction are far less than double those for the smaller.

Of course, as the size of the quantities purchased increases, a point is eventually reached beyond which there is little, if any, further reduction in unit costs. But the savings made possible by large-scale buying furnish economic justification for the policy of allowing quantity discounts. Second only to cash discounts, allowances for quantity are probably the most generally used of all features of price structure.

Quantity discount systems may be of several types. There may be a single quantity bracket within which the allowance is made or there may be several successive brackets with a different percentage deduction applying against each of them. Thus the seller may allow 5 percent off list on amounts of 100 or more units but charge list price for all quantities of less than 100 units. This type of arrangement most frequently applies to carload and less-than-carload lots. It may apply to the dollar amounts of the order, such as 5 percent off on all orders totalling $100 or more. An example of a two-or-more discount bracket system is one in which the seller gives 10 percent off on amounts of more than 500 units each, and 15 percent on lots of more than 1,000 and so on. Quantity discounts may be "noncumulative" and apply solely to individual transactions, or they may be offered on a so-called "cumulative" basis and apply to the total purchases made by a customer during a period, such as a month or a year.

An example of the noncumulative, or single-transaction, quantity-discount system is furnished by a firm manufacturing and selling a breakfast food, which gave the following allowances:

Amount Bought in One Order	Percent of Discount
Less than one case	no discount
1 to 5 cases	2 percent
6 to 10 cases	5 percent
11 to 25 cases	7½ percent
Over 25 cases	10 percent

While this type of system stimulates customers to purchase in larger orders and thereby makes possible the savings described above, it also tends to induce retailer and wholesaler buyers to overstock. This often results in serious disadvantages to them and to the manufacturer in the form of slower turnover, high storage costs, spoilage, and losses of sales due to stale and unattractive merchandise.

A company manufacturing crackers and biscuits at one time used the following rather elaborate cumulative, or period, quantity-discount system:

Amount Bought Per Month	Percent of Discount
Less than $15	no discount
$16 to $30	5 percent
$31 to $60	7½ percent
$61 to $120	10 percent
$121 to $250	12½ percent
$251 to $500	15 percent
Over $500	17½ percent

This system has very little, if any, tendency to induce buyers to overstock. During the discount period it gives the company that uses it a measure of monopoly of the patronage of individual customers. A retailer whose business justifies purchases of crackers and biscuits amounting to slightly more than $60 a month will not divide his orders among several sources because by so doing he may cause himself to fall from the 10 percent to the 7–½ percent, or even the 5 percent discount class.

Since under this system a customer may pursue a hand-to-mouth buying policy through purchasing very frequently and in small amounts, while still enjoying the same discount percentages as one who takes much larger orders, this system does not always result in all the marketing savings which the quantity discount generally yields to its user. It is apt to enable him to make some savings in manufacture by stabilizing the demand for his output, thus making it possible for him to regularize his production schedules.

Functional Discounts

In many trades it is common for the manufacturer to sell at different prices to outlets at different levels in the marketing channel. In this way, for example, he may differentiate between wholesalers and retailers. This is usually done by allowing different discounts from the list price. Since the types of customers receiving these allowances usually perform different functions in the marketing process, these differentials are commonly known as *functional discounts.*

A functional discount system might look like this:

Type of Buyer	*Price Paid*
Consumer...................	List
Retailer.....................	25 percent off list
Wholesaler.................	25 percent and 15 percent off list

The list price is usually the price appearing in the seller's catalog. If the list price of an article sold under the above discount system were $1.00, the retailer who bought direct would pay 75¢ and the wholesaler would pay 75¢ less 15 percent of 75¢ (11¢), or 64 cents.

Under such a system the list is often the price at which the retailer is expected to resell to the consumer. The wholesaler will not be able to sell to the retailer for much, if any, above 75¢; if he tries to go much above that figure the retailer will buy direct. The system means that the manufacturer has decided that the retailer needs about 25 percent of his selling price to cover his costs and profit, while the wholesaler can cover his costs and make a profit on a gross margin of 15 percent.

When a manufacturer uses a functional discount system the matter of definition becomes very important. Certain firms do both a wholesale and a retail business. If such a house is defined as a retailer, it will be forced out of the wholesale part of its business. If it is classed as a wholesaler, it enjoys a distinct advantage in its retailing operations which may tempt it to cut price. If the manufacturer tries to allow it the wholesale discount on its jobbing volume and the retail discount on its sales to ultimate consumers, he is apt to find it hard to keep the two kinds of business separate.

Is a chain store system that accepts shipments at a central warehouse and buys in quantities as big as or bigger than most wholesalers to be defined as a wholesaler or a retailer? Some manufacturers set up a separate discount for such buyers which is sometimes greater and sometimes less than the wholesaler's discount. The functional discount often causes as many problems as it solves.

Cash Discounts

The cash discount or some other variation of the terms of payment equals or exceeds the quantity allowance in the frequency with which it is used as a feature of price structures. In one respect the former is a species of contingent discount; its granting is dependent upon the performance of a certain act by the buyer after the date of purchase-payment within the time limit. The administration of such allowances sometimes involves a certain amount of friction with customers who persist in deducting them, even though not properly earned. Cash discounts are usually stated as a part of the terms of payment; for example, "2 per cent 10 days, net 30 days" (sometimes expressed "2/10, n/30"), which means that the buyer who pays within 10 days after the date of the invoice is authorized to deduct 2 percent from the total net sum.

The precise amount of a cash discount, like that of a quantity allowance, presumably bears some relation to the differences in the cost of handling the type of transactions involved. It may be thought of as a payment which the seller is willing to make for speed and certainty in the settlement of the bill. In this sense it is purely a financial matter. In some trades, however, the percentage customarily granted is entirely out of relation to any possible saving in expenses resulting from selling for cash rather than on credit. In such cases the cash discount amounts to a competitive selling device used to get the business. *sometimes.*

Delivery Terms

Terms of delivery constitute another important feature of all price structures. Whether the seller is to make delivery, or the buyer is to call for the merchandise, or which of the two is to pay the costs of transportation when the merchandise is carried to its destination by a third party, must be stated or understood clearly in a contract of purchase and sale in order that the transaction may be completed smoothly. Within the same market area various wholesale grocers, for example, may choose to follow divergent policies in this regard, each appealing to a different section of the retail trade. Most of the business is usually done by those who undertake to deliver goods without charge to the buyer's place of business. It is generally understood that the cost of this service is included in the prices they charge for the merchandise instead of being separately itemized.

In the same market a considerable volume of sales is apt to be made by cash-and-carry jobbers to retailers who are willing to forgo the delivery service in order to get the lowest possible prices. It is not at all certain that the retailer can actually perform this service himself more cheaply than his supplier can, but the fact remains that, from the standpoint of price structure, the variation in the demand for different services from the wholesalers is one of the factors that cause some of them to quote different prices for the same product in the same market.

The vendor may offer to sell the product either with or without delivery, and may set up a price differential sufficient to cover the cost of rendering that service to those who wish it. This practice has been tried, with some success, even by retailers. Usually, however, the seller makes no such adjustment, simply stating his delivery terms and charging the same price to all buyers, even though some of them come and get the merchandise.

Much more complicated elements of price structure are involved when delivery is made through a third party; for example, a railroad or a trucking company. The freight charges for certain bulky commodities make up a considerable part of their total delivered costs. Such products are often sold at a basic selling price plus freight, the transportation charges being paid to the carrier by the seller but collected by him from the purchaser. Thus the delivered cost to different buyers varies according to how far they are away from the shipping point.

Sellers of other products on which freight charges are heavy attempt to equalize the cost of transportation to all customers regardless of location. The practice of freight absorption by the seller and of quoting delivered prices, particularly in such special forms as the basing-point system, have attracted much public interest. It is argued that it is unfair to require customers located near the point of shipment to pay part of the cost of transporting merchandise to those in more distant places. But it is equally valid to argue that it is unjust to penalize certain buyers because they are not located near the point of production.

When the shipper absorbs the freight on commodities of small bulk and high value, the practice is never questioned. The amount of the freight charge is usually such a minor item in the delivered cost of such an article that it is more than offset by the saving in trouble and accounting expense achieved by selling to all at an equalized delivered price instead of billing each separately for the small amount represented by transportation costs or of requiring each to pay the freight charges directly to the carrier. Consumers' goods sold direct to the retailer offer many instances of this practice. There is an additional advantage to the seller of such merchandise in his being able to name in his advertising a price that is not subject to adjustment for freight charges.

The practice of freight equalization or absorption has been most severely criticized in connection with the use of basing-point systems. Under such a plan, every member of an industry quoted prices on its product delivered from a single shipping point (known as the basing point, usually a leading production center) even though many of the plants making it were located elsewhere. At one time the steel industry used Pittsburgh as its sole basing point, which gave rise to the phrase "Pittsburgh plus." Thus a steel manufacturer, regardless of where his plant was situated, quoted prices to his customers, wherever they were located, on an f.o.b. Pittsburgh basis, which meant that the freight from Pittsburgh to the point of delivery had to be added to the quoted price in order to obtain the net delivered price. This was true even though the steel was furnished from a nearby plant and was shipped only a few miles.[3]

This plan was based primarily on the theory that the principal competition faced by steel manufacturers in Chicago and other centers was from the steel plants located in Pittsburgh, and that the customers, wherever located, naturally measured quoted prices against the cost of obtaining the same product from Pittsburgh, the best known and largest producing center. It was also a recognition of the fact that since

---

[3]Also consider the following hypothetical example: A farm implement manufacturer, located in the western part of Chicago, placed with a steel company in the Chicago district an order for a certain steel product the basing point of which was Pittsburgh. The price that he paid for the steel delivered to his plant was a flat rate per ton plus the freight rate from Pittsburgh to his factory on his order, even though it was shipped to him from the Chicago district.

D. E. Montgomery in "Basing-Point Prices" (*National Marketing Review*, Vol. I, No. 1) illustrates the operation of this system very clearly and discusses certain theoretical implications.

the steel plants in markets other than Pittsburgh ordinarily did not produce enough of the commodity to satisfy local demand, certain consumers in these markets were forced to buy from Pittsburgh, which always produced a surplus. The price everywhere thus tended to be fixed by the central market. Therefore it was a convenience for everyone involved that all prices should be stated in a way that permitted ready comparison with those quoted by Pittsburgh producers.

The steel industry at one time used numerous basing points, the list varying with the different products of the industry.[4] Basing points were also used in several other industries, among them cement and lime. This pricing system offers one of the most illuminating examples of the way in which the elements of a price structure evolve as a result of the efforts of sellers to find a broad policy adjusted to suit the varying circumstances or requirements of different classes of customers. The use of trade or industry basing points was declared illegal by the Supreme Court, although the language of the decision indicates that a single firm may establish its own basing points.

Many firms use a form of freight equalization that is closely akin to the basing point system but does not suffer from its legal disabilities. This arises when Firm X, with a plant in Yonkers, New York, has a branch warehouse in St. Louis, from which it delivers to customers in the Chicago area (where a competitor has a factory). In selling to customers in the Chicago area this firm equalizes freight with Chicago. This means that a customer in Elkhart, Indiana, pays freight from Chicago to Elkhart on goods shipped from St. Louis or Yonkers, and Firm X pays the rest of the cost of transportation. This enables Firm X to compete on equal delivered price terms with its competitor in Chicago. In the meantime, the competitor in Chicago is probably equalizing freight with St. Louis and Yonkers in order to compete on equal terms with Firm X in those markets. The ramifications of all these arrangements can become infinitely complex.

Miscellaneous Price Allowances

The major aspects of price structure so far mentioned have been quantity and functional allowances, cash discounts and credit arrangements, and terms of delivery. Other features include arrangements governing the rendering of installation or maintenance service, guarantees concerning price or quality, the return of merchandise, and promotional allowances.

[4]Thus all firms, wherever located, quoted prices on Product A as f.o.b. Syracuse; on Product B, f.o.b. Gary, Indiana; on Products C and D, f.o.b. Pittsburgh, etc.

Price Guarantee.   Some consideration of the practice of price guarantee may prove helpful. It takes several forms: 1.   The seller may guarantee that during a given period after an order is sold and delivered,
the price at which he vends his goods will not fall below that at which
he sold them to the buyer to whose purchase the guarantee applies. If
within the specified time his price declines below that figure, the difference is rebated to the customer or credited to his account. If the seller's
price advances, the amount of the purchaser's bill remains unchanged.

2.   The vendor of an order for future delivery may guarantee that
the price at which he sells on the market will not decline before the
delivery date. If it does so, the buyer gets the benefit of the change. The
seller may guarantee against the decline of his own price, that of a
specific competitor, or that which prevails in the market.

This practice is used to make sure that there will be a continuous
demand for the vendor's merchandise during periods of price uncertainty, when buyers would otherwise purchase hand-to-mouth or withdraw from the market entirely. It is also employed by manufacturers of
goods which are either produced seasonally or demanded by buyers only
at certain times of the year. Without this device the makers of such
merchandise find it practically impossible to induce wholesalers, retailers, or industrial consumers to purchase it ahead of the time when
they can resell it or use it.

The privilege is also sometimes granted by sellers as a competitive
device. This use occurs mainly during periods when prices are falling
or when business is bad. It may be supplemented by forward or seasonal
dating, whereby the invoices for goods that are delivered in December
or January, for instance, are dated March 1 and are therefore not due
and payable until after that time.

The so-called escalator clauses that prevailed during and after World
War II were simply price guarantee arrangements in reverse. The buyer
of an order for future delivery agreed that if the seller's price or costs
increased before delivery, the price would be adjusted accordingly.
Escalator clauses tend to prevail only during periods when goods are
very scarce.

Sales Promotional Allowances.   Promotional allowances are based
upon the claim of important retail and wholesale firms that they are in
a position to sell distribution services to the manufacturers with whom
they deal, as well as to buy goods from them. Such concessions have
been demanded and given to cover the cost of advertisements featuring
the producer's goods in local newspapers, the installation of window,
counter, or shelf displays, payments to salespeople for "pushing" the

manufacturer's merchandise, the wages of special clerks engaged in demonstrating his products in retail stores, and various other promotional activities. Frequently such selling services have been performed in a perfunctory fashion, or not at all; the amount of the allowance constituting in reality nothing more than a reduction in the price of the merchandise upon which it was granted.

For a number of years widespread complaints arose from competitors who did not receive such discounts. The pressure for regulation of this practice led to Congressional investigations and finally to the passage of the Robinson-Patman Act, which establishes rules governing the granting of promotional differentials (among other aspects of price structure) in what is claimed to be an attempt to eliminate unfair discrimination among buyers. As a result, most manufacturers no longer grant flat or percentage promotional allowances but tie them to specific services whose rendering can be checked.

Chain store systems, mail order houses, and large department stores were especially active in demanding and receiving such special concessions, as were also cooperative groups of retailers and wholesalers.

Chain Discounts.   In some trades it is the practice to grant chain discounts. As many as 14 or 15 percentages have been quoted to be applied, one after another, to the reduction of the original list price[5] The final net price has been known to be less than 20 percent of the stated list amount. This method is sometimes used to preserve as a trade secret the actual figure at which retailers or wholesalers buy their goods, at the same time permitting the printing of catalog and list prices that may be shown to the general public. This secrecy also facilitates discrimination among buyers, according to their purchasing power or bargaining ability. Its employment makes unnecessary the frequent reprinting of expensive catalogs. The list prices mentioned in such a publication remain unchanged over long periods of time. Each salesman carries a discount sheet which lists for each commodity the percentages that must be deducted from the catalog figure to obtain the current price. These lists may be changed as often as desired.

For some types of products the net price in each sale must be computed by applying a complicated formula which varies with the specifications of the article required. One such commodity is heavy electric cable. The salesman vending it is usually an engineer and is provided with a

---

[5]For instance, if the list price is $1.00 and the chain discount quotations are 50-20-30-15-10 percent, the net price actually paid by the customer will be 17¢. The net price is found by subtracting 50 percent of $1.00 from $1.00, then subtracting 20 percent from this 50¢, which leaves 40¢, and so on until all the percentages have been applied.

list of formulas rather than a price book. In quoting on any particular order he once had to take into account 13 separate factors, such as the diameter of the copper core, the thickness of the covering layer of lead, and the nature of the insulating wrappings. This system is still common in the metals trades.

Reasons for Price Variations

No matter how strange any given feature of price structure may seem, the observer will do well to approach its study with the attitude that there is—or once was—a reason for it. Usually the price system of a commodity is constructed to suit the various ways in which it is distributed. In some cases, however, the original justification for a given element has disappeared, so that it is like a vestigial organ, reflecting the history of the trade rather than its actual present needs.

Hybrid forms of price structure sometimes arise when a firm that is accustomed to handling one type of merchandise begins to produce and sell another, and, in distributing the new articles, uses the same price system it found effective in vending the old. Thus a maker of electric batteries or fuses may start to manufacture radio tubes or transistors and may seek to sell them without changing his pricing plan. Such a procedure tends to create confusion, distrust, and ill will. In the long run the seller is likely to find that it is good policy to make his price structure conform in its general outlines to the prevailing pattern of the industry.

The general outlines of the price structure which will prove most effective in any given situation are determined pretty largely by the character of the commodity to be marketed and the types of distributors who handle it. In a sense the different features of such a system usually represent a recognition of the principal cost- or risk-generating functions involved in distributing the article or in serving the various classes of customers who buy it. Thus an elaborate method for handling freight charges, such as the basing-point system, is more likely to grow up in the marketing of heavy commodities, like steel or cement, than of articles like diamonds, whose weight is very little in relation to their value.

The elements of a price structure may also be determined by the pressures exerted upon the seller by various types of customers seeking special favors. A class of customers, or the more aggressive customers, may point to certain economies which the seller enjoys in dealing with them and insist so strenuously upon a proportionate price adjustment that it is granted. Once such a differential is allowed to one or more members of a class, the same consideration must be given to all buyers belonging to the group.

Such demands for special allowances are not based on cost differences alone. A customer or class of buyers may urge the seller to grant discounts because of special marketing services which he or it offers. Thus chain store systems have been able to gain concessions by promising that window displays, counter displays, and other types of promotional material featuring the seller's brands will be installed in each of the outlets they operate or, by contract, assuring the seller a certain volume of sales.

The aggressive buyer may also ask for a price arrangement different from that which the seller allows to the general run of his customers because he finds it more convenient or is able to meet the discount requirements more easily under such a special arrangement. Thus chain store systems have generally sought to obtain quantity discounts instead of to qualify for the functional discounts allowed in some trades to wholesalers. Their pressure has sometimes been sufficient to cause a general shift from a functional to a quantity discount basis.

The convenience of certain buyers may also lead to modifications of the credit terms of a vendor. If a firm sells on 2/10, n/30 terms, a large purchaser who finds it convenient to pay every 15 days is likely to be allowed to do so and to take his cash discounts, even though by so doing he violates the credit terms.

Before the passage of the Robinson-Patman Act a customer might secure unusually low prices simply because of the size of his business, even though there were no differences in cost or other considerations to justify the favor. Such a differential might be based not on the quantity of purchases actually made by such a customer, which sometimes was small, but on the potential volume that might eventually be secured from him.

In some instances the differential allowed seemed to be designed primarily to induce a large customer to buy the product rather than to make it for himself and thereby become a potential competitor of the supplier in disposing of his surplus output. In such a case the seller offered the article at a price so low that the buyer could not profitably undertake its production. The supplier sometimes was willing to make such sales without profit.

Such a purchaser was sometimes more than a potential competitor; for example, a large grocery chain system might roast and sell coffee and, at the same time, buy large quantities of it already roasted from independent producers. Such a firm was in a position to exercise a profound influence on the price structures and policies of every independent concern engaged in supplying roasted coffee, not only in connection with its sales to that concern but generally throughout the trade. In order to curry favor with the chain buyer as a customer, the coffee house, in its capacity as a competitor, must conform to his wishes. In determining the price policy for his own brand, the roaster must take into account the probable effect of his actions on the chain system's problems in selling its private brand.

Some buyers won special price concessions as a result of the exercise of superior bargaining ability. Complete ruthlessness in squeezing the last penny of allowance out of a harassed or financially embarrassed seller, adroitness in the finer details of the great art of bluffing, and finesse in the game of threat and counterthreat all bore fruit in the shape of discounts not enjoyed by those purchasers not blessed with a full measure of these talents. Many of these advantages have now been nullified by the Robinson-Patman Act, although many of them still have some effect, either openly or secretly.

PRICE POLICIES

Despite the general market and legal factors which determine the broad limits within which the price structure of a seller must be erected, there remains a considerable area inside which he may establish his own policies. For example, although the nature of a commodity may determine the elements of cost which must be recognized in price differentials among buyers of it, its seller has a great deal of discretion as to the precise amount of the differentials allowed and the details of terms and conditions. The general price structure of an industry may make allowance, in some degree, for the conflicting interests of two or more types of customers, while two sellers within that industry may pursue very different policies in the extent to which they favor or encourage one buying group over another.

Such policy decisions may affect the entire future of the business whose managers make them. One marketing executive may be staking the fortunes of his firm on his judgment that a traditional type of distributor will survive and prevail, while another commits the future of his house to his belief that a new type of outlet is rising to dominance. One company may be so situated that it must place great reliance on certain promotional facilities offered by its larger customers, while another acts on the theory that it is strong enough to get along very well without such aid.

General Objectives of Price Policy

Any one or more of several general objectives may determine the policies that a given manufacturer follows with regard to his price structure. Perhaps the most logical attitude for a producer is to view the entire group of retailers, wholesalers and agents handling his product as members of a distribution team working with him. He prefers aggressive rivalry to exist among them but is anxious to avoid the kind of friction or suspicion that makes one or a group of them withhold cooperation from the rest or actively obstruct the others in the performance of their interdependent functions.

For instance, the maker of a food or drug product may hope for healthy competition between chains and independents but seek to prevent his product from becoming the subject of any bitterness or animosity between the two groups. Fairness and openness are primary requirements of price policy in such a situation, and the rules must be so definitely formulated and clearly stated that the members of each group know exactly what they can expect. Such a system can be kept elastic to meet changing conditions, but any modification of its details must be carefully worked out and fully explained to all who have any stake in the matter. The seller who proceeds on this theory must recognize that, through it, he becomes the arbiter of fair competition among those who handle his products and is thereby undertaking a very formidable task.

In setting up his price policy the producer may choose to interest himself not so much in assuring competitive balance among his distributors as in sharpening the keenness of their competition. Some manufacturers believe that their responsibility for their products ceases as soon as the goods leave their hands and that their distributors should be allowed to sell them for whatever they can get in free competition. Others actively endeavor to stir up price rivalry in the resale of their goods.

For example, a manufacturer may offer subsidies or other inducements to his most aggressive distributors to influence them to cut the price of his product, or he may bring additional competitive pressure to bear upon its market in other ways. Such an arrangement can frequently be made between a large seller and a large buyer, to their mutual benefit, since it permits each to gain a competitive advantage at his own level.

The members of a third group of manufacturers seek control over the competition among wholesalers and retailers, usually with the purpose of favoring or preserving a particular type of outlet. The seller may prefer a certain variety of outlet because of some special services its members perform. Manufacturers of plumbing equipment, for instance, accept certain weaknesses in their marketing setup because they feel that it is highly important to retain the goodwill of the master plumbers who exercise such a direct and potent influence over the final sale and installation of these fixtures. A particular class of distributors may be favored because of some long-range consideration, such as the superior loyalty or stability its members are believed to exhibit. Thus a manufacturer may sell entirely through independent drugstores, or protect them as to price, because he believes that the independent retail druggist furnishes the most certain and dependable outlet for his goods. In pursuance of this policy he may forgo a considerable volume of business which he might obtain from such buyers as syndicates, department stores, supermarkets and chain systems.

Policy concerning price structure is intimately related to that having to do with price levels. One phase of this relationship may be illustrated by reference to the three plans of action just outlined. Each reacts in its own way upon the price level. The first, which seeks balanced distribution with the avoidance of friction and irritating forms of competition among distributors, tends to cause the manufacturer to maintain a constant, or standard, price-quality combination for each product which brings the greatest number of dollars into the market for its purchase. Those who follow it emphasize the need for teamwork in the performance of the joint function of marketing and also recognize that the ultimate sale of the commodity to the consumer must produce the total fund out of which all those cooperating in its production and distribution are to be paid. It is to the mutual advantage of all sharing in it that this fund be as large as possible.

Each of the other two policies may result in a final price which yields less than this maximum. The practice of stimulating the intensity of competition among dealers may lead to consumer prices so low that the income to the industry as a whole is reduced. The manufacturer seeks to build his own monopoly power by stimulating excessive rivalry among his distributors. He may suffer in the end when losses impel them to demand a revision of his price level that will give them a greater portion of the total return from the output, which, along with their share, has been progressively curtailed because of his policy. They may even refuse to handle his product, or may give it only "under the counter" treatment.

The third practice, protecting a given type of distributor at all costs, is likely to lead to unusually high prices. Outlets so protected tend to grow less efficient through lack of competitive stimulus. Although competition may remain keen in connection with such matters as the multiplication of costly services, the total income of the industry is liable to be curtailed because an ever-smaller number of consumers is willing to pay for them. The effect of such a price policy by the original seller and of its abuse by the middleman it protects will be in the direction of monopoly, which will tend to favor primarily the intermediaries. Such practices are liable to bring about this result when they are carried so far that actual control of price policy is lodged in the hands of the protected middlemen.

Resale Price Maintenance

The device that is most commonly used by manufacturers to protect certain groups of their distributors is resale price maintenance, often referred to as "price maintenance." This practice involves the attempt by a manufacturer to fix the price at which buyers of his product —chiefly retailers—shall resell it. It is usually applied only to goods that are distributed under the manufacturer's brand.

Many producers of branded articles prefer to have them sold to all ultimate consumers at uniform prices. The manufacturer of a branded product may suffer several types of injury when retailers cut its price.

1. Price cutting at retail tends to reduce the storekeeper's margin of gross profit on the involved item and to lead him to demand a reduction in the figure at which the manufacturer sells it to him. When the producer is forced to comply with such a demand, he must choose to reduce his costs of operation, which is not always possible, to be satisfied with a smaller profit, or to lower the quality of his product.

2. It is also urged that the prevalence of different prices for the same brand of an article in the retail market tends to undermine its prestige and that of its maker in the minds of ultimate consumers. There is considerable evidence to indicate that long public familiarity with retail price cutting has brought about the practical elimination of this tendency.

3. Price cutting discourages some retailers from activity promoting the sale of goods under the maker's brand. A few of them even go so far as to drop from their stocks certain items which are footballs of competition. When a chain system, a supermarket, a department store, or a discount house makes deep and long-continued cuts in the price of Brand X, for example, many competing independent stores follow the practice of putting their stocks of this item under the counter and

selling it only when it is specifically called for. Some even go so far as to try to substitute goods under other labels when consumers ask for Brand X. This apathy or hostility of retailers is the chief injury that manufacturers stand to suffer from retail price cutting.

These factors led manufacturers to attempt to reduce or to eliminate price cutting at retail. In order to accomplish this it was first necessary for them to set up an accurate definition of the activity they sought to prevent or to limit. This they attempted to do by establishing and advertising certain suggested or approved prices at which the retailer was supposed to resell products under the makers' brands. In the second place they sought to eliminate price cutting on their brands by bringing pressure to bear upon the dealer to prevent him from selling them at figures lower than those suggested or specified. This process is resale price maintenance.

Several devices have been employed to enforce this policy.

1. One method involves the exercise of the manufacturer's right to select his customers. He can refuse to sell to those who resell at less than his suggested price. This is a fairly satisfactory method if the manufacturer sells direct to the retailer; but if he sells through wholesalers the problem of policing the policy may be very difficult unless the wholesalers cooperate wholeheartedly.

2. A fairly satisfactory means of effectuating this policy consists in granting exclusive franchises to certain wholesalers and retailers. As has been explained, these grants do not create agencies in the legal sense of the term; they are simply marketing agreements whereby the producer promises not to sell through other dealers in the trading area of the holder of the privilege, and the latter contracts to promote the sale of the article actively. The holder of such a privilege knows that price cutting on his part is apt to result in the loss of the franchise. This device, while perfectly legal if properly used, can be successfully employed in the marketing of only a small number of commodities.

3. A third method of enforcement, which is effective but rather expensive, involves the consignment by the manufacturer of his merchandise to the retailer. Under this arrangement the goods belong to the producer until the storekeeper sells them. This practice results in a tremendous increase in the manufacturer's inventories and a loss of accounting control over them.

4. What would seem to be the most effective means of enforcing price maintenance is the employment of a system of contracts in which those who buy the manufacturer's product for resale agree to resell it at a specified price. Such a system may involve a direct agreement

between the producer and each retailer who sells his brand, or it may consist of the use of the so-called fair-trade laws.

Most states of the Union have statutes which provide that a manufacturer within the state may execute a contract with one or more retailers in the state establishing the minimum price at which the retailer shall resell his branded product. He may then notify all other retailers in the state of the existence of this contract and they become bound by its provisions. If one of them resells at a lower price he is guilty of "unfair trading" and is subject to penalty. This is known as the "nonsigners' clause." Federal law extends this machinery to interstate transactions if both the manufacturer and the retailers affected are in states having fair-trade laws.

The social and economic desirability of price maintenance has been the subject of much bitter debate. It is argued that when a manufacturer sells his branded product to a retailer, he really vends not one thing but two. First, he disposes of the tangible article itself; second, he authorizes the use of his brand or trademark (such as Camel or Winston) in reselling the tangible commodity. The trademark is his. He does not convey it to the retailer along with the physical product, he merely authorizes its use. Therefore he has a right to control the conditions under which that use takes place. Since the price at which the physical commodity is sold at retail may change the value of the brand, the fixing of that price is an appropriate and reasonable means of exercising such control.

The proponents of this practice also justify it on the ground that it prevents indiscriminate, uneconomic price cutting among dealers which may both destroy healthy competition and cause the elimination of small wholesalers and retailers. It is urged that a relatively small group of price cutting sellers—often fly-by-nights—can bring about a market's complete demoralization. Also, large, well-financed distributing concerns, handling a variety of merchandise or operating over a wide area, by drastically reducing their prices on specific groups of products or in particular districts, can drive their more specialized or local competitors, who have smaller pocketbooks, out of business.

Those who oppose resale price maintenance urge that the proper method to cope with this evil is legislation which fixes a floor—presumably bearing some relation to the dealer's costs of operation and what he pays for his merchandise—below which prices shall not be reduced.

There can be little quarrel with the logic of either of these arguments, but there may be reasonable doubts as to their inclusiveness.

They are based entirely upon the concept of the rights of individual manufacturers and dealers. The matter of the influence of the practice of price maintenance upon the general social welfare and upon the economic position of the ultimate consumer is left entirely out of account by those who urge these considerations to the exclusion of all others.

The opponents of price maintenance argue that its practice entirely eliminates price competition among retailers in the sale of the articles to which it is applied. It makes no allowance for price reductions that might be offered by different retailers on the basis of the variations in the auxiliary services with which they surround the sale of the products to which the practice applies. Under this plan, for example, it is impossible for a self-service store to recompense its customers for forgoing the usual services with lower prices. Nor can the large retail establishment (which, because of the tremendous quantities in which it buys, is able to obtain its merchandise at unusually low prices) pass on these reductions to its ultimate consumer-patrons.

Price maintenance likewise tends to prevent the purchasers of protected articles from sharing the savings in the costs of handling them that unusually efficient store managers may make through superior skill. As a corollary it is pointed out that these three types of retail establishments—the self-service store, the large firm, and the concern with unusually efficient management—are handicapped by the practice.

Those who oppose price maintenance contend that, in the case of merchandise sold under a manufacturer's brand, its use by him implements and lends effectiveness to a species of semi-monopoly that he enjoys by reason of his use of the trademark. They point out that if brands and the extensive advertising of them accomplish their obvious purpose, they effect a sort of partial monopoly for the manufacturer. If, in the mind of the average ultimate consumer, X soap ceases to be merely a variety of cleansing agent and becomes a separate commodity, "X SOAP," its maker possesses a semi-monopoly of its production and sale. If a user is sold on X SOAP its producer can, within certain limits, hold its price higher than it should be without serious danger of losing that user's patronage. Resale price maintenance allows him to extend that monopolistic control into the field of retail selling.

Of course, this power exists only within the rather narrow limits fixed by the added amount over and above the usual price of the commodity which the average ultimate consumer is willing to pay for X SOAP by reason of his conviction of its greater desirability. If the maker attempts to push his price beyond that limit, he meets the competition of the producers of other branded soaps and will lose volume as a result.

It is argued that the manufacturer carrying out a policy of price maintenance will tend to set a retail price somewhat higher than that which would prevail under competition. Since one primary purpose of the plan is usually to achieve distribution through the maximum number of retail outlets, the retail price fixed by the producer will tend to be one that will make it profitable for the less efficient storekeepers to handle the article. This also tends to prevent the normal but cruel forces of competition from eliminating these ineffectives from the distribution system and to saddle upon the ultimate consumer the cost of the waste resulting from their lack of skill.

This argument is vigorously denied by the proponents of price maintenance who urge that, as a result of its application, the retailer is able to make a reasonable profit on each item he handles and is no longer under the wasteful necessity of making up, by exorbitant returns upon the less competitive items, the losses he sustains upon those that are the subjects of the price cutting efforts of his less discriminating or more fortunately situated rivals.

There is considerable evidence that even if almost all legal obstacles to the practice of this policy were removed, its use is not likely to be widespread. During the years when "fair-trade" laws were unchallenged, it was applied extensively in only a few industries, chief among them drugs, cosmetics and toilet preparations, books, household appliances, and alcoholic liquors.

The manufacturer who employs price maintenance to fix a price on his brand that is materially higher than it should be must be prepared to meet considerable competition from the proprietary brands of distributors. The chain store systems, mail order houses, and certain large department stores have been especially active in this direction, and even the orthodox wholesaler or independent retailer is not always averse to turning an honest dollar or two of volume on his private brands by making invidious comparisons between the prices of his own and the manufacturer's products.

Effects of General Price Levels on Price Policy

General price trends, or levels, constitute another major problem of policy determination for the primary seller. In the case of unbranded staples this problem centers around seasonal and cyclical fluctuations. Price policies of firms making such articles tend to be influenced by the nature of the production process and the cost structure of the industry. In the petroleum business, for example, individual concerns are under considerable compulsion to go on producing and selling, whatever the price may be, because it is impossible to shut off flowing wells and because crude oil is perishable and protective storage facilities highly expensive. Copper producers, on the other hand, can cease selling and retain vast stocks of the commodity in storage until prices are more favorable. They may even continue production for a period and increase their inventories rather than sell the output at reduced prices.

On the other hand, if a large percentage of a firm's costs are of the overhead variety, as is likely to be the case in highly mechanized industries, it will sometimes find it desirable to sell its output at a price that is less than the total expense of producing it. To manufacture and sell at any price above the direct costs of production, so that some portion of the receipts will be left to apply against overhead expenses, is better than to discontinue operations entirely and lose all the overhead.

The maker of a price policy for a branded product must be influenced by the probable history of the article throughout its future existence. The manager of a firm which invests in specialized equipment to produce such a commodity must try to visualize not only what it will sell for today but the price it is likely to bring eight or ten years from now. His expectation is that consumers will "buy the plant" bit by bit in the form of depreciation and obsolescence charges made against each unit of output sold to them. He is interested, therefore, in the probable conditions influencing volume and price during the entire period over which he must attempt to amortize the cost of the plant or any part of it.

The expenditure of funds for advertising to develop a market for a product may be considered as an investment. Nice judgment is required to determine just how rapidly and to what extent a market will respond to price reduction alone and the degree to which sales promotional forms of cultivation are required. If consumers must continually be taught or induced to use the commodity, the cost of doing so must be included in its current price. Too drastic a reduction of price may absorb the funds potentially available for financing such work. Meritorious products have often been hampered in their market development because the seller relied on lower prices alone to expand his market. The reduction of its price will not induce people to buy an article if they have not yet learned of its use and been convinced of its desirability. The marketing manager must at all times maintain a nice balance between the use of the price appeal and of the various methods of sales promotion as devices for sustaining and increasing his volume.

Knowing when and how to make a price cut is also of vital importance to the seller. Vast promotional value often lies in the mere act of reduction itself—aside from the influence of the new level which is established—if the cut is wisely timed and cleverly dramatized. For this reason it is usually better to make one substantial slash at some time during the course of a period—and thus gain considerable consumer attention—than to make a series of small cuts at frequent intervals which are apt to pass unnoticed.

In establishing and administering his price policy and in managing his own relations with his outlets and their relations with each other, the manufacturer must consider the pricing problems and practices of his wholesalers and retailers.

Let us discuss first the situation and behavior of the retailer in this respect. He sells a complex bundle of utilities, consisting of both goods and services. In vending merchandise (except that sold under his own brand) he really acts as a part of the marketing machinery of the manufacturer or supplier from whom it came. His own service is the thing he offers for sale in his capacity as a retailer. From his viewpoint the merchandise that he handles is nothing more than a vehicle to carry the retail service, which he really wants to sell and must sell if he is to be successful.

In pricing a commodity he must determine whether he will make his selling policy merely an extension of that followed by its manufacturer, or, in accordance with the dictates of his own interests, will place himself in opposition to the producer in an attempt to control his part of the price structure of the article. Close coordination with the manufacturer's price policy is perhaps the easiest solution so long as the retailer does not have too large a stake in those commodities in his stock whose distribution is controlled by their producers.

Small retailers may have no choice other than to distribute such products in conformance with the selling policies pursued by the manufacturer. If the storekeeper handles such an article at all, he must buy it at the discounts offered by the producer or wholesaler and sell it at or near the price established by competition. Even the small merchant, however, in the absence of price maintenance, may exercise some degree of discretion in setting his selling price if the immediate competitive pressure is not too great. For instance, if he is located in a somewhat isolated neighborhood he may sell a commodity on a convenience basis at a figure above the level prevailing generally in the market, even though he thereby fails to achieve his full volume possibilities.

A retailer may be willing to sell below the usual price. In theory, the storekeeper who handles a variety of commodities is interested primarily in securing an adequate gross profit on his entire volume and is less concerned with the percentage of margin he enjoys on any particular article. Thus if a certain manufacturer is able to exercise sufficient control of the market so that he can oblige retailers to handle his product, even though they enjoy less than the average percentage of gross profit, they may accept this situation without too much protest if there are other articles in their stocks with margins sufficiently great to net a satisfactory return on their volume as a whole.

In practice, however, the retailer usually objects to accepting an unusually narrow margin on a product because he does not realize that this loss can be balanced by higher gross profits on other products or because he distrusts his ability to obtain such augmented gross profits. Nor is he always convinced by the argument that since such a product costs him less to handle, he can afford to accept a smaller margin on it. For it is not impossible for the producers of most of the other articles he stocks to put them on the same basis and to make similar demands for decreases in his operating margins. The retailer wants, first of all, a sufficient amount of gross profit to enable him to maintain his service capacity and leave him something for net profit. But low-cost distribution involves a decreased service standard, and hence a decreased demand for his services, and is liable to mean a lower level of net earnings for him.

In making allowance for the value of his own services in the process of fixing his selling prices, the retailer must consider the psychology of his customers. Many consumers seem willing to forgo retail services if the cost of each service is computed and announced so that they can choose whether to buy or not to buy it. Numerous stores have experimented with two price levels: one sufficiently high to cover the cost of rendering the full retailing service and the other designed to meet the cost of supplying a minimum of service. The usual result of such experiments has been that large numbers of consumers tend to buy at the lower figure, forgoing service, and to avoid that for which they would receive the greater service content. The retailer may feel that this is contrary to his best interest since he is primarily engaged in the sale of his services and, presumably, would like to sell as many of them as possible.

An increasing number of retailers, such as supermarkets and discount houses, find it profitable to dispense with such services as credit, delivery and salespeople, and to compensate customers for their lack by lower prices. In conformity with the do-it-yourself spirit of the times they throw upon their customers the performance of several of the time-honored retailing functions. In order to support the expensive floor space and parking facilities necessary to do this they must have sales volume. Not too long ago a grocery store with an annual sales volume of $100,000 was a large one. Today there are many whose annual sales volume is in the millions of dollars.

A most potent tool in building such volume is price. In many lines of trade, therefore, the manufacturer who wishes his product to be handled by the retail outlets with the biggest volume must make it possible for them to offer the price appeal. In building his pricing policy he must somehow seek to reconcile in it the low price, low margin needs of these concerns with the higher margin, higher price requirements of the smaller outlets. The grocery manufacturers seem to have learned how to do this reasonably well. Producers in other fields, such as household appliances and clothing, are in the process of learning.

The retailer's exercise of price policy in buying is largely for the purpose of bringing pressure to bear upon his suppliers to force them to accord him an improved status as a purchaser; for example, to grant him wholesale discounts or special advertising allowances. In attempting to accomplish this objective he may depart from the prevailing price level or method of sale in a variety of ways. The attempt to understand such practices in detail must be based upon a consideration of the price structure as a whole, and upon a study of the interplay of pressure and strategy among all the groups having claims upon the amount the consumer pays for the goods which they participate in making and distributing.

The selling price policies of the wholesaler are a mixture of those of the manufacturer and the retailer. His position is in some respects similar to that of the producer in that he is distributing to various types of customers and must attempt to keep their demands upon him in balance. His situation resembles that of the retailer since he handles a wide range of commodities and is interested primarily in receiving compensation for the services he renders in so doing.

One feature of the position of the wholesaler that has no exact parallel in the case of either the producer or the retailer arises entirely from his function as a middleman. Manufacturers and retailers tend to deal with each other directly whenever they cease to believe that the jobber can perform the intermediary services more cheaply for them than they can for themselves. Any given wholesale house, then, is in competition not merely with other similar concerns but also with producing firms and retailing establishments which are operated on the theory that they can perform the jobbing functions less expensively and more efficiently.

More than any other distributive agent the wholesaler is obliged to justify his existence from day to day on the basis of his cost of operation and the skill with which he performs his services. His prices are taken as evidence of both.

PRICING AND THE LAW

In making his decisions the pricing executive must at all times think in terms of the laws that govern his work. Most of these laws are federal, although a few industries (such as liquor, and in some states the gasoline business) are affected by state pricing regulations as well.

The federal statutes that affect pricing are known as the antitrust laws. The underlying theory of most of these statutes is that competition must be maintained and protected. If competition is active and aggressive the consumer will reap the benefits of protection against excessive prices and quality depreciation, and, in addition, may enjoy the fruits of the technological and managerial improvements business concerns develop and apply in the struggle for competitive advantage.

A legal corollary to this theory seems to be that the quality of competition depends primarily on the number of competitors. In a general sort of way this corollary is probably true; certainly there is less chance of a thousand competing firms agreeing on a price policy or practice than of three or four doing so. But this auxiliary theory overlooks the fact that in many of our industries only the large plant can be efficient and only the big firm can pay for the expensive brains and facilities to develop technological improvements or can afford the costly equipment to capitalize upon them for the mutual benefit of itself and its customers. The net result of this corollary has been that, to a "man up a tree," many of the actions and decisions of the enforcement agencies look more like attempts to protect competitors, particularly the small ones, than measures to protect competition or benefit consumers.

Another corollary of the basic theory underlying the antitrust laws seems to be that price is the chief weapon of competition. The statutes themselves and the administrative and court decisions interpreting them recognize other bases of competition, to be sure, but price seems to hold the center of the enforcement stage. So, more than any other business executive, the man who makes pricing decisions must do his work with the Federal Trade Commission and the Department of Justice looking over his shoulder, and occasionally jiggling his elbow.

Certain specific pricing activities are especially to be avoided.

Collusion

If competitors agree on the prices they will charge, their action is clearly illegal. The penalties for violation of the antitrust laws are fine and imprisonment. It is impossible to imprison a corporation and a bit difficult to fix complete responsibility for a particular corporate act on any one person in the corporation, so the usual and expected penalty for many years was a fine assessed against the corporation found guilty of violation. In general, corporate executives, except so-called "three-time losers" were not penalized. The fines inflicted—even Judge Kenesaw Mountain Landis' famous $29 million judgment against the Standard Oil Company—probably were a cheap price to pay for the fruits of collusion. In 1961, however, the federal courts found several companies producing and selling electrical equipment, and their price-making executives, guilty of collusion, and not only fined the companies but imposed fines and jail sentences on the executives involved. An added penalty of a violating firm is its liability to pay triple the proven damages to customers and competitors.

While positive collusion in fixing prices is probably rare, the hidden variety, in the shape of informal understandings, is not uncommon. The existence of such understandings, even of positive collusion, is hard to prove.

Predatory Price Cutting

Price cutting for the purpose of injuring a competitor or driving him out of business tends to injure competition, and so is illegal. This also is very difficult to prove since real proof lies in the motive of the price cutter. Unless the price-making executives of a firm are incredibly careless or outspoken, evidence of intent is not easy to come by. A reasonable assumption of intent may arise from the nature of the price cut and the circumstances in which it is made, but such evidence can rarely establish it beyond reasonable doubt.

It is very hard to tell when the process of getting business turns into that of "getting" a competitor. Almost every price reduction has as one of its purposes taking business away from a rival. Almost inevitably, when A takes business away from B, B is hurt and his effectiveness as a competitor is damaged in some degree. At what point does the damage become so severe as to be illegal? It is hard to say. Partly because of these uncertainties, comparatively few prosecutions under the antitrust laws have been based on this violation alone.

As a result of the attempts of the Department of Justice to prove monopoly, collusion, or illegal price cutting in specific cases, the pricing executive is faced with a real dilemma. If his price is the same as that of his competitors, this fact is evidence of collusion. If his price is below those of his competitors, it constitutes evidence that he is trying to drive them out of the market and to injure competition. If he prices his product above competition, that is evidence that he has a monopoly for otherwise he could not get away with it. All three of these situations have been adduced as evidence in antitrust cases. About the only legally safe procedure for a pricing executive would seem to be to pull numbers out of a hat in the presence of witnesses of unassailable integrity.

Price Discrimination

The Robinson-Patman amendment to the Clayton Act prohibits price discrimination that impairs competition, except under certain conditions. In the early cases decided in administering this law, the courts showed a tendency to assume that the mere proof of price differentials to different customers was adequate evidence of injury to competition. More recently they have leaned toward the notion that to establish a *prima facie* case of price discrimination the Department of Justice must prove that the differential actually impairs or injures competition.

Once a *prima facie* case of discrimination that injures competition is established the burden of proof is on the defendent to show that his pricing action comes under one of the permitted exceptions. If he can do so, he avoids the penalties of the law.

a) He may attempt to show that the products sold at different prices are not of "like grade and quality." Not much has been done with this as a defense. It is still an open question, for example, whether the same product, one in the manufacturer's package bearing his label and brand and another in an unidentified package for private branding, is of "like grade and quality."

b) He can try to prove that one customer, by the method or quantity in which he bought, made savings possible in the cost of manufacture, sale, or delivery at least equal to the price differential. At first this seemed to promise the best way out, since a big customer buying a large quantity of a product on a long-term contract made it possible to spread a fixed amount of overhead costs over many more units. But the courts held that such reductions in overhead were attributable to the volume taken by *all* customers, not merely the large one.

The justification of quantity discounts is confined pretty narrowly to the savings in marketing costs they make possible. Even the differentials so justified may be limited by the Federal Trade Commission, which has charge of administering the law. The commission has exercised this power very sparingly but its threat is constantly present.

Both the commission and the courts have required cost accounting analyses conducted according to accepted accounting principles to establish the amount of such savings. One of the real managerial benefits of the law has been to encourage the practice of marketing cost analysis.

c) The defendant may show that the price differential was granted in response to changing market conditions or changing marketability of the goods, such as perishability, seasonal obsolescence, or distress sales.

d) He may seek to prove that the price differential was granted to a customer to meet an equally low price of a competitor. At first the commission and the courts tended to take a dim view of this plea. But in recent years it has become probably the most widely used defense under the act. The firm claiming it must present convincing evidence that a competitor actually did offer to sell the favored customer at the lower price. The concession granted cannot be more than enough merely to meet the price, and must not go below it. Any firm that is subject to the competition of quonset hut or garage operators can probably use this defense to cut its price in almost any major market where it seems desirable.

The law also forbids the granting of allowances (such as advertising allowances) and the supply of marketing services (such as point-of-sale promotional material or demonstrators) to a customer unless they are made available to all customers on "proportionally equal terms." The courts have not yet clarified the precise meaning of this language. It is so obscure and the activities it seeks to cover are so diverse as to arouse serious doubts about their ever being able to do so.

The act prohibits the allowance of brokerage fees to large customers who buy direct. For example, many food products are sold through brokers or manufacturer's agents. Large chains that bought direct from the manufacturer formerly claimed that they were performing the agent's functions and were entitled to his commission. To get their business many manufacturers agreed. This is no longer legal.

Legal Costs

Many practices are probably legal under the antitrust laws that have not been declared so by the courts. This is because of the cost of getting a judicial decision. If a well known firm is sued by the Department of Justice the news of the suit is likely to make the front pages of most newspapers. By and large, readers are apt to assume that the company is guilty. Incalculable goodwill may be lost. If the firm at long last wins a clearance from the charges, the news is likely to find a place somewhere back in the financial section, which few customers read. Many firms prefer to forgo what may well be effective and perfectly legal marketing activities rather than run the risk of this sort of loss.

Even when loss of goodwill is not involved it may not be worthwhile for a firm to run the risk of a suit to establish the legality of a pricing action. Once the government brings a suit it seldom stops short of the highest court. To fight a case through to a Supreme Court decision is apt to cost a quarter to a half a million dollars, and more if much evidence has to be compiled. To these costs should be added the risk of customer suits for triple damages if the firm loses; this is particularly true in a price discrimination case.

Before it is profitable for a management to spend this kind of money in a suit it must be able to see in the action involved profit possibilities amounting to at least twice the probable cost of the suit. Except when really vital issues are involved, the average management prefers to pay its legal staff to keep it out of pricing lawsuits rather than to fight them. For this reason the pricing executive will be wise to consult legal advice with respect to any pricing action that follows too closely or too exactly a competitor's action, that involves different prices for different customers, that represents an unusually drastic change, or that involves any sort of inducement for dealer cooperation in the manufacturer's sales promotion program.

Fixing Resale Prices

The system of so-called fair trade laws grew out of the persistent hostility of the federal courts to resale price maintenance. They declared that contracts between a manufacturer and his wholesalers or retailers, fixing the price at which the latter should resell the former's products were illegal, (with the exception of the unwieldy and expensive consignment contract by which the producer consigned his products to his outlets, thus retaining ownership until they were finally sold to the ultimate consumer). Under the antitrust acts they outlawed most of the devices by which a manufacturer could spot and refuse to sell to price-cutting dealers.

Chiefly as a result of the lobbying and pressure activities of wholesalers and retailers, especially in the drug trade, many state legislatures passed fair-trade laws during the 1930's, most of them containing the controversial "nonsigner's clause." At one time more than 40 states had such legislation on their statute books. Such a law suffered from the drawback that its mechanism could be used only by manufacturers located within the state in marketing to outlets also within the state. It could not be applied to goods that moved in interstate commerce. The same kind of lobbying pressure finally induced Congress to pass a law, later amended by the McGuire Act, which provided that any manufacturer located in a state having a fair-trade law could utilize the provisions of the fair-trade law of any other state in dealing with his outlets in the latter state. A manufacturer in a fair-trade state could legally practice price maintenance in all but a few of the states of the Union.

During the late 1940's and 1950's many of these laws were subjected to judicial examination or legislative reconsideration. Some of them were declared invalid; others were repealed or modified. The nonsigner's clause proved especially vulnerable to attack in both the courts and the legislatures. Now many of the states which once had such laws are without them; in others the law has been emasculated by the removal or invalidation of the nonsigner's clause. The marketing manager who plans to control the retail price of his product should seek legal advice to find out just what machinery is available for doing so in each state.

The growth of the discount house and other types of retail outlets which rely heavily on price appeal has forced many manufacturers to take a sober second look at the whole subject of resale price maintenance. To a very considerable extent the large margins the manufacturer had to build into his price maintenance system (to enable the less efficient retailers to handle his product profitably) helped the discount outlet grow by enabling it to make invidious comparisons between the fixed price and its own much lower prices.

In response to the pressure of the regular retailers many manufacturers spent large sums of money in trying to police their fair-trade contracts. In the main, they were unsuccessful. Many of them also realized that if they persisted in such attempts they would not only incur heavy legal expenses but shut themselves out of outlets that sold a large volume of their kind of merchandise and place themselves under severe handicaps in competing with rivals who did not fair-trade their merchandise.

It is probable that at the present time most of the pressure for price maintenance comes from the retailers and not from the manufacturer. Much of this pressure is clearly illegal. Anyone who has observed what goes on during a retailers' campaign to induce or force a producer to fair-trade his merchandise must recognize that the threats of retail substitution of other brands, putting the victim's merchandise "under the counter" or in the back room, "talking it down," and various other devices are all features of a combination or conspiracy in restraint of trade. These actions cannot occur coincidentally in many retail stores over a wide area without some sort of agreement. Probably the only thing that has prevented antitrust actions against them is the fact that they have been committed by small businessmen who are the particular darlings of politicians because they control or can influence large numbers of votes.

Marketing Planning and Control

We come now to the two functions of planning and control. We have chosen to treat them together even though, theoretically, planning comes at the beginning and control at the end of the marketing process. Our decision is based on the facts that (*a*) in the well managed firm both marketing planning and control go on constantly in coincidence with operations and (*b*) the two functions lean heavily on each other, planning being guided by information disclosed by control, and control relying on planning to supply standards of measurement. These functions are alike also in that the raw material of each is information. The planner starts with a problem and facts about it, and winds up with a program of action. Control starts with facts from which it constructs standards of performance, gathers facts to check actual performance with the standard, and ends up with a measurement of action. The control executive's standards must to a large extent be drawn from the planner's plans, and the wise planner grounds future courses of action largely on the success or failure of past and current operations as measured by control.

So we will start our study of planning and control with a chapter outlining the kinds, and sources, of information needed in marketing management. We will follow this with a chapter on marketing research dealing with the collection of facts, most of which are *external* to the firm, and another chapter on marketing cost analysis designed to marshall information that is to be found *in* the company's records. This will be followed with a chapter devoted to the methods and problems of marketing planning, and then by a chapter dealing with the techniques and purposes of control and the spirit in which it should be applied to marketing activities.

CHAPTER 18

Marketing Intelligence*

INTRODUCTION

Information is power. It's as critical to successful marketing operations as military intelligence is to warfare. As Marion Harper, Jr. put it in the 1960 Parlin Memorial Lecture, which honors the father of marketing research: "To manage a business well is to manage its future; and to manage its future is to manage information."

Today's marketing can be characterized as neither art nor science; it is a bit of both. But if marketing is to become more scientific in the future, management must learn to use more timely, accurate, pertinent, and significant information than it has been content with in the past. In short, decision making in marketing will have to become more informed and less intuitive.

Marketing executives haven't always appreciated the need for marketing intelligence. Many have been rightfully accused of operating in the dark and "flying by the seat of the pants." Production, engineering, and financial executives transferred to marketing posts have often been appalled at the paucity of facts and figures with which they had to work. The marketing director of a local brewery, when asked to explain what accounted for his company's success in achieving the Number 1 market position for its brand, replied: "We just don't know; I wish we did. All we're sure of is that we won't *change* our strategy one iota as long as we're on top!" Small wonder that many marketing leaders have been toppled from their perches. Inadequate, incorrect, and misinterpreted information lies at the roots of many collossal marketing failures.

Authors' Note: We are particularly indebted to two men for many of the ideas expressed in this chapter: Mr. Robert J. Williams, Director of Marketing Intelligence for the Edward Dalton Co., a division of Mead Johnson & Co., and Mr. Robert Prather, Manager of Marketing Research, Chemical Division, Merck and Co., Inc.

Marketing research, to be sure, has long been regarded as a key function by prudent marketers. Throughout this book we have repeatedly high-lighted the role of information and research in decision making and in formulating marketing policies. Yet even where marketing research has been widely applied it has too often been used only in piecemeal fashion to help solve isolated marketing problems. A broader perspective on the information management function is needed if we are to properly evaluate marketing results and promptly revise and redirect our programs and strategies as conditions change.

WHAT IS "MARKETING INTELLIGENCE"?

Marketing intelligence can be defined as the purposeful, systematic, broad-gauge, on-going search for facts to serve as decision making premises in marketing. In functional terms it involves the entire process of specifying, selecting, collecting, creating, organizing, processing, translating, transmitting, presenting, using, safeguarding, and storing information aimed at improving both short-term and long-range marketing operations.

Marketing intelligence is information, but it isn't mere *data-gathering*. A distinction may be drawn between data and information. Marketing information refers to elements of knowledge which are *useful* in decision making and which serve as bases for rational marketing action; it is possible to have tons of marketing data without possessing an ounce of information. To become information, raw data must be made to take on managerial significance. This often requires data translation or processing of one sort or other. For instance, information can often be extracted from data through statistical procedures which reveal useful interrelations between bits of data which, alone, would be meaningless or operationally sterile.

Nor does marketing intelligence deal only with undisputed facts and statistics. Assumptions, emotional reactions, attitudes, opinions, concepts, theories and premises, as well as fact, may all be grist for the intelligence mill.

Marketing intelligence is also a broader and more inclusive field than marketing research. Marketing intelligence *embraces* marketing research but extends *beyond* it. Marketing research is typically conducted on an *ad hoc* basis to assist management in solving specific marketing problems. But marketing intelligence is as much a problem *prevention* business as a problem *solving* business. It incorporates *all* useful marketing information, whether systematically obtained by objective research and experimentation, derived from mathematical manipulation of data, or generated by other means of surveillance, reconnaissance, monitoring, and reporting.

Many of the standard tools and techniques of marketing intelligence, such as sales reports, marketing research, sales analysis, and distribution cost analysis are discussed elsewhere in this book. In this chapter we will focus on issues such as these: *What is the role of intelligence in managing the marketing function? What kinds of information are needed, and from what sources can they be acquired? What are the costs and benefits involved? How can we effectively manage the intelligence function in marketing?*

Establishing Intelligence Needs

Clearly, a marketing executive's judgment is no better than his information. Facts, figures, and estimates of many kinds must be systematically gathered to accurately reflect the ever-changing dimensions of the marketing function. Indeed, some observers claim that the gathering and presenting of marketing information is fast becoming the single most important factor in marketing success or failure. Why are marketing directors becoming increasingly dependent upon more and better information and altogether new kinds of intelligence?

In part, the answer lies in the increasingly tight vise of the cost-profit squeeze in which many marketers have found themselves. This bind has sharply reduced the margin of marketing error which can be tolerated in many companies. Whereas the old-style marketing executive often got a pat on the back if 51 percent of his decisions turned out to be correct, the modern manager may be severely chastised for registering a batting average below 70 or 80 percent.

A Broad Perspective on Intelligence Requirements

A moment's reflection reveals many general uses for marketing intelligence. In each of the substantive areas of marketing—in segmenting markets, pricing, product planning, channel management, distribution, personal selling, advertising and sales promotion—marketing intelligence definitely plays a key role.

In planning and executing overall marketing strategies and tactics, intelligence must supply the triggers to action, help in pinpointing objectives, and assist in identifying the limits within which action can be taken. Like military intelligence, marketing intelligence involves the collection of information used both in generating strategies and in the tactical direction of activity toward desired goals. Intelligence also suggests occasions when we must depart from plan and move opportunistically to cash in upon uniquely favorable transient market circumstances. Intelligence also incorporates the feedback principle in auditing marketing results at all links in the distribution setup, and, as a basis for taking corrective action, the marketing executive needs a continuous playback on the critical aspects of current marketing performance. Competitors are ready to pull the marketing rug from under us the moment we suffer a lapse in marketing intelligence.

From the procedural point of view, marketing intelligence cuts across all of the so-called processes organic to administration: planning, organizing, and controlling. It provides the early warning signals which tip off the need for new planning and supplies valuable input data for matching means to ends. Information is also needed to adjust programing assumptions as marketing plans are executed. Information, in short, is the key resource in rational planning. Information also affects organization structures and control systems. Lack of information, for example, is often cited as a major obstacle to delegation. Marketing intelligence has many functions in connection with staffing, supervision, and other executive activities, but its chief usefulness lies in preventing marketing problems from arising and in facilitating sound decision making when they become unavoidable.

Information in Marketing Decision Making

"We aren't given enough information to solve the problem." To the ears of instructors who have used the case method of teaching marketing, these words have a familiar ring. One of the favorite "outs" of the student who is reluctant to make a decision in the face of uncertainty is to say: "We need more facts than the case supplies. I recommend marketing research." When the instructor inquires into such matters as precisely what form of research is needed, what the research is to find out, what the student proposes to do with the information it discloses, what it will cost and whether it will be worth the cost, the student becomes much less positive and vocal. Similar attitudes are also characteristic of seasoned business executives, and one often encounters much the same vagueness as to the real informational objectives, decision making usefulness, and costs of marketing intelligence.

Such experiences suggest that management by and large still has much to learn about the management of marketing information. Two key questions calling for early resolution are *What intelligence do we really need?* and *How can we begin to measure its value against the cost of getting it?* A step toward answering the first of these questions is to recognize the kinds of decision situations in the handling of which marketing intelligence can be useful to managers. Decision situations in marketing seem to fall into at least five basic types with respect to identifying intelligence needs.

1. Do we have a marketing problem, and if so exactly what is it? What's the score? Am I doing well or badly? Which problems should I look into first? The marketing manager may feel that things are not going just right but may not be able to put his finger on the precise part of his operation that generates his feeling of uneasiness. Strangely enough, unexpected good fortune may also raise this question.

For example, when a marketer of an industrial good finds that a customer is buying a volume greatly in excess of his known or estimated usage of the item, the marketing manager begins to wonder whether his information system is as good as it should be, whether a new use is being developed that he doesn't know about, or whether the customer is buying for resale to an unknown user to whom the marketer should be selling direct at greater profit. Marketing intelligence, therefore, can contribute to problem awareness and diagnosis.

2. What can we do in a given situation? In this case, the marketing manager realizes that he has a problem and feels that he knows what it is, but is not sure that he has uncovered all possible ways of dealing with it. He is especially doubtful that he has found the *best* way of solving it. In this situation the objective of marketing intelligence is the discovery of alternatives or of information that will point the way to alternative courses of action.

3. Shall we do a particular thing or not do it? This is probably one of the decision situations in which marketing intelligence is most often useful. Examples of the kinds of things that are attempted or walked away from are the introduction of a new product, the entering of a new market, the adoption of a new marketing policy, or the launching of a new promotional campaign.

4. If we do a particular thing, shall we do it this way or that way? Of the many ways of doing something, which is best? For example, in carrying out a certain project shall we rely chiefly on personal selling, or on advertising, or on some form of sales promotion? How effective a marketing tool is price in this situation? That is also a type of decision in which marketing intelligence is commonly found useful. Rational choice among identified alternatives depends upon selection criteria unearthed by marketing intelligence.

5. Shall we go on doing what we are now doing, or shall we stop it, or shall we modify the way we are doing it? This is a decision situation arising out of the control function and one in which marketing intelli-

gence is used primarily to facilitate control. In part, this question is simply another form of the first one, "Do we have a problem?" in part, any marketing intelligence work in connection with it is a search for alternative courses of action in addition to the one now in use; and in part, such information is expected to help in appraising the performance of the alternative currently being carried out.

An important step toward establishing intelligence requirements in marketing is to understand the potential contribution of information to these decision situations. Concrete problem areas need to be cataloged and classified in terms of their relative importance to the company, the frequency with which they arise, and the way in which decision making responsibilities for marketing are distributed in the company's organization. But more than a mere list of short-run and long-range decision situations is required.

Marketing intelligence cannot be limited to the search for information pertaining to current crises or sources of difficulty. If the marketing manager is to be both forewarned and forearmed, the eyes and ears of his intelligence system must also monitor areas of strategic importance to the firm in terms of *potential* opportunity or trouble. Furthermore, one of the functions of marketing intelligence is to provide negative advice to marketing managers; that is, to indicate what *not* to do in order to avoid trouble. Certain aspects of *timing* in marketing management must also be considered when estimating intelligence requirements. In introducing a new product, for instance, one company decided to break its advertising when distribution coverage hit the 40 percent figure—not earlier nor later. Accordingly, marketing intelligence was assigned the responsibility of monitoring the market and informing management when the base figure was being approached. Thus, *marketing intelligence sometimes involves the continuous tracking of variables* that will identify the proper moment for releasing preplanned activity.

A moving picture, not just a static snapshot of marketing operations, is often called for. It is primarily in this sense that marketing intelligence is distinguished from the narrower field of marketing research. Marketing research is often done on a one-shot basis to meet one or more of the five decision situations described above. Marketing intelligence also incorporates various types of permanent or continuous monitoring to trigger action or to avoid problem areas altogether.

Intelligence Auditing

A possible line of attack for further clarifying concrete marketing intelligence requirements is to conduct a crude form of supply-and-demand analysis. Disparities between the demand for and the supply of marketing information in a company signal the need for changes in the intelligence system currently employed.

Most companies do not have a "marketing intelligence department" as such. However, they can assess the informational outputs of their marketing research departments, economic forecasters, controllers, sales analysts, field sales reporters, and other individuals or organizational units specifically charged with performing portions of the marketing intelligence function. The aim is to identify the information which enters the company and is made available to marketers. A summary statement of this information *supply* which reflects the standards to which intelligence suppliers, such as market researchers presumably attempt to conform, might be assembled. This statement could then be compared with a counterpart document put together by executive users of information to highlight the *demand* for marketing intelligence within the company. The latter would reflect the standards by which suppliers of marketing intelligence are in fact being evaluated by the users of their services. It is to be expected that the two intelligence summaries would differ in some respects, thereby revealing a possible communication failure within the company.[1]

Attempts could then be made to trace the origin of the failure to specific intelligence units, to responsible line executives, or to the organizational arrangements within which both the users and suppliers of marketing information function.

The intelligence supply may be deficient for any number of reasons. It may be inadequate in terms of subject coverage. It may not be timely, either in terms of reporting frequency or in terms of lags and delays. It may be presented in inappropriate or unusable form. Its reliability may be held suspect. The volume of intelligence may be too great (drowning and paralyzing executives with excessive data) or too little (starving them for knowledge). Information may prove to have been routed to the wrong receivers or, worse yet, locked away in inaccessible files. A critical evaluation of the existing intelligence system of the average firm would probably reveal such supply deficiencies.

Intelligence estimates can also err on the demand side. In assessing intelligence needs it is well to remember that information is costly and that its generation must be purposeful. Thus we must visualize uses and benefits when making demand estimates for the marketing intelligence

---

[1]For a similar approach and viewpoint see Robert E. Sessions, "A Management Audit of Marketing Research," *Journal of Marketing,* January, 1950, pp. 563–71.

function. Cost factors alone prohibit us from generating information strictly on an "it would be nice to know" basis. Thus information gathering and analysis must be goal-directed and tied to reality. The key test for estimating the value of any bit of information is this: Will it make a significant contribution to decision making and marketing action?

Information, then, is not an end in itself. Yet marketing executives often place nonfunctional demands upon suppliers of intelligence. Here are some of the more common reasons for deficient information demand analyses:

1. Some executives foolishly try to keep informed about everything, get swamped in details, and create unreasonable demands for intelligence.

2. An executive may be aware of the latent power of control over information and hoard it from others in the organization.

3. Some executives are totally impatient with details and fail to use essential data even if it is made available, preferring to place greater reliance on private hunches and assumptions. One purpose of an intelligence audit is to reappraise the validity of underlying expectations, attitudes, opinions, concepts, beliefs, and values which function as unseen decision making premises in day-to-day marketing operations.

4. Executives may ask for the wrong kinds of intelligence; for example, ordering qualitative information when quantitative facts are really needed, or overstressing information directed to methods for increasing sales volume while undervaluing intelligence about marketing costs, or asking for mere data rather than real information.

5. An executive may let his intelligence system grow like a weed patch, permitting it to get out of touch with changing market conditions by failing to prune out unnecessary data from time to time.

6. Some executives, preoccupied with the past and present, overvalue historical and current operating data to the detriment of rational estimates and forecasts of future conditions.

Such biases on the demand side should be rooted out in auditing true intelligence requirements. They act as blinders and as stiflers of ingenuity and creativity, and they increase information costs.

Questions each marketing executive should ask himself in defining intelligence requirements are: What information do I need to carry out my assigned responsibilities? What information must I supply to others in the company? Why do we really need it? When do we have to have it? How will it be used?

For long-range marketing, management needs fundamental information touching upon the survival and growth needs of the company. Therefore informational needs hinge on the answer to the classic question: "What business are we in?" An analysis of basic objectives is a useful step in assessing intelligence requirements, for the value of much information is ultimately weighed in terms of its contribution to profit objectives and other goals.

As situations and goals change so do intelligence requirements. Short-range marketing operations are grounded in more specific situations and their solution calls for different information inputs. Planning manuals, containing written objectives, policies, procedures, methods, programs, and timetables; and control systems, containing relevant indices and standards for evaluating performance data, should be examined for clues to intelligence requirements.

There are some things a marketing manager simply must know, e.g., whether sales volume is high or low in a key market. Negatives, as well as positives, are important. For instance, intelligence which pinpoints trade channels where a product is *not* moving, areas where competitive price pressures are strongest, and consumer dissatisfactions as well as satisfactions with product performance may highlight marketing weaknesses to be corrected. In short, attention-directing, problem-preventing, problem-solving, score-card, and corrective-action intelligence are all required. Both latent and manifest problems are involved.

Information is of little value unless it gets into the hands of decision makers in intelligible form and is readily related to planning and control issues. Before placing the responsibility for marketing intelligence deficiencies on individual suppliers or users of information, the manager must first examine the organization structure. Since an organization can be viewed as a communications network, organizational analysis may be useful in locating communications trouble spots.

We must see that the intelligence system is geared to organizational arrangements. Each executive's information needs must be examined to ensure that he is supplied with an adequate and timely flow of decision making premises. In part, this can be done by studying available job descriptions, organization charts, and personnel policy manuals. Communications centers need to be identified to clarify the information-interest of all key marketing people and to assure that marketing intelligence is distributed properly within the organization. Specially prepared flow diagrams can highlight routing sequences and reporting responsibilities with reference to the flow of information between people in the marketing department.

Interdivisional communications analysis within the company is also necessary. For example, in new product work the engineering department may be dependent upon marketing for information which will help it produce designs for maximum consumer acceptance. Marketers may need estimates on plant capacity or production runs from the manufacturing division to help them set marketing objectives.

In approaching the intelligence audit through organization analysis it is also worthwhile to recall the description of marketing channels from earlier chapters in this book. The distribution system is really an external arm of the company organization. When appraising the flow of information in a marketing system care must be exercised to ensure that information is secured on every important segment and link in channels of distribution, as well as on the end-use market segments and competitive environments toward which each channel extends. A smooth movement of goods at high velocity throughout the system, from plant to pantry, is heavily dependent upon a flow of marketing information. Intelligence of merchandise flow is available for purchase in many cases.

To sum up this discussion of the intelligence audit we have suggested that intelligence can be assessed from the supply side or from the point of view of the internal demand for it, and that this analysis can be extended through many organizational levels in a marketing system. This approach should reveal what information is needed but not currently available, and also what intelligence is being needlessly generated. The audit should help define intelligence objectives, clarify information needs and critical intelligence functions, reveal obstacles to communication flow, establish priorities for different kinds of information, and adjust intelligence means and resources to desired ends.

The marketing manager is now ready to turn to a quite different set of issues. How he will get the needed information is a question of *method* or technique. Where he can find it is a question of being familiar with *sources* of information. What he is willing to pay for marketing intelligence raises the issue of *costs*. Let us consider the cost question first.

INTELLIGENCE COSTS[2]

Little has been written to guide managers on the economics of marketing intelligence. Yet the intelligence function must ultimately be evaluated in terms of both costs and benefits. How can a marketing manager decide when getting marketing intelligence is worthwhile? In theory the answer is very simple. Marketing intelligence is worthwhile whenever the cost of getting it is less than the costs, risks, and consequences of not getting it. For example, in the five types of decision sit-

[2]This section reproduces much material in an article by R. S. Alexander, "Let's Have a Marketing Research Done, *Journal of Business,* Seton Hall University, December, 1963.

uations outlined earlier in this chapter the worth of marketing intelligence consists almost entirely of the added soundness of decision it makes possible. If, to be more specific, without the facts disclosed by marketing intelligence services, management has a 60–40 chance of making the right decision, while *with* those facts its chances of doing so have improved to 70–30, the value of the intelligence is measured by the dollar value of the added 10 chances in every 100 which management has of making the right decision.

With respect to the five decision situations described, the ratio between the cost of having marketing intelligence and the cost of not having it in any decision situation depends chiefly on three things: (1) the difficulty of getting the needed information, (2) the stakes involved in the decision, and (3) the chances of making a mistake in the decision. The harder the information is to get the more it is apt to cost. If the decision involves possible sales amounting to $10 million, promising 20 percent net profit on sales, the stakes are greater than with one that involves a volume of only $100,000 at any conceivable rate of net return.

The chances of making a mistaken decision because of lack of information depend on the kinds of facts we lack and the density of our ignorance about them. If the missing facts are vital to the issue and the decision maker is completely in the dark about them, the chances of mistake are greater than when the absent information is only ancillary to the issue and enough fragments are known so that an astute management can guess at the rest.

The cost of not engaging in marketing intelligence work is the cost of making a mistaken decision times the difference between the chances of making a mistake with and without the information it may supply. How can a marketing manager appraise ahead of time the costs of making a wrong decision in a given situation? Very rarely, if ever, can this be done with any degree of exactitude. Any figures set down will almost invariably be in the nature of estimates made on a very tenuous factual basis. But we can at least try to isolate the cost elements conceptually. Then, perhaps, by estimating the dollar value of each element separately we may arrive at a total that will be somewhere near the mark.

Consider the decision to do a certain thing or not to do it. If we decide to do it and should not have done it, the cost of our mistake includes at least (*a*) the cost of doing it, minus any gross cash inflow resulting from doing it, (*b*) the loss of the added net cash inflow and other benefits that would have resulted from spending the same amount of money, time, and effort on some other project, i.e., opportunity cost, (*c*) the value of the loss of prestige and customer confidence that results from the "blooper," and (*d*) the value of the loss of morale among our own personnel that we sustain from their knowledge that we "pulled a boner."

If, on the other hand, we do not do it and should have done it, our conceptual cost elements will be at least (*a*) the profits we would have made from doing it, minus the cost of doing it, (*b*) the loss of improvement in market position we would have gained by doing it, and (*c*) the loss of internal morale because of what is sooner or later likely to be recognized as an opportunity ignored.

Consider also a decision as to the way in which a certain thing should be done. If we decide to do it the wrong way we must pay at least the following conceptual cost elements:

1. The cost of doing it the wrong way, minus the cost of doing it the right way
2. The value of the results we would have got by doing it the right way, minus the value of whatever results we got by doing it the wrong way
3. The loss of market position resulting from the ineffective use of a marketing tool or handling of a marketing opportunity
4. The loss of morale that our people will suffer when they realize they are being made to do it the hard way.

Let us assume for the moment that we are able to assign reasonably accurate figures to these conceptual costs of a yes-or-no decision situation in which certain information, which is now unknown, may be disclosed through marketing intelligence if management decides to authorize it. We might have an analysis that looks something like this:

Estimated cost of making a mistake.............	$100,000
Chances of making a right decision:	
If we tossed a coin.................................	50–50
With known facts and no further marketing intelligence...	60–40
With additional facts disclosed by new marketing intelligence....................................	75–25

The mistake-making-cost per decision of this kind then becomes

If we toss a coin.............................	$50,000
If we do not use new marketing intelligence......	40,000
If we use new marketing intelligence............	25,000
Saving from using new marketing intelligence.....	15,000

It seems clear that in making decisions of this kind and under these assumptions we may expect by using additional marketing information to avoid making mistakes that will cost us an average of $15,000 per decision. If, then, we can get the information for less than $15,000, it will pay to do so. As its cost approaches or exceeds $15,000, its use becomes uneconomic.

At this point we may flatter ourselves that we have developed a nice exercise in decision theory. But has it any practical value? The only figure in the analysis which we can really document in the average decision situation is the cost of getting the marketing information. We can, for instance, get cost estimates from marketing research firms. All the others may usually be the sheerest "guesstimates."

But let us examine the way in which decisions to get or not to get marketing information are all too often made. The marketing manager feels the need for additional information in a specific situation. He decides what facts he would like to find out and asks his marketing research man for an estimate of the cost of getting them. He then decides that the added information is or is not worth what the research man says it will cost. Or he submits the estimate of the cost of the research, with a description of the project and some indication of what he proposes to use its results for, to the executive charged with the responsibility of approving such expenditures. If the boss approves he has really said "It is worth the cost"; if he turns the project down he has really decided that the information is not worth the cost of getting it.

The point is that the decision as to whether the information expected is worth what it will cost must be made every time marketing intelligence is considered. The *sole* question is *how* it shall be made: on the basis of a subconscious and often cursory casting up of the values involved, or after a conscious and systematic attempt, however crudely made, to reduce those values to their conceptual elements and assign dollar figures to each of them? May it not be possible that the kind of analysis involved in the latter process will result in sounder decisions as to when marketing intelligence is needed and significantly increase its usefulness as a function of marketing management?

Moreover, the process of making decisions about the use of marketing intelligence on the basis of subconscious reaction or a casual casting up of the values can be improved only through the slow development of managerial "feel" for the situation. One of the chief ways in which this feel is developed is by making mistakes. This is an expensive way, especially since in a firm committed to the policy of growing its executives from within it is likely to happen that about the time an executive has developed this particular type of sensitivity he is ready to be promoted to another job where he may not have the opportunity to use it.

But if a manager makes decisions about this matter on the basis of a theory he recognizes as sound, or by a process that is definite and detailed, or through the employment of tools that he has learned to use, the road is open to him to constantly reexamine the soundness of his theory and to seek to improve the process and sharpen the tools. Moreover, theories, processes, and tools can readily be passed on by one executive to another in training to succeed him, a thing that cannot be done with "feel."

It is not our purpose to deprecate the importance of feel in marketing decision making; anyone who has experienced it or seen it operate cannot be without a vast respect for subjective or personal judgment. But it is a rare quality and not all of us have it who think we do. Furthermore, it is not something that can be passed on from one person to another. So it is probable that the farther managers can travel along the road to decision by conscious analysis before beginning to rely on feel, the better their decisions will be.

Nor is it our purpose to suggest that any large percentage of the marketing intelligence efforts now being performed are not worth their cost, although there are undoubtedly some of which that is true. From the standpoint of marketing intelligence functions and the persons engaged in them, it would be better if many were never carried out. The more precisely marketing intelligence can be made to operate as a managerial function and the greater the skill management develops in its use, the more valuable it becomes and the stronger grows the position of those assigned intelligence responsibilities.

As a matter of fact, it is not unlikely that many marketing intelligence tasks that should be done are not done because a properly convincing case cannot be made for them on the basis of a casual, subconscious casting up of intangible values. This is especially likely to be the case in firms whose organization structures are such that significant appropriations for such projects must be approved by financial officers or by top management. The reviewing officer is more inclined to take a sympathetic attitude toward a proposal that is documented with an honest attempt to indicate the value of the information the company may expect to get for the money it is asked to spend than when no such attempt is made. It is true that this documentation must consist largely of estimates that sometimes approach the quality of guesses. But these same executives are accustomed each year at budget making time to bet the company bankroll on sales estimates, usually originating in the marketing area, which, in the final analysis, have a lot of guesswork in them. Why should they gag at making decisions to commit much smaller sums on the basis of estimates, even though made on much more tenuous factual bases, originating in the same area?

It is not unlikely that more rather than less marketing intelligence work would be done if its proposals, instead of being couched in some such terms as "Let's spend X dollars for marketing research," were phrased something like this: "If we spend X dollars on marketing research, we may expect to get X plus Y dollars in return." In general, then, marketing intelligence costs must be weighed in terms of the uses to be made of information and the consequences resulting from incomplete or erroneous facts.

The true cost is also a function of the reliability of information. Cut-rate research can truly turn out to be expensive. Costs will also be affected by choices made with respect to research design, alternative methods for generating intelligence, and the sources from which it is drawn.

For example, as far as marketing intelligence is concerned, the sales-force is often a "lost battalion" because research men fail to communicate its role in the intelligence function to the line sales manager. Because of the large number of factors affecting the costs and effectiveness of intelligence, marketing information services must be purchased by skilled buyers. This may pose a problem, since the intelligence specialist often tends to become more closely identified with the tools of his craft than with the business problem he helps to solve. Some researchers become wedded, through bias and habitual usage, to a particular technique. A "good survey man," for instance, may continually use survey methods even when observational, experimental, or other techniques of intelligence might be more effective and cheaper.

How can we overcome the problems of the specialist without destroying his usefulness? The answer seems to lie in staffing intelligence services with both generalists and specialists. A strong case can be made out for the argument that marketing intelligence should be headed by a managerially oriented generalist with specialists reporting to him. It may also be desirable to see that the intelligence "generalist" is a staff-man not directly responsible to the line marketing executives whom he serves. This could be argued in terms of disparities of perception between suppliers and users of intelligence.

The unit cost of marketing intelligence also goes down if we can distribute it over many applications. Multi-use information is less expensive than single-purpose intelligence. For example, basic data on market potentials is usually both a high priority and a low cost intelligence item because it is useful in virtually every major decision faced by marketing executives. Highly specialized data may be used just once and discarded, rather than put into storage for future use. If we buy information on a continuous basis we may pay less per marketing action than if we buy it on a strictly *ad hoc* basis—provided we can visualize multiple uses for it and realize the potential payoff on the investment.

The possibility of multiple uses for a single variety of intelligence, of course, raises problems in distributing its costs to particular uses and to organizational units. The problem can be very complicated in large-scale marketing programs or campaigns which may contain literally hundreds of interlocking individual decisions in complex means-end chains.

Intelligence costs also vary with the degree of difficulty involved in obtaining information. This, in turn, is dependent on the availability of data. For instance, food marketers have come to take the availability of consumer panel and store audit data for granted. Their strong interest in velocity and routinization of transactions (historically linked to the old greengrocer's adage, Sell It or Smell It!) has led to a strong demand for marketing intelligence and fostered the commercial development of such services.

By way of contrast, marketers of television sets and other consumer durables have often not demonstrated a capacity for changing marketing plans quickly because they simply haven't had fast, accurate reporting on what the consumer was doing. The scarcity of field information in durables industries grows out of such difficulties as

1. *High Unit-of-Sales Price.* The dealer plays his cards close to his chest when the items he is selling run to $200 or more. He feels that the best way to keep information from his competitor is not to tell anybody.

2. *Slow Turnover.* While total durable goods sales are enormous, the average dealer's turnover on a single item is slow and therefore hard to measure economically.

3. *Traffic Builders* vs. *Price Lines.* If a dealer is using a well known line to build store traffic, but using items paying a longer discount to switch the buyer after he enters the store, he does not want such practices traced to him.

4. *Indeterminate Market.* Each family becomes a prospect for a single item of durable goods at very long intervals. Only a tiny fraction of the public is interested at any given time. This fraction is difficult to locate, hard to measure, and is continually changing.

5. *Thin Distribution.* The larger number of brands and models available in durable goods and the relatively few dealers which many manufacturers have in many important markets make ordinary methods of sampling a very difficult and unreliable means of market measurement.[3] A good deal of work has been done and must continue to be done to overcome such barriers to low-cost marketing intelligence.

---

[3]"Control of Consumer Durables Inventory," *Proceedings, Twenty-Sixth Boston Conference on Distribution,* Retail Trade Board, Boston Chamber of Commerce, 1954, p. 99.

The generation of marketing intelligence consumes scarce resources; it ties up manpower, time, money, and facilities. Mismanagement of the information function can lead to unnecessary fragmentation or duplication of effort with corresponding decreases in effectiveness and increases in costs. Since the cost of information is high, the marketing intelligence system must be designed and managed to be as efficient as any other cost generating function in marketing. Effort should be directed toward establishing rational intelligence programs and budgets aimed at assuring good results.

There are interesting analogies to be pursued between information management and advertising management. Advertising and intelligence services are both intangibles, for instance, and both functions typically depend at least partially on outside service agencies for assistance. Therefore, much of the topical material covered in the chapters on advertising management probably applies with equal force and validity to intelligence management. For example, in establishing a marketing intelligence program it should be possible at the beginning of the year to forecast crudely the major issues, decisions, and applications likely to require informational guidance and assistance.

Sound management principles would seem to prohibit intelligence administration (in at least the larger companies) purely on a job-to-job and hand-to-mouth basis. Control is essential, and it is preferable to set up an intelligence budget representing an overall judgment of the annual value of marketing intelligence to the company.[4] Perspectives on budgeting and other aspects of planning and administration for the intelligence function can be gleaned by carefully rereading the chapter on advertising and by translating and reinterpreting it in terms of the information management function.

SOURCES AND TYPES OF MARKETING INFORMATION

Marketing managers must ultimately set criteria for information structures. Toward this end, we must be thoroughly familiar with the various kinds of intelligence important to marketing and the sources from which each type can be secured. As a start toward systematizing the information management function we might try to classify information into some kind of meaningful framework.

Information Classification

There are many ways in which marketing information can be classified for analysis. It can be classified functionally; that is, by the way in

---

[4] See "How to Buy Marketing Research," *Cost and Profit Outlook,* October, 1951, p. 3.

which it will be used. It can be classified according to where it is likely to be found, according to sources. It can also be classified according to the methods used to generate it. There are so many possible classification methods that no single scheme is likely to prove useful under all marketing conditions. However, the following list of two-way classifications should help to highlight the variety of intelligence inputs to be considered:

1. Primary and Secondary	6. *Ex Ante* vs. *Ex Post Facto*
2. Internal and External	7. Multi-Purpose and Single-Use
3. Qualitative and Quantitative	8. Overt and Covert
4. Cost and Revenue Information	9. Plum-Picking vs. Derivation
5. Continuous vs. Intermittent	10. Miscellaneous

Primary and Secondary.   Secondary data is already available and is often in published form. Primary information must be generated by the direct collection of previously unavailable material. Since it is usually less costly to tap secondary sources than primary sources, marketers should learn how to fully exploit the lode of readily available specialized marketing literature[5] and other kinds of data before conducting original research. In some circumstances, however, greater emphasis must be placed on primary information. Secondary information is available to all competitors at the same time, and there may be inaccuracies in published information due to such things as injection of editorial opinions, untruthful or half-truthful reporting, time lags, and other distortions. The chapter on marketing research which follows is chiefly concerned with methods for generating primary information through original field work.

Internal and External.   Some kinds of information can be found inside the company while others must be sought outside. Internally, marketing information can be gleaned from accounting records, routine and special reports, sales order analysis, talks with members of other departments, and so on. External information includes intelligence secured from government sources, trade associations, distributors, and others. Internal sources should usually be exhausted before tapping external ones. This helps to reduce duplication of known data and to cut travel and communications costs; and it saves time when interviewers assigned to gather external information have already been saturated with inside information.

Qualitative and Quantitative.   While financial and manufacturing executives are prone to say "Give me the *figures!*" marketing people

---

[5]For a list of 46 basic sources see "Where to Find Marketing Facts," *Harvard Business Review,* September-October, 1962, pp. 44ff.

often display a distaste for numbers. In part this is because marketing rests more heavily on influencing people rather than things and, consequently, involves many intangible and unmeasurable factors. Yet marketers should strive to express data in numerical and financial terms whenever possible so that the power of mathematical and statistical analysis can be brought to bear more fully on marketing matters. Statistics from the Bureau of the Census, from *Sales Management's* "Survey of Buying Power," and from other sources are widely used to supplement qualitative judgments in marketing.

Cost and Revenue Information. Many marketers exhibit a strong tendency to be "volume happy" and ignore many of the costs involved in revenue generation. But obviously both the cost and the revenue sides of the profit coin need to be considered. Subsequent chapters deal with tools for both sales analysis and distribution cost analysis.

Continuous vs. Intermittent. Some types of marketing information are generated only periodically; other kinds are produced on a continuous-flow basis. Sales records, consumer diaries, panels, and store audits provide data for continuous monitoring. Continuous reportage presents a dynamic picture and usually permits more depth of analysis than does static and intermittent intelligence. Continuous tracking may be necessary for auditing routine and repetitive operations and for picking up fugitive or transient information of a highly strategic nature about the marketing environment; for example, information about changing technology, competitive conditions, and legal regulations which may call for changes in marketing strategy. Of course, continuous surveillance is often more costly than equivalent periodic reports. One cannot help but get some information continuously, whether he wants it that way or not. Certain research firms, for instance, will not sell their information except as an on-going service, and there is a continual trickle of marketing information from company salesman and the elusive grapevine in most cases.

Ex Ante and Ex Post Facto Information. *Ex ante* data enters the planning process and involves information about the future; for example, market trends. *Ex post facto* information is backward looking and plays a key role in the control process. A balance of both kinds is needed in marketing management.

Multi-Purpose and Single-Use Intelligence. Single-use intelligence is used for solving nonrecurring problems. Multi-use intelligence is used for both recurring issues and for a range of dissimilar problems requiring similar information inputs. Most basic *market* data, for instance, is multi-purpose information because it enters into pricing decisions, product decisions, distribution plans, advertising campaigns, and many other areas of *marketing*. Multi-use information may lie dormant on microfilm, in files, or in other forms of storage between active applications.

Overt vs. Covert Intelligence. Overt information is obtained through "open intelligence," such as the reading of widely available trade papers. Covert information is obtained by clandestine means. It may be necessary to conduct certain kinds of intelligence functions by covert means to avoid tipping one's hand to a competitor. Some marketers, for example, may be reluctant to test-market a new product for fear of prematurely informing a rival. Other methods of covert competitive intelligence and counterintelligence are not unknown to marketing executives.

Plum-Picking vs. Data Derivation. Some information can be almost "picked off the floor;" that is, collected in such form that it is ready for instant use. Other data may have to be collected and processed with the expectation that it may yield significant implications for marketing management. Every forward step made by statisticians, accountants, operations researchers, marketing theorists, computer experts, and financial ratio analysts in perfecting their tools increases the potential gain to be achieved through data manipulation aimed at producing useful bits of marketing information through inductive and deductive processes.

Miscellaneous. There may be many other useful distinctions to be drawn when classifying marketing intelligence by type or source. For instance, in some cases it is useful to distinguish between accessible and inaccessible information, although this is usually a matter of degree. Information retrieval problems in research and development, for instance, are brought to mind here, as are secrecy and security matters associated with all the things that one businessman typically refuses to tell another. The essence of military intelligence lies in problems of access, and one can profitably carry this notion over into marketing. Another distinction might lie in differences between detailed information and general information. This might be useful in the organizational work of marketing managers. Top-level marketing executives, as an example, should not usually be supplied with the detailed information going to subordinate marketing personnel. The reader can doubtless think of many other approaches to pragmatic information classifications in marketing.

Basic Criteria for the Information Structure

Success in the entire marketing intelligence function depends largely upon the prompt, efficient, and rational *assembling* of scattered and heterogeneous bits of information into a complete *structure* of decision premises and situational variables which will adequately support a total marketing effort. This, in turn, depends upon an adequate *cross section* of intelligence sources and information types. There is great danger in unduly stressing a single source or type of information: it may be as garbled and unreliable as a rumor mill and will rarely provide the depth and range of material that is essential. Additional sources are required to fill intelligence gaps, and multiple sources can serve (*a*) as cross-checks on each other to verify reliability, (*b*) as benchmarks to reveal the true significance of isolated bits of data, and (*c*) as a means to discover important relationships between different kinds of marketing information. There must, as we have noted, also be an efficient order or sequence for seeking marketing information both inside and outside the company.

An effective intelligence program requires proper planning and administration, and a wise early step is to determine the proper design criteria for the information structure. Five guidelines, suggested by S. A. Spencer of McKinsey and Company, offer food for thought:

1. Information should highlight the critical factors controlling the company's success.
2. Information should be keyed to the individuals responsible.
3. Information should include nondollar or causal factors, as well as dollar results.
4. Information should cover the external environment as searchingly as it deals with internal factors.
5. Information should be presented in brief, to-the-point, easy-to-use form. This means using computers, where appropriate, to distill the points requiring action out of masses of data.[6]

TECHNOLOGICAL AIDS IN MARKETING INTELLIGENCE

Within the past decade or two, science and technology have increasingly come to aid the marketing executive in his intelligence work. For instance, new tools have been developed in the fields of motivation and operations research. New office machines, photographic and printing techniques, recording devices, telephonic and closed-circuit television services, and other aids have also been made available. It is in the electrical and electronics areas, perhaps, that the more revolutionary and near-revolutionary breakthroughs have occurred to the real or potential benefit of marketing intelligence.

Specifically, electronic computers are coming to enjoy more wide-

---

[6] S. A. Spencer, "The Dark at the Top of the Stairs: What Higher Management Needs from Information Systems," *Management Review*, July, 1962, p. 11.

spread use in the marketing area.[7] To be sure, marketers have not been able to put the computer to such a range of applications as one finds in accounting, finance, or production. This is because much less is known about cause-and-effect relationships in marketing, many significant marketing variables having proved difficult to quantify, and some external forces impinging upon marketing defy not only measurement but observation. Much computer usage has been devoted toward simply improving the efficiency of routine operations, as in processing papers like orders and invoices, or toward developing more and faster marketing information of rather conventional types: reporting, summarizing, and appraising field sales results with less time lag.

There have been fewer attempts to use the computer to provide really new marketing information not previously available by other means, such as extending operations research techniques to a wide range of marketing problems. But this by no means suggests that computer applications are confined to exceptional or isolated cases of purely academic interest. What is the extent of present computer usage in the key marketing areas of manufacturing concerns?

There has been substantial use in order processing and physical distribution planning. A number of producers, for instance, have turned to the computer to help resolve problems relating to the optimum number and location of warehouses. Sales forecasting has seen fairly heavy computer application, with multiple correlations being much easier to undertake than they used to be with manual methods of computation. Moderate computer usage has been seen in the area of field salesforce management. The processing of sales and profit reports, of course, has lead to faster and more accurate performance measurement.

Decisions on the size of the salesforce and on how salesmen should allocate their time to territories, customers, and products have also been made easier by turning to the computer. Product and product line management has also seen a moderately heavy use of the computer, perhaps moreso by consumer goods than by industrial product concerns.

The evaluation of product mix, new product screening and evaluation, and the scheduling and controlling of development projects have yielded to the computer in many instances. Computers have been used less frequently for pricing decisions, although there are a number of industrial goods manufacturers who have achieved important results in

---

[7]In preparing this section we have drawn heavily from a special report entitled "What Every Intelligent Marketing Man Should Know about Computers," *Printers' Ink,* July 13, 1962. Additional references to marketing and the computer may be found in the bibliography.

this area. Although advertising has been slow to yield to the inroads of the computer, budgeting and media scheduling are promising areas for further development.

It will undoubtedly require some time to bring the computer to bear fully on systemwide problems of marketing planning and control, but there is now some promise of achieving more progress toward that end.

Some companies, particularly the industrial goods giants, have already applied electronic assistance to broad areas of marketing intelligence and communications. A survey conducted by *Sales Management* magazine in 1958, for instance, reported a growing trend toward the use of private wire electronic communications networks to reduce customer inventories, replenish warehouse stocks, coordinate dealers and distributors, speed deliveries, expedite billing, trace orders, link production to distribution, and forestall the day when companies need to decentralize their marketing organizations. Republic Steel, Alcoa, Olin Mathieson, The Carborundum Company, National Electric Products Corporation, and Clark Equipment Company are examples of firms pursuing such a course. As an illustration of one of the more modest of these rapid communications systems, Clark's 13,000-mile leased wire Dealer Network System was originally opened to connect 101 independent Clark equipment dealers with all Clark plants, sales offices, and with each other.[8]

As this brief introduction suggests, marketing intelligence is simultaneously becoming both easier and more complicated. It is rapidly coming to be recognized as a specialization in its own right and to be elevated in status to a separate subfunction of marketing management.

Marketing intelligence is by no means limited or restricted to the widely known techniques of marketing research, sales analysis, and distribution cost analysis. This chapter will have served its purpose if it provides a broad backdrop against which we can examine and appraise some of the more representative tools of the marketer's kitbag in closer detail.

---

[8]Nathaniel Gilbert, "Winning Customers with Order Automation," *Sales Management,* June 6, 1958, pp. 106-10.

CHAPTER 19

Marketing Research

The preceding chapter established the broad structure of a marketing intelligence or information system designed to aid management in its whole range of decisions on marketing activities. This chapter will consider marketing research as one of the most important means of providing information for the total marketing intelligence system. It will include first a review of the growth of marketing research over recent years. The second section will consider the problems of managing the marketing research function within a firm and possible relationships with external research organizations to which some of the work may be assigned. Next will be a consideration of some of the more important sources of published information useful to marketing managers. This will be followed by a brief description of the various steps required in making a marketing research study, and, finally, we will discuss some of the fundamental types of research assignments which have multi-use as opposed to single-use application.

GROWTH OF MARKETING RESEARCH

Although a few companies were using marketing research in the 1920's or even earlier, substantial growth did not start until the 1930's and has been particularly dramatic since the end of World War II. This growth is indicated in Table 19–1, which has been adapted from data in a survey of American Marketing Association members,[1] plus data which a group of companies added to fill out the sample.

Thirty percent of the 57 publishing and broadcasting companies and 23 percent of the 93 advertising agencies responding in this survey had departments prior to 1938. In contrast, only 15 percent of the consumer products manufacturers had been long-time users, and 2 percent of the

---

[1] "A Survey of Marketing Research," American Marketing Association, 1958, Chart 6, p. 18.

industrial goods manufacturers. This disparity between the use of marketing research departments by consumers' goods manufacturers, as compared to industrial goods manufacturers, has since been changed, and today the proportion of industrial goods producers making use of marketing research is approximately equivalent to that of manufacturers of consumers' goods. Table 19–2 shows this comparison, as well as the high incidence of use by advertising agencies and media. Less than half of the retailers and wholesalers answering had departments, as was also true for the All Other group.

TABLE 19–1

NEW MARKETING RESEARCH DEPARTMENTS
(Formed by Five-Year Periods)

Period	Number of Departments
1953–1957	273
1948–1952	174
1943–1947	116
1938–1942	44
1933–1937	43
1928–1932	18
1923–1927	12
1918–1922	9
Before 1918	3

SOURCE: See Footnote 1.

TABLE 19–2

COMPANIES USING MARKETING RESEARCH

Type of Company	Number Answering	Formal Department	One Person Assigned	No One Assigned
Advertising agencies	132	71.9%	18.2%	9.9%
Publishing and broadcasting	85	71.8	14.1	14.1
Manufacturers of consumer products	315	62.2	15.6	22.2
Manufacturers of industrial products	480	59.1	22.3	18.6
Retailing & wholesaling	63	46.0	17.5	36.5
All others	139	46.8	21.6	31.6
All companies answering this question*	1,214	60.1	19.2	20.7

*Excludes market research and consulting firms.
SOURCE: *Ibid.*, adapted from Chart 3, p. 12.

As might be expected, a higher proportion of large than of small firms have formal marketing research departments. For companies with sales volumes of over $500 million annually, 93 percent of the 58 answering had such departments. For mid-range companies, between $100 and $199 million, the percentage was 83.1; for companies between $5 and $24 million, the percentage was 55.0; and for those under $5 million it was 30.4 percent. This overall relationship between size and the proportion of companies having marketing research departments holds for manufacturers of consumer products and industrial products, and for retailers and wholesalers. For advertising agencies, however, 42 percent with billings under $5 million annually have departments, 90 percent of those with billings between $5 and $25 million have departments; and all agencies in size classes above this have such departments.

Somewhat less dramatic, but generally similar, is the picture for publishers and broadcasters, with 55 percent of companies under $5 million a year reporting departments; between $5 million and $25 million, 85 percent; $25 to $50 million, 90 percent; and for the two largest classes, 80 and 100 percent, respectively. In addition to having more marketing research departments, large advertising agencies and publishers and broadcasters have more marketing research employees than small ones do. Median figures range from 2.9 to 51.0 for advertising agencies, and 3.0 to 4.9 for publishers and broadcasters—from the smallest sized groups to the largest. However, the largest publisher reporting was in the size group $25 to $50 million, and the largest advertising agency was in the $50– to $100–million bracket. Manufacturers of industrial goods reported median employees of 2.5 for under $5–million firms, to 10.4 for over $500–million firms. The range for consumers' goods manufacturers started at 3.6 for the $5– to $25–million category, and went up to 11.3 for over $500 million.

Along with the growth of marketing research departments within manufacturing, distributive, and service organizations, specialized companies have developed to conduct various types of marketing studies. These organizations are set up to undertake many types of marketing research studies and it is difficult to classify them into any very meaningful or consistent categories. Their growth reflects the general increase in demand for marketing information by business executives. Clients of such organizations include both companies which have marketing research departments but follow the practice of subcontracting some part of their work, and companies which do not have formal marketing research staffs.

One difference between research organizations which has some validity is the extent to which they operate on a problem solving or study-by-study basis, as contrasted with gathering certain predetermined types of information on a continuing basis. In the latter category, for example, is to be found the store audit type of operation in which field men visit a sample of retail stores and measure movement across the retail counter by product classes and by individual brands.

The A. C. Nielsen Company for many years has conducted store audits in the food and drug field, and has been active in the broadcast media area in measuring exposure. Nielsen more recently has undertaken exposure measurements in the magazine and newspaper fields. There are also other companies which operate in one or more of these fields.

A second type of continuous study is the consumer purchase panel in which housewives submit weekly or monthly diaries showing their purchases of particular classes of products. The Market Research Corporation of America is one of the best known companies in this general field. Some research companies tend to do most of their work in the consumers' goods field, while others handle both consumer and industrial studies. A relatively small number of firms specialize on industrial marketing problems and measurements.

Scope of Marketing Research Activities

As was shown in the previous chapter, there is a wide range of information needed by marketing executives to aid them in making better decisions. It is apparent from every study of organized marketing research that has been made in recent years that these departments carry out an extremely wide range of different types of studies. Table 19–3, adapted from the American Marketing Association survey,[2] confirms this breadth of scope and provides a breakdown by consumers' goods and industrial goods manufacturers. It also shows which activities tend to be done by the marketing research department—as contrasted with another department within the company, or by an outside firm.

We can see from the table that there are differences in frequency of use by consumers' goods vs. industrial goods companies. For example, consumers' goods companies, as might be expected, engage more often in test marketing and store audits, in studies of "deals" and premiums, in product testing, in the use of motivation research, and in "make or buy" analysis. The marketing research department, by its major role both in consumers' and industrial goods situations, participates in the actual conduct of all 29 types of activities, except for a few categories in which other departments are active. For example, make or buy analysis quite logically might be done in the purchasing department; forecasting

---

[2] *Ibid.*, Charts 13, 14, 15 and 16.

of personnel requirements by a personnel department; product testing at times by research and development; and media studies and copy research certainly are often done by advertising agencies.

TABLE 19–3

MARKETING STUDIES BY COMPANIES WITH MARKETING RESEARCH DEPARTMENTS
(Consumers' Goods vs. Industrial Goods)

Market and Sales Research Activities	Done by Department		Done by Outside Firms		Done by Another Dept.		Total	
	Con- sumers'	Indus- trial	Con- sumers'	Indus- trial	Con- sumers'	Indus- trial	Con- sumers'	Indus- trial
Development of market potentials......	83%	84%	1%	0	7%	4%	91%	88%
Sales analysis...............	74	66	1	0	13	13	88	79
Share-of-market studies.......	75	81	10	0	2	4	87	85
Determination of market characteristics.................	74	73	6	1%	4	1	84	75
Establishment of sales quotas...	54	47	1	0	29	25	84	72
Establishment of sales territories......................	46	50	1	0	37	25	84	75
Studies of market changes......	66	66	6	0	4	3	76	69
Channels of distribution and distribution cost studies......	39	38	2	0	21	14	62	52
Studies of methods of paying salesmen...................	24	23	1	1	36	23	61	47
Test markets—store audits.....	44	9	10	2	6	3	60	14
Studies of "deals" and premiums.	35	6	1	1	12	2	48	9
Forecasting of personnel requirements......................	15	16	1	0	31	28	47	44
Studies of export markets......	10	23	0	0	31	18	41	41
Product Research								
Potential of new products......	69	72	6	2	9	9	84	83
Present products vs. competition.	62	65	6	1	14	16	82	82
Research on competitors' product....................	47	39	6	1	21	26	74	66
Packaging research, design or physical characteristics.......	33	14	12	3	21	23	66	40
Product testing...............	42	10	8	2	13	11	63	23
Studies of length of "line"......	38	32	2	0	14	9	54	41
"Make or buy" analysis........	9	10	0	0	17	15	26	25
Business Economics								
Short-range forecasting........	72	70	0	1	16	15	88	86
Long-range forecasting........	59	68	2	1	15	11	76	80
Studies of business trends......	58	68	1	2	12	9	71	79
Profit analysis...............	24	22	1	0	37	38	62	60
Plant and warehouse locations..	22	31	0	0	31	19	53	50
Purchases of companies or sale of divisions...............	16	31	0	1	30	18	46	50
Advertising Research								
Media studies...............	16	13	27	13	18	20	61	46
Copy research...............	18	7	26	13	13	17	57	37
Use of projective techniques motivation research.........	23	5	19	6	6	10	48	21

Expenditures for Marketing Research

Marketing research expenditures by manufacturers are generally a fraction of 1 percent of annual sales volume, and the percentage decreases as the size of the company increases. Table 19–4 presents data for consumers' goods and industrial goods manufacturers which demonstrate this relationship with volume in both series. Within each size classification, however, there is a fairly wide dispersion in budgets. Among consumers' goods manufacturers with annual sales of $100 to $200 million, for example, the median budget was 0.10 percent of sales, while the upper quarter spent more than 0.23 percent, and the bottom quarter less than 0.07 percent of sales.

TABLE 19–4

MANUFACTURERS' MARKETING RESEARCH BUDGETS AS A PERCENTAGE OF SALES
(Consumers' Goods vs. Industrial Goods)

Annual Sales *(Millions)*	*(1)* *Number* *Responding*	*(2)* *Median* *Budget*	*(3)* *One Quarter* *Spent More* *Than*	*(4)* *One Quarter* *Spent Less* *Than*
Consumers' goods:				
$ 5–$ 25..............	41	0.18 %	0.50 %	0.10 %
25– 50..............	32	0.185	0.32	0.10
50– 100..............	34	0.165	0.28	0.08
100– 200..............	17	0.10	0.23	0.07
200– 500..............	25	0.055	0.105	0.02
Over $500..............	14	0.025	0.08	0.019
Industrial goods:				
$ 5–$ 25..............	66	0.21	0.30	0.10
25– 50..............	46	0.10	0.20	0.06
50– 100..............	38	0.06	0.10	0.05
100– 200..............	36	0.043	0.07	0.02
200– 500..............	25	0.025	0.042	0.014
Over $500..............	15	0.028	0.0425	0.01

SOURCE: *Ibid.*, p. 30.

The three-to-one relationship of these last two figures holds for seven out of the total of twelve observations in the two groups. In one instance it is lower and in the other four it is higher. This high variability in the amount of money spent among manufacturers within the same size class, both by consumers' goods manufacturers and industrial goods manufacturers, is partly a result of variation in the scope and complexity of the marketing function in the different companies. It also undoubtedly reflects the extent to which management has really accepted marketing research activity as a significant form of assistance in making marketing decisions.

Advertising agencies, publishers, and broadcasters spend more than manufacturers. The median expenditure for agencies was 1.0 percent for those with annual billings of under $5 million, ranging down to 0.36 percent for those in the $25- to $50-million range, and then rising slightly to 0.50 percent for the top firms reporting in the $50- to $100-million group. A few larger agencies reported in the survey but the sample was too small to include any figures. Publishers and broadcasters showed a somewhat similar pattern.

MANAGING THE MARKETING RESEARCH FUNCTION

It is most common for marketing research activities to be handled as the full-time responsibility of a specialized department or individual. This was true in nearly two-thirds of the replies to a survey made by Richard D. Crisp. Next most common is the assignment of part-time responsibility to a line executive in about one fifth of the cases, and to a staff executive in 7 percent of the companies.

Since the purpose of the marketing research department is to provide information of immediate help in making marketing decisions, organizational placement under the chief marketing executive has compelling logic. The subject matter of the department's information generating activities is concentrated on marketing problems, and access to the chief marketing executive should assure that there is a genuine desire to secure and use relevant marketing information. The department's scope of activity and ability to report its findings fully and frankly need not be limited by fear that such studies will uncover situations casting discredit upon the chief marketing executive; for in many companies today the critical need for placing highly competent people in these top marketing positions has become widely accepted. The growing understanding of the marketing manager concept, with its customer-oriented approach, has undoubtedly helped in this regard.

The Crisp study showed that 39 percent of the heads of marketing research departments reported to marketing executives of vice presidential level, while 24 percent reported to other sales or marketing executives. Eleven percent were under the president of the company, while 3 percent reported to an executive vice president, or vice president and general manager. Fourteen percent of the department heads reported to a variety of nonmarketing executives, with some limited concentration evident in finance and control positions. Preliminary reports of a study made by the American Marketing Association in 1963 indicate that the percentage of marketing research directors reporting to top management has declined and that an increased proportion of them report to the chief marketing executive. The American Marketing Association survey shows very much the same distribution of reporting relationships.

The most important factors in establishing a climate in which marketing research can generate its maximum contribution is that the executive to whom the department reports be genuinely interested in the gathering of information to improve decision making, should know how to use this information effectively, and should have sufficient power within the organization framework to achieve the action indicated by the studies. If this person is the president or executive vice president, the department may very well be placed under him. However, if the top executives are not basically oriented to the value of such information but have tolerated the organization of the department because it is believed to be the fashionable thing to do, a basic ingredient to a favorable climate is certainly lacking and the problem of gaining company-wide acceptance for the marketing research department is compounded. This is especially true if the department is new and has to make its way (as all new departments do) against the inertia, suspicion, and fear of mid-zone executives.

The head of a new department usually finds out quickly that the ability to do competent work is not enough. There is an important problem of communication and salesmanship within the organization for which his professional training usually has not prepared him. These communication and selling skills are needed in building acceptance for the department's work, yet they must be subtly handled to avoid arousing apprehension and resistance. The marketing research director and his assistants are distinctly staff people and exist for the contribution which they can make to operating executives. They must be willing to let others take credit where this will facilitate the acceptance and use of their work, and must become skillful in the technique of planting ideas which can be picked up and championed by other operating executives.

For a new department, a modest scale of initial operations is desirable with a director, senior analyst, statistical clerk and secretary. Because of the limited amount of work which a small group can do, the first projects to be undertaken should be selected with special care. These should be of very real interest and significance to management, and wherever possible have a reasonably high probability of generating tangible benefits of a "dollars in the cash register" type. Successful completion of a few assignments of this kind are of great help to the new department in getting off to a running start.

Also of importance is a modest scale of the departmental budget—which is less likely to attract attention if an economy wave should develop. Another benefit of a limited scale of operations in the beginning is that the backlog of projects waiting to be started will not only force hard choices as to which should have top priority because of their fundamental importance to the company, but will provide the most tangible and believable evidence of the need for larger marketing research expenditures.

Compensation levels for directors of marketing research tend to increase with the size of the company. The American Marketing Association study in 1958 found median figures ranging from $7,000 for companies under $5 million sales to $19,500 for companies over $500 million sales among manufacturers of consumers' goods. For industrial goods producers the median was $10,000 each for the three size classes of companies up to $50 million dollars per year, and then it rose to $17,600 for companies of over $500 million sales. The dispersion of figures around the median was quite wide within the size classes. For example, the 34 companies in the $50- to $100-million size bracket reported a median payment to their directors of $15,300, but one quarter of the companies paid their men over $20,000 and one quarter less than $11,000. Similar ranges also appeared among manufacturers of industrial products.

In starting a marketing research department the company has the choice of bringing in a man with suitable qualifications and experience from the outside as director, or of putting a company man in charge whose knowledge of company problems and internal stature within the organization will expedite the acceptance of the new activity. This latter approach, of course, does not provide the full benefits of a man with an outside point of view, free of the preconceptions and habit patterns of those who have been with the company for some time. However, there may be many circumstances in which the use of the internal man is very wise and necessary to make maximum progress. But such a man will rarely have the necessary professional competence to handle the job and he needs to be backed up by a second-in-command who possesses this training.

An important aid to the efficient operation of the marketing research department is to provide that the director be represented on management committees which are related to the work of the department. Even though it may not be feasible for him to cast an actual vote in the decision process, his presence is vital if he is to understand trends in management thinking with sufficient lead time so that he can guide the work of his department most effectively.

In multi-division companies a problem is posed in the organization of the marketing research function. Some companies utilize a centralized department containing individuals or groups who concentrate on the problems peculiar to the several divisions. A variant of this is to have branch units of the centralized department physically located in the divisions but reporting to the central market research director. At the other end of the spectrum are separate marketing research departments in each division which are completely autonomous in their operation. A common arrangement is to have separate divisional departments which report administratively to divisional management but which operate under the general guidance and consulting assistance of a headquarters marketing research staff.

The central department has some advantages in greater specialization and efficiency in use of personnel, but it suffers from the fact that divisional executives may not view the group as really being on their team. They may also believe, and sometimes with justification, that they cannot get the help they need as promptly as they would like it. The best arrangement seems to be units within divisions reporting to divisional management and operating with an informal but regularly maintained relationship with the central department. The central staff helps out on particularly troublesome assignments, aids in the recruitment and screening of personnel, and, perhaps most important, exercises a type of persuasive quality control in terms of research methods and standards.

A final comment concerns the desirability of avoiding routine assignments. There are times when the department should take the leadership in setting up certain types of information flow and feedback which have not been part of the company's reporting system. However, when such reports have proved their worth and are to be prepared on a regular basis, they should be turned over to the appropriate department for repetitive handling. Not to do this will result in limiting the work capacity of the marketing research department and tend to introduce a lower grade of personnel than is desirable.

Subcontracting of Marketing Research Assignments

Most companies spend substantial fractions of their marketing research expenditures in purchasing service from outside organizations. Among consumer products manufacturers in the American Marketing Association study an average of 48 percent of the total budget was so spent. In contrast, industrial goods producers averaged only 13 percent, while advertising agencies reported 35 percent and publishers and broadcasters 41 percent devoted to outside research. Some of the research assignments which are subcontracted could be carried on by the marketing research department, but because of the unevenness of work load overtime, it has been found cheaper to use this approach even though costs per study are sometimes higher than if they were done by the company. Other reasons may be to bring in an outside point of view or to use research agencies which have developed special competence and unusual experience in particular types of studies.

The first step here is to identify the most promising research organizations in terms of the particular problem or study. Knowledge of these companies and their strengths and limitations is usually part of the stock in trade of the director of marketing research, but in any particular situation it may be desirable to go further and check with clients of the concerns being considered.

When the field has been narrowed to just a few, preliminary meetings should be set up to discuss the problem with them. These meetings will be much more effective and take less time if the client provides written information in advance describing the company, its method of doing business, and the particular problem or problems at issue. This has the benefit of supplying a sort of standardized stimulus to each research company being considered and therefore permits a more accurate judgment as to how well each grasps the situation and its needs.

At the preliminary meeting questions should be answered frankly and full discussion encouraged. Even though management may feel very certain as to the nature of the problem it faces and the kinds of information needed, openmindedness at this stage of the game costs little and can result in a variation in approach or even in an entirely new approach which is more appropriate to the fundamental issues at stake.

A request for proposals is the next step—normally at the expense of the research agency. Sometimes, however, a really worthwhile proposal requires a very substantial amount of work, more than could be reasonably expected without pay. Under these circumstances, with a truly difficult problem and high stakes riding on the decision that is finally made, it may be worthwhile to negotiate proposal writing contracts with two or more of the most likely prospects. The effect of this would be a sharing of expense with the agencies and much more carefully prepared proposals.

Definite due dates should be set for proposals, bearing in mind that insistence on too short a time is likely to cut quality but that an excessively long time is unlikely to improve quality. Unless a substantial amount of fieldwork or other time-consuming work is necessary, a range of two to four weeks is reasonable. During the proposal preparation period, all reasonable requests for additional data should be granted.

After the proposals are in and have been studied carefully, further meetings should be held. Sometimes proposals seem to be so wide of the study objective that there is a temptation to eliminate the research company without a meeting. In general this is poor policy, not only because each agency is entitled to a hearing if it has made a sincere effort to develop a program, but because out of what will undoubtedly be a spirited discussion may come some approaches and ways of conceptualizing problems that have been overlooked.

During the meetings one of the important questions is to determine who in the research organization will be available to work on the study and the amounts of time that they will be able to devote to it. Although some research organizations prefer not to commit themselves too far in this direction because of the inevitable stresses and strains of their work, it is a reasonable request on the part of the client and may at times have a very significant bearing on the quality of the work which is performed. Taking a strong negotiating position on this topic implies that the company either knows the individuals already through previous work or some other contact, or has learned enough about their competence to feel sure that their work will be good.

Once the decision has been made to select a particular research agency, a timetable for different parts of the work and a schedule of meetings should be set up. There is more than ample evidence to indicate that difficulties which at times develop between the research company and the client are usually traceable to the failure to have sufficiently frequent and full two-way communication. This is an absolute must for best results. The proposal has presumably spelled out the research methodology, including sample design (if one is involved), means of collecting data, types of analyses to be performed, and the like. Nonetheless it is quite appropriate and even vital that the client be in a position to monitor the research plan as it develops and, when it seems desirable, to exercise quality checks at crucial points.

As will be pointed out later, there are real problems in maintaining quality levels for fieldwork. Although this is most noticeable in consumer market studies, the complexity of many industrial marketing situations also introduces problems of interviewer training, content of interviews, and interpretation of results. The kind of relationship envisioned here between the client and a research company of course assumes that the client has a sophisticated marketing research staff. A manufacturer without such a staff would not be in a position to follow through in the course of a study.

SOURCES OF PUBLISHED INFORMATION

The preceding chapter classified information in several ways. Let us first look at what is available from published sources. Some of these publications may be had for the asking without charge, as is true of various studies offered by advertising media to describe the size and characteristics of the markets which they reach, while other publications carry a price determined by the publisher. Much of the material issued by the federal and state governments bears a nominal price tag and the average book is not overly expensive. Some of the published data to be considered, however, are the result of special compilations on a continuing basis and consist of such information as movement of merchandise through retail stores, purchases by families, volume of advertising placed in different media, exposure to advertising, and other types of information which may be helpful in the planning and control of marketing. Since the cost of generating information published in these services is very heavy, correspondingly high prices are placed upon them.

Secondary data sources are in general far less costly than attempts to generate comparable information through new research and, therefore, deserve very careful attention in undertaking a marketing study. Unfortunately, business literature is not well codified, and while the volume of abstracting is growing, still a great deal of the effort required in a comprehensive literature search consists of setting up and putting into effect a careful search routine, and winnowing through bushels of chaff to get relatively few grains of good wheat.

There are certain cautions which should be kept in mind in using any published information. For one thing, the competency of the author or issuing organization, as well as the stated and the unstated objectives it seeks, need to be carefully evaluated. Much business data is issued by organizations with a product or service to sell and they may not be as wholeheartedly and consistently objective as would be desirable. In such cases direct contact with the issuing organization and some questions asked regarding methodology may shed enough light to determine how far reliance can be placed upon the information in terms of the particular problem under study. At times it may be impossible to learn much about how a particular study was made, and in such instances one has to decide whether the reluctance to disclose is because of legitimate unwillingness to talk about a technique which is a trade secret or whether it is because a factual report of method would cast doubt upon the basic validity of the data.

Indexes are an important finding device in searching for published data. Examples are the *Cumulative Book Index, Business Periodicals Index, Public Affairs Information Service, New York Times Index,*

Wall Street Journal Index and others specializing in particular subject matter fields, such as medicine, engineering, psychology, and sociology. Bibliographies of various types help to pinpoint a wide variety of useful secondary data and include such articles and publications as *Where to Find Marketing Facts*[3], *A Basic Bibliography on Marketing Research*[4], *Current Sources of Marketing Information*[5], and *A Basic Bibliography on Industrial Marketing*[6]. *How and Where to Look It Up*[7] is a book with good coverage of business sources and an extensive topical list of reference sources. "Marketing Articles in Review," a regular feature of the *Journal of Marketing,* contains summaries of selected current articles from approximately 175 periodicals of interest to marketing managers. These are organized under 23 topical headings.

The federal government generates vast quantities of data, much of which is of direct use to marketing managers. In fact, the scope of the government publication program is so broad that some skill is required in locating the information most pertinent to a particular problem and in being sure that nothing of importance has been overlooked. Some of the reference sources of value in locating governmental information are *Governmental Statistics for Business Use*[8], *The Monthly Catalogue of U.S. Government Publications*[9], *Marketing Information Guide*[10], *Statistical Services of the U.S. Government*[11], and the *Federal Statistical Directory.*[12]

The Department of Commerce is a major source of information with its censuses of population, business, manufacturers, mineral industries, transportation, agriculture, housing, and governments. Most of these censuses are taken every five years, except that of population, which is taken every ten years. The Bureau of the Census gathers certain information annually on a sampling basis for the years between the censuses.

---

[3]Steuart Henderson Britt and Irwin A. Shapiro, September-October, 1962, *Harvard Business Review.*

[4]Hugh G. Wales and Robert Ferber (rev. ed.; Chicago: American Marketing Association, 1963).

[5]Edgar G. Gunther and Frederick A. Goldstein (Chicago: American Marketing Association, 1960).

[6]Thomas A. Staudt and William Lazer (Chicago: American Marketing Association, 1958).

[7]Robert W. Murphey (New York: McGraw-Hill, 1958).

[8]Philip Hauser and William R. Leonard (rev. ed.; John Wiley and Sons, 1956).

[9]Available from the Superintendent of Documents, Washington, D.C.

[10]Published monthly with brief annotations on selected current materials by the Business and Defense Services Administration, Washington, D.C.

[11]Office of Statistical Standards, Bureau of the Budget, Washington, D.C., 1959.

[12]Published annually by the Office of Statistical Standards; contains names of personnel in governmental agencies and the types of statistical work in which they are engaged.

Other government agencies issuing data of much value to marketers include the Bureau of Labor Statistics, the Bureau of Mines, the Department of Agriculture, and the Tariff Commission. The *Standard Industrial Classification Manual,* published in 1957 by the Bureau of the Budget, is used by many government agencies to achieve standardization among the statistical reports issued. This classification has been adopted widely by business firms and is used in the reporting of much marketing data.

Commercial Services

An important type of secondary data consists of the various commercial services which have developed in response to the need for marketing information on a continuing basis. The A. C. Nielsen Company was one of the earliest firms to measure the flow of food and drug products at the retail store level by product groups and by brands within product classes. Field auditors visit a sample of food and drug stores every 60 days, analyze invoices covering receipts of merchandise during the period since the last field visit, and take a physical inventory of the goods on the shelves and in the back room. These data, used in conjunction with inventory figures from the preceding visit, provide a measurement of product and brand movement into the hands of consumers. The samples of approximately 1,600 food stores and 750 drugstores are projected to a total figure for the country, and are also presented for such breakdowns as regions, city-size, and store-size groups.

One of the limitations of a store audit covering specific trade channels is that many consumer products have multi-channel distribution, some of which may not be covered by the service. There seems to be a tendency recently for some of the auditing services to move in the direction of obtaining reasonably complete coverage of the channels important to a particular product group. As channels shift in relative importance and as new types emerge, the store audit procedure must be adapted to provide comprehensive and accurate information. Undoubtedly, audits will develop to cover the discount store which has become so important in recent years.

A second method of measuring consumer purchases is that provided by the consumer purchase panel, usually consisting of from 5,000 to 7,000 families, which represents a sample of the United States population. The housewife in each family of such a panel fills out a weekly diary, recording information on family purchases of specified product classes. She reports separately on each item bought, indicating the date of purchase, the size of the package, the price paid, the number of units bought, and the store in which the purchase was made. This is the basic building block of marketing information and is normally used to generate a tabulating card. The transition from cards to tape is under way, but the basic concept of detailed purchase information by items for each family will, of course, be maintained.

The strength of the store audit procedure in measuring consumer purchases by products and brands is, primarily, greater accuracy because the sample of the stores covers a substantially larger number of families than can be included in the typical consumer panel. Also of importance is the fact that it does not require any cooperation or participation by the housewife or other members of the household, and thus avoids the danger of getting information from consumers who may become "professional" panel members. Likewise, the store audit method avoids any problems which might arise from over- and under-reporting and the difficulty of including in a purchase panel sufficient numbers of members of different racial and social groups and of high and low income classes.

The strong point of the consumer panel is that purchase patterns can be identified with specific families, and profiles of socioeconomic characteristics can be studied to learn whether there are differences in buying patterns between brands and product types. Furthermore, the purchase history of brands is available consecutively over time, enabling detailed studies of brand loyalty and brand switching, and an appraisal of the effect of special price promotions upon purchasing patterns.

The basic need for the kinds of data provided by the store audit and the consumer purchase panel stems from the existence of inventory pools at the wholesale and retail levels in the distribution of consumers' goods.

Another type of commercial service is a distribution check of a sample of stores to determine the availability of brands and the extent of store exposure. This, of course, does not give a measure of actual sales but, if done on a regular basis, indicates the availability of brands in retail outlets, an important contributing factor to sales results.

Measurement of exposure to advertising through various techniques comprises a third type of continuous marketing research carried on by commercial research agencies. Perhaps the best known of these are the ratings of television and radio programs issued by the American Research Bureau, Nielsen, Pulse, and others. In some instances this is a measure of the tuning of sets to different frequencies as provided by electronic devices; in others it consists of the results of telephone calls made during the period in which the program is on, and in others by questioning for memory recall of programs to which respondents had been exposed during a block of time prior to the interview. As part of a Congressional investigation of the rating services the American Statistical Association was asked to evaluate the statistical methods used in securing the broadcast ratings. This analysis was printed as a report of the Harris Committee on Interstate and Foreign Commerce.[13]

In the magazine field measurements are made by field interviewing techniques involving different types of exposure to advertisements. Some of the companies active in this field are Starch, Gallup, Robinson, Nielsen, and W. R. Simmons.

MARKETING RESEARCH TECHNIQUES

In order to contribute to the growth and profitable operation of his company the marketing manager must continuously try to expand markets and to run its marketing program as efficiently as possible. The variety of subject matter fields in which marketing research departments have contributed to better decision making for marketing executives has been portrayed earlier in this chapter. In providing such assistance for decision makers, marketing research has been concerned with the gathering of information and its analysis to yield insight and guidance on specific problems.

During much of the period of growth and use of marketing research more emphasis was placed upon fact gathering than upon analysis. There was so much that the manufacturer did not know about his markets, his competition, trade channel structures and behavior that great value was derived simply from an examination of the descriptive data without much in the way of formal analysis. There were exceptions to this, of course, and we find some early pioneers in the field of multivariate analysis. Dr. L. D. H. Weld at Batten, Barton, Durstine and Osborne, drawing from his background in the use of statistics for agricultural research, developed a county buying power index for the United States, based upon multiple correlation analysis of retail sales and certain economic factors. Donald R. G. Cowan in his book, *Sales Analysis from the Management Standpoint,* similarly urged the use of such techniques in establishing sales potential figures for territories and in planning marketing campaigns. Interest in quantitative approaches has been growing sharply in recent years, partly aided by the increased

[13]87th Congress, 1st Session, Report No. 193, *Evaluation of Statistical Methods Used in Obtaining Broadcast Ratings,* Report of the Committee on Interstate and Foreign Commerce, submitted by Mr. Harris, Chairman (U.S. Government Printing Office, Washington, D.C., 1961).

use of men trained in operations research and generally well grounded in mathematical and statistical techniques. Another factor which cleared the way for more sophisticated analysis was the explosion in computer technology which makes entirely feasible an amount and complexity of computation which could not even have been considered a few years ago.

It is important that a marketing research study be designed specifically to supply the decision making needs of management. There is an obvious interaction between the data gathering process and the analytical aspect of the work. The characteristics of the data to be gathered, while affected primarily by management problems, are to a degree dependent upon the analytical approach to be used. Conversely, the analytical method which is most efficient and appropriate may itself impose certain requirements both on the types and amounts of data to be collected. Because the research design itself is so important in determining the contribution which a marketing research can make, it highlights the necessity for real understanding of the problem at hand and the kind of assistance which management will find most helpful.

Unfortunately, this is by no means an easy matter. Even if the assignment seems to be unequivocal (for example, to determine actual retail use of a new point-of-purchase display stand four weeks after it has been distributed to retailers), a host of questions arise before the project should be started.

For example, what would be the meaning of finding that 40 percent of the stores were in fact making use of the display? Is this good, poor, or so-so? If it is judged to be poor, is it poor because the retailers thought the display was unattractive to their customers, or because it was too big or difficult to assemble? What part do wholesaler salesmen or company salesmen play in this situation? Did the displays reach the retail stores on the scheduled dates? Even more fundamental, perhaps the real question is not whether the display had wide or limited acceptance but whether, in fact, this was the part of the marketing program that should be investigated.

Possibly the basic symptom is that sales are lower than forecasted goals and it is the opinion of someone in management that the most likely culprit is the point-of-sale material. In this latter type of situation an exploratory investigation among key home office marketing personnel, field salesmen, branch managers, and knowledgable dealers, coupled with analysis of sales records and industry-wide sales experience, would aid in defining the real problem more precisely.

The best research design is clearly of little avail if it is focused upon the wrong problem, and it is for this reason that the exploratory investigation occupies an important position in the list of research investigation steps to be discussed shortly. Basically, of course, an overriding objective of most marketing research studies is to learn about causal relationships between one or more independent variables and a controllable variable. With knowledge of the existence and nature of such causal relationship, prediction of results of managerial action becomes possible.

The three general techniques for data gathering are *survey, observational,* and *experimental.* The survey method consists of asking questions of various individuals and groups within the market place. The observational method involves a broad scope of data. For example, it may consist of utilizing established series of statistical information published by the government or by trade associations, or perhaps of sales records of the company itself. It also may include a purposeful program of observation, as when a motion picture camera has been put within a retail store to take one picture frame every few seconds and in this way permit an analysis of the flow of customer traffic and behavior in the purchase of merchandise.

The final major method consists of experimentation, in which there is usually deliberate intervention by the company in the processes of the marketplace. However, careful observation of market data will often reveal experiments conducted by others which can be analyzed to yield useful information without company intervention. The experimental method has great appeal as the most truly scientific of all, yet in point of fact it has not had wide application. The reasons are that it is always difficult to implement and, in many situations, impossible. Furthermore, it can be quite expensive. On the other hand, it does permit a sophisticated research design which makes it possible to gather information concurrently on the effects of several variables. We will discuss these methods briefly in the next section.

Marketing Research Procedure

The various steps involved in a typical investigation of a marketing problem are listed below, and will then be discussed briefly point by point.

1. Definition of the problem and tentative statement of specific objectives sought by the study.

2. Exploratory investigation of company records and, among informed persons both inside and outside the company, checks upon the validity and completeness of the preliminary objectives and the true significance of the problem itself in terms of apparent company needs.

3. Determination of the types of data needed, the method to be used in gathering the data, and the analyses to be made. At this point a "dummy" report can be prepared with an outline of topics, and tables and titles with row and column headings (but of course no data). This serves as a vehicle for an important planning session for the executives who will later be using the results. It is an effective way of achieving a real meeting of minds on the scope of the survey and the results to be gained, and serves as an important "preselling" step to later usage. This is the last point in the investigation process at which any significant change can be made in the research design.

4. Collection of required data.
    A. Gathering data from secondary sources such as published material and internal company records.
    B. Gathering data from primary sources.
        1. Survey approach through personal interviews, telephone interviews, or mail questionnaires.
        2. Observational approach.
        3. Experimental approach.

5. Analysis of data collected.

6. Presentation of solution of the problem in the manner that will achieve most effective implementation of the results.

7. Follow-up to learn about the effectiveness of the study and the experience in implementing it.

1. *Tentative Statement of Objectives.* As was pointed out above, it is very important to make sure there is a clear understanding of the problem which is troubling the executive and the nature of the study which is necessary to help solve the problem. The first step here is to set down, in written form, a statement of the objectives of the study in as much detail as possible. This will involve a careful discussion between the marketing research man and the executive or executives involved. It also will serve to uncover whether there is any real doubt as to whether the proper problem is being attacked. If there is, there may be need for further work to identify and define the problem more exactly before starting a study.

2. *Exploratory Investigation.* This stage is a means of both sharpening and at times challenging the validity of the tentative statement of objectives. It consists of contact in depth with a limited number of key sources of information. Often within the company there are highly relevant sales records or past studies, or, in the experience of certain individuals, there is a storehouse of knowledge which can contribute to an understanding of the situation. Likewise, the field sales personnel and key wholesalers and dealers can be most helpful. Trade paper editors are usually well informed in their particular fields and often can be of great assistance.

One of the functions of the exploratory investigation is to see if specific hypotheses or statements of relationships between two or more variables can be formulated and used as a guide to the design of the study.

When the study involves the purchase of products by ultimate consumers the exploratory investigation may be of particular value in uncovering promising hypotheses to test. The purpose here is not to cover a representative sample of consumers (although in the limited group studied there should be a spectrum of types) but rather to gain as much insight as possible into the way they buy and view the product, and insight into any element of the whole situation which might have a bearing on the company problem. Some of the techniques and skills of motivation research can be particularly valuable here.

For reasons which are hard to understand, many studies shortchange this exploratory step or eliminate it entirely. The statement of the problem, objectives, and hypotheses can be investigated with much greater assurance and in greater detail than could have been done in the beginning. Further conferences may be needed here to communicate any new information from the exploratory phase and to make any changes that are indicated in the direction and details of the study.

3. _Development of the Research Plan._ The research plan can be developed from the final statement of the problems and objectives as they been crystalized from the exploratory investigation. With an explicitly defined problem and key hypotheses to be tested, decisions can be made concerning types and sources of information needed and methods by which it can be obtained. A budget of anticipated costs can be prepared and a definite timetable set up.

In most marketing problems it is necessary to learn more about the behavior of various groups of individuals and businesses. These groups may, for a widely used consumer product, be the general public, or various segments of the public who are thought to have particular special needs and buying practices. In industry, examples might be the steel industry as a market for oxygen generators, or insurance companies as a market for computers. The groups may also be internal to the company, such as the salesforce or company branch offices. A third type of group may be a particular type of trade channel such as supermarkets or discount or department stores.

Whatever the group involved, there is the problem of efficient gathering and analysis of data needed for the problem at hand. Fortunately, it is not necessary to make a complete census of the groups to be studied, which would be prohibitively expensive for most companies, since a properly designed sample will yield results which are accurate within known limits. Such a design is called a probability sample because all units have a known probability of being included in the sample. Thus, a simple random sample would be one in which the marketing analyst has a list of the various units in the universe and then picks a sample of, say, 500 units by using a table of random numbers or some other technique.

If the data needed on each unit have already been gathered and published by some other organization and the only problem is to secure a representative sample, this method of sample design is quite efficient. However, if primary data gathering is involved and the units on the list are scattered geographically, the travel costs of reaching them by personal interviews can be prohibitively high and some method must be found of clustering contacts so as to get greater travel efficiency for field interviewing without doing violence to the probability design. This last point is important since the ability to construct confidence limits and, within these, to estimate the sample size required to achieve a desired plus or minus reliability in the study results depends upon adhering to the probability design.

The simple random sample treats the universe as one big group without regard to the existence of segments or strata which might conceivably behave differently from one another. Thus a second type of sample design is called a stratified random sample, in which certain characteristics of units within the universe are known in advance and are believed to have a significant effect upon the purchasing behavior of people in this segment. This opens the possibility of breaking the universe up into different subuniverses or strata. Assuming that the sample size in each stratum is sufficient to provide individual estimates within the desired range of reliability, information will be available on the various segments and this may be an important feature of the total research design.

However, there may also be reasons for stratification quite aside from the desire to learn about the segments. If behavior turns out to be homogeneous within each stratum, but with a high variance between strata, this will provide a better estimate than the use of a simple random sample. So the problem of the analyst here is to weigh the possible gains of efficiency, if things turn out as described above, against the extra costs of planning the details of the stratified sample and such complications as it poses in the administration of field work and analysis of results.

Another reason for stratification is to be found in the size distribution characteristics of many of the universes or populations with which marketing managers must work. In a universe of business organizations there is likely to be a fairly heavy concentration of total sales, production, number of employees or whatever size measure may be used among a relatively small number of the total companies in the group. Thus a study of retail food chains or steel producers would show that from 10 to 25 or 30 percent of the firms represented from 70 to 80 percent or more of the business. In such a skewed distribution a simple random sample might very well miss some of the large users and end up with a poorer estimate of the universe than could be secured by a sample design which was stratified into size classes, and in which the size of sample in each stratum was large enough to offset the possibility of significantly different behavior among the large users. While a stratified random sample is an improvement over simple random sampling, it still requires the existence of lists of the units in each stratum and poses the same difficulty of excessive travel costs because the units chosen may be widely separated geographically.

Another important class of probability sample designs involves the sampling of clusters of the units in the universe, as opposed to the selection of individual units in the design. With clusters, the sample design really shifts from a sample of individual units to a sample of clusters. The statistical soundness of the sample will be greatest in situations in which the characteristics of the units within the clusters sampled are highly unlike one another, and will be least when they are very similar.

Since area sampling, which is a common approach for the probability sampling of human populations, inevitably makes use of clusters, such as blocks within cities, and since often there is reasonable similarity among the households within a given block, the statistical efficiency of area sampling might seem to be undesirably low. This might be true except for the important economic advantage which area sampling provides in the ability to cluster fieldwork assignments and thus avoid the extremely expensive work of trying to reach the units drawn from a simple random sample. When economic efficiency is considered, the area sample scores higher than either the simple random sample or the stratified random sample.

Area sampling is usually a multi-stage process. A two-stage process can be illustrated in an analysis for one city in which the first stage consists of a random selection of blocks, and the second stage a random selection of dwelling units within the blocks which were chosen in the first stage. The latter process might either consist of an actual enumeration of families or it might be achieved through some sort of systematic random sampling of the dwelling units located in the blocks chosen. As we move from one-city studies to national studies, three or even four stages may be required.

The discussion so far has dealt with probability type samples which are used in many studies where known precision of results is an important factor. Many marketing studies, however, are still employing sample designs which are nonprobability in nature. In this category one of the commonest types is termed judgment sampling, in which the analyst selects a sample which he believes to be best for a particular study. Such samples may be extremely valuable for certain studies as a means of limiting the amount of fieldwork necessary to yield important information. However, a very real danger is that such a sample will not necessarily be representative; this procedure may presume more knowledge of the universe and its characteristics than the analyst actually possesses.

A second variant of nonprobability sampling methods is quota sampling. This involves selecting certain characteristics, usually of a socioeconomic nature. These really result in strata and are often called "control characteristics." This means that up-to-date information must be available concerning the distribution of these characteristics within the universe. Also, it is desirable to select characteristics which are believed to be closely related to the main objective of the study. Typical characteristics chosen might be age, income, size of family, and the like. When these have been chosen it is possible to assign quotas to each interviewer calling for so many interviews from families with a certain income, so many interviews with a certain age distribution, and so forth. Under this kind of sample design the interviewer is usually left free, within the general area assigned, to seek out respondents who qualify under each quota. Even with the best intentions on the part of interviewers it is likely that the more accessible and cooperative people will be reached. Also, there can be real difficulties for the interviewer in identifying accurately the presence of the particular characteristics desired. Neither age nor income are easy to estimate or to secure from direct questions.

The quota sample is a nonprobability sample. As such, it is not proper to use statistical measures of reliability within given confidence limits, although this is often done. Sometimes a sample is "validated" by taking the characteristics reported by respondents other than those on which the quotas were established and comparing the sample distribution of these characteristics to their known distribution in the total universe. If the correspondence is close it is alleged that this must be a representative sample for the purposes of the study. Although this is a persuasive line of reasoning, it is unsound unless there is conclusive evidence that the characteristics so used are directly related to the purpose of the study. However, such validation procedures can be useful in indicating limitations of a particular sample.

Probability samples have some significant advantages over quota and judgment type samples: they do not depend upon recent and comprehensive knowledge about the characteristics of the universe, precision limits can be calculated for the results, and they furnish an objective basis for calculating the sample design which will yield the highest economic efficiency. Despite these very solid advantages they are not used as widely as would be expected or as seems desirable. The explanation often is that cost per completed interview is normally higher than with a quota sample. This comparison is unduly unfavorable to the probability sample simply because there is rarely any valid way in which the quality of the information in a quota sample can be objectively judged, and so economic efficiency comparisons are of little real value.

A second difficulty is that some substantial planning time is necessary to get ready for a probability sample unless the agency conducting it is regularly engaged in such work and has up-to-date maps and other necessary data. A third difficulty is that a multi-stage area sample requires personnel who are skilled and experienced. There are not too many such people in marketing research departments of manufacturers and even among the specialized research agencies they tend to be concentrated in the organizations which do a lot of national survey work.

A final point may be the feeling that there is greater possibility of serious error in the fieldwork stage of surveying respondents than in sample design. This may be true, but it is no defense of a sample design which falls far short of representative coverage of the universe being studied.

All told, these barriers are substantial and it is understandable why, with the pressures that exist on marketing research departments for quick response at minimum cost, nonprobability sample designs continue to be widely used. Even within these designs, however, it is possible to adapt certain features of probability sampling with real benefit. Perhaps most rewarding would be steps to remove from the hands of the interviewer decisions as to where and whom to interview. Usually it is possible to assign blocks and to work out a definite detailed procedure for calling on a systematic random sample of dwelling units within each block. Further, if the blocks themselves are chosen at random, a wider coverage of area and population types will be obtained than would be the case under a quota system of sampling.

Although this discussion of sample design may have seemed to be directed largely at consumer marketing studies, the same principles apply to industrial market investigations. Here, of course, concentration of business among a relatively few companies in the industry is quite common and experience has shown that the variance in behavior between such large users is often very high even within the same industry. This means that stratification is essential in sample design and that in the large size brackets it is necessary to make practically a complete census if the full picture is to be known.

Another factor causing difficulty in the design of industrial market survey samples is the multiple purchasing influence structure for industrial products. The sample must include not only enough of the right kind of companies but it must plan for adequate coverage of different job positions within each organization. The large multi-division companies also often pose special problems, as their breadth of product line may be such that they actually belong in several industries. One useful source for identifying branch plants and some information about the products they make is the *Fortune* directory of the 500 largest manufacturing companies.

4. *Collection of Required Data.* Since there was considerable discussion earlier of secondary data sources and their uses, further treatment is not necessary here and we can move directly to the problems of gathering data from primary sources. For this the survey, observational, or experimental methods can be used. The most common by far is the survey. The three major methods of securing information by the survey method are (1) personal interviews on a face-to-face basis, (2) telephone interviews, and (3) mail questionnaires. While there are many elements of interchangeability, each has its primary field of usefulness.

Surveys. Personal interviewing can be done by regular staff members of the marketing research department although there are very few companies that maintain a substantial staff for this purpose, largely because the workload tends to be too uneven. Occasionally there is some use of other company personnel, such as salesmen, although in general this has not worked out too well. A second alternative is to hire, train, and supervise part-time workers when there is a job to be done. Finally the interviewing may be "farmed out" to a specialist research organization. The research agency may conduct only the fieldwork, using the questionnaire developed by the company and turning the interview reports over to the company for analysis, or it may undertake the entire job or some in-between scope of assignment.

There is no question whatever that the weakest spot of much marketing research lies in the quality of the fieldwork, and it is not easy to pinpoint responsibility for this. Most important, perhaps, is the fact that fieldwork is inherently expensive and business executives may not be sufficiently aware of the importance of the quality control problem to be willing to pay the extra price. Part and parcel of the problem is the fact that, since research organizations generally cannot afford to have full-time personnel in the field, they draw upon the pool of supervisors throughout the country, who in turn have contact with resident interviewers. These supervisors, as well as the interviewers, usually work for several agencies.

Another factor is that research agencies generally prefer to treat their supervisors as independent contractors rather than as employees in order to avoid the burden of costly record keeping, tax payments, and fringe benefits. However, to maintain this relationship under the rules of the Internal Revenue Service an agency must be very careful to avoid providing much supervision or instruction. Thus the obvious good standards of fieldwork administration are very likely to be considered a violation of the contractor relationship. Another difficulty, again related to cost, is that interviewers are not paid very much ($1.50 to $1.75 per hour) and this makes it difficult to secure competent people.

Before the interviewing can start a suitable interviewing guide or questionnaire has to be prepared which will develop the information needed for the particular study. This requires a high degree of skill and experience, plus the willingness to test out the questionnaire in the field to make sure that it has reached its maximum potential. Failure to do adequate testing and development of the questionnaire is often a primary reason for poor quality in field surveys. Questions may be poorly phrased, so that they are confusing to the respondent; they may tend to lead the respondent in a certain direction and thus bias the results; the order of the questions may not be the best, and a whole host of other difficulties may arise which can be avoided through an adequate program of testing. Because the amount of supervision which field workers get is likely to be quite limited, the written instructions for the interviewer are highly important and deserve the greatest care in preparation and testing.

When field training and supervision are feasible, a variety of methods may prove useful. These include such things as lecturers, role playing, class discussion, and a number of practice interviews in the field. The latter is of particular importance in getting a survey off to a good start. In fact, the ideal fieldwork situation includes the possibility of meeting with the field group for a few minutes at the start of each day, after having reviewed questionnaires prepared during the preceding day or two. This allows for the clearing up of ambiguities while they are still reasonably fresh in the interviewer's mind, and it enables a better than normal check on any individuals who are doing a poor job.

A very serious form of poor quality work involves the falsification of question responses or, in some cases, entire questionnaires. The so-called problem of "cheaters" has been discussed for many years and has not been completely solved. It is too costly to send another interviewer as a follow-up. Postcard checkups are of some value, but may be misleading because they may be answered by an individual in the household who knows nothing about the matter. Telephone callbacks are better because, in the case of a negative answer, they give an opportunity to determine whether someone else in the household had been interviewed. Some marketing research practitioners feel that the problem has been magnified out of its true proportions and that some of the blame for what falsification does exist should be placed on poorly designed and incomplete questionnaires and instructions which leave the interviewer confused and uncertain as to what to do.

Another difficulty is that many people are not found at home when the call is made. In normal daytime calls on housewives, 40 percent or more will be away from home on the first call. This means that callbacks must be made if these units of a sample are to be included, and, as a result, the interviewer faces the problem of making the most effective use of callback effort. Resourceful interviewers will contact neighbors and any other local sources of information as to the most probable times of finding the individual at home.

In average neighborhoods (except those which are big city or heavily apartment) a callback will usually add 15 to 20 percent of respondents, or 65 to 75 percent of the total. A third call (the second callback) will often obtain another 10 to 15 percent, or a total of 75 to 80 percent. Because of the high cost of callbacks, ingenious approaches have been developed to combine a limited number of callbacks with a means of estimating the probability of finding people at home and assigning heavier weights to those less likely to be found at home. This is done by asking whether each respondent would have been at home had the interviewer called the same time the preceding day, the same time the day before that, and so on, backward through the time span of one week.

The most active possible individual under this approach would be one who was to be found at home only the one day of the week he or she was interviewed. In other words there was a one-to-seven probability of including such an active person, and his responses can be assigned a heavier weight than those of someone whose probability of being located at that time of day was 5/7ths. Properly carried out, this combination of limited callbacks and the development of a weighting scheme is a reasonably economic solution to the not-at-home problems, although it assumes that the responses of the limited number of hard-to-catch persons actually interviewed accurately represents those who "escaped."

Another source of difficulty is that some individuals will be traveling, sick, or temporarily located at another address (including a few who are involuntary guests of the state). There is no weighting technique or other approach to hypothesize the responses of this segment of the sample. Equally lost is the group who refuses to cooperate with the interviewer. This refusal may take the form of unwillingness to be interviewed at all, or unwillingness to answer certain questions which are regarded as impertinent or involving confidential information. The rates of refusal encountered vary somewhat depending upon the sensitivity of the type of study being made, the nature of the neighborhood where the interviews are being conducted, and, most importantly, the skill of the interviewer. Rates at times run to 10 or 20 percent, and even higher, but a skilled interviewer can hold them to substantially lower levels. Whatever the fraction may be in a particular study, it represents a "hole" in the information yielded by the sample.

Interviewing in the industrial market requires a higher degree of knowledge, intelligence, and maturity than in the typical consumer survey. Because of the more complex character of many industrial marketing studies and the variability of conditions encountered among different respondent organizations, it is not practical to develop as highly structured a questionnaire as in most consumer studies. Generally an interview guide is prepared which provides a listing of the topics to be discussed and a general pattern of approach. It is pretty much agreed that the industrial interviewer should not attempt to take detailed notes during the interview, except for occasional vital data which might otherwise be forgotten or remembered erroneously. The information gained in the interview should be recorded at the earliest possible moment after leaving the presence of the respondent, and preferably before any further interviews are undertaken. Almost inevitably there will be some confusion as to who said what in writing up a series of interviews several hours or days later. It is important that whoever does the interviewing should have, by training and background, enough understanding of the respondent's problems to promote effective discussion. Interviews of 30 to 45 minutes are usual, and many run much longer, especially if the inquiry is complex.

If a company has a well developed call-report system, salesmen regularly enter on these forms much information of value for marketing executives. But it is generally agreed that salesmen do not make good interviewers for marketing research. Few of them are research minded by temperament, and they are particularly fearful of jeopardizing, through questioning, the good relationships they have with their customers. Furthermore, salesmen are an expensive marketing instrument, and to use them as interviewers may be a misallocation of company resources. Well-trained field workers should be available for substantially less wages than the average salesman.

Telephone interviewing in marketing surveys has increased sharply in the last several years. For one thing the use of the telephone has extended very broadly across our society, and the figure for telephones in metropolitan area homes now runs at 75 percent. In suburban areas of higher-than-average income it is close to 100 percent. Assuming that recent directories are on hand for the areas in which the study is to be made, the picking of a good telephone sample is fairly simple by using either random number tables or a systematic random sample approach. There are some problems, however. No directory is completely correct even though it has just come from the printer, and the longer it has been in use, the more errors it has.

In general, interviews over the phone cannot be as long as those conducted face-to-face. If the respondent becomes impatient there is more chance that he or she will hang up than that a personal interview will be terminated under like circumstances. While there is direct feedback to the interviewer in the form of verbal responses, there are no visual clues to the interviewer's behavior, attitudes, or intensity of feeling (other than tone of voice), and therefore the telephone interview is not quite as revealing as personal contact. On the other hand, it is definitely cheaper because it eliminates the travel time of interviewers both on initial calls and on callbacks. Busy signals, of course, require callbacks. One difficulty is that it is not always possible to distinguish homes from business establishments in the telephone listing, and this may interfere with the soundness of the sample design.

Telephone interviewing has been quite successful in many industrial marketing surveys. There seems to be surprisingly little resistance on the part of businessmen to telephone interviewing, and a large part of the time which in personal interviewing might be spent in waiting rooms is saved. Of course, it is not practical to conduct long or detailed discussions over the phone, and particularly discussions which might require the respondent to gather data from his records. One technique involves writing a letter in advance asking for cooperation, describing the data needed, and setting up the time for a telephone call a few days later. This has the advantage of identifying the organization making the study and, to this extent, might tend to generate more cooperation. On the other hand, there is no chance for the give-and-take of conversation, and the skillful interviewer probably has a better chance of persuading a reluctant respondent to agree to gather the information when face-to-face than the most carefully composed letter.

One of the important problems of using the mail questionnaire is that the groups of people who do not respond may be quite large, and may be quite different in its behavior from the group that does. For example, there is a tendency for people who are interested in the particular subject to answer while those without interest may not. If the answers received are considered representative of the market, the figures as to usage and attitudes are, clearly, vastly overstated. Thus it becomes necessary, in making use of the mail questionnaire, to provide some means for subsampling the characteristics of the nonrespondents. Of course there may be no difference in these characteristics. However this must be definitely proven by firm evidence before it can be accepted and before the precaution of studying the nonrespondents can be dropped.

To check the characteristics of nonrespondents readily, we must be able to distinguish the people who returned the questionnaire from those who did not. This can be troublesome at times since it may be desirable not to request names in the questionnaire and to promise anonymity to the cooperating individual. If the questionnaire is coded, and the code is obvious, this may cause some disbelief and apprehension unless it is handled very skillfully. If the coding is done covertly it may be discovered by some of the more observant and suspicious people who are apt to be critical of what appears to be deception. If there is no identification at all, a subsampling can take place only by using the entire sample and apologizing to those who have already responded.

However, to send this out by mail will not necessarily improve the representation of the nonrespondent group because the same self-selection process will take place as that which originally occurred. Thus it will be necessary to use either telephone or personal interviews and to follow these up with callbacks until questionnaires have been secured from a group of people who had ignored the initial mailing. If this group constitutes a sample of sufficient size, inferences can be drawn as to its characteristics and compared with the characteristics of those who sent back the questionnaire.

Observational Method. The observational method does not ask questions of people; it involves making a record of events as they occur. This clearly has the advantage of reducing response bias on the part of a person who is asked a direct question and it also tends to eliminate difficulties due to the misunderstanding of questions. An example of the use of the observational method is the Nielsen Audimeter, which makes a continuous timed record of the use of TV sets and the channels to which each is tuned. Another example is a count of the flow of customers through check-out stands in supermarkets, or a count of the size and location of display spaces for a particular brand of product inside retail stores. The term can also apply more broadly to encompass sales results of an industry, a company, or a product. In effect, these represent observations of what happened over a series of time periods.

An obvious limitation of the observational method is that it cannot provide data directly on the personal characteristics and attitudes of individuals. As such, it cannot be of much help in learning why an individual behaves in a certain way. Although many observational studies can be designed so that the subjects are not aware that they are being observed, this is not true of all of them. When observation is obvious it is possible that some degree of bias may creep into the data because the behavior of the subjects is likely to be conditioned by the realization of being watched. However, some investigations of this problem suggest that it may not be too serious. For example, in the tape recording of interviews it is usually found that after a period of getting used to the fact of being recorded the behavior of the person studied reverts to normal patterns.

Even under ideal circumstances, where subjects are unaware of the fact of observation, there remains the possibility of error on the part of human observers. While some sort of machine surveillance may circumvent this, still it is true that the great bulk of observational situations require the use of people.

A final limitation is that of cost, since it is necessary to be where action takes place and wait until it does take place—as would be true in observing buying behavior for a specified product in a retail store. Of course it is possible to try out certain things in laboratory situations, and, with proper design of the research method, this can be a very effective approach. To observe the behavior of people and things in the marketplace itself, however, involves a great deal of idle time.

Experimental Method.   Experimentation has been defined as "the collection of data in such a way as to permit clear and unconfused conclusions as to the correctness of a hypothesis which involves cause and effect relationships."[14] Usually, but not always, this involves intervention on the part of the company to achieve the necessary controls for testing the hypothesis which has been established. Experiments can be developed to test advertising campaigns, packaging changes, new products, and variations in store or window displays. The logic underlying conclusions drawn from experiments is two-fold: 1) If the introduction of the experimental variable does not bring about a change in the variable being studied, the experimental variable cannot be viewed as a cause of it; 2) If a change in the variable under study occurs without the introduction of the experimental variable, the latter cannot be the cause of the change.

In the usual experiment two groups of subjects are selected who have similar characteristics so far as the purposes of the experiment are concerned. The variable being tested is introduced into the experimental group and is not introduced into the other or control group. If sales change within the experimental group, but not in the control group, it may be concluded that there is a causal relationship between the variable and the result. However, if there is no change in sales in the experimental group, or if sales to both groups change in about the same degree and direction, it may be concluded that the variable did not cause the change.

While this is the general pattern of experimental designs, there are a number of variations which have been used. One is sometimes called the "before-after" design, which uses the same individuals as both the experimental and the control group. There is a measurement of the behavior of the group before the experiment is started and a measurement after the experimental variable has been introduced. The effect of the variable is assumed to be the difference between the measurements afterwards and before.

This design has the limitation that, since it is spread over a time period, uncontrolled external variables may be largely responsible for the changes. This can be remedied by introducing a control group into the structure, in which there are advance measurements, with both

---

[14] Harper W. Boyd and Ralph Westfall, *Marketing Research* (Homewood, Ill.: Richard D. Irwin, Inc., 1956), pp. 79–80. This discussion of experimental design has been based largely on pp. 79–100 of this book.

the experimental group and the control group. Then the experimental variable is introduced with the experimental group (and not with the control group) and there are measurements at the end of the experiment for both groups. Any difference between the before and after measurements of the control group can be viewed as a result of uncontrolled variables, while the difference between the measurements of the experimental group is the result of the experimental variable plus the same uncontrolled events that influenced the control group.

One difficulty with this design arises if the people in the groups are aware they are being measured in various ways. This fact of measurement can cause results in behavior and attitudes which will affect the validity of their responses. For example, the before measurements of one group might easily lead to sensitizing them to the particular subject matter and therefore make them more vulnerable to effects from the stimulus of the experimental variable.

In order to get around this difficulty a more elaborate design is sometimes used, although its expense is a real barrier. This involves two experimental groups and two control groups, one set of which is not measured prior to the introduction of the experimental variable. All four groups are preselected, so that they are equal. Because of the heavy expense of this "ideal" design, a simplified design, entitled "after only with control group," is often used. Here there is no "before" measurement of either group, but an "after" measurement of both groups and the effect of the experimental variable is determined by computing the difference of the two measurements taken at the end.

The "ex post facto" design is a variation of the "after only design" in that the experimental and control groups are selected after the experimental variable is introduced instead of before. This has the advantage that the test subjects cannot know that they are to be tested since they have been exposed before being selected for the sample. Another benefit is that the experimenter can let the experimental variable be introduced at will and need control only his observations.

5. *Analysis of Data.* As indicated earlier, a well planned study is not only pointed directly toward the management decisions at issue, but it also provides a definite structure which encompasses the data to be gathered, the important variables to be studied, and the ways in which the relationships between these variables are to be analyzed. We cannot do more than mention some of the most useful of these methods of analysis. Standard statistical texts and the growing literature of quantitative approaches to marketing are available to the interested reader.[15]

---

[15]Ronald E. Frank, Alfred A. Kuehn, and William F. Massy, *Quantitative Techniques in Marketing Analysis* (Homewood, Ill.: Richard D. Irwin, Inc., 1962).

Fundamentally, the purpose of much analysis is to measure the degree and character of association between one or more variables. From these associations, plus a skilled interplay of experience and intuitive insight, it may be possible to infer that certain causal relationships exist. About the only cases in which causal relationships can be directly postulated are those in which an experiment has been designed for this express purpose and other variables have been held constant.

A simple way to see whether there appear to be relationships between variables is to set up the data in the form of an array. An example would be to plot two variables on a graph to make a scatter diagram. Another method is to use cross-classification tables which can handle up to four or five variables before becoming unwieldy. Such arrays can be made by relatively unskilled personnel and, if correctly specified and prepared, can be evaluated by executives who have a knowledge of the marketing problem being investigated but who are not skilled in statistical methods. Even though the relationships so determined are gross in nature, the advantages of comprehension are powerful, and such exhibits are often included in reports even when much of the analysis has been made by more sophisticated methods.

Two of the most important methods of studying relationships between variables are *correlation* and *regression*. Correlation analysis measures the degree of linear dependence between two variables. The correlation coefficient presents a summary measure of this association and indicates the degree to which the points on a scatter diagram tend to lie on a straight line. Regression analysis, by providing information on the slope of the linear relationships, makes possible the preparation of estimates which can be used in various forecasting problems. Multiple factors can also be taken into account in regression analysis.

Factor analysis is a means of compressing an extensive body of data into more compact form.[16] It is a process for discovering a smaller number of variables which will summarize a larger original set.

6. *Presentation of the Report.* In a well managed study the presentation of the report is a capstone on a series of working relationships between the marketing research staff and the executives who are responsible for the problem being studied and the type of positive action to be taken. This does not say that it does not require a high order of writing, visual, and oral skill. Rather, the real process of ensuring use of the findings starts with early involvement of the executives concerned. As explained briefly in the outline above, the "dummy report" is a

---

[16]Harry Harmon, *Modern Factor Analysis* (Chicago: University of Chicago Press, 1960).

valuable tool in portraying the types of information to be developed in the study and in facilitating effective two-way communication between the marketing research staff and the executive. This two-way communication should be maintained throughout the study, as occasions may arise when some change in direction or emphasis should be made.

7. *Follow-Up*. Although the implementation of the recommendations of a research report is the best evidence of its true acceptance by executives, this is no reason why the marketing research staff should forget the project, even if the recommendations are followed. It is highly desirable for them to have a regular system of follow-up to learn how the recommended solution actually works out. In many respects this is the best test of the validity of the original analytical approach. Such a review may at times be very unsettling as it may indicate that some important factors, which would have changed the final result substantially, had not been taken into consideration. This kind of feedback may also be valuable in checking out the appropriateness of the analytical method used and in making possible greater planning sophistication in later studies of the same type. However, the chief emphasis in this follow-up and review is not so much that of methodological improvement as it is the sharp focusing on executive acceptance and implementation of research findings, a problem that haunts research consultants and marketing research staffs alike.

FOUR IMPORTANT TYPES OF MARKETING RESEARCH STUDIES

As pointed out earlier in the chapter, marketing research departments conduct a wide range of studies. Four of these are of particular importance because the information they provide is multi-use in the sense of contributing to two or more management decision areas. In the remainder of the chapter we will briefly discuss

1. Sales analysis
2. Measuring the size of markets
3. Studying customers' buying patterns and characteristics
4. Measuring competitors' marketing strategies and tactics

Sales Analysis

Sales made by a company are one of the most important results of the whole complex of marketing activities, and, along with dollars of gross margins and of marketing expenses, have a very important effect upon the net profits earned by the business. Various standards of sales volume accomplishment at a company-wide, divisional, salesman, and sometimes even customer level are developed in marketing planning and control activities, and comparisons are made at regular intervals with actual results. These comparisons show where performance is substandard and remedial action is needed.

It is difficult to think about the sale of a product without viewing purchasing action of a customer as the necessary other side of the shield. Thus it is helpful in thinking about both sales analysis and measures of market size to realize that the smallest possible unit of information is the sale of the specific lot of a product to a specific customer. If this information is available in the normal course of a firm's operations, as would be true for an industrial goods producer who sold his entire output directly to customers through his own sales force, complete flexibility exists. These product-market units of information can be rearranged to provide meaningful data at the customer level for whatever breakdowns of products or customers, or cross-classifications of the two, may be desired. Actually, many companies do some grouping of items in the sales records system because individual item reporting is bulky and hard to interpret.

In addition to analyzing sales by product and market classifications, we can sort them by geographic area. For example, the total purchases of all of the customers falling within the territory of a particular salesman represent his sales volume. Similarly, salesmen's territories can be grouped to show district totals, and so on, until figures for the complete marketing area of a company are accumulated. The units for sales analysis are dollars or physical units of the product—or in many cases both. If the price of the product fluctuates widely, it is hard to interpret sales figures which are shown only in dollars unless price indexes are used to adjust for the effect of price changes. Many product lines have models which vary substantially in price, and once again it is helpful to know the number of physical units represented in sales dollars.

The source of information on sales is frequently the invoice prepared at the time a shipment is made to a customer. The usual invoice contains several items, and normally each line on the invoice generates a separate tabulating card or other data processing unit. However, there may be various reasons why it is not feasible to ship merchandise at the time the order is received. For example, if there is any particular change in the product made at the customer's request, there will be a time lag before shipment. Similarly, if there is a strong seller's market, and orders are outrunning factory capacity, there will also be a time lag.

In such instances it is common to analyze unfilled orders as well as shipments. Not all of these, of course, will actually be shipped, because there may be cancellations. This is especially likely if orders have been pyramided by customers because of tight supply. As soon as the market softens—and it is often said the difference between a seller's market and a buyer's market is just one unit of the product in question—cancellations are apt to be heavy.

Sales analysis reports commonly compare current sales with sales of the preceding year for the same time period, with sales budgets, or with some other standard which has been set up in the marketing plan. On monthly sales reports, usually, the cumulative figure for the year to date is also provided. Other types of reports may reach back several years in order to provide a trend picture. The frequency of issuing reports depends upon the need of the manager to act quickly. One of the problems is to make sure that management is getting the information it needs and is using what it receives. An essential part of an effective sales analysis system is regular pruning out of reports which have outlived their usefulness.

Needless to say, the reports should be very clear in their meaning, and the key story they have to tell should be easy to understand. The basic principle is to make it as easy as possible for management to use the information in its regular decision work.

This discussion of sales analysis has assumed that the manufacturer is in a position to know from his own shipping records the specific products which were sold to specific customers, who are also their end-users. Although there are some industrial goods manufacturers who practice 100 percent control over marketing operations to their final customers, most companies, even in the industrial goods field, also make use of one or more types of middlemen. And in the consumers' goods field it is a most unusual situation to sell direct to ultimate consumers.

When sales are made through retailers, or through wholesalers and retailers, the sales records reflect the flow only to those levels. This may or may not parallel sales to ultimate users because there are inventories at both wholesale and retail levels which can absorb a substantial amount of fluctuation in consumer demand without reflecting it perfectly in their restocking behavior. For manufacturers in this situation there is real need for supplementing the information available through company records by some direct knowledge of ultimate user buying rates. In the consumer field, this information may be available through purchase of commercial services which operate store audit or consumer purchase panels. It can also be estimated in sufficient detail and accuracy for many purposes by means of survey techniques.

Measuring Size of Markets

Information derived from sales analysis becomes most meaningful for executive decision when it can be compared with appropriate standards of performance. The use of company performance during a comparable time period in the preceding year as a standard of comparison is interesting but not necessarily relevant. A healthy increase over last year of 50 percent is pleasant to contemplate, but no one can be sure it should not have been 100 percent—or perhaps 200 percent.

Thus there is need for measuring the size of the total market for various products. At the same time it is often possible to develop information about the relative importance of various segments of the market which purchase the product. Such measurements enable management to know what share of the total market each product line is securing and whether market development is more or less evenly distributed over the various segments or is heavily concentrated in a few. Without knowledge of the total market and the ability to calculate share-of-market figures, the absolute sales performance of the company is impossible to interpret. There are times when gradually declining sales volume might represent outstanding performance for the company because the total industry sales volume had declined very much faster. Conversely, growth in absolute sales volume for the company may lead to a feeling of optimism and self-confidence which is not at all justified because competitors' volume is growing much faster.

The problem of measuring market size is intimately related to the length of time that the product has been on the market and its approximate position on the growth curve. A product that has been marketed for many years and aggressively promoted by a number of suppliers will have established a sales history and a current sales performance level which can often be ascertained from commercial services, trade association, or government statistics. The longer a product has been established in the market the more information is available about it.

Many trade associations collect statistical information on production and sales from members and circulate it as totals of industry activity. Each member thus knows the total output of his industry and can calculate his own share of the market, but data is not given for individual members. Some of these figures can be extremely useful, but should be carefully evaluated. One limitation is that sometimes one or two large producers are not members of the association and their figures are not in the total. Also, the statistical methodology used should be carefully checked and a sincere effort made to be sure that the data are reasonably valid.

Trade magazines often publish annual statistical issues which assemble estimates of product output, shipments, and market segments which can be very useful for marketing planning and control purposes. Directories which list producers (and sometimes distributors) in particular industries contain a lot of information about individual companies, and frequently arrange them geographically. A company itself may well have internal sources of data which yield useful estimates of market size. The purchasing department, for example, should be well informed in a number of fields and may have relevant information. The research and development department may have some very well informed people on certain product or market situations. Needless to say, it is the responsibility of the marketing research department to have a thorough inventory of such internal sources and to make sure that no stone is left unturned in searching for information.

If the needed data on market size cannot be found from published sources, and if there are no commercial services available which do the job adequately, it may be necessary to make a special study which usually involves field investigation. Estimates of total industry sales, without benefit of solid statistical figures, are at best informed opinion. However, by cross-checking various sources it is often possible to put together a rough measure of market size which results in information that is much better than guesses or no information at all.

So far discussion has been limited to measurement of total market size. Actually, a very important use of market size measurements is to indicate the relative fertility of different geographical areas, particularly salesmen's territories, sales districts, and divisions. These figures are very important because they provide a basis of allocating effort to market opportunity. Unfortunately there are very few statistical reporting systems which provide industry sales data by small geographic areas. One exception to this is the appliance industry, which has a statistical interchange of sales to retailers by counties.

Most companies face the problem of developing some sort of index or series of indexes by which the total market can be distributed among area units small enough to be used in laying out sales territories. Such indexes inevitably involve a number of assumptions which may or may not be generally true. Some of these indexes can be specific to the product in the sense of having a demonstrable causal relationship to it, such as new housing starts and building materials, but these are few and far between. Most of them are general purpose indexes, which sometimes have a high correlation with past sales and sometimes must be used in the absence of something better, always with the pious hope that they provide a reasonable indication of market opportunity. One general consumers' goods index that is widely used is that of *Sales Management* magazine, which is available for counties and metropolitan districts throughout the United States.

Discussion to this point has concerned products which have been on the market for some time and for which it can be assumed that there has been a reasonable stimulation of demand as a result of competitive efforts by several suppliers. When a product is in the beginning of its growth curve, the number of producers is few and marketing effort is uneven and limited in scope. As we move from established products to new products, the difficulties of measuring probable market size are greatly increased. Industry sales, even when known, offer only a partial indicator of market opportunity, and the concept of market potential has to be introduced. Market potential can be said to represent an estimate of the total possible purchases (within a given time period) of buyers who have a use for a given product and might purchase it if it were effectively brought to their attention. While the need for market potential measurements is greatest during the early part of the growth cycle of a new product, the concept can be useful for established products as well, whose potential is usually not much different from total industry sales.

Customer Buying Patterns and Attitudes

Knowledge of customer buying patterns and attitudes is vital information in planning effective marketing programs for both industrial and consumer products. The manufacturer of consumers' goods, because he normally has no contact with users unless he makes a special study, is particularly likely to be uninformed. He is interested in such things as variations in amount purchased, the degree of brand loyalty demonstrated, the willingness of consumers to use private brands, the relationship of socioeconomic factors to the purchase of his type of product, and the "reasons why" underlying customer purchasing behavior. This information is of particular importance because, with the steady growth of self-service in retail stores, there is less and less opportunity for feedback of consumer behavior through retail sales personnel. Thus it is possible for a manufacturer to be using a marketing program which is quite wide of its real target simply because he knows so little about consumers.

In the past several years interest has grown in learning more about the motivations that impel consumers to buy or to ignore various product types and brands. As a result of this interest, motivation research became a popular approach to the study of many marketing problems. In such studies fairly small samples of people are interviewed and heavy use is made of various projective techniques whose purpose is to circumvent the bias that would be present in answers to direct questions about sensitive areas of purchasing behavior. The method caused wide discussion among marketing men and pitched battles occurred between its protagonists and its critics, some of which generated more heat than light. It appears, in retrospect, that one of the reasons for the high degree of interest was the intriguing nature of concepts which emerged from depth interviewing of individuals on an exploratory nondirective basis, utilizing such projective devices as the thematic apperception test, the sentence completion test, the Rorschach inkblot test, and the like.

Sometimes it seemed that executives became bemused by the new and intriguing procedures and did not always ask themselves what could be done operationally with the results. In other cases some of the ideas are indeed promising and deserve careful testing to determine how, and how often, they can be used in the marketplace. A balanced point of view would seem to suggest that the motivation research cycle demonstrated the importance of the exploratory investigation in the marketing research procedure, a step which too often has been conspicuous by its absence. Experience has also made it pretty evident that there is much more to psychological and social science research than the mere use of projective techniques, and that there are many ways of approaching the highly important problem of motivation.

In the industrial market it is important to know which functional activities within a customer firm are affected sufficiently by the purchase of a product, so that the executives in charge of them have some voice in the buying decision. The role played by these men in the purchase procedure should be known, as well as the language they understand most easily and the appeals which are likely to influence them. From all this effective ways of communicating with them can be devised. If salesmen are to be used, what kind of men should they be and what kind of training should they have? If advertising is to be used, what buying appeals should be employed to best meet the particular situation, and what media should be used?

Another aspect is the matter of service needs for the product both during the selling process and after it has been purchased. There have been some general studies of industrial purchasing procedure but they are not specific enough to help a particular company very much in a marketing strategy problem. Much information is available, as a result of salesmen's call-reports and field contacts with executives, but reliable and extensive information will undoubtedly require some fieldwork. Needless to say, the heavy concentration of purchasing among the larger units in the average industrial market means that careful attention should be paid to these. Sellers of noncompetitive products used by the industry market in question may also be helpful.

Studies of Competitors

While the product and program decisions made by a marketing executive can have a profound effect upon the market at times, especially if he introduces a successful innovation, in most cases a company has to adjust skillfully to the environment of the marketplace. A very important variable in this environment is represented by the group of companies which are significant competitors in the sense that they vend roughly comparable products, selling to at least some of the same market groups. It would seem obvious that as much information as possible should be assembled about these competitors and from a great variety of sources. Yet this is not always done on a really careful basis, nor is it necessarily kept up to date as skillfully as it should be. Such knowledge is particularly important today because of the stepped-up pace of research and development and the greater variety of new products. It is of particular importance to try to understand the real strengths and weaknesses of each competing firm and as much as possible about their habit patterns. Many decisions will hinge upon the probable reaction of one or more competitors and any information which would shed light on this key factor is extremely valuable. A useful list of questions, which indicates the wide scope of desirable information about competitors, is given below:[17]

1. How many competitors do we have (including competitive materials and products outside your industry, if applicable)?
2. How much of the market do they have (including trends and forecasts)?
3. How have they fared over the past five years?
4. What are their marketing objectives?
5. Where are their manufacturing facilities?
6. Where are their warehouses?
7. What distribution systems do they use?
8. What are their current products?
9. What are their prices?

---

[17] From Alfred B. De Passe and J. Stewart Fleck, "How to Keep Track of Your Competition," *Sales Management,* November 10, 1959.

10. What are their standard discounts and terms?

11. How are their deliveries?

12. Is any one competitor concentrating on a particular segment of the market?

13. What future products are they planning?

14. What is their reputation in the industry?

15. What do customers think of them?

16. How are they organized for selling and marketing?

17. How many persons in the home office?

18. How many in the field?

19. What types of people do they have?

20. How is their personnel turnover?

21. What kind of sales training do they practice?

22. How do they pay their people (including base salary, incentives, fringe benefits, etc.)?

23. Are they planning any acquisitions or mergers?

24. Are they building new plants?

25. Are they opening new sales offices?

26. What kind of new equipment are they buying?

27. How profitable are their operations (gross and net)?

28. How much authority do their salesmen have (on deliveries, special discounts, etc.)?

29. How do they support their salesmen (top-echelon contacts, financial assistance to customers, factory visits, 13-unit dozens, "push money," etc.)?

30. What are their billing practices?

31. What kinds of sales promotion activity do they have (direct mail, promotional, personnel, etc.)?

32. What is their advertising program (theme, budget, publications, national or regional media used, cooperative programs, etc.)?

33. What is their returned-goods policy?

34. What are their warranties and guarantees?

35. What are their field service policies and practices?

36. How important is our market to their total business?

37. How much total selling power (direct sales plus advertising and promotion plus staff) does each competitor have?

38. How does the total selling power of each compare with its share of the market?

39. How much do they know about us?

The financial results of competitors' operations are of great interest and value, although in these days of diversified product lines it is extremely difficult to find out about the results definitely traceable to a particular product or group of products. However, by gathering a wide range of information estimates can sometimes be made as to probable production and marketing cost levels. Concerns which are closely held are particularly difficult to research and great ingenuity may be required to develop useful information. A search of court cases, of government proceedings, and of hearings before various regulatory agencies may sometimes provide very useful data. Of very great importance is any and all information that can be gathered about the probable direction of competitors' growth and technical development. Despite the difficulty of this kind of study, a continuous and comprehensive effort will yield very useful information without engaging in practices that would violate commercial espionage legislation or accepted ethical standards.

It is almost certain that in the minds and contacts of its employees the average firm has access to much more information about its competitors than it uses. This material will become available only if some system is devised to mobilize it and to train employees to observe and report fragments of information that, when fitted together, become significant and to provide incentives for them to do so.

CHAPTER 20

Marketing Cost Analysis

Many corporate operating statements list among the expense items the inclusive entry "Marketing (or Sales) and General Administration." Since such statements are for general publication, management prefers that they report expenditures in large and heterogeneous lumps to avoid helping competitors find out what the firm is doing and how much it costs to do it. Others issue their reports in this way because their executives have not yet recognized the managerial uses of analyzing internal accounts in such a way as to determine how much marketing costs are or what they are spent for.

A generation ago the entry quoted above represented the entire sum total of the knowledge most managements had of their marketing costs. The development during the past several decades of a better understanding of the managerial importance of marketing planning and control has led to a growing interest in the application of cost accounting techniques to the expenses of marketing. Basic factors in every marketing plan are how much it will cost to execute and what benefits we may expect to get from doing so. An increasing number of firms use costing techniques to analyze marketing expenses so as to aid their executives in planning their marketing work more intelligently and directing it more efficiently.

Essentially, these techniques involve assigning to each of the marketing functions the costs it generates, to each customer or customer group the costs to which his or its business gives rise, to each product or group of products the expenses involved in marketing it, to each sales area the costs that arise from marketing in that area, and sometimes to each transaction or type of transaction the costs it creates.

Some marketing executives tend to look darkly upon cost analysis for marketing, regarding it as a top management check on their operations. This is not a true picture of its purpose. Its primary use should be to supply the marketing manager a tool with which he can plan and control the operations of his organization so as to achieve more profitable results for his company or gain its objectives more efficiently. This simple concept is a hard one to get across to the sales manager of the old school, who clings firmly to the belief that sales and more sales are the only salvation of himself and his company.

DISTRIBUTION COST ANALYSIS IS DIFFERENT

The techniques of cost accounting were first developed and applied in the field of production. They were well formulated and refined in that area before any serious or widespread attempt was made to apply them to marketing activities. When this attempt began, it was found that the problems in the two areas were so different that some of the methods used in production cost accounting could not be applied to distribution, others had to be modified, and some new techniques had to be developed. These differences are of several kinds.

a)   The production manager deals with *things,* most of which are tangible: materials, machines, and the men who work them. The various elements are readily subject to counting and detailed study. On the other hand, the marketing manager deals largely with intangibles, such as sales appeals, what the salesman says during his calls, and customer attitudes and reactions, which are not easy to count or measure. By the very nature of his operations, he has less control over the elements of the cost structure than does the manager of production.

b)   The units of product of the manufacturing operation are uniform or at least standardized within certain classes or groups of products, each unit of which is practically identical with every other. If we think of the order as the product unit of the marketing operation it immediately appears that each one differs from every other in physical bulk, value, composition, shipping arrangements, and the circumstances under which it is obtained and handled.

c)   The cost results desired from distribution accounting analysis are much more varied than those of production. The results sought in production cost accounting are chiefly the expenses of each process and for each unit of product. The marketing manager may need costs by product, by customer, by function, by order, by channel of distribution, by salesman, by kind or size of transaction, and by geographical area. Some of these can be derived by combinations of others, but a number of them must be computed separately.

d)   Joint costs are much more prevalent in marketing than in production. This is true of much order handling and order filling expense, some of the cost of advertising, salesmen's salaries and expenses and, to some extent, even commissions and supervision expenses, to mention only a few. A much smaller portion of marketing expense can be charged directly and logically to a cost result than is the case with production costs, and a much larger portion must be allocated on some basis that has at least an element of arbitrariness in it.

STEPS IN THE PROCESS OF COST ANALYSIS

Traditionally, a firm's expenses are classified into such accounts as salaries and wages, interest, rent or occupancy costs, insurance, taxes, depreciation, etc. Each of these is likely to contain expenditures generated by marketing activities. Before marketing cost analysis work can be done these expenditures must be distilled out of the customary accounts and assigned to a new order of accounts, each representing the costs generated by a specific marketing activity or function.

Therefore the first task of the distribution cost analyst is to make a list of the marketing activities or homogeneous groups of marketing activities that his firm carries on. This list is apt to vary somewhat from company to company, and it should be made to fit and completely cover the marketing operations of the specific company. By no means should it be copied from another company or from a book or article on the subject.

The accounts which represent these activities we may call functional accounts. Those that are apt to be common to most firms are: carrying finished inventory, order handling, salesmen's compensation and expenses, advertising, sales promotion, delivery. In addition, such categories as marketing research, marketing planning, customer and sales correspondence, technical service, field supervision, packaging, marketing overhead, and others may be established. Practically all of these have in them wages, salaries and rent, and several of them include an element of interest, insurance, or depreciation.

The analyst must sort out of each traditional expense account the part that belongs to marketing and allocate it to the appropriate functional account or spread it among several of them. A simple form may be used in this work. Figure 20–1 shows such a form, in which the usual items of outlay are listed down the left hand margin of the page and the names of suggested functional-cost groups across the top.

In using this form the analyst considers each of the customary expense items separately, dividing the total amount of each item into the parts that apply to the several functions and entering each amount so obtained in the appropriate functional column. After all the customary

TABLE 20-1

ANALYSIS OF DISTRIBUTION COSTS

Customary Expense Accounts	Total Dollars	Functional-Cost Groups								
		Marketing Research	Inventory Carrying Cost	Physical Handling	Order Routine	Personal Selling	Advertising	Sales Promotion	Delivery
Salaries and wages									
Interest									
Rent									
Delivery									
Sales expense									
Insurance									
Taxes									
Office supplies, etc.									
Depreciation									
Accounting									
Heat, light, etc.									
Telephone									
Correspondence									
Miscellaneous									
TOTALS									

expense accounts have been thus distributed, the columns are added vertically to give totals for each functional-cost group. A few expense items can usually be assigned without breakdown to a single functional column. Some can be broken down by reference to the individual entries behind the total in the ledger. Payments for salaries and wages, for instance, can often be distributed by computing the total wage paid to each employee and assigning it to the cost group arising from that part of the firm's activities in which he was engaged. For example, if a man works entirely in the advertising department his entire salary can be assigned to the advertising column. If his activities are spread over two or more functional areas, his wage can be divided among them on the basis of a time and motion study of his activities or of an analysis of the various things he does and an estimate of the time he spends in doing each of them.

Expense items, however, must often be distributed on the basis of a more arbitrary analytical procedure. Allocation of rent depends in part upon measurements of the space utilized by each of the functions, and in part on the location of that space. The distribution of the expense of supervision may call for an arbitrary assumption that the supervisor divides his time equally among his subordinates, or that he apportions it among them in a manner roughly proportionate to his appraisal of the relative importance of their tasks, or on the basis of his estimate of how much time he actually spends with each. The selection of arbitrary allocation factors calls for an intimate knowledge of the business and a nicely balanced judgment.

Whether interest on investment should be treated as a distribution cost is a problem. The weight of accounting opinion is against its inclusion in production-costing. But it is difficult to see how the costs of a mercantile business can be accurately computed at all if this item is excluded. The real difference between profitable and unprofitable commodities may lie in the interest on the inventory investments in them; and the real distinction between customers that are good and those that are bad, from a profit standpoint, may be found in the differing amounts of interest costs generated by their accounts outstanding. The analyst of distribution costs should urge the inclusion of interest as an operating expense, for it can scarcely be disputed that each element in the business should make at least this minimum return over and above conventional operating expenses.

The functional-cost groups shown in Figure 20–1 are by no means standard; the list is offered merely as a suggestive one. The operating structure of any given business should, in the last analysis, determine the division of its distribution costs into functional classes.[1]

Whatever functional cost groups the analyst may find it desirable to use for his firm, he will be wise to define them carefully. If he fails to do so he runs the risk of counting some cost items more than once and of having others fall between two cost groups without being counted at all. If the cost groups are to be kept to a manageable number they will certainly tend to overlap each other to some degree and may not cover all marketing activities. Here again, the analyst will be wise not to use the standard definitions set up in the writings on distribution cost analysis but to prepare definitions that fit the operations of his firm. He will probably wind up with a set of definitions that will, in general, conform to the standard ones, but will differ in certain particulars that are important in preparing a usable picture of the marketing cost structure of his company.

The functional cost groups we mentioned earlier generally include the following items:

a) *Carrying inventory* includes the costs of warehouse or storeroom space, of moving goods into storage, of keeping records of merchandise in storage, of financing their value while there, of insurance, and perhaps obsolescence or depreciation while in storage.

b) *Order handling* includes the expenses generated by editing orders, pricing them, making working copies of them if necessary, picking merchandise off the storage floor or shelves, moving it to the shipping platform, packing it for shipment, moving it into the truck or railroad car, and sometimes of preparing bills of sale or invoices.

c) *Personal selling* embraces amounts paid to salesmen as compensation, expenses, and allowances.

d) *Advertising* includes all the expenses of the advertising department of the firm. The composition of this item may vary widely. Some companies include as advertising many of the activities that we have described in this book as sales promotion. In some trades the work of preparing copy, layout, and procuring space or time may be done by the agency and be hidden in the cost paid for space or time. In others, especially in the industrial goods area, the firm may not use an agency and these expenses may appear as separate items in the records of the company.

e) *Sales promotion* is another uncertain item and needs the same

---

[1] The number of functional-cost groups varies widely; Longman and Schiff list 34. See D. R. Longman, M. Schiff, *Practical Distribution Cost Analysis* (Homewood, Ill.: Richard D. Irwin, Inc., 1955).

kind of special definition as that suggested for Advertising. Both these items include the cost of the office space occupied in carrying on the activities involved.

f) Delivery is sometimes called *transportation,* and ordinarily its chief items are freight bills paid to common carriers such as railroads or trucking companies. If the firm operates its own trucks to perform this service, this item includes wages of truckers and porters and costs of truck operation.

g) Marketing overhead certainly includes the salaries and other costs generated by the marketing executives. It may or may not embrace the expense of marketing planning, field supervision, and customer and salesmen's correspondence. Whether these are set up as separate functional cost groups depends largely upon how large they loom in the whole marketing cost picture.

Allocating Functional Expenses to Cost Results

We must now develop methods to allocate the functional group expenses to the cost results we seek. A cost result is something we want to find out. We may wish to know how much it costs to perform a certain marketing function, in which case the functional group figure may tell the story, unless we seek to break the general functions into minor subfunctions; for example, the expense of participating in trade shows as a part of the general sales promotion activity. We are most apt to want to know how much it costs to market specific products or groups of products, or what is the cost of marketing to individual customers or groups of customers. We may find it desirable to learn the expense of handling orders of different sizes. We may want to compare the cost of handling business on an individual order basis with that of handling it on the basis of contracts covering six months or a year. We may wish to know how much we spend to market our products in New England or in California. All these are cost results.

If we are able to assign costs to functions, to products, and to customers we can, by a process of addition, obtain many other cost results. For example, the cost of a geographic area is the summation of the expenses of marketing to the customers in the area.

The approach to the process of allocation is in most cases that of computing the cost per unit of work or activity that is involved in each function, obtaining the number of such units involved in the cost result and then multiplying one by the other. Such units of work may be a salesman's call, an order edited, a line extension of an order processed, a case lot of merchandise removed from the floor or the shelf, a letter written, or an hour of technical service provided. Perhaps the best way to gain a clear understanding of this process and the difficulties met in carrying it on is to describe briefly some of the methods used in allocating each of several functional cost groups to products and to customers.

Inventory Maintenance. The costs generated by this function are essentially of three, perhaps four, kinds: the expenses involved in providing warehouse or storeroom space, including heat, light, and similar items; those arising from the wages of people and equipment costs to keep inventory records and to move goods into that space; the cost of financing goods while in storage; and perhaps incidental services, such as insurance, while in storage. These costs may be assigned to products in the following ways:

a) Cost per square foot of space used can be computed for any period by dividing the total space expenses by the average number of square feet occupied by merchandise during the period. The average number of square feet used by each product during the period is then the space reserved for it or may be computed from its dimensions and the average amount of it held in storage. This average is multiplied by the cost per square foot to get a total cost for the product. This is then divided by the number of units of the product passing through storage during the period to get a cost per unit.

b) The cost of financing an inventory of a product is a function of the amount of money the firm has invested in it during the time of storage. This will usually be factory cost plus transportation cost from factory to warehouse if it is stored at a distance from where it is made. The financing cost may be computed on the basis of either the current interest rate or the rate of profit the firm enjoys on investment. The financing charge per unit of product sold during any period may be computed by applying either of the above rates to the average investment in the inventory of the product, and then dividing this result by the total number of units of the product marketed during the period.

c) The costs of warehouse record keeping can be allocated to products by the formula: total costs of record keeping divided by total number of record entries equals cost per entry. Cost per entry times number of entries for Product A equals record keeping cost for Product A. The expense of moving goods into and within the storeroom may be allocated by establishing a handling unit (such as a case, a drum, or a pallet) and dividing the total costs of this work by the number of units handled to get a handling cost per unit. This can then be applied to the number of units of Product A handled so as to get the total cost of handling Product A.

Probably the most practical way of allocating inventory carrying costs to customers is by obtaining an inventory carrying cost per unit for each product by the above methods and multiplying this factor by the number of units of each product the customer buys. Occasionally a marketer may agree to carry a specified amount of stock earmarked for a particular customer. The cost of doing so can then be allocated directly to the customer.

Order Handling. This cost results from two kinds of activities, the paper work involved in processing an order and the work of physically assembling the order from racks, shelves, or floor, moving it to the shipping platform, preparing it for shipment, and moving it into the truck or freight car.

The paper work involved is of two kinds, (1) that which is common to all orders regardless of size, such as checking the name and address of the buyer, preparing or checking shipping instructions, and checking credit, and (2) that which pertains to each item or product line on the order, such as checking the name of the product, the amount of it ordered, entering its unit price, multiplying the unit price by the number of units, and adding the results to get a total price for the order.

Studies can be made to determine how much of the clerical force's working time is used in doing the things that must be done to each order, regardless of whether it includes one line or several pages, and how much is devoted to the work that is associated with the lines themselves. In this way total order costs and line costs can be derived. Dividing the former by the total number of orders received during a period yields a cost per order. The same process applied to the line data gives a cost per line. One company found that these cost factors were $1.40 per order and 40¢ per line.

Order processing costs can be allocated to customers by multiplying the order factor by the number of orders submitted by each customer, and the line factor by the number of lines in those orders. Since each line involves one product, the line costs for a product can be obtained by a similar process of multiplication, and order costs can be allocated by spreading them among the various products according to the total number of times each product appears on all orders.

Physical handling costs can be allocated by a similar process. An order may call for a carload, a pallet, a drum, a case, a loose piece, or any multiple of these units. By studying the work of order handlers, the analyst can determine the portion of their activities devoted to each type of unit, thus obtaining a total cost for handling carloads, drums, cases, or loose pieces. Dividing each of these totals by the number of the appropriate units handled during a period yields a cost per unit. A company which delivered in bulk containers, cases, and loose pieces found that its cost factors were bulk containers, 56¢; cases 40¢; and loose pieces 12¢ each. Handling costs can then be allocated to products by multiplying each of the cost factors by the number of the several handling units through which it moves out of the warehouse. The same technique can be applied in assigning physical handling costs to customers.

These techniques can also be used in computing the costs of processing and filling orders of different sizes. For example, one company found that if it sold a certain product—whose purchasers bought nothing else from the company—in less than 500-pound drums, the order processing and handling costs alone exceeded the gross profit.

Personal Selling. Personal selling costs are hard and expensive to allocate. If the salesman works on a commission basis it might seem easy to charge each customer with the commissions paid on his business and each product with the commission on its volume. If the firm pays the salesman's expenses this item might be allocated among customers and products in the same proportions as commissions. This is not strictly accurate since some products are harder to sell than others and some customers require more of a salesman's time than others. Adjustments might be made on the basis of a time and motion study of the salesmen's activities, but this is very expensive and of doubtful accuracy since a salesman tends to behave differently under observation than when he calls alone.

If the salesman is paid a salary and expenses, time and motion techniques might supply some basis for allocation. But it is doubtful if the added precision would pay for the cost of the study. Most firms probably allocate the salesman's cost to customers on the basis of an average expense per call factor, and to products on the basis of the portions of his calling time he spends on various products, estimated on information obtained through conversations with him about the emphasis he puts on the several products. Admittedly this is inaccurate, but it is doubtful if added accuracy would be worth its cost.

Advertising. The cost of direct mail advertising that features a single product can be allocated direct to the product and to the customer who buys it. If it features several products it may be allocated direct to customers and to products according to the space devoted to each product in the advertisement.

A journal or TV or radio advertisement that features one product may be charged direct to that product, and through that charge to customers who buy the product. If more than one product is featured, its cost can be allocated among them on the basis of the portion of total time or space devoted to each.

General advertising designed to build goodwill for or recognition of the firm or its line presents a more difficult problem. Probably the most usual treatment of its cost is to close it into the general overhead of the advertising department and allocate it on the basis of the percentage of the directly allocable advertising costs assigned to different products and customers.

All of these methods suffer from the difficulty that they throw upon the customers the burden of the firm's attempts to reach and influence possible buyers who are not customers. Perhaps, if management has a clear understanding in its marketing objectives of the extent to which it proposes to use advertising to retain old customers and to capture new ones, the expense of this activity could be divided into these two categories—and the first allocated and the second disregarded in the customer costing system.

Sales Promotion. The problems here are just about the same as those encountered with Advertising, and the methods of allocation are about the same.

Delivery. If goods are shipped fob shipping point, without freight allowance or equalization, there is no problem of allocating delivery costs for there are no delivery costs. If they are sold at a delivered price or shipped fob destination, transportation costs can be allocated to both customers and products on the basis of freight bills. If a freight allowance is granted or a basing point or equalization system is used, allocation is more difficult but still can be accomplished with substantial accuracy. But if the firm makes delivery through its own trucks, the problem becomes highly complex. Probably the most sensible approach is to compute a cost per transportation unit, such as a pound-mile (one pound carried one mile) or hundred-pound mile—although this may have to be varied for products of great bulk in relation to weight. Once this is done costs can be allocated directly to products and customers on the basis of how much is carried and how far.

Marketing Overhead. Occasionally some parts of this expense can be charged directly to customers or products, but most of it must usually be allocated on an arbitrary basis. For example, it may be possible to make a reasonably close estimate of the portion of an executive's time that is devoted to specific customers or groups of customers, or to particular products or product groups. In such a case the expense of the executive and his immediate supporting staff can be allocated in the same proportions. If any part of marketing overhead can be allocated in this way it is probably not highly inaccurate to allocate the rest of it in the same way.

If no such basis of allocation exists, marketing overhead is often charged to products and to customers according to dollar volume of sales or according to the distribution of directly allocable marketing costs. For example, if Product A is charged with 10 percent of all directly allocable marketing costs, 10 percent of marketing overhead will be allocated to it.

It is our hope that this brief description will give a general understanding of the method by which marketing expenses are allocated to cost result groups and of some of the bases on which allocations are made. We should emphasize again that the seven marketing cost classes we have used to illustrate this procedure are by no means standard. Such classes should be set up to fit the kinds of marketing activities the firm conducts. Some cost analysts use many more than we employed. In general, the more detailed the classification the more likely it is that a reasonable basis can be found on which each cost class can be allocated directly. (Also the more expensive the whole operation will be.)

We have described the process as it must be carried on under the conventional accounting system. When machine accounting is used many parts of it may be telescoped. For example, many cost items can be card-punched or tape recorded in such a way that allocations can be made in one operation. Items can be broken down in much greater detail than was formerly possible. The whole operation is much less expensive and the results can be made available much more currently. In a firm whose accounting is automated there is no excuse for the marketing manager who fails to know what his costs are. In order to do so he does not need to know how the computer system operates, although he does have to know what cost results will help him manage and what marketing activities generate the costs.

General Considerations

Certain general observations may be made about the work of analyzing marketing costs.

Since many marketing executives are suspicious of the application of cost accounting techniques to distribution and tend to regard it solely as a device of top management to check on their activities and clip their spending wings, the analyst has the job not only of analyzing but of selling his whole procedure and its results to the people whose operations he is analyzing. The manager who proposes to introduce a system of cost analysis for marketing will be wise to choose an analyst who has the ability to do both these things.

The people in the marketing area must be assured that the purpose of the analysis is not to take customers, products or dollar volume away from them but to supply them with facts they can use in directing their efforts to increase volume and to get more sales dollars that have big profit margins in them and relatively fewer sales dollars that yield little or no profit. The net effect of the proper managerial use of cost results may very well be that the marketing department will be given more dollars rather than fewer to spend in its work.

These results may supply the marketing manager a sound basis on which to evaluate the sometimes imaginative proposals of his subordinates to spend company money on pet programs. Their use also tends to put him in a strong position in proposing expenditures to his superiors because they soon discover that he knows what he is doing cost-wise, and their confidence in him and his judgment is apt to be increased accordingly. If the analyst convinces the marketing executives of these advantages, he will find his work much easier and his results will be more realistic.

The analyst can also capture the confidence of the marketing executives by consulting them with respect to the various assumptions he has to make in the course of his work. Every distribution-costing job involves a whole series of assumptions, some of them wholly or partly supported by facts, others based on the best-informed opinion as to how things are really done. The best-informed opinion about most of the areas, where assumptions are necessary, is that of the maketing executives. By constantly checking with them with respect to the details of departmental activities the analyst not only gains accuracy for his results but convinces the marketing managers of their reliability.

The cost analyst must constantly weigh against the benefits of great accuracy in his results the cost of getting that accuracy. For example, by carefully counting the miles between customers and computing the time and cost of traveling those miles the analyst may get a much more accurate figure for the cost of calling on each customer than he can obtain by the usual method of dividing the amount the firm pays to and on account of each salesman by the number of calls he makes, thus deriving an average cost per call which is multipled by the number of calls made on any given customer so as to arrive at a cost of personal selling to charge against that customer. But the expense of doing the job by the more careful method would probably far exceed any losses the firm might possibly sustain from wrong decisions made because of lack of accuracy in this particular item of information. Perfectionists should not do distribution cost analysis work.

USES OF MARKETING-COST DATA

Marketing-cost results have three chief uses. They may be employed in the determination of prices and price policies. An attempt may be made to reprice products if cost analysis shows that at present levels the firm is incurring either a net loss or an unusually lush net profit. Such action is of course limited by the necessities of competition, and sometimes it is impossible. When this is true the results of cost analysis may be used to obtain reasonable earnings for an entire group of related products, even though competition will not permit a "break-even" price on some of them.

The second major use of cost analysis lies in discovering guides for operating policies. It may disclose that the handling of certain commodities or lines of goods is unprofitable and that they should be dropped or the methods of marketing them should be modified. It may show that entirely too much stock of certain items is being carried. It may demonstrate that the business of certain customers is unprofitable to the house and that their patronage should no longer be solicited, or that they should be solicited and served in a different manner from that now used. It may demonstrate that the same situation exists with regard to the firm's business in a whole geographic area, and may indicate the remedies to be applied.

But the value of the results of cost analysis does not lie wholly on the side of the restriction and limitation of present operations. Such results may also indicate new types of business that may profitably be cultivated. The discovery and study of profitable customers, commodities, territories, or techniques suggests other markets or methods which may prove equally worthwhile if cultivated or utilized. Avenues of extension for the business may be sought on the basis of its existing profit pattern. Consider the case of the wholesaler who found, generally speaking, that the part of his business that returned a profit was that done with customers located within 100 miles from his warehouse, and that the part which was sold to those farther away resulted in a loss. The program of action indicated by such a cost result is not merely to cease to cultivate business outside the profit radius but to solicit orders inside that limit more intensively.

Finally, a minimum of cost analysis work is necessary for all firms that may be called upon to defend their price-discount systems under the Robinson-Patman Act.

In the course of deciding the various complaints that come before it under this law, the Federal Trade Commission and the courts are developing a series of precedents with respect to the costing methods approved for use in computing the differences in the expenses of distributing to different customers, upon which price differentials must be based under the act. Manufacturers who use the quantity discount and the promotional allowance as parts of their pricing structures find it necessary to base their decisions as to the amounts of such differentials on some defensible system of cost accounting for distribution. The system developed for this purpose must meet the approval not only of the controller of the firm but of the company attorney as well.

LIMITATIONS ON THE USE OF MARKETING-COST DATA

The material presented in the preceding pages indicates that cost analysis can be of great importance in improving the management of marketing, but it should not be regarded as the answer to the marketing manager's prayer. Its application is subject to very real handicaps and difficulties, and its usefulness is rather narrowly limited.

In the first place, the process of computing unit costs of distribution for customers, commodities, salesmen, orders, or territories is liable to be exceedingly complicated and difficult. A considerable part of the marketing expenses of the typical company cannot be allocated directly to any of the above-mentioned units on any basis that is logical, obvious, or simple. Many of the costs of marketing tend to behave like overhead or joint expenses in that there is no clear-cut, obviously reasonable, or readily discoverable factor according to which they may be charged to individual units. The work of developing a technique for allocating them is often a long, laborious, expensive process requiring much tedious research.

Consider, for instance, the task of distributing the salary and expenses of a salesman for a manufacturing firm among the articles which it handles. To simplify our problem, let us suppose that the firm sells only two items: A, of which the salesman vends $70,000, and B, on which his volume is $30,000 in the year under analysis. At first blush it seems logical to assign 70 percent of this salary and expenses to Product A and 30 percent to B.

But a somewhat closer examination shows that Product A is a nationally advertised, mature article which, because of the sales momentum and consumer demand generated for it by the manufacturer's publicity, makes its appearance automatically on the want list of the average retailer-customer. Product B, on the other hand, is a new item and, since it is not well known and has not been heavily advertised, does not of its own motion appear on the order blank but must be put there by the efforts of the salesman in spite of buyer prejudices and inertia. To make sure that it will move off the dealer's shelves into the hands of ultimate consumers, the salesman must induce him to use inside displays, handbills, window posters and displays, and local advertising featuring the product.

Obviously, then, the salesman spends more time in selling a dollar's worth of item B than of A. But how much more? The answer can be found only by research and field investigation. The salesman may be asked to fill out a job ticket for each call, indicating the length of time spent in promoting each item. He is liable to resent such a request and to be careless in his compliance. Also, in the heat of selling, his sense of time is likely to be highly inaccurate. Special investigators may travel with salesmen from time to time and hold stopwatches on them, thereby seeking to glean the desired information, but since the salesman is a man and not a machine and is therefore likely to behave differently under observation than in the normal course of his business, results derived from this method are none too accurate.

Consider, also, the problem of allocating a salesman's time and expenses among his customers. On his route are Town X, in which are Customer A who is very large and B who is small; Town Y, in which is Customer C who is small; and Town Z with Customer D who is big. The accompanying map will help us visualize the situation.

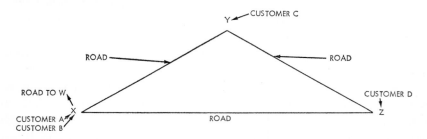

In allocating the salesman's salary (which is a function of time) and his expenses (which are largely a function of distance) among the four customers in these three towns, the analyst runs into such questions as: How much of the cost of getting the salesman from W to X should be charged against Customer A and how much against Customer B? Should it be split equally? Or, since the salesman would have to go from W to X anyhow to see big Customer A, should not small Customer B, whom he might otherwise have passed by, get a free ride?

Should Customer C be charged the entire cost of the time and travel from X to Y, or, since the salesman would have gone from X to Z to call on Big Customer D anyway, should he be allocated only the difference between the expense of going straight from X to Z and that of going by way of Y?

This is a good example of the influence of joint costs and suggests why many (probably most) firms work on the basis of an average cost per call, especially since the total amount per customer involved is small to begin with.

Out of the intricacies and difficulties involved in the work of applying cost accounting techniques to the expenses of marketing arises another limitation upon its usefulness—the fact that, if carried on continuously, it is often exceedingly expensive. It necessitates the keeping of numerous and costly records. It involves the collection and analysis of multitudinous items of detailed information. It often requires considerable outlays for fieldwork and research. Much of it demands the use of machines for record keeping and statistical sorting and analysis. This precludes the possibility of its use by many small concerns whose volume of sales is not sufficient to support the cost of using such equipment. The development of electronic data recording and processing equipment has materially reduced the expense of marketing cost analysis for firms able to make use of it.

Experience has shown that many companies can save much of this effort and expense by conducting complete cost studies at intervals only, instead of attempting to maintain such detailed records as a regular part of their accounting work. The results of a careful study of a firm's costs by commodities or by customers, completed today, will probably be substantially representative of its experience for a considerable period of time to come, unless, of course, there is a significant change in its method of operation. Such studies, conducted on a research basis at intervals of one, two, or three years, may give sufficient information to guide the firm's activities. During the intervening periods, one or two criteria which can be compiled currently, such as rate of stock turnover or size of order, may often be found which will serve as indications of the amount and direction of change.

Nor do sales costs always furnish an entirely adequate and satisfactory basis upon which marketing decisions may be made. Sales facts often behave like bowling pins: the disturbing of one may knock over another, or a whole series. Suppose, for instance, that we discontinue handling article A because our cost records show that it is netting us a loss instead of a profit. But we find that its disappearance from our catalog does not reduce the size of our warehouse or cut down the number of orders we receive or of bills we send out; our salesmen remain just as numerous as before and they travel just as many miles and consume just as much time and money in travel and in calling; and we must maintain the same staff of order pickers and porters we have always had.

In this particular case most of our distribution costs behave like overhead. They go on just the same after we abandon article A as they did before, but there no longer remains the same volume over which to spread these expenses. The marketing cost per dollar of sales on the remaining items therefore is liable to increase, and certain items which we formerly found profitable now become unprofitable. We may also find that this action increases production costs per unit, owing to the necessary reallocation of factory burden over a smaller number of units of output.

Proper management, however, may completely neutralize this tendency. If the marketing executive sees to it that his salesmen apply the time and effort which they formerly spent in promoting article A to the sale of the most profitable remaining items, he may be able to avoid any increase whatsoever in unit costs and to increase the firm's net gain. This happy result will not be enjoyed, however, without careful planning and active supervision on his part.

The same results may flow from dropping unprofitable customers or groups of customers from a firm's prospect list. The small loss of volume resulting from such action may cause a considerable change in the cost structure of a business. A firm that drops an unprofitable item from its product mix may find that it is needed by a customer who buys large orders of other highly profitable articles and who, because he can no longer buy the "dog" from his old supplier, proposes to shift a substantial portion of his patronage elsewhere. In making any specific modification of existing practice, however minor it may be and however soundly it may seem to be justified by cost analysis, the marketing manager must consider the probable repercussions of that change upon other elements of the enterprise.

Someone has said that it is the imponderables that win battles and tip the scales of victory in war. The same thing is almost equally true of marketing campaigns. Factors which cannot be valued or expressed numerically are often decisive. The marketing executive who persists in eliminating items and customers simply because a cost analysis shows them to be individually unprofitable is liable to find himself eliminated.

On the other hand, an article or an account that is shown by such a

study to net the firm a loss rather than a gain ought at least to be regarded with suspicion by those charged with the management of the
affairs of the concern. When such facts are placed before an able executive, sooner or later he finds a way to do something about them.
In a few cases he may decide to drop an item or a customer, but he is
much more likely to find some means of transposing a losing element
in his business to the profitable side of the ledger.

It is surprising how frequently it is possible once the facts are known
to find some change in the method of handling an unprofitable article
that will lower the expense it entails. This may be done by securing
a more rapid turnover or by rearranging the method of selling, storing
or delivering it. For example, an analysis of a wholesale drygoods house
in the Middle West showed that certain items in the hosiery department
were turning over ten times a year, while the stock of certain other
articles in the same department was sufficient to last five years at the
current rate of sale. On the latter items the firm was suffering a net
loss. The method of buying was at fault. By changing this method, and
by a series of clearance sales, the manager of the firm was able to transform many of these slow-moving items into profitable articles.

It is also possible to convert into profitable accounts many customers
whose business nets the house a loss rather than a gain. By good salesmanship, or by some special inducement, they may be prevailed upon to
buy in larger amounts, to purchase the full line of the firm's merchandise instead of a few selected items, or in other ways to change the nature of their patronage so as to become profitable. Without a cost
analysis the manager would never have realized that he was losing
money on his sales to them.

The average business with an extensive product line handles a relatively large number of items on which it enjoys a net profit; on others,
however, it suffers a loss. The able executive knows this and endeavors
to make certain that in the course of the year the profitable transactions
completed by his firm will balance those that are carried out at a loss
and leave a satisfactory net gain on all transactions. This is the essence
of good management. The information gleaned from careful cost analysis serves to guide the executive in putting added stress upon the profitable elements of the business.

Theoretically, the sale of every item to every customer should return
a net profit when all costs are charged against it. But this is not always
possible. A wholesale grocery house must handle sugar whether or not
it makes a profit on it. Ordinarily, in many parts of the country, wholesalers just manage to break even on their sugar business or they lose

slightly on it. It sometimes pays a firm to sell an article on which it sustains a loss in order to hold old customers or to attract new ones who buy profitable merchandise in considerable quantities. A cost analysis discloses the accounting facts about a company but it cannot show whether or not the firm's loss on a specific item reflects its performance of this kind of sales promotional function. This decision must be left to the common sense and experience of the manager.

Marketing cost analysis can never take the place of good managerial judgment. It must remain in its proper sphere, affording a factual background against which that judgment can be exercised intelligently. It will pay rich dividends to the business whose executives use it consistently in this manner.

CHAPTER 21

Marketing Planning

The manager who acts without plan must learn to live without profit, and the marketing manager is by no means an exception to this truism. As a matter of fact, the changing nature of our economic structure constantly serves to throw increasing emphasis on the importance of planning the marketing work of the firm.

So long as our economy operated in a seller's market, the planning work of the typical firm could start with production and be based on the theory that it was the function of the marketing unit to sell what it seemed economical for the company to make. With the shift to an economy that is governed primarily by the wants and purchasing attitudes and habits of the buyer the situation has not been reversed, but the change has thrown greater emphasis on planning for marketing. Company plans must now at least start with the expected outflow of physical units of product into the market which governs the rate and timing of production operations and with the expected inflow of sales dollars out of which must come the funds to pay for all the activities of the firm with something left over for profits.

Before the processes of management were as well understood as they now are, it was assumed that if each functional unit of a business performed its specialized task efficiently the enterprise would be profitable. That is, if marketing sold as much as it could, and production made things as efficiently as it knew how, and finance carefully guarded and preserved the company funds, any failure of the business to achieve a profitable outcome could be blamed on a malignant fate or uncontrollable outside forces.

With a better understanding of the true function of management came an appreciation of the fact that the enjoyment of profits comes from the performance of every unit of the firm according to a plan designed to achieve the best results for the whole enterprise. The function of marketing is recognized to be not simply to sell, but to sell those products to those customers, by those methods, and in those quantities that will be in the best interest of the business. This concept was emphasized by the growth in the size of the average business establishment, the diversification of the products it makes and the markets it serves, and the almost incredible increase in the influence of technology on business operations, all of which augmented the complexity of the enterprise and the delicate interdependence of its parts.

The result of these changes is not only that it is much more difficult to plan marketing activities than it once was, but it is much more vital to the company's welfare that they be planned carefully and well. It is fairly simple to plan to sell all you can of one or two or even half a dozen kindred products. It is an entirely different matter to plan to market half a hundred different products to ten or a dozen different kinds of customers while also trying to balance out such distracting and often contradictory factors as the influence of productive capacity or the size of production runs on factory cost, the relative profitability of different products and different customers as affected by the several methods by which they may be contacted or served, the relative costs and effectiveness of the different marketing channels and tools available, the financial strengths and needs of the company, and the interaction of sales volume and the direct costs generated in the process of getting it and servicing it, on the one hand, and overhead costs on the other.

Why discuss planning here? Strict logic might suggest that in a book such as this marketing planning should be treated at the beginning instead of near the end, since, if planning is to be at all useful, it must come before action. We did not follow this scheme of organization for two important reasons.

In the first place, it is hard to plan until you know what it is you are planning for. Plans are apt to be highly unrealistic unless the planner knows something about the environment in which they must be carried out, the tools that must be used, the kinds of difficulties the operating units will face in trying to put his plans into effect, and the kinds of problems for which they must provide solutions. For these reasons we feel that to try to discuss marketing planning with the student before he has as much understanding of marketing processes as we are able to give him would be uninteresting and without challenge and would probably fail to achieve its purpose.

In the second place, marketing planning is not a process that is done at a particular time and then allowed to lie in abeyance until the plans are carried out. It must be a continuous process because the conditions on which plans are based change constantly. The marketing manager is in much the position of the captain of a tramp freighter who operates according to an overall plan for his voyage but who must constantly make minor, sometimes major, shifts in response to information about storms, icebergs, opportunities to secure cargo, and other factors that were unpredictable when the original voyage plan was made. Add to this the necessity of preparing, when one voyage is little more than half over, an overall plan for the next voyage, and you get some idea of the continuity and complexity of the process. It is our hope that the location we have chosen for this chapter will help the student acquire a workable understanding of the process of planning for marketing.

THE NATURE OF MARKETING PLANNING

In its essence, planning is the making of a series of decisions. These are of two basic types. The first centers around the question, What shall we try to do? The second involves seeking answers to the question, How shall we try to do it? The first is basic and fundamental, and results in the formulation of an objective or a series of objectives or policies. The second is more a matter of detail, involving the manipulation of ways and means, and its outcome is usually a program of action or schedule of specific things to be done. The first type should always involve the participation of the chief marketing executives and usually of the top management of the company. Decisions of the "how" type tend to be made within the marketing area, many of them by the managers of specialized units such as personal selling, advertising, sales promotion, or customer service.

On the basis of the time involved, three types of plans can be distinguished. These differ markedly in the methods employed in making them and in the managerial uses they serve.

Long-Range Plans

Any plan that covers more than one year is usually regarded as long-range. There is a growing tendency to try to project the business of the company five or ten years into the future and to make at least rudimentary marketing plans for these periods. Obviously, the farther the planner tries to peer into the future the more obscure his vision becomes and the less accurately he can foresee and provide for the details of operation. Long-range marketing plans are therefore usually confined to estimates of demand, prices, probable sales of the more important products of the firm, costs of production, overall marketing costs (calculated without much attention to detail), and probable resulting profits or losses. To this picture may be added an estimate of the effects likely to be exercised on all these factors by new products that are far enough along in research to offer reasonable promise of being added to the product mix during the period.

The long-range plan is of limited usefulness to the marketing manager. It may afford him some idea of the marketing manpower that will be needed during the coming period. If the marketing job of the firm is at all complex, the manpower to handle it five years from now must be recruited and trained during the coming four years. If the advent of new products can be foreseen, plans for their marketing can be made at leisure and, if they are of a technical nature, their progress through reseach can be followed sufficiently closely so that when the time comes to market them the marketing area may know enough about their technical features to avoid most of the mistakes that otherwise might be made.

The long-range plan is useful mainly to the executives in charge of providing production capacity, personnel, and the funds needed to finance the developments expected. It may also be helpful in guiding research and allocating research emphasis. From these observations it is apparent that the five- or ten-year plan is apt to be much more helpful to top management in trying to shape the long range future of the firm than to the managers of its functional units. But the marketing manager is bound to be in the middle of such planning work.

Short-Range Plans

Any plan that projects one year or less into the future is usually designated as short-range. The budget is the most common type of short-term plan, usually drawn to cover one year in the future. From the management viewpoint the budget has two general uses: to provide a framework and an incentive for planning, and to supply a standard of performance for use in control. If the budget is simply a financial document it will fail to serve either of these purposes. If it is to be useful for these ends, the final document must be simply a summary dollar expression of careful and detailed plans originally prepared in physical units.

For example, the marketing part of the budget must be initially prepared, on the income side, in terms of pounds or tons or cases of products we will try to sell and, on the expense side, in salesmen man-years, units of advertising space or time, sales promotion pieces, technical service time, and other activities we propose to use in order to sell and distribute the physical units of sales volume we select as our target. These factors are then priced out to get the marketing budget. If this is not done the budget is worse than useless. The work of preparing it is a waste of valuable time and manpower.

Short-range marketing plans, exemplified by properly drawn budgets, serve a number of managerial purposes.

a)   They tend to reduce to a minimum what may be called "crisis management." In the absence of such plans, decisions tend to be made in response to emergencies as they develop. And if emergencies are allowed to develop they are liable to assume the proportions of crises. The manager is then forced to make decisions with time breathing hotly down his neck and catastrophe jogging his elbow. This is hardly conducive to clear thinking or sound decision.

If planning is done properly many of these emergencies can be foreseen and aborted, or decisions can be made as to what to do about them if they occur. These decisions can be made in an atmosphere of relative calm and are apt to be sounder than those arrived at under pressure.

b)   The preparation of a marketing plan endows the personnel, from manager to clerk, with a sense of direction and purpose. In such an atmosphere many things can be delegated that would otherwise demand the attention of the top manager. For example, once the advertising part of the plan is approved the advertising unit can take over the task of carying it out, unless unforeseen difficulties occur which demand its revision. To some extent the marketing executive can enjoy the advantages of management by exception, or variation.

c)   A properly drawn marketing plan can be used by the production group in scheduling its activities. It should also provide a guide to the purchasing unit in planning its purchases and making long-run buying commitments. The extent to which these uses can be made of the marketing plan depends upon the ability of the marketing group to prepare plans that work out with a reasonable degree of accuracy and to break down the annual sales estimate into monthly or quarterly amounts. Its usefulness for these purposes can sometimes be increased by monthly or quarterly revisions, or by a policy of revision whenever variances threaten to be so great as to undermine its reliability for scheduling production and purchasing.

d)   The marketing part of the budget plan may also be very useful to the chief financial executive in managing working capital—which typically flows from cash into inventory to service production and sales, then into accounts receivable resulting from sales and, finally, back into cash. The amount, timing, and rate of this flow may dictate the short-term borrowings of the firm and the availability of cash for special projects.

Project Plans

It seems worthwhile to distinguish this third type of marketing plan. Examples of projects that might justify separate plans are the introduction of a new product, the penetration of a new market, and the creation or modification of a public or trade attitude. Because some of these projects require more than one year to complete, plans for them might be classed as long-range. Those that can be achieved within a year will undoubtedly be included in the budget and could belong to the short-range group. To set them apart as a separate type may seem to smack of classification for classification's sake, but there seems to be sound managerial justification for doing so.

Such projects are usually of great importance to the company. But if the plans for achieving them are simply closed into the long-range plan or marketing budget, they are apt to "get lost in the shuffle." Management fails to bestow upon them the attention their importance justifies. Perhaps an example will serve to illustrate the point.

Some years ago the management of a firm decided to enter a new field and win a significant market position there. As an entering wedge it made the mistake of buying a small company in the field with an annual sales volume of about $1½ million and a line of products composed of "cats and dogs." Careful planning and drastic managerial action were necessary to carry out the project. It was closed into the operations of a marketing department of the company with a sales volume of about $20 million. No separate plans for it were prepared; it was automatically provided for in the long-range plan and budgets of the department. The result was that the project failed to receive the careful and dynamic attention of top management that it required because top management tended to look on it as an insignificant part of the whole departmental budget.

No progress was made until the departmental manager was asked to prepare a separate plan for it to cover a number of years and to result, at the end of that time, in a volume of about $10 million. Annual parts of this long-range plan were to appear as separate parts of the succeeding departmental budgets. The result was that the project began to receive the attention and consideration its potential sales volume justified, and management began to make the decisions, some of them costly, needed to capture a satisfactory part of that potential.

Project plans may be looked upon as a recognition of the fact that the men who must make the final top-level decisions are, after all, human in their habits of thought.

METHODS AND PROBLEMS OF PLANNING

Planning cannot be done in a vacuum. It must be carried on in the rush and flow of a fluid situation, and within the bounds of an economy and an industry complex that is constantly on the move. The plans that a firm evolves must to some extent conform to and take advantage of what is happening and will happen in the entire economy and in the industry to which the planning unit belongs. To some extent they must be designed to modify the effects which future changes of the economy and the industry will otherwise have on the welfare of the firm. Therefore a first step in marketing planning must be to try to forecast the changes in the economy and the industry which will occur during the planning period and the effects these changes will tend to have on the sales and profits of the firm. The planner must also endeavor to foresee what effect the planned marketing activities of the firm will have on its welfare in the forecasted economic and industry climate. Forecasting is therefore one of the most important steps in marketing planning.

Forecasting

Inevitably, the process of forecasting consists essentially of projecting the conditions and observed trends of the present into the future on the basis of the experience of the past. We know that the conditions of today are the outgrowth of certain conditions of yesterday, so we feel justified in assuming that the shape of tomorrow will derive from the features of today. The trick of forecasting lies largely in judging which of the present features will persist in the future, which will no longer exist, and which will be altered and in what way and by how much.

For example, suppose that when we make our forecast our sales and those of the industry are increasing by an annual rate of 10 percent. Will this trend continue? And if so, at the same or a higher rate, or at a lower rate? Or will it spend itself during the early months of the forecasting period and turn into a decline? And if so, when will this happen and how steep will be the drop?

There are three chief methods by which sales forecasts may be made, (1) the overall or statistical method, (2) the marketing research method, and (3) "bottom-up" or "grass roots" method.

1. *The Statistical Forecast.* The making of a statistical sales fore-

cast is generally a process of projecting trends with due allowance for the behavior of similar trends in the past. For example, a secular trend may be expected to change its direction or pitch very slowly, while some notion of the future behavior of a cyclical trend can often be obtained by comparing it with past cyclical fluctuations and trying to determine where we are on a curve of such trends that is often fairly typical and fast-moving.

A very common kind of statistical forecast is one which depends on a relationship that appears to be constant between a firm's sales and some other variable factor, such as gross national product, disposable income, or number of people employed. By the use of correlation techniques the forecaster seeks to discover some such factor or statistical series which varies with some consistency; that is, according to the same pattern as that of his company's sales. Then, by a variation of the equation, he projects his sales into the future.

We need not discuss these statistical techniques here. The marketing manager who has the facilities and skills of a marketing research or economic analysis unit would be wise to rely on it for this work. In the absence of such a unit he can usually find someone on his staff with mathematical skills who can do a better job of it than he can. His chief task is to see that the work is done and to seek for special or unusual factors that are likely to cause the trends or his sales to behave in an abnormal manner. He must also seek for market information that may provide a "tip-off" as to their future behavior and to see to it that proper allowance is made for such factors and data in the figures finally arrived at.

If the forecaster is lucky he may find some statistical series whose fluctuations are the same as those of his sales but which lead them in point of time. If a probable causal relationship can be found to explain this coincidence, he is on fairly firm ground in assuming that it will persist in the future. If no such causal explanation can be found, but the relationship has been consistent in the past, he can hardly rely upon it with the same degree of confidence, but it may be useful nevertheless.

The forecaster may be less lucky but still find a series that varies along with his sales, paralleling them in point of time, and that can be more accurately predicted than his own sales volume. If in such a situation he has sound grounds for reasoning that the fluctuations of both arise from a common complex of causes, he may apply his statistical predictive tools with some degree of assurance. If no such common causal factors can be found, his tools may still be useful but they must be employed with greater caution.

The statistical method of forecasting has certain advantages and limitations.

a) It is likely to be relatively inexpensive. While it may involve considerable calculation work, this can be done by fairly inexpensive help once it is laid out. If it is desirable that the overall forecast be broken down by product or customer groups, or by geographical divisions of the marketing department, the work of computation and its expense are greatly augmented.

b) Usually an overall statistical forecast loses accuracy when it is broken down by product or customer groups. This is especially likely to be true of assignments to geographical units, because neither the overall figure nor the breakdown technique is apt to take account of local conditions that may cause wide variations of sales in small areas without having much effect on the total figure.

c) The method is not usually applicable in forecasting sales of new products since there is no past or present experience that can be projected for them. If a new product is a substitute for an old one the method may have some usefulness, although the behavior of a new product does not always follow the pattern of the one it supersedes. If the new product is entirely new, statistical methods somewhat different from those mentioned above may be used to estimate its ultimate total possible sales or potential but they may afford little help in forecasting what actual sales will be during the immediate coming period.

d) The statistical method rests on the assumption that a relationship that has been observed to prevail in the past will persist in the future. This assumption is apt to be more reliable if the relation is pretty clearly one of cause and effect, but new and unexpected causes have a habit of interjecting themselves and may upset the relationship. Even if such unwelcome forces fail to destroy the general tendency of sales and the predictive series to fluctuate in the same direction, they are apt to cause changes in the extent of the variations of one or the other of them, with the result that the forecast is liable to lose accuracy.

e) The statistical method usually results in a sales forecast that does not embrace the results of changes in the marketing efforts of the firm. In some cases it is possible to include this factor. For example, if the primary purpose of advertising is to bring immediate sales, it may be that statistical techniques can be used to determine with reasonable accuracy the effect which different amounts and kinds of advertising have had on sales volume in the past. The ratios developed from such an analysis may be used to modify the forecast based on trends alone.

The same thing is true of personal selling work if the primary function of the salesman is to get immediate orders.

2. *The Marketing Research Method of Forecasting.* This is sometimes called the sample method. It is especially applicable to certain kinds of industrial goods and durable consumers' goods whose unit price is high enough to cause their purchase to be the subject of considerable planning by the buying units.

In the industrial goods field it usually takes the form of trying to establish arrangements with customers to disclose their purchasing expectations during a coming period. On the face of it this would seem to be a fairly reliable procedure; in practice it does not work out as well as might be expected. If a firm tries to contact its customers directly through its own salesmen or marketing research men, the customer is apt to be hesitant about supplying the information, probably feeling that the figure mentioned possesses some of the aspects of a commitment. This hesitancy is less with respect to a new, hitherto unknown product than with an old familiar one, the market for which is highly competitive. If an outside agency collects the data, the figures are apt to be general and serious mistakes are liable to be made in trying to translate them into share-of-the-market terms.

In the consumer durable goods field much pioneer work has been done by the Survey Research Center of the University of Michigan, already referred to. A two-pronged approach has been used. A panel of consumers are asked to record their intentions to buy or not to buy a list of durable goods items during a coming period. They are also asked to indicate their expectations during the period as to the security of their jobs, changes in their incomes, changes in business conditions, and other attitudes that may be indicative of a general atmosphere of optimism or foreboding. The results of both of these procedures have been checked against actual purchasing behavior during the periods surveyed and have been found to be fairly predictive.

While individual firms can use this technique and marketing research agencies can probably profitably offer a service based on its use, it has not been widely employed. This may be because its effectiveness has only recently been demonstrated.

But the marketing research method of forecasting sales also has several handicaps.

a) It is not particularly adapted to use in the field of nondurable goods or durable articles of moderate or low unit price.

b) It is expensive. The cost of a single forecast is not excessive, but forecasting, if it is to be useful, must be a more or less continuous process. Many firms employ a "rolling" forecast, estimating each month the sales for the succeeding twelve months, or, each quarter sales for the next four quarters. When this is desirable, the cost of marketing research to implement it is apt to be a significant figure.

c) In the industrial goods field, and with many kinds of consumers' goods that have a status implication, the responses received may be somewhat less than candid. Or, if candid, the respondents may not be entirely representative of the general market.

3. *The Grass Roots Forecast*. The grass roots forecast is a composite of estimates of future sales made by the men nearest the customer: the field salesmen. A typical example of the way this system works is supplied by a company making and marketing a line of industrial materials through a salesforce of about 100 men who call on using firms. During August of each year every salesman was supplied a form something like that shown in the accompanying exhibit.

Customer	Sales Year before Last	Sales Last Year	Budgeted Sales This Year	Sales to Date This Year	Sales Objective Next Year	Number of Calls to Make Objective
XYZ Company						
Product A						
Product B						
Product C						
MNO Company						
Product A						

The field manager also received a copy of this form for each salesman reporting to him. All columns except the last two were filled in by the central office. During the month of August the field manager was expected to spend at least one day with each man going over this form and filling in the man's sales objective—the physical units of each product he really expected to be able to sell—during the coming year to each customer. The summation of these estimates supplied the forecast for his territory, and the summation of the objectives of all the salesmen was the forecast for the company.

Prior to the deliberations of the salesman and his manager the central office supplied them with a forecast of the price fluctuations of each product, a summary of the executive expectations as to general business and industry conditions during the forecast period, a general indication of managerial objectives with respect to product emphasis and overall company volume, and a very general idea of managerial intentions as to the direction and volume of company advertising and sales promotion during the coming period. The central office reviewed each man's objectives in some detail. Very rarely were changes ordered in individual objectives, although explanations were commonly asked for items that appeared to be unrealistic.

This method, or some modification of it, is especially useful in the marketing of industrial goods where the number of accounts served by the individual salesman is likely to be relatively small and the number of salesmen limited. Its use is not unknown, however, in the consumers' goods field. For example, several oil companies are reported to employ it with salesmen servicing filling stations.

Like its statistical and research rivals, the grass roots method has its own advantages and limitations.

a) If applied to a salesforce of 500 or 1,000 or more men, servicing tens of thousands of customers, it is apt to be cumbersome and to lack accuracy. Executive review can be, at best, sketchy.

b) In most cases it is more expensive than its statistical counterpart. Much of this cost is hidden in the time of salesmen spent in setting objectives instead of selling to customers, and of executives reviewing the objectives, but it is real nevertheless. The larger the salesforce and the more numerous the customers, the greater the cost becomes.

c) A possible limitation that does not always eventuate lies in the likelihood that the salesman will be something less than completely objective in making his estimates. The shrewd man might be expected to try to set his objective low in order to look good when he exceeds it, with the result that the overall company forecast will be less than it should be. In actual practice this has not been found to be a serious defect since the typical salesman is apt to be an optimistic soul who expects to be able to do more than he actually can perform. Rigorous and intelligent executive review of salesmen's estimates can usually eliminate most of the effects of both uncandid shrewdness and unrealistic optimism.

d) The grass roots method is perhaps the best way of achieving a high degree of personal commitment to the marketing plan throughout all levels of the organization. A statistical estimate made at headquarters and broken down among the operating functional or area segments of the organization is likely to be regarded by the average sales-man as "home office blue-sky stuff"; i.e., unrealistic. And however well it may be done it is almost certain, in some segments, to be ex-actly that. On the other hand, a salesman is apt to regard his own esti-mate as his own creation and his ego is at stake in making it work out. The best way to sell a man on a plan is to get him to help prepare it.

This method tends to combine to some extent a forecast of what the natural trend of demand will be and what effect intended marketing activities are apt to have on the firm's part of that demand. It is almost impossible for a salesman to estimate the volume he expects to get from a customer next year without, at the same time, thinking about what he intends to do to get more of the customer's business and with-out estimating the probable effect of his efforts. He may be optimistic in his estimates of both these matters, especially the latter, but the fact remains that the grass roots forecast reflects to some extent the effect of marketing effort, while the statistical and marketing research mehods usually do not.

Jury of Executive Opinion. A modification of the grass roots method is the jury of executive opinion. This involves the averaging or reconciliation by compromise of individual sales estimates made by a number of the marketing executives of the firm. The executives invited to engage in this exercise may include district or regional managers, sales supervisors, managers of product or customer sales groups, and other functional or staff heads.

Unless this procedure involves extended conferences for discussion and debate to effect a meeting of the minds among the participating executives, it is apt to be fairly inexpensive. But if a man knows that his estimate will not be required to stand on its own feet and meet the test of open criticism or comparison with actual performance, but will instead be lost in the anonymity of averaging, he will not spend much time or thought on it. This method is neither as scientific as sta-tistical or marketing research forecasting nor as thorough as the grass roots procedure, and, in consequence, may be expected to be somewhat inaccurate. This lack of accuracy may be offset somewhat by the fact that the method makes maximum use of executive "feel" or "seat-of-the-pants" judgment, which are not to be ignored as determinants of sound management decisions.

Some firms use more than one of these methods and match the re-sult of one against that of the other. If the application of two methods brings about the same result, the agreement adds to the confidence man-agement can place in the forecast. If the results of two methods differ materially, the discrepancy suggests the need for a reexamination of both to determine why they differ. The search for the causes of difference may shed light on their relative reliability.

The Use of Inventories in Forecasting

If sales forecasts are to be of maximum use as guides to the scheduling of production and purchasing they must be made, or revised, periodically during the budgetary period. How often they are needed depends chiefly on the length of the production cycle (the time between the dates when materials are started in the production process and when they emerge as finished goods) and on the purchasing "turnaround time" (the time between the dates when an order is placed and delivery may be expected). In most industries production must turn out enough products to maintain an inventory of finished goods adequate to service sales. If the inventory gets bigger than that, carrying charges mount; if it becomes too much less, sales are lost. If the production cycle is 60 days, the amount of materials put into process today determines the amount of finished product that will come out two months from now. So it is vital to have a reasonably accurate forecast of what sales will be during the next 60 days.

The firm that markets through distributors, or wholesalers and retailers, may use their inventories as a means of forecasting its own sales during short periods. For example, a concern that made a covering for kitchen counters, and marketed it through wholesalers and local installation contractors, made arrangements with its wholesalers to make weekly telegraphic reports of sales. From these and from factory shipments it was possible to compute wholesalers' inventories and a typical pattern of wholesalers' stock-carrying practices, as well as the rate of flow-through into the kitchens of consumers. If wholesalers typically carried around 60 days' stocks, and the company a like amount, it thus obtained a highly reliable forecast of its sales 60 days hence. This plan can probably be worked with considerable success by firms using franchise dealers or maintaining very close relationships with outlets.

The information supplied by this sort of forecasting may also enable management to change or abandon mistaken marketing programs long before their ineffectiveness would otherwise have become apparent.

Accuracy of Forecasts

In general, the more numerous the consumers or buying units of a firm's product, and the more diversified they are, the more accurately can its sales be forecast. Large bodies of people tend to shift their purchasing habits and patronage preferences slowly. The fewer the users or buying units of an article, the less certain its marketer can be about the accuracy of his sales estimates.

This means that, as a general rule, consumers' goods marketers can forecast their sales more accurately than those engaged in distributing industrial goods. For example, a producer of a certain industrial material had five customers who took 90 percent of his total sales volume, one of whom took about 35 percent of it. If this single buyer changed his patronage or his buying behavior the effect on the supplier's planned operations would be catastrophic. When the chief purchasing officer of this customer firm died his demise engendered in the supplier's marketing executives not only personal grief but a disturbing commercial unease as well. On the other hand, many makers of goods that are used by the 180 million consumers habitually estimate their sales within a margin of error of 1 or 2 percent, or less.

The question may well be asked: If forecasts of the sales of some goods are of such doubtful accuracy, why go to the trouble and expense of making them? When the potential annual volume of a product's sales is small and it has no great strategic importance in the firm's product mix, there probably is little or no justification for doing so. But if the stakes are big and the customers are few, the efforts to capture or retain the business of each customer take on the aspect of a separate campaign, often enlisting the activities of executives high up in the supplying company. Since these efforts are so important, they must be carefully planned. Requiring a forecast of sales is one way of making sure this planning is done. This alone makes the forecasting process worthwhile, even though its result is of limited use as a guide to production or financial scheduling.

Forecasting and the Marketing Mix

The forecasting methods we have been talking about result in sales estimates that represent, mainly or entirely, the sales volume that can be expected without regard to the effect of the marketing activities of the firm, or, perhaps more exactly, on the assumption that those activities will continue as in the past. This estimate may be modified by the marketing work the firm proposes to do during the period involved. The assignment of this work to the various tools available to the marketing manager, such as advertising, sales promotion, personal selling, customer service, technical service, etc., results in what is called the marketing mix. In the process of preparing the budget—as an example of a marketing plan—the managers of the firm may prepare a number of marketing mixes, estimate the effect of each on forecasted sales and costs, and select for adoption the one that promises a satisfactory profit or, ideally, the maximum possible profit.

This is a thing that is more easily described than done. The crux of the difficulty lies in trying to forecast what the effect of a given marketing mix will be on the sales of the firm during the budgetary period and beyond. As we have seen, the only basis on which we can attempt to do this is by observing the effect which the various tools of marketing have had on our sales or on the attainment of our other marketing objectives in the past and then projecting those effects into the future with due regard for the conditions we expect will prevail.

This business of measuring the effects of advertising, various sales promotion devices, personal selling, technical service, and the several features of customer service on our past marketing performance is one of the most nebulous and difficult processes in the whole field of management. In spite of the vast amount of work that has been done on it, it still remains largely in the realm of executive judgment, feel, and "seat of the pants" instinct. While managerial feel or judgment, which is the distilled essence of experience, is not to be sneered at in this or any other field, much can be done to channel it and afford it solid ground on which to operate. Mathematical techniques are now available to help in doing this in some areas. In other areas about the most that can be done is to segregate and define the concepts involved so as to channel executive thinking where it can be most effective. This process is really a part of control, the next general subject we shall discuss. But it seems that some discussion of it here is necessary to enable us to understand the planning of marketing.

Perhaps the best way to approach the subject is to consider the problem of measuring the effectiveness of the two activities on which the average firm spends most of its marketing money, personal selling and advertising. A necessary first step in conceptualizing the problem of measuring the effect of either of these tools is to establish in some detail the objective or objectives of its use. Then, perhaps, methods can be devised for measuring the extent to which each objective has been achieved and the contribution of the tool to its achievement.

Personal Selling

a) If the sole or primary purpose of personal selling is to get immediate orders, the problem is not too difficult. Mathematical analyses can be made of the number and size of orders correlated with salesmen's calls, and indexes of effectiveness under varying conditions can be developed. This approach is especially adapted to the marketing work of house-to-house marketers and of manufacturers who sell direct to large numbers of retail stores. The results will never supply a completely reliable basis for planning because all the conditions affecting the harvesting of orders can never be known. But it can provide an approach to accuracy.

b) If the chief or only objective for which management uses personal salesmanship is to induce retailers (or others in a position to influence resale) to push the sale of the manufacturer's product, the problem is more difficult. This use of personal selling is characteristic of some firms that employ missionary salesmen through whom they try to reach around the wholesaler to the retailer, or, in the drug business, around both wholesaler and retailer to the physician, or, in the building materials trade, around the retailer and contractor to the architect or building owner.

In this kind of selling it is not always possible to trace the flow of goods through the marketing channels so as to make mathematic analysis possible. For example, when a manufacturer sells a bill of goods to a wholesaler, he may not be able, except at great expense, to find out where they go thereafter. But it is often possible, by varying the amount and intensity of sales effort within certain market areas that are more or less self contained, to observe variations in the amounts of the product flowing to wholesalers serving those areas, and, from the resulting data, to obtain at least a rough check of its influence on total sales. This is apt to be expensive, but at least part of the added cost is likely to be recouped in added sales.

c) If management proposes to use personal selling to achieve less tangible objectives; for example, to build or change a company image or to create confidence in the firm or to familiarize channel members or users with a product or with the services offered by the firm, then the problem of measurement is even more difficult. All of these ends express themselves in the attitudes as well as in the actions of the persons or firms the salesman contacts. Changes in such attitudes can be checked by attitude surveys, but when such a change is observed by marketing research it is very difficult to determine how much it is worth to the firm that brought it about.

d) Many of the other tasks management relies on the personal salesman to perform are hard to measure in terms of cost and results. Some of them, such as the distribution or installation of display or promotion materials, securing the participation of dealers in special deal projects, maintaining contact with customers, and persuading prospects to become customers, can be checked through observation or counting, but their evaluation in terms of costs and volume is hard to achieve. Others, such as arranging special services for customers or helping them with technical or promotional advice, are difficult both to check and evaluate. But by breaking the personal selling job down into its component parts and dealing with each part separately, management may be able to get a more accurate idea of its effectiveness and the results that may reasonably be expected from money spent on it than would otherwise be possible.

Advertising

Most of the techniques that have been used in trying to check the effectiveness of advertising have been based on an attempt to measure its intermediate results instead of the final effects that really count.[1] This is true of such activities as finding the number of people who have seen an advertisement or who are able to recognize or recall it. These matters bear little relationship to what the people who see, recognize, or recall an advertisement actually feel or do about the ideas it presents. The little boy in the story had undoubtedly seen spinach, he could recognize it, and he certainly could recall it, but all of these things had an adverse rather than beneficial effect on his consumption of the green, which was the real objective sought. Perhaps a better approach would be for a manager to define the jobs he wants his advertising to do and then try to develop some devices to measure the effectiveness with which it does them.

a) If a primary purpose of advertising is to make immediate sales, there are mathematical techniques to measure the relationships between the two.[2] This is the chief objective of most retail advertising and of firms selling by mail. It is probably a secondary purpose of the advertising of most firms marketing widely distributed consumers' goods.

b) If a firm's advertising has as a primary purpose the stimulation of inquiries which may be followed up either by letters or personal salesmen in the attempt to turn them into sales, it is possible to get some idea of its effectiveness by counting the inquiries and computing the dollar volume of the sales made to the prospective customers who sent

---

[1]C. E. Eldridge, "Advertising Effectiveness: How Can It Be Measured?" *Journal of Marketing*, January, 1958.

[2]Vidale and Wolfe, "An Operations Research Study of Sales Response to Advertising," *Operations Research*, June, 1957.

them. If marketing costs and net profit can be computed on this business, a fairly accurate evaluation may result.

c) If the principal objective of a firm's advertising is to create a public image or influence a group attitude, its effectiveness in doing so can be measured by attitude survey techniques. While this enables the marketing planner to estimate the extent to which a proposed advertising program can be expected to create or influence an attitude, it offers no help in calculating the value of the attitude to the firm. To the best of our knowledge, no generally useful method of doing this has been developed. On the other hand, when management decided upon such an objective it must have estimated that the benefits of achieving it were worth the estimated expense; so the attitude survey method should give management a reasonably accurate measure of the extent to which the advertising is providing and will continue to provide the benefits expected.

d) If advertising has as its objective the paving of the way for the salesman by arousing the interest of the customer, this too can be measured to some extent by attitude surveys, by inquiries received, or by sales made per salesman's call. Admittedly all of these measures fall far short of complete accuracy, but they may afford some basis for marketing planning.

e) If advertising has the purpose of providing an argument which salesmen may use to induce dealers to stock a new product or to participate in a special promotion, some idea of its effectiveness can be gained by comparing the results obtained by salesmen who use it intelligently with those who do not employ it wisely or who fail to use it at all. Every salesforce of any size will include representatives of both groups. The effectiveness of this use of advertising can also be checked by market testing campaigns.

Advertising has other objectives, for some of which effectiveness tests—appropriate to their nature and the surrounding conditions—can be devised. From both this discussion and that of personal selling it is obvious that there are many possible tests of the effectiveness of marketing tools that have been used but little—or not at all. This disregard of available measures probably arises mainly from four causes.

1. The history of marketing planning is really very short and the planners have by no means completely explored either its possibilities or the means needed to do it well.

2. In the area of advertising and, to a lesser extent, with other marketing tools as well, the measurers of effectiveness have been primarily absorbed in measuring the intermediate reactions—seeing, recogniz-

ing, recalling—and have tended to ignore the idea of trying to measure final effects.

3. In part, at least, this has been due to the failure of marketing managers and planners to set specific objectives for or to determine specific uses to which they propose to apply the various marketing tools included in their plans. Many frankly confess that they maintain certain levels of advertising and personal selling effort because they are afraid not to do so. Many have yet to grasp and act upon the idea of breaking down the overall marketing objective (and the complex of intermediate steps that must be taken to achieve it) into groups or kinds, and then to assign these steps or groups of steps as subobjectives to the various marketing tools available.

4. Many marketing managers feel that the increased precision in planning that might be gained by a program of seeking and applying methods of measuring the effectiveness of marketing tools would not be worth the cost of such a program. In many cases this decision is sound. If it is to be reliable, a program of measuring effectiveness must be continuous, and some features of it are highly expensive. On the other hand, it is probably true that many firms have information in their sales records and reports which, if properly analyzed, would provide some such measures at minimal cost.

This is an area in which much research, experimentation and improvement may be expected during the coming years.

Basic Concepts in Planning the Marketing Mix

Our discussion has now led us to two questions that are basic in the process of marketing planning: (1) How can a manager decide how much money his firm should spend on marketing work? (2) How can a marketing manager decide how much of the total marketing expense budget he should spend on each marketing tool?

Both of these questions must be answered in relation to the overall objectives of the company. For example, if in a coming budget period the primary objective of the firm is to maximize profits earned during the period, the answers to both questions will be different than they would be if the chief goal of the company were to gain the maximum possible share of the market during the period. Both sets of answers would in turn be inapplicable if the company objective were either to maximize profits over the next five or ten years or to capture the largest possible share of the market over the same period.

In all of these cases, however, the marginal concept is likely to be found useful in marketing planning. Let us apply this principle to these situations and see where it leads us.

If the objective is to maximize profits over the coming budgetary period, top management should spend money on each functional area, such as production, research, marketing, up to the highest point (within the firm's available resources) at which an additional dollar spent on any one of them may be expected to return the same added net profit during the year as an additional dollar spent on any of the others.

If maximum market position at the end of the year is the thing desired, the same principle applies—except that the final dollar spent on any of the activity areas should return the same added sales volume as the final dollar spent on any other area.

If either of these objectives is set on a ten-year basis the theoretical procedure will be about the same, except that the long-run rather than the short-run effects would be decisive. Such activities as research, production process improvement, and marketing activities having a delayed effect would probably account for much more of the total expense budget than under the short-term assumptions.

The same concept applies to the marketing planner's task of dividing the marketing share of the expense budget among the tools he has to work with, such as personal selling, advertising, sales promotion, technical service and customer service, and among the various subareas into which these can be segmented. Each should be supported to the highest point within the budget expense limitation at which its beneficial effect toward the objective is the same as that of any other.

It is understood, of course, that in actual practice this principle cannot be applied with any high degree of precision. One thing that complicates its application is the fact that most firms have multiple rather than single objectives, and that these are often contradictory. A marketing mix designed to achieve one will tend to defeat another. The conflict between net profit and market share, in the short run at least, is an example. This can be offset, to some extent, by weighting the several objectives according to the importance management attaches to each and using these weights to resolve conflicts in planning the allocation of marketing effort.

By far the greatest handicap in applying the concept, however, lies in the difficulty of measuring with any degree of exactness the past and present effectiveness of the marketing tools, thereby providing a basis on which to forecast their future results. Its precise or scientific application must wait on the development of methods of making such measurement. In the meantime it seems not improper to suggest that, even though the methods of measurement are imperfect, if the manager understands thoroughly the theory according to which he should allocate funds to the elements in the marketing mix, his thinking will gain precision and his decision making processes will be channeled along more realistic lines—instead of being nebulous and without sense of direction, as is too often the case when they lack the guidance of a basic concept. Moreover, the recognition and acceptance of the concept itself tends to generate attempts to provide the tools to make the principle really useful.

THE PRODUCTS OF MARKETING PLANNING

The products of marketing planning may assume several forms. Let us glance briefly at the most common.

Objectives. No plan, marketing or otherwise, can exist without an objective, a goal. It is useless to plan to do something without a clear idea of what you hope to accomplish by doing it. Examples of marketing objectives are: "$100,000,000 sales by 1965," "to increase our market share from 20% to 22% during the coming year," "to win the loyalty and cooperation of our dealers," or "to establish ourselves as a dominant element in the electronic materials market." An objective may be capable of achievement within a few months or within a budgetary period, or its realization may extend five or ten years into the future; but it usually involves the time element.

The marketing objectives of a business should conform to and aid the accomplishment of its general company-wide objectives. For this reason they are usually subject to approval by top management even though the chief marketing executive is almost always responsible for developing and recommending them. Objectives imposed from the top, without first coming up in detail from below, are rarely effective, however. They tend to lack the realism which comes from close contact with and knowledge of the market conditions in which the firm must operate and the tools it must use. Objectives that originate within the operating units and pass upward for approval are apt to possess a realism and to command widespread loyalty and personnel commitment that rarely attach to those handed down from above.

If properly drawn, marketing objectives lend the organization a sense of purpose, afford junior executives and staff personnel guidance in making decisons, serve as tools for coordination, and provide an incentive for marketing activities. They also serve both as a starting point and as a point of arrival in the planning process, for the guiding principle in that process should be the development of plans that will accomplish the objective—and the test of the adequacy of a plan is "Will it, if successful, achieve the broader objective?"

In determining objectives, the adage "hitch your wagon to a star" is of limited validity. They should be attainable, but with reasonable effort. Shooting at an impossible, or remotely possible, result tends to make plans fuzzy and unrealistic and leads to misunderstanding and frustration.

When marketing plans are written out, as almost invariably they should be, the objective should be clearly stated as part of the plan. Its expression tends to call attention to any features that may creep into the detailed planning process that are not pointed pretty sharply and directly toward the achievement of the goal.

Marketing Policies. The problems which arise for decision in managing the marketing efforts of a firm are likely to fall into groups. Those in each group conform to a pattern or possess many fundamental factors in common. Because of this similarity, the basic principle or principles governing the solution of one of the problems may also be followed in solving the others. These general guiding principles, applicable to the making of decisions in many similar situations, may be expressed as marketing policies.

Examples of marketing policies are: "We will be competitive in price but not be a price-cutter"; "We will rely on the wholesaler-independent retailer channel of distribution as the backbone of our marketing system"; "We will make our appeal primarily on the basis of the quality of our product"; "We will offer our customers the most complete and comprehensive technical service we are able to supply"; and "The customer is always right."

A policy may be a short-run affair designed to facilitate the achievement of a specific objective, or it may be an abiding guide to decision that influences the determination of a series of objectives. Marketing policies serve several highly important managerial purposes, all of which bear directly on the problems of planning and control.

a) It makes possible more carefully considered and, hence, sounder managerial decisions. Without policies each problem represents a crisis situation, with respect to which the manager makes a decision with time breathing down the back of his neck and competitive pressures jittering his nerves. If a firm uses policy as a management tool its managers can work out quietly and without disturbing pressures the *kind* of decision to make in each *kind* of situation. The resulting course of action is likely to be sounder, better thought out, and more consistent with the resources and objectives of the firm than that which follows the crisis type of decision.

b) The use of policy enables management to delegate authority much farther down the chain of command than is otherwise possible.

As a matter of fact, only rudimentary decentralization of authority can be achieved without an adequate system of policies.

c) The <u>determination and promulgation of policies by top management goes far to relieve middle and junior management of much of the fear of mistakes and to increase their willingness to make decisions.</u> Policies set guide lines or determine limits within which decisions must be made, and should diminish the danger of really serious mistakes at the lower levels.

Policies, unless frequently reviewed, have a habit of becoming fossilized and of straitjacketing management thinking long after conditions that gave rise to them have disappeared. When policies are set, managers all too often, especially at the middle level where the spadework of planning is done, tend to quit thinking. For these reasons policies should be reexamined frequently, certainly whenever long-range plans are reviewed, and perhaps annually when budgets are drawn.

Once company or departmental policies are adopted they usually are not included in successive written marketing plans, but their applicability is taken for granted. Those, however, which are pointed at the achievement of specific short-run or project objectives should be included as part of the plans made to bring them about.

Marketing Programs. The typical <u>marketing program is the document, or a member of the series of documents, from which the marketing budget is drawn</u>. In essence it is an orderly list of things that are to be done to achieve a stated objective or group of objectives. Sometimes it may designate who is to take each action and when. When the costs of these activities during a fiscal period are estimated and summarized under appropriate group headings, and the sales results are estimated and priced out, the resulting document is the marketing budget. If the budget is prepared in sufficient detail and the dollar figures in it are the outcome of the costing and pricing of planned activities and physical unit sales results, it may become an adequate marketing plan. If it is adopted without this preliminary spadework in planned physical units of input and expected output, the budget is probably a waste of time and paper.

The Completed Marketing Plan

The forms of completed marketing plans are as varied as the firms that prepare them. The long-range plan will probably consist mainly of estimates of yearly or quarterly sales in physical units of products, forecasts of changes in prices and their timing, the pricing out of estimates of sales by time periods, and probably estimates of marketing costs in dollars.

The short-term plan needs to be much more detailed. Product sales should be estimated in physical units, probably by months, with price changes forecasted and sales income priced out. Marketing activities should be scheduled in some detail. Some firms, especially in the industrial goods field, find it worthwhile to plan the number of salesmen's calls on each of their most important customers. Many plan varying call rates on different groups of customers, usually classified according to their volume of actual or potential purchases of the planning firm's products, or according to their growth possibilities. It is usually desirable to schedule advertising and sales promotional activities in considerable detail because commitments must be made for these long before the dates of their appearance. The result is apt to be an accurate time schedule of the things the marketing group proposes to do.

This does not mean that the plan, once it is adopted, will be carried out blindly and as a matter of course. Such things as changes in business conditions and competitive activity may justify or force reconsideration and revision from time to time. The more probable of these events may have been foreseen, and alternative reactions to them may have been determined upon and integrated into the original plan.

All this involves a lot of work and expense, but an increasing number of firms find it worthwhile.

CHAPTER 22

The Control Function in Marketing Management

"How well are we doing?" is an exceedingly difficult question for the marketing manager to answer, much more so than it is for the manager of production.

Basically production is an engineering operation, involving the application of energy through machines or other tangible equipment to tangible materials to create tangible or readily measurable products. The physical and time limits within which most types of equipment will operate, or chemical processes will take place, are known, and these limits set the maximum or optimum capacity of any production complex. Of course the human factor has an influence, but it merely modifies productivity and is not the sole determinant of it.

The efficiency of marketing operations, on the other hand, is almost entirely a matter of the human factor. Moreover, it is affected by the actions of several groups of people over most of whom the marketing manager has no control. The effectiveness of the marketing activity of a concern is influenced not only by the people it hires to carry on that activity but by the consumer buyers to whom its products are finally sold, by the intermediaries through whom they are marketed, by the competitors against whose opposition they must be sold, and by the elements in the population that create the economic and emotional atmosphere within which they must be marketed. The result is that marketing management is constantly struggling with intangible factors the extent or intensity of which it is difficult if not impossible to gauge. The marketing manager must try to measure how well he is doing by or against the pressure of forces he cannot measure. He knows that he cannot do a really good job of measuring performance, but good management dictates that he try.

NATURE OF THE CONTROL FUNCTION

Purposes

In seeking the answer to "How good a job are we doing?" the marketing manager usually has a purpose in view beyond the mere satisfaction of his curiosity. Of course it is inevitable that a man whose job is not to do things himself but to get others to do them will tend to feel isolated and will have a sense that he "does not know what is going on." So it is that the purpose of control work is almost certain to involve, to some degree at least, the personal reassurance of the manager who directs it and the satisfaction of his curiosity. But a knowledge of how well the operation is going serves other, more objective purposes for the marketing manager. A brief outline of these purposes seems desirable here to help us understand the nature of the function. Later we will explore them in much more detail.

1. *Planning.* Practically all planning of marketing activities must be done on the move, so to speak; that is, it must be done while marketing is going on. But it is difficult to decide where to try to go and how to try to go there unless you know where you are, in what direction you are headed, and how fast you are progressing. Control work supplies or should supply this information, or most of it.

2. *Stopping Mistakes.* When an operation continues over a period of time and mistakes are made in its conduct, control work may disclose them and permit their rectification before they have gone far enough to threaten disaster. For example, when a new product is introduced it sometimes happens that the reaction of wholesalers and retailers is enthusiastic, leading them to stock up heavily, while consumer response is something less than favorable. If an adequate control system discloses this situation early enough, changes may be made in production schedules to prevent the building up of excessive inventories, or the advertising or sales promotion may be changed to move stocks off the retail shelves, or the product may even be modified to make it more attractive to consumers.

3. *Salvage Operations.* When an operation goes wrong, and control information shows the nature and extent of its failure, steps may be taken to salvage at least something from the debacle, whereas if such steps were too long delayed the loss would be complete.

4. *Prevent Recurrence.* Good controls should not only disclose the occurrence of mistakes or failures of performance but should afford some clues as to why they happened. As a result, steps may be taken to prevent their happening again. As a matter of fact, one of the prime

purposes of control work should be to uncover the *why* of performance failures. This is perhaps its most constructive use.

5. *Blame.* Too many managements still regard fixing the blame for failure as the primary purpose of the control function. This use is of doubtful desirability. It leads employees at all levels to spend an exorbitant portion of their time in thinking up and documenting excuses for failures both actual and imagined. It puts a premium on the art of "buck-passing." It tends to create an atmosphere of "sit-tight-and-keep-your-neck-in," with the result that initiative is stifled and the will to decision is paralyzed.

6. *Incentives.* Controls may be used to provide incentives. When they are employed to fix blame they provide a powerful stimulus to avoid the failures to which blame will be attached, but they may also supply a positive stimulus when they afford goals or objectives for the people or units in the organization. The most common example is the salesman's quota. When properly set, the quota offers a target for the salesman to shoot at, from the achievement of which he may get a "psychic income," and, if the quota forms a part of the compensation system, a monetary one as well.

A review of these uses or purposes of the control function suggests that its effective performance is more important in marketing than in most of the other functional divisions of the business. A mistake or failure in production results in loss of current output, but very rarely will its damaging effects extend beyond a few months. If the personnel manager makes a mistake in hiring a man it can be rectified by "unhiring" him, provided it is discovered early enough. But a marketing mistake or failure is very apt to alienate customers, the loss of whose business may damage the company for years to come. So it is especially important in the marketing area that failures be spotted as early as possible and that remedial steps be taken promptly.

Steps in Control

In order to find out whether we are doing a good job in managing the marketing work of our firm we must first know what, under the conditions in which we operate, a good job is. In other words, we must set up standards of performance against which we can measure what we actually accomplish.

Having set standards of performance, we must develop and operate devices by which we can find out what really happens. Such tools may be as simple as personal observation, or they may take the form of elaborate systems of reports that require much time and effort to compile.

As a third step we must compare the information we thus obtain—what actually happens—with the standards so as to disclose wherein actual performance falls short of the standard. This step also may be very simple, as when a supervisor observes a salesman in operation and compares what the man does with his own mental picture of what he should do. Or it may involve highly sophisticated statistical analysis of sales figures.

Finally, the manager must take action to cause performance to conform to the standards, or to nullify or ameliorate the damaging effects of lapses or failures.

It must not be assumed that these steps are as sharply differentiated in practice as we have made them here, or that they follow each other in the exact sequence we have set up. Often two or more of them are performed simultaneously. This is especially likely to occur with the collection of control information and its measurement against standards. The supervisor is apt to observe the salesman's performance and compare it with the standards in the same instant. Or he may observe and later analyze, compare, and take corrective action in a single conversation with the salesman. A good report form is so constructed that it presents a record of what happened, and a comparison with the standard, in one document.

STANDARDS OF MARKETING PERFORMANCE

It is especially difficult to set standards of marketing performance because of three chief reasons. First: so much of the work of marketing is of an intangible nature. For example, the salesman of industrial goods really does not sell goods but *benefits in use,* while the man selling consumers' goods really sells the *satisfactions* to be enjoyed from the ownership or use of commodities, rather than the goods themselves. In essence, marketing is the purveying of *ideas* instead of tangible things, and intangibles are hard to define, let alone measure.

Second: much marketing work is designed to bring about future rather than current results. Thus it must be directed toward the preservation or creation or intensification of an attitude or a conviction. It is hard even to detect the existence of an attitude or a belief, let alone measure its changes in intensity.

Third: the results of marketing effort are influenced to a marked degree by forces outside the marketing firm, such as changes in general business conditions, shifts in the industry in which it operates, and the actions of competitors. It is often almost a hopeless task to try to determine how much of a given sales result is the outcome of the efforts of the marketing group and how much is due to fortuitous circumstances entirely beyond managerial control.

These factors exercise a marked influence on the kinds of performance standards that can be used, and they tend to subtract from the reliability of those actually employed. In spite of these difficulties a number of such standards have been developed. Some of them are peculiar to the firms that use them and arise from the special circumstances in which those firms operate. Others are more general and are used widely. We shall confine our discussion to the latter.

Past Performance

To compare what you do *now* with what you did *then* is a very natural procedure. Even in firms (and there are many of them) which do not use a comparison of sales this year with sales last year—or during several preceding years—as a part of their formal control procedure, it is probable that most of their marketing executives, more or less as a matter of course, match this month's results with last month's or with the same month last year. So it is not surprising that past results was one of the earliest standards of performance used in controlling marketing activities, nor that its use continues to be widespread.

It is one of the most commonly used standards in the department store business, where comparison is often made on a daily basis, today's sales being matched against those for the same day last year with appropriate adjustment for differences in the weather, the day of the week, and other factors likely to influence customer behavior. Very few marketing managers of manufacturing firms find it worthwhile to make the comparison on a daily basis, but many make monthly comparisons. It is usually not the only control standard used by such firms but it is apt to be followed quite closely by management.

Past sales can hardly be said to be the best of all performance standards in controlling marketing activities. Where we were yesterday or last year gives no sound indication of where we should be today—or of where we should have been yesterday or last year, for that matter. If such a comparison shows that we have progressed, it supplies no assurance that we have improved as much as we should have, nor does it even indicate whether the improvement was our own doing or the result of forces outside the firm for which its managers are in no way responsible. The use of this standard presumes that all the factors affecting sales volume are constant except our own efforts. This is never the case. In fact, the only sure thing in marketing is that the market of today is *different* from that of yesterday.

The result is that this standard supplies no stable benchmark against which the marketing manager can measure the performance of the unit he heads. About the best that can be said for it is that, if no *better* standard can be found, past performance is probably better than no standard at all.

Market Potential

Market potential is defined in at least two ways. It may be regarded as the entire volume of sales for all marketers that would result if every consumer bought and consumed an amount of the product that would give him the maximum satisfaction or benefit from its use. For example, consider a preparation which when sprayed on grape vines in the optimum amount brings about an increase of 20 percent in the yield of grapes. According to the definition stated above, its potential for the grape market would be the price of the amount of the product needed to spray an acre of vines times the total number of acres of grape vines at the fruitbearing age. The market potential for lipstick would be the total volume of the product that all manufacturers of it would sell if every woman used enough to maintain her maximum labial attractiveness during waking hours.

Obviously this is an ideal concept that will never be actualized. An ideal concept is usually not a good standard of performance; it is better to seek something that is realistic. If a firm sets as its standard a performance that no company or combination of companies can attain, its people are likely to take the attitude "What's the use of trying?" The very fact that it is not realistic casts doubt on its validity.

Then, too, it will often happen that the gap between standard and actual performance will be so great that significant variations in actual performance are obscured. If one has to go far down in the percentage scale to describe the relationship between the standard and the realistically attainable, one must go well out into the decimal places to express variations in actual performance in relation to the standard. Their significance thus tends to be obscured.

Another much more useful definition of market potential is the total amount of the product that would be sold if all its manufacturers did a reasonably good job of marketing it. This concept is usually almost identical with the total amount which actually is sold by all competitors. Sometimes this latter figure can be obtained without great difficulty. For example, new automobiles must be registered before they can be used and such registrations are a matter of public record. A tax must be paid on all sales of gasoline and the total amount of tax paid is also a matter of public record.

Sometimes the figure must be pieced together from fragments of information gathered from various sources. Consider the example of a company making a material that was used by pharmaceutical firms in compounding a certain end product. The market research department of this company collected samples of the end products made by all compounders. The labels showed the amount of the material in each unit of each end product. The sales records of a sample of the drugstores of the country enabled the marketing research department to compute total unit sales of each brand of each end product. From this information it was possible to compute the amount of the material used by each compounder and the total used by all compounders. In a few cases it was possible to check the accuracy of the estimates computed for customers who were known to buy all or a certain percentage of their requirements of the material from the company or who were willing to disclose their total purchases of it.

Market potential presents the advantages of a standard that in no way depends on either the previous performance of the marketing unit of the firm using it or on the judgment or aggressiveness of the management of the firm. It is an independent although shifting benchmark, against which the marketing results of the company can be measured, that will go far toward really answering the question "How well are we doing?"

Market Share

Market share is a derivative of market potential. It is the portion, usually expressed as a percentage, of the total sales of a product by all competitors that is made by a firm. The market share, used as a standard of performance, may not be the share actually sold by the firm but the share its managers hope or expect or intend to achieve. Thus a firm making and marketing gym clothing, which during a given year sold 10 percent of the total volume of that product, set as its goal for the succeeding year a market share of 12 per cent and used this as its performance standard.

It will be observed that market share is a relative figure. When it is used as a standard, an increase in actual sales resulting from a general increase in total industry volume (of which the firm actually captures a decreasing share) is not likely to beguile management into thinking that all is well. On the other hand, the use of the market-share standard will give an accurate picture of the marketing job being done by a firm whose sales are declining at a rate less rapid than the volume of the market as a whole. Both these situations are apt to mislead the management that relies too heavily on past performance as a standard.

Neither market share nor past sales, if used as a sole standard of marketing performance, contains any reflection of changing costs and so may mislead management instead of affording sound guidance.

There are three chief ways in which a firm can increase its market share. It may improve its product; it may cut price; or it may increase the amount of advertising, sales promotion, and sales effort. Two of these increase costs and the other reduces gross profit. It may easily happen that, in the process of increasing its market share, a company generates such an outflow of cost dollars, or so decreases the inflow of gross profit dollars, that net profits are reduced. It may be meeting its marketing performance standard admirably but heading for bankruptcy by doing so.

Marketing Objectives

Marketing objectives may sometimes be used as standards of performance. If objectives have a time limit and are short-run, they may be very useful for this purpose. A long-range objective is much less useful since the conditions that affect its achievement may change drastically during the period it covers. Also, it is desirable that performance be measured at frequent intervals, and unless a long-range objective can be broken down into a series of short-run parts, it can be used as a standard only when, at the end of the period, it either has or has not been accomplished. A long-run objective may be used as a standard against which to measure the system of short-run objectives designed to achieve it.

Moreover, most firms and most marketing units have more than one objective, so that two or more objectives may be in conflict. For example, a firm may be seeking both to increase its rate of net profit on sales and to increase its share of the market. It costs money to augment market share and the achievement of this end may for a time actually subtract from net profit instead of add to it. Even when multiple objectives are not in conflict the resources available may not be enough to achieve them all. An attempt to realize all of them may result in the achievement of none.

Unless management is willing to weight multiple objectives in the order of the importance of their achievement, objectives are not likely to be very useful as standards of performance. When objectives are of unequal value, a proper balance of the efforts to accomplish them is, in iself, an element of performance.

In general it is probably safe to say that in marketing, as in other functional areas of business management, objectives usually afford a source from which control standards of performance can be drawn rather than that they constitute such standards themselves. But this is not *always* true.

Marketing Policies

Policies may themselves be used as standards of marketing performance or they may be the sources from which such standards are drawn. If a policy is quite specific (as that of a leading oil company which for years followed the policy of being the third firm to change price in response to the action of the price leader in the areas where it did not exercise price leadership) it can function very well as a standard of performance. If, on the other hand, the policy is general, it may be of little use as a standard unless it happens that certain specific things must be done in order to effectuate the policy. Then these may be used as standards.

If the marketing department is organized on a decentralized basis, so that the heads of units in it exercise wide discretion, policies offer one of the few means of control. They may be used to set guide lines within which unit heads are allowed to exercise their discretion. Conformance to or departure from them may serve as a useful indication of the performance of the unit manager in his semi-autonomous position.

While marketing policies promise a highly useful measure of performance, their employment for this purpose poses several problems and opens the door for certain dangers. If they are to be effective as standards, they must be specific enough so that nonconformance can be readily observed. But the more specific a policy is the more it hamstrings the originality and judgment of the men who work under it, and the more liable it is to become outdated. Moreover, if policies are to be specific they must apply to details instead of to general courses of action. And if a general course of action is to be controlled it must be broken down into a number of policies, each so specific that conformance can easily be measured. The danger is that under differing, changing conditions, which demand freedom of action, they will become rules of procedure that limit such freedom.

Moreover, if policies are framed in general terms they require interpretation in specific situations. The interpretation of the executive whose job is to measure performance, is apt to differ from the interpretation of his subordinate who must operate under the policies. Control then becomes nonexistent or degenerates into conformance to a series of interpretations, each of which assumes the aspect of a separate specific policy, with all the drawbacks of such a multiplicity of policies.

Both of these faults suggest the necessity of a periodic reevaluation of marketing policies since the conditions that gave rise to them may change or cease to exist. But the very purpose of management by policy tends to discourage changes. The use of policy is an attempt to guide individual decisions by the setting up of general principles—and the setting of such principles tends to engender a false sense of security that has the effect of causing management to put off the reexamination of existing policies. The result is apt to be that operating executives act under outdated rules of the game.

In general, policies (like objectives) are a source from which performance standards can be developed; they should rarely, of themselves, function as such standards.

Marketing Plans

As was pointed out in the preceding chapter, the complexity of our economy and its dynamic character make it necessary for a management, hoping to operate successfully, to plan its marketing activities carefully and in detail. The elements of such a plan usually afford standards by which to measure marketing performance.

A long-run plan covering five to ten years is generally not very useful to the marketing manager as a standard of control. It is likely to be drawn in terms that are too general to serve as checks on current performance. Such a plan may enable the marketing executive to measure his actual performance against what it has to be if he is to complete the long-range plan on time, but it is not apt to be very effective as a standard against which to measure the day-to-day or month-to-month performance of his department or any unit of it.

If the marketing part of the budget plan is prepared initially in physical units of sales and activities to be carried on, it may serve as an effective standard of performance. It will then contain a list of specific things we propose to do in order to bring about certain results. As the budgetary period passes the manager may observe whether the units of his organization are doing these things and whether the expected results are being achieved. If he delegates broadly he must, in making such checks, allow for minor variances that will result from his subordinates' exercise of the privilege of doing things their own way.

In its ultimate form a project plan is likely to consist of a list of processes or actions that are to be completed, and perhaps a schedule of when each will be begun and finished. If control reports or observations are geared to such a schedule they afford the manager an excellent means of learning how the projects involved are going.

The use of objectives and marketing plans (often in the form of budgets) as control standards of performance is very common throughout industry. They probably constitute one of the best kinds of performance standards, but they have one serious drawback. This system of standards contains no built-in check on the excellence of the plans or of the objectives themselves. The firm that checks its actual performance against a poor plan, based on objectives that are too modest or cautious, is liable to find itself falling behind in the competitive race. If the objectives on which marketing plans are based represent a goal of profits or share of the market, their soundness as performance standards is somewhat improved. But the question still remains: "What profit performance or market share should a company shoot for?" This is a question to which no one has developed a pat answer. It remains a matter of managerial judgment, initiative, and ambition.

List of Activities

Lists of activities or things to be done may be used as performance standards. A salesman may be expected to average a certain number of calls per day, for example, or he may be given a target of X number of demonstrations of the product for every 100 calls, or he may be obligated to make a specified number of calls per year on each customer, according to the customer's potential. A sales supervisor may be expected to spend X number of days a year traveling in the field with each veteran salesman, and Y number of days with each new man. A sales manager may be expected to spend one third or one half of his annual working days in the field with his men.

Such "activity list standards" are usually the outgrowth of the marketing plan, and they may represent an attempt to use a few key factors of the plan, instead of all its details, as controls. In such a case their use as a control standard is simply an extension of the use of the marketing plan for the same purpose. Sometimes, though, they are of long standing and have little relationship to any sort of short-range or long-range plan or project.

Standard Costs

By the ingenious use of cost accounting techniques it is sometimes possible to develop standard costs for some marketing activities. This is especially likely to be true of the costs generated by the order handling and physical distribution parts of the marketing operation.

Even in these areas the validity of standard costs as criteria of marketing performance varies with the basis on which they are constructed. Standard costs may be the result of an attempt to construct the costs as they would be if the operations that generate them were carried out with faultless efficiency. This results in an ideal figure having something of the nature of an ideal market potential. It is a standard that can never be achieved and, like market potential, is not to any great extent under the control of those managing the activity. Standard costs may also be constructed mainly as an extension of past costs, in which case they suffer the defects of all standards that are geared to the past.

In general, marketing managers have not found standard costs too useful as measures of performance. This does not mean that marketing cost analysis results are not highly useful both in the planning and control of marketing activities. Their value is that they provide the marketing manager information as to what the costs of specific activities or operations are, either as an initial step to trying to reduce them or in emphasizing those activities that yield unusual returns in relation to outlays. We will explore some of the methods employed in doing this when we consider the checking of performance.

Profits

Since the making of profits is almost always a prime objective of a firm, and control standards are best when they bear a close and direct relation to objectives, it might be expected that profits would be a widely used standard of marketing performance. This, however, is not the case, although the use of some sort of profit figure for this purpose seems to be increasing.

Many managements are not willing to incur the risks resulting from the wide dissemination of cost and profit information among employees (implicit in the use of cost-and-profit marketing performance standards). While this attitude is more often shortsighted than is generally realized, it is probably fully justified for many companies. Another limiting factor upon the use of profit figures for this purpose arises from the fact that profits are the result of the activities of the *whole* business and are not primarily derived from the work of any part of it. Undoubtedly though, it is the obligation of the marketing part of the business to emphasize the sale of those products to those customers whose volume returns, or promises to return, the highest net profit to the whole operation. Even when management is debarred from making a complete disclosure of profit figures it is often possible to devise a marketing performance standard that is based on the relative profitability of products and customers.

Some firms make extensive use of profit figures in controlling marketing performance. For example, a company which markets materials to five different industrial groups of customers has a separate force of salesmen calling on each customer group and operating under a separate marketing manager (with his own staff organization) who buys advertising, sales analysis work, marketing research work, and other services from a group of staff service units under the direction of a general marketing manager. Each of these customer-group marketing managers receives goods from the production department at standard factory cost and is responsible for the net profit realized on his operations.

Subject to the advice and approval of general management, he prepares his own budget and determines the profit figure he will shoot for during the coming year. His profit performance is then measured against the budgeted net result. This method has caused the marketing managers to become extremely conscious of costs and the relative profitability of products and customers. Nor can they afford to lose sight of volume as a means of keeping down overhead costs per dollar of sales. This scheme can be modified to allow some of the profit to appear as a result of the operations of the production part of the business by charging goods to the marketing managers at a figure somewhat above factory cost. Production can then augment its share by achieving reductions in actual costs below estimated or standard factory cost.

When this complete disclosure of costs and profits to operating executives is not feasible or desirable, some substitute for them, often in the form of points per unit of product sold, varying according to profitability, may be used. Or goods may be turned over to the marketing department at factory cost *plus* all other allocable costs (except those of marketing) *plus* expected company profit. The marketing department is then expected to pay the expense of its operations out of the difference between this figure and selling price. By economic and efficient operation it may show a profit on its activities.

Or merchandise may be charged to marketing at expected selling price less a commission graduated according to the profitability of the several products. The marketing department can then show a profit out of this commission either by expanding volume and reducing costs through efficiency of operations, or by emphasizing the sale of high-profit and high-commission items. All these plans, and others of a similar nature, make use of profit as an instrument of control without disclosing the actual amount of the profit figure to the personnel controlled.

In spite of the natural and logical suitability of profit as a standard of performance for an organization dedicated to the making of profit, its use poses certain problems. How much profit should constitute the standard to be set as a target? On what grounds should it be determined? Inevitably, the amount of profit to be striven for by the marketing department, as well as by other parts of the business, is the result of the plans and objectives of the management. So it will be a good or an inadequate standard according to the imagination, courage, ambition, and soundness of judgment of the management. If the management is timid and without vision or confidence in itself and its people, the standards it sets will be inadequate. If it is overly ambitious or so lacking in soundness of judgment that it allows itself to be carried away by impossibly optimistic dreams of accomplishment, its standards will be unrealistic and unattainable.

For these reasons profit is often used as an instrument of control without actual standards being set. When this practice is followed in the marketing field the marketing manager's profit performance is judged by comparison with an informal and often nebulous concept of what it should be under the particular set of competitive and other conditions in which he had to operate during the control period. Often profit performance during a current period is compared with profit performance during a previous period. This practice suffers from the same defects as do all attempts to judge present performance by comparison with the results of the past. It has the advantage, though, that the measurement is made on the basis of the prime objective of the enterprise.

By this time you may have concluded that there is no absolute or perfect standard by which marketing performance can be measured, and you are correct in this conclusion. But this does not mean that all attempts to set and apply such standards are useless. Often a system of standards that applies to different activities involved in marketing can be devised that will prove highly effective. Such a system must grow out of the conditions under which the marketing manager operates, the jobs he must do, and the overall goals of the business to which he belongs. A set of control standards that serves one firm well is likely to be entirely unsuited to the needs of another.

CHECKING PERFORMANCE

The second step in the managerial control of marketing activities includes observing or recording what happens in the marketing process and analyzing the information thus obtained so as to compare actual performance with the standards previously set. The devices commonly used to check marketing performance do not differ markedly from those employed in other functional areas. The nature of the marketing activity, however, causes marked variances in the way in which these devices are used. The chief sources of marketing control information are sales analysis, reports, observation, marketing research, and cost analysis.

Sales Analysis

In the process of servicing customers, records of sales can readily be kept. These are compiled either from orders received or invoices submitted, often from both. Sales analysis involves abstracting from these records, or from the original documents from which they are drawn, the information that can be used in control, then processing it to facilitate comparison with performance standards.

Sales analyses may be very simple. For example, the sales manager of a firm that makes and markets industrial materials has in his desk drawer a loose-leaf notebook in which his secretary keeps a record of orders received from the 25 customers who take about 60 percent of the company's sales volume. Most of them order not more than twice a month, some of them only once. By studying this record he finds that most of these customers have distinctive order patterns: the Uno Company orders twice a month, a small order about the 15th and a large amount about the 25th; the Duo Company orders once a month, somewhere between the 25th and the 28th; the Trio Company places three orders a month, on or near the 5th, the 15th, and the 25th.

If our notebook-keeping sales manager observes that the 27th of the month has come and gone, bringing no order from the Duo Company, he telephones the salesman who handles the account and suggests that something may be wrong and that it might be wise for somebody to do something about it. One outcome of this procedure is that most of his salesmen now keep their own notebooks, with the result that the sales manager usually receives explanations of departures from the norm before he gets around to inquiring about them.

Sales analyses may also be very complex. They are often compiled by customers, by territories, by products, and with various cross-classifications that may provide useful information. Such analyses are most helpful when they provide comparisons of actual sales with the standard against which performance is to be measured—the sales plan, the budget, or the quota. As the operating period passes the analysis may show current results for the month, day, or week, together with cumulative results for the period, as in the accompanying illustration.

Month	Sales This Month	Cumulative for Year to Date	Budget for Year	Percent of Budget to Date	Percent of Budget This Month
January					
February					
March					

The period covered by a sales analysis depends on the circumstances and nature of the business. If customers are many and orders are small and numerous, and conditions change rapidly, it may be worthwhile to make such analyses daily or weekly. Department stores, certain types of wholesalers, bakeries, and manufacturers of food and cleansing products, selling directly to retailers, find it pays to do this. For most makers of industrial goods it is profitable to do this only on a monthly basis. In general, it is not worthwhile for the manager to receive such information more often than he can do something to try to correct the lapses from standard. Control information that is not or cannot be used is a waste.

The reports of sales analyses should be prepared so that comparison with performance standards is easy. The analysis report that requires the manager to use a slide rule or a comptometer to compute relationships or trends is not properly prepared. Items of information that need to be compared should be put adjacent to each other so that comparison is hard to avoid. Many standard forms for sales analysis reports have been prepared, and entirely too often they are adopted without change by individual firms. Usually this is not good because the form should be suited to the control problem and the control system of the firm that uses it. Really, there is no reason why it should not be suited to the working habits and convenience of the man who uses it most.

Reports

Reports of the activities of individuals or operating units constitute a very widely used tool by which to check marketing performance. It is probable that practically every marketing organization, except the very small ones, requires periodic performance reports of the operating units into which it is divided. The call report, submitted by the individual salesman, is a standard tool of sales control.

A surprising number of marketing managers, however, do not require call reports from their salesmen. Some of them, whose men work entirely on a commission basis, find it difficult to enforce such a requirement because the men feel that they are really in business for themselves and that how they spend their time is none of the company's business. This attitude is apt to be especially strong when the salesman is expected to pay his expenses out of the commission. Other managers feel that the salesman's job is to sell and not to do paperwork. Others see no profitable use they could make of the information a call report would supply. Still others say "Our men are individualists. We want them to be that way. They would resent our trying to look over their shoulders." The benefits visualized by the managers holding these attitudes may be real or illusory, but there is no question that they lack control in an area where it counts heavily.

The salesman's call report may be very simple or it may assume the proportions of a rather formidable document. It may involve little more than a listing of the persons or firms called upon during the period. On the other hand, it may involve the discovery and reporting of detailed information designed to establish the credit position of the customer or disclose his methods of operation, the products he makes or plans to make, who his other sources of supply are and what portion of his needs he buys from them, and other similar detailed data.

A few firms, usually those whose sales are made in very large lumps and to only a few customers, require what is sometimes called a "he sez and I sez" report. This sort of document is a running summary of the interview, outlining the attitudes expressed by the customer, his description of his needs, and what the salesman feels the firm can do to get his business. Such a reporting system is justified only if the fieldman needs a great deal of supporting work done or material supplied by the home office staff.

Many reports are oral. This is true even of the salesman's reports. For example, if a salesman in the course of his work uncovers a situation that is "hot," such as a highly dissatisfied customer whose complaint requires executive action, or an important prospect for whose business the salesman needs a little reinforcement by the "brass," he is apt to report the particulars by phone.

Most of the day-to-day reports of the marketing executives of the average firm are made face-to-face or by interoffice telephone. A marketing manager charged with distributing the products of his firm to a certain group of customers under a director of marketing put it this way: "If it is something the boss doesn't have to decide, I do it and then phone him I've done it and how it came out. If it is something I must get his clearance for, I walk down the hall and tell him I'm going to do it. If he says O.K. I go ahead, and then tell him what happens." Of course, these informal oral reports are usually supplemented by more formal annual, quarterly, or monthly written reports.

The general dictum "The fewer reports the better" has unusual applicability in the marketing area, especially with respect to the written reports of field salesmen. The salesman is apt to feel, and rightly so, that his job is to sell. He is likely to resent the time and energy he must devote to preparing reports; he regards this work as unproductive. It seems banal to say that no report should be required whose information is not used: surely, no marketing manager will be so stupid as to require his men to make reports that are not used. But reports, once embedded in a control procedure, display a survival tenacity that is incredible even though the situation that gave rise to the need for them has long since passed. They will not be eliminated unless they are periodically reexamined and deadwood is ruthlessly pruned out.

The same thing is even more true of unneeded items in reports that, as a whole, are still valuable parts of the control system. To drop them the entire report form must usually be redesigned, the supply of old forms discarded and new ones printed. This often irritates the economy nerve of the office manager or procedures clerk beyond its point of endurance. Here, too, a certain amount of managerial ruthlessness is needed if unused items of information are to be kept out of salesmen's report forms.

The report form should also be designed so that the maximum amount of information may be communicated with the minimum of work—by check marks, for example. Most managers find that by operating on this principle they can get the maximum amount of usable control information with the minimum of grumbling. Some firms that need reports of the "he sez and I sez" variety find it worthwhile to equip their salesmen with dictating machines, the tapes or discs of which are mailed to the home office for transcription. This also recognizes the fact that the average salesman talks much better than he writes and would much rather talk than write.

Observation

Much marketing control information is gathered by observation. By observing how his subordinate executives handle themselves in their day-to-day contacts with each other and with executives in other parts of the business, the marketing manager can gain a pretty sound notion of their performance in a vital part of their jobs.

Observation is a much less effective tool for gathering information about the field salesman's performance. While the marketing manager's immediate subordinates are more or less constantly under his eye, and in consequence their performance cannot be one thing when he is watching them and something else when he is not, the salesman must operate most of the time without direct observation. When a supervisor visits a salesman the man is apt the try to adjust his normal method of operation to what he thinks the supervisor would like it to be.

He can never be entirely successful in doing this. Telltale details of behavior are apt to escape his attention and give his show away. Then, too, the reaction of the customer often affords clues. For example, the drug salesman who is allowed behind the customer's prescription counter is "in." Customer unfamiliarity with the sales program that has been under way during several previous visits of the salesman suggests that our man has not been pushing the program as we would like him to do. So in spite of its inherent weaknesses, personal observation is one of the chief methods of gathering control information about the performance of the field salesmen.

Marketing Research

One of the common uses of marketing research is to find out how programs are going. It may be especially useful in checking on the effectiveness of advertising and sales promotion activities. For example, when the objective of an advertising campaign is to change a customer attitude, create a brand or company image in the customer's mind, or communicate to customers certain facts about a product, successive customer attitude or information surveys may be very useful in showing how effective the campaign is. When a new product is being introduced, or a new promotional campaign is under way and the goods must be marketed through wholesalers and retailers, marketing research of the store audit type, designed to disclose the rate of flow-through at the retail level, may be very revealing in showing whether the campaign is moving our products off the retail shelves into the hands of consumers—or that they are piling up in wholesalers' warehouses and retailers' stockrooms.

These are only a few of the many ways in which marketing research can be used to gather marketing control information. It is apt to be a costly method, but when the needed performance data cannot be obtained by any less expensive means it may be more costly *not* to get the information than to pay for the marketing research needed to obtain it.

Marketing Cost Analysis

During recent years an increasing number of firms have been applying the techniques of cost accounting to the task of analyzing marketing costs. Because of the complexity of this process and the special problem it presents, we have devoted a separate chapter to its discussion.

USING CONTROL INFORMATION

The final step in the use of marketing controls is taking the managerial action indicated by the information and analysis. Such action may be of at least six types.

1. As a result of data disclosed by the control devices the marketing manager may stop a going project that seems not to be working well, or may change the way in which it is being carried out. For example, a firm may inaugurate a special deal or other promotional program for a product. During its early stages wholesalers stock the article heavily in anticipation of expected demand and, when retailers do likewise, reorder to replenish their inventories. The program seems to be working well. But a store audit indicates that the goods are not moving off the retailers' shelves. This control device has indicated that something is wrong with the program. If the marketing manager can diagnose the trouble quickly and remedy the defect, he may be able to modify his plans so as to make them work. If he cannot find the trouble he will probably be wise to call the whole thing off before wasting any more of his firm's money.

2. Control information may enable the marketing manager to salvage something from the wreck of plans that go wrong. In the case outlined above, for example, the manager must do something about the excessive stocks of his product that have piled up in the hands of wholesalers and retailers in order to avoid ill will in his marketing channels. He probably has, or will soon have, excess inventories in

his own warehouse. Obviously, one possible step is a cutback in production. Perhaps some sort of special advertising or point of sale promotion or special allowance permitting price reductions at the retail level may relieve channel overstocks. At least, the early discovery of the difficulty enables him to make plans to deal with the results of the debacle before the situation gets out of control. Such plans are almost always sounder than those thrown together under heavy stress.

3. Controls may provide a powerful incentive to subordinates. A salesman who knows the standards by which he is to be judged and receives regular comparisons of his performance with the standard is likely to take steps on his own to match performance to standard. He can be expected to do this only if he accepts the standard as fair and reasonable. The manager of a marketing unit which is a cost-profit center, and who works against an accepted profit plan, is apt to become as conscious of costs and profits as his boss, and just as anxious to learn what is happening so he can deal with performance lapses before they add up to failure.

4. Good control information, properly followed up, may prevent the recurrence of failure. For example, over a period of years an industrial goods house put out several new products that "went sour" on the market. These cut seriously into the profits of successful new products introduced during the same period. A careful analysis of the causes of the failures disclosed at least two marketing mistakes that were common to the history of all the unsuccessful products. This knowledge enabled the marketing manager to avoid these mistakes in putting future new products on the market and substantially improved the company's new product batting average. The important fact here is not that the product failed but *why it failed*. This is certainly one of the most fruitful and constructive uses that can be made of control techniques and information.

5. This use of the control function can be broadened into its employment as a general aid in marketing planning. If we know from our control information and analysis that a certain marketing technique, device, or policy is working satisfactorily, we can, with some assurance, include it in our future plans. If our control work indicates that a marketing method is not working well, we know that we should either leave it out of our future plans or modify it to remove the "bugs." How well we are performing in the achievement of our objectives during the current operating period indicates to a great extent what they should be for the coming period. Probably the most constructive use of control information is as a guide in planning.

6. Probably the least constructive use of control work, and certainly the most disturbing one to those controlled, is fixing responsibility or finding who is to blame for failure. Of course a certain amount of this is necessary to provide information to serve as a guide in promotions, transfers of personnel, separations, and adjustments of duties, but if it is regarded as the primary purpose of the control function, if control standards are used as whipping posts in the punishment of those who fail, or if the comparison of performance with standards serves mainly as a point of departure for hectoring and browbeating the poor unfortunates who fail to achieve the norm, controls become a destructive force in the organization. This use causes backbiting, "buck passing," reluctance to act for fear of making a mistake, and the waste of infinite time and energy in concocting excuses (often prepared before the event) for failure.

On the other hand, if control information is used as the starting point for stopping failure before it becomes final, or for finding out why it occurred so that it can be avoided in the future, the control function can become a constructive force aiding men to enlarge their natural capacities and to work together to achieve things beyond their individual capabilities. Control can be the constructive force that binds men to a common effort instead of a disruptive force that puts men at each other's throats.

PROBLEM AREA VII

Matters of Right and Wrong

CHAPTER 23

Ethics and the Marketing Manager

If we accept as sound the classical economists' theory of free untrammeled competition, we must look upon business as a realm governed by the law of the jungle. Greed—or its less unlovely synonym, the "acquisitive instinct"—must be accepted as the businessman's conscience, and the tooth and claw as his socially approved instruments.

As a matter of fact, though, the number of men committed to greed as the sole or even the consistently dominating instinct is, and for a long time has been, narrowly limited. This has made it necessary for society to establish laws to protect the mass of mankind, motivated by other instincts, from their purely predatory fellows. Many of these laws apply to business relationships. By and large they probably reflect the lawmakers' interpretation of the generally accepted concepts of right and wrong in those relationships.

But the law alone cannot be the keeper of a man's conscience, nor can it cover all the questions of right and wrong that arise to plague the different groups that make up the society the law governs. There remains an area within which the group or each person in the group must create and live by some extra-legal standard of right behavior. This is the area of personal or group morals.

In our society one of the most important groups for which such extra-legal standards of behavior exist is business or, more exactly, business management. Since most problems of moral behavior arise from human relationships, and most business activities involve human relationships, questions of morals or ethics are highly pervasive and important in the business area.

More than any other functional area of management, except possibly personnel, marketing is a matter of the relationships between either individuals or groups. As a result the marketing manager, more often than most of his fellow executives, finds himself in situations which require him to decide, for himself and for his firm, what is right or wrong, fair or unfair, proper or improper. In addition, the moral problems he faces are apt to be more complicated than those met by his fellow managers. The on-the-job human relationships of other functional executives are mainly, or entirely, with people inside the firm, while his are with customers—people outside the firm—as well. The marketing manager is liable to find himself and his ethical code in the middle, between the conflicting interests of the firm and the people in it on the one hand, and of his customers on the other.

MORAL BEHAVIOR TO WHOM?

The concept of a moral principle or standard contemplates the existence of a duty or obligation to a person or a group of persons, such as the employees or customers of a firm; or to a thing, such as the firm itself, insofar as it may be said to have a separate entity, or as the system of competitive free enterprise. The groups or types of persons or things to which the marketing manager may owe such duties is highly varied. They may include

His superiors in the firm
The firm itself, as an entity
His fellow functional executives
His subordinates
All employees of the firm whose jobs depend on the sales his department makes
His competitors and their executives with whom he comes in contact
The extra-firm members of his marketing channels
The ultimate users of the products he markets
Auxiliary service organizations he uses, such as advertising agencies, warehouse firms, etc.
The industry to which his firm belongs
The social and economic order in which he functions
The governments which make rules to control his activities

From this list it is not hard to see the wide variety and heterogeneity of the group interests which may create moral problems for him, nor is it difficult to understand the extent to which his obligations to these groups conflict with each other. When a person or occupational group owes obligations in only one direction, or when the importance of one relationship heavily outweighs that of every other, the resolving of ethical problems is simplified, and codes of morals, both professional and personal, can be fairly definite and even rigid. Examples are physicians, whose duty to the patient outweighs all others, and members of the legal profession, whose obligations to the client are paramount.

When the duty pattern is as varied and complex as that of the marketing manager, it is exceedingly difficult to draw hard and fast rules, and, if they can be drawn, they will apply much less universally.

This is one of the reasons why marketing managers lack a code of ethics in any way comparable with those guiding physicians and lawyers, and why, when attempts are made to draw such codes, they tend to be so broad as to be almost meaningless and so are often honored in the breach rather than in the observance. It also explains why we will not attempt to put together a moral code for marketing managers but will be content with indicating some of the more common issues of right and wrong which the marketer faces—and with some very general suggestions as to how he may go about resolving them.

Perhaps some discussion of the obligations the marketing manager owes to the groups listed above may help to illuminate the nature of the moral problems with which he must deal.

The Firm

The marketing manager's obligations to the firm that employs him are much the same as those of any other executive in its organization. Like human beings, the firm possesses a will to live and a sense of immortality. If the human being faces facts he must realize that, in his corporal form, his span of life is definitely limited. This is not true of the firm. By its legal nature it may live as long as the society and the legal system under which it was set up, and social structures and legal systems have a way of surviving changes and even revolutions that upset the governments that express them and are supposed to administer them.

It is undoubtedly the duty of the marketing manager to help provide for the continuity of the firm that employs him. In a dynamic society or economy, continuity can be achieved only by change and growth to conform to a fluid environment. Therefore the marketing manager must constantly be planning ways in which the distribution activities of the firm can be adapted to conditions that may be expected to prevail in the future, sometimes long after he ceases to be marketing manager. This is an ethical obligation that is usually not written out in his contract of employment.

The corporation also possesses a personality which reflects itself in a public image. In his activities and those he directs within his span of control and influence the marketing manager is under the obligation to refrain from doing things or having things done that violate the firm's personality or impair its image. He shares this duty with his fellow executives, but it bears more heavily upon him than upon most of them because he commands the firm's most widely flung system of contacts with the general public. To consumers and to the personnel of the distribution system his actions and those of the people he directs are the actions of the firm. To them he is *the* firm.

His Superiors in the Firm

To top management the chief marketing executive owes just about the same moral obligations as do other heads of functional divisions. It is his duty to advise and help in formulating overall company objectives, policies, and plans that will be to the best interests of the firm. In doing this he is obligated to think in terms of the whole company and to subordinate the interests of his functional area to those of the firm. It is his duty to leave no doubt in the minds of top management as to the effects proposed decisions are likely to have on marketing activities, but once a decision is made, he should be willing to live with its effects in the interest of the company welfare.

Once top management decides upon an objective, a policy, or a plan the marketing manager has two ethical alternatives if he is convinced that it is wrong. He may resign or he may devote his best efforts to making it a success. It does not seem morally inconsistent with the latter course of action to bide his time and, at the proper moment, attempt to get the decision reversed. The all-too-prevalent practice of "dragging his feet" in carrying out the decision, in an attempt to defeat its efficient execution, is at best of doubtful moral justification.

His Fellow Executives

To his fellow functional top executives the marketing manager owes candor and cooperation. To the chief of production he owes the most accurate and honest estimate he can make of future needs for finished products. The financial officer is entitled to his best estimate of cash income from sales. To the chief of research and development he owes the most reliable information he can supply regarding the marketability of proposed new products.

But his obligations go beyond this. Functional mistakes are bound to be made and functional emergencies are certain to occur. When an overstock develops, or demand is out of alignment with optimum production cost rates, or when sudden needs for cash arise, or when shifts in demand threaten employment changes that may disturb labor relations, the chiefs of production, finance, and personnel have a right to expect that he will make an honest attempt to adjust marketing efforts to help overcome the difficulty.

His Subordinates

The ordinary obligation of a boss to treat fairly those who work under his direction is probably intensified in the case of marketing managers because of the nature of their work. This is because so much of their effectiveness and work satisfaction depends on imagination, enthusiasm, and the expression of personality, qualities which are apt to be dampened by the uncertainty and frustration that unfairness generates. This also emphasizes, in the marketing area, the obligation of the chief to provide leadership. Likewise it intensifies the importance of the common duty of executives to provide an atmosphere and environment in which the subordinate can develop and use his powers to the maximum. The marketing manager who fails in these relations with the people under him, an obligation which can not be adequately expressed in his contract of employment or position description, defaults in his ethical duty to them.

The Employees of the Firm

The marketing operation is the chief source from which the company derives the cash needed to pay the wages of its employees. If the marketing work of a firm is not well done, the jobs of all its employees are insecure. Some years ago the president of a firm set a deadline when he proposed to close out a segment of its business in which 250 people were employed, and which provided $5 million of annual sales on which the company was losing half a million. Aghast at the idea of 250 people losing their jobs the marketing manager and his department, by imaginative and energetic planning, developed and had in operation before the deadline a program which within two years turned the half-million loss into a $600,000 profit. The ethical obligation to make secure those jeopardized jobs had been there for at least four or five years: the marketing manager just had never risen to it until forced from above to face it.

Marketing Channel Members

The firm's relations with the wholesalers, distributors, retailers, and agents in its channels of distribution are the peculiar province of the marketing manager. This is also an area fraught with ethical implications, many of which center around the question: What is the proper basis on which to determine fair treatment of the several units in the marketing channel?

Should all be treated alike, regardless of the volume of the manufacturer's product they handle, the marketing functions they perform, and how well they perform them?

Or does the path of fairness lie in the direction of providing special rewards to those who market unusually large quantities of the producer's goods, or render more varied marketing services, or render them more efficiently?

The Robinson-Patman Act offers some guidance in resolving this major question. As we have seen, it limits variations in prices to savings achieved by reason of the quantities purchased and certain exigencies of competition. It requires that rewards and aids in sales promotion must "be available to all" on proportionately "equal terms" (whatever that means). But many promotional rewards and aids are of such a nature that they can be earned only by the large or well managed outlet. Should the marketing manager, in conformance with what might seem to be the spirit of the law, forgo the use of these promotional devices? Should he, as a matter of ethics, extend this principle of availability and proportionality to matters in the channel relationship not covered by the law?

His answers to these questions may be colored by a reasonable doubt as to whether this part of the law really expresses moral standards that are above challenge. In an attempt to protect small and inefficient retailers and wholesalers against abuses of the power which size or skill places in the hands of large or well managed retailers, those who made and interpreted the law have made it illegal for the manufacturer to reward the big retailers, and those who are more efficient and better managed, for the amount and quality of marketing service they are able to render. This violates an ethical principle for which we have Biblical authority, "The laborer is worthy of his hire."

Many firms have been guilty of such questionable ethical procedures as (a) using manufacturer's agents and franchise wholesalers and retailers to build demand, then depriving them of the fruits of their efforts by cancelling the relationship and marketing to all outlets, (b) selling direct, as house accounts, to the largest customers in an outlet's territory, (c) using the power resulting from the demand developed by heavy advertising to beat down dealers' gross profit margins.

Perhaps all of these are entirely ethical if the outlet clearly understands the terms of the deal when the manufacturer-outlet relationship is established. Complete candor, resulting in information and understanding on both sides, is certainly the beginning of fairness in the channel relationship, but not all of it. A retailer or a wholesaler may know that the terms on which he is asked to buy a product are unsatisfactory but he is forced to buy it anyway because the manufacturer's advertising has created such a demand for it that customer pressure compels him to stock it.

The marketing manager probably owes the members of his marketing channel the duty of exercising restraint in the use of the superior power he often has, and of offering them terms upon which they may handle his product at a reasonable profit. The line between doing this and coddling the inefficient members of the channel with too liberal terms is hard to draw. Perhaps the hard goods manufacturers (before the coming of the discount house) actually owed it to their retailers to reduce their obese margins and puncture the slothful complacency that made them the prey of a newer, more austere, aggressive retail outlet.

Auxiliary Service Organizations

The marketing manager has a debt of fair treatment to various auxiliary concerns from which he buys services, such as advertising agencies, marketing research firms, and warehouse companies. What constitutes ethical behavior in his relations with such firms varies according to the nature and service of each firm. It seems, therefore, hardly worthwhile to try to go into greater detail.

The Consumers

There has probably been more public discussion about this area of business ethics than any other. The chief reason for this is that from the standpoint of society as a whole the satisfaction of the consumer is the final justification of business activity, and how well business enterprise performs this function is a central core of interest to those critics who would be keepers of the business conscience. For the same reason management cannot for long afford to ignore it. The marketing manager does not bear full responsibility for his firm's ethical behavior toward the consumer: many decisions affecting it are not his to make; but his advice is usually listened to regarding them and it is his job to offer responsible advice on behalf of consumers. These obligations to the consumer center around several factors.

1. *The Product.* The marketer owes the consumer a product that will work; that is, one that will do the thing it is supposed to do when used not only as it should be used but as the typical consumer actually

will use it. This warranty is substantially implicit in any contract of sale. But the typical consumer is not litigious and the makers of many products could, with reasonable safety and considerable profit, ignore the warranty within discreet limits. In doing so they would rely on the consumer's ignorance, or "forgiving inertia," and thereby display a pretty shoddy standard of morals. This is apt to be an area in which the marketing manager may exercise influence but lacks the power of decision; the extent of his personal ethical obligation is debatable.

2. *The Truth*. The marketer is obligated to tell consumers the truth in his communications to them but there are several grey areas in the implementing of this obligation. Is he obliged to tell the *whole* truth? and, if so, to place equal emphasis on all parts of it? To what extent is he morally responsible for implications consumers may draw from what he says? Both state and federal laws prohibit misrepresentation in advertising and sales promotion material, but this legislation leaves much to the marketer's individual judgment of right and wrong.

3. *The Whole Truth*. If a product, when used carelessly (as the average consumer is apt to use it), is dangerous, the marketer's moral obligation seems clear. Not long ago a manufacturer put on the market a small hand-portable electric water heater so constructed that if the user touched the water being heated, or a metal container in which it was being heated, he was liable to receive a shock that might be lethal. A small tag was attached warning against this; but was this enough?

The law requires that containers of preparations with lethal chemical ingredients be conspicuously labelled "Poison." The manufacturer of the heater was at least obligated to supply equivalent warning to users of his product. Probably he was morally obligated not to put it on the market at all. The makers of necessary drugs, insecticides, and disinfectants can not avoid the use of dangerous ingredients, but hand electric water heaters can be insulated so as to be safe. If not, electrical manufacturers should allow people to get along without them.

Cases like these seem to be pretty clear-cut, but further application of the principle rapidly carries us into the land of "maybe yes—maybe no." For example, just what should the management of a tobacco company do about cigarettes and lung cancer: go out of the cigarette business, state in their advertising that a respectable body of medical opinion holds that the product causes lung cancer, advise smokers not to inhale, or limit their radio and TV advertising to programs scheduled after nine in the evening so as to avoid appealing to youngsters? There is evidence that some of the companies have not faced up to all the moral implications involved in this situation. Again, many people are killed in automobile accidents each year. Are the motor manufacturers and the oil companies morally obligated to include in each of their advertisements a warning against reckless driving?

4. *Emphasis.*   When a product has certain defects that may be frustrating, disappointing or unpleasant, many marketers extol its virtues and neglect to mention its faults, or, if they do so mention them in very muted language printed in small type. If a marketer is asked point-blank about the limitations of his product, there is no question about his ethical obligation to tell the truth. This is one of the reasons why manufacturers of industrial goods tend to stick to provable claims in all their selling work; they know they will be asked about the weaknesses of their products by people who can check the answers. But such queries are very scarce in the consumers' goods field.

It is not impossible that it may be good business (as well as sound ethics) for the marketer to inform consumers about the drawbacks of his product in tones at least as stentorian as those in which he describes its virtues. Selling can make little headway without winning the confidence of the customer in the seller; therefore the believability of his communications must be established. It may be that if he tells the bad along with the good, the good may be believed more readily. This is a very debatable area commercially as well as ethically, and the marketing manager is in the middle of it. It is definitely within his decision making province.

5.   *Implication.*   Some years ago the maker of a preparation advertised, in many well chosen words, that it would "remove dandruff." So will soap and water, but the average reader or listener interpreted this language to mean that the product would *prevent* or *cure* the annoyance. He told the exact truth but in such a way that, intentionally or unintentionally, he conveyed a false impression. This sort of thing is probably much more common than outright misrepresentation—and just as effective. Its moral justification is, to say the least, debatable. And the marketing manager is usually responsible for it.

6.   *Short-Filling.*   A common complaint is that the marketer is less than ethical in his packaging. This offense does not take the form of claiming a weight or cubical measurement of the contents not in the package but of using a package larger than needed, or of shaping or decorating the container so as to cause it to look bigger than it is. (The use of an oversize package is not always the fault of the marketing manager, however; its genesis may lie in the production or purchasing area which may be caught with a stock of containers—and machines built to fill them—when a cost-price squeeze forces a decrease in the amount to be

sold at a standard widely advertised price.) But the marketing manager cannot escape moral responsibility for advertising as a "new money-saving offer" a package containing 5 ounces and priced at 91 cents which formerly contained 6 ounces and sold for 99 cents. And he must live with a conscience "elastic" enough to condone selling his company's product in a package designed to cause the consumer's eye to deceive her into thinking it is bigger than it actually is.

7. *Honest Quality.* The common consumer attitude that "you get what you pay for" expresses a confidence in the marketer's price—quality honesty that, in turn, throws upon him an obligation to justify that confidence by maintaining a fair relationship between the quality of his product and the price he charges for it. This does not mean that he is obliged to ignore the forces of demand in setting his price or to entirely forgo the principle of charging what the traffic will bear, but it does suggest that if he prices his product at a premium (in comparison with others like it) he should see to it that it offers some quality differential sufficient to justify the premium. While the final decision in this area does not always rest on the marketing manager, he usually has something to do with it.

The Industry

To a large extent the marketing manager's ethical obligations to the industry to which his firm belongs consist of things that the marketing group must do if his company is to behave properly in its relation to its industry. For example, a manufacturer is under some obligation to help develop and improve the technology and product offering of his industry, and this involves research and pioneering in both processes and products. A firm can make money with modest risk by riding on the research and development coattails of other companies in the same industry that are more progress-minded, but the rest of the industry is apt to view its behavior with a rigidly restrained enthusiasm, based on the realization that if every firm in the industry confined its operations to capitalizing on improvements made by others there would shortly be no improvements, and in due course no industry.

The marketing manager's part in meeting this obligation consists in doing what he can to guide the research and development activities of his firm into channels that will be both useful and profitable, in building markets for new products, and in developing or helping develop and administer a pricing structure to support the cost of the necessary research and development work.

Most industries find it desirable to carry on certain cooperative activities such as the interchange of nonconfidential information, the improvement of techniques, and the development of codes of ethical behavior. Usually these are organized through the trade association; sometimes they are conducted informally. Here again the marketing manager's ethical obligation consists in contributing in his functional area and in conforming to the commonly accepted patterns of behavior. The degree and nature of his participation is usually determined by the attitude of top management.

Competitors

It might be assumed that since competition is a species of commercial warfare and since we have pretty reliable authority that "all's fair in love and war," one competitor owes no ethical obligations to another. But in actual practice rules of the game are *not* inconsistent with the deadliest competition. Even the most ruthless professional gunman of the old west was outside the pale if he shot a man in the back or perforated an unarmed man. Rules of ethical behavior are apt to be more than usually rigid when life-and-death issues are at stake.

It follows that among any group of business rivals there are certain things that are "not to be done." These vary from trade to trade, but most of them have to do with matters of marketing. It behooves the marketing manager, therefore, to know what they are and to conform. In this respect he has the ethical standing of his firm among its fellows in his keeping.

The members of some trades have tried to formalize these general understandings into codes of ethics, often developed under the leadership of the trade association. Some of these codes represent an honest effort to make the common conscience of the group the guide of its every member. Others are mere pious professions of faith, so general in their terms or so idealistic that no one pays any attention to them. Many of the activities dealt with in these codes lie in the marketing area, and the marketing manager almost certainly owes his industry the obligation of trying to make its code as realistic and meaningful as possible and of doing all in his power to cause his firm to support the code and comply with its marketing provisions.

Probably the best known attempt to apply ethics in business—and the one nearest the consumer—is the Better Business Bureau, which is a cooperative project of retailers and local advertising media to police the honesty of merchants and advertisers. The bureau necessarily operates on a local basis. Most large cities in the country have such bureaus that are loosely tied together in an association, which results in some degree of uniformity in standards throughout the country.

Since, through its tie-up with the advertising media of a city, the Better Business Bureau is in a position to withhold advertising services from offending merchants, it has considerable power to enforce its standards. And although each bureau is financed by the contributions of local merchants and media, contributors in most communities have learned to keep hands off the detailed operations of the bureau, and to confine their participation to financing and setting general policies and standards.

The marketing manager of a manufacturing firm certainly owes the retailer members of his distribution channel every encouragement in their participation in this project. He also should feel obligated to see to it that his marketing programs—and especially all the advertising copy and promotion material his firm supplies his retail outlets conform to the ethical standards of the bureaus.

In addition to this impersonal responsibility the marketing manager is apt to owe certain generally recognized obligations to his opposite numbers in competing firms. For example, if an official of a competitor asks about the qualifications and performance of a former sales employee, the marketing manager usually has the option of telling the truth as he sees it or of refusing to answer—which in itself is apt to be vastly enlightening to the inquirer. In some trades it is regarded as proper to exchange price information except with respect to specific bids. Personal ethics usually require that the marketing manager keep competition at the company level and not seek to injure his opposite number in a rival firm—except insofar as the gaining of a competitive advantage in and of itself undermines the latter's position.

The Social and Economic Order

In spite of the incursions of the welfare state our social structure is still built around the central concept of individualism and the paramount importance of the freedom of the individual and of his self-development, and our economic order may be described as one of regulated free enterprise and free competition. This fact explains the importance of several things we have emphasized over and over in this book; for example: the dominant role of the customer, his freedom of choice in all marketing planning and action, and the extent to which the marketing manager must depend on persuasion and leadership rather than on orders and penalties to accomplish his objectives.

To this part of the American system the business manager owes an obligation that extends far beyond that expressed in the law or in his employment contract. On his shoulders rests the responsibility of making the economic part of this system work and accomplish its objectives, one of the most important of which is to improve our productive and distributive technology so that our economy may grow and, through its growth, may broaden and enrich the pattern of satisfactions enjoyed by all our people.

Much has been said and written to emphasize the role of the government in achieving the objective of economic growth, but the effectiveness of governmental action in this area has yet to be proved. It is reasonably certain that the soundest and most enduring growth of our economy takes place as the result of improvements in processes and technology and the development of new products in response to competitive pressures and expressed or latent consumer demand.

The marketing manager is in the middle of this situation. Every scandal that breaks in the marketplace and every justifiable criticism, public or private, of marketing activity undermines public confidence in the free enterprise system. Every new product or marketing innovation opportunity that is ignored (or fumbled in the execution) subtracts from the healthful growth of the gross national product. These things are all within the ethical province of the marketing manager.

The Government

It is the function of the government, insofar as possible, to codify and administer the generally accepted rules of business conduct. A large segment of business legislation deals with marketing activities. We have described these laws at appropriate points throughout the book.

It might seem that when the law has spoken with respect to any business activity it has defined the marketing manager's ethical obligations in the matter. He needs but to obey the law. But this is an over-simplification. Any law has a purpose or an objective which is, or reflects, its spirit. It is also drafted in statutory language which often does not adequately express the spirit. The manager's obligation clearly embraces obedience to the letter of the law, but does it extend beyond that to conformance with the spirit? If so, how can he be sure what the spirit really is?

Even obedience to the letter of the law is not always easy. Most of the statutes regulating marketing had to be drawn in very general terms in order to cover the welter of heterogeneous relationships and activities that make up any marketing practice. For example, the Sherman Act, passed in 1890, prohibits "contracts, combinations, or conspiracies in restraint of trade." To this day the courts are still engaged in interpreting what these words mean in specific situations.

The Department of Justice can usually be depended on to seek to enforce the most inclusive interpretation. Should the business manager accept this, and thereby perhaps subject himself and his fellows to restrictions not intended by those who passed the law? Or should he (at a cost of perhaps a quarter or half a million dollars to his company) fight a case through to the Supreme Court to establish the rights of his own firm and those of other firms in the same situation? Is he ethically justfied in spending stockholders' money in this way? The marketing manager rarely, if ever, has this decision to make, but he is apt to be in on the preliminaries and in the middle of the case if it develops.

The marketing manager is apt to be involved in whatever lobbying activities his firm conducts because many of the ends the lobbyist seeks arise from marketing activities or have marketing implications. In some firms he has charge of lobbying activities, more generally—and in some cases more accurately—called "government relations."

The term lobbying has a sinister implication, and in some cases this is justified. Certainly an industry and its individual firms have a right to seek to influence pending legislation by presenting their side of the case and by offering information and opinions regarding it. The same is true with respect to the establishment and interpretation of specific regulations and procedures under general legislation. This usually involves personal contact with the people in the regulatory body. In some cases, if this is to be effective, it must be venal. When this is true it may pose a serious ethical question for the marketing manager.

For example, if in order to market and deliver materials or equipment to be installed in a building the marketer has to "grease the palms" of the bribe-hungry petty inspectors of a venal city administration, should he swallow his conscience and his pride and submit to their extortions; allow their demands to exclude him from the market they control; or try to "fight the system"? Certainly the latter is most admirable, but it is apt to be hopeless for the individual firm because, to win, it must oust the venal administration that fosters "chiseling" inspectors. If all competing suppliers band together to fight the system, they take the risk of running afoul of the antitrust laws.

On the other hand, anyone who has had experience in a regulatory body knows that an honest Washington lobbyist can often be most effective and influential by offering the regulator information he does not have ready access to and by explaining and clarifying trade conditions and practices. He thus performs not only an honest but a necessary function. This whole matter of government relations is one in which it is not easy to distinguish rigidly between what is right and what is wrong. It is also an area in which the marketing manager is almost certain to be involved to some extent.

This brief outline of the nature of the obligations the marketing manager owes to each group or institution that has a moral claim on him should serve to emphasize the complexity of the ethical problems he must face. This arises from the conflicting claims to right and privilege resulting from the opposing interests of the various parties with whom the marketing manager must have contact in the course of his work. He must constantly balance his obligation to one against his duty to another.

ACTIVITIES CREATING ETHICAL PROBLEMS

Another way to look at the marketing manager's ethical problems is from the standpoint of the activities that generate them. In our previous discussion we have dealt with some of these activities that are closely associated with what might be called particular "moral claimants." Perhaps it might be worthwhile to note a number of activities that generate ethical problems which do not apply to specific institutions or groups of people.

Pricing

This is an activity that is very fertile in the production of moral dilemmas. We have already examined some of them; several others seem to deserve our attention.

Relation of Price to Cost. Most of these dilemmas center around the concept that there should be some sort of normal relation between price and cost. This may have its genesis in the economist's notion of "normal price," the idea that over the long run the price of an article tends to approach its true cost. This true cost includes not only the conventional accounting costs but a profit sufficient to call forth enough supply to satisfy the demand. The Tudor regulations of prices suggest that its origin goes back even farther than that and the attitudes expressed recently by the governmental officials conducting the Kefauver investigations show that it is still very much alive.

What the Traffic Will Bear. These very words carry the implication of unethical practice. Put in economic terms the expression means that when a seller has an advantage because demand is strong and supply is scarce, he prices on the basis of demand instead of cost. If we accept the moral validity of the basic economic principle that price is a function of the relationship between supply and demand, we may expect that when demand is strong and supply is weak, price will be high, and when the reverse is true price will be low. And we must accept the moral validity of this concept so long as we depend on the forces of the market to provide the balance wheel of our economy. But still the expression "what the traffic will bear" sounds bad, and the manager must wrestle with the ethical question: How far am I really justified in allowing the principle to guide me in my pricing work?

Cost Advantage. When a firm has a cost advantage, this dilemma becomes especially acute. In such a case, is management justified in pushing price competition to the point of eliminating high-cost competitors? As a matter of fact, since our economy is officially a competitive one, can the manager ethically adopt any other course? The problem is complicated by the fact that there is both in business and among the general public at least a rudimentary ethic of "live and let live."

Line Pricing. The multi-product firm meets this problem head on in adjusting the prices of the several articles in its product mix. If it prices all its products to economic cost, some of them are very likely to return no profit, or even a loss, since the market will not permit recouping complete cost, and those on which it has a cost advantage will contribute nothing to compensate for this drain. If the firm drops the noncontributing products it thereby reduces the supply of them and buyers must pay more for them. Just where does the ethical obligation of the firm lie?

Skimming Pricing. This problem is very acute for a firm in a growth industry with a rapidly improving technology and a growing product line. On many new products it has a temporary market advantage which approaches monopoly. On the other hand, many of its products are partially obsolescent and their profit margins low. Growth and technological improvement require heavy research and development expenditures that, because of the risk involved, can be safely financed only out of a high profit rate.

These characteristics mean that if the manager fails to price on the principle of what the traffic will bear, his company has no funds for research and development and he violates his ethical obligation to do his part to bring about improvement. If he prices the products on which he has an advantage so as to provide funds for research and development, he will be guilty of setting a spread between cost and price that may be fantastic. No one has yet worked out a code of behavior that satisfies the nebulous, confused, and uncertain ethical notions of the politicians and the idealists and that still conforms to the realities of the needs of the situation.

Advertising and Selling

This activity gives rise to more public criticism than any other phase of marketing. This is probably due not only to the fact that it is the most conspicuous and widely observed function in marketing but because it touches more closely and at more points the common ideas of what is right and wrong than does any other marketing activity. Several aspects of this ethical conflict seem worth our examination.

Specific Attacks. Most marketing managers join the general public in the feeling that to attack competitors or their products by name is not the thing to do. There is some doubt about the propriety of attacks on types of products without mention of specific names, as have occurred recently in the pain reliever preparation trade. Another fuzzy area is illustrated by the dilemma of the salesman whose customer asks a question about the behavior of a competitor or the performance of a competitor's product. It seems pretty clear that the salesman should not initiate such discussions, but to what extent should he participate in them?

This "reticence ethic" subtracts somewhat from the performance of the function basic to both advertising and salesmanship, that of conveying information to the customer and the consumer. But the practice of specific comparisons, even though initially confined to facts, is almost certain to degenerate quickly into irresponsible name-calling and backbiting and become intolerable to all parties. To mention only one difficulty, different competitors may have conflicting ideas as to just what the facts are and how much emphasis they deserve.

Emphasis on Nonessentials. In the form in which Galbraith sets it in his *Affluent Society,* this is a crime against mankind in that it involves the wastage of our scarce and irreplaceable resources in making and marketing things that are of trifling importance. There seems little room to doubt that those who make the decisions under a system of free enterprise owe that system the obligation of managing business activity in such a way as to promote the general welfare rather than to impair it. This is easier said than implemented in specific cases.

Many of the critics seem to find it not difficult to decide what products and services are socially worth making and marketing and which represent waste. Who should make this decision: the critics, the politicians, or the people—through their market acceptance or rejection of a series or pattern of tentative decisions made initially by individual business managers? Certain it is that if free enterprise, working through myriads of individual decisions in the factory and the market place, fails to make an allocation of resources that conforms to the general concept of the public benefit, the politicians, probably advised by the critics, will take it over. This suggests the nature of the moral obligation business management owes the system of free enterprise in this matter. The obligation is primarily that of top management but the marketing manager shares in it because he controls the firm's contact points with the market.

Even though a firm uses resources to produce a product that is indubitably in the public interest, is the marketing manager justified in emphasizing its trivial, nonessential features in advertising and selling it? Or has our technology and ethics of production advanced to such a point that the buyer can count on any manufacturer's output to deliver the essential services and basic satisfactions of the product, and can distinguish between the offerings of rival suppliers only on the basis of relatively less essential features? If so, how far is it ethically justifiable for management to go in using scarce resources to create such features, and to what extent is it morally acceptable for the marketing manager to emphasize them? At least part of this problem lies in the lap of the marketing manager.

Emotional Appeals. The theory of free enterprise presumes that the buyer will make his product choices on the basis of a somewhat cold-blooded analysis and appraisal of the relative satisfactions offered by the goods of different suppliers. To what extent is the marketing manager ethically justified in seeking to get the customer to substitute emotional motives for this sort of analysis?

The answer to this question depends, to some degree at least, on the nature and sources of consumer satisfaction. Some satisfactions, such as warmth, allaying hunger pangs, and slaking thirst, are almost entirely physical. Others are predominantly psychological; their sources lie in the emotions. If the satisfactions flowing from supplying the physical wants, such as hunger, thirst, or the desire for warmth, are better or on a higher moral plane than those associated with emotional drives, it is not a long step to the conclusion that selling appeals based on the physical uses of products are entirely ethical and that appeals to the consumer's emotions are at best of doubtful morality. But it would be a bold moralist who would contend that physical satisfactions are good and emotional satisfactions are bad.

Perhaps the moral problem involved here is basically one of emphasis: when the marketer overemphasizes emotional appeals, he violates ethical standards; when he uses them with proper restraint, his conduct remains within such standards. Perhaps it may be a matter of the kind of emotions he appeals to: an appeal based on love, kindness, or family affection may be ethical; one directed to such emotions as hate, pride, or greed may be reprehensible. On the other hand, it has been urged that the prostituting of the lovelier human emotions to the ends of commerce is unforgivable. Just what constitutes ethical behavior in this area remains pretty much a matter of debate. The conscientious marketing manager will find little in the way of a commonly accepted code of behavior to guide him.

Good Taste. This is closely akin to the problem of emotional appeal. A man probably owes his fellows the duty of avoiding behavior that offends their collective sense of propriety and good taste. This probably attains the status of an ethical obligation, or something very near to it, but for this kind of problem the marketing manager can get little guidance from the codes propounded by the Emily Posts and the Amy Vanderbilts. Perhaps, though, if in his dealings with matters of good taste he follows the basic concept of *nobless oblige* that underlies their codes of polite behavior, he will not be far afield. The fact remains, however, that in this area the marketing manager is very much on his own.

We have outlined most of the general areas in which the marketing manager is likely to meet problems of ethics. In only a few of them have we been able to suggest specific patterns of behavior that are clearly and indisputably ethical. Too many of his problems arise in the gray area where his moral obligations to different groups of people conflict or where no generally accepted canons of behavior exist.

Perhaps the surest guide the writers of books like this can offer young men and women who may become marketing managers is Polonius' advice to Laertes, his son: "To thine own self be true." A man can cut his ties to everyone else on earth, but he *must* live with himself. He can be nothing but supremely unhappy if, in this one person with whom he must abide until the end, he sees a man for whose motives and conduct he has no respect. Position and money are poor substitutes for the consciousness of having tried to do the right as one sees the right.

APPENDIX A

Marketing Definitions*

A

Accessories; see Equipment.

Advertising. Any paid form of nonpersonal presentation and promotion of ideas, goods, or services by an identified sponsor. It involves the use of such media as the following: *magazine and newspaper space; motion pictures; outdoor (posters, signs, skywriting, etc.); direct mail; novelties (calendar, blotters, etc.); radio and television; cards (car, bus, etc.); catalogs; directories and references; programs and menus, and circulars.*

This list is intended to be illustrative, not inclusive.

> *Comment.* Advertising is generally but not necessarily carried on through mass media. While the postal system is not technically considered a "paid" medium, material distributed by mail is definitely a form of presentation that is paid for by the sponsor. For kindred activities see Publicity, and Sales promotion.

Advertising research; see Marketing research.

Agent. A business unit which negotiates purchases or sales or both but does not take title to the goods in which it deals.

> *Comment.* The agent usually performs fewer marketing functions than does the merchant. He commonly receives his remuneration in the form of a commission or fee. He usually does not represent both buyer and seller in the same transaction. Examples are: broker, commission merchant, manufacturers agent, selling agent, and resident buyer.
>
> The Committee recommends that the term functional middleman no longer be applied to this type of agent. It is hardly logical or consistent in view of the fact that he performs fewer marketing functions than other middlemen.

Assembling. The activities involved in concentrating supplies or assortments of goods or services to facilitate sale or purchase.

> *Comment.* The concentration involved here may affect a quantity of like goods or a variety of goods. It includes the gathering of adequate and representative stocks by wholesalers and retailers.

---

*Reprinted from *Marketing Definitions: A Glossary of Marketing Terms,* Committee on Definitions, (Chicago: American Marketing Association, 1960) by permission of the American Marketing Association.

Automatic selling. The retail sale of goods or services through currency-operated machines activated by the ultimate-consumer buyer.

> *Comment.* Most, if not all, machines now used in automatic selling are coin-operated. There are reports, however, of promising experiments with such devices that may be activated by paper currency; machines that provide change for a dollar bill are already on the market.

Auxiliary equipment; see Equipment.

B

Branch house (manufacturer's). An establishment maintained by a manufacturer, detached from the headquarters establishment and used primarily for the purpose of stocking, selling, delivering, and servicing his product.

Branch office (manufacturer's). An establishment maintained by a manufacturer, detached from the headquarters establishment and used for the purpose of selling his products or providing service.

> *Comment.* The characteristic of the branch house that distinguishes it from the branch office is the fact that it is used in the physical storage, handling, and delivery of merchandise. Otherwise the two are identical.

Branch store. A subsidiary retailing business owned and operated at a separate location by an established store.

Brand. A name, term, sign, symbol, or design, or a combination of them which is intended to identify the goods or services of one seller or group of sellers and to differentiate them from those of competitors.

> *Comment.* A brand may include a brand name, a trademark, or both. The term brand is sufficiently comprehensive to include practically all means of identification except perhaps the package and the shape of the product. All brand names and all trademarks are brands or parts of brands but not all brands are either brand names or trademarks. Brand is the inclusive general term. The others are more particularized. See also National Brand and Private Brands.

Brand Manager; see Product Management.

Brand Name. A brand or part of a brand consisting of a word, letter, group of words or letters comprising a name which is intended to identify the goods or services of a seller or a group of sellers and to differentiate them from those of competitors.

> *Comment.* The brand name is that part of a brand which can be vocalized—the utterable.

Broker. An agent who does not have direct physical control of the goods in which he deals but represents either buyer or seller in negotiating purchases or sales for his principal.

> *Comment.* The broker's powers as to prices and terms of sale are usually limited by his principal. The term is often loosely used in a generic sense to include such specific business units as free-lance brokers, manufacturer's agents, selling agents, and purchasing agents.

Buying Power; see Purchasing Power.

C

Canvasser; see House-to-House Salesman.

Cash and Carry Wholesaler; see Wholesaler.

Chain Store, Chain Store System. A group of retail stores of essentially the same type, centrally owned and with some degree of centralized control of operation. The term "chain store" may also refer to a single store as a unit of such a group.

> *Comment.* According to the dictionary, two may apparently be construed to constitute a "group."

Channel of distribution. The structure of intracompany organization units and extracompany agents and dealers, wholesale and retail, through which a commodity, product, or service is marketed.

> *Comment.* This definition was designed to be broad enough to include (a) both a firm's internal marketing organization units and the outside business units it uses in its marketing work, and (b) both the channel structure of the individual firm and the entire complex available to all firms.

Commercial auction. An agent business unit which effects the sale of goods through an auctioneer who, under specified rules, solicits bids or offers from buyers and has power to accept the highest bids of responsible bidders and thereby consummates the sale.

> *Comment.* The auctioneer usually but not always is a paid employee of an auction company which is in the business of conducting auctions.

Commission house. (sometimes called Commission merchant). An agent who usually exercises physical control over and negotiates the sale of the goods he handles. The commission house usually enjoys broader powers as to prices, methods, and terms of sale than does the broker, although it must obey instructions issued by the principal. It generally arranges delivery, extends necessary credit, collects, deducts its fees, and remits the balance to the principal.

> *Comment.* Most of those who have defined the commission house state that it has possession of the goods it handles. In its strict meaning the word "possession" connotes to some extent the idea of ownership; in its legal meaning it involves a degree of control somewhat beyond that usually enjoyed by the commission merchant. Therefore, the phrase "physical control" was used instead. The fact that many commission houses are not typical in their operations does not subtract from their status as commission houses.

Commissary store; see Industrial store.

Commodity exchange. An organization, usually owned by the member-traders, which provides facilities for bringing together buyers and sellers of specified commodities, or their agents, for promoting trades, either spot or futures, or both, in these commodities.

> *Comment.* Agricultural products or their intermediately processed derivatives are the commodities most often traded on such exchanges. Some sort of organization for clearing future contracts usually operates as an adjunct to or an arm of a commodity exchange.

Company store; see Industrial store.

Consumer research; see Marketing research.

Consumers' cooperative.   A retail business owned and operated by ultimate consumers to purchase and distribute goods and services primarily to the membership; sometimes called purchasing cooperatives.

> *Comment.* The Consumers' Cooperative is a type of cooperative marketing institution. Through federation, retail units frequently acquire wholesaling and manufacturing institutions. The definition confines the use of the term to the cooperative purchasing activities of ultimate consumers and does not embrace collective buying by business establishments or institutions.

Consumers' goods.   Goods destined for use by ultimate consumers or households, and in such form that they can be used without commercial processing.

> *Comment.* Certain articles, for example, typewriters, may be either consumers' goods or industrial goods, depending upon whether they are destined for use by the ultimate consumer or household, or by an industrial, business, or institutional user.

Convenience goods.   Those consumers' goods which the customer usually purchases frequently, immediately, and with the minimum of effort in comparison and buying. Examples of merchandise customarily bought as convenience goods are tobacco products, soap, newspapers, magazines, chewing gum, small packaged confections, and many food products.

> *Comment.* These articles are usually of small unit value and are bought in small quantities at any one time, although when a number of them are bought together, as in a supermarket, the combined purchase may assume sizeable proportions in both bulk and value. The convenience involved may be in terms of nearness to the buyer's home, easy accessibility to some means of transport, or close proximity to places where people go during the day or evening, for example, downtown to work.

Cooperative marketing.   The process by which independent producers, wholesalers, retailers, consumers, or combinations of them act collectively in buying or selling, or both.

D

Dealer.   A firm that buys and resells merchandise at either retail or wholesale.

> *Comment.* The term is naturally ambiguous. For clarity, it should be used with a qualifying adjective, such as "retail" or "wholesale."

Department store.   A large retailing business unit which handles a wide variety of shopping and specialty goods, including women's ready-to-wear and accessories, men's and boys' wear, piece goods, small wares and home furnishings, and which is organized into separate departments for purposes of promotion, service and control. Examples of very large department stores are Macy's, New York; J. L. Hudson Co., Detroit; Marshall Field & Co., Chicago; and Famous, Barr of St. Louis. Two well-known smaller ones are Bresee's of Oneonta, New York, and A. B. Wycoff of Stoudsburg, Penn.

> *Comment.* Many department stores have become units of chains, commonly called "ownership groups," since each store retains its local identity, even though centrally owned. The definition above stresses three elements: large size, wide variety of clothing and home furnishings, and departmentization. Size is not spelled out in terms of

either sales volume or number of employees since the concept keeps changing upwards. Most department stores in 1960 had sales in excess of $1 million.

Direct selling. The process whereby the firm responsible for production sells to the user, ultimate consumer, or retailer without intervening middlemen. The Committee recommends that when this term is used it be so qualified as to indicate clearly the precise meaning intended (direct to retailer, direct to user, direct to ultimate consumer, etc.).

> *Comment.* The phrase "firm responsible for production" is substituted for "producer" in the old definition so as to include the firm that contracts out some or all of the processes of making the goods it sells direct; for example, the drug house that has its vitamin pills tableted by a contractor specializing in such work.

Discount house. A retailing business unit featuring consumer durable items, competing on a basis of price appeal, and operating on a relatively low markup and with a minimum of customer service.

Discretionary fund. Discretionary income, enlarged by the amount of new credit extensions, which also may be deemed spendable as a result of consumer decision relatively free of prior commitment or pressure of need.

> *Comment.* These are the definitions of the National Industrial Conference Board, which publishes a quarterly Discretionary Income Index Series: Discretionary income is calculated by deducting from disposable personal income (*a*) a computed historical level of outlays for food and clothing; (*b*) all outlays for medical services, utilities, and public transportation; (*c*) payment of fixed commitments such as rent, home owner taxes, net insurance payments, and installment debt; (*d*) homeowner taxes; and (*e*) imputed income and income in kind.

Discretionary income. That portion of personal income, in excess of the amount necessary to maintain a defined or historical standard of living and which may be saved with no immediate impairment of living standards, or which may be, as a result of consumer decision, relatively free of prior commitment or pressure of need.

Disposable income. Personal income remaining after the deduction of taxes on personal income and compulsory payment, such as social security levies.

> *Comment.* This is substantially the Department of Commerce concept.

Distribution. The Committee recommends that the term "distribution" be used as synonymous with "marketing."

> *Comment.* "Distribution" is also sometimes used to refer to the extent of market coverage. In using this term marketing men should clearly distinguish it from the sense in which it is employed in economic theory, that is, the process of dividing the fund of value produced by industry among the several factors engaged in economic production. For these reasons marketing men may be wise to use the term sparingly.

Distribution cost analysis; see Marketing cost analysis.

Distributor. In its general usage this term is synonymous with "wholesaler."

> *Comment.* In some trades and by many firms it is used to designate an outlet having some sort of preferential relationship with the manufacturer. This meaning is not so widely used or so standardized as to justify inclusion in the definition. The term is sometimes used to designate a manufacturer's agent or a sales representative in the employ of a manufacturer.

Drop shipment wholesaler; see Wholesaler.

E

Equipment. Those industrial goods that do not become part of the physical product and which are exhausted only after repeated use, such as machinery, installed equipment and accessories, or auxiliary equipment. *Installed equipment* includes such items as boilers, linotype machines, power lathes, bank vaults. *Accessories* include such items as gauges, meters, and control devices. *Auxiliary equipment* includes such items as trucks, typewriters, filing cases, and industrial hoists.

Exclusive outlet selling. That form of selective selling whereby sales of an article, or service, or brand of an article to any one type of buyer are confined to one retailer or wholesaler in each area, usually on a contractual basis.

> *Comment.* This definition does not include the practice of designating two or more wholesalers or retailers in an area as selected outlets. While this practice is a form of selective selling, it is not exclusive outlet selling. The term does not apply to the reverse contractual relationship in which a dealer must buy exclusively from a supplier.

F

Fabricating materials. Industrial goods which become a part of the finished product, and which have undergone processing beyond that required for raw materials—but not as much as finished parts.

> *Comment.* Examples are plastic molding compounds.

Facilitating agencies in marketing. Those agencies which perform or assist in the performance of one or a number of the marketing functions, but which neither take title to goods nor negotiate purchases or sales. Common types are banks, railroads, storage warehouses, commodity exchanges, stock yards, insurance companies, graders and inspectors, advertising agencies, firms engaged in marketing research, cattle loan companies, furniture marts, and packers and shippers.

Factor. (1) A specialized financial institution engaged in factoring accounts receivable and lending on the security of inventory. (2) A type of commission house which often advances funds to the consigner identified chiefly with the raw cotton and naval stores trades.

> *Comment.* The type of factor described in (1) above operates extensively in the textile fields but is expanding into other fields.

Factoring. A specialized financial function whereby producers, wholesalers, and retailers sell their accounts receivable to financial institutions, including factors and banks, often on a nonrecourse basis.

> *Comment.* Commercial banks, as well as factors and finance companies, engage in this activity.

Fair trade. Retail resale price maintenance imposed by suppliers of branded goods under authorization of state and federal laws.

> *Comment.* This is a special usage of the term promulgated by the advocates of resale price maintenance and bears no relation to the fair practices concept of the Federal Trade Commission; nor is it the antithesis of unfair trading outlawed by the antitrust laws.

G

General store. A small retailing business unit, not departmentized, usually located in a rural community, and primarily engaged in selling a general assortment of merchandise of which the most important line is food. The more important subsidiary lines are notions, apparel, farm supplies, and gasoline. These stores are often known as "country general stores."

> *Comment.* This is, roughly, the Bureau of the Census usage.

Grading. Assigning predetermined standards of quality classifications to individual units or lots of a commodity.

> *Comment.* This process of assignment may be carried on by sorting. This term is often defined so as to include the work of setting up classes or grades. This work is really a part of standardization.

H

House-to-house salesman. A salesman who is primarily engaged in making sales direct to ultimate consumers in their homes.

> *Comment.* The term "canvasser" is often employed as synonymous with house-to-house salesman. Due to its extensive use in fields other than marketing this usage is not recommended.

I

Independent store. A retailing business unit which is controlled by its own individual ownership or management rather than from without, except insofar as its management is limited by voluntary group arrangements.

> *Comment.* This definition includes a member of a voluntary group organization. It is recognized that the voluntary group possesses many of the characteristics and presents many of the same problems as the chain store system. In the final analysis, however, the members of the voluntary groups are independent stores, cooperating, perhaps temporarily, in the accomplishment of certain marketing purposes. Their collective action is entirely voluntary and the retailers engaging in it consider themselves to be independent.

Industrial goods. Goods which are destined to be sold primarily for use in producing other goods or rendering services, as contrasted with goods destined to be sold primarily to the ultimate consumer. They include equipment (installed and accessory), component parts, maintenance, repair and operating supplies, raw and fabricating materials.

> *Comment.* The distinguishing characteristics of these goods is the purpose for which they are primarily destined to be used, in carrying on business or industrial activities rather than for consumption by individual ultimate consumers or resale to them. The category also includes merchandise destined for use in carrying on various types of institutional enterprises. Relatively few goods are exclusively industrial goods. The same article may under one set of circumstances be an industrial good, and under other conditions a consumers' good.

Industrial store. A retail store owned and operated by a company or governmental unit to sell primarily to its employees. Nongovernmental establishments of this type are often referred to as "company stores" or "commissary stores." In certain trades the term "company store" is applied to a store through which a firm sells its own products, often together with those of other manufacturers, to the consumer market.

Comment. Many of these establishments are not operated for profit. The matter of control over and responsibility for these stores, rather than the motive for their operation, constitutes their distinguishing characteristic.

Installed equipment; see Equipment.

J

Jobber. This term is widely used as a synonym of "wholesaler" or "distributor."

Comment. The term is sometimes used in certain trades and localities to designate special types of wholesalers. This usage is especially common in the distribution of agricultural products. The characteristics of the wholesalers so designated vary from trade to trade and from locality to locality. Most of the schedules submitted to the Bureau of the Census by the members of the wholesale trades show no clear line of demarcation between those who call themselves jobbers and those who prefer to be known as wholesalers. Therefore it does not seem wise to attempt to set up any general basis of distinction between the terms in those few trades or markets in which one exists. There are scattered examples of special, distinctive usage of the term "jobber." The precise nature of such usage must be sought in each trade or area in which it is employed.

L

Limited function wholesaler; see Wholesaler.

Loss leader. A product of known or accepted quality priced at a loss (or no profit) for the purpose of attracting patronage to a store.

Comment. This term is peculiar to the retail trade; elsewhere the same item is called a "leader" or a "special."

M

Mail order house (retail). A retailing business that receives its orders primarily by mail or telephone, and generally offers its goods and services for sale from a catalogue or other printed material.

Comment. Other types of retail stores often conduct a mail order business, usually through departments set up for that purpose, although this fact does not make them mail order houses. On the other hand, some firms that originally confined themselves to the mail order business now also operate chain store systems. For example, Sears, Roebuck and Company and Montgomery Ward and Company are both mail order houses and chain store systems.

Mail order wholesaler; see Wholesaler.

Manufacturer's agent. An agent who generally operates on an extended contractual basis; often sells within an exclusive territory; handles noncompeting but related lines of goods; and possesses limited authority with regard to prices and terms of sale. He may be authorized to sell a definite portion of his principal's output.

Comment. The manufacturer's agent has often been defined as a species of broker. In the majority of cases this seems to be substantially accurate. It is probably more accurate in seeking to define the entire group not to classify them as a specialized type of broker but to regard them as a special variety of agent since many of them carry stocks. The term "manufacturer's representative" is sometimes applied to this agent. Since this term is also used to designate a salesman in the employ of a manufacturer, its use as a synonym for "manufacturer's agent" is discouraged.

Manufacturer's store. A retail store owned and operated by a manufacturer, sometimes as an outlet for his goods, sometimes primarily for experimental or publicity purposes.

Market. (1) The aggregate of forces or conditions within which buyers and sellers make decisions that result in the transfer of goods and services. (2) The aggregate demand of the potential buyers of a commodity or service.

> *Comment.* The businessman often uses the term to mean an opportunity to sell his goods. He also often attaches to it a connotation of a geographical area, such as the "New England market," or of a customer group, such as the "college market" or the "agricultural market." Retailers often use the term to mean the aggregate group of suppliers from whom a buyer purchases.

Market analysis. A subdivision of marketing research which involves the measurement of the extent of a market and the determination of its characteristics.

> *Comment.* See also *Marketing research.* The activity described above consists essentially of exploring and evaluating the marketing possibilities of the aggregates described in (2) of the definition of Market.

Market potential (also Market, or Total market). A calculation of maximum possible sales opportunities for all sellers of a good or service during a stated period.

Market share (or Sales potential). The ratio of a company's sales to the total industry sales, on either an actual or potential basis.

> *Comment.* This term is often used to designate the part of total industry sales a company hopes or expects to get. Since this concept usually has in it a considerable element of "blue sky," this usage is not encouraged.

Marketing. The performance of business activities that direct the flow of goods and services from producer to consumer or user.

> *Comment.* The task of defining Marketing may be approached from at least three points of view.
> 1. The *legalistic,* of which the following is a good example: "Marketing includes all activities having to do with effecting changes in the ownership and possession of goods and services." It seems of doubtful desirability to adopt a definition which throws so much emphasis upon the legal phases of what is essentially a commercial subject.
> 2. The *economic,* examples of which are: "That part of economics which deals with the creation of time, place, and possession utilities," and "That phase of business activity through which human wants are satisfied by the exchange of goods and services for some valuable consideration." Such definitions are apt to assume somewhat more understanding of economic concepts than are ordinarily found in the marketplace.
> 3. The *factual or descriptive,* of which the definition suggested by the Committee is an example. This type of definition merely seeks to describe its subject in terms likely to be understood by both professional economists and businessmen without reference to legal or economic implications. This definition seeks to include such facilitating activities as marketing research, transportation, certain aspects of product and package planning, and the use of credit as a means of influencing patronage.

Marketing budget. A statement of the planned dollar sales and planned marketing costs for a specified future period.

> *Comment.* The use of this term is sometimes confined to an estimate of future

sales. This does not conform to the general use of the term "budget," which includes schedules of both receipts and expenditures. If the marketing budget is to be used as a device to facilitate marketing control and management, it should include the probable cost of getting the estimated volume of sales. The failure to allow proper weight to this item in their calculations is one of the most consistently persistent and fatal mistakes made by American business concerns. It has led to much of the striving after unprofitable volume that has been so costly.

A firm may prepare a marketing budget for each brand or product, or for a group of brands or products it sells, or for each group of customers to whom it markets. See also *Sales budget.*

Marketing cooperative; see Producers' cooperative marketing.

Marketing cost accounting.   The branch of cost accounting which involves the allocation of marketing costs according to customers, marketing units, products, territories, or marketing activities.

Marketing cost analysis.   The study and evaluation of the relative profitability or costs of different marketing operations in terms of customers, marketing units, commodities, territories, or marketing activities.

> *Comment.*   Marketing cost accounting is one of the tools used in marketing cost analysis.

Marketing function.   A major specialized activity or group of related activities performed in marketing.

> *Comment.*   There is no generally accepted list of marketing functions, nor is there any generally accepted basis on which the lists compiled by various writers are chosen. The reason for these limitations is fairly apparent. Under this term students of marketing have sought to squeeze a heterogeneous and nonconsistent group of activities. Some of them are broad business functions with special marketing implications; others are peculiar to the marketing process. The function of assembling is performed through buying, selling, and transportation. Assembling, storage, and transporting are general economic functions; selling and buying are more nearly individual in character. Most of the lists fail sadly to embrace all the activities a marketing manager worries about in the course of doing his job.

Marketing management.   The planning, direction, and control of the entire marketing activity of a firm, or division of a firm, including the formulation of marketing objectives, policies, programs and strategy, and commonly embracing product development, organizing and staffing to carry out plans, supervising marketing operations, and controlling marketing performance.

> *Comment.*   In most firms the man who performs these functions is a member of top management in that he plays a part in determining company policy, in making product decisions, and in coordinating marketing operations with other functional activities to achieve the objectives of the company as a whole. No definition of his position is included in this report because there is no uniformity in the titles applied to it. He is variously designated Marketing Manager, Director of Marketing, Vice President for Marketing, Director or Vice President of Marketing and Sales, General Sales Manager.

Marketing planning.   The work of setting up objectives for marketing activity and of determining and scheduling the steps necessary to achieve such objectives.

> *Comment.*   This term includes not only the work of deciding upon the goals or results to be attained through marketing activity but also the determination, in detail, of how they are to be accomplished.

Marketing policy. A course of action established to obtain consistency of marketing decisions and operations under recurring and essentially similar circumstances.

Marketing research. The systematic gathering, recording, and analyzing of data about problems relating to the marketing of goods and services. Such research may be undertaken by impartial agencies or by business firms or their agents for the solution of their marketing problems.

> *Comment.* Marketing research is the inclusive term which embraces all research activities carried on in connection with the management of marketing work. It includes various subsidiary types of research, such as (1) *Market analysis,* which is a study of the size, location, nature, and characteristics of markets, (2) *Sales analysis* (or *research*), which is largely an analysis of sales data, (3) *Consumer research,* of which *motivation research* is a type, which is concerned chiefly with the discovery and analysis of consumer attitudes, reactions, and preferences, and (4) *Advertising research,* which is carried on chiefly as an aid to the management of advertising work. The techniques of *operations research* are often useful in *marketing research.* The term "market research" is often loosely used as synonymous with "marketing research."

Merchandising. The planning and supervision involved in marketing the particular merchandise or service at places, times, prices, and quantities which will best serve to realize the marketing objectives of the business.

> *Comment.* This term has been used in a great variety of meanings, most of them confusing. The usage recommended by the Committee adheres closely to the essential meaning of the word. The term is most widely used in this sense in the wholesaling and retailing trades. Many manufacturers designate this activity as Product Planning or Management and include in it such tasks as selecting the article to be produced or stocked and deciding such matters as the size, appearance, form, packaging, quantities to be bought or made, time of procurement, and price lines to be offered.

Merchant. A business unit that buys, takes title to, and resells merchandise.

> *Comment.* The distinctive feature of this middleman lies in the fact that he takes title to the goods he handles. The extent to which he performs the marketing functions is incidental to the definition. Wholesalers and retailers are the chief types of merchants.

Middleman. A business concern that specializes in performing operations or rendering services directly involved in the purchase and/or sale of goods in the process of their flow from producer to consumer. Middlemen are of two types, *merchants* and *agents.*

> *Comment.* The essence of the middleman's operation lies in the fact that he plays an active and prominent part in the negotiations leading up to transactions of purchase and sale. This is what distinguishes him from a marketing facilitating agent who, while he performs certain marketing functions, participates only incidentally in negotiations of purchase and sale. This term is very general in its meaning. It also possesses an unfortunate emotional content. Therefore the Committee recommends that whenever possible more specific terms be used, such as agent, merchant, retailer, wholesaler.

Missionary salesman. A salesman employed by a manufacturer to call on customers of his distributors, usually to develop goodwill and stimulate demand, to help or induce them to promote the sale of his employer's goods, to help them train their salesmen to do so, and, often, to take orders for delivery by such distributors.

Motivation research. A group of techniques developed by the behavioral scientists which are used by marketing researchers to discover factors influencing marketing behavior.

> *Comment.* These techniques are widely used outside the marketing sphere; for example, to discover factors influencing the behavior of employees and voters. The Committee has confined its definition to the marketing uses of the tool. Motivation research is only one of several ways to study marketing behavior.

N

National brand. A manufacturer's or producer's brand, usually enjoying wide territorial distribution.

> *Comment.* The usage of the terms "national brand" and "private brand" in this report, while generally current and commonly accepted, is highly illogical and non-descriptive. But since it is widespread and persistent, the Committee embodies it in this report.

P

Personal selling. Oral presentation in a conversation with one or more prospective purchasers for the purpose of making sales.

> *Comment.* This definition contemplates that the presentation may be either formal (as a "canned" sales talk) or informal, although it is rather likely to be informal —either in the actual presence of the customer or by telephone, although usually the former, either to an individual or to a small group, usually the former.

Physical distribution. The management of the movement and handling of goods from the point of production to the point of consumption or use.

Price cutting. Offering merchandise or a service for sale at a price below that recognized as usual or appropriate by its buyers and sellers.

> *Comment.* One obvious criticism of this definition is that it is indefinite. But that very indefiniteness also causes it to be more accurately descriptive of a concept which is characterized by a high degree of indefiniteness in the mind of the average person affected by price cutting. Traders' ideas of what constitutes price cutting are so vague and indefinite that any precise or highly specific definition of the phenomenon is bound to fail to include all its manifestations. If you ask a group of traders in a specific commodity to define price cutting you will get as many conflicting formulas as there are traders. But if you ask those same traders at any particular time whether selling at a certain price constitutes price cutting, you will probably get a considerable degree of uniformity of opinion. It is precisely this condition which the definition is designed to reflect.

Price leader. A firm whose pricing behavior is followed by other companies in the same industry.

> *Comment.* The price leadership of a firm may be limited to a certain geographical area, as in the oil business, or to certain products or groups of products, as in the steel business.

Private brands. Brands sponsored by merchants or agents as distinguished from those sponsored by manufacturers or producers.

> *Comment.* This usage is thoroughly illogical since no seller wants his brand to be private in the sense of being secret—and all brands are private in the sense that they are special and not common or general in use. But the usage is common in marketing literature and among traders. Therefore the Committee presents it in this report.

Producers' cooperative marketing. That type of cooperative marketing which primarily involves the sale of goods or services of the associated producing membership. It may perform only an assembly or brokerage function, but in some cases, notably milk marketing, extend into processing and distribution of the members' production.

> *Comment.* Many producers' cooperative marketing associations also buy for their members. This fact does not subtract from their status as producers' cooperatives. This is especially true of farm cooperatives. This term does not include those activities of trade associations that affect only indirectly the sales of the membership. Such activities are the maintenance of credit rating bureaus, design registration bureaus, and brand protection machinery.

Product line. A group of products that are closely related either because they satisfy a class of need, are used together, are sold to the same customer groups, are marketed through the same type of outlets, or fall within given price ranges. Example: carpenters' tools.

> *Comment.* Sublines of products may be distinguished, such as hammers or saws, within a product line.

Product management. The planning, direction, and control of all phases of the life cycle of products, including the creation or discovery of ideas for new products, the screening of such ideas, the coordination of the work of research and physical development of products, their packaging and branding, their introduction on the market, their market development, their modification, the discovery of new uses for them, their repair and servicing, and their deletion.

> *Comment.* It is not safe to think of product management as the work of the executive known as the Product Manager, because the dimensions of his job vary widely from company to company, sometimes embracing all the activities listed in the definition and sometimes being limited to the sales promotion of the products in his care.

Product mix. The composite of products offered for sale by a firm or a business unit.

> *Comment.* Toothpaste is a product. The 50¢ tube of Whosis ammoniated toothpaste is an item. Toothpastes and powders, mouth washes, and other allied items compose an oral hygiene product line. Soaps, cosmetics, dentifrices, drug items, cake mixes, shortenings and other items may comprise a product mix if marketed by the same company.

Publicity. Nonpersonal stimulation of demand for a product, service or business unit by planting commercially significant news about it in a published medium, or obtaining favorable presentation of it upon radio, television, or stage that is not paid for by the sponsor.
> *Comment.* Retailers use the term to denote the sum of the functions of advertising, display, and publicity as defined above.

Purchasing power (buying power). The capacity to purchase possessed by an individual buyer, a group of buyers, or the aggregate of the buyers in an area or a market.

R

Rack jobber. A wholesaling business unit that markets specialized lines of merchandise to certain types of retail stores and also provides the special services of selective brand and item merchandising and arrangement, maintenance, and stocking of display racks.

> *Comment.* The rack jobber usually, but not always, puts his merchandise in the store of the retailer on consignment. Rack jobbers are most prevalent in the food business.

Resale price maintenance. Control by a supplier of the selling prices of his branded goods at subsequent stages of distribution by means of contractual agreement under fair trade laws or other devices.

Resident buyer. An agent who specializes in buying, on a fee or commission basis, chiefly for retailers.

> *Comment.* The term, as defined above, is limited to agents residing in the market cities who charge their retail principals fees for buying assistance rendered, but there are resident buying offices that are owned by out-of-town stores and some that are owned cooperatively by a group of stores. The former are called *private* offices and the latter *associated* offices. Neither of them should be confused with the central buying office of the typical chain where the buying function is performed by the office directly, not acting as a specialized assistant to store buyers.
>
> Resident buyers should also be distinguished from apparel *merchandise brokers* who represent competing manufacturers in the garment trades and have as customers out-of-town smaller stores in search of fashion merchandise. These brokers are paid by the manufacturers, to whom they bring additional business, on a percentage of sales basis.

Retailer. A merchant, or occasionally an agent, whose main business is selling directly to the ultimate consumer.

> *Comment.* The retailer is to be distinguished by the nature of his sales rather than by the way he procures the goods in which he deals. The size of the units in which he sells is an incidental rather than a primary element in his character. His essential distinguishing mark is the fact that his typical sale is made to the ultimate consumer.

Retailer cooperative. A group of independent retailers organized to buy cooperatively either through a jointly owned warehouse or through a buying club.

> *Comment.* Their cooperative activities may include operating under a group name, joint advertising, and cooperative managerial supervision.

Retailing. The activities involved in selling directly to the ultimate consumer.

> *Comment.* This definition includes all forms of selling to the ultimate consumers. It embraces the direct-to-consumer sales activities of the producer whether through his own stores, by house-to-house canvass, or by mail order. It does not cover the sale of industrial goods by producers or industrial supply houses—or by retailers to industrial, commercial, or institutional buyers for use in the conduct of their enterprises.

S

Sales agent; see Selling agent.

Sales analysis. A subdivision of marketing research which involves the systematic study and comparison of sales data.

Comment. The purpose of such analysis is usually to aid in marketing management by providing sales information along the lines of market areas, organizational units, products or product groups, customers or customer groups, or such other units as may be useful.

Sales budget. The part of the marketing budget which is concerned with planned dollar sales and planned costs of personal selling during a specified future period.

Sales forecast. An estimate of sales, in dollars or physical units, for a specified future period under a proposed marketing plan or program, and under an assumed set of economic and other forces outside the unit for which the forecast is made. The forecast may be for a specified item of merchandise or for an entire line.

Comment. Two sets of factors are involved in making a sales forecast: (1) those forces outside the control of the firm for which the forecast is made, that are likely to influence its sales, and (2) changes in the marketing methods or practices of the firm that are likely to affect its sales.

In the course of planning future activities the management of a given firm may make several sales forecasts, each consisting of an estimate of probable sales if a given marketing plan is adopted or a given set of outside forces prevails. The estimated effects that several marketing plans may have on sales and profits may be compared in the process of arriving at that marketing program which will, in the opinion of the officials of the company, be best designed to promote its welfare.

Sales management. The planning, direction, and control of the personal selling activities of a business unit, including recruiting, selecting, training, equipping, assigning, routing, supervising, paying, and motivating, as these tasks apply to the personal sales force.

Comment. These activities are sometimes, but not generally, designated Sales Administration or Sales Force Management.

Sales manager. The executive who plans, directs, and controls the activities of salesmen.

Comment. This definition distinguishes sharply between the manager who conducts the personal selling activities of a business unit and his superior, the executive, variously called Marketing Manager, Director of Marketing, or Vice President for Marketing, who has charge of all marketing activities. The usage of this form of organization has been growing rapidly during recent years.

Sales planning. That part of the marketing planning work which is concerned with making sales forecasts, devising programs for reaching the sales target, and deriving a sales budget.

Sales potential; see Market share.

Sales promotion. (1) In a specific sense, those marketing activities, other than personal selling, advertising and publicity, that stimulate consumer purchasing and dealer effectiveness, such as display, shows and exhibitions, demonstrations, and various nonrecurrent selling efforts not in the ordinary routine. (2) In retailing, all methods of stimulating customer purchasing, including personal selling, advertising, and publicity.

Comment. This definition includes the two most logical and commonly accepted usages of this much abused term. It is the suggestion of the Committee that, insofar as possible, the use of the term be confined to the first of the two definitions given above.

Sales quota.   A projected volume of sales assigned to a marketing unit for use in the management of sales efforts. It applies to a specified period and may be expressed in dollars or in physical units.

> *Comment.*   The quota may be used in checking the efficiency, stimulating the efforts, or remunerating individual salesmen or other personnel engaged in sales work. A quota may be for a salesman, a territory, a department, a branch house, a wholesaler or retailer, or for the company as a whole. It may be different from the sales figure set up in the sales budget. Since it is a managerial device, it is not an immutable figure inexorably arrived at by the application of absolutely exact statistical formulas.

Sales research; see Marketing research and Sales analysis.

Selective selling.   The policy of selling to a limited number of customers in a market.

Self selection.   The method used in retailing by which the customer may choose the desired merchandise without direct assistance of store personnel.

Self-service.   The method used in retailing whereby the customer selects his own merchandise, removes it from the shelves or bulk containers, carries it to a check-out stand to complete the transaction, and transports it to the point of use.

Selling.   The personal or impersonal process of assisting and/or persuading a prospective customer to buy a commodity or a service or to act favorably upon an idea that has commercial significance to the seller.

> *Comment.*   This definition includes advertising, other forms of publicity, and sales promotion, as well as personal selling.

Selling agent.   An agent who operates on an extended contractual basis, sells all of a specified line of merchandise or the entire output of his principal, and usually has full authority with regard to prices, terms, and other conditions of sale. He occasionally renders financial aid to his principal.

> *Comment.*   This functionary is often called a "sales agent."

Service wholesaler; see Wholesaler.

Services.   Activities, benefits, or satisfactions which are offered for sale or are provided in connection with the sale of .goods. Examples are amusements, hotel service, electric service, transportation, the services of barber shops and beauty shops, repair and maintenance service, the work of credit rating bureaus. This list is merely illustrative and no attempt has been made to make it complete. The term also applies to the various activities, such as credit extension, advice and help of salespeople, and delivery, by which the seller serves the convenience of his customers.

Shopping center.   A geographical cluster of retail stores collectively handling an assortment of goods varied enough to satisfy most of the merchandise wants of consumers within convenient traveling time and, thereby attracting a general shopping trade.

> *Comment.*   During recent years the term has acquired a special usage in its appli-

cation to the planned or integrated centers developed in suburban or semi-suburban areas, usually along main highways and featuring ample parking space.

Shopping goods. Those consumers' goods which the customer, in the process of selection and purchase, characteristically compares on such bases as suitability, quality, price, and style. Examples of goods that most consumers probably buy as shopping goods are millinery, furniture, dress goods, women's ready-to-wear and shoes, used automobiles, and major appliances.

> *Comment.* It should be emphasized that a given article may be bought by one customer as a shopping good and by another as a *specialty* or *convenience good.* The *general classification* depends upon the way in which the average or typical buyer purchases. See comment under *Specialty goods.*

Specialty goods. Those consumers' goods with unique characteristics and/or brand identification for which a significant group of buyers are habitually willing to make a special purchasing effort. Examples of articles that are usually bought as specialty goods are specific brands and types of fancy foods, hi-fi components, certain types of sporting equipment, photographic equipment, and men's suits.

> *Comment.* Price is not usually the primary factor in consumer choice of specialty goods although their prices are often higher than those of other articles serving the same basic want but without their special characteristics.

Specialty store. A retail store that makes its appeal on the basis of a restricted class of shopping goods.

Standardization. The determination of basic limits or grade ranges in the form of uniform specifications to which particular manufactured goods may conform, and uniform classes into which the products of agriculture and the extractive industries may or must be sorted or assigned.

> *Comment.* This term does not include grading, which is the process of sorting or assigning units of a commodity to the grades or classes that have been established through the process of standardization. Some systems of standardization and grading for agricultural products are compulsory by law.

Stock or inventory control. The use of a system or mechanism to maintain stocks of goods at desired levels.

> *Comment.* Such control is usually exercised to maintain stocks that are (*a*) representative in that they include all the items the customer group served expects to be able to buy from the firm involved, (*b*) adequate in that a sufficient quantity of each item is included to satisfy all reasonably foreseeable demands for it, and (*c*) economical in that no funds of the firm are held in inventory—beyond those needed to serve purposes (*a*) and (*b*)—and in that it facilitates savings in costs of production.

Storage. The marketing function that involves holding goods between the time of their production and their final sale.

> *Comment.* Some processing is often done while goods are in storage. It is probable that this should be regarded as a part of production rather than of marketing.

Superette; see Supermarket.

Supermarket. A large retailing business unit selling mainly food and grocery items on the basis of low margin appeal, wide variety and assortments, self-service, and heavy emphasis on merchandise appeal.

Comment. In its bid for patronage the supermarket makes heavy use of the visual appeal of the merchandise itself. The Committee realizes that it would be foolhardy in this day of rapid change to try to indicate how large a store must be to be a supermarket. At the time of this report the latest figures indicate that the average store recognized by the Supermarket Institute as belonging to the class has annual sales of somewhat under $2,010,000, and that about 45 percent of them sell more than that amount each year. Both of these figures have been changing rapidly and may continue to do so. A *superette* is a store somewhat smaller than a supermarket but possessing most of the same characteristics.

T

Trademark. A brand or part of a brand that is given legal protection because it is capable of exclusive appropriation; because it is used in a manner sufficiently fanciful, distinctive, and arbitrary; because it is affixed to the product when sold; or because it otherwise satisfies the requirements set up by law.

Comment. Trademark is essentially a legal term and includes only those brands or parts of brands which the law designates as trademarks. In the final analysis, in any specific case, a trademark is what the court in that case decides to regard as a trademark.

Trading area. A district whose size is usually determined by the boundaries within which it is economical (in terms of volume and cost) for a marketing unit or group to sell and/or deliver a good or service.

Comment. A single business may have several trading areas; for example, the trading area of Marshall Field for its store business is different from that for its catalog business.

Traffic management. The planning, selection, and direction of all means and methods of transportation involved in the movement of goods in the marketing process.

Comment. This definition is confined to those activities in connection with transportation that have to do particularly with marketing, and form an inseparable part of any well organized system of distribution. It includes control of the movement of goods in trucks owned by the marketing concern as well as by public carrier. It does not include the movement of goods within the warehouse of a producer or within the store of a retail concern.

Truck wholesaler; see Wholesaler.

U

Ultimate consumer. One who buys and/or uses goods or services to satisfy personal or household wants rather than for resale or for use in business, institutional, or industrial operations.

Comment. The definition distinguishes sharply between industrial users and ultimate consumers. A firm buying and using an office machine, a drum of lubricating oil, or a carload of steel billets is an industrial user of those products, not an ultimate consumer of them. A vital difference exists between the purposes motivating the two types of purchases, which, in turn, results in highly significant differences in buying methods, marketing organization, and selling practices.

V

Value added by marketing. The part of the value of a product or a service to the consumer or user which results from marketing activities.

Comment. There is urgent need of a method or formula for computing "value added by marketing." Increased attention is being devoted to developing such a formula. At present, none of those suggested have gained enough acceptance to justify inclusion in this definition or comment.

Variety store. A retailing business unit that handles a wide assortment of goods, usually in the low or "popular" segment of the price range.

Comment. While some foods are generally handled, the major emphasis is devoted to nonfood products.

Voluntary group. A group of retailers, each of whom owns and operates his own store and is associated with a wholesale organization or manufacturer to carry on joint merchandising activities, and who are characterized by some degree of group identity and uniformity of operation. Such joint activities have been largely of two kinds: cooperative advertising and group control of store operation.

Comment. A voluntary group is usually sponsored by a wholesaler. Similar groups, sponsored by retailers, do not belong in this category. Groups of independent stores sponsored by a chain store system are usually called "agency stores."

W

Wholesaler. A business unit which buys and resells merchandise to retailers and other merchants and/or to industrial, institutional, and commercial users, but which does not sell in significant amounts to ultimate consumers. In the basic materials, semi-finished goods and tool and machinery trades merchants of this type are commonly known as "distributors" or "supply houses."

Comment. Generally these merchants render a wide variety of services to their customers. Those who render all the services normally expected in the wholesale trade are known as *service wholesalers;* those who render only a few of the wholesale services are known as *limited function wholesalers.* The latter group is composed mainly of *cash and carry wholesalers,* who do not render the credit or delivery service; *drop shipment wholesalers,* who sell for delivery by the producer direct to the buyer; *truck wholesalers,* who combine selling, delivery, and collection in one operation; and *mail order wholesalers,* who perform the selling service entirely by mail.

This definition ignores or minimizes two bases upon which the term is often defined: (1) the size of the lots in which wholesalers deal and (2) the fact that they habitually sell for resale. The figures show that many wholesalers operate on a very small scale in small lots. Most of them make a significant portion of their sales to industrial users.

APPENDIX B

Case Reference Chart

This chart is intended to help those instructors who may wish to use cases in conjunction with this book. By cross-referencing chapters in this text with six popular casebooks in marketing management, we sought to facilitate the assignment of case problems.

To illustrate how the chart is designed to work: for Chapters 16 and 17 of this text, which deal with pricing, cases 40, 41, 42, 43, 44, 45 and 46 of the Westfall and Boyd casebook might be used as supplemental teaching aids.

Dynamic Management	Marketing Casebooks*					
	C[1]	F[2]	L–D[3]	T[4]	W–B[5]	B–E–M[6]
1........	1	1	2, 3			
2........	2, 10		6–8, 10–11, 86	1–3, 5–6	5, 6, 8	2–3
3–4......	3, 7, 11	17–25, 28	52, 55–64, 87	9–11, 36–37	7, 9, 22–30	4
5–6–7....		5–10, 26, 38 58, 82	1, 9, 13–15, 17 19, 21, 24, 28 48–49, 51, 53 70, 73, 75–76	7–8, 22–29 32, 47–48	10–12, 53	
8–9......		27, 44, 48, 51 72, 85	20, 50, 54	20, 52–53		
10.......	24–25	29–36, 39 41–43, 45–47	16, 18, 22–23 25–27, 29–37 67, 98	12–17, 19 21, 38, 45	31–39	5
11–12.....	27	49–50, 52, 57	5, 65–66, 72 74		59–62 63–81	
13–14.....		59–68, 70–71 73–76	77–79, 88	30–31 33–35 39, 54	47, 49–52 54–58 82–85	6
15.......	28–29				86–89	
16–17.....	12–16	16, 77–79 81, 84, 86	38–47, 92–93 97	49, 55	40–46	7
18–19–20...	8	3, 11 ,15		40, 42–44 50–51	4, 13–15 91	8
21–22.....	9, 17–23, 26	87–91	4, 68–69, 71 80, 82–83, 85		1–3 16–21, 90 92–98	9
23........	30–32		89–91, 94 96, 100			

*Numerals in *Dynamic Management* and "B–E–M" columns are *chapter* numbers; all other numerals are specific *case* numbers.

[1]C: E. Raymond Corey, *Industrial Marketing: Cases and Concepts* (Englewood Cliffs, N. J.; Prentice-Hall, 1962).

[2]F: David E. Faville, *Selected Cases in Marketing Management* (Englewood Cliffs, N. J.: Prentice-Hall 1961).

[3]L–D: Lawrence C. Lockley and Charles J. Dirksen, *Cases in Marketing* (2d ed.; Boston: Allyn and Bacon, 1959).

[4]T: George R. Terry, *Marketing: Selected Case Problems* (2d ed.; Englewood Cliffs, N. J.: Prentice Hall, 1956).

[5]W–B: Ralph Westfall and Harper W. Boyd, *Cases in Marketing Management* (Homewood, Ill.: Richard D. Irwin, Inc., 1961).

[6]B–E–M: Milton P. Brown, Wilbur B. England, and John B. Matthews, Jr., *Problems in Marketing* (3d ed.; New York: McGraw-Hill, 1961).

APPENDIX C

Bibliography

CHAPTER 1

GENERAL BIBLIOGRAPHIES ON MARKETING MANAGEMENT

KELLEY, EUGENE J., *et. al. Marketing Management: An Annotated Bibliography*. Chicago: American Marketing Association, 1963.

MERTES, JOHN E. *The Management of Marketing: A Graduate Course Syllabus and Reading List of Current Literature in Managerial Marketing*. Norman, Okla.: University Book Exchange, University of Oklahoma, 1961.

STAUDT, THOMAS A., AND LAZER, WILLIAM. *A Basic Bibliography on Industrial Marketing*. Chicago: American Marketing Association, 1958.

BOOKS

ALDERSON, WROE. *Marketing Behavior and Executive Action*. Homewood, Ill.: Richard D. Irwin, Inc., 1957.

ALEXANDER, RALPH S.; CROSS, JAMES S.; AND CUNNINGHAM, ROSS M. *Industrial Marketing*. Rev. ed. Homewood, Ill.: Richard D. Irwin, Inc., 1961.

COX, REAVIS, AND ALDERSON, WROE (eds.). *Theory in Marketing*. Homewood, Ill.: Richard D. Irwin, Inc., 1950.

HANSEN, HARRY L. *Marketing: Text, Cases and Readings*. Rev. ed. Homewood, Ill.: Richard D. Irwin, Inc., 1961.

HOWARD, JOHN A. *Marketing Management: Analysis and Planning*. Rev. Ed.; Homewood, Ill.: Richard D. Irwin, Inc., 1963.

LAZER, WILLIAM, AND KELLEY, EUGENE J. (eds.). *Managerial Marketing: Perspectives and Viewpoints*. Rev. ed. Homewood, Ill.: Richard D. Irwin, Inc., 1962.

MCCARTHY, EUGENE J. *Basic Marketing: A Managerial Approach*. Rev. Ed.; Homewood, Ill.: Richard D. Irwin, Inc., 1964.

NYSTROM, PAUL H. (ed.). *Marketing Handbook*. New York: The Ronald Press Co., 1954.

PHELPS, D. MAYNARD, AND WESTING, J. HOWARD. *Marketing Management*. Rev. Ed.; Homewood, Ill.: Richard D. Irwin, Inc., 1960.

ARTICLES

ALLISON, HARRY. "A Framework for Marketing Strategy," *California Management Review,* Fall, 1961, pp. 74–95.

"Are More Marketing Men Getting the Top Posts in Company Management?" *Printers' Ink,* May 20, 1960, pp. 22–26.

BARNET, EDWARD M. "Showdown in the Market Place," *Harvard Business Review,* July-August, 1956, pp. 85–95.

BUND, HENRY, AND CARROLL, J. W. "The Changing Role of the Marketing Function," *Journal of Marketing,* January, 1957, pp. 268–325.

DOSCHER, F. K. "The Vice President for Marketing: What Kind of Man Must He Be?" *The Marketing Concept: Its Meaning to Management.* Marketing Series No. 99. New York: American Management Association, Inc., 1957, pp. 17–30.

FELTON, ARTHUR P. "Conditions of Marketing Leadership," *Harvard Business Review,* March-April, 1956, pp. 117–27.

HOUSER, T. V. "The True Role of the Marketing Executive," *Journal of Marketing,* April, 1959, pp. 363–69.

MCLEAN, J. C. "The New Responsibilities of Marketing Management," *Journal of Marketing,* July, 1958, pp. 1–8.

VERDOORN, P. J. "Marketing from the Producer's Point of View," *Journal of Marketing,* January, 1956, pp. 221–35.

CHAPTER 2

BOOKS

CLARK, LINCOLN H. *Consumer Behavior: Volume II: The Life Cycle and Consumer Behavior.* New York: New York University Press, 1955.

DEAN, JOEL. "Demand Analysis," *Managerial Economics.* Englewood Cliffs, N.J.: Prentice-Hall, Inc., 1951, pp. 134–246.

Fortune, The Editors of. *Why Do People Buy?* New York: McGraw-Hill Book Co., Inc., 1953.

———— *The Changing American Market.* Garden City, N.Y.: Hanover House, 1953.

HAMILTON, DAVID. *The Consumer in Our Economy.* Boston: Houghton Mifflin Co., 1962.

LIFE Study of Consumer Expenditures, Vol. I. New York: Time, Inc., 1957.

KATONA, GEORGE. *Psychological Analysis of Economic Behavior.* New York: McGraw-Hill Book Co., Inc., 1951.

———— *The Powerful Consumer.* New York: McGraw-Hill Book Co., Inc., 1960.

MAZUR, PAUL. *The Standards We Raise.* New York: Harper and Bros., 1953.

WESTING, J. H., AND FINE, I. V. *Industrial Purchasing.* New York: John Wiley and Sons, 1955.

ARTICLES AND PAMPHLETS

ALEXANDER, R. S. "Some Aspects of Sex Differences in Relation to Marketing," *Journal of Marketing,* October, 1947, pp. 158–72.

AUSTIN, DAVID F. "How to Make a Market Your Market," *Sales Management,* January 4, 1957, p. 29ff.

BAYTON, J. A. "Motivation, Cognition, Learning: Basic Factors in Consumer Behavior," *Journal of Marketing,* January, 1958, pp. 282–89.

DRURY, J. G. "Is Your Problem Overproduction—Or Underproduction of Markets?" *Printers' Ink,* July 5, 1957, pp. 19–22ff.

DUNCAN, D. J. "What Motivates Business Buyers," *Harvard Business Review,* Summer, 1940, p. 448ff.

FERBER, ROBERT. "Our Changing Consumer Market," *Business Horizons,* Spring, 1958, pp. 49–66.

"The Future of Business Lies in Understanding the Buyer," *Printers' Ink,* November 15, 1957, pp. 36–47.

"Geographic Data in Census of Manufacturers Help Pinpoint Your Market—Economically," *Printers' Ink,* September 14, 1956, pp. 35–41.

HOBART, D. M. "Stimulating Consumer Demand through Manufacturing Customers," *The 1957 Turck Lecture Series on Marketing and Distribution.* New York: National Association of Manufacturers, 1957, pp. 32–36.

KELLEY, EUGENE J. "The Importance of Convenience in Consumer Purchasing," *Journal of Marketing,* July, 1958, pp. 32–38.

KLEIN, L. R., AND LANSING, J. B. "Decisions to Purchase Consumer Durable Goods," *Journal of Marketing,* October, 1955, pp. 109–32.

LEVY, SIDNEY J. "Symbols for Sale," *Harvard Business Review,* July-August, 1959, 117–24.

LOEB, B. S. "The Use of Engel's Laws as a Basis for Predicting Consumer Expenditures," *Journal of Marketing,* July, 1955, pp. 202–7.

MARTINEAU, PIERRE. "Social Classes and Spending Behavior," *Journal of Marketing,* October, 1958, pp. 121–30.

MORTIMER, C. G. "Two Keys to Modern Marketing: One Old, One New," New York: Updegraffe Press, Ltd., 1955.

NEWMAN, J. W. "New Insight, New Progress for Marketing," *Harvard Business Review,* November-December, 1957, pp. 95–102.

"1970 Markets: Where and How Big," *Printers' Ink,* September 6, 1957, pp. 87–90.

"The Odd Case of the Consumer," *Business Week,* September 6, 1958, pp. 123–26.

REED, V. D. "Changes in Consumer Markets as a Guide to Marketing Management," *Changing Structure and Strategy in Marketing,* R. V. MITCHELL (ed.). Urbana, Ill.: University of Illinois, 1958, pp. 47–65.

"Relating Company Markets to SIC," *Journal of Marketing,* April, 1963, p. 42ff.

CHAPTERS 3 AND 4

BOOKS

BERG, THOMAS L., AND SHUCHMAN, ABRAHAM (eds.). *Product Strategy and Management,* New York: Holt, Rinehart and Winston. Inc., 1963.

COREY, E. RAYMOND. *The Development of Markets for New Materials.* Boston: Harvard Graduate School of Business Administration, 1956.

DEAN, JOEL. "Cost," *Managerial Economics.* Englewood Cliffs, N.J.: Prentice-Hall, Inc., 1951, pp. 247–347.

DREYFUSS, H. *Designing for People.* New York: Simon and Schuster, Inc., 1955.

HILTON, PETER. *Handbook of New Product Development.* Englewood Cliffs, N.J.: Prentice-Hall, Inc., 1961.

LIPPINCOTT, J. GORDON. *Design for Business.* Chicago: Paul Theobald, 1947.

MARTING, ELIZABETH (ed.). *Developing a Product Strategy.* New York: American Management Association, 1959.

PHELPS, D. MAYNARD. *Planning the Product.* Homewood, Ill.: Richard D. Irwin, Inc., 1947.

WALLANCE, DON. *Shaping America's Products.* New York: Reinhold Publishing Corp., 1956.

PAMPHLETS AND MONOGRAPHS

Establishing a New Product Program. AMA Management Report #8. New York: American Management Association, 1958.

How to Plan Products That Sell. AMA Management Report #13. New York: American Management Association, 1958.

LARSON, GUSTAV. *Developing and Selling New Products.* Washington, D.C.: U.S. Government Printing Office, 1949.

MEGATHLIN, DONALD E., AND HARTNETT, EDWARD J., JR. *A Bibliography on New Product Planning.* AMA Bibliography Series No. 5. Chicago: American Marketing Association, 1960.

New Product Development: I, Selection-Coordination-Financing. Studies in Business Policy, No. 40. New York: National Industrial Conference Board, Inc., 1950.

New Product Development: II, Research and Engineering. Studies in Business Policy, No. 57. New York: National Industrial Conference Board, Inc., 1952.

New Product Development: III, Marketing New Products. Studies in Business Policy, No. 69. New York: National Industrial Conference Board, Inc., 1954.

Organizing for Product Development. AMA Management Report #31. New York: American Management Association, 1959.

ARTICLES

ANSOFF, H. I. "A Model for Diversification," *Management Science,* July, 1958, pp. 392–414.

ASPINWALL, LEO V. "The Characteristics of Goods Theory," *Managerial Marketing: Perspectives and Viewpoints.* Rev. ed. WILLIAM LAZER AND EUGENE J. KELLEY (eds.). Homewood, Ill.: Richard D. Irwin, Inc., 1962, pp. 633–43.

———— "The Parallel Systems Theory," *Managerial Marketing: Perspectives and Viewpoints.* Rev. ed. WILLIAM LAZER AND EUGENE J. KELLEY (eds.). Homewood, Ill.: Richard D. Irwin, Inc., 1962, pp. 644–52.

BERENSON, CONRAD. "Pruning the Product Line," *Business Horizons,* Summer, 1963, pp. 63–70.

BLACK, C.. "Product Differentiation and Demand for Marketing Services," *Journal of Marketing,* July, 1951, pp. 73–79.

BOWMAN, BURTON F., AND MCCORMICK, FREDERICK E. "Market Segmentation and Marketing Mixes," *Journal of Marketing,* January, 1961, pp. 25–29.

CONRAD, GORDON R. "Unexplored Assets for Diversification," *Harvard Business Review,* September-October, 1963, pp. 67–73.

COPELAND, M. T. "Relation of Consumers' Buying Habits to Marketing Methods," *Harvard Business Review,* April, 1923, pp. 282–89.

CUNNINGHAM, ROSS M. "Brand Loyalty: What, Where, and How Much?" *Harvard Business Review,* January-February, 1956, pp. 116–28.

———— "Customer Loyalty to Store and Brand," *Harvard Business Review,* November-December, 1961, pp. 127–37.

DALZELL, R. W. "Diversification: Watch the Pitfalls," *Iron Age,* August 16, 1956, pp. 22–26.

DEAN, JOEL. "Product-Line Policy," *Journal of Business,* October, 1950, pp. 248–58.

ENZIE, W. H. "Planning Your Package," *Modern Packaging Encyclopedia, 1962: Modern Packaging,* November, 1961, pp. 26–29.

GARDNER, B. B., AND LEVY, S. J. "The Product and The Brand," *Harvard Business Review,* March-April, 1955, pp. 33–40.

HOLTON, RICHARD H. "The Distinctions between Convenience Goods, Shopping Goods and Specialty Goods," *Journal of Marketing,* July, 1958, pp. 53–56.

HOUFEK, LYMAN J. "How to Decide Which Products to Junk," *Printers' Ink,* August 1, 1952, pp. 21–23.

JOHNSON, SAMUEL C., AND JONES, CONRAD. "How to Organize for New Products,"*Harvard Business Review,* May-June, 1957, pp. 49–62.

KLINE, C. H. "The Strategy of Product Policy," *Harvard Business Review,* July-August, 1955, pp. 91–100.

LADIK, FRANK; KENT, LEONARD; AND NAHL, PERHAM C. "Test Marketing of New Consumer Products," *Journal of Marketing,* April, 1960, pp. 29–34.

LEVITT, THEODORE. "Marketing Myopia," *Harvard Business Review,* July-August, 1960, pp. 45–56.

MANDELL, MELVIN. "Product Testing: Everybody's Doing It," *Dun's Review and Modern Industry,* April, 1958, pp. 40–42 and 137–39.

McMurry, Robert N. "How to Pick a Name for a New Product," *Sales Management,* August 15, 1954, pp. 102–5.

O'Meara, John T., Jr. "Selecting Profitable Products," *Harvard Business Review,* January-February, 1961, pp. 83–89.

Patton, Arch. "Top Management's Stake in a Product's Life-Cycle," *The Management Review,* June, 1959, pp. 3–26.

Randle, C. Wilson. "Selecting the Research Program: A Top Management Function," *California Management Review,* Winter, 1960, pp. 9–15.

Roberts, Alan H. "Applying the Strategy of Market Segmentation," *Business Horizons,* Fall, 1961, pp. 65–72.

Smith, W. R. "Product Differentiation and Market Segmentation as Alternative Marketing Strategies," *Journal of Marketing,* July, 1956, pp. 3–8.

Staudt, Thomas A. "Program for Product Diversification," *Harvard Business Review,* November-December, 1954, pp. 121–31.

Stewart, John B. "Functional Features in Product Strategy," *Harvard Business Review,* March-April, 1959, pp. 65–78.

Stillson, P., and Arnoff, E. L. "Product Search and Evaluation," *Journal of Marketing,* July, 1957, pp. 33–39.

"Success in a Segmented Market," *Printers' Ink,* September 18, 1959, pp. 21–28.

Tallman, Gerald B. "Planned Obsolescence: The Setting; the Issues Involved," *Advancing Marketing Efficiency,* Lynn H. Stockman (ed.). Chicago: American Marketing Association, 1959, pp. 27–39.

Wasson, Chester R. "What Is 'New' About a New Product?" *Journal of Marketing,* July, 1960, pp. 52–56.

"What New Products Mean to Companies: Growth, a Longer Life, Bigger Profits," *Printers' Ink,* June 13, 1958, pp. 21–28.

"Why Modern Marketing Needs the Product Manager," *Printers' Ink,* October 14, 1960, pp 25–30.

CHAPTERS 5, 6, AND 7

Books

Barker, C. W.; Anderson, I. D.; and Butterworth, J. D. *Principles of Retailing.* New York: McGraw-Hill Book Co., Inc., 1956.

Brown, D. L., and Davidson, W. R. *Retailing Principles and Practices.* New York: The Ronald Press Co., 1953.

Cassady, Ralph. *Competition and Price Making in Food Retailing: The Anatomy of Supermarket Operations.* New York: The Ronald Press Co., 1962.

Charvat, Frank J. *Supermarketing.* New York: The Macmillan Co., 1961.

Duncan, Delbert J., and Phillips, Charles F. *Retailing: Principles and Methods.* 6th ed. Homewood, Ill.: Richard D. Irwin, Inc., 1963.

Emmet, B., and Jeuck, J. E. *Catalogues and Counters.* Chicago: University of Chicago Press, 1950.

Hollander, Stanley C. (ed.) *Explorations in Retailing.* East Lansing, Mich.: Bureau of Business and Economic Research, Michigan State University, 1959.

JONES, F. M. *Retail Merchandising.* Homewood, Ill.: Richard D. Irwin, Inc., 1957.

KELLEY, E. J. *Shopping Centers: Locating Controlled Regional Centers.* Saugatuck, Conn.: The Eno Foundation for Highway Traffic Control, 1956.

MARSHALL, MARTIN V. *Automatic Merchandising.* Boston: Harvard Graduate School of Business Administration, 1954.

McKINLEY, WILLIAM. *Bibliography of Self-Service Discount Department Stores.* Boston: Boston University Department of Geography, 1962.

SCHREIBER, G. R. *Automatic Selling.* New York: John Wiley and Sons, 1954.

WINGATE, J. W., AND CORBIN, A. (eds.). *Changing Patterns in Retailing.* Homewood, Ill.: Richard D. Irwin, Inc., 1956.

WINGATE, JOHN W., AND WEINER, J. DANA. *Retail Merchandising.* 6th ed. Cincinnati: South-Western Publishing Co., Inc., 1963.

ZIMMERMAN, M. M. *The Super Market: A Revolution in Distribution.* New York: McGraw-Hill Book Co., 1955.

ARTICLES

ALEXANDER, R. S. "The Changing Structure of Intermediate Markets and Manufacturers' Marketing Strategy," *Changing Structure and Strategy in Marketing,* R. V. MITCHELL (ed.). Urbana, Ill.: University of Illinois, 1958, pp. 66–79.

ALEXANDER, R. S. AND HILL, R. "What To Do About the Discount House," *Harvard Business Review,* January-February, 1955, pp. 53–65.

"Another Look at Census of Business Retail Data," *Journal of Retailing,* Spring, 1963, p. 32ff.

APPLEBAUM, WILLIAM, AND CARSON, DAVID. "Supermarkets Face the Future," *Harvard Business Review,* March-April, 1957, pp. 123–35.

"Automatic Vending Goes National," *Printers' Ink,* September 2, 1960, pp. 18–22.

BALDERSTON, F. E. "Assortment Choice in Wholesale and Retail Marketing, *Journal of Marketing,* October, 1956, pp. 175–83.

BLACK, W. "Nonfoods in Supers," *Printers' Ink,* June 28, 1957, pp. 19–21ff., and July 5, 1957, pp. 30–36.

BLISS, PERRY. "Non-Price Competition at the Department-Store Level," *Journal of Marketing,* April, 1953, pp. 357–65.

——— "Price Determination at the Department-Store Level," *Journal of Marketing,* July, 1952, pp. 37–46.

CAIRNS, JAMES P. "Suppliers, Retailers, and Shelf Space," *Journal of Marketing,* July, 1962, pp. 34–36.

"Competitive Strategy for the Independent Store," *Stores,* April, 1963, p. 18ff.

"Discounting: "Why It's Tougher Now," *Printers' Ink,* March 22, 1963, p. 19ff.

GAULT, E. H. "The Future of Small Retailing—Will It Survive?" *Michigan Business Review,* November, 1956.

GILCHRIST, F. W. "The Discount House," *Journal of Marketing,* January, 1953, pp. 267–72.

GORDON, HOWARD L. "How Important Is the Chain Store Buying Committee?" *Journal of Marketing,* January, 1961, pp. 56–60.

HILEMAN, DONALD G., AND ROSENSTEIN, LEONARD A. "Deliberations of a Chain Store Buying Committee," *Journal of Marketing,* January, 1961, pp. 52–55.

HOLLANDER, S. C. "The Discount House," *Journal of Marketing,* July, 1953, pp. 57–59.

———— "The Wheel of Retailing," *Journal of Marketing,* July, 1960, pp. 37–42.

HORN, J. D. "Merchandising Non-Food Items through Super Markets," *Journal of Marketing,* April, 1954, pp. 380–86.

"How Far Can a Producer Retail?" *Business Week,* January 21, 1961, p. 77ff.

"How to Get Into the Supers," *Sales Management,* September 2, 1960, pp. 87–92.

"The Independent Retailer Fights Back," *Advertising Age,* July 23, 1962, p. 80.

"Is Your Major Retail Outlet Still Number One?" *Advertising Age,* May 29, 1961, p. 62.

Journal of Retailing. (This, the professional journal on retailing published quarterly by New York University, contains much information on retailing that is of interest to distribution managers in manufacturing concerns.)

MARTINEAU, PIERRE, "The Personality of the Retail Store," *Harvard Business Review,* January-February, 1958, p. 47ff.

MERTES, J. E. "The Shopping Center: A New Trend in Retailing," *Journal of Marketing,* January, 1949, pp. 374–379.

NORDSTROM, GUSTAV L. "How to Win—or Retain—Shelf Space against 6,000 New Items Each Year," *Sales Management,* March 7, 1958, pp. 86–90.

OAKS, C. L. "Organizing for Retail Decentralization," *Journal of Marketing,* January, 1956, pp. 255–61.

REGAN, WILLIAM J. "Full Cycle for Self-Service?" *Journal of Marketing,* April, 1961, pp. 15–21.

SHEPPARD, E. J. "The Growing Importance of the Small Town Store," *Journal of Marketing,* July, 1955, pp. 14–19.

TALLMAN, GERALD B., AND BLOMSTROM, BRUCE. "Retail Innovations Challenge Manufacturers," *Harvard Business Review,* September-October, 1962, pp. 130–41.

"Variety Stores in '61," *Sales Management,* April 7, 1961, p. 82ff.

"Will Manufacturers Go Into Retailing?" *Advertising Age,* December 31, 1962, p. 35.

WITTREICH, WARREN J. "Misunderstanding the Retailer," *Harvard Business Review,* May-June, 1962, pp. 147–59.

CHAPTERS 8 AND 9

BOOKS AND PAMPHLETS

BECKMAN, T. N., AND ENGLE, N. H. *Wholesaling.* 2d ed. New York: The Ronald Press Co., 1949.

HILL, RICHARD M. *Wholesaling Management: Text and Cases.* Homewood, Ill.: Richard D. Irwin, Inc., 1963.

History Defines the Food Broker. Washington, D.C.: National Food Brokers Association, n.d.

REVZAN, DAVID A. *Wholesaling in Marketing Organization.* New York: John Wiley and Sons, Inc., 1961.

SHIRK, A. V. *Marketing through Food Brokers.* New York: McGraw-Hill Book Co., Inc., 1939.

WARSHAW, MARTIN R. *Effective Selling through Wholesalers.* Michigan Business Studies, Vol. XV, No. 4. Ann Arbor, Mich.: University of Michigan, 1961.

ARTICLES

ALDERSON, WROE. "Scope and Function of Wholesaling in the United States," *Journal of Marketing,* September, 1949, pp. 145–91.

BRENDEL, L. H. "What Distributors Want to Know before They'll Take Your Line," *Sales Management,* October, 1951, 76ff.

——— "Where to Find and How to Choose Your Industrial Distributors," *Sales Management,* September, 1951, p. 128ff.

COLLINS, J. H. "How to Find and Appraise Qualified Sales Agents," *Sales Management,* September 15, 1948, p. 65ff.

CONVERSE, P. D. "Twenty-Five Years of Wholesaling: A Revolution in Food Wholesaling," *Journal of Marketing,* July, 1957, pp. 40–53.

HART, L. C. "Essentials of Successful Marketing: A Case History in Manufacturer-Distributor Collaboration," *Journal of Marketing,* October, 1948, p. 195ff.

KARAS, M. R. "The Historical Development of the Wholesaler during the Past 150 Years," *Successful Marketing at Home and Abroad,* W. D. ROBBINS (ed.). Chicago: American Marketing Association, 1958, pp. 402–8.

LEWIS, E. H. "Comeback of the Wholesaler," *Harvard Business Review,* November-December, 1955, pp. 115–25.

LIVESEY, C. A. "Appraising the Mill Supply Distributor," *Readings in Marketing.* 2d ed., M. C. MCNAIR AND H. L. HANSEN (eds.); New York: McGraw-Hill Book Co., Inc., 1956, pp. 282–99.

MARSHALL, C. "What Distributors Want from Manufacturers," *Industrial Marketing,* September, 1957, p. 202ff.

MARSTELLER, W. A. "Can Manufacturers' Agents Outsell Salesmen?" *Industrial Marketing,* February, 1951, p. 33ff.

MCFARLAND, S. W. "The Marketing Position of Industrial Distributors," *Journal of Marketing,* April, 1953, p. 394ff.

"New York Buying Offices: One-Stop Marketing Centers," *Sales Management,* September 2, 1960, p. 39ff.

SAWYER, H. G. "How to Sell through Industrial Distributors," *Industrial Marketing,* May, 1960, pp. 61–75.

SHEERAN, J. J. "The Role of the Rack Jobber," *Journal of Marketing,* July, 1961, pp. 15–21.

SNITZLER, J. R. "How Wholesalers Can Cut Delivery Costs," *Journal of Marketing,* July, 1958, pp. 25–31.

STAUDT, T. A. "How to Know When to Use Manufacturers' Agents," *Industrial Marketing,* October, 1952.

THOMAS, P. E., "Making a Good Contract with a Manufacturers' Agent," *Industrial Marketing,* February, 1950, p. 56ff.

CHAPTER 10

BOOKS AND PAMPHLETS

CLEWETT, RICHARD M. (ed.). *Marketing Channels for Manufactured Products.* Homewood, Ill.: Richard D. Irwin, Inc., 1954.

COLE, R. H.; DEBOER, L. M.; *et al. Manufacturer and Distributor Brands.* Urbana, Ill.: University of Illinois, 1955.

COLE, R. H.; MURCHISON, C. T.; *et al. Vertical Integration in Marketing.* Urbana, Ill.: University of Illinois, 1952.

CURTICE, H. H. *Distribution Policies and Practices of General Motors.* Washington, D.C.: Senate Interstate and Foreign Commerce Committee, U.S. Government Printing Office, 1956.

Dealer Margins. Studies in Business Policy, No. 42. New York: National Industrial Conference Board, Inc., 1950.

HEWITT, C. M. *The Development of Automobile Franchises.* Bloomington, Ind.: Bureau of Business Research, Indiana University, 1960.

MIGHELL, RONALD L., AND JONES, LAWRENCE A. *Vertical Coordination in Agriculture.* Agricultural Economic Report No. 19, U.S. Dept. of Agriculture. Washington, D.C.: U.S. Government Printing Office, 1963.

Organization behind the Salesman. Marketing Series No. 64. New York: American Management Association, 1946.

PALAMOUNTAIN, J. C., JR. *The Politics of Distribution.* Cambridge, Mass.: Harvard University Press, 1955.

Training Dealers. Studies in Business Policy, No. 48. New York: National Industrial Conference Board, Inc., 1950.

ARTICLES

BERG, THOMAS L. "Designing the Distribution System," *The Social Responsibilities of Marketing,* WILLIAM D. STEVENS (ed.). Chicago: American Marketing Association, 1962, pp. 481–90.

BRUNER, DICK. "How Do You Get Them into National Distribution?" *Printers' Ink,* June 1, 1956, pp. 21–23.

"The Changing Channels of Distribution," *Printers' Ink,* July 11, 1958, pp. 21–30.

CHRISTIAN, RICHARD C. "Three-Step Method to Better Distribution Channel Analysis," *Journal of Marketing,* October, 1958, pp. 191–92.

Cox, Reavis. "The Channel of Marketing as a Unit of Competition," *Successful Marketing at Home and Abroad,* W. D. Robbins (ed.). Chicago: American Marketing Association, 1958, pp. 481–90.

—— and Goodman, Charles. "Marketing of Housebuilding Materials," *Journal of Marketing,* July, 1956, pp. 36–61.

Curran, K. F. "Exclusive Dealing and Public Policy," *Journal of Marketing,* October, 1950, pp. 133–44.

Daggett, F. K. "Planning the Distribution of a New Product," *Developing a Product Strategy,* Elizabeth Marting (ed.). New York: American Management Association, 1959, pp. 243–53.

De Loach, D. B. "Competition for Channel Control in the Food Industry." *Conference of Marketing Teachers from Far Western States.* Berkeley, Calif.: University of California, 1958, pp. 119–28.

Duncan, D. J. (four articles). *Marketing by Manufacturers,* C. F. Phillips (ed.). Chicago: Richard D. Irwin, Inc., 1951, pp. 173–264.

Evans, K. J. "When and How You Should Sell through Distributors," *Industrial Marketing,* March, 1959, pp. 41–44.

"Franchising Is Wave of Future for Ad Agencies," *Advertising Age,* September 5, 1960, p. 80.

Hewitt, C. M. "The Furor over Dealer Franchises," *Business Horizons,* Winter, 1958, pp. 80–87.

Hill, W. C., and Scott, J. D. "Competition between Different Types of Retail Outlets in Selling the Same Commodity," *Harvard Business Review,* July, 1933.

Lebow, Victor. "Our Changing Channels of Distribution," *Journal of Marketing,* July 1948, pp. 12–22.

McVey, Phillip. "Are Channels of Distribution What the Textbooks Say?" *Journal of Marketing,* January, 1960, pp. 61–65.

Murphy, J. A. "What Type of Distribution Set-Up for the New Product?" *Sales Management,* April 1, 1948, pp. 44–50.

Newman, William H., and Berg, Thomas L. "Managing External Relations," *California Management Review,* Spring, 1963, pp. 81–86.

Ridgeway, Valentine F. "Administration of Manufacturer-Dealer Systems," *Administrative Science Quarterly,* March, 1957, pp. 464–83.

Rost, O. F. "The Shift in Manufacturer-Distributor Relationships." Proceedings of Boston Conference on Distribution, 1936.

Scott, J. D. "Selected Distribution Defined and Described." *Readings in Marketing.* 2d ed., M. P. McNair and H. L. Hansen (eds.). New York: McGraw-Hill Book Co., Inc., 1956, pp. 300–316.

"Selective Distribution," *Electrical Wholesaling,* November, 1959, pp. 71–94.

Smith, C. W. "Exploring New Channels of Distribution." Proceedings of Boston Conference on Distribution, 1958, pp. 43–45.

Williams, W. A. "Manufacturer and Dealer Responsibilities in Automobile

Marketing," *Marketing's Role in Scientific Management.* ROBERT L. CLEWETT (ed.). Chicago: American Marketing Association, 1957, pp. 17–24.

CHAPTERS 11 AND 12

BOOKS AND PAMPHLETS

ASPLEY, J. C., AND HARKNESS, J. C. *The Sales Manager's Handbook.* 9th rev. ed. Chicago: The Dartnell Corp., 1962.

BENGE EUGENE. *Manpower in Marketing.* New York: Harper and Bros., 1945.

CANFIELD, B. R. *Sales Administration: Principles and Problems.* 4th ed. Englewood Cliffs, N.J.: Prentice-Hall, Inc., 1961.

Checklists of Sales Essentials. New York: Printers' Ink Publishing Co., 1954.

DAVIS, JAMES H. *Handbook of Sales Training.* Englewood Cliffs, N.J.: Prentice-Hall, Inc., 1954.

DAVIS, ROBERT T. *Performance and Development of Field Sales Managers.* Boston: Harvard Graduate School of Business, 1957.

The Field Sales Manager. Management Report No. 48. New York: American Management Association, 1960.

GRIEF, EDWIN CHARLES. *Modern Salesmanship: Principles and Problems.* Englewood Cliffs, N.J.: Prentice-Hall, Inc., 1958.

HAAS, K. B. *How to Develop Successful Salesmen.* New York: McGraw-Hill Book Co., Inc., 1957.

LAPP, C. *Successful Selling Strategies.* New York: McGraw Hill Book Co., Inc., 1957.

LESTER, B. *Selling to Industry.* New York: The Industrial Press, 1952.

MANDELL, MILTON M. *A Company Guide to the Selection of Salesmen.* Research Report No. 24. New York: American Management Association, 1955.

PEDERSON, CARLTON A., AND WRIGHT, MILBURN D. *Salesmanship: Principles and Methods.* 3d ed. Homewood, Ill.: Richard D. Irwin, Inc., 1961.

STANTON, WILLIAM, AND BUSKIRK, RICHARD. *Management of the Sales Force.* Homewood, Ill.: Richard D. Irwin, Inc., 1959.

STILL, RICHARD R., AND CUNDIFF, EDWARD W. *Sales Management: Decisions, Policies, and Cases.* Englewood Cliffs, N.J.: Prentice-Hall, Inc., 1958.

TOSDAL, HARRY R. *Introduction to Sales Management.* 4th ed. New York: McGraw-Hill Book Co., Inc., 1957.

———— *Selling in Our Economy.* Homewood, Ill.: Richard D. Irwin, Inc., 1957.

———— AND CARSON, WALLER. *Salesmen's Compensation* (2 vol.) Boston: Harvard Graduate School of Business, 1953.

ARTICLES

BAUER, R. A. "Limits of Persuasion," *Harvard Business Review,* September-October, 1958, pp. 105–10.

BERG, THOMAS L. "How to Run a One-Shot Crew Operation," *Sales Management,* November 17, 1961, pp. 75–80.

BURSK, EDWARD C. "Opportunities for Persuasion," *Harvard Business Review,* September-October, 1958, pp. 111–19.

DAVIS, R. T. "Sales Management in the Field," *Harvard Business Review,* January-February, 1958, pp. 91–98.

FOX, W. M. "Four Ways to Route Salesmen," *Printers' Ink,* November 12, 1954, pp. 78–80.

"Functions of the Sales Executive," *Readings in Marketing.* 2d ed. M. P. MCNAIR AND H. L. HANSEN (eds.). New York: McGraw-Hill Book Co., Inc., 1956, pp. 414–42.

KELLEY, E. J., AND LAZER, WILLIAM. "Basic Duties of the Modern Sales Department," *Industrial Marketing,* April, 1960, pp. 68–74.

LAPP, C. L. "Are Your Sales Job Descriptions Adequate?" *Sales Management,* June 6, 1958, pp. 90–93.

MCMURRY, R. N. "The Mystique of Super-Salesmanship," *Harvard Business Review,* March-April, 1961, pp. 113–22.

SEMLOW, W. J. "How Many Salesmen Do You Need?" *Harvard Business Review,* May-June, 1959, pp. 126–32.

SHUCHMAN, ABRAHAM, AND KAHN, GEORGE. "Specialize Your Salesmen," *Harvard Business Review,* January-February, 1961, pp. 90–98.

SIMMONS, HARRY. "Check List of Functions of Modern Sales Management," *Printers' Ink,* January 23, 1948, p. 40ff.

STICKNEY, RICHARD W. "Deploying Multi-Line Salesmen," *Harvard Business Review,* March-April, 1960, pp. 110–12.

TALLEY, WALTER J. "How to Design Sales Territories," *Journal of Marketing,* January, 1961, pp. 7–13.

CHAPTERS 13 AND 14

BOOKS

ASPLEY, J. C. (ed.). *Sales Promotion Handbook.* Chicago: The Dartnell Co., 1960.

BARTON, ROGER. *Advertising Agency Operations and Management.* New York: McGraw-Hill Book Co., Inc., 1955.

——— *Advertising Handbook.* New York: Prentice-Hall, Inc., 1950.

BERNAYS, E. L. *The Engineering of Consent.* Norman, Okla.: University of Oklahoma Press, 1955.

BORDEN, NEIL H., AND MARSHALL, MARTIN V. *Advertising Management: Text and Cases.* Homewood, Ill.: Richard D. Irwin, Inc., 1959.

BROWN, LYNDON O.; LESSLER, RICHARD S.; AND WEILBACHER, WILLIAM. *Advertising Media.* New York: The Ronald Press Co., 1957.

CANFIELD, B. R. *Public Relations.* Homewood, Ill.: Richard D. Irwin, Inc., 1956.

CAPLES, JOHN. *Tested Advertising Methods.* New York: Harper and Bros., 1961.

DUNN, S. WATSON. *Advertising: Its Role In Modern Marketing.* New York: Holt, Rinehart and Winston, Inc., 1961.

FREY, ALBERT WESLEY. *How Many Dollars for Advertising?* New York: The Ronald Press Co., 1955.

———— *Advertising.* 3d ed. New York: The Ronald Press Co., 1961.

GROSS, ALFRED. *Sales Promotion.* 2d ed. New York: The Ronald Press Co., 1960.

HATTWICK, MELVIN S. *How to Use Psychology for Better Advertising.* New York: Prentice-Hall, Inc., 1950.

HEPNER, HARRY WALKER. *Modern Advertising: Practices and Principles.* New York: McGraw-Hill Book Co., Inc., 1956.

KIRKPATRICK, C. A. *Advertising.* Boston: Houghton Mifflin Co., 1959.

KLEPPNER, OTTO. *Advertising Procedure.* 4th ed. Englewood Cliffs, N.J.: Prentice-Hall, Inc., 1950.

LUCAS, DARRELL B., AND BRITT, STEUART H. *Advertising Psychology and Research.* New York: McGraw-Hill Book Co., Inc., 1950.

MARTINEAU, PIERRE. *Motivation in Advertising.* New York: McGraw-Hill Book Co., Inc., 1957.

MAYER, MARTIN. *Madison Avenue, U.S.A.* New York: Harper and Bros., 1958.

MEREDITH, GEORGE. *Effective Merchandising with Premiums.* New York: McGraw-Hill Book Co., Inc., 1962.

OGILVY, DAVID. *Confessions of An Advertising Man.* New York: Atheneum, 1963.

PACKARD, VANCE. *The Hidden Persuaders.* New York: David McKay Co., Inc., 1957.

ST. THOMAS, CHARLES E. *How to Get Industrial and Business Publicity.* Philadelphia: Chilton Co., 1956.

SANDAGE, C. H., AND FRYBURGER, VERNON. *Advertising Theory and Practice.* 6th ed. Homewood, Ill.: Richard D. Irwin, Inc., 1963.

SIMMONS, H. *Successful Sales Promotion.* New York: Prentice-Hall, Inc., 1950.

WEDDING, NUGENT, AND LESSLER, RICHARD S. *Advertising Management.* New York: The Ronald Press Co., 1963.

WHITTIER, CHARLES L. *Creative Advertising.* New York: Henry Holt & Co., 1955.

WHYTE, W. H. *Is Anybody Listening?* New York: Simon and Shuster, 1952.

WISEMAN, MARK. *The Anatomy of Advertising.* New York: Harper and Bros., 1959.

ARTICLES

"Ad Budgets: A Growing Science," *Printers' Ink,* December 16, 1960, p. 16ff.

ADLER, LEE. "How Marketing Management Can Make Sounder Media Decisions." *Marketing Keys to Profits in the 1960's,* W. K. DOLVA (ed). Chicago: American Marketing Association, 1960, pp. 149–56.

"Advertising: Capital Investment or Current Expense?" *Industrial Marketing,* March, 1959, pp. 138–42.

BERG, THOMAS L. "Managerial Aspects of New-Product Promotion," *The Business Quarterly,* Spring, 1963, pp. 52–61.

"Coordination of Advertising with Display and Personal Selling," *Journal of Retailing,* Fall, 1956.

DEAN, JOEL. "How Much to Spend on Advertising," *Harvard Business Review,* January, 1951, pp. 65–74.

DEAN, SIDNEY W., JR. "Fission in Markets: It Calls for a New Strategy in Media Buying," *Sales Management,* November 10, 1959, pp. 58–62.

DELANO, LESTER A. "Creative Advertising Planning," *Marketing's Role in Scientific Management,* R. L. CLEWETT (ed.). Chicago: American Management Association, 1957, pp. 335–41.

ELDRIDGE, CLARENCE. "The Job of the Advertising Manager," *Effective Marketing Action,* D. W. EWING (ed.). New York: Harper and Bros., 1958, pp. 319–28.

"How to Sell the Ad Budget to Management," *Industrial Marketing,* September, 1956.

KLAW, SPENCER. "Advertising: The Battle of 15 Per Cent," *Fortune,* October, 1956, p. 142ff.

KOFRON, J. H. "Pinpointing Industrial Advertising Targets." Proceedings of 5th Annual Conference of ARF. New York: Advertising Research Foundation, 1959, pp. 53–59.

LEWIS, E. H. "Use of Principles in the Management of Advertising," *Journal of Marketing,* January, 1955, pp. 258–60.

LUSK, R. E. "How to Pick an Advertising Agency: Finding the Agency That Fits Your Needs," *Dun's Review and Modern Industry,* October, 1958, p. 52ff.

MCMURRY, R. N. "How to Win or Lose Sales at the Point of Purchase," *Journal of Marketing,* July, 1959, pp. 41–49.

OGILVY, DAVID. "The Image and the Brand: A New Approach to Creative Operations," *Advertising Age,* November 14, 1955, pp. 113–14.

"Organization of the Advertising Department," *Printers' Ink,* October 23, 1953, pp. 51–54.

PETERSON, ELDRIDGE. "Why Management is Reappraising Advertising," *Dun's Review and Modern Industry,* October, 1958, p. 49ff.

"Planning Ad Budgets: A New Model, *Printers' Ink,* June 17, 1960, pp. 67–69.

POLITZ, ALFRED. "The Dilemma of Creative Advertising," *Journal of Marketing,* October, 1960, pp. 1–6.

ROBINSON, F. D. "The Advertising Budget," *The Controller,* August, 1958, p. 368ff.

RUBEL, I. W., "Toward Better Advertiser-Agency Relations, *Harvard Business Review,* March-April, 1958, pp. 107–14.

"What Factors Determine the Choice of Media," *Printers' Ink,* January 23, 1953, pp. 33–35.

CHAPTER 15

BOOKS AND PAMPHLETS

BROWN, ROBERT G. *Statistical Forecasting for Inventory Control.* New York: McGraw-Hill Book Co., Inc., 1959.

Industry's Terms and Conditions of Sale. Studies in Business Policy, No. 26. New York: National Industrial Conference Board, 1948.

IRONS, WATROUS, H. Commercial Credit and Collection Practice. 2d ed. New York: The Ronald Press Co., 1957.

MAGEE, JOHN G. *Production Planning and Inventory.* New York: McGraw-Hill Book Co., Inc., 1958.

Management of the Physical-Distribution Function. Management Report No. 49. New York: American Management Association, 1960.

NYSTROM, PAUL H. (ed.) *Marketing Handbook.* Section 5: Service Policies. New York: The Ronald Press Co., 1954, pp. 183–215.

SMYKAY, EDWARD J.; BOWERSOX, DONALD J., AND MOSSMAN, FRANK. *Physical Distribution Management.* New York: The Macmillan Co., 1961.

Technical Service in the American Economy. Ann Arbor, Mich.: University of Michigan Bureau of Business Research, 1962.

ARTICLES

BABIONE, F. A. "Marketing Equipment by Lease," *Journal of Marketing,* October, 1950, 205ff.

"The Case for 90 Per Cent Satisfaction," *Business Week,* January 14, 1961, pp. 82–85.

DENENHOLZ, R. S. "Physical Distribution as a New Staff Function in Marketing, *The Frontiers of Marketing Thought and Science,* F. M. BASS (ed.). Chicago: American Marketing Association, 1960, pp. 95–101.

FORRESTER, JAY F. "Industrial Dynamics: A Major Breakthrough for Decision Makers," *Harvard Business Review,* July-August, 1958, pp. 37–66.

GILBERT, NATHANIEL. "Winning Customers with Order Automation," *Sales Management,* June 6, 1959, pp. 106–10.

"The Great Credit Pump," *Fortune,* February, 1963, p. 122ff.

"How to Make 'Service' Mean Something," *Industrial Distribution,* October, 1954, p. 108ff.

"Integrating Your Transportation for Profit," *Dun's Review and Modern Industry,* June, 1959, pp. 60–62.

"Is Your Credit Man a Member of Your Sales Team?" *Sales Management* January 18, 1957, p. 42ff.

KIRCHHOFER, K. F. "Your Service Can Also Sell—Make Sure That It Does," *Industrial Marketing,* March, 1952, p. 86ff.

LAIRD, D. A. "The Service Emphasis Takes Over Modern Selling," *Management Review,* August 1951, p. 496ff.

MADDOCK, S. "Industrial Financing and Its Role in Distribution," *Advanced Management,* February 1957, p. 11ff.

MAFFEI, RICHARD B., AND SHYCON, HARVEY N. "Simulation: Tool for Better Distribution," *Harvard Business Review,* November-December, 1960, pp. 65–75.

MAGEE, JOHN F. "The Logistics of Distribution," *Harvard Business Review,* July-August, 1960, pp. 89–101.

MANDELL, MELVIN. "Boosting Sales with Faster Delivery," *Dun's Review and Modern Industry,* February, 1960, pp. 44–45.

MORGAN, JAMES I. "Questions for Solving the Inventory Problem," *Harvard Business Review,* July-August, 1963, pp. 95–110.

"Product Warranties: Are They Worth Their Cost?" *Industrial Marketing,* February, 1956, p. 61ff.

"Service Sells the Salesman," *Industrial Distribution,* October, 1948, p. 92ff.

THOMAS, R. S. "Product Service: How Much is Enough?" *Industrial Marketing,* December, 1957, p. 53ff.

"What Does Service Mean?" *Industrial Distribution,* April, 1954, 94ff.

CHAPTERS 16 AND 17

BOOKS

BACKMAN, JULES (ed). *Price Practices and Price Policies.* New York: The Ronald Press Co., 1953.

———— *Pricing: Policies and Practices.* Studies in Business Economics, No. 71. New York: National Industrial Conference Board, 1961.

BERGFELD, ALBERT J.; EARLEY, JAMES S.; AND KNOBLOCK, WILLIAM R. *Pricing for Profit and Growth.* Englewood Cliffs, N.J.: Prentice-Hall, Inc., 1962.

Competitive Pricing. Management Report No. 17. New York: American Management Association, 1958.

Current Pricing Practice. Chicago: The Dartnell Co., 1957.

DEAN, JOEL. *Managerial Economics.* Englewood Cliffs, N.J.: Prentice-Hall, Inc., 1951, 395-547.

KAPLAN, A. D. H.; DIRLAN, J. B.; AND LANZILOTTI, R. F. *Pricing in Big Business.* Washington, D.C.: The Brookings Institution, 1958.

OXENFELDT, A. R. *Industrial Pricing and Market Practices.* New York: Prentice-Hall, Inc., 1951.

———— *Pricing for Marketing Executives.* Belmont, California: Wadsworth Publishing Co., Inc., 1961.

SAWYER, ALBERT E. *Business Aspects of Pricing under the Robinson-Patman Act.* Boston: Little, Brown and Company, 1963.

ARTICLES

ADELMAN, M. A. "Pricing by Manufacturers," *Conference of Marketing Teachers from Far Western States.* Berkeley, Calif.: University of California, 1958, pp. 146–158.

AUSTIN, R. W. "Let's Get Cost Pricing out of Our Laws," *Harvard Business Review,* May-June, 1954, pp. 67–72.

BOCK, BETTY. "Regional Price Differentials," *Business Record,* November, 1959, pp. 521–25.

COREY, E. RAYMOND. "Fair Trade Pricing: A Reappraisal," *Harvard Business Review,* September-October, 1952, pp. 47–62.

DEAN, JOEL. "Cost Forecasting and Price Policy," *Harvard Business Review,* January, 1949, pp. 279–88.

———— "Problems of Product-Line Pricing," *Journal of Marketing,* January, 1950, pp. 518–28.

DEARDEN, JOHN. "Interdivisional Pricing," *Harvard Business Review,* January-February, 1960, pp. 117–25.

FOY, FRED C. "Creative Pricing: Policy or Accident?" *Business Record,* November, 1957, pp. 520–24.

GRIFFIN, CLARE E. "When Is Price Reduction Profitable?" *Harvard Business Review,* September-October, 1960, pp. 125–32.

HAWKINS, E. R. "Price Policies and Theory," *Journal of Marketing,* January, 1954, pp. 233–40.

HOLLANDER, S. C. "The 'One-Price System': Fact or Fiction?" *Journal of Retailing,* Fall, 1955, pp. 127–44.

IDE, E. A. "How to Use Marketing Analysis in Price Determination," *Marketing's Role in Scientific Management,* R. L. Clewett (ed.). Chicago: The American Marketing Association, 1957, pp. 198–214.

KARGER, THEODORE, AND THOMPSON, G. CLARK. "Executives Report on Pricing Policies and Practices," *Business Record,* September, 1957, pp. 434–42.

MCNAIR, M. P., AND MAY, E. G. "Pricing for Profit," *Harvard Business Review,* May-June, 1957, pp. 105–22.

OXENFELDT, A. R. "Multistage Approach to Pricing," *Harvard Business Review,* July-August, 1960, pp. 125–33.

ROBBINS, W. DAVID. "Is Competitive Pricing Legal?" *Harvard Business Review,* November-December, 1957, pp. 83–89.

SCHELLING, THOMAS C. "An Essay on Bargaining," *American Economic Review,* June, 1956, pp. 281–306.

"Who Pays List Price?" *Fortune,* June, 1952, pp. 104–6.

"Who Sets Prices in Industry?" *Business Week,* July 5, 1958, pp. 48–51.

CHAPTER 18

BOOKS AND PAMPHLETS

ALDERSON, WROE, AND SHAPIRO, STANLEY J. (eds.). *Marketing and the Computer.* Englewood Cliffs, N.J.: Prentice-Hall, Inc., 1963.

The Coming Electronic Communications Revolution—And Its Impact on the Total World of Marketing. New York: Doyle, Dane, Bernbach, Inc., 1956.

Current Sources of Information for Market Research: A Selected and Annotated Bibliography. Chicago: American Marketing Association, 1954.

ARTICLES

BALDERSTON, FRED. "Communication Networks in Intermediate Markets," *Management Science,* January, 1958, pp. 154–71.

BONI, G. M. "Evaluating the Information Used in the Marketing Function," *Analyzing and Improving Marketing Performance.* New York: American Management Association, 1959, pp. 72–81.

BRITT, STEUART H., AND SHAPIRO, IRWIN A. "Where to Find Marketing Facts," *Harvard Business Review,* September-October, 1962, p. 44ff.

BURLINGAME, JOHN F. "Information Technology and Decentralization," *Harvard Business Review,* November-December, 1961, pp. 121–26.

CLARKE, GEORGE T. "The Art of Using Facts," *Effective Marketing Action,* DAVID W. EWING (ed.). New York: Harper and Bros., 1958, pp. 227–32.

DANIEL, D. RONALD. "Management Information Crisis," *Harvard Business Review,* September-October, 1961, pp. 111–21.

DePASSE, ALFRED, AND FLECK, STEWART. "How to Keep Track of Your Competition, *Sales Management,* November 10, 1959, pp. 18–21.

ECKLER, A. ROSS. "A Guide to Census Statistics," *Effective Marketing Action,* DAVID W. EWING (ed.). New York: Harper and Bros., 1958, pp. 242–53.

ESTES, B. E. "Where to Go for Data," *Effective Marketing Action,* DAVID W. EWING (ed.). New York: Harper and Bros., 1958, pp. 233–41.

EVANS, MARSHALL K., AND HAGUE, LOU R. "Master Plan for Information Systems," *Harvard Business Review,* January-February, 1962, pp. 92–103.

GILBERT, NATHANIEL. "Winning Customers with Order Automation," *Sales Management,* June 6, 1959, pp. 106–10.

HAGEN, ROGER C., AND MAXWELL, DENNIS G. "Filling in the Gaps in Published Data," *Effective Marketing Action,* DAVID W. EWING (ed.). New York: Harper and Bros., 1958, pp. 254–60.

HARPER, MARION, JR. "Communications Is the Core of Marketing," *Printers' Ink,* June 1, 1962, pp. 52–53.

LADD, H. O. "Practical Benefits of Marketing Facts to Corporate Profits," *What Modern Marketing Means to Corporate Success,* New York: National Association of Manufacturers, 1958, pp. 18–21.

LANGHOFF, PETER S. "Marketing Intelligence and Planning," *Distribution Costs: A Key to Profits,* Marketing for Executives Series, No. 5. Chicago: American Marketing Association, 1958, pp. 22–27.

LINDSAY, FRANKLIN A. "Find Out—or Flounder!" *Sales Management,* April 6, 1962, p. 41ff.

———— "Marshall Your Marketing Information," *Business Horizons,* Summer, 1962, pp. 53–60.

LONGMAN, DONALD R. "The Role of the Marketing Staff," *Journal of Marketing,* July, 1962, pp. 29–33.

McDONALD, JOHN. "Strategy of the Seller—or What Business Won't Tell," *Fortune,* December, 1952, pp. 124–127ff.

SEARES, A. N. "Marketing Intelligence," *The 1957 Truck Lecture Series on Marketing and Distribution.* New York: National Association of Manufacturers, 1957, pp. 17–25.

SESSIONS, ROBERT E. "A Management Audit of Marketing Research," *Journal of Marketing,* January, 1950, pp. 563–71.

SHUCHMAN, ABE. "The Marketing Audit: Its Nature, Purpose and Problems," *Analyzing and Improving Marketing Performance,* Management Report No. 32. New York: American Management Association, 1959, pp. 11–19.

SPENCER, S. A. "The Dark at the Top of the Stairs: What Higher Management Needs from Information Systems," *Management Review,* July, 1962, p. 11ff.

THOMAS, PAT. "Market Intelligence—What to Look For, Where to Find It, How to Obtain It," *DATA Magazine,* July, 1960, pp. 5–7.

THURSTON, PHILIP H. "Who Should Control Information Systems?" *Harvard Business Review,* November-December, 1962, pp. 135–39.

WEST, HERBERT. "How to Fit Facts into a Master Strategy Blueprint," *Advertising Agency Magazine,* April 12, 1957, pp. 60–64.

———— "How to Select Facts for a Master Planning Blueprint," *Advertising Agency Magazine,* March 15, 1957, pp. 60–62.

"What Every Intelligent Marketing Man Should Know about Computers," *Printers' Ink,* July 13, 1962, pp. 21–30.

CHAPTER 19

BOOKS AND PAMPHLETS

BOYD, H. W., AND WESTFALL, R. *Marketing Research: Text and Cases.* Homewood, Ill.: Richard D. Irwin, Inc., 1956.

BROWN, LYNDON O. *Marketing and Distribution Research.* 3d ed. New York, The Ronald Press Co., 1955.

CHURCHMAN, C. W., AND ACKOFF, R. L. *Introduction to Operations Research.* New York: John Wiley and Sons, 1957.

CRISP, RICHARD D. *Company Practices in Marketing Research.* New York: American Management Association, 1953.

———— *Marketing Research.* New York: McGraw-Hill Book Co., Inc., 1957.

———— *Marketing Research Organization and Operation.* New York: American Management Association, 1958.

Criteria for Marketing and Advertising Research. New York: Advertising Research Foundation, 1953.

FERBER, R., AND WALES, H. G. *Motivation and Market Behavior.* Homewood, Ill.: Richard D. Irwin, Inc., 1958.

FOX, WILLARD M. *How to Use Marketing Research for Profit.* New York: Prentice-Hall, Inc., 1950.

Marketing, Business, and Commercial Research in Industry. Studies in Business Policy, No. 72. New York: National Industrial Conference Board, 1957.

Marketing Research in Action. Studies in Business Policy, No. 84. New York: National Industrial Conference Board, 1957.

NEWMAN, J. W. *Motivation Research and Marketing Management.* Boston: Harvard Graduate School of Business, 1957.

SMITH, GEORGE HORSLEY. *Motivation Research in Advertising and Marketing.* New York: McGraw-Hill Book Co., Inc., 1955.

ARTICLES

ANSHEN, MELVIN. "Fundamental and Applied Research in Marketing," *Journal of Marketing,* January, 1955, pp. 233–43.

BOGART, LEO. "How to Get More out of Marketing Research," *Harvard Business Review,* January-February, 1956, pp. 74–84.

BRITT, S. H. "Should You Fit the Research to the Budget?" *Journal of Marketing,* April, 1956, pp. 401–3.

BROWN, LYNDON O. "Marketing Research Foundations for Changing Marketing Strategy," *Changing Structure and Strategy in Marketing,* R. B. MITCHELL (ed.). Urbana, Ill.: University of Illinois, 1958, pp. 94–104.

JEUCK, J. E. "Marketing Research: Milestone or Millstone?" *Journal of Marketing,* April, 1953, pp. 381–87.

MARSTELLER, W. A. "Putting the Marketing Research Department on the Executive Level," *Journal of Marketing,* July, 1951, pp. 56–60.

MARTINEAU, PIERRE. "It's Time to Research the Consumer," *Harvard Business Review,* July-August, 1955, pp. 45–54.

MORRIS, W. W. "What Marketing Research and Planning Can Do for Marketing Management," *Successful Marketing at Home and Abroad,* W. D. ROBBINS (ed.). Chicago: American Marketing Association, 1958, pp. 180–88.

NEWMAN, JOSEPH W. "Put Research into Marketing Decisions," *Harvard Business Review,* March-April, 1962, pp. 105–12.

NICHOLAS, G. P. "Marketing Research Needn't Be Expensive," *Sales Management,* March 20, 1959, p. 82ff.

POLITZ, ALFRED. "Science and Truth in Marketing Research," *Harvard Business Review,* January-February, 1957, p. 116ff.

ROBERTS, H. V. "The Role of Research in Marketing Management," *Journal of Marketing,* July, 1957, pp. 21–32.

ROSBERG, J. W. "A Minimum Program for Marketing Research," *Industrial Marketing,* January, 1960, pp. 125–29.

TASKER, G. W. "No Research Is Better Than Bad Research," *Sales Management,* February 19, 1960, pp. 105–10.

CHAPTER 20

BOOKS AND PAMPHLETS

CULLITON, JAMES W. *The Management of Marketing Costs.* Cambridge, Mass.: Harvard Graduate School of Business Administration, 1948.

Distribution Costs: A Key to Profits. Marketing for Executives Series, No. 5. Chicago: American Marketing Association, 1958.

HECKERT, J. B., AND MINER, R. B. *Distribution Costs.* Rev. ed. New York: The Ronald Press Co., 1953.

LONGMAN, DONALD R., AND SCHIFF, MICHAEL. *Practical Distribution Cost Analysis.* Homewood, Ill.: Richard D. Irwin, Inc., 1955.

SEVIN, C. H. *Distribution Cost Analysis.* Economic Series, No. 50. Washington, D.C.: Bureau of Foreign and Domestic Commerce, 1946.

——— *How Manufacturers Reduce Their Distribution Costs.* Washington, D.C.: U.S. Department of Commerce, 1948.

ARTICLES

BAUMOL, W. J., AND SEVIN, C. H. "Marketing Costs and Mathematical Programming," *Harvard Business Review,* September-October, 1957, pp. 52–60.

COWAN, D. R. "High Cost of Selling—Under Fire Again," *Printers' Ink,* July 16, 1954, p. 37ff.

——— "Marketing Critics Ask Again 'Distribution Costs Too High?'" *Sales Management,* February 1, 1956, p. 30ff.

CRISP, R. D. "How to Boil the Fat out of Sales Costs," *Industrial Marketing,* March, 1949, p. 33ff.

DOW, L. A. "Marketing Costs and Economic Theory," *Journal of Marketing,* April, 1955, pp. 346–50.

HOUFEK, L. J. "How to Find and Forget Unprofitable Customers," *Management Review,* June, 1952, p. 379ff.

HOUGHTON, DALE. "Marketing Costs: What Ratio to Sales?" *Printers' Ink,* February 1, 1957, p. 23ff.

LAIRD, D. A. "Costs of Distribution," *Purchasing,* December, 1953, p. 119ff.

LONGMAN, DONALD R. "Recent Developments in Distribution Cost Analysis," *Conference of Marketing Teachers from Far Western States.* Berkeley, Calif. University of California, 1958, pp. 60–74.

MAZUR, P. M. "Does Distribution Cost Enough?" *Fortune,* November, 1947, p. 138ff.

MITCHELL, W. J. "The Sales Department's Place in Cost Reduction," *Printers' Ink,* January 6, 1950, p. 33ff.

"Sales Costs *Can* Be Controlled," *Management Review.* October, 1954, p. 677ff.

TOMLIN, S. "How Engineering Know-How Can Improve Distribution," *Management Review,* August, 1951, p. 29ff.

"The Values and Uses of Distribution Cost Analysis," *Journal of Marketing,* April, 1957, pp. 395–400.

WATSON, R. H. "Bases for Allocating Distribution Costs," *Journal of Marketing,* July, 1951, p. 29ff.

"Why So Little Data on Distribution Costs?" *Distribution Age,* December, 1953, p. 17ff.

CHAPTER 21

BOOKS AND PAMPHLETS

CRAWFORD, C. M. *Sales Forecasting: Methods of Selected Firms.* University of Illinois Bulletin, Vol. 52, No. 46. Urbana, Ill.: University of Illinois, 1955.

Economic Factors in Market Planning. New York: American Management Association, 1949.

Evaluating and Using Business Indicators. Management Report No. 25. New York: American Management Association, 1959.

Forecasting Sales. Studies in Business Policies, No. 106. New York: National Industrial Conference Board, 1963.

FREY, A. W. *The Effective Marketing Mix.* Hanover, N.H.: The Amos Tuck School of Business, Dartmouth College, 1956.

LUCAS, DARRELL B., AND BRITT, STEUART HENDERSON. *Measuring Advertising Effectiveness.* New York: McGraw-Hill Book Co., Inc., 1962.

MASSY, WILLIAM F. *Planning in Marketing: A Selected Bibliography.* Cambridge, Mass.: The M.I.T. Press, 1962.

WRIGHT, WILSON, *Forecasting for Profit.* New York: John Wiley and Sons, Inc., 1947.

ARTICLES

ANDERSON, R. C. "Organization of the Planning Process," *Advanced Management,* May, 1958, pp. 5–11.

BORCHERDT, G. T. "Design of the Marketing Program for a New Product," *Marketing's Role in Scientific Management,* R. L. CLEWETT (ed.). Chicago: American Marketing Association, 1957, pp. 58–73.

BORDEN, N. H. "Note on Concept of the Marketing Mix," *Managerial Marketing: Perspectives and Viewpoints,* E. J. KELLEY AND WILLIAM LAZER (eds.). Homewood, Ill.: Richard D. Irwin, Inc., 1958, pp. 272–75.

BOULDEN, JAMES B. "Fitting the Sales Forecast to Your Firm," *Business Horizons,* Winter, 1958, pp. 65–72.

BROWN, G. H. "Strategy and Long-Range Planning in Marketing Management," *Changing Structure and Strategy in Marketing,* R. V. MITCHELL (ed.). Urbana, Ill.: University of Illinois, 1958, pp. 11–16.

BUELL, VICTOR P. "Better Management through Planning," *Effective Marketing Action,* DAVID W. EWING (ed.). New York: Harper and Bros., 1958.

BUND, H. "Economic Forecasting," *Advanced Management,* January, 1953, p. 64ff.

COLM, G. "Economic Projections: New Tool for Top Management," *Sales Management,* November 10, 1955, p. 54ff.

DAVIDSON, G. W. "Why You Should Blueprint Your Marketing Plan," *Printers' Ink,* April 19, 1957, pp. 31–33.

ETCHEVERRY, B. E. "Long Range Planning for Markets," *The Broadening Perspectives of Marketing.* Chicago: American Marketing Association, 1956, pp.126–31.

FERBER, ROBERT. "Sales Forecasting by Correlation Techniques," *Journal of Marketing,* January, 1954, pp. 219–32.

——— "Sales Forecasting by Sample Surveys," *Journal of Marketing,* July, 1955, pp. 1–13.

FERRELL, R. W. "Marketing Planning, A Vital Part of Long-Range Business Planning," *The Broadening Perspective of Marketing.* Chicago: American Marketing Association, 1956, pp. 113–19.

HANSEN, H. L. "Creative Marketing Strategy," *31st Annual Conference on Distribution.* Boston: Boston Conference on Distribution, 1959, pp. 54–57.

HOUFEK, L. J. "Short-Term Sales Forecasting: Top Job for the Marketing Team," *Printers' Ink,* February, 1952, p. 80ff.

JAMES, C. C. "How To Plan and Set Up An Effective Marketing Program," *Advanced Management,* June, 1957, pp. 14–17.

"Marketing Strategy for the Small Guy," *Printers' Ink,* October 19, 1956, p. 44ff.

McDONALD, JOHN. "A Theory of Strategy," *Fortune,* June, 1959, pp. 100–109.

McKAY, E. S. "How to Plan and Set Up Your Marketing Program," *Blueprint for an Effective Marketing Program,* Marketing Series, No. 91. New York: American Management Association, 1954, pp. 3–17.

OXENFELDT, ALFRED R. "The Formulation of a Market Strategy," *Managerial Marketing: Perspectives and Viewpoints,* E. J. KELLY AND WILLIAM LAZER (eds.). Homewood, Ill.: Richard D. Irwin, Inc., 1958, pp. 264–272.

PEARSON, A. E. "An Approach to Successful Marketing Planning," *Business Horizons,* Winter, 1959, pp. 74–82.

SARGENT, J. R. "Marketing Management's Key Responsibility: Effective Strategy," *Marketing Keys to Profits in the 1960's,* W. K. DOLVA (ed.) Chicago: American Marketing Association, 1960, pp. 57–66.

SHEPHERD, GEOFFREY. "The Analytical Problem Approach to Marketing," *Journal of Marketing,* October, 1955, pp. 173–77.

"Strategy Behind the Marketing Plan," *Advertising Agency Magazine,* November 11, 1955, pp. 56–57.

STRONG, LYDIA. "Sales Forecasting Comes of Age," *Management Review,* August, 1956, p. 687ff.

"Ten Steps in Forecasting Sales," *Management Review,* April, 1956, p. 261ff.

TILLES, SEYMOUR. "How to Evaluate Corporate Strategy," *Harvard Business Review,* July-August, 1963, pp. 111–21.

WEST, HERBERT. "The Four Basic Parts of a Master Strategy Blueprint," *Advertising Agency Magazine,* February 15, 1957, p. 69ff.

——— "How to Get an OK On a Marketing Plan," *Advertising Agency Magazine,* September 13, 1957, pp. 20–22.

——— "How to Plan a Master Strategy Blueprint," *Advertising Agency Magazine,* July 5, 1957, pp. 18–21.

———"How to Use a Marketing Plan," *Advertising Agency Magazine,* October 11, 1957, pp. 24–26.

————"How to Write Objectives of a Master Strategy Blueprint," *Advertising Agency Magazine,* August 16, 1957, pp. 20–23.

———— "Who Should Write a Master Strategy Blueprint?" *Advertising Agency Magazine,* June 7, 1957, pp. 58–60.

———— "Why You Need a Master Strategy Blueprint," *Advertising Agency Magazine,* January 18, 1957, p. 57ff.

WILLETT, R. P. "A Model for Marketing Programming," *Journal of Marketing,* January, 1963, pp. 40–45.

CHAPTER 22

BOOKS AND PAMPHLETS

Analyzing and Improving Marketing Performance. Management Report No. 32. New York: American Management Association, 1959.

Aspects of Modern Marketing: Tools, Techniques, and Market Trends. Management Report No. 15. New York: American Management Association, 1958.

COWAN, D. R. G. *Sales Analysis from the Management Standpoint.* Chicago: University of Chicago Press, 1938.

CRISP, RICHARD D. *Sales Planning and Control.* New York: McGraw-Hill Book Co., Inc., 1961.

EASTWOOD, R. P. *Sales Control by Quantitative Methods.* New York: Columbia University Press, 1940.

GORT, MICHAEL. *Stability and Change in Market Shares.* Chicago: Graduate School of Business, University of Chicago, 1963.

HUMMEL, FRANCIS E. *Market and Sales Potentials.* New York: The Ronald Press Co., Inc., 1961.

JEROME, WILLIAM TRAVERS, III. *Executive Control: The Catalyst.* New York: John Wiley and Sons, Inc., 1961.

Report Forms and Procedures for Successful Sales Administration. Special Report No. 2. New York: American Management Association, 1955.

SMITH, CHARLES W. *Making Your Sales Figures Talk.* Small Business Administration, Management Series No. 8. Washington, D.C.: U. S. Government Printing Office, 1953.

ARTICLES

"Better Selling through Sales Analysis," *Industrial Distribution,* May, 1948, p. 81ff.

BRENDEL, L. H. "How to Determine Potentials and Set Quotas for Distributors," *Sales Management,* February 15, 1952, p. 121ff.

CRISP, R. D. "How to Develop Sales Control Facts from Your Own Company Records," *Industrial Marketing,* October, 1948, p. 33ff.

"Executives Tell Why They Use Quotas—and Why Not," *Industrial Marketing,* June, 1951, p. 40ff.

"Five Yardsticks for Measuring a Salesman's Efficiency," *Sales Management,* March 1, 1947, p. 37ff.

"Harris-Seybold Grades Prospects, Matches Sales Push to Potentials," *Sales Management,* September 18, 1959, pp. 40–46.

HERZOG, D. R. "Use of Sales Quotas by Manufacturers," *Advanced Management,* September, 1956, pp. 23–26.

HUMMEL, F. E. "Market Potentials in the Machine Tool Industry," *Journal of Marketing,* July, 1954, p. 34ff.

KIDDER, N. R., AND HUMMEL, F. E. "How to Find, Classify, Contact Your True Market Potential," *Sales Management,* July 15, 1955, p. 57ff.

LONGMAN, D. R. "Control of Marketing Operations," *Marketing by Manufacturers,* C. F. PHILLIPS (ed.). Chicago: Richard D. Irwin, Inc., 1951, pp. 591–622.

MCDANIEL, R. "Why Not Let Charts Control Your Sales Force?" *Sales Management,* August 15, 1955, p. 102ff.

"Measures of Productivity," *Industrial Distribution,* May, 1950, p. 109ff.

NEOKOM, J. G. "Executive Coordination of the Marketing Program," *Conference of Marketing Teachers From Far Western States.* Berkeley, Calif.: University of California, 1958, pp. 129–133.

OXENFELDT, ALFRED R. "How to Use Market Share Measurement," *Harvard Business Review,* January-February, 1959, pp. 59–68.

RUSSELL, J. "A System of Sales Analysis Using Internal Company Records," *Journal of Marketing,* April, 1950, p. 675ff.

"Trends in Sales Quota Setting," *Printers' Ink,* February 15, 1952, p. 42ff.

WILLETT, R. P. "The Control of Firm Marketing Activity," *A New Approach to Marketing Theory,* Indiana Readings in Business, No. 18. Bloomington, Ind.: University of Indiana School of Business, 1957, pp. 99–112.

CHAPTER 23

BOOKS

BORDEN, NEIL H. *The Economic Effects of Advertising.* Homewood, Ill.: Richard D. Irwin, Inc., 1942.

BROWN, COURTNEY C. (ed.). *The Ethics of Business: Corporate Behavior in the Market Place.* Columbia Business School Series, No. 2. New York: Columbia University Graduate School of Business, 1963.

EELLS, RICHARD, AND WALTON, CLARENCE. *Conceptual Foundations of Business.* Homewood, Ill.: Richard D. Irwin, Inc., 1961.

HODGES, LUTHER H. *The Business Conscience.* Englewood Cliffs, N.J.: Prentice-Hall, Inc., 1963.

MCGUIRE, JOSEPH W. *Business and Society,* New York: McGraw-Hill Book Co., Inc., 1963.

PATMAN, WRIGHT. *Complete Guide to the Robinson-Patman Act.* Englewood Cliffs, N.J.: Prentice-Hall, Inc.. 1963.

SIMON, M. J. *The Law for Advertising and Marketing.* New York: W. W. Norton and Co., 1956.

SPURRIER, WILLIAM A. *Ethics and Business.* New York: Charles Scribner's Sons, 1963.

STEVENS, WILLIAM D. (ed.). *The Social Responsibilities of Marketing.* Chicago: American Marketing Association, 1962.

ARTICLES

BERG, THOMAS L. "The Role of Belief in Human Relations," Business Quarterly, Spring, 1962, pp. 38–46.

DRUCKER, PETER F. "Marketing and Economic Development," *Journal of Marketing,* January, 1958, pp. 252–59.

Index

This book has been set on the Linotype in 12 and 10 point Garamond No. 3, leaded 1 point. Chapter numbers are in 14 point Garamond No. 3 caps and chapter titles are in 24 point Deepdene italics. The size of the type page is 27 by 46½ picas.